THE GREAT WAR SEEN FROM THE AIR

BIRGER STICHELBAUT
PIET CHIELENS

THE GREAT WAR *SEEN FROM THE* AIR

IN FLANDERS FIELDS, 1914–1918

MERCATORFONDS

IN COOPERATION WITH
IN FLANDERS FIELDS MUSEUM, YPRES
IMPERIAL WAR MUSEUMS, UNITED KINGDOM
THE ROYAL MUSEUM OF THE ARMED FORCES AND OF MILITARY HISTORY, BRUSSELS

DISTRIBUTED BY YALE UNIVERSITY PRESS, NEW HAVEN AND LONDON

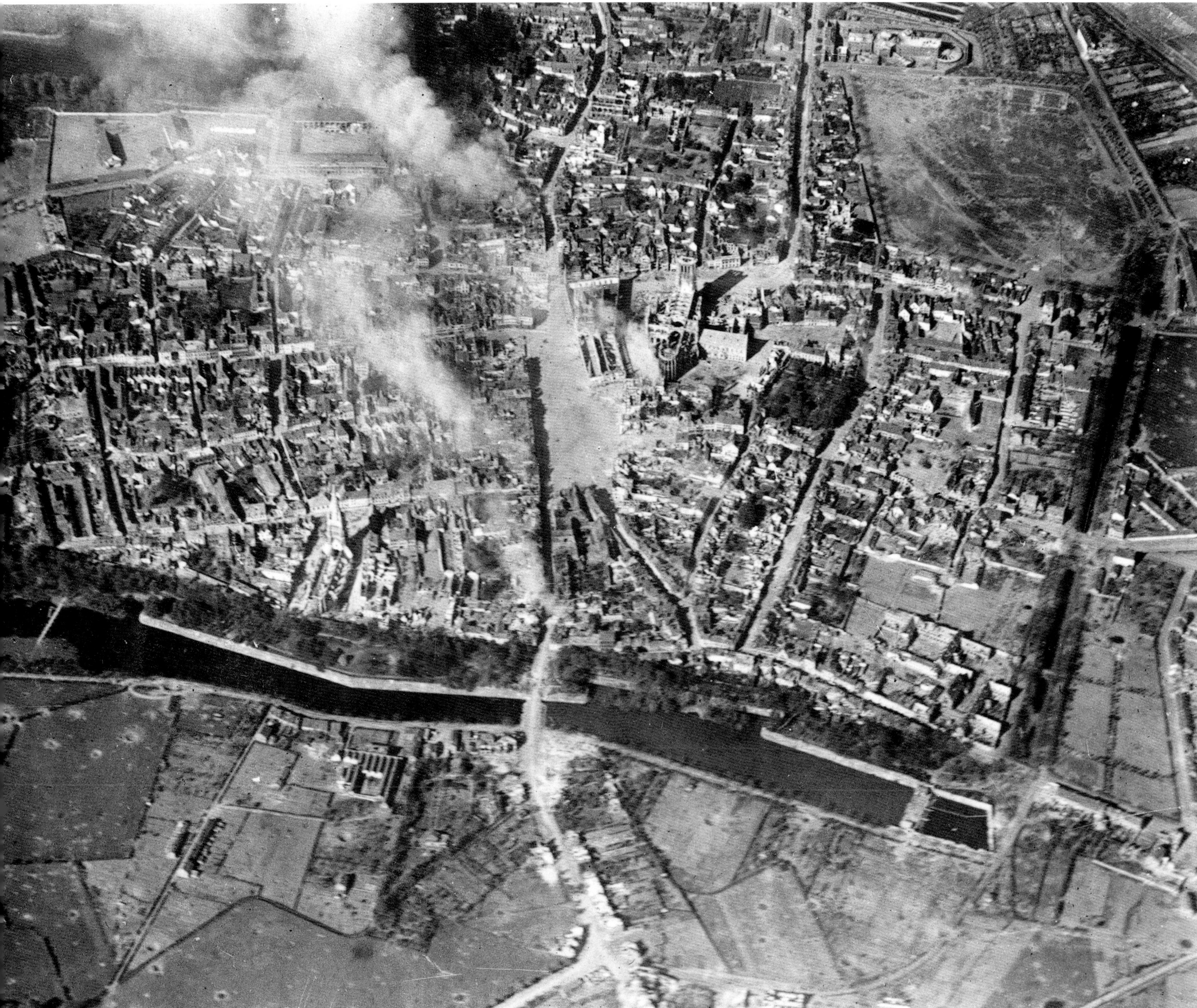

PUBLISHER
Mercatorfonds, Brussels
under the direction of Bernard Steyaert

IN COOPERATION WITH
In Flanders Fields Museum, Ypres
Imperial War Museums, UK
The Royal Museum of the Armed Forces
and of Military History, Brussels

AUTHORS
Birger Stichelbaut
Piet Chielens

TEXT EDITING AND TRANSLATION
First Edition, London

PROOFREADING
Kate Bell

DESIGN
Janpieter Chielens, Tijdgeest, Ghent

PRODUCTION
Tijdsbeeld & Pièce Montée, Ghent
under the direction of Ronny Gobyn and Rik Jacques

COORDINATION
Barbara Costermans, Tijdgeest, Ghent
Bregje Provo, Tijdsbeeld & Pièce Montée, Ghent
Ann Mestdag, Mercatorfonds, Brussels

PRE-PRESS, PRINT AND BINDING
New Goff, Ghent
Printed on LuxoArt Samt 150 g

TYPEFACES
Bulmer by William Martin
Halis by Ahmet Altun

www.mercatorfonds.be
www.inflandersfields.be
www.iwm.org.uk
www.klm-mra.be

ACKNOWLEDGMENTS

This book is based on research carried out since 2004 at Ghent University (Department of Archaeology), in close coordination, from 2009, with the In Flanders Fields Museum and the Province of West Flanders. The project was developed by Tijdsbeeld & Pièce Montée: thanks to Ronny Gobyn and Janpieter Chielens we are able to present the aerial photographs in this fine and beautifully designed book. We are also particularly grateful to Bregje Provo and Barbara Costermans for all their work, suggestions, and, above all, patience in the realisation of this complicated project.
Nor would this book have been possible without the support of the archive institutions and museums in which the aerial photos are kept. With their kind cooperation we have had full access to their rich collections. Our thanks also go to the following (in alphabetical order): Dominiek Dendooven, Anne Godfroid, Dominique Hanson, Sandrine Smets, Barry Smith, Lieven Stubbe, Annick Vandenbilcke, Alan Wakefield and Mark Whitmore.

BIRGER STICHELBAUT AND PIET CHIELENS

Distributed in Belgium, the Netherlands, and Luxembourg
by Mercatorfonds, Brussels
ISBN 978-94-6230-026-2
D/2013/703/35

Distributed outside Belgium, the Netherlands, and Luxembourg
by Yale University Press, New Haven and London
yalebooks.com/art
yalebooks.co.uk
ISBN 978-0-300-19658-0
Library of Congress Control Number: 2013955407

PHOTOGRAPHS COVER
FRONT: 'Trench of Death', Diksmuide, 4 November 1917 (see p. 187)
BACK: Captured German trenches, Boezinge,
5 August 1917 (see p. 158)

PHOTOGRAPH PAGE 3
Flight above Ypres, May 1915 (see p. 16)

PHOTOGRAPH PAGE 9
Gotha bomber over Flanders (see p. 302)

IN ASSOCIATION WITH
UNIVERSITEIT GENT
ArcLand HERITAGE · DATA · KNOWLEDGE

CONTENTS

Preface

JEAN BOURGEOIS
Department of Archaeology, Ghent University

2014 will without a doubt be the year of remembrance. A century ago, after decades of mounting nationalism, a cataclysm was unleashed and for four long years, from Nieuwpoort to the Swiss border, and in numerous other parts of the world, the so-called civilised nations found the resources and energy for a display of incredible human stupidity which was to cost the lives of millions of men and women, civilians and military. This war, which some called the 'war to end all wars', made its mark on our memories as much as on our landscape.
The forms of commemoration will be legion, in our country and elsewhere, and it is to be hoped that they will stress the immense impact this war had on our world. Why then another project presenting the war – in a sense – from the air, at times even an almost sanitised version, since it overlooks the many dead or wounded soldiers, the animal carcases, the human and animal suffering? The aerial photographs this work takes as its starting point show the suffering of the countryside, the way in which it was affected by the war. It is another way of looking at the conflict, certainly no less dramatic than a collection of photographs taken on the ground.
From the North Sea to Comines-Warneton, Belgium saw the front line of the war take root in its countryside. Without wishing to minimise the importance of the human losses and suffering, which were the most tragic consequences of war, the four years of conflict also left a profound mark on the land, not only in the form of the linear traces of the trenches of the warring parties, but also in the depths of the country, dozens of kilometres behind the front. The troops in the trenches had to have places for supplies of arms and men; the wounded soldiers had to be moved out to be cared for in dressing stations and then hospitals or, too often, to be buried; as for the civilians, they had often already abandoned their farms and villages and even their towns that in certain cases – and here Ypres is their iconic symbol – had, so to speak, been razed to the ground; at the front trenches and dugouts were excavated, concrete shelters constructed and mines detonated in order to breach the enemy lines. These actions left deep scars on the landscape, many traces of which can be seen today. These vestiges of war are, to use the expression coined by a fine exhibition organised in 2006 – the 'last witnesses of the war'.
One of the effects of the first world conflict in our regions was the capture of the landscape on tens, or hundreds, of thousands, if not more, of photographic negatives or plates. Barely a decade after the first piloted and motorised flight by the Wright brothers in 1903, these photographs were taken from primitive aeroplanes with photographic apparatus that was continually improved throughout the war, ceaselessly creating 'superb' pictures of these war-torn landscapes, these landscapes of hell. It is hard to believe, but every inch of the front area and its hinterland was photographed at least once. It may seem heartless, but, thanks to the war, we now have an impressive documentation of the landscape of our regions as it was a century ago and of the development endured by this area during the conflict, which ultimately left parts resembling the Moon's surface rather than that of our Earth.
The photographs presented in this book are limited to 129 episodes. The aerial photographs have been deconstructed, analysed and, in a sense, brought alive again. The episodes chosen demonstrate the considerable documentary quality of aerial photography for those wishing to understand the landscapes of yesterday and today.
Whereas aerial photographs traditionally served above all as illustrations – numerous books on the First World War contain one or two aerial photographs but no more – thanks to digital imaging techniques and geographical information systems they have now come into their own as a documentary source of the first order. I would even say that they are a more objective source than the many photographs taken on the ground, since they were, for example, not of Allied bodies but only those of the enemy: more objective than the best novels or war diaries, refined by the filter of literary creation; more objective than trench maps, always of course drawn up without the

↑
Oblique aerial photograph of Polygon Wood, early 1915.

knowledge of the enemy. This book represents an important step in the appreciation of the value of these aerial photographs. Anyone who wishes to find out more should visit the In Flanders Fields Museum in Ypres, or consult the aerial photograph archives of the The Royal Museum of the Armed Forces and of Military History in Brussels or the Imperial War Museum in London.

This book gives us an impressive but tragic picture of the life on the war front in our regions, while showing us at the same time the extent to which the land can be altered by man, at a speed and on a scale unknown in its 'normal' evolution. Everywhere in the world landscapes tend to develop and change to the rhythm of the decades, centuries, even millennia. Here four years sufficed. Unimaginable. And if our minds can also visualise in this landscape living beings, allies or enemies, civilians or military, the idea of war becomes even more of a nightmare.

1

INTRODUCTION

'Aerial photographs were the eyes of our armies, as the cavalry had been in the past, but now how much more penetrating and precise!'[1]

GENERAL DUVAL, 1921

'The surface scars of the Great War are a secret language requiring knowledgeable translation.'[2]

D. WINTER, 1978

An untold wealth of wartime data

The First World War broke out in Europe in August 1914. What was expected to be a short, sharp series of military manoeuvres turned into a stalemate lasting years, not only in the trenches of the Western Front but, soon after, on many other fronts besides. Over time, war-torn terrain stretched from the North Sea in Belgium to the Franco-Swiss border and from the Black Sea in the south to the Baltic in the north. It encompassed parts of Italy and Slovenia, as well as more distant theatres of war, such as Gallipoli in Turkey and even Palestine.

An untapped resource

It was during the First World War that aerial photographs were first taken on a large scale. This was done on all fronts with the photographs serving as a source of military information – they were taken in order to obtain additional information concerning the enemy's position and intentions. Nowadays, these exceptional eyewitness records document territory under conflict during the First World War from a unique perspective. They depict a cultural landscape, remnants of which sometimes still remain as scars on the terrain, though often discernible only to eagle-eyed experts. These aerial photographs are now being revealed for the first time as a primary source of information for archaeologists, historians and landscape researchers.

In any story about the history and evolution of aerial photography, some reference is always made to the First World War. It is a story that has its beginnings in the nineteenth century – when the hot-air balloon was still the means of elevation – and which ends for now in the present day with high-resolution satellite photography. Many authors have already pointed to the importance of the First World War regarding the rapid, wholesale development of aviation, cameras and technology in general, but the subject is seldom studied in detail. In the eyes of the general public, the history of aviation in the First World War is dominated by heroic aerial battles performed by the famous 'flying aces', successful fighter pilots such as Albert Ball, Georges Guynemer and Manfred von Richthofen.[1] By comparison, aerial photography has all too often been treated as a somewhat lacklustre activity, quite literally lacking in colour.

When we look at the vast quantity of aerial photographs taken during the brief period between 1914 and 1918 – little more than a decade following the very first flight of an aeroplane on 17 December 1903 – the enormous significance of aerial photography soon becomes clear. There were quite literally millions of aerial photographs and to this day hundreds of thousands of these are still preserved in archives and museums throughout the world. These photographic archives hold an extraordinary and as yet unknown potential in terms of the information they contain.

About this book

The intention of this book is to awaken interest in these images and to reveal the wealth of information that they contain. As expressed by the scholars Bewley and Raczkowski: 'Unlocking these (historical) archives is perhaps the single most important development which would dramatically improve our understanding and knowledge of Europe's historical environment'.[2] At the end of the book (from p. 340 on), readers are provided with an appendix containing descriptions of the world's largest collections of First World War aerial photographs. By drawing attention to the museums and archives where these images can be viewed and studied, we aim to increase public awareness and access to these unique collections. Using this information, anyone with an interest will be able to consult aerial photographs of the Western Front for themselves in the original preserved archives. They are well worth being put at the disposal of the general public.

This book is divided into two parts. First, there is a general introduction concerning aerial photography during the First World War. We outline a succinct frame of reference and explain the context within which aerial photography appeared and developed during the war. This is not intended to be a complete history of aerial photography over the course of those four years. For such a study, we would encourage readers to consult Terrence J. Finnegan's *Shooting the Front*, the first and – at present – the only comprehensive review of the subject. Our own, more concise account of the birth of aerial photography begins with the first airborne photographic

↑ **A crossroads in the vicinity of Kortrijk (Courtrai) in the German hinterland. This is a rare aerial photograph where the eye is drawn immediately to the presence of people on the ground.**

experiments of the nineteenth century. This is followed by a deeper analysis of the use of aerial photographs for military intelligence and an outline of the most important ways in which the images have been used, both in the past and today. We will give brief explanations of what can be seen in the photographs, not only from an archaeological and topographical point of view, but also from a human perspective. Although aerial photographs may appear at first glance to be 'devoid of detail', stripped of any human presence, on closer inspection they reveal a complete overview of human activity in a war; what we see is invariably the record of humanity at work. When combined with other historical records, these images supply us with a unique insight into the fate of the people who lived, fought and died on and around the front.

All of this is substantiated in the second section of the book, which contains 129 case studies of the First World War in Belgium. For the first time, this historical subject will be approached from a bird's-eye view. Our intention is neither to rewrite the story of the First World War nor to provide a complete illustration of it. Far too many historical publications have employed aerial photographs simply for the sake of having some 'diverting pictures'. Very often these will include stereotypical images, such as overhead aerial views of the village of Passchendaele before and after heavy bombardment. This book adopts a reverse approach. The aerial photographs are the starting point. They supply information about a particular location or event. (That said, some images are so expressive or singular that they have been included purely for their visual impact.)

Wherever possible, we have placed the case studies in chronological order; they show the course and evolution of the First World War up to its conclusion. A conscious decision was made to adopt a geographically wide-ranging approach to the material. Not only do we highlight the trenches on the front lines and the no-man's-land lying in between, but we also focus attention on areas in the hinterland. The zones at the front are typified by the extraordinary density of trenches, bunkers and other military reinforcements. However, when we cast our gaze wider to take in areas extending well beyond the fields of combat, we are presented with a vast range of differing sites; a picture begins to emerge that includes airfields, storage depots, hospitals, port facilities and even a base for Zeppelins and bombers.

Furthermore, the armistice of 11 November 1918 did not signal the end of the story of the First World War from the air, even if the military dimension ceased from that moment. Some rare aerial photographs allow us to see reconstruction of the 'devastated region'. Even now, one hundred years later, the effects of the war remain tangibly present in the Westhoek region of western Belgium and northern France. Now that there are no longer any witnesses of the war still living, only the landscape is left to present its enduring, silent testament to the conflict.

The selection of the photographs

The aerial photographs selected for this book derive from a data set of more than 20,500 images that over the past few years has undergone academic research and study. We have the archives to thank for enabling us to bring these images together for this visual analysis. The wealth of material made it possible for us to select from among the most striking, fascinating and original photographs.

Interpreting an aerial photograph requires expertise and specialist knowledge. Consequently, to make them accessible to the layperson, we have annotated a large number of the photographs using transparent overlays that help to 'translate' our visual analysis. Often, it is the position of a piece of terrain in a photograph that is important; reference is made to the GPS coordinates[3] of the sites under discussion, thus making it possible to visit the location. Moreover, notes are provided in the margin to indicate distances from relevant population centres. We have also displayed several sites photographed at different times in order to show the development of the war and its impact on the landscape. Where it has seemed useful, aerial photographs have been included alongside photographs taken at ground level, historical maps and personal testimonies.

A town in its death throes

YPRES IN THE FIRST YEAR OF THE WAR

An intense feeling of presence

Somewhere within the pages of many of the personal photograph albums kept by German officers would be found an aerial photograph of Ypres. Very often, the town could be seen in the distance with the battle lines in the foreground. These photographs give us a sense of the feeling that must have weighed on any German commander who had been posted to that front for any length of time: so tantalisingly near and yet so frustratingly far.

Occasionally, there is a second photograph: a low pass over the town, never a vertical shot but, instead, oblique and quickly taken – a stolen glance at the devastation and suffering below. These are the most poignant of images, because aerial photographs give the impression of providing a view of reality caught in the here and now. It is the only medium to succeed in doing this. Time solidifies in photographs taken from the ground and thus they are always rooted in the past. Panoramas freeze the wind blowing across the landscape and turn the world into an icy stasis. However, aerial photographs are at once both far removed from what is happening and yet able to provide a bird's-eye view of it. And it is that bird's-eye view that is responsible for an intense feeling of presence in relation to the events that took place there. The distance means that, although you cannot, of course, see any motion, you still sense it as if it were there.

Visitors to the research centre at the In Flanders Fields Museum are sometimes in search of the place where an ancestor went missing in action or was given temporary burial. If an aerial photograph of that place happens to exist, taken perhaps only a few days or weeks after the date in question, such visitors will often remark that 'he's in the picture', even if a grave can hardly ever be discerned, let alone identified. This is not unusual for photographs taken at such a height. Nevertheless, they are right – 'he' *is* still *in* the picture.

Ypres: From bustling centre to ghost town

Aerial photographs of Ypres taken in the first year of war reveal the gradual death of the town as a result of the conflict. The oldest images date from after the burning of the medieval Cloth Hall and St Martin's Cathedral on 22 November 1914. The fire-ravaged buildings were left as skeletal shells among other structures that were still standing, where people had either taken shelter or continued to live.

→ **The centre of Ypres after the fire of 22 November 1914.**

→ **Oblique aerial photograph of a fragment of the Ypres Salient, autumn 1915. In the foreground is the front line at Bellewaarde and Hooge and in the distance the ruins of Ypres.**

Three photographs of Ypres from the south-west, spring 1915

The photographs of the south-western part of the town were taken between the First (19 October – 22 November 1914) and Second Battle of Ypres (22 April – 25 May 1915). As yet, the neighbourhood around the station square and the esplanade has hardly been damaged, apart from the unfortunate café Het Torretje (A2-B2) on the corner of the imposing neo-Gothic terrace along the north side of the park (B2). Fresh bursts of shelling evident in the photograph on p. 14 have already been extinguished in the one on p. 15, apart from in the public gardens. The popinjay mast (p. 14, B4-C4) belonging to the venerable archers' guild, next to the gunpowder magazine (p. 14, B4), is still standing bolt upright and ready for use.

←
Oblique general view from the south-west. The moat of the Vauban fortifications is quite easily visible. At the top is the market with the Cloth Hall.

↑
Shell holes in C3 and C4 on the photograph above have been filled in on the photograph to the right (p. 15, B1 and p. 15, E1 respectively).
A smaller station building (B3) is shown intact on the photograph above and has bomb damage on the photograph to the right (p. 15, B1). In both cases the popinjay mast is untouched.

The popinjay mast of the archery club
in the middle of the gunpowder magazine site.

Flight above Ypres by aerial observer Freiherr Dietrich von Kanne, 11(?) May 1915

The last of the town's inhabitants were evacuated a few days before this reconnaissance flight. A great many of the public buildings have already been gutted by fire, although most of the walls are still standing; St Martin's Cathedral and the Cloth Hall had already gone up in flames on 22 November 1914; St James's Church burned from 23 to 25 April 1915, St Nicholas's Church and the school behind it on 6 and 7 May. Moreover, in the weeks between 22 April and 8 May hundreds of soldiers and civilians in the town were killed by the bombardments. The last remaining citizens were evacuated by military order on 9 May 1915.
When Camiel Delaere, the pastor of St Peter's Church, and Gustave Delahaye, warden of the Sacred Heart Institute, returned to Ypres on 11 May with a few lorries from the Friends Ambulance Unit, to salvage any valuables still remaining, they observed that there were fires burning in five or six places and that – in contrast to the activity undertaken in previous weeks – nobody was taking the trouble to put them out any longer. The plumes of smoke in this series of photographs confirm this. In the days to follow a large part of the historic town centre would burn to the ground, street by street.

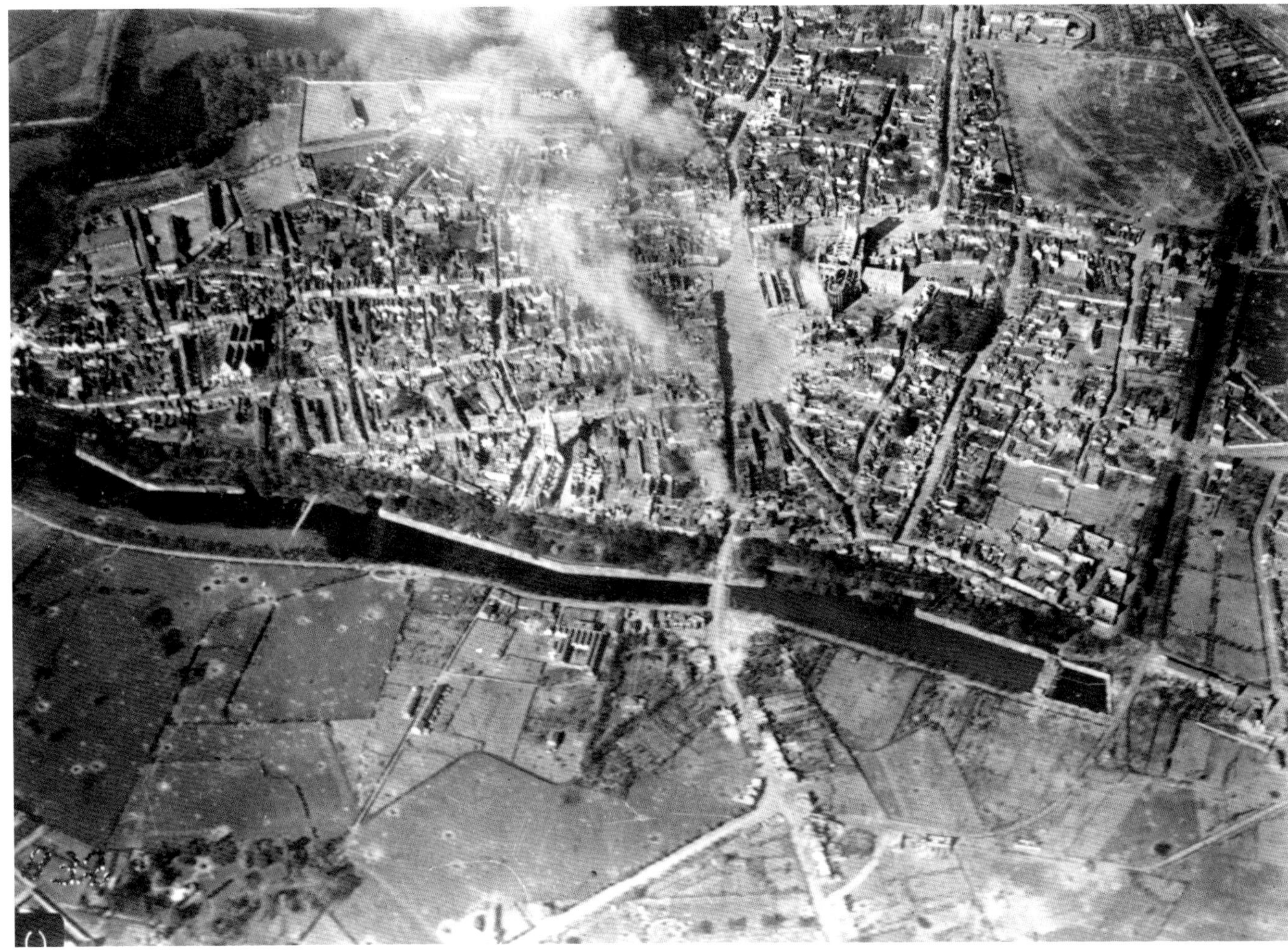

Two photographs taken from the north-east, 11(?) and 13(?) May 1915

Many accounts attest to the fact that, for as long as people remained living in the town, every effort was made to isolate and quell each centre of conflagration, even when the fire brigade had already fled. However, once the population was gone, the flames were able to take their destructive course, burning down one street after another.

The photograph above is part of a series taken by the aerial observer Freiherr von Kanne on 11(?) May. Although we cannot be absolutely certain, the photograph to the left may also have been taken by him, given that the flight path is precisely the same. By that time, the fire had been raging for several days. Menenstraat is completely ablaze, and Cartonstraat (almost intact in the photograph above, D1-E1) has already burned itself out, as have a number of buildings surrounding St Martin's Cathedral.

The south-western part of the town, spring 1916

The two photographs from the spring and summer of 1916 show how comprehensive the devastation has been in the interim. After each bombardment, fire has continued to rage across the ghost town that Ypres has become. All of the houses in Stationsstraat and the esplanade, as well as in the district to the north, are burnt-out shells. Even the sturdy infantry barracks has sustained damage. And the popinjay mast has finally collapsed – not thanks to an archer's skill, but because of enemy artillery.

→ **The popinjay mast now taken down, and the infantry barracks.**

←
The collapsed popinjay mast.

Aerial photography and the war: a brief history

Earliest beginnings

It should go without saying that the beginnings of aerial photography were closely associated with developments in photography and aviation. The invention of the daguerreotype by Louis Daguerre in 1839 ensured that photography could be made quite widely accessible for the very first time.[1] Attempts were soon also made to take photographic images from the air. In 1858 photographs were taken of Paris from a hot-air balloon[2] by Gaspard Félix Tournachon,[3] who went by the pseudonym of Félix Nadar. One year later he offered his services to Napoleon III and went on to provide reconnaissance at the Battle of Solferino using aerial photography. In 1845 the French officer Aimé Laussedat was the first to try to convert the information contained in aerial images into accurate cartographic material.[4] For the purpose of this photogrammetry, Laussedat used photographs that had been taken from balloons, kites and the roofs of buildings. The oldest surviving aerial photographs show the American city of Boston. They were taken around 1860 by the American photographer James Wallace Black.

Many early shots taken from the air were connected with major military conflicts. Following Nadar's aerial photographs of the Austrian troops at the Battle of Solferino in 1859,[5] further photographs were taken during the American Civil War (1861–65)[6] of the battle lines between Richmond and Petersburg (Virginia).[7] These were followed by photographs of the Franco-Prussian War of 1870 and the Spanish-American War of 1898.[8] This usually involved photographs being taken from hot-air balloons, which were used as an elevated platform from which to gain military information about the enemy.

Of equal importance were developments in the photographic process. The daguerreotype was followed from 1851 onwards by the use of collodion on glass-plate negatives, which reduced exposure times to a few seconds.[9] The process required the glass plates to be wet both when taking the photograph and when developing it, all of which necessitated a portable darkroom. In 1871 Richard Maddox was the first to use a dry plate. A coating of gelatine emulsion containing silver nitrate and cadmium bromide[10] was applied to the glass-plate negative. This made the plates significantly more light-sensitive, which in turn made it possible for exposures to last less than one second. Moreover, this dispensed with the need for a mobile darkroom, because the photographer was able to develop the plates much later after exposure.

Althrough the earliest aerial photographs were taken from hot-air balloons or airships, experiments were also performed using unmanned cameras mounted to kites, projectiles or even carrier pigeons.[11] All of this was changed for ever after 17 December 1903. The 12-second flight at Kitty Hawk (USA) of the *Wright Flyer*, the aeroplane built by the brothers Wilbur and Orville Wright, signified the birth of modern aviation. Wilbur Wright would also go on to be the first person to take an aerial photograph from an aeroplane, an event that occurred on 24 April 1909 in Italy.[12] Further experiments were undertaken in the years that followed; however, the great breakthrough for aerial photography was to take place in the First World War.

Aerial photography and the First World War

When Germany invaded Belgium on 4 August 1914, aerial photography had not yet been fully developed within the aviation services of Europe's opposing forces. Aviators were sent out on missions to report artillery positions and troop movements. These reconnaissance airmen made sketches of their observations or simply made mental notes of what they had seen. The first reported British aerial photographs were taken at the Aisne front[13] by Lieutenant Prettyman on 15 September 1914, while the first Belgian aerial photographs date from 23 September. On that occasion, Lieutenant Deschamps and Captain Schmidt were in command of a Henry Farman HF.20 reconnaissance aircraft and photographed German positions near Antwerp.[14] It was quickly realised that aerial photographs contained far more information than aerial observers were capable of retaining during their flights. At the very least, this was documentary evidence in black and white capable of confirming their reports.

Following the Battle of the Yser (18 October – 11 November 1914) and the First Battle of Ypres (19 October – 22 November 1914), warfare employing tactical manoeuvres turned into trench warfare. From that point forward, the traditional 'eyes' of the army – the cavalry and espionage – were no longer able to furnish the information required. Opportunities now rested with aerial observation and aerial photography.[15] What during the first few months had been the domain of a handful of enthusiastic aviators quickly turned into an entirely new discipline that was developed and employed on a grand scale by all the combatants. In addition to technical advances made in performing aerial photography (improved lenses, longer focal lengths, a semi-automatic plate changing system, stereo photography, etc.), great advances were also made in reading and interpreting the photographs.[16]

As described by a French military manual in 1916, the most important reason for taking aerial photographs was to discover 'the precise nature of the enemy's positions' and to establish 'their reason for being there'.[17] First, an attempt was made to analyse in detail the various components of a defensive position: bunkers, trenches, shelters, artillery positions and so forth. Next, this information was considered from a tactical perspective in order to understand the enemy's intentions.[18] In this way, aerial photography yielded up a vast quantity of information and its impact was considerable. As a result, we can concur with Finnegan that the First World War was 'the first information and intelligence war of the modern era'.[19] For the first time, troops were able to advance with prior knowledge about the concentration of enemy troops and the terrain.[20] Visual information was available far beyond the limits of natural sight with which people on the ground had previously had to contend.[21] Aerial photography can be employed for all types of military strategy, but in trench warfare the comparison of photographs taken on different dates supplies far more information than one image alone.

←
A sergeant of the Royal Flying Corps demonstrates a Type C aerial reconnaissance camera mounted to the fuselage of a BE2c aircraft, 1916.

Aerial photographs: dimensions, quality and types

DIMENSIONS

The reconnaissance flights carried out by all of the combatants produced millions of aerial photographic prints. Their dimensions depend on the size of glass-plate negative used. The prints are almost always the same size as the negative, although sections from some aerial photographs were also enlarged. Different formats were used for different purposes and in cameras from different manufacturers.

Early aerial photographs, prior to 1915, come in a variety of sizes because standard cameras were not available at the time. During the first months of the war some observation teams purchased their own photographic equipment. Consequently, a variety of formats can be found held in collections. Photographs from 1914 and 1915, and sometimes up to the spring of 1916, often have a negative measuring 13 × 18 cm. This format was used for cameras with 26-cm lenses. Later aerial photographs frequently measure 18 × 24 cm and could be used for cameras with various focal lengths: 26 (wide-angle lens), 50 or 52, and 120 cm (telephoto lens). These cameras produced greater detail in the photographs and made them easier for people to interpret. The surface being photographed is relatively large when using a short lens. A much smaller area is visible when using a 120-cm telephoto lens.

French cameras had negatives measuring 13 × 18 or 18 × 24 cm.[22] These cameras were also in general use by Belgian and American aerial observers. The British, on the other hand, had already developed special cameras for aerial photography prior to the war, such as the Watson aerial camera, which used negatives measuring 4 × 5 inches (10.2 × 12.7 cm).[23] This type remained in use throughout the war both for ordinary shots and for composites of aerial photographs pasted alongside each other.[24] Many other British aerial photographs measure 6½ × 8½ inches (16.5 × 21.6 cm). There is no real connection between focal length and the size of the negatives. In 1918 a number of British cameras were converted to an 18 × 24-cm format in order to achieve a standard format for all Allied aerial photographs.[25]

The negatives consisted of a glass plate coated with a silver bromide emulsion.[26] Tests were also done using flexible film, albeit not in great quantities. Among the French, these photographs retained the 18 × 24-cm format;[27] with regard to the Royal Flying Corps, and later the Royal Air Force, this was 4 × 5 inches (10.2 × 12.7 cm).[28] Less was published about German aerial photography in the First World War. Research at the Bavarian Main State Archive in Munich indicates that at least five different negative formats were in use. These ranged from small to large: 9 × 12, 10 × 15, 16 × 16, 13 × 18 and even 24 × 30 cm.[29] The focal lengths were very similar to those used by the Allies, ranging from 25 to 50, 70 and 120 cm.[30]

QUALITY

The quality of aerial photographs from the First World War depends on a great many factors. First of all, one needs to consider the camera optics. Germany possessed a major advantage in that regard; it had control over the high-quality lenses produced by Carl Zeiss. The sole manufacturer in any way capable of standing up against Zeiss was Parra-Mantois[31] in France. Consequently, Belgian, British and American aerial photographers were largely dependent on the French for their lenses. It was not uncommon for specimens of poorer quality to be used. Even at the time, there was no shadow of doubt concerning the importance of good-quality lenses. Indeed, on occasion, the conflict was referred to as the 'war of the lenses' given that 'good aerial photography [was] the basis for good artillery'.[32]

↓ **Three Belgian aerial cameras with focal lengths of (from right to left) 26, 52 and 120 cm. The glass-plate negatives and contact prints measure 13 × 18 and 18 × 24 cm.**

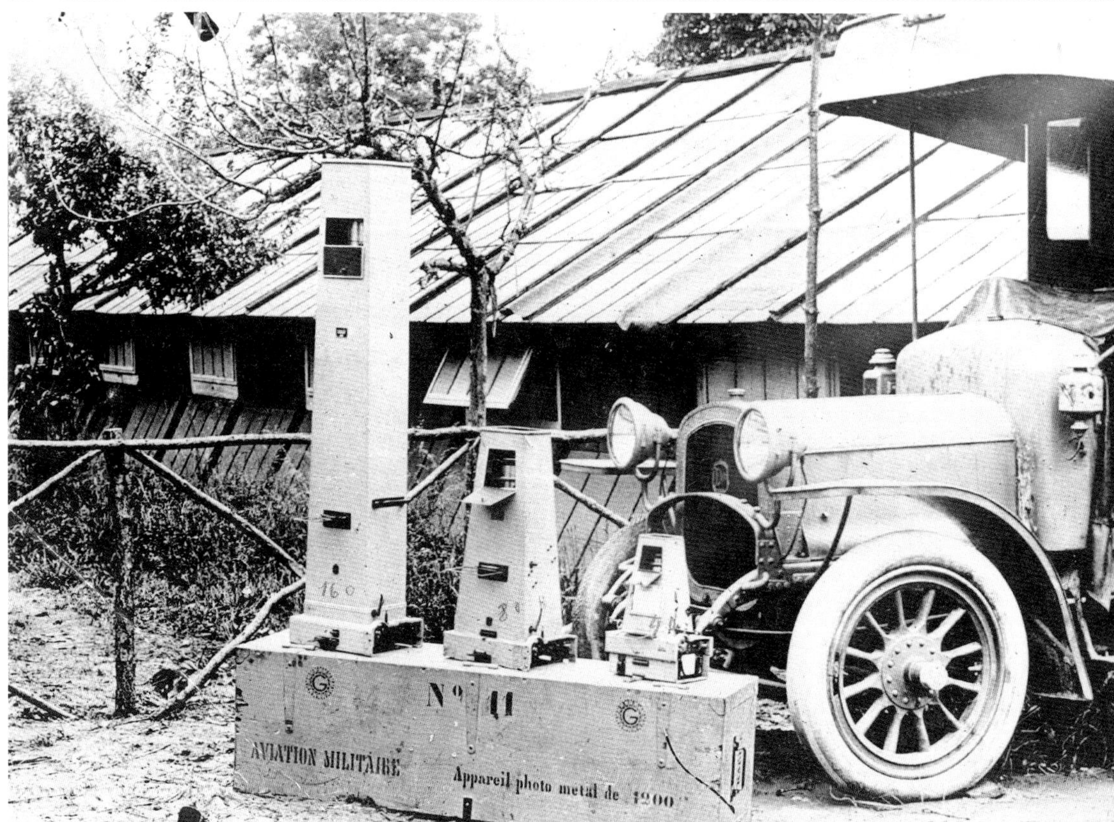

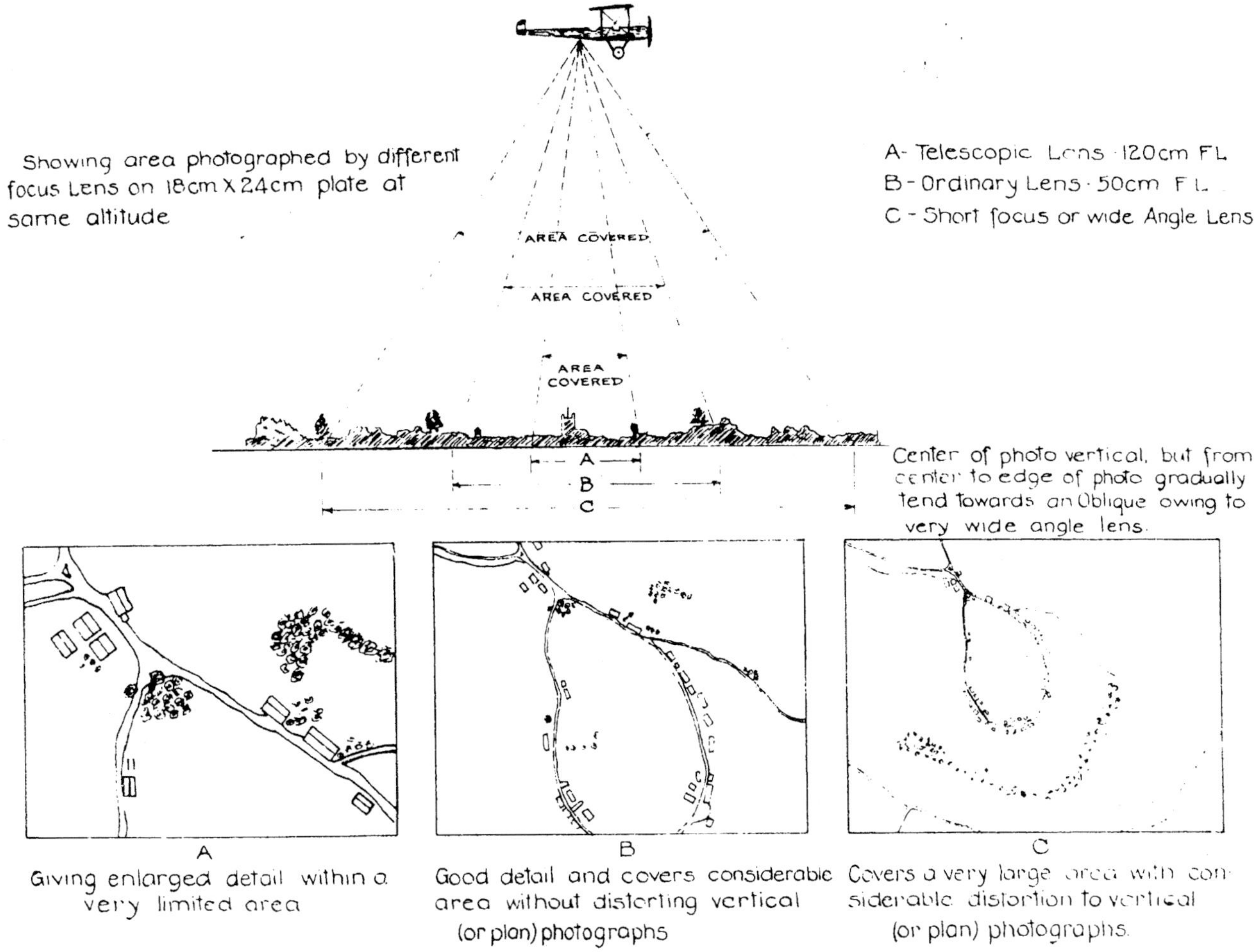

↑
Differences between the areas photographed when using different focal lengths.

A somewhat more subjective parameter was that of image clarity. For the purposes of interpretation, the most serviceable images are ones that are clear without being under- or overexposed. Moreover, the climatological conditions under which aerial photographs were taken are also significant. An overcast sky produces darker, greyer images with little contrast or clarity. Other photographs contend with scattered shadows cast by clouds, which obscure parts of the photograph and thus make them more difficult to interpret. On the other hand, photographs of snow-covered terrain are of particular interest to analysts.
One final factor of significance is the use of specific emulsions for developing and printing photographs. A variety of products were used depending on the information required and the time available to yield it up. Some photographs were ordered, taken and printed within three to four hours, which was obviously far from ideal for a good result. When it was possible to work with less haste, it was more usual for photographs to be more detailed and clearer.[33]

TYPES OF AERIAL PHOTOGRAPH AND THEIR INTERPRETATION

There are three types of aerial photograph: vertical, oblique and panoramic.[34] In the case of vertical shots, the camera's optical axis is at right angles to the target surface. Experience is needed to interpret aerial photographs; otherwise these images can be difficult to read owing to their two-dimensional representation of a three-dimensional reality, just as in the case of a map. If the camera's optical axis is angled in relation to the target surface, the result is an oblique aerial photograph.[35] This is easier for the layperson to read because its perspective is more akin to how we normally observe the world. Nevertheless, oblique aerial photographs are of only limited use for conversion into cartographic data.[36] Panoramic aerial photographs have an optical axis that runs more or less parallel with the horizon. They usually depict the terrain and some sky above it.[37] Their greatest advantage is in displaying a region's entire battle front plus the geographic relief in one image.
Looking from the perspective of a bird's-eye view is essential to the study and interpretation of aerial photographs. However, this is not the normal way in which human beings perceive their environment, and it is not at all how we are accustomed to looking at military fieldworks or structures in a battle front system. Oblique photographs provide a slightly distorted image, although they can yield a great deal of information to the unskilled viewer. Their chief importance is in helping to understand the terrain's topography and its military installations. The image they create is similar to that obtained by looking down from the top of a hill.[38]
Vertical aerial photography is far more important in relation to map-making. This is made clear by the two aerial photographs that follow on pages 24 and 25 below. The oblique (angled) perspective is similar to a person's natural vision. You can clearly see the above-ground earthen ramparts of the old fortifications near Nieuwpoort. Tree stumps, ruined dwellings and sluices can also be readily identified. These features are much more difficult to discern from a vertical image of the same area. The outlines of the fortification and the moat remain easy to spot. Nevertheless, the same is not the case for the trees, which you can make out only by the shadows they cast on the ground. On the other hand, many military features across the terrain, such as the crenellated trenches, can be seen far better in the vertical image. This perspective closely resembles that given by a ground plan or map.
Whatever the case, aerial photographs are not metrically precise documents that employ a uniform scale in every image. Different lenses will have been used and perspective distortions occur. Nor do these photographs bear a legend as on a map in which all of the features are provided with set definitions and 'forms of representation'. Instead, each separate image requires us to make new interpretations, each time giving fresh meaning to the texture, the shadows and the subtle variations in tone.

A diverse range of objectives

COMPREHENSIVE INFORMATION

The first aerial photographs were taken during the first months of the war. In these cases, observers would hand-hold their amateur cameras and point them over the edge of the cockpit towards the land below. Consequently, most of these photographs were oblique and served to confirm visual observations. The Belgian military required three aircrews to corroborate gathered information before putting the aerial photographs to use, which led inevitably to a loss of both time and human lives.[39] Aerial photographs taken during reconnaissance flights proved to be more detailed and accurate than the hasty notes and sketches jotted down previously, and the information they contained was comprehensive.

When the conflict turned into trench warfare, a proportion of the photographs continued to be comprised of oblique or panoramic shots, even once it became technically possible to take almost vertical aerial images. Panoramic photographs where the optical axis was pointed in the direction of the enemy position[40] provided the infantry with an idea of the terrain for their own trenches. Images such as these were easy for the layperson to interpret and supplied the opposing side with information about the land across which they might launch an attack and the obstacles that they might encounter along the way.[41] The photographs were also annotated and interpreted for the purposes of the infantry, which had no experience of aerial photography interpretation techniques.[42]

THE ARTILLERY'S EYES

The artillery played a pivotal role in trench warfare. Naturally enough, they were able to launch an effective attack on enemy positions only once they possessed precise knowledge about such targets and about the results of artillery fire. Thus it was essential for aerial observers and the artillery to work in partnership.

One of the tasks of military aviation consisted of tracing out artillery targets by means of aerial photography. Photographing enemy positions was relatively straightforward during the first few months of the war. Even in 1915 and 1916 little effort was yet being made to keep concealed from aerial observation. Therefore, as expressed in a British aerial photography manual in 1918, aerial photographs were able to 'locate with certainty some enemy batteries; determine exact position of batteries approximately located by other means; give, in certain cases, suggestions in regard to probable occupation of battery, average firing direction, method of construction, and consequent means for destroying it.'[43]

Gradually, artillery positions became more difficult to detect. All manner of camouflage techniques complicated the job of the aerial observer. Ultimately, photographic interpreters were able to master the challenge posed by camouflage thanks only to the technique of stereo aerial photography.

Aerial photographs were also used repeatedly in order to determine the result of artillery fire. They showed the destruction of enemy positions following preliminary bombardments and counter-fire directed towards enemy artillery batteries. Photographs taken in the hours immediately preceding a major offensive gave commanding officers the opportunity to aim their fire directly at any unexpected resistance still remaining.[44]

MILITARY CARTOGRAPHY

The First World War's trench warfare created an unprecedented demand for continually updated and detailed trench emplacement maps at scales of up to 1:200 and for maps of larger areas at scales of up to 1:1,000,000 for strategic planning.[45] Peter Chasseaud observes that 'aerial reconnaissance

→
British vertical aerial photograph showing at the centre of the traced-out crosshairs a German artillery position at ‘Potsdam’ between Frezenberg and Zonnebeke in the Ypres Salient. The photograph was taken on 1 May 1917, perhaps during an aerial reconnaissance mission for the purpose of directing British counter-artillery fire.

→
Belgian oblique aerial photograph of the Yser (IJzer) near Nieuwpoort, showing the complex of sluice gates at Ganzenpoot (centre) and the old fortifications of Palingbrug (left foreground). The photograph was taken during a low pass. It is undated but may have been taken in the spring of 1917.

←
German vertical aerial photograph of Fort Palingbrug to the north of Nieuwpoort. The image was taken on 23 April 1916 using a 50-cm aerial camera at an altitude of 2,100 metres.

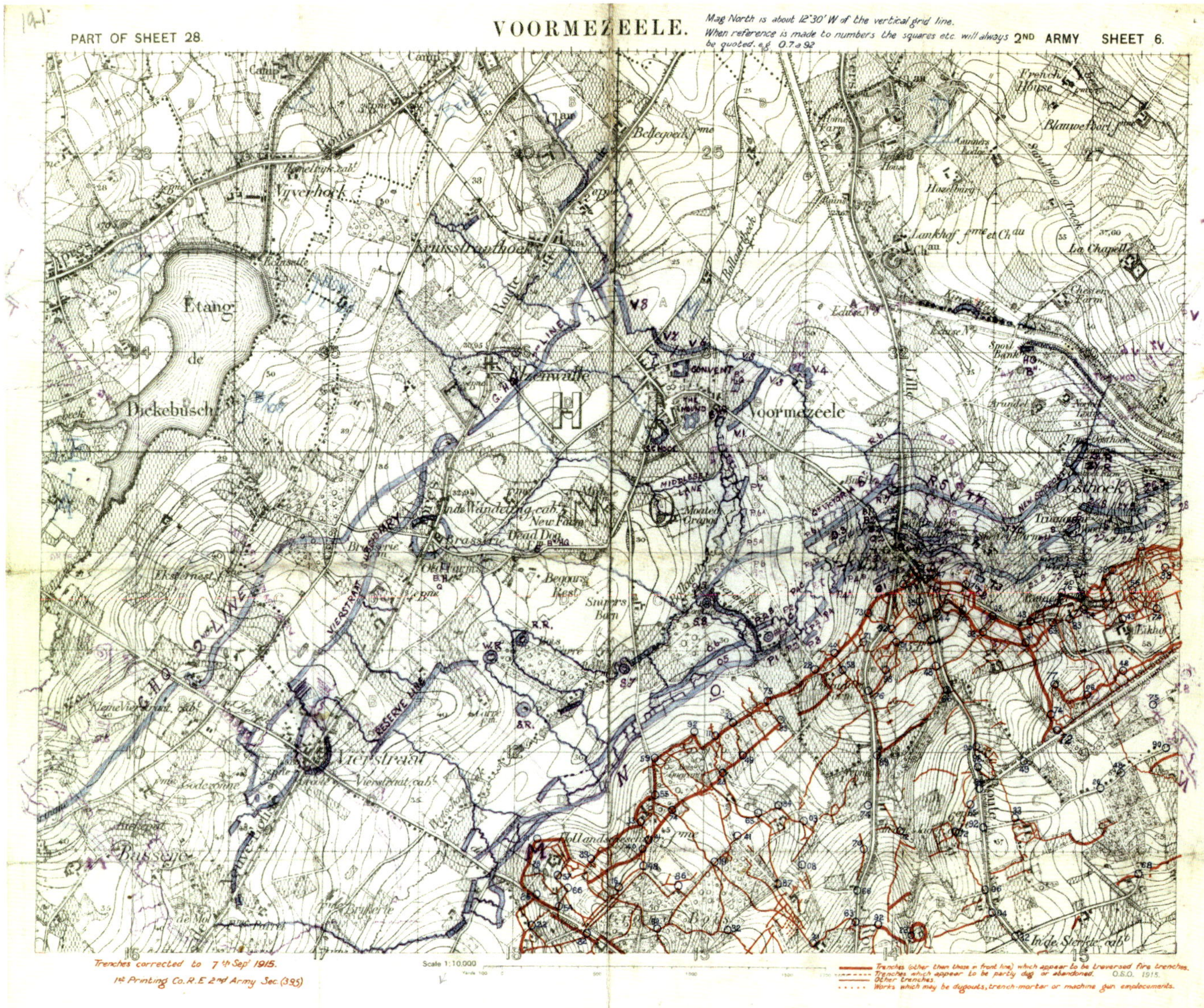

←
British trench map (Sheet 28 NW4 + SW2) dated 7 September 1915 and relating to the British-German front at Sint-Elooi just to the south of Ypres. The German trenches have been marked in red.

became the most important development for military cartography of the war'.[46] A cursory comparison of an aerial photograph and a topographical map of the same area might lead one to conclude that they were virtually identical and that the aerial photograph was a more detailed version of the information shown on the map. However, that impression would be false; aerial photographs are not metrically accurate documents and the images are subject to distortion.[47] A photograph needed to undergo conversion using photogrammetry techniques before its data could be transferred to a map.

For interpretation purposes, it was important to know what was visible in an aerial photograph. Map-making ensured that each point observed in the photograph was placed in an exact location on the map. Parts of the Western Front were mapped out on the basis of this technique, even during 1914. By the end of the war, automatic aerial photography cameras had been developed thereby ending the need to change glass-plate negatives manually. The German Reihenbildner camera, for instance, was capable of producing a stereoscopic record of a surface area of 2.4 × 60 km by taking approximately 250 pictures during the course of one flight.[48]

Aerial photographs intended for map-making were usually taken using wide-angle cameras capable of capturing large expanses of terrain. Photographs were also taken at different dates and then compared in order to discern changes to the enemy defences. Moreover, it was not only the enemy's system of trenches that was photographed, but also that of one's own side. There were several reasons for this. In the first instance, it was a means by which to document one's own defensive organisation and the progress of essential maintenance work. Additionally, it made it possible to gauge how effectively camouflaged one's own concealed structures were: for example

↑
Aerial photographs were sometimes assembled to create large composite images. American students from a school of aerial photography can be seen here creating just such mosaics.

→
German troops set off a flare in order to show their position to a German aerial observation crew. Analysis of the subsequent aerial photograph would then be able to reveal the position of offensive troops.

bunkers, artillery positions, dugouts and tunnel entrances. Lastly, it was a way of monitoring the destruction of one's own defensive system by enemy fire.

PREPARING FOR OFFENSIVES

Aerial photographs were important source material when preparing for offensives. They provided military command with all the information needed to draft orders and helped troops in the field to identify plotted targets quickly.[49] Commanding officers had to have a detailed knowledge of enemy defences and thus, according to Captain de Bissy, it was impressed on photographic interpreters that they should 'penetrate the minds of the German commanders, understand the lives of the men in the trenches and anticipate the action they would take instinctively in the event of an offensive'.[50]

Preparations began with orders to take aerial photographs of both the front line and the hinterland in order to identify strengths and weaknesses in the enemy's system of defences. These would be used to draw up a plan of attack. In the days and hours just before the offensive, new aerial photographs would be taken to assess the extent of the artillery's success in eliminating enemy trenches, barbed-wire barriers and artillery batteries. This enabled final adjustments to be made to the plan of attack and made it possible for any supplementary instructions to be given to the artillery. One striking example of this type of operation was that of French preparations for an attack on Fort Douaumont near Verdun on 22 May 1916.[51] Approximately 40 minutes before the offensive, a French aircrew took photographs of the Germans' fortifications. The glass-plate negatives were quickly developed and prints were then transferred by air to headquarters. A few minutes before the signal for attack, the plan was adjusted in order to avoid certain German zones that had been insufficiently destroyed and thus from which resistance could still be expected. A precondition for these types of mission was an efficiently operating aerial photography unit that – not least – was capable of developing negatives at speed.

Finally, aerial photography was employed during the offensive in order to determine how successful a bombardment had been and to identify new supply routes and artillery positions.[52]

After the offensive, it was important to verify accurate new positions as quickly as possible,[53] sometimes even by using special location panels on the ground. The fact was that the new front line could end up in shell craters or in wire entanglements within fire or communication trenches.[54] Aerial photographs could also be used to anticipate possible counterattacks. With that in mind, particular attention was paid to the hinterland in order to identify places where concealed fortifications might be located.

GETTING WIND OF THE ENEMY'S INTENTIONS

Another of aerial photography's applications was to detect preparations for enemy action. The front and rear lines were photographed at regular intervals to gauge the opponent's intentions. After all, knowing where and when enemy activity would occur was of vital importance. This was deduced from a number of factors: increased numbers of troops on the front line, more trenches for communications and launching attacks ('jumping off trenches'), the construction of new airfields, roads and railway tracks, and so on. Each change might herald an impending enemy offensive. Not only was it important to detect these changes, but it was also necessary to make the correct interpretation. This was not always a straightforward matter, because it was to the enemy's advantage always to maintain the element of surprise. As far as possible, preparations were kept concealed while also misleading the enemy to the greatest possible extent.

→ **Belgian aerial photograph of a downed German Albatros.**

↓ **Belgian aerial photograph used for debriefing purposes following an assault launched on a fortified position close to Mangelare.**

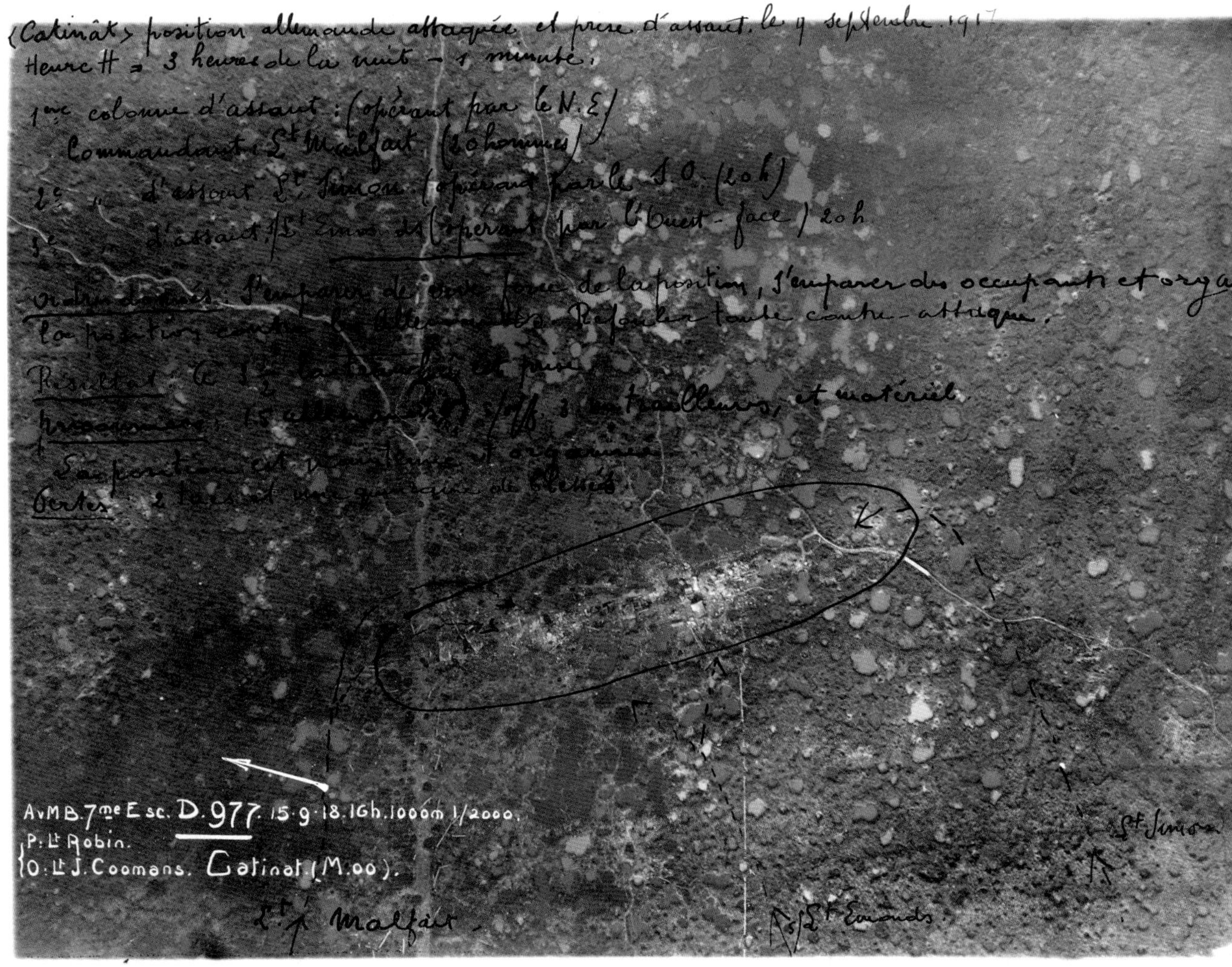

OTHER USES

A small number of aerial photographs were not associated with any of the aforementioned categories. On occasion, aerial observers would take photographs of crashed enemy aircraft as proof of an aerial victory, which the military command could then acknowledge. If an enemy fighter crash landed on home turf, then, naturally enough, the ground troops there would be able to confirm the fact. However, this was not the case when an aeroplane was shot down over enemy territory, and reliance on the testimony of other pilots was deemed insufficient. Aerial photography was able to supply a definitive answer in such instances, as in the case of the German Albatros brought down by the Belgian air ace Adjutant André De Meulemeester on 4 November 1917. The aircraft went down behind German lines on the Yser front. The aerial photograph that the Belgian observer Lieutenant Robin and his pilot, Lieutenant Heyvaert, made on the very same day provided the evidence for official recognition of the fighter pilot's aerial victory.[55]

Yet another instance was the use of aerial photographs to evaluate an offensive. Just such a photograph taken on 15 September 1918 near Mangelare to the north-east of Bikschote was annotated to indicate and describe the result of a small-scale Belgian infantry attack mounted on the previous 9 September. The target had been a fortified position with bunkers in the midst of a ravaged landscape of craters. The Belgians attacked in three groups, each numbering twenty men, and the routes they took were plotted on the aerial photograph. The planned objectives were achieved – the position was captured and reorganised as a new position of their own; counter-attacks were repulsed – at the cost of two fatalities and twelve casualties. The annotated aerial photograph was used for debriefing purposes.

Interpretation

During the First World War aerial photographs were used and interpreted differently from how they might be handled today. The images were originally taken within the context of an exclusively military assignment. Nowadays we scrutinise them within the context of archaeological and historical research, and they can also be used as source material when studying cultural and national heritage.

STAGES OF ANALYSIS

The observer's role was not at an end once the reconnaissance aircraft had landed. He would have been responsible for the first interpretation of the aerial photographs, thus simplifying the work of the photographic services team on the ground. The observer helped in identifying the photographed terrain.[56] Further interpretation went on to determine the nature, value and importance of the enemy's field defences. Studies were sometimes conducted in respect of one's own trench system.

Immediately after landing, the negatives were developed and contact prints made, rinsed and dried. Afterwards, the photographed area was identified and the print was annotated.

During the First World War, the analysis of an aerial photograph progressed through four stages.[57] First, the photograph was 'read'. All of its details, natural or man-made, were scrutinised. This was then followed by an analysis or investigation of the importance and significance of those details. Significant features were subsequently indicated on topographical maps as precisely as possible. It was only once this had been done that analysts proceeded to the final and most important stage: the interpretation and review of all of the information obtained within the general context of the situation at the front.[58] A French manual from 1921 reduced these four stages to three: seeking out and clarifying the details, transferring the data to a topographical map, and sketching or indicating findings on the aerial photograph itself. An attempt to discern the enemy's intentions would be made on the basis of analytical comments.[59] Another manual summarises the process as one of interpretation, resitution and utilisation.[60]

In practice, aerial photographs were studied using a magnifying glass.[61] The entire surface of the photograph was scanned, and photographs taken on different dates were compared.[62] The photographed terrain was then identified in relation to a topographical map, which made it possible to gauge the scale of the photograph. The direction of the sun was important for determining the height of the terrain and of the features present on it connected with warfare. This was achieved by measuring shadow lengths. Instead of displaying north at the top of a photograph – as on a map – the image was turned so that the shadows shown on it pointed towards the photographic interpreter.[63] The interpreter transferred the information to tracing paper using a series of agreed symbols. These interpretations could then be placed on top of new photographs of the same area at a later stage, which made it easy to spot any differences. Afterwards, the interpretations were passed to the cartographic section, which transferred the data on to new artillery and trench maps.

Orienting a photograph so that its shadows point towards the viewer enables its areas of elevation or depression to be read correctly.[64] Photographs in the second part of this book have been oriented with the publication's design in mind and according to features in photographs that we have chosen to emphasise. The direction of the sun can be deduced from the shadows that are cast; it may sometimes help the reader if he or she views the photographs in the correct orientation as was used for interpretation. The example above shows the same photograph twice but with a rotation of 180 degrees in one instance. The image is of the British–German front at Sint-Elooi, a sector where tunnels had been dug repeatedly below enemy positions, filled with explosives and then detonated. The explosions caused deep mine craters up to 60 metres across. The left print shows north at the top as on a map. However, because of this orientation, the shadows point away from the viewer,

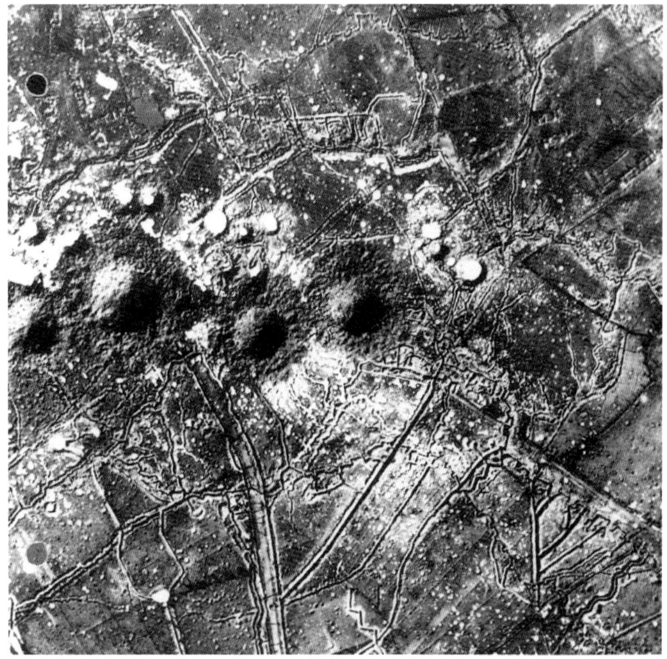

↑
German aerial photograph of mine craters at Sint-Elooi. The photograph's orientation is to the north; consequently, the shadows point away from the viewer and give a false impression of the terrain.

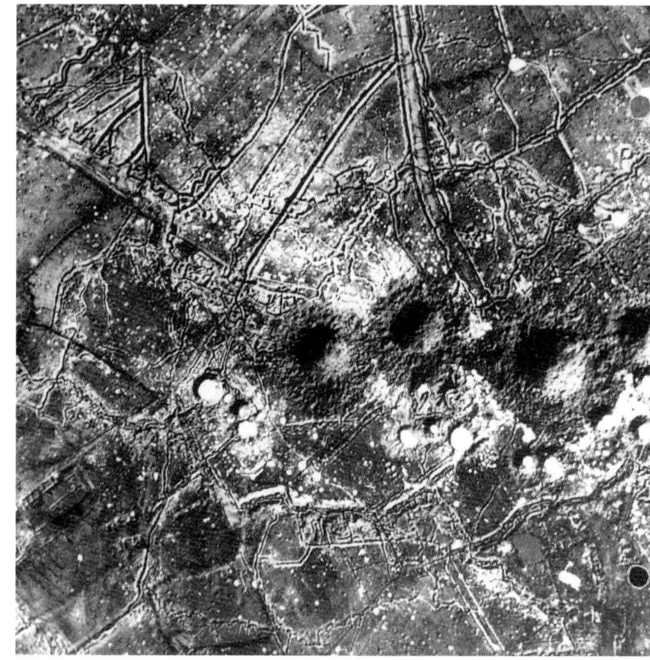

↑
The same aerial photograph correctly oriented. The shadows point towards the viewer, showing the cratered landscape at Sint-Elooi after the mine explosions of 27 March 1916.

→
Members of an RAF Mobile Photographic Section washing glass-plate negatives in a stream.

→
Drying aerial photograph prints.

giving us the impression of a series of small mounds or bulges in the landscape. In the right print, the shadows point towards the viewer. This allows us to focus clearly on the large, circular craters in the picture.

CAMOUFLAGE AND STEREOSCOPY

The intensity of photo-reconnaissance missions from 1915 onwards compelled ground troops to conceal their intentions and positions to the greatest possible extent. This made it essential for them to adopt camouflage techniques. One of the simplest and most efficient of these was to take up position next to existing rows of trees: the shade of trees acted as camouflage for anything beneath.[65] As far as possible, artillery batteries and other fieldworks were covered with vegetation, painted canvas or debris. Fake positions and fieldworks were also simulated.

A new technique was introduced in order to win the increasingly intense 'battle' between aerial reconnaissance above and the camouflage below: stereoscopy. This was not a First World War invention; however, it was innovatory as far as its use in aerial photography was concerned.

Early stereo photographs on the ground were usually taken using a camera with two lenses side by side in order to create an overlapping section between the two images.[66] Owing to the high altitude at which the aircraft flew, such a system was not feasible in flight. Instead, an interval was taken between two consecutive shots to achieve partially overlapping images by that means. The two-dimensional plane of the vertical photograph would then take on a three-dimensional appearance. Elevations and depressions were accentuated in the stereoscope by exaggerating the contours at ground level.[67] A British manual explained that the best results were to be gained if there was an overlap between two photographs of approximately two to three inches.[68] The surface relief would not appear when the overlap was less than this, while, if it were any greater, the surface relief would be out of proportion.

The time required between the two exposures was calculated through the use of tables and diagrams.[69] The flying altitude, the camera's focal length, the negative's dimensions and the aircraft's flight speed all had to be taken into account. Consequently, 6 seconds was the ideal overlap time between two exposures when using a 50-cm camera at an altitude of 1,000 metres and at a speed of 140 km per hour.

Subsequently, the two photographs also required analysis using a stereoscope. An American manual provided the following instructions: '(1) Superpose the common parts of the two photos. (2) Find the line connecting centres of the two photos (prick with pin, if necessary). (3) Keep this line continuous. (4) Separate the two photos on above line to a distance equal to that between the eyes. (5) Place the stereoscope (adjusted as to separation) upon the photos, parallel to line of centres, with parts to be studied arranged symmetrically in the two eyepieces. (6) Place the eyes on the stereoscope and raise them until the two images (at first seen separately) resolve into one, giving effect of relief.'[70] This approach was followed by all aerial photography services and is described in many manuals.[71] An interesting footnote to this concerns the creation of the first Belgian stereoscope, which was made using material that came from a crashed aeroplane. Two magnifying lenses were attached to a copper tube from the fuel tank. The first Belgian stereoscope manufactured on a large scale was built using just such rudimentary components.[72]

The role played by stereoscopy in the First World War cannot be underestimated. After the war, magazines such as *Popular Mechanics* even went so far as to describe it as the 'deadliest weapon in the war'.[73]

↓ **According to an American handbook the two overlapping photographs have to be held in this position in order to provide a stereoscopic view.**

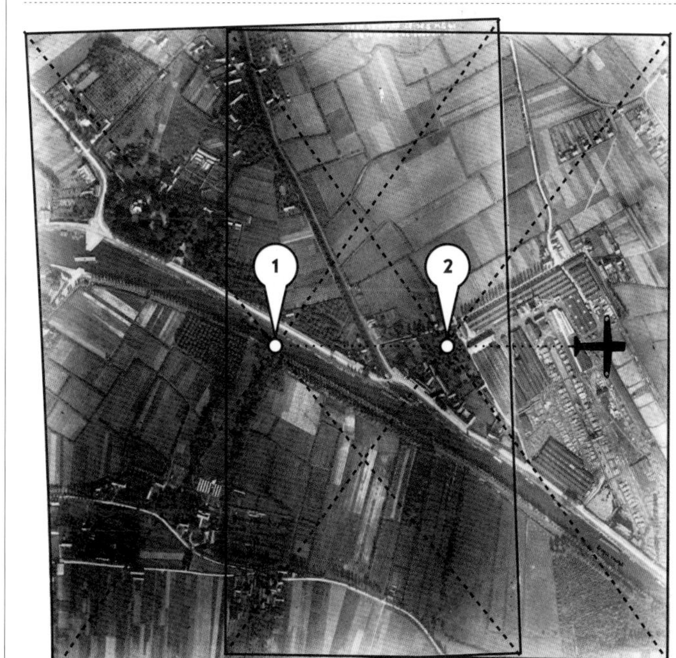

Multi-layered landscapes

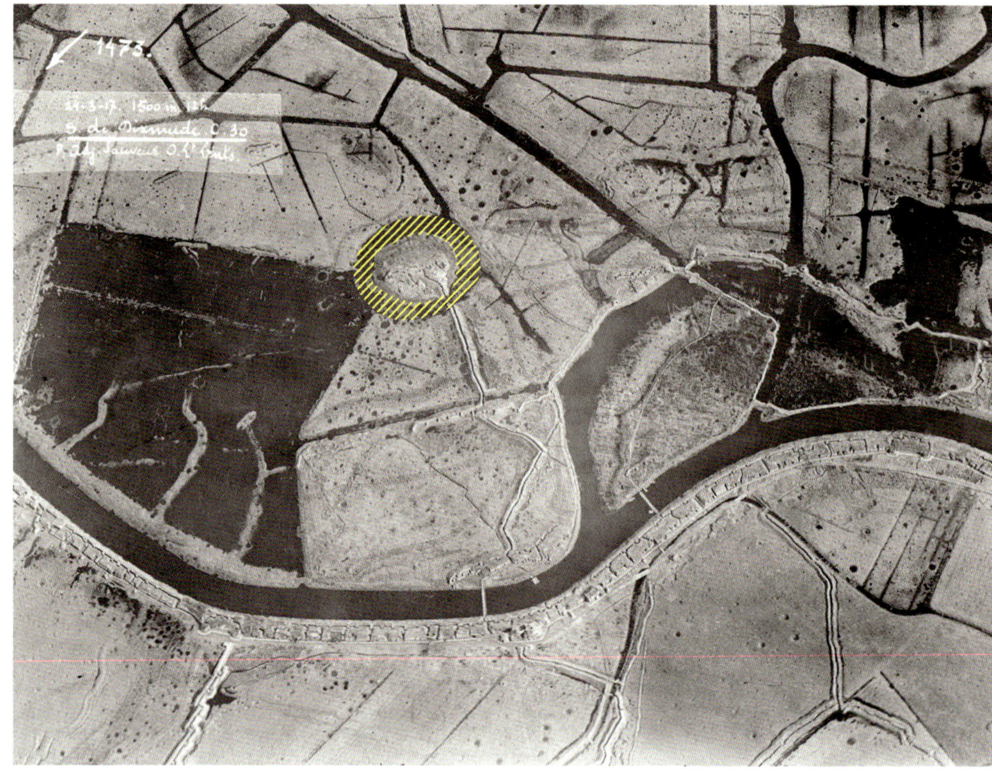

Archaeological landscape

MEDIEVAL MOATED SITE

When First World War aerial photos are examined in detail, it becomes clear that these sources provide us with a multi-layered landscape. The aerial photographs show much more than the obvious features of a military landscape – they reveal how different aspects of the landscape interact with each other and are interwoven. They allow us, for example, to detect hitherto unknown archaeological sites, offering 'a view which registers a palimpsest of past activities', as Nicholas Saunders points out.[1]

A new source

If the photographs are studied closely, archaeological sites can be discovered hidden in the fields. However, because of the high altitude at which the reconnaissance normally took place – mostly between 2 and 5 km – recognising these archaeological traces is far from easy. On the other hand, the continual artillery fire destroyed the field patterns. This fact, combined with the deliberate inundation of some of the rivers (such as the Yser) for strategic purposes, provides ideal circumstances for the detection of watermarks. These archaeological features can be identified because of the different levels of humidity in places where ditches or moats were once situated. In the area covered by this book, literally hundreds of medieval moated sites can be detected.[2] This is important because many of them were destroyed during the war and are now no longer visible. Medieval and post-medieval city walls and fortifications can also be studied in many aerial photographs.

A second important asset of the aerial photographs is their importance in studying the landscape at the beginning of the last century. In most cases, the early aerial photographs of the war are the oldest aerial photos of these landscapes. They can show us what the countryside looked like a century ago more effectively than maps. They reveal the terrain in all its aspects and inform us in great detail about its every feature: its structures, land use, development, economic and aesthetic values. They also reveal traces of older field systems. It can be claimed that these pictures are a forgotten – and therefore new – source for landscape specialists.[3] This pre-1914 landscape can be best seen in the earlier pictures, dating before the major offensive actions, which were accompanied by abundant artillery barrages. These bombardments gradually forced the pre-1914 aspect into the background, while, in some places, everything was simply reduced to a lunar landscape.

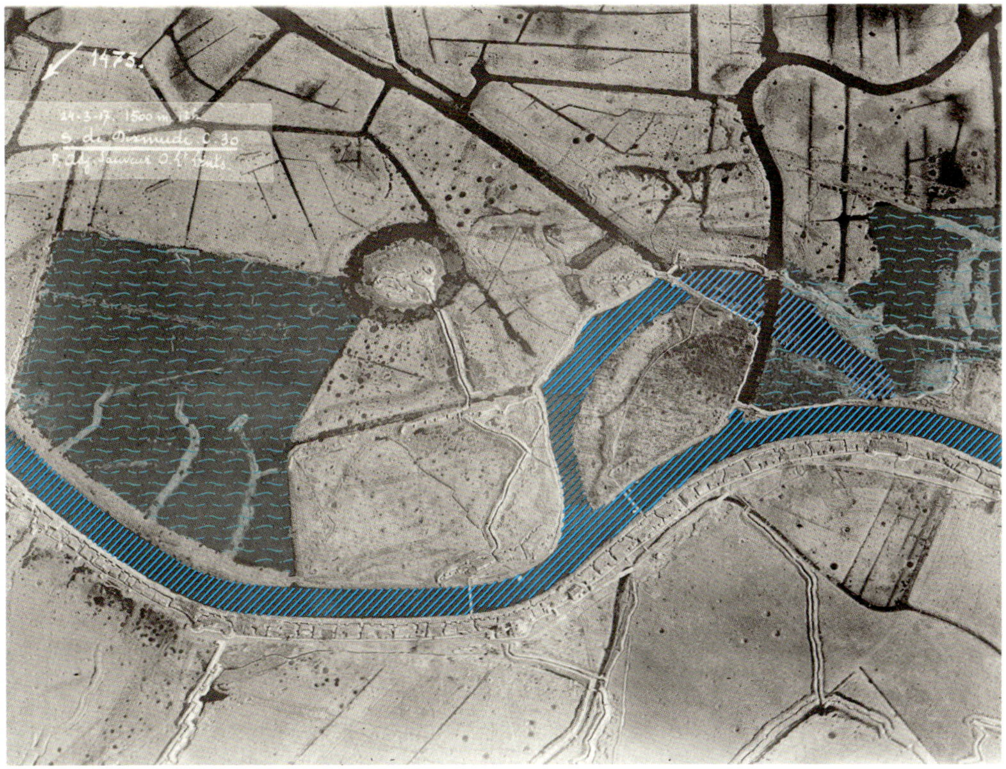

↑
Natural landscape

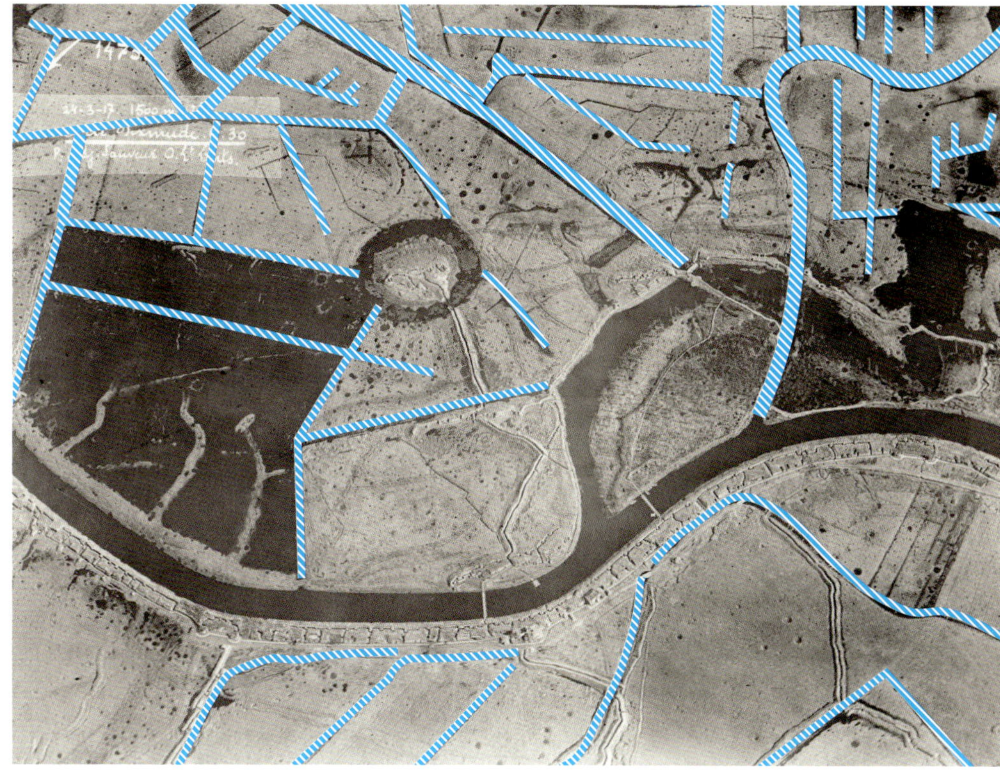

↑
Historical landscape

NATURAL WATERCOURSE

DRAINAGE CHANNELS

INUNDATED AREA

Reading aerial photographs

When we look at aerial photographs from the First World War, we can see straight away the more recent nature of the vast majority of the visible features and their connection with the war. This military landscape extended over an important part of Europe. The main components (ubiquitous trench lines, belts of barbed wire and bunkers) are the same, but regional differences can be observed. Two different entrenchment systems can be seen, separated only by a small stretch of land in-between: no-man's-land. Several successive lines of defence were constructed, linked by communication trenches. At first sight, this complex seems to have been laid down in a random manner. However, if we look more closely, certain patterns and practices can be noted. Early developments of front-line systems are connected to the pre-war features in the landscape, such as waterways, woods and ridges. On a much more detailed level, they are also defined by roads, houses and farm buildings, ditches, hedges and rows of trees. When we focus on those areas further away from the front line, we can observe artillery zones, scattered with gun pits and camouflaged positions. Military camps, railways, ammunition dumps, railway stations and aerodromes make up the majority of visible features.

The interaction between these layers is visible on an aerial photograph taken on 14 March 1917, just south of the Belgian town of Diksmuide. In the centre of the photograph a medieval moated site can be observed (the *archaeological* landscape). The large circular moat is filled with water and immediately draws the viewer's eye. The Yser meanders through the foreground, and the photograph shows us what the landscape looked like at the beginning of the twentieth century (the *natural* landscape). Field and property boundaries are clearly visible and reflect a post-medieval rural landscape (the *historical* landscape). When the photograph is examined closely, many military features can be identified (the *military* landscape). The photograph provides an oblique aerial view of the Belgian front-line trenches on the west bank of the Yser. Some advanced listening posts on the other bank of the river are discernible – these were reached by a number of wooden bridges and small rafts that were used to ferry soldiers to the opposite side of the river. The German front line is located just east of the area shown in the photograph. The military landscape is literally laid on top of the natural, archaeological and historical landscapes. Trenches are, for instance, dug on top of

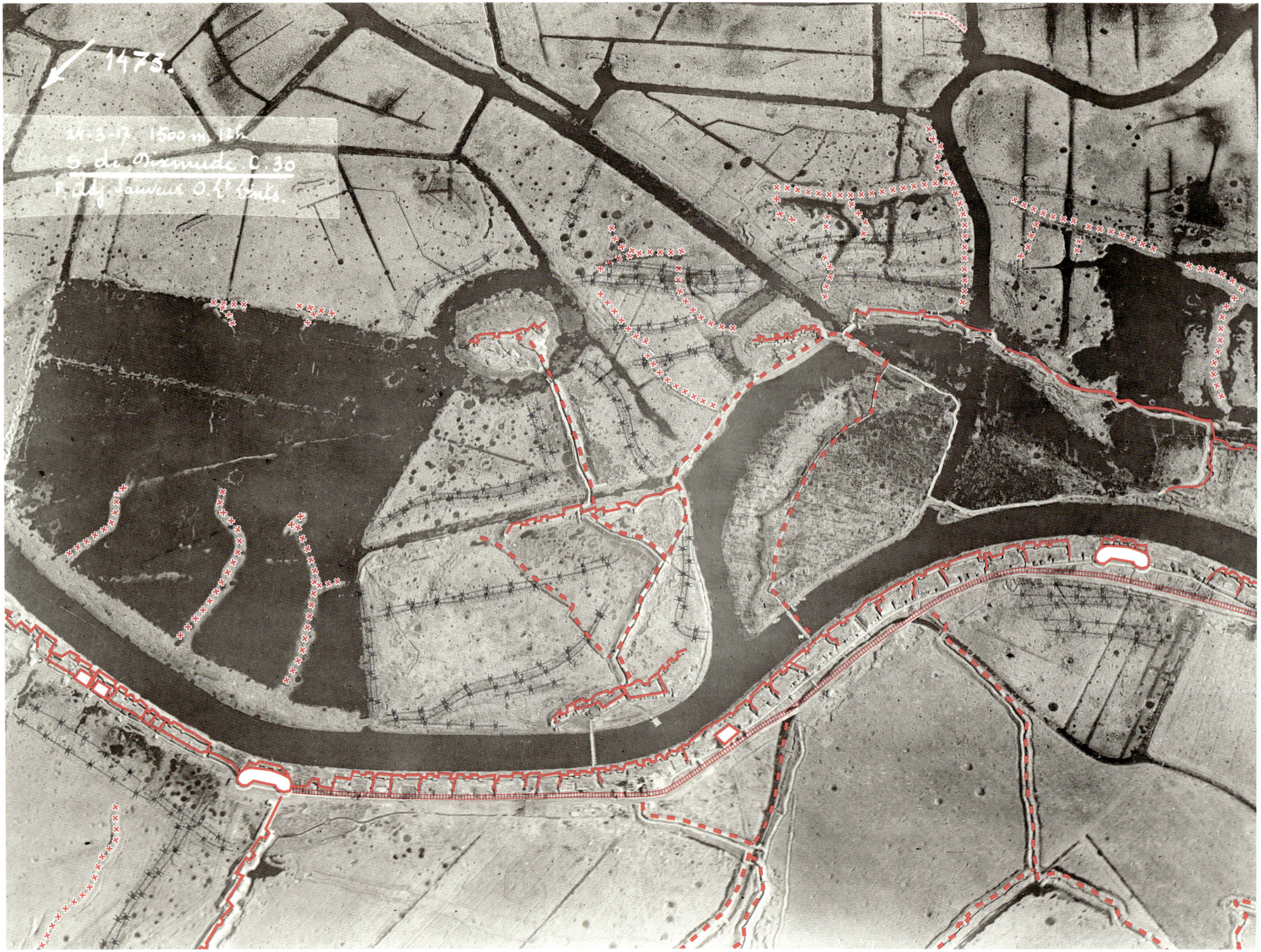

↑
Military landscape

FIRE TRENCHES

COMMUNICATION TRENCHES

ABANDONED TRENCHES

BARBED WIRE

BUNKER OR SHELTER

NARROW-GAUGE RAILWAY

the archaeological site – because the latter forms an elevated position in the flat landscape – and in relation to the river, which formed a natural line of defence.

Reading aerial photographs and interpreting the traces visible on them often requires specialised knowledge and an understanding of landscapes and military field defences. The case studies in the second part of this book focus on the in-depth reading and interpretation of aerial photographs. However, because of its complexity and because few people have experience of this approach to historical aerial photographs, this needs some introduction. This part of the book hints at the diversity of information that can be gathered from the images and provides some basic interpretative keys for reading the natural, historical and military layers of the landscape.

Oblique aerial photograph of Polygon Wood, early 1915 **(see also pp. 6-7)**

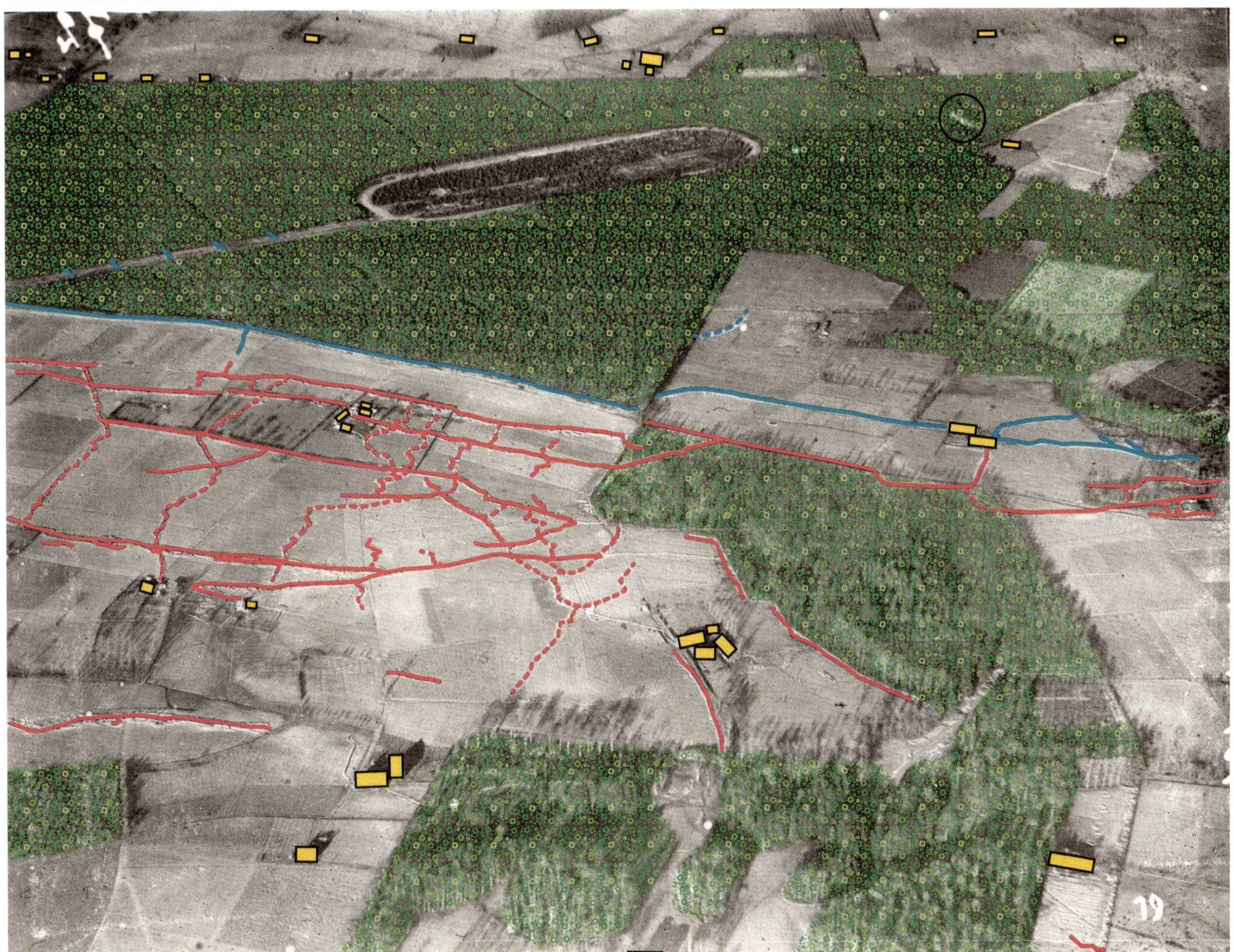

Reading the landscape

A German aerial photograph (early 1915) shows the area between Zonnebeke and Geluveld, two villages east of Ypres. The oblique image is one of the earliest aerial photographs of this region and provides a unique insight into the pre-war landscape of the Ypres Salient. Although many military features are already visible in the image, the landscape remains almost intact. The higher ridges around Ypres were still largely wooded when the war broke out. The large wood in the background is Polygon Wood (Polygoonbos), a small remnant (70 ha) of the much larger 'Nonnebossen' area of woodland that was reclaimed for agriculture at the beginning of the nineteenth century. The wood was first employed as a military training area during the Dutch period. After Belgian independence a shooting stand with an earthen ramp to catch bullets and a large oval horse-racing track were added. The latter was used by the equestrian school of the Belgian cavalry, which had been based at Ypres since 1860. In the foreground is one of many landscaped gardens that were laid out around the nineteenth-century country houses of the elite. Château Polderhoek is one of more than thirty country estates that were built between the end of the eighteenth century and 1900 in the Ypres area. Following the French Revolution, the monastic lands and properties were confiscated and sold to a wealthy new industrial elite. On the northern edge of the château's park runs the small brook known as the Reutelbeek. The Polygoonbeek has its source on the eastern edge of Polygon Wood. Most trees in the Polygon Wood are conifers, while most trees in and around Château Polderhoek are deciduous. The front lines seen here were established from 11 November 1914 onwards, in the final phase of the First Battle of Ypres (19 October – 22 November 1914). Allied troops (first British, up to 11 November 1914, then French, and then British again from early April 1915) dug a line of rudimentary trenches along the edges of the wood, and used its cover to reach this front line. Their German opponents, on the other hand, constructed a more elaborate network of fire and communication trenches on the open slopes to the south of the wood.

GERMAN TRENCHES

ALLIED TRENCHES

WOOD

BUILDING

Reading the war landscape

As soon as the war of movement became a war of entrenchment, the landscape in the western part of Belgium became a part of operations. The topography of the battlefields helped shape the conflict. The trench warfare of the flat polder landscape between Nieuwpoort and Diksmuide is different in every way from the field defences of the landscape near Ypres with its small ridges and hills. Moreover, on a micro level the pre-war landscape was optimally used and adapted for military purposes. Trenches were often concealed in woods and behind hedges. Higher ground was extremely valuable for observation purposes. Barracks were constructed under the protective cover of trees and gun emplacements were positioned behind ridges to conceal them from the enemy's trenches. The opposite is true as well – four years of intense trench warfare also shaped the landscape. Gradually, the pre-war landscape was destroyed, and villages, trees and cultivated fields disappeared under the welter of intensive artillery fire.

By the end of 1914 the entire landscape along the Western Front between the North Sea and the Franco-Swiss border was militarised. On both sides of a narrow no-man's-land two almost continuous networks of field defences were constructed. An example of such a network of trenches can be detected on an aerial photograph taken north of Hollebeke on 28 February 1915 (see pp. 39, 41). A German photographic interpreter annotated the photograph, marking the Allied and German front-line trenches as dotted lines, with the no-man's-land located between them. Château Mahieu, an ostentatious country estate built between 1901 and 1903, and the landscaped gardens around it, dominate the foreground. During the war Allied soldiers nicknamed the house the 'White Château' because of the distinctive white sandstone used for its walls. Kilometres of trenches were cut through the rural countryside, often carefully located behind hedges and rows of trees. The dark shadow in the centre of the trenches shows that the trenches have been dug deep into the soil. The light shade of the excavated earth, by contrast, indicates that many of them have only recently been constructed and are not yet overgrown with weeds and grasses. On the right-hand side of the image, the front crosses the former Ypres–Lys (Leie) Canal.

In 1915 and 1916 this military landscape expanded rapidly – more and more lines of trenches were dug and field defences, bunkers and artillery emplacements were ingeniously concealed. Gradually, the intensity of artillery fire also increased, destroying the pre-war landscape and field defences and turning it into a lunar-like landscape peppered with countless shell holes. This is a typical view of the battlefields starting from the summer of 1917. The preparatory artillery barrages for the Third Battle of Ypres, for example, transformed the landscape in a startling manner. This had, of course, an effect on the character of the war and the tactics and strategy deployed. Instead of making use of a network of trenches for defence, shell holes were occupied and converted into strongholds and used defence in depth.

Images of such devastated landscapes are even more difficult to read because every recognisable landmark has simply been erased. Houses and farms have been destroyed by the shelling, field boundaries and hedges have faded away and sometimes even roads can hardly be identified. The image below is a typical example. This German aerial photograph was taken in the northern part of the Ypres Salient on 10 September 1917, more than a month after the start of the Third Battle of Ypres. Thousands of shell holes scar the landscape and have turned it into a muddy swamp. A number of large concrete pillboxes have survived the shelling. Small tracks lead from one bunker to another, indicating they are occupied by troops. Because of the high water level, only shallow trenches can be dug into the soil over short stretches. In the centre of the photograph, a German photographic interpreter has circled a crashed aircraft.

↑
The 'White Château', 1915.

↓
Typical aerial photograph of the Ypres Salient during the Third Battle of Ypres, 10 September 1917.

→
Australian troops in the trenches, Garter Point, 27 September 1917.

It is not only near the front lines that the military layer is visible. The industrial scale of the conflict needed a war machine to keep the front supplied. On both sides of the front line this military landscape extends over dozens of kilometres. Trenches, bunkers and gun pits gradually give way to barracks, hospitals, cemeteries, airfields, ammunition and storage dumps and to other, more unusual military features such as submarine and Zeppelin bases. A British aerial photograph taken on 2 April 1916 (see p. 43) shows the hinterland near Kruiseke, a hamlet just south-east of Geluveld. At this point in time the photographed area was located almost 7 km behind the German front line. The aerial photograph shows a lot of activity. Unsuccessful efforts are being made to conceal barracks by constructing them within small copses. Such efforts are being immediately undermined by the building of new military roads connecting the two groups of barracks. The roads and the building activity are instantly apparent because of the light shade of the raised earth. Dozens of artillery emplacements are more subtle features within the photograph. Many of these horseshoe-shaped earthen embankments and covered casemates are positioned close to or behind strips of woodland and hedges; an early attempt to provide them with camouflage. A German line of trenches runs from Kruiseke to Zandvoorde, its trace determined by the local topography or the altitude lines on a trench map. An 8-metre-wide wire entanglement is visible in front of this trench as a very subtle difference in tonality. Telephone and communication cables ensured that units were in touch with their commanders and that orders were passed on. To protect them against artillery fire they were buried in straight cable trenches.

A second aerial photograph (see p. 45) gives an oblique view of the activities behind the front line at Geluwe in the autumn of 1918. Geluwe was located behind German lines from the end of 1914 until the final offensive in 1918. When this aerial photograph was taken (late 1918) the front was 12 km away. The aerial photograph at first sight seems to show a completely deserted and abandoned village and landscape. This is a constant in aerial photography – because of the scale of the photographs and the flying altitude the human element recedes into the background. However, aerial photographs do in fact have very personal stories to tell. The evidence provided by German soldiers indicates the presence of a field hospital in a windmill, which was locally known as the 'Goemaeremolen'. The emblem of the Red Cross ideally served to protect hospitals from artillery fire and aerial bombardment. The most striking feature in the photograph is a German military cemetery. The 'Ehrenfriedhof Gheluwe' is located close to the civilian graveyard but is clearly separated from it. Two tracks lead directly from the hospital to the cemetery. Detailed photo-interpretation reveals that the cemetery was built in three phases, since it repeatedly proved to be too small to accommodate the numbers of soldiers dying from their injuries in the hospital. The oldest part of the hospital is located the furthest away from the road. All graves have large white crosses, while small plants and bushes decorate the cemetery. This part of the cemetery was carefully landscaped and attention was paid to symmetry. The first extension of the cemetery took place towards the road. These graves are grouped in rows of five, six or seven fallen soldiers. This extension soon proved insufficient and the area of the cemetery was doubled and a new access road was constructed. In a third extension, the soldiers are buried in rows of up to fifteen graves and are much more closely packed. The graves are much smaller and there are no longer any individual crosses marking the graves. The fourth part of the cemetery is not yet in use, but by looking at the large open space it is clear that many more casualties are expected. This is a different kind of aerial photo-interpretation – instead of identifying and dating military features it provides narratives about the people who are in some sense within the photographs. In this instance, what at first sight looks like an inconsequential aerial photograph in fact shows a changing attitude towards the burial of soldiers. Originally, a high degree of attention was given to the design of the cemetery as well as to the individual graves, but gradually this decreased as the number of burials increased.

Other parts of the image are also of interest, showing important military activity in the hinterland. Military roads, tracks and narrow-gauge railways crisscross the area around Geluwe, ensuring that stocks of ammunition, building materials and other supplies can be distributed to the front. Large numbers of prefabricated railway tracks are stacked up next to roads, ready to be assembled. Because of the high level of detail in this photograph, it is even possible to identify electricity and telegraph poles. Some of them lead towards a two-storey building close to the main road, which can be identified as a German power station.[4] A second mill, located towards the back of the photograph but nonetheless close to the front, was used as a German observation post. Although the village is located at some distance from the front, the buildings are in ruins. Besides some isolated shell holes, there are few traces of artillery fire to be seen. The village was evacuated between 30 June and 10 November 1917. From that moment onwards, the houses were pillaged and stripped for building materials and wood. Witnesses describe how houses had their roofs removed. The wood was used in the construction of field defences at the front and as firewood.[5] This oblique aerial photograph is also interesting from the perspective of the historical landscape. It shows a small relict landscape just south of the village centre. Each of the compact fields is surrounded by hedges and narrow bands of woodland; this was typical for the area around Ypres and is a remnant of the small-scale agriculture of the nineteenth century.

↑
German camouflaged artillery emplacement near Zandvoorde.

↓
Typical scene in the Ypres Salient showing large water-filled shell holes and a number of the sturdy pillboxes.

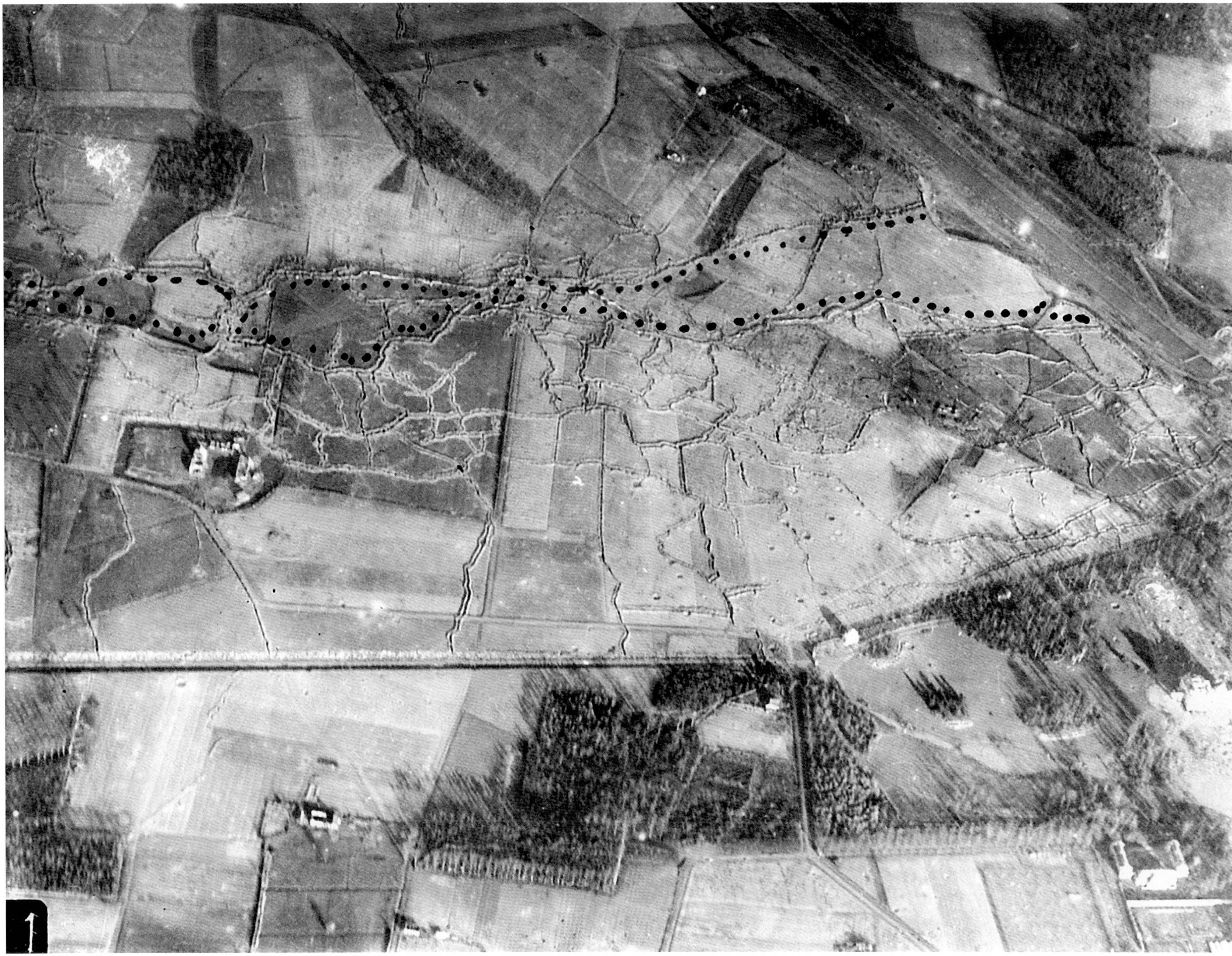

↑
Hollebeke. Front lines near the 'White Château' and the Ypres-Lys Canal.

Reading the landscape

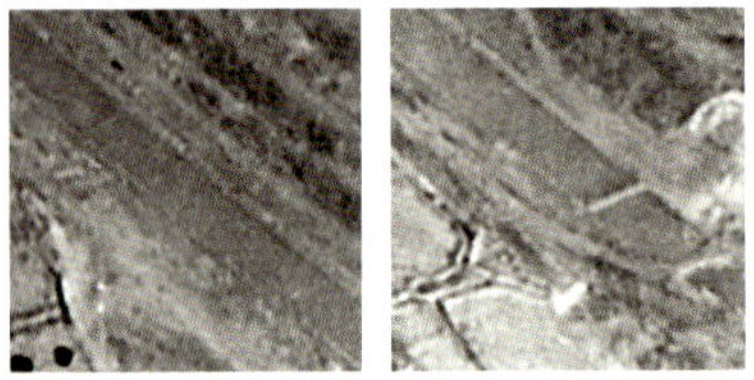

WATERWAYS → G2, H3

Topographical features such as rivers and waterways are easy to observe on aerial photos. Rivers tend to have a mainly irregular trace and a uniform dark, even black, shade; this is because water absorbs light and does not reflect it. Canals are identifiable by their linear nature, while smaller brooks and creeks have a sinuous course. Inundated ground appears as dark areas.

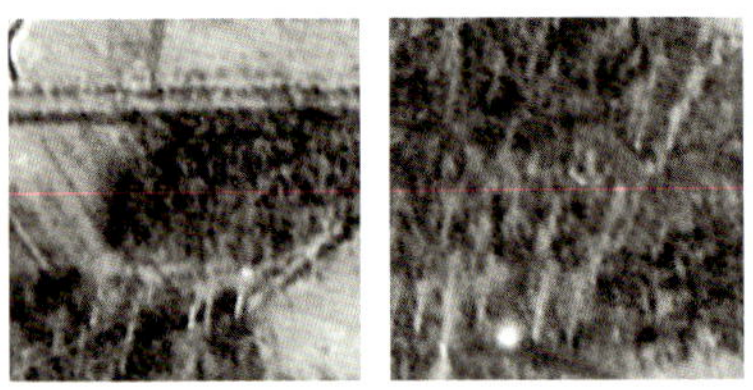

WOODS → E5, D6

Stretches of woodland can be easily identified on aerial photographs as a darker area. On large-scale photographs, the tops of individual trees can be seen. The best results are obtained when woodland areas are studied using photographs taken in winter or even during late autumn or early spring. At such times the foliage is less dense and some ground features may be visible.

FIELDS MEADOWS → B1, C4

Patchworks of fields and meadows can be seen everywhere in the aerial photographs. Their shade depends on the soil type and the vegetation growing there. In the areas close to the front line, agriculture was discontinued during the conflict (for obvious reasons). The fields were abandoned at the time of the first military actions and were not returned to agriculture until the front line moved further away, in some cases only four years later. The photographs show an interesting variety of field systems, property boundaries and landscape elements such as hedges, woods and willows as well as evidence of farming practices – manure heaps, haystacks and crops.

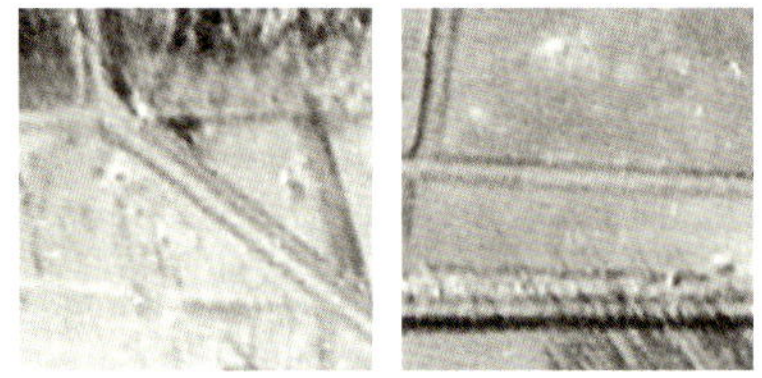

ROADS → F6, D4

Roads can be identified as pale lines on aerial photographs. In the western part of Belgium, they are often bordered by trees, the shadows of which are visible in the surrounding fields. On photographs of snow-covered landscapes, the roads are black. The snow in these photographs has melted as a result of heavy traffic. The configuration of the roads is very helpful in identifying the photographed area.

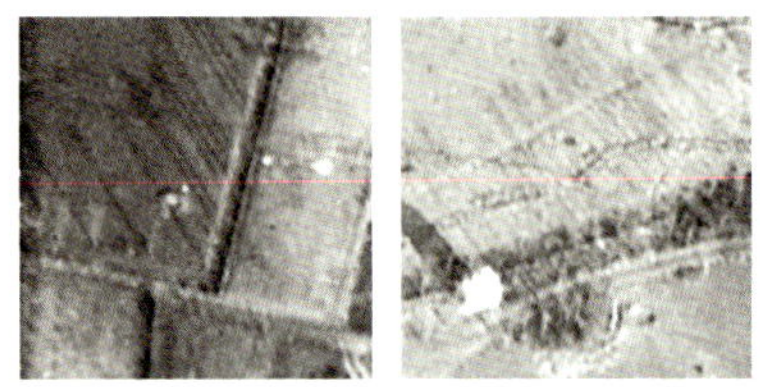

STANDS OF TREES AND HEDGES → A3, F4

On many aerial photographs, rows of trees, hedges and woods are visible and can be identified as dark linear features. Their shadows may be visible but should not be confused with the actual trees. Shadows of trees are an ideal feature for orienting the aerial photographs correctly. On a small-scale aerial photo, hedges should not be confused with water-filled field boundaries; both have a dark tone.

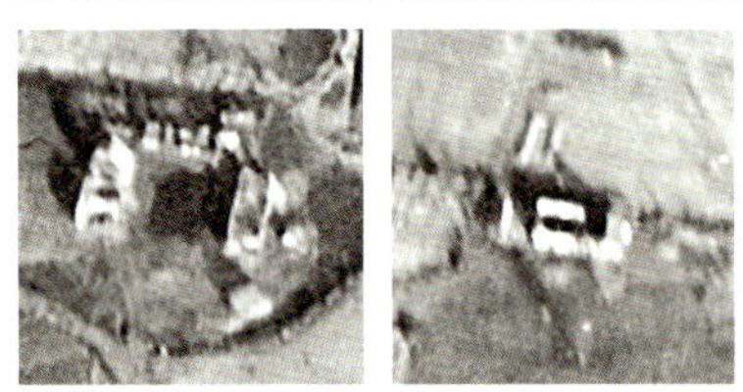

DWELLINGS → B3, C6

Dwellings can be observed as rectangular features, often with a saddle roof, one side of which is frequently illuminated by the sun while the other part is in the shade. In the areas around the front line, houses were a target for artillery fire because many bunkers were constructed inside them (as camouflage); basements were often used to house troops, too. As the war progressed, dwellings sustained ever more significant damage. Many of the rooftops simply disappeared and thus the houses became even more visible because of the white outlines of the (destroyed) walls.

Reading the war landscape

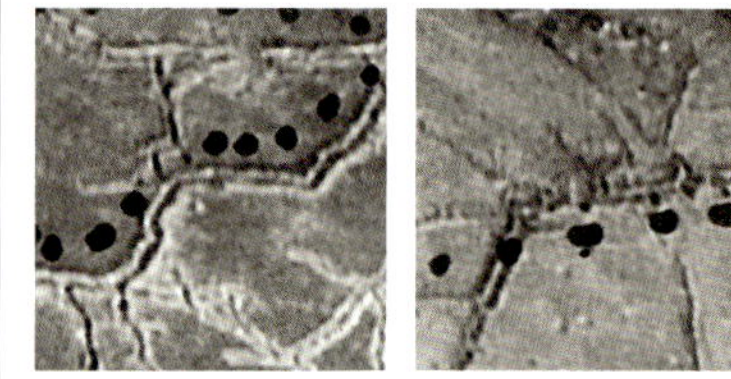

FIRE TRENCHES → C3, F2

The trace of a trench is outlined on an aerial photograph as a narrow dark line, cast in shadow, beside a bank of excavated earth, which has a lighter shade. Trenches can be spotted most easily in an aerial photograph if they are newly constructed because the contrast between the vegetation on the ground and the excavated earth is at its most defined. The longer trenches have been in use, the darker their tone becomes as the excavated earth becomes overgrown with vegetation. The shape and trace of trenches can vary a great deal. Trenches were built with alternating fire bays and traverses. Fire bays are the parts of a trench facing the enemy. Traverses, on the other hand, are the parts receding in the opposite direction. In this way, soldiers in a traversed trench were protected against fire from the flanks, while the effect of exploding shells was confined. Sometimes it was impossible to dig trenches into the soil. Where the water table was high, trenches were constructed as surface breastwork and were located almost entirely above ground.

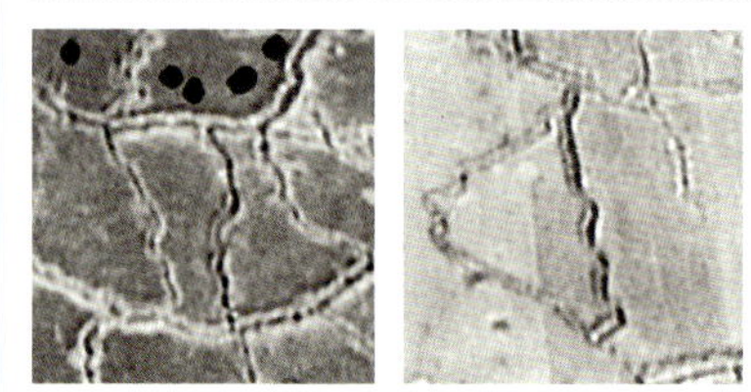

COMMUNICATION TRENCHES → C3, E4

Communication trenches link the fire trenches and connect them with zones in the rear, thereby tying together the whole system of field defences. The most typical communication trenches have a zigzag or sinuous trace.

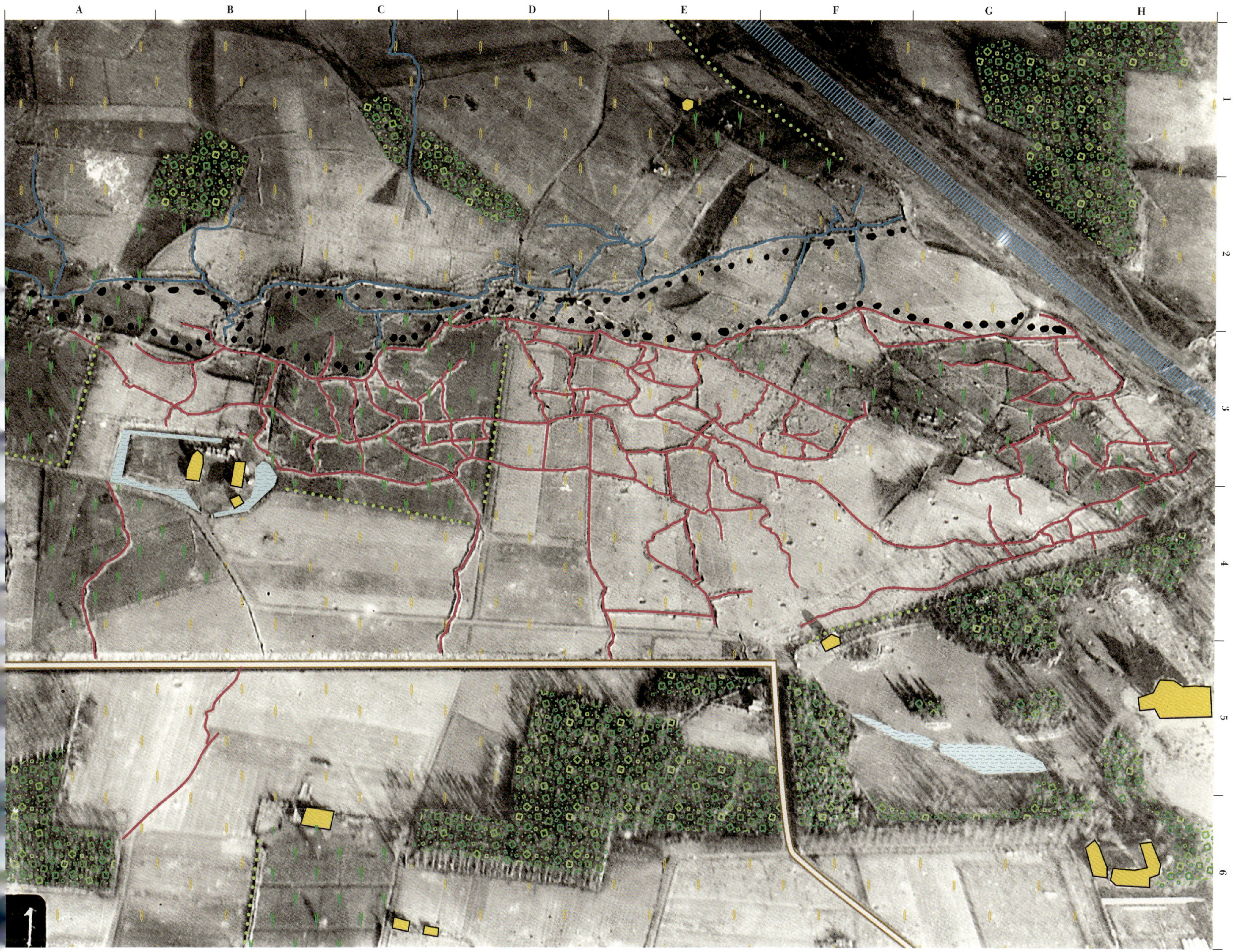

↑
Hollebeke. Front lines near the 'White Château' and the Ypres-Lys Canal.

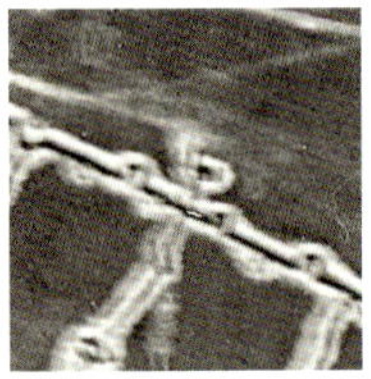
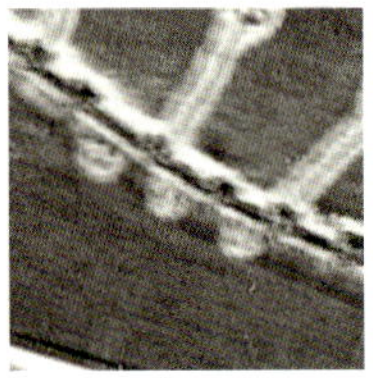

SHELTERS → E1, D1/E1

Along the front line, thousands of shelters were constructed to protect soldiers from artillery and gunfire. Some provided protection only from the rain, shrapnel and small shell fragments. In many instances, these are dug into the sides of trenches. It was possible to construct them completely underground, or in the breastwork of a trench. The best way of spotting them was by using oblique aerial photographs. On some of these, the entrances to the shelters can be observed.

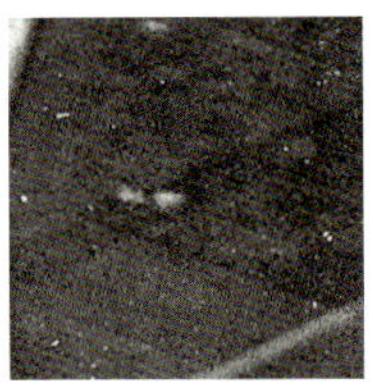

BARBED-WIRE ENTANGLEMENTS → D1, H2

Barbed wire is sometimes visible on an aerial photograph as a grey- or even black-shaded ribbon. Entanglements are often found in front of trenches. They are usually located parallel to the trenches but can also be found throughout the landscape at intervals between positions or trench lines. In aerial photographs, it is often possible to observe gaps in the wire, which provided access for working parties and counter-attacking troops. In rear areas, the presence of wire is often made visible by the different tonalities found in the aerial photographs, since, of course, farmers were unable to sow or harvest crops in these areas.

NEW MILITARY ROADS → C3

BURIED CABLES → A2

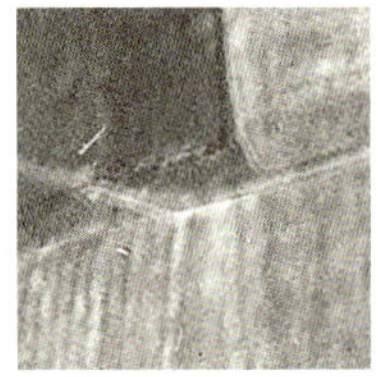

NARROW-GAUGE RAILWAYS → E3, G2

In order to supply and distribute a variety of goods (building materials, ammunition, water and food supplies, etc.) to the front as efficiently as possible, a network of narrow-gauge railways was set up. The visibility of such railways varies enormously. While in open fields they are easily legible because of their curved trace, where they have been constructed alongside an existing road, their detection is much more difficult and relies mainly on the availability of large-scale aerial photographs showing the rails and cross-beams.

BUNKERS → p. 44 D3, p. 36 B1

Many protective structures are made of concrete. These are called bunkers, concrete shelters or pillboxes. In general, these concrete structures can be identified – where they are not hidden from aerial observation – as bright squares or rectangles in stark contrast with the natural soil. Yet, many bunkers are effectively camouflaged. However, they become more visible when they are the target of artillery fire, destroying the camouflage and exposing the concrete walls and ceiling.

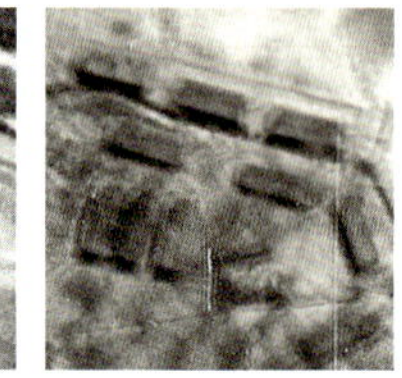

BARRACKS → H1, C2

Large military camps and quarters were impossible to camouflage as a result of the intense movement of ground troops. Therefore, barracks can be clearly seen in the aerial photographs as rectangular buildings with a regular layout. These constructions are mainly lightly coloured because they are made of wood. Barracks were often grouped together and the layout of such a group depended, in many cases, on field boundaries and the presence of hedges and stands of trees. Vegetation provides significant cover from aerial observation if the barracks are situated in its shadow. In many cases, woods were used to conceal groups of barracks, which were very hard to spot beneath dense foliage.

ARTILLERY EMPLACEMENTS → F3, G3

The massive amount of artillery fire was a prime characteristic of the First World War, and typical of a war of position. The first few kilometres of a region's defensive organisation are strewn with very diverse artillery emplacements forming a network of batteries. Sometimes a battery of heavy artillery was fired in the open without any field defences. However, in the aerial photographs a large number of gun pits can be detected.
The least developed and therefore most basic type of artillery emplacement consists of open gun positions. Many of them take the form of a horseshoe and are arranged in batteries of up to six emplacements. Another type consists of covered gun emplacements. Usually, these are well camouflaged and covered with a trapezoidal casemate made of earth and probably wooden beams and girders.

→
German camp between Nieuw-Kruiseke and Oud-Kruiseke.

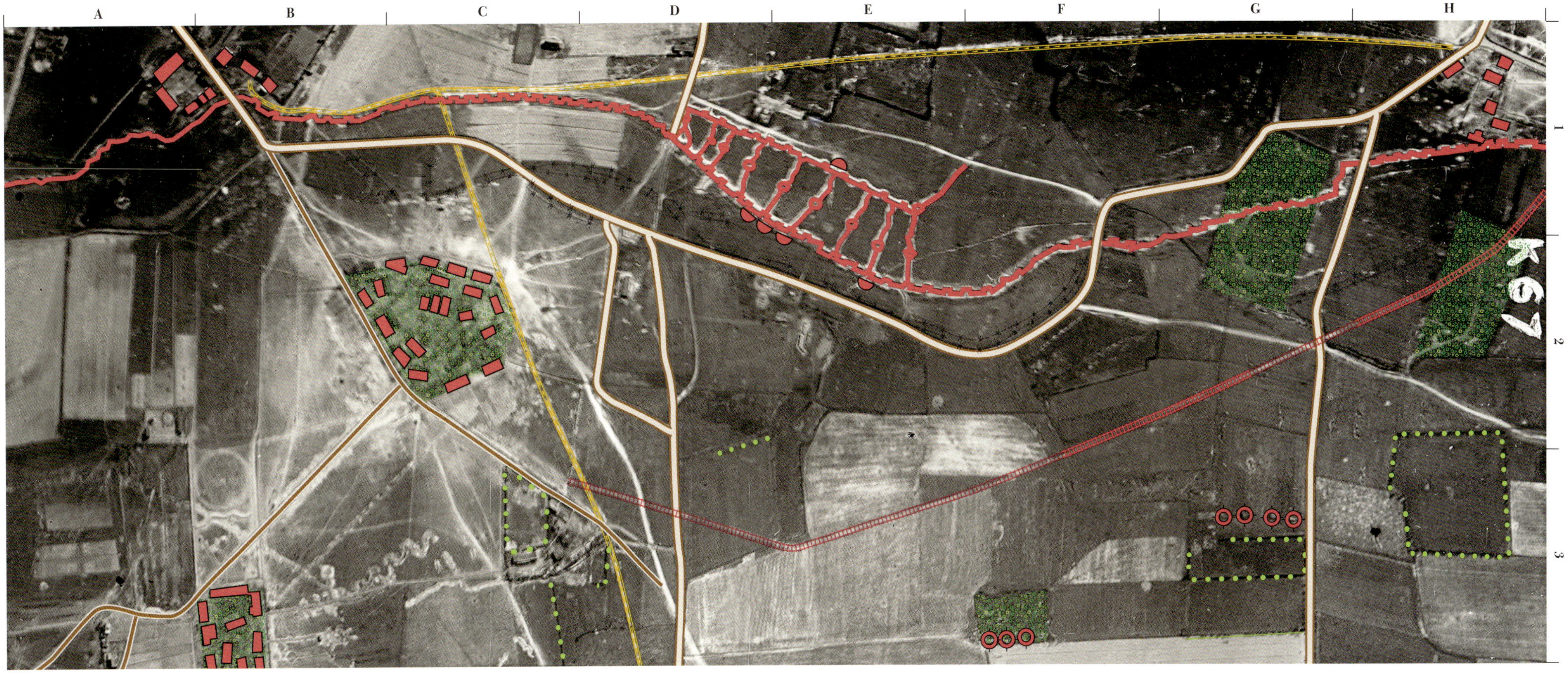
A
B
C
D
E
F
G
H
1
2
3
K67

1
2
3
K67

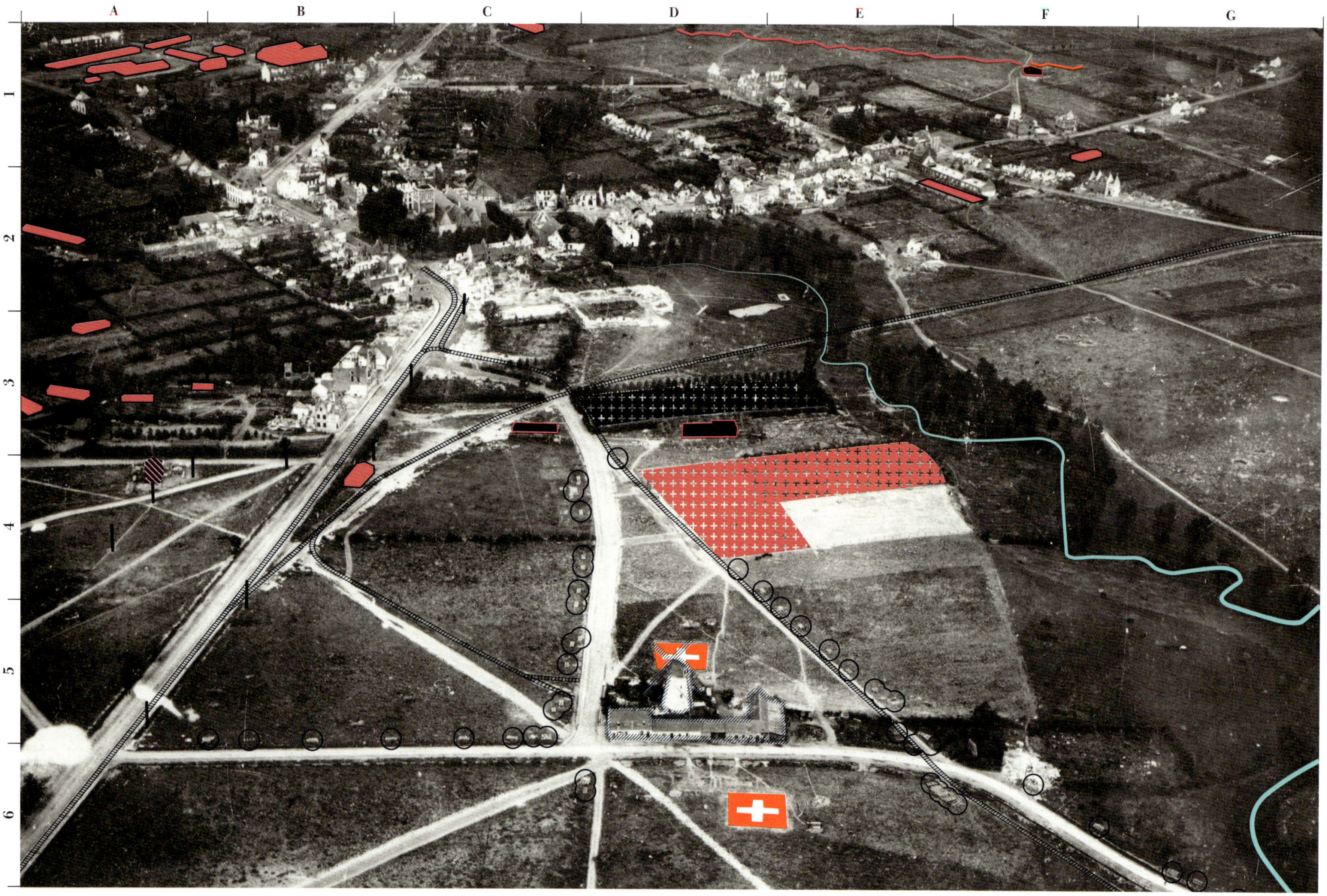

	SHED OR BARRACKS	→ A1
	BUNKER	→ C3
	ELECTRICITY AND TELEGRAPH POLES	→ A4
	GERMAN ELECTRICITY STATION	→ A4
	CIVIL CEMETERY	→ D3
	MILITARY CEMETERY	→ D4
	NARROW-GAUGE RAILWAY	→ B4
	GOEMAEREMOLEN (MILL)	→ D5
	STREAM	→ F4
	GROUND MARKINGS OF FIELD HOSPITAL	→ E6
	MATERIALS FOR NARROW-GAUGE RAILWAY UNDER CONSTRUCTION	→ C5

←
Goemaeremolen, taken on 9 May 1917,
before it was used as a field hospital.

‹←
German military cemetery in Geluwe –
the Goemaeremolen (mill) is visible in the distance.

↑
Oblique aerial photograph, Geluwe 1918.

2

THE GREAT WAR SEEN FROM THE AIR

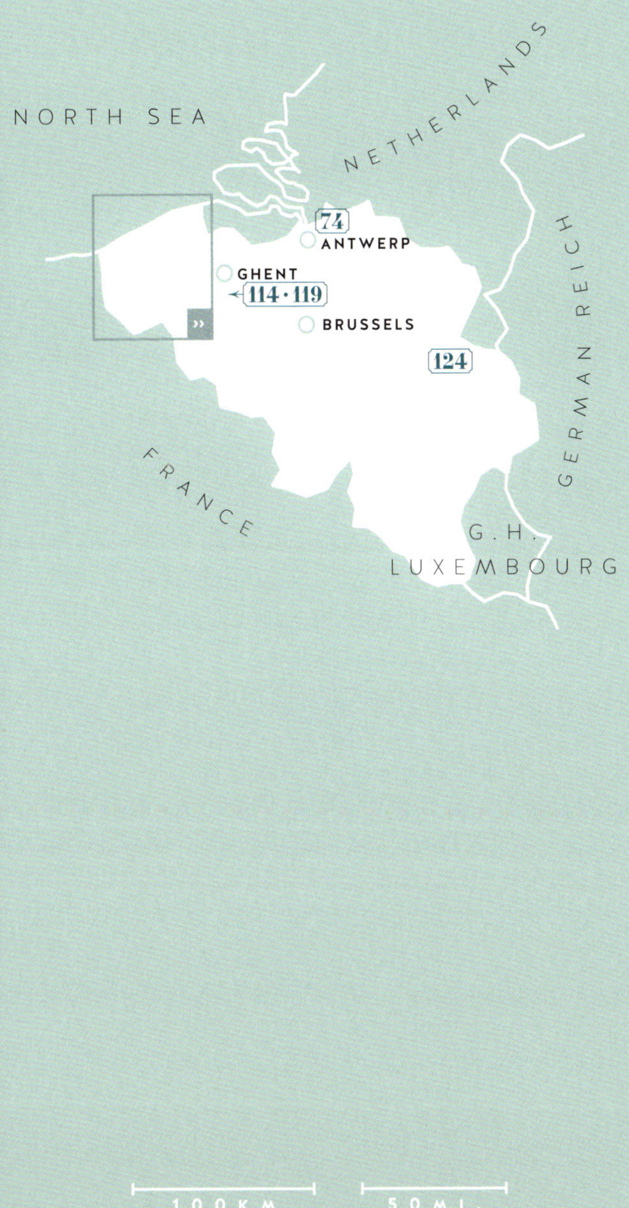

› BELGIUM ‹

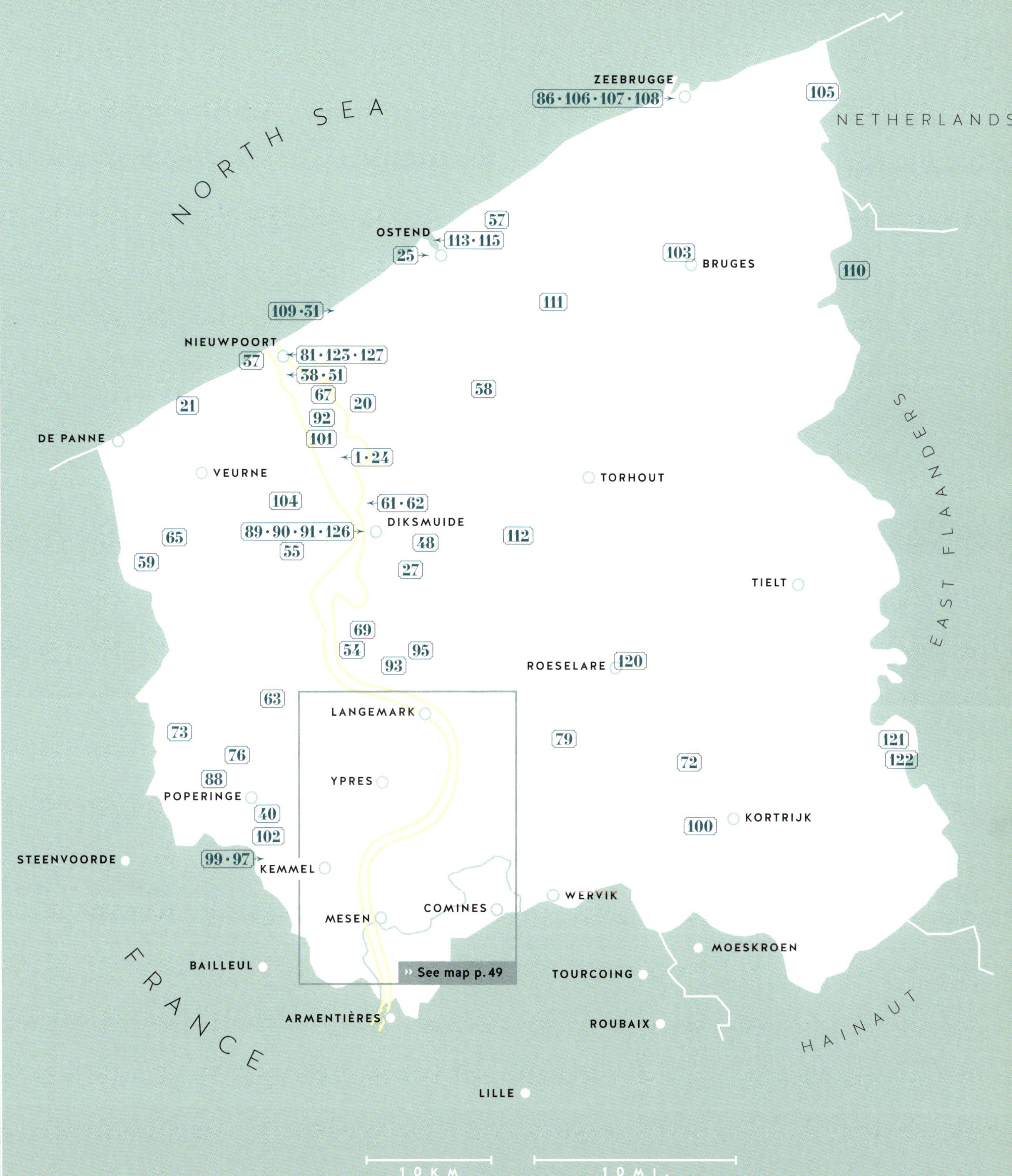

» See map p.49

› WEST FLANDERS, 1914 ‹

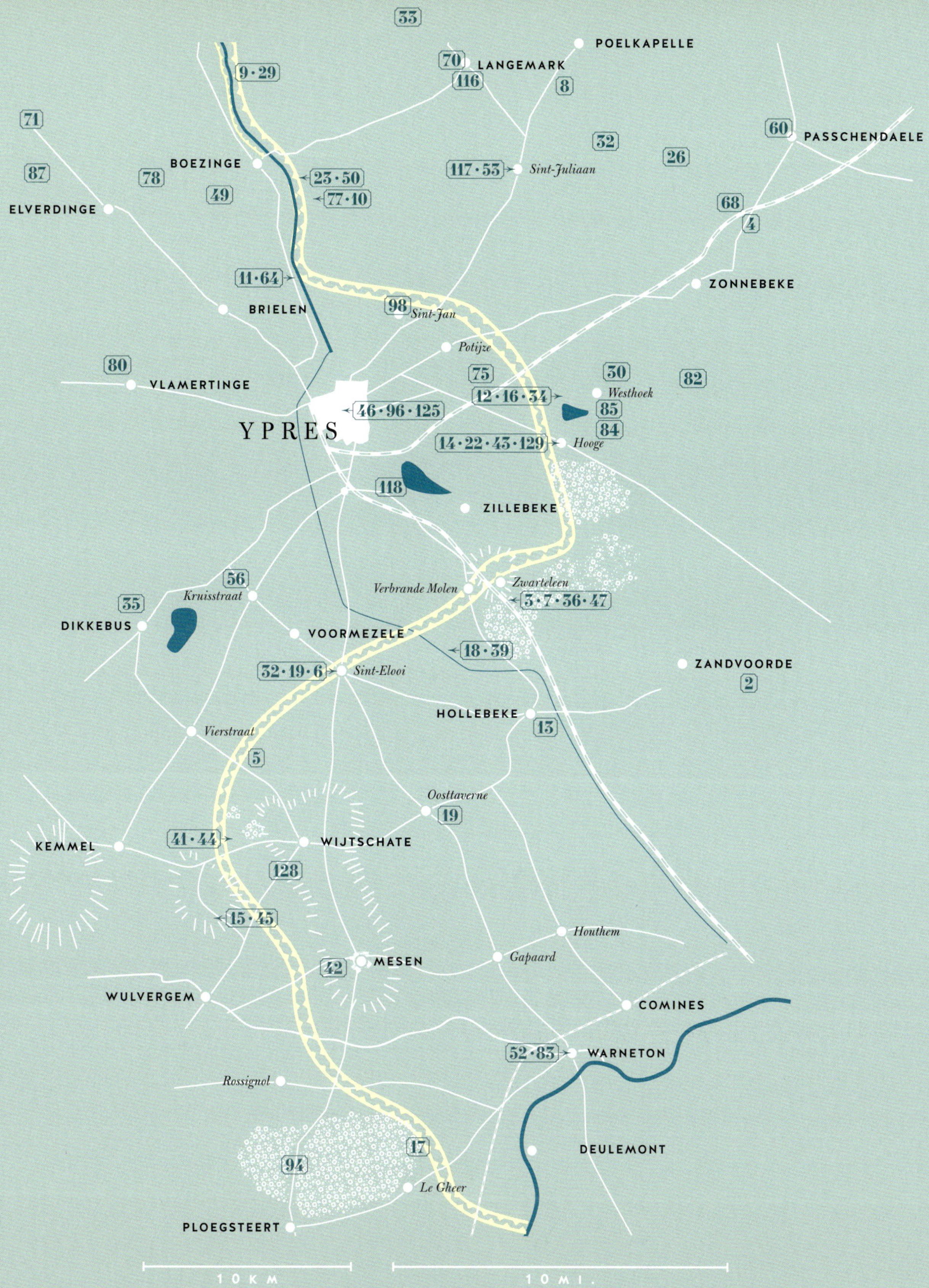

› Y P R E S S A L I E N T, 1 9 1 5 - 1 9 1 7 ‹

HOW TO USE THIS BOOK

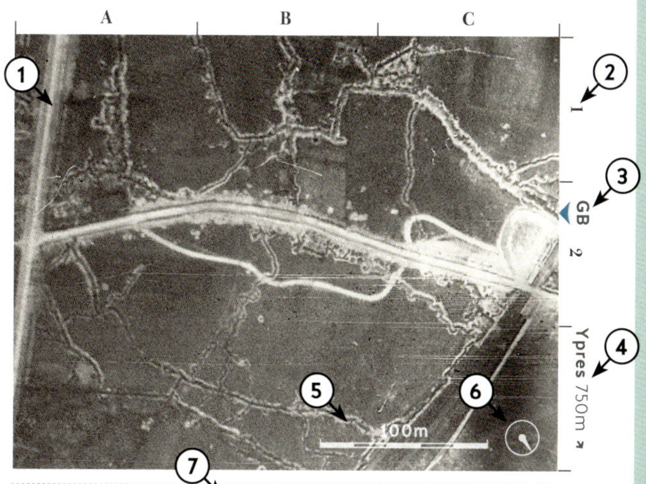

7

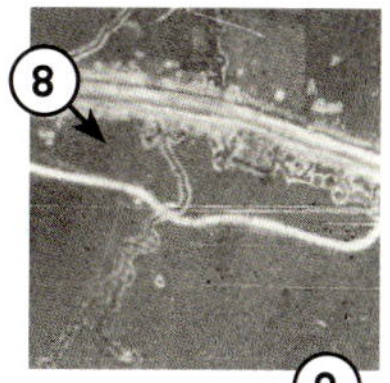

B2

GERMAN TRENCH

The German trench runs from the earlier Franco–British line (just to the north above the road) and the German line on a level with the cemetery.

9

» **SEE ALSO** 68 TYNE COT

10

SYMBOLS

ALLIED FRONT LINE AND TRENCHES

1. THE AERIAL PHOTOGRAPH (ALWAYS ON THE RIGHT-HAND PAGE)
2. DIVISION OF THE AERIAL PHOTOGRAPH INTO SQUARES DENOTED BY LETTERS (HORIZONTAL) AND NUMBERS (VERTICAL)
3. POINT WHERE THE FRONT LINE CROSSES THE EDGE OF THE PICTURE – THE ABBREVIATIONS INDICATE THE RESPECTIVE ARMIES:

G	German Reich	F	France	ANZAC	Australia and New Zealand
GB	Great Britain	B	Belgium	CAN	Canada

4. NAMES OF PLACES AND DISTANCES SHOWN IN THE MARGIN, e.g. Ypres is situated 750 metres from the aerial photograph, in the direction of the arrow.
5. SCALE
6. THE ARROW IN THE COMPASS INDICATES NORTH
7. REFERENCE TO A SQUARE, e.g. the German trench is in square 'B2'.
8. DETAIL OF A PLACE INDICATED ON THE AERIAL PHOTOGRAPH
9. REFERENCES TO ANOTHER AERIAL PHOTOGRAPH ARE INDICATED BY THE NUMBER OF THE PHOTOGRAPH IN A BOX
10. MARKS ON TRACING PAPER ARE EXPLAINED IN A SEPARATE KEY TO SYMBOLS

The first months of the war

ON 4 AUGUST 1914 GERMAN troops invaded Belgium near Liège. The Belgian divisions had been positioned all over Belgian territory, ready to counter an attack from any direction. However, they were no match for what would soon become three German armies. French and British support was unable to stop a proportion of the German troops sweeping into France. A month and a half later the remainder of the German troops took Antwerp, Belgium's principle stronghold. From October, the Belgian field army, and the British and French troops who had sped to their aid, fell back westwards. On the way there was more fighting at Melle, near Ghent.

Meanwhile, with every day that passed, more German, French and British troops poured into the area around Ypres, as the two opposing sides sought to outflank each other. The last phase of the mobile war began. The Westhoek – the extreme western corner of Belgium between the North Sea and the River Lys – became the theatre of a double confrontation. On 18 October the Battle of the Yser flared up, and one day later the First Battle of Ypres began.

The Belgian defence on the Yser soon ran into difficulties despite French help. At Diksmuide, there were French marine fusiliers and four infantry divisions whose ranks included colonial troops, Zouaves and *tirailleurs* from North and West Africa. Starting on 25 October the defending army retreated behind the Diksmuide-Nieuwpoort railway embankment and, by opening the sluices, carried out a successful inundation of the polder on the left bank of the Yser (27–29 October). At Ramskapelle, the last German attempt to break through was defeated. Diksmuide finally fell only on 10 November. During this time a second inundation was carried out to the south of the town – now two large areas of water separated the armies.

Near Ypres there had been a large presence of French and British cavalry since the beginning of October. Seven British and eleven French infantry divisions – along with colonial support from India and North Africa – arrived every day. For a month and a half they fought a bloody war against two German armies and in the opening days alone some 3,000 young German recruits met their death at Langemark. On 22 November 1914 Ypres was set on fire. Finally two salients were formed curving around Ypres and Armentières. The no-man's-land between the lines was narrow and dangerous. In the two pitched battles at Yser and Ypres more than 80,000 lives were lost. This was the end of the mobile warfare on the Western Front and the beginning of almost four years of trench warfare, in which the observation of every single movement and position was of capital importance for winning or losing, living or dying.

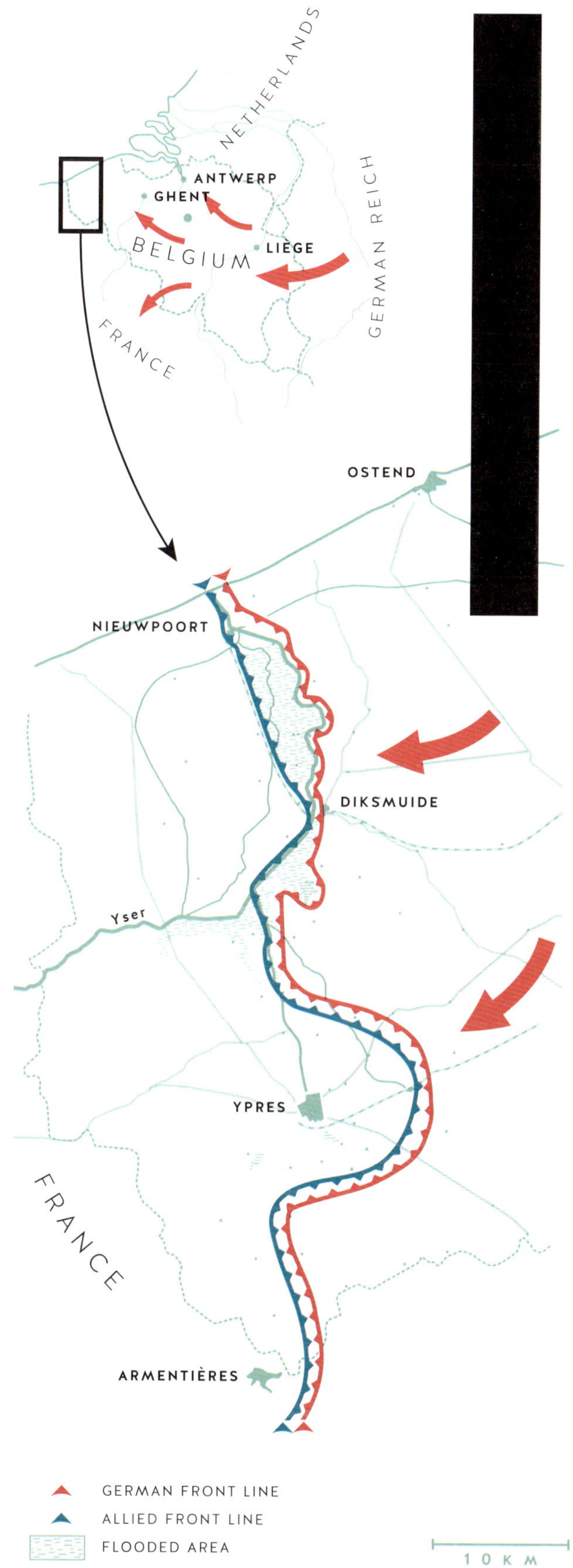

←
German assault on Belgian positions near Hoegaarden, Flemish Brabant, 10 August 1914.

1
TERVATE BATTLE OF THE YSER
(photograph 18 December 1917)

From mid-October 1914 the British, French and Belgians took up positions behind the Yser and in the vicinity of Ypres. They hastily dug shallow trenches: it was generally assumed that the war would soon be over. The Battle of the Yser began on 18 October 1914 but as yet there was no sign of the immense networks of trenches for which the First World War would become notorious. At most, the soldiers took cover against enemy fire in shallow foxholes. Aerial photographs from this initial period are extremely rare but later photographs, such as this one taken on 18 December 1917, sometimes still show whole lines of these primitive shelters. These provide a good picture of the battle positions and the progress of the war in Flanders during the first few months of the war.

GPS 51°04'53.88"N 2°50'29.43"E

→ **SMALL SHELTER**

Two German soldiers take cover in a foxhole; their equipment shows that this is an early photograph.

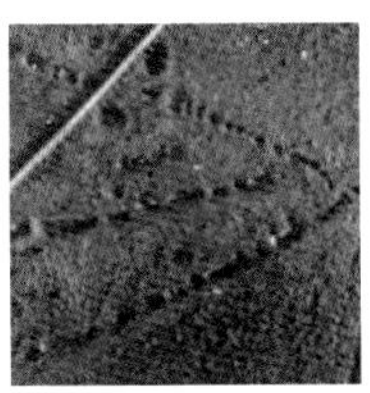

D4-D5
FOXHOLES

The bridge over the Yser at Tervate was the scene of fierce fighting. On 22 October 1914 German units managed to cross the Yser and form a bridgehead on the left bank. Traces of foxholes there date from that time.

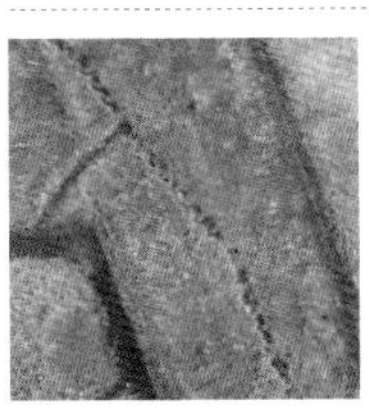

A5
A LINE OF FOXHOLES

Foxholes were dug out in lines. Later they would develop into extensive, complex networks of interconnected trenches.

→ **BRITISH FOXHOLES**

Soldiers of the 2nd Battalion of the Scots Guards in their hastily dug foxholes near Ghent, 9 October 1914. The mounds of excavated earth provided low cover for the upper body.

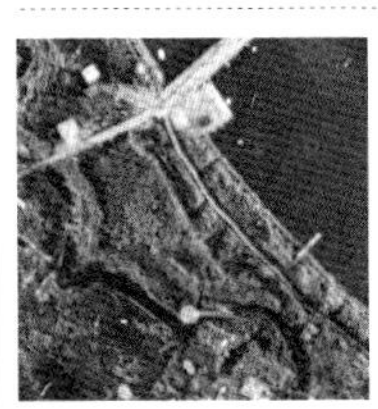

F3
THE BANKS OF THE YSER

After the Battle of the Yser both parties dug themselves in. The Germans make good use of the elevated Yser dyke.

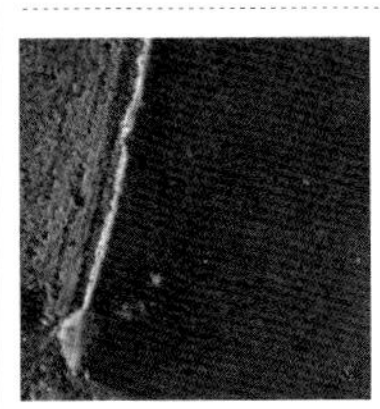

E5
INUNDATION

From the end of October 1914 large areas west of the Yser were flooded to provide a 'natural' barrier to the advance of the German army.

A
B
ditch filled with water
D
E
Yser
F
G
H
1
2
Diksmuide 5km
3
narrow railway
Yser
5
inundation
6
50m
wooden footbridge
8km Nieuwpoort
3km Pervijze

2
ZANDVOORDE FIRST BATTLE OF YPRES
(photograph 18 September 1915)

At the start of the war aerial photography was still in its infancy and it was only after mid-1915 that the use of aerial photographs increased. These early pictures show the still-intact landscape around Ypres, as yet untouched by heavy bombardment. This British photograph of 18 September 1915 shows traces of the earliest British defence fortifications in the Ypres Salient between Zandvoorde and Kruiseke. From 19 October the British 7th Division held the Zandvoorde–Kruiseke–Geluveld line, supported – from 25 October – by the 6th and 7th Cavalry Brigades. The line fell on 29 October. Almost a year later the field defences are still visible but no longer in use. They are nothing like the greatly expanded networks of trenches that were constructed in the Ypres Salient after the front came to a standstill in November 1914.

↑ **PRISONERS OF WAR**

German prisoners of war are taken into town during the First Battle of Ypres. Menin Road, October 1914.

↑ **YPRES FIRE**

The first large plumes of smoke rise from Ypres early in 1915. German oblique aerial photograph taken by the aerial photographer Freiherr von Kanne.

↑ **NORTHUMBERLAND HUSSARS**

Northumberland Hussars (7th Division) near Ypres, November 1914. The ground is undamaged. These pictures are in stark contrast to later photographs.

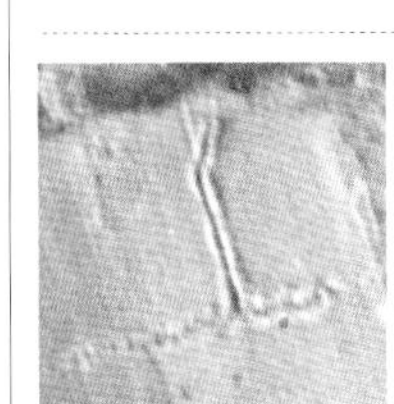

B6-C6
BRITISH FRONT LINE

Rudimentary trenches indicate the position of the front line in October 1914. This position was defended by the Gordon Highlanders.

F4
FOXHOLES

In some places the trenches are nothing more than shallow pits offering only a modicum of protection to one or more soldiers.

A
B
C
D
E
F
G
H
↑ 2 km Geluveld
↑ 770 m Kruiseke
1
2
3
4
5
6
100 m
← 650 m Zandvoorde
↓ 1.2 km Ten Brielen

3
ZILLEBEKE – HILL 60
DECEMBER 1914

Some 4 kilometres south-east of Ypres lay 'Hill 60', an artificial hill created by spoil from excavation work for the building of the Ypres–Comines railway line. The hill was only 60 metres high but afforded an unbroken, strategically important view over Ypres. An early German photograph taken in December 1914 shows the as yet untouched area between Hill 60 and Zillebeke. The woods are still intact, the roofs of the houses undamaged and there is scarcely a trench to be seen. The front comprises a single line of irregular trenches, with only a few communication trenches leading into the area behind the front. This photograph was taken after the Germans had taken Hill 60 on 10 December and before the French exploded the first mines under the hill on 29 December.

» **SEE ALSO** 7 36 47 HILL 60

→ **PANORAMA OF YPRES**

The strategic importance of Hill 60 is apparent from this German photograph. From the top of Hill 60 the Germans had a view over large parts of the Ypres Salient.

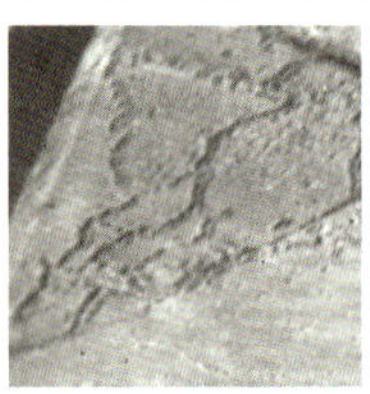

B3
HILL 60

The 200-metres-wide Hill 60 lay on the northern side of the railway cutting. On this aerial photograph it forms a distinctive triangle.

B2-B3
'THE DUMP'

'The Dump', known by the French as 'La Butte des Tirailleurs' (the riflemen's hillock), was a pile of excavated earth next to the railway line. It served as a good lookout point for the Allies.

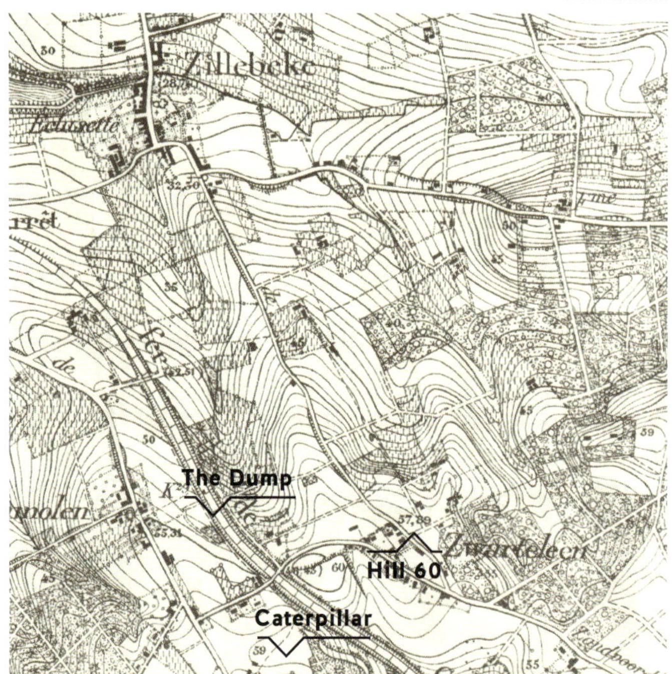

← **TOPOGRAPHICAL MAP**

The spoil from the excavations for the Ypres–Comines railway line was left on both sides of the track. To the north of the railway, between Zwarteleen and Verbrandemolen, a 60-metre-high hill arose that was christened 'Hill 60'. To the south of the railway was the 59-metre-high 'Caterpillar' and, a little further north, the smaller 'Dump'.

SYMBOLS

- ALLIED FRONT LINE AND TRENCHES
- GERMAN FRONT LINE AND TRENCHES
- RAILWAY
- WOOD

GPS 50°49'26.03"N 2°55'45.20"E

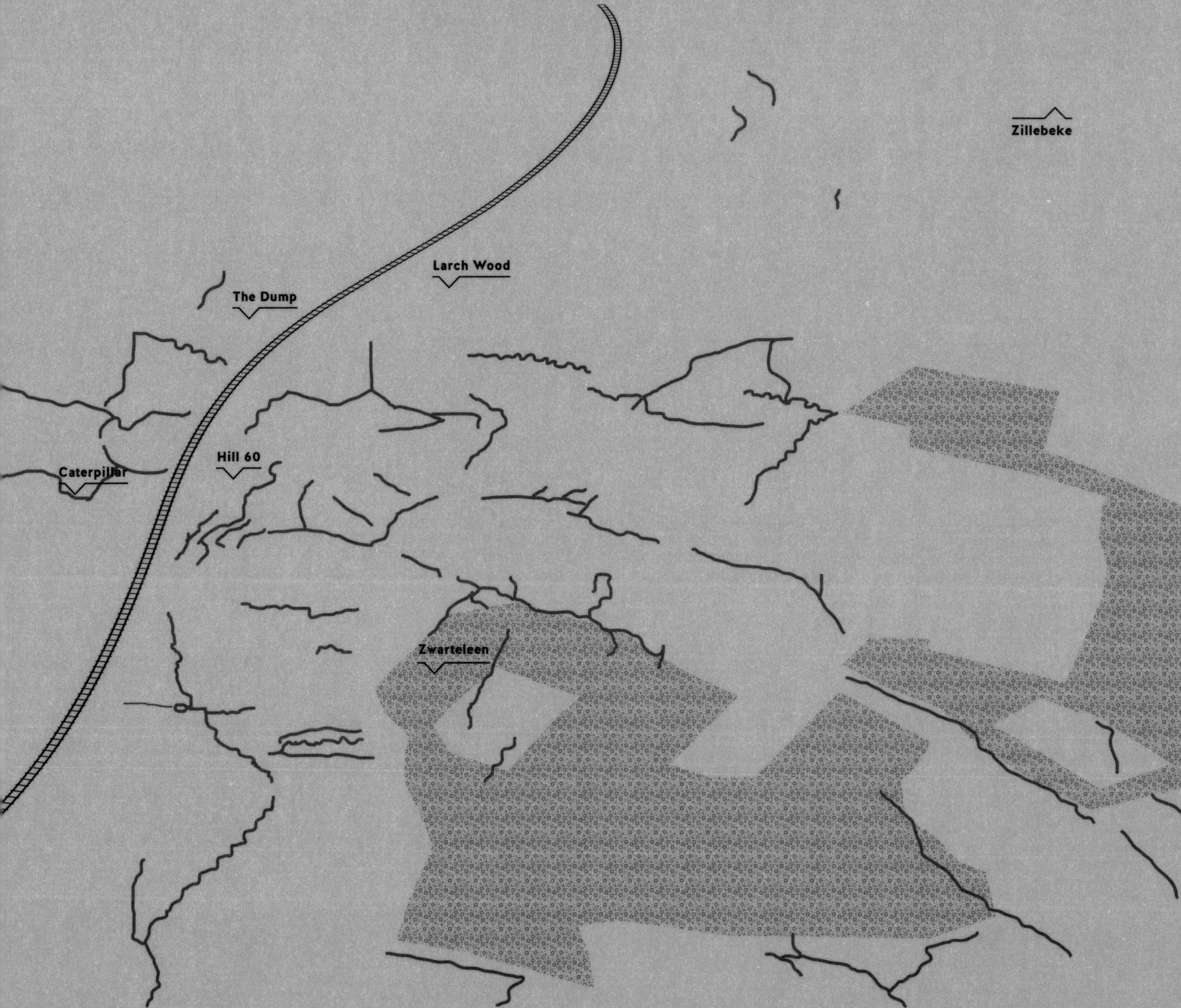
Zillebeke
Larch Wood
The Dump
Hill 60
Caterpillar
Zwarteleen

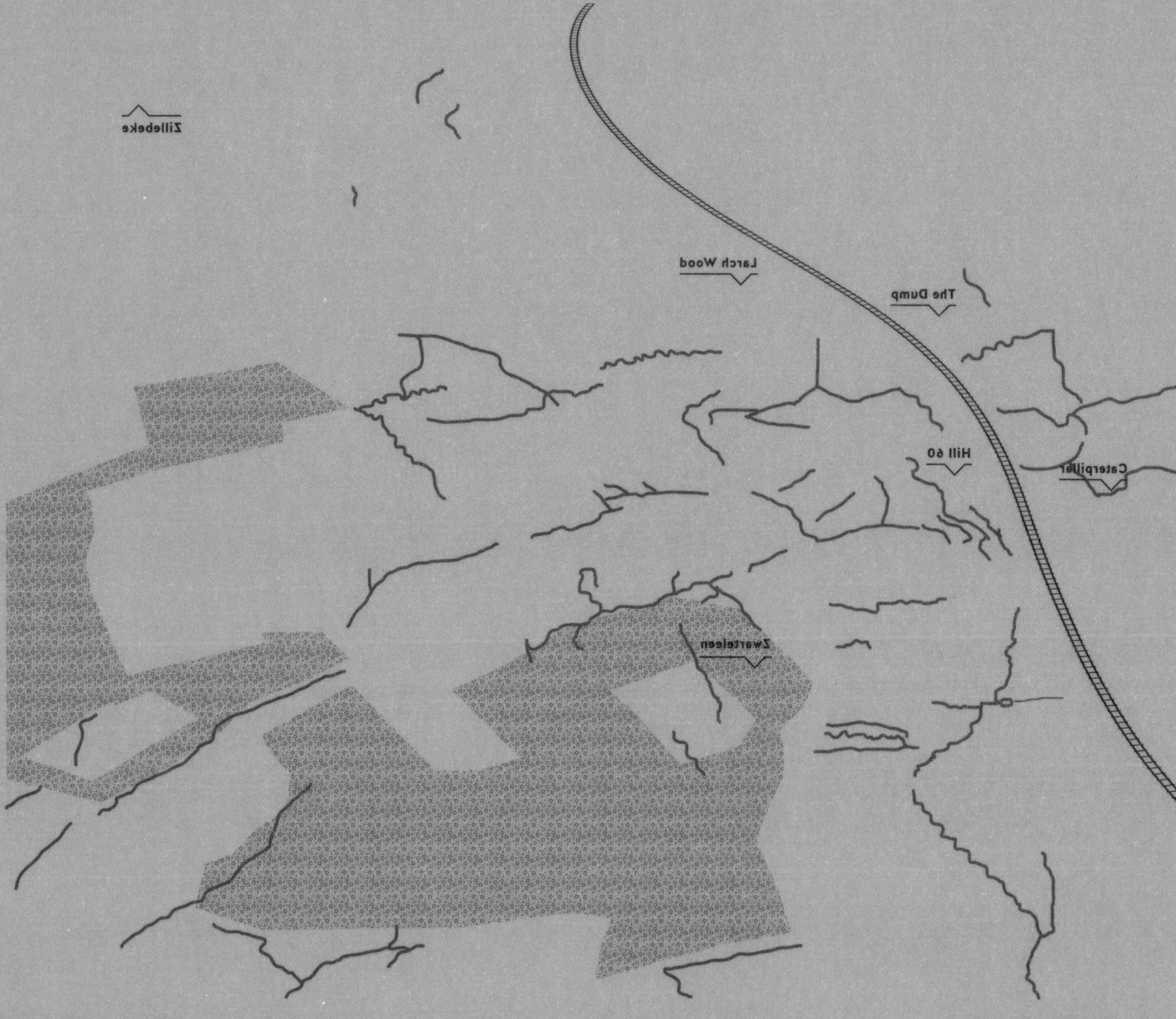

Zillebeke
Larch Wood
The Dump
Hill 60
Caterpillar
Zwarteleen

A
B
C
D
↑ railway to Ypres
F
↑ 3km **Ypres**
G
H
1
2
3
↓ Armagh Wood
5
↓ Mount Sorrel
↓ 400m **Klein Zillebeke**

4
ZONNEBEKE - TYNE COT
SPRING 1915

Following the First Battle of Ypres the French, British and Germans dug in along a wide arc around Ypres, some 8 kilometres from the town. In the winter and spring of 1915 the front was not yet being systematically photographed from the air. For this reason there are only a few early aerial photographs scattered across the archives. During the Second Battle of Ypres the Germans advanced a few kilometres towards Ypres, with the result that the existing battlefields were left stranded far behind the front. On a vertical aerial photograph taken almost a year later, on 10 April 1916, the Franco-British and German positions can still be made out. Shortly after the Second Battle of Ypres the Germans built trenches to connect the ground they had won. This makes it difficult at first sight to make out the no-man's-land of the time. The three oblique pictures present an unusual view of the positions during the first months of trench warfare. They are undated but were presumably taken in the second half of 1915.

» **SEE ALSO** 68 TYNE COT

GPS 50°53'01.19"N 3°00'20.77"E

→ A1-B1 to A3-B3

THE FRONT, NOVEMBER 1914 - APRIL 1915

Oblique aerial photographs of the German-British front line at Nieuwemolen taken before the Second Battle of Ypres by the German aerial photographer Freiherr von Kanne. At the time of his reconnaissance flight the trenches were deserted, the front having been pushed westwards as a consequence of the Second Battle of Ypres. The aerial photographs were taken over the Nieuwemolen crossroads and look southwards towards Broodseinde, with the crossroads in the background. The German front line is situated 75 metres to the right of Nieuwemolen. Note the numerous recesses in the sides of the trenches - these were shelters for the soldiers.

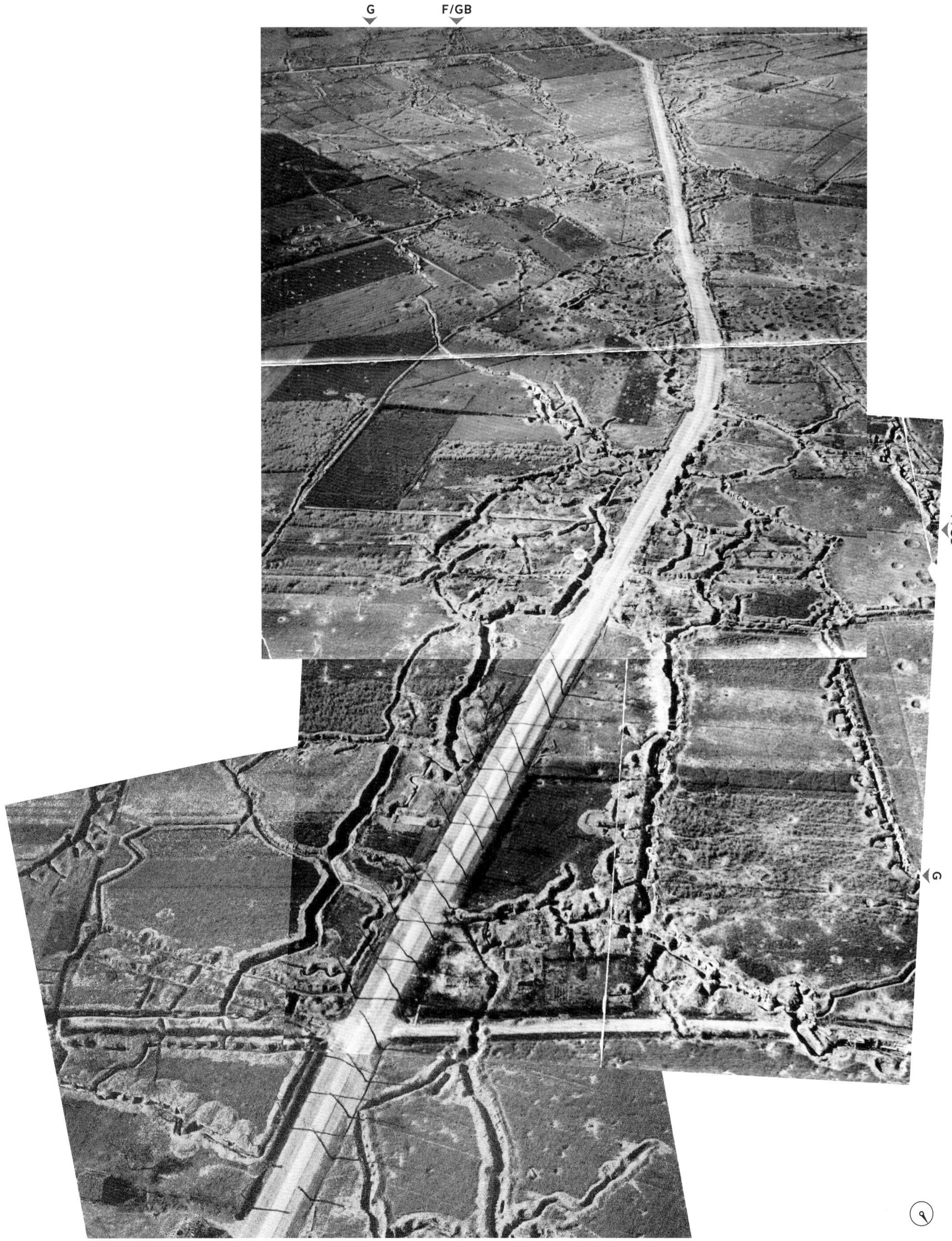

D5

NO-MAN'S-LAND

The narrow strip of land separating the Franco–British and German front lines was known as 'no-man's-land'.

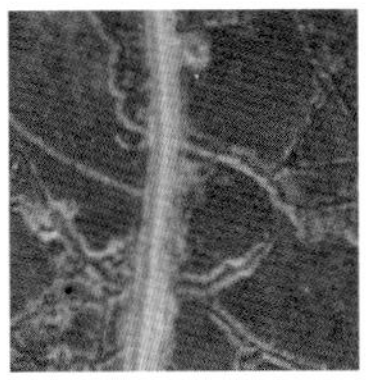

B2

FRANCO-BRITISH FRONT LINE

Here the British front line crosses the road from Zonnebeke to Passchendaele. The German trenches were situated only 45 metres further up the road.

B3

GERMAN TRENCH

The German trench runs from the earlier Franco–British line (just to the north above the road) and the German line on a level with the cemetery.

C4-C5

GERMAN CEMETERY

The German military cemetery at Keerselaarhoek. The trenches just to the west of the cemetery show the German front line as it was from November 1914 up to the Second Battle of Ypres in April 1915. Two hundred metres to the west (E4) is the famous British cemetery known as Tyne Cot, which dates from the end of 1917.

5 WIJTSCHATE – HOLLANDSE SCHUUR 4 FEBRUARY 1915

At the end of the First Battle of Ypres trench warfare was taking shape. The Germans had dug in on the strategic heights that surround Ypres in an inverted S configuration. After the taking of Mesen (Messines) and Wijtschate at the end of October / beginning of November 1914 French troops dug their first positions opposite the Germans on the ridge. Two German aerial photographs taken on 4 February 1915 show the battlegrounds between Sint-Elooi and Wijtschate. At this period, the impact on the landscape of hundreds of small bomb craters was still minimal. Control of the Allied front had passed two days earlier from the French 31st Division to the British 28th Division. The front line is still formed of scattered fragments of trenches, some of which are connected to each other by long zigzagging trenches. The two parties would systematically expand the trench system over the next few years.

↓ AERIAL PHOTOGRAPH ON RELIEF MODEL

An oblique reproduction of the aerial photograph laid over a digital terrain model provides a three-dimensional view of the ridge. Hollandse Schuur Farm is on the extreme right at the top of the hill. The German position is indicated by a dotted line. The Allied trenches are in the valley.

B6

HOLLANDSE SCHUUR FARM

The German trenches can be seen around the farm buildings. On 7 June 1917 three deep mines were exploded under this elevated position.

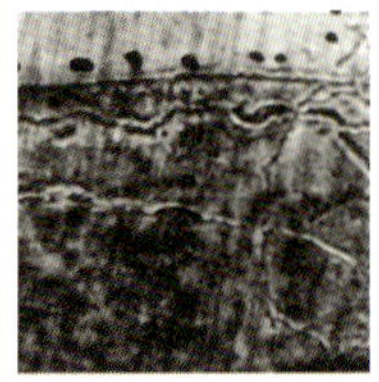

H4

BAYERNWALD

This wood, built up into a heavily strengthened position, was called 'Bayernwald' by the British. Saps, or approach trenches, run from the wood to advanced listening posts in no-man's-land.

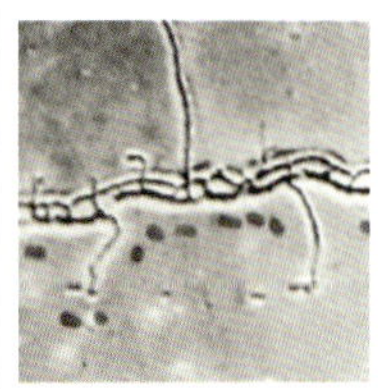

A3

EARLY TRENCHES

The earliest trenches were built on a somewhat random pattern. They often consisted of two parallel ditches connected with each other at irregular intervals. Gradually, the trenches were planned more systematically, with standardised square or semicircular traverses.

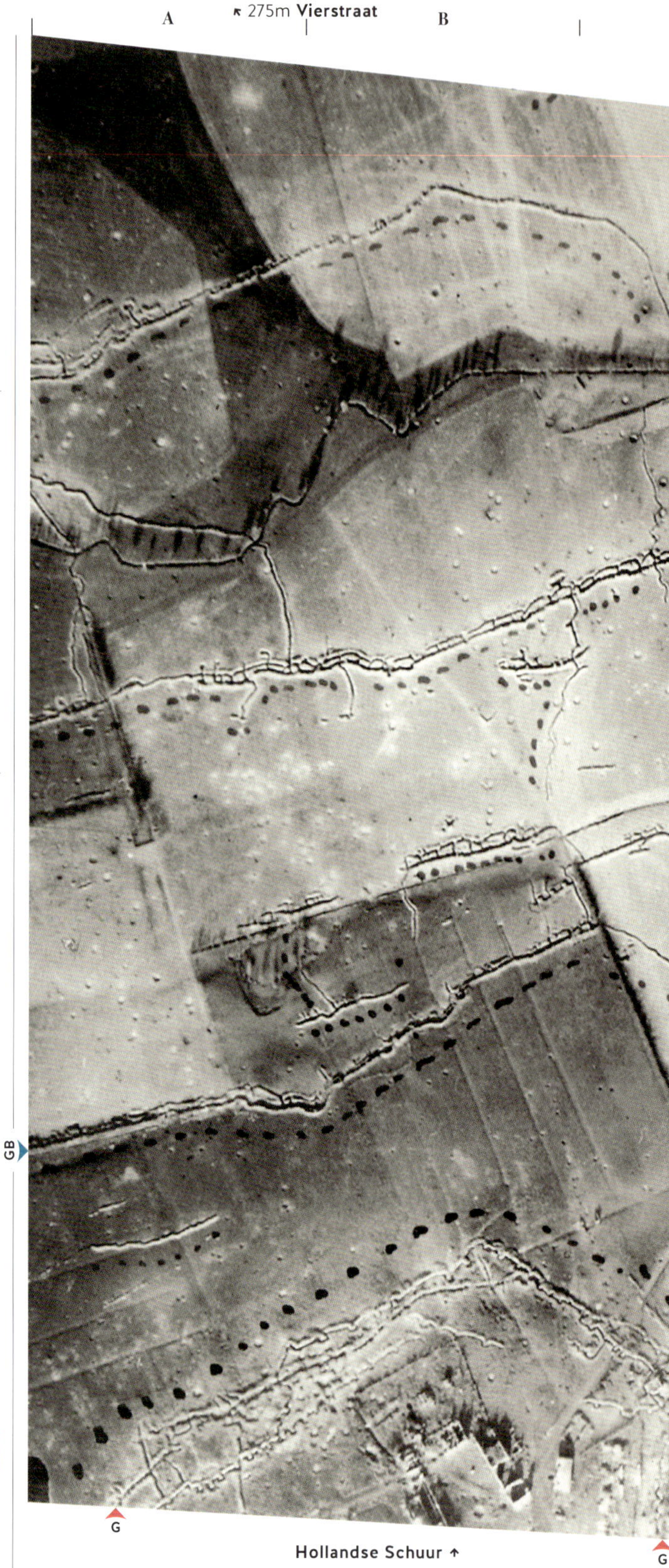

GPS 50°47'56.56"N 2°52'22.08"E

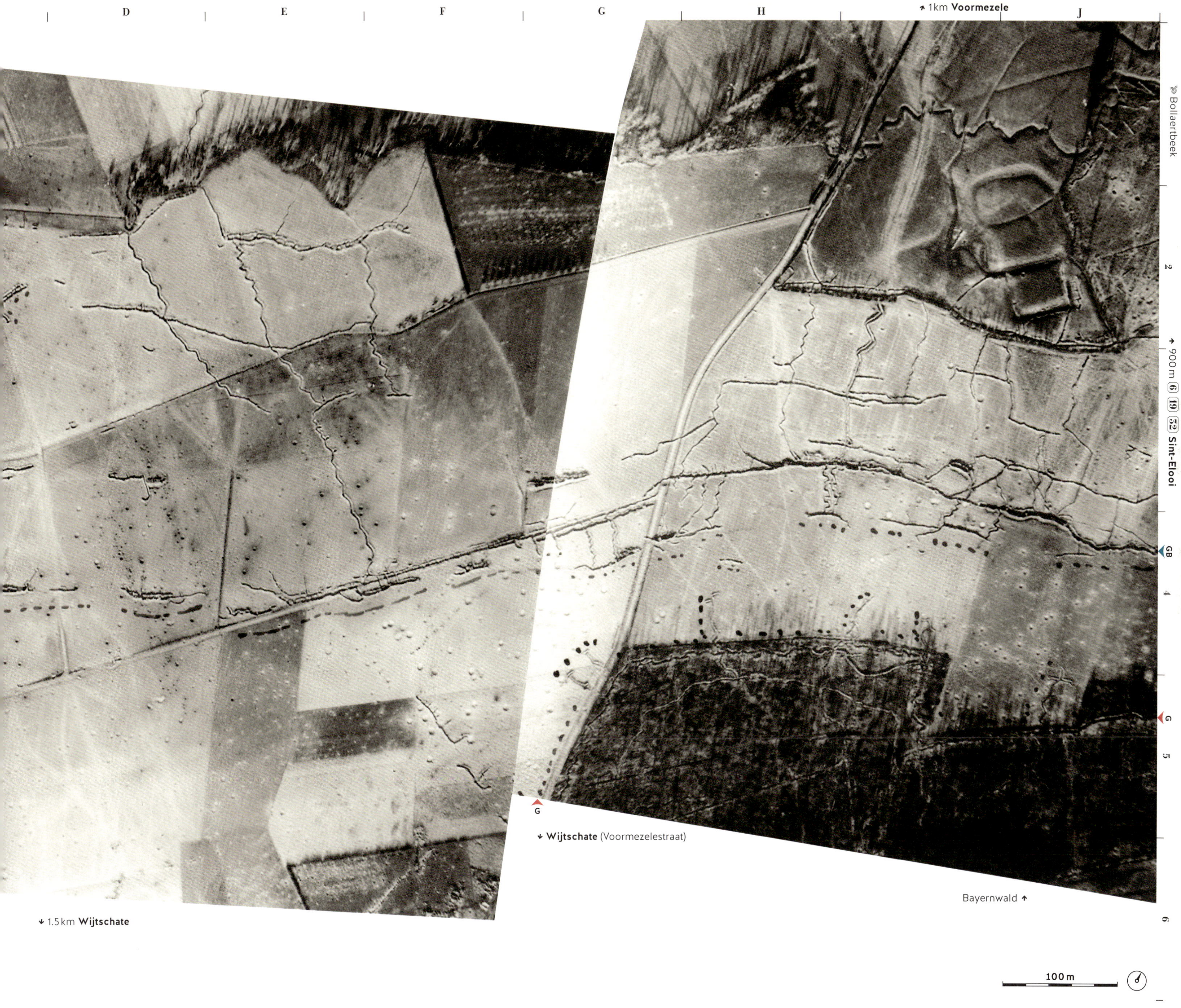
D
E
F
G
H
J
↑ 1km Voormezele
Bollaertbeek
2
↑ 900 m 6 19 52 Sint-Elooi
GB
4
G
5
6
G
↓ Wijtschate (Voormezelestraat)
Bayernwald ↑
↓ 1.5 km Wijtschate
100 m

6

SINT-ELOOI – THE MOUND

4 FEBRUARY 1915

In autumn 1914 French and German units were already fighting hard for The Mound at Sint-Elooi (E5). This heap of clay residue from a small brickyard was an excellent observation post. A German aerial photographic interpreter's comments on a series of aerial photographs included an indication of the position of the Allied and German front lines. Early in February 1915 the British took over from the French, and on 4 February The Mound was still in British hands. It was a thorn in the flesh of the Germans, who made plans to tunnel under it – this marked the start of years of competition between the Allied Tunnelling Companies and the German Pioneers.

» **SEE ALSO** 19 52 SINT-ELOOI

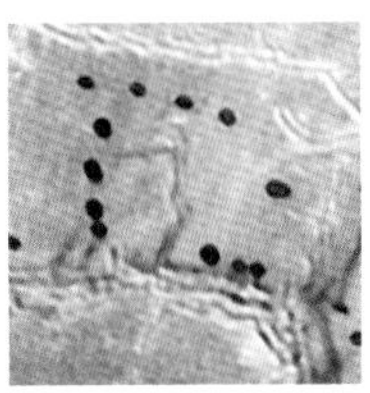

B4

APPROACH TRENCHES

Approach trenches (saps) run from the German front line through the no-man's-land and towards the Allied lines.

↓ **THE MOUND**

Detail from a British panoramic photograph taken from Voormezele on 20 March 1915. On the left, The Mound towers above the surrounding landscape.

↑ **SINT-ELOOI, FEBRUARY 1915**

Detailed photograph of Sint-Elooi, 4 February 1915. The no-man's-land between the British and German trenches is indicated by a double dotted line. On the top of the hill an observation post towers high above the German lines.

↑ **SINT-ELOOI, MARCH 1915**

On 14 March 1915 the Germans exploded two mines and took part of Sint-Elooi.[1] The explosion blew away most of The Mound and the British troops were pushed back 150 metres. On this German oblique aerial photograph of 31 March dotted lines indicate the most forward German lines.

GPS 50°48'33.71"N 2°53'30.98"E

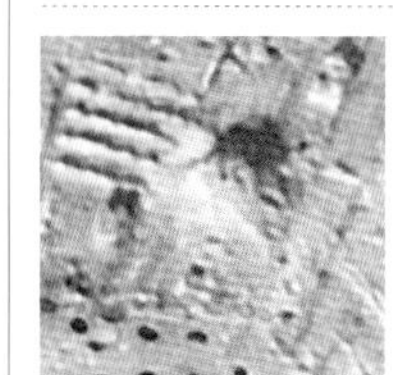

F4

THE MOUND

The Mound at Sint-Elooi was an old mill base built up with clay from the nearby brickworks. It served as an excellent observation post.

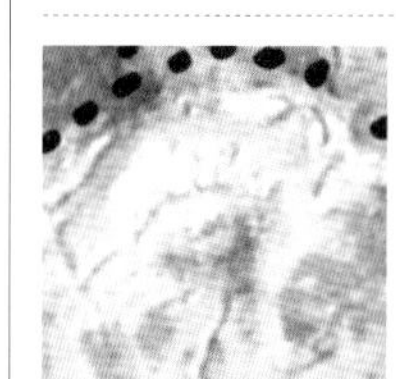

bIV

CRATER

German mines destroyed most of The Mound. This photograph shows the first of a long series of craters caused by explosions at Sint-Elooi.

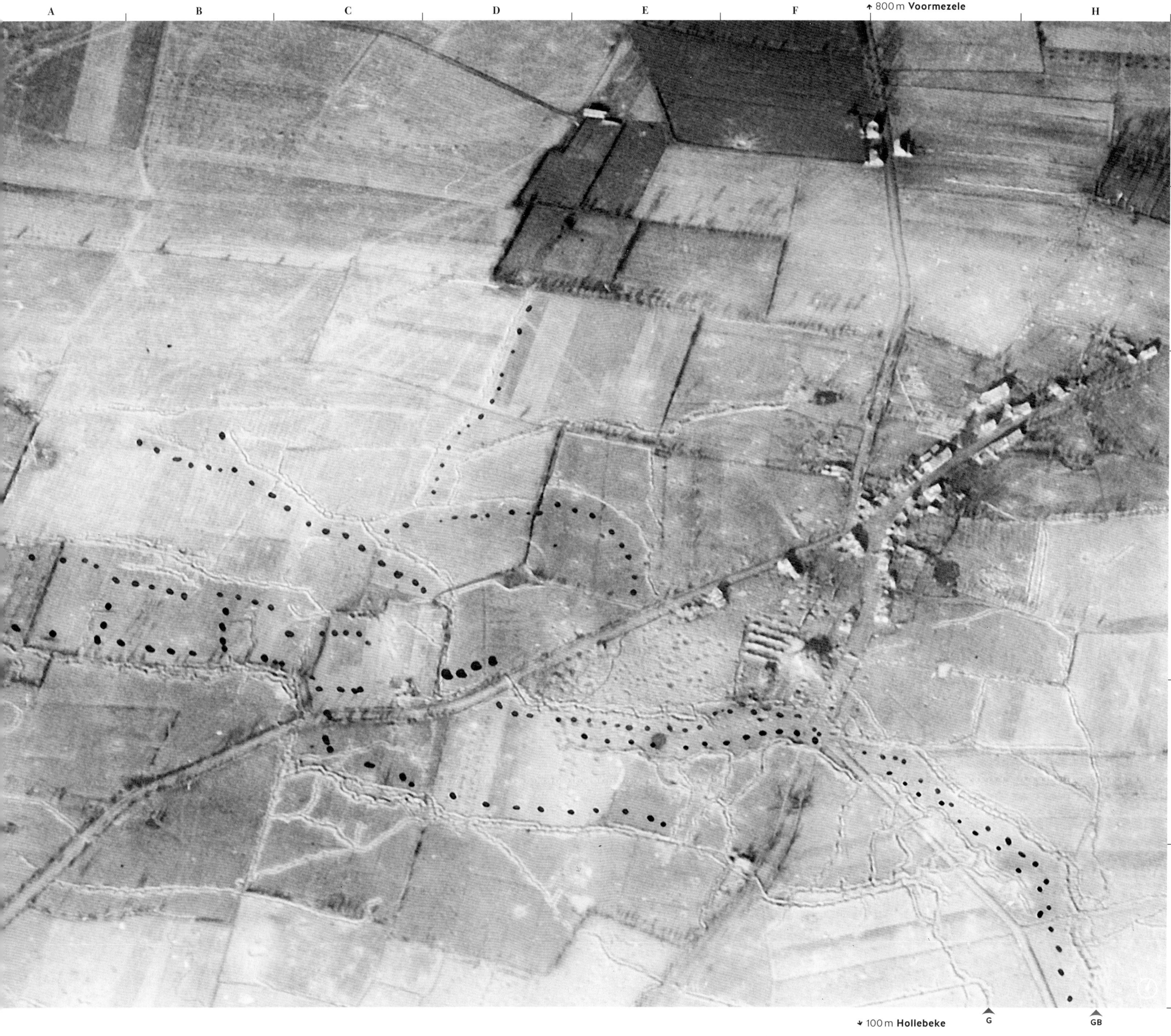

A
B
C
D
E
F
↑ 800 m Voormezele
H
1
2
↑ 1.7 km Ypres
↑ 3 km Hill 60 5 7
↑ 1.7 km 18 59 The Bluff
5
6
↓ 100 m Hollebeke
G
GB

7
ZILLEBEKE – HILL 60 MAY 1915

Immediately after the Germans took Hill 60 on 10 December 1914 the French started undermining the hill. From 17 December the engineers of the 42nd Infantry Division began to construct shallow galleries under enemy lines and on 29 December 1914 they exploded charges of 500 and 350 kilograms.[2] No infantry attack followed, however. In February the British took over from the French and in turn prepared to win Hill 60 back. On the evening of 17 April, British troops exploded five depth mines under Hill 60, leaving deep craters. The British thereupon attacked and took the landmark. After inflicting two gas attacks on the Allies on 1 and 5 May 1915, the Germans retook it. A German aerial photograph shows the crater landscape on Hill 60 shortly after the explosion of the British mines. The battle for Hill 60 is clearly in full swing. Visible are the communication trenches running towards Hill 60 from the British lines – an attempt to consolidate the ground won. Casualties were high: 800 from the German XV Army Corps and more than 3,000 from the British 5th Division.

» **SEE ALSO** [5] [36] [47] HILL 60

↓ **PANORAMA**

British panoramic photograph taken from the top of The Dump, 10 April 1915. Hill 60 is on the left of the railway track. Visible on its flank are traces of the early French mine explosion. The British front line is just before the bridge over the railway.

↑ E3
MINE CRATER 1915

German troops digging in one of the British mine craters. In the foreground is the entry to an underground shaft.

↗ B5
GERMAN TRENCH

German trench on the flank of the railway cutting, 150 metres behind the front line.

→ D5
GERMAN TRENCH

German soldiers in a trench on the side of the railway cutting, 350 metres behind the front line.

SYMBOLS

- ALLIED FRONT LINE AND TRENCHES
- GERMAN FRONT LINE AND TRENCHES
- COMMUNICATION TRENCHES USED TO CONSOLIDATE THE CRATERS
- YPRES–KORTRIJK RAILWAY
- FRENCH CRATER
- BRITISH CRATER
- GERMAN CRATER

GPS 50°49'26.03"N 2°55'45.20"E

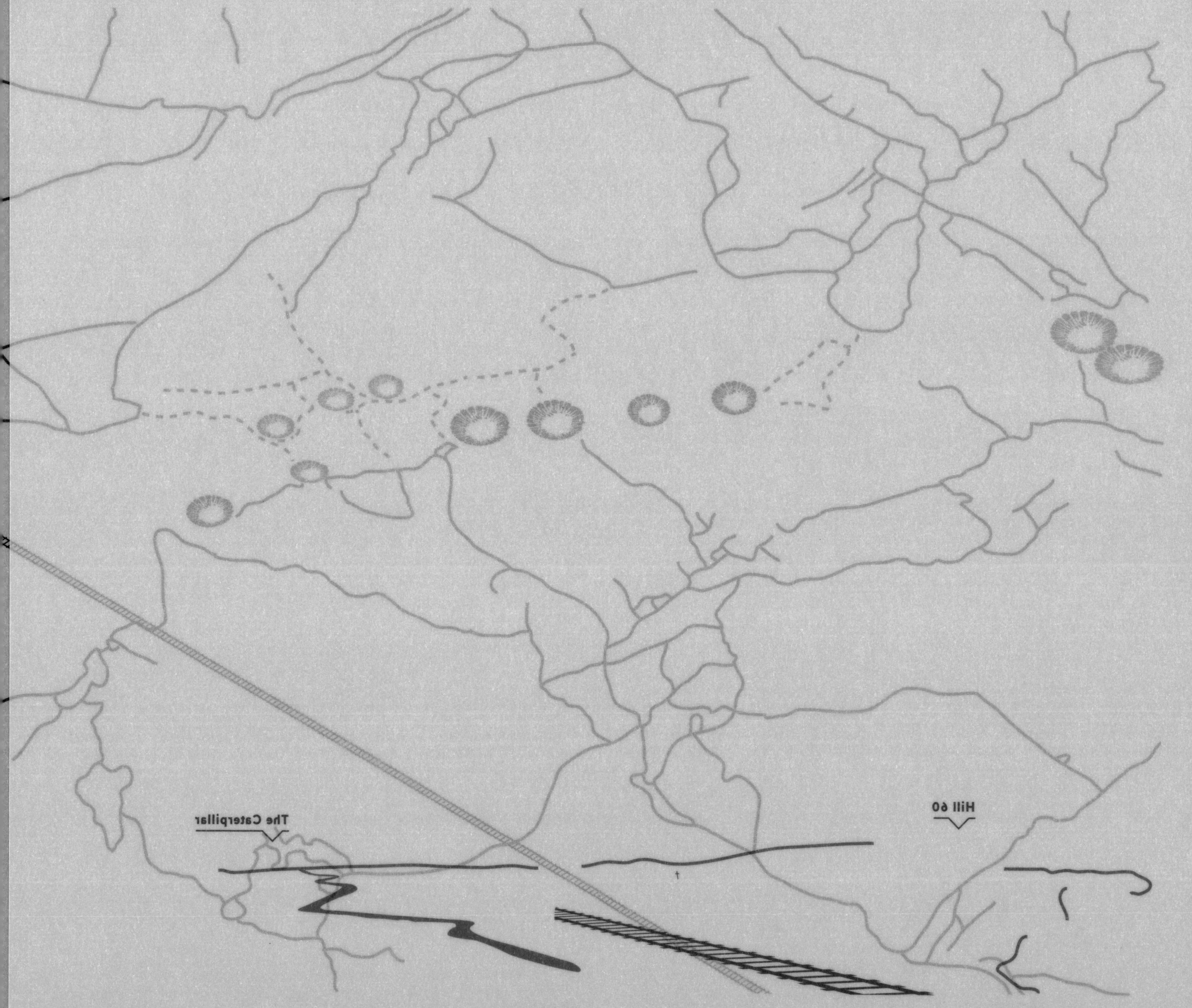
The Caterpillar
Hill 60

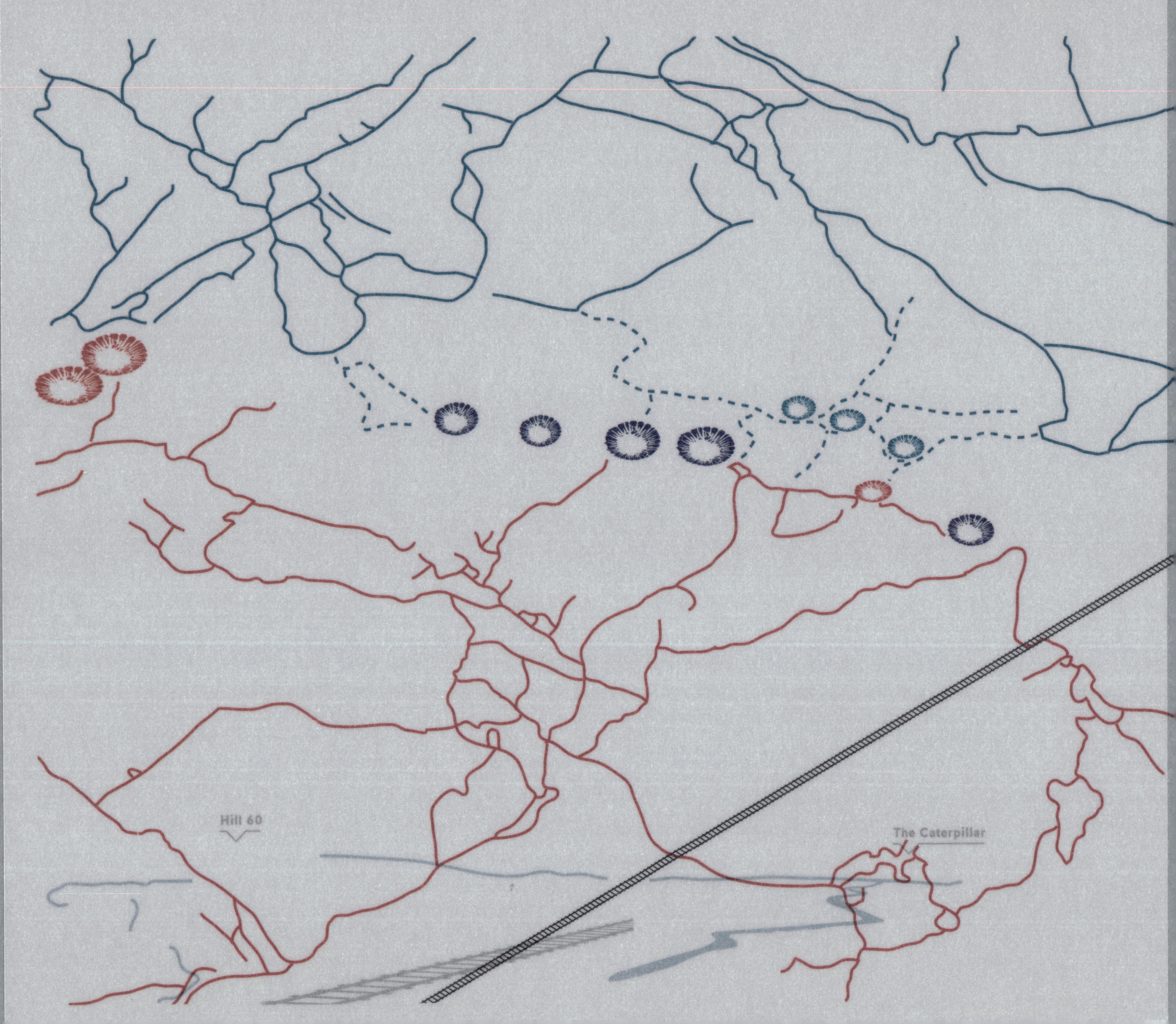

Hill 60
The Caterpillar

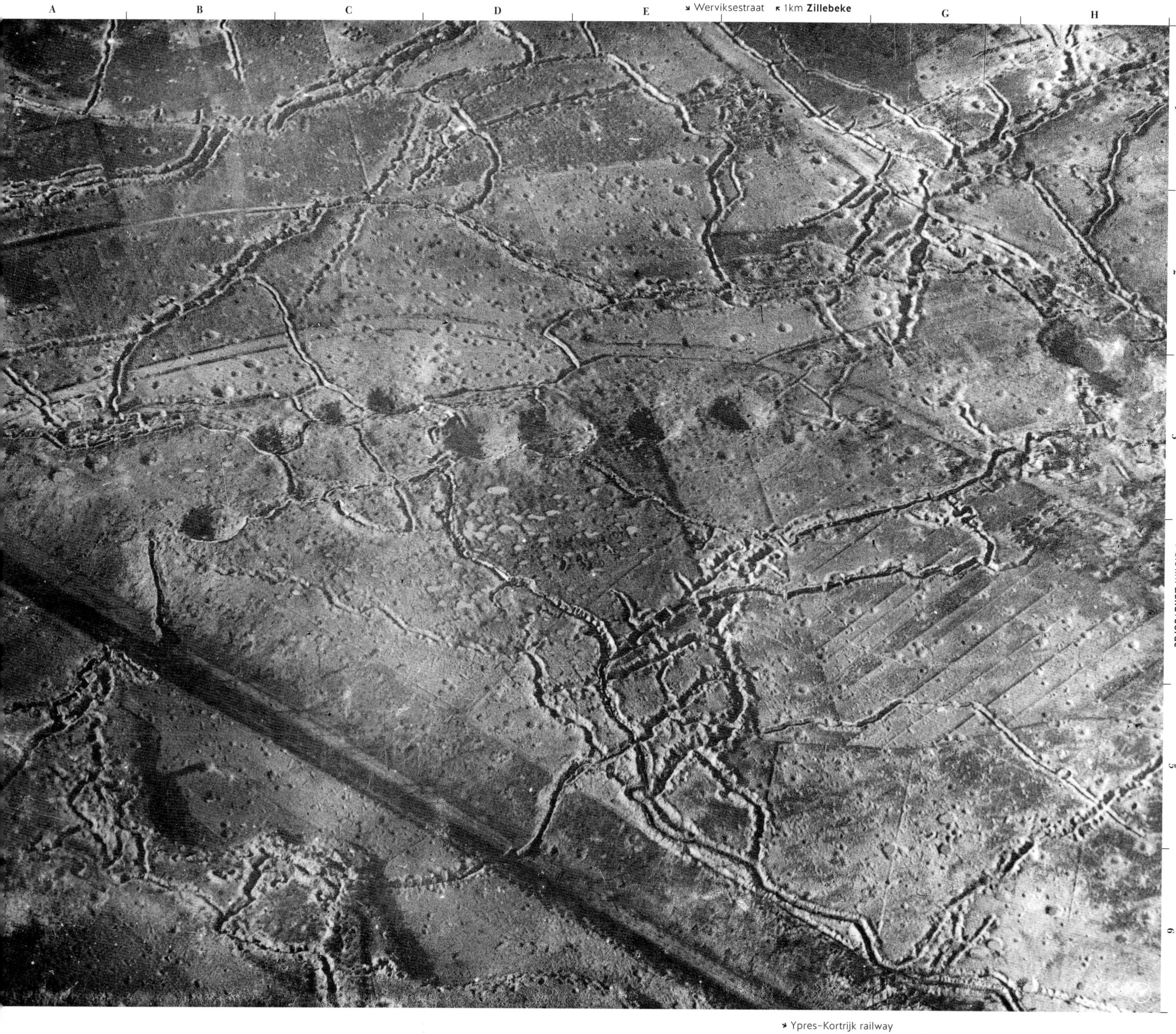
A
B
C
D
E
↘ Werviksestraat
↖ 1km Zillebeke
G
H
1
↗ Zwarteleen
2
3
↗ 3.6km Zandvoorde
4
5
6
↘ Ypres-Kortrijk railway

The Second Battle of Ypres and trench warfare

AFTER THE FIRST WINTER of war both parties decided to break the deadlock on the Western Front. The British and French frontal attacks in northern France had not been successful, and on 22 April 1915 the Germans deployed chlorine gas for the first time. The chlorine gas attack over the French trenches between Steenstraat and Schreiboom (Langemark) opened up a breach of 4–8 kilometres. For a whole month the Germans tried to capitalise on their surprise attack. The Ypres Salient shrank at both ends and was now only 4 or 5 kilometres from the town centre, but Franco-British resistance remained resolute.

Heavy fire from the artillery and machine-gunners claimed many victims. More than 40,000 soldiers died in the fighting. Only a small part of this heavy toll was accounted for by poison gas. The great shortage of Allied artillery and the fairly unprotected position of the French and British in defence and counter-attack were the cause of most of the deaths. For more than two years, up to the beginning of June 1917, the positions remained unchanged. But there was a tactical battle for every favourable position on the ground.

By the end of 1914 trench warfare was already considered a fact of military life. Tunnelling under enemy positions was the most frequent weapon of attack. Tunnels were dug from the friendly line to the enemy line and mines set off – the explosion was sometimes followed by an above-ground attack, sometimes not. Both parties used miners who literally 'undermined' each other's efforts. The most northerly mines on the Western Front exploded on the low ridge at Bellewaarde. Between 1915 and 1917 there was what amounted to an 'underground war' at five points on the Ypres Salient: at Bellewaarde, Hooge, Hill 60, The Bluff and Sint-Elooi.

There were two more relatively big infantry attacks: between June and September 1915 the British tried in vain to shift Germans from the highest positions in Bellewaarde and Hooge. The German attack of 2 June 1916 surprised the Canadian Corps, but in the course of the following ten days the corps regained the lost ground near Hill 62.

On the Yser front, both sides built up their outposts in the inundated area. Large-scale attacks were not possible but the German artillery on the coast and inland tried hard to inflict severe damage on Allied supplies.

Aerial observation, now used by all the armies, provided decisive assistance for the trench warfare on the ground.

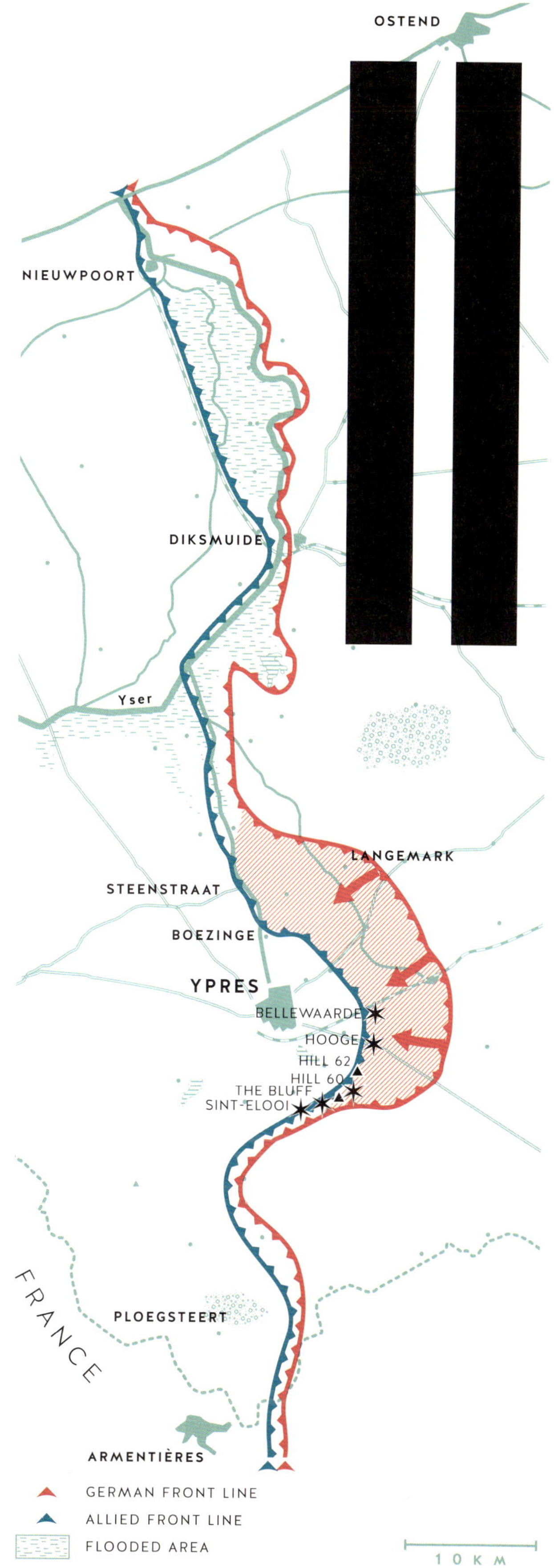

←

German soldiers in a trench in Sint-Elooi.

8 LANGEMARK APRIL 1915

An oblique German aerial photograph from mid-April 1915 shows a view of the northern part of the Ypres Salient. The Franco–German front line runs north-west of Langemark. The village itself lay just behind the line where, on 22 April 1915, the Germans released more than 5,500 cylinders of lethal chlorine gas. At the time there was no known means of protection against the gas and the panic that arose enabled German troops to advance several kilometres in one go. The photograph shows French trenches all around the village. Positions consist of fragments of trenches that are hardly connected to each other. The German lines ran some hundreds of metres to the north of the top right-hand corner of the photograph. Although the picture was taken early in the war, the landscape is already severely damaged. The church is in ruins and the village is surrounded by bomb craters several metres wide. It was only in the summer of 1917 that Langemark was returned to the Allies.

» **SEE ALSO** 29 LANGEMARK-NORD

↗ **CAPTURED TRENCH**

German photograph of a trench captured during the Second Battle of Ypres. Two dead soldiers lie among the rubble.

→ **WOUNDED IN LANGEMARK**

Wounded and dead North African soldiers from the French 45th Division at Langemark.

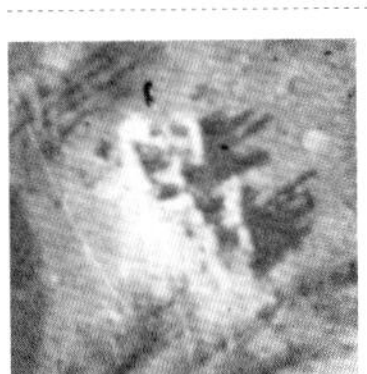

D5
CHÂTEAU DE PATIN

The ruins of the Château de Patin set amid the château grounds with a lake.

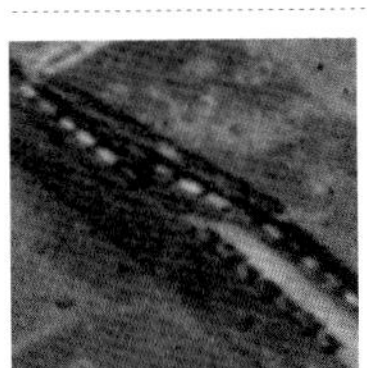

C2
RAILWAY

The railway between Ypres and Torhout, with wagons abandoned on the track.

GPS 50°54'48.17"N 2°55'08.90"E

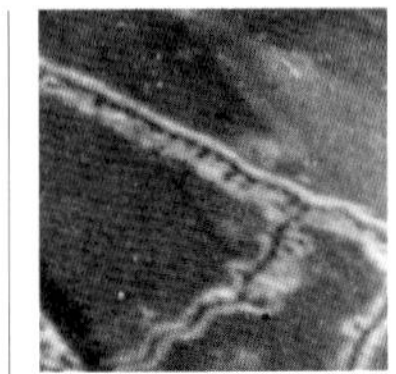

H3-H4
FRENCH TRENCH

Allied fire trench. Small niches were dug out of the parados – the rear-side of the trench – to make a primitive shelter.

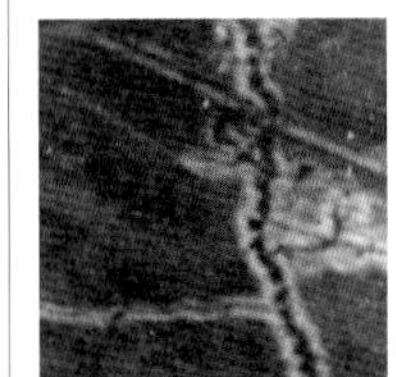

H1-H2
FRENCH TRENCHES

French trenches near the front. The German front line is a few hundred metres to the north.

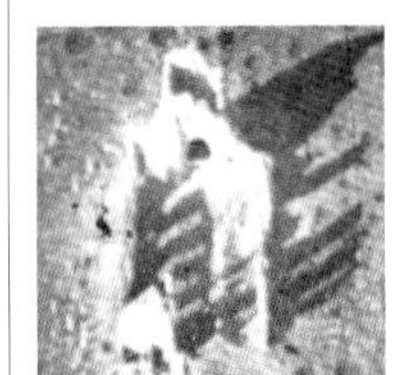

B6
LANGEMARK CHURCH

The photograph shows the silhouette of the ruined church of St Paul's. The building was reduced to ruins early in 1915.

↖ 3.2 km 10 Fusilier Farm
B
C
D
↑ 3.8 km 9 Boezinge – Het Sas
↗ 3.2 km Bikschote
G
H
1
↑ 1 km 35 Broenbeek
2
3
↑ 300 m German front ↑ 300 m 29 Langemark-Nord
5
Ypres-Torhout railway ↗
Zonnebekestraat ↗

9

BOEZINGE – HET SAS

28 APRIL 1915

After the gas attack of 22 April 1915, Prussian regiments succeeded in crossing the Ypres–Yser Canal at Steenstraat and Het Sas (Boezinge lock). That evening they reached their planned destination. Instead of profiting from the circumstances and advancing towards Ypres, they immediately started work on establishing a bridgehead on the western bank of the canal. That week saw fierce fighting to repel the Germans at Steenstraat and the hamlet of Lizerne. On 28 April the German aerial photographer Freiherr Dietrich von Kanne took pictures of the consolidation of the German position between Het Sas and Lizerne. German trenches formed a bridgehead on the western bank of the canal. The French defence forces retained roughly the area to the west of the road from Boezinge to Lizerne. The area was marked by hundreds of shell holes, presaging what was to follow in the years to come. On 16 May the Germans were driven back to the eastern bank of the canal and years of stalemate began.

» **SEE ALSO** 28 BOEZINGE – HET SAS

F4-F5

BOEZINGE SAS

Seventeenth-century lock on the Ieperlee. The Germans reached their outposts over the canal, just to the right of the lock.

A5-H4

YPRES-YSER CANAL

German trenches dug into the bank of the Ypres–Yser Canal.

C3

LAMOTTE FARM

When this aerial picture was taken Lamotte Farm was in French hands and under heavy fire from German artillery.

↑ **SKETCH BY RUDOLF LANGE**

Sketch of Boezinge Sas by the German officer Rudolf Lange.

E4-F3-G2

GERMAN FRONT LINE

Solidly built trench on the canal's western bank. On 16 May it was taken by French colonial troops.

F4-F5

ST NICHOLAS FORT

Visible on the aerial photograph are traces of the hornwork of the old Vauban fortification around the lock.

→ **MAP OF GAS ATTACKS**

German map showing the area captured during the German gas attack on 22 April 1915. The Germans succeeded in crossing the canal at both Steenstraat and Het Sas and establishing a bridgehead on the canal's western bank.

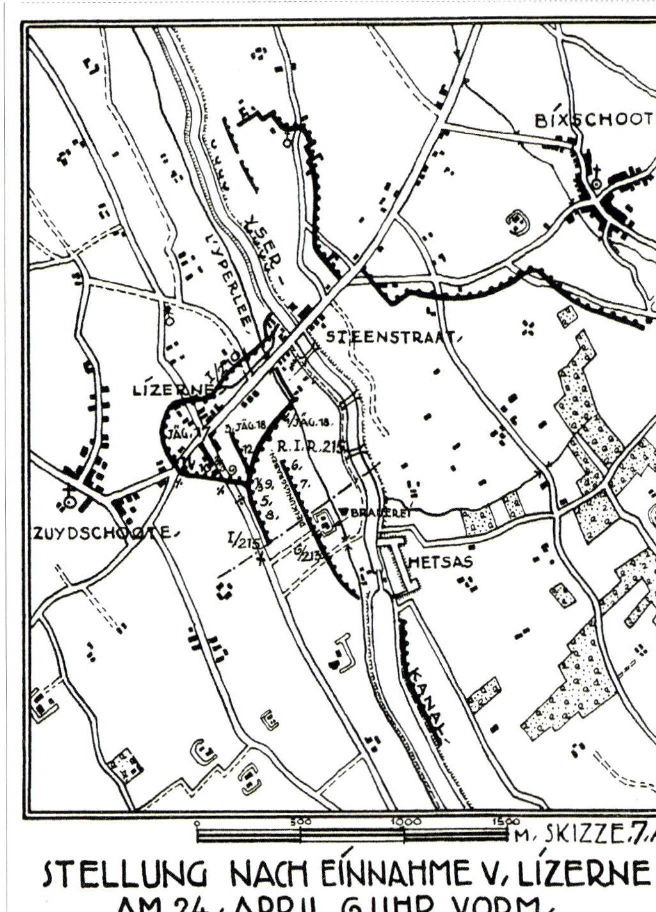

A
B
C
D
600 m Zuidschote
E
F
F
G
H
G
300 m Lizerne
2
3
Ieperlee
5
6
Sasstraat

10
YPRES – FUSILIER FARM
28 APRIL 1915

The gas attack of 22 April 1915 caused the French front between Steenstraat, Langemark and Keerselaar to collapse. In the gathering dusk the Germans dug themselves in near Pilkem, just past the highest point on the slope facing Ypres. At the same time the French front line formed to the north of the Kleine Poezelstraat between the night of 22 April and 28 April 1915. German aerial photographs by Freiherr Dietrich von Kanne are primary sources for the astonishingly rapid creation of the famous salient around Ypres. Within just a few days the basis was created for a front line that would remain unchanged for more than two and a quarter years.

GPS 50°53'01.65"N 2°53'04.27"E

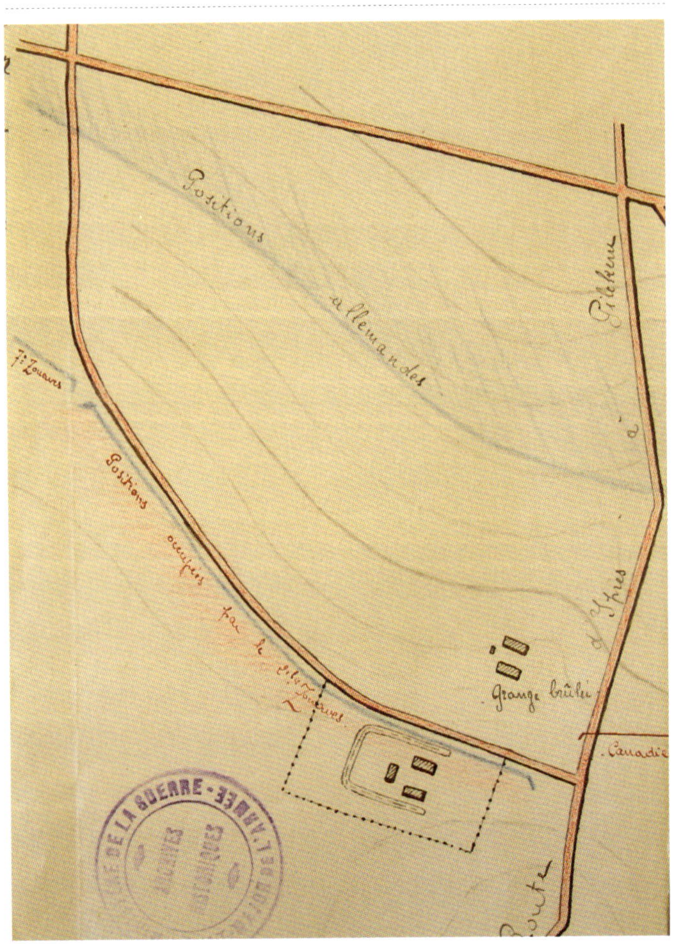

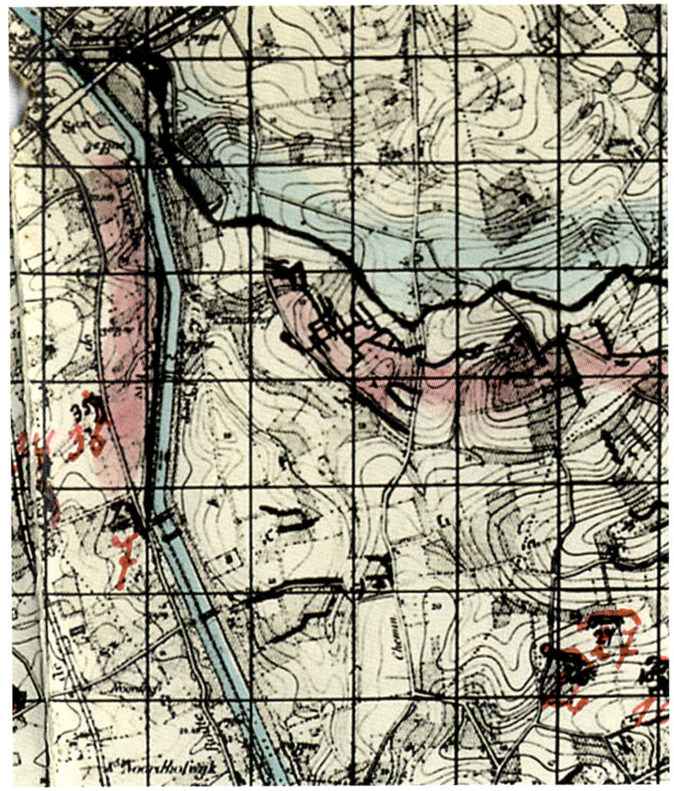

↑ OBSERVER MAP, 25 APRIL 1915

The German observer Freiherr von Kanne mapped the enemy positions from aerial photographs. The positions on the Kleine Poezelstraat are at the centre of this picture.

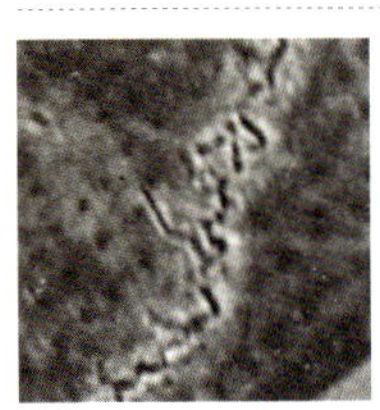

D1
GERMAN TRENCHES

The siting of the German defences was determined by the situation on the ground. Contours were the first consideration. Small natural elements such as rows of trees and hedges were also important factors in determining where trenches should be.

← FRENCH ZOUAVES, 23 APRIL 1915

A French map shows the position of the Zouaves on 23 April 1915, dug in behind the Kleine Poezelstraat.

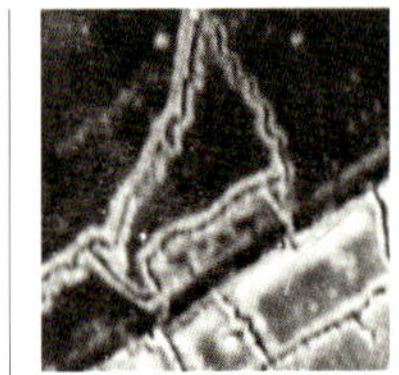

D4
FRENCH TRENCHES

On 22 April the French retreated to behind the Kleine Poezelstraat. In the days after this they regained territory and, trench by trench, moved further towards the German lines.

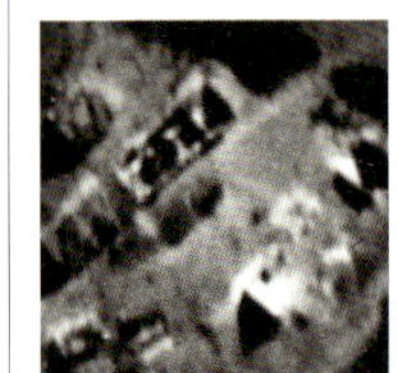

G2
FUSILIER FARM

This moated farm was reduced to a ruin in this phase of the war.

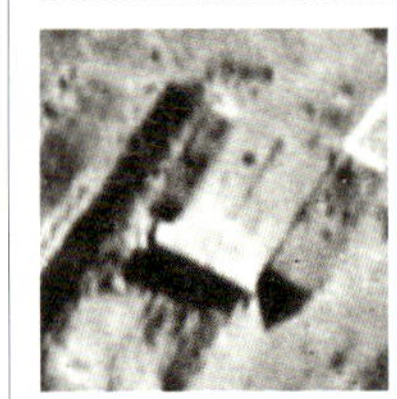

H3
LANCASHIRE FARM

In the following years the front line was expanded and reinforced. Beneath this farm the British built a large underground dugout in 1917.

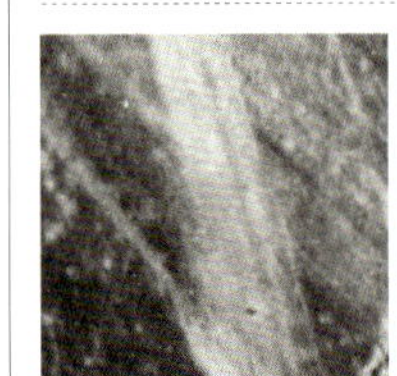

B4-B5
TRACES OF TROOP MOVEMENTS

The vegetation shows traces of intensive troop movements in the period immediately preceding the digging of lines.

SYMBOLS

- ALLIED TRENCHES
- GERMAN TRENCHES

Vijfwegen

Vijfwegen

A
B
Pilkemseweg
D
G
E
F
F
G
H
1
Kleine Poezelstraat
3
3.2 km 46 96 125 Ypres
5
6
100m
F
1.2 km 11 64 Essex Farm

11
ESSEX FARM END OF APRIL 1915

The German observer-photographer Freiherr Dietrich von Kanne was active over the Ypres Salient during the Second Battle of Ypres. In the last week of April he photographed the canal sector just north of Ypres. It was in this area that, on 3 May 1915, the Canadian doctor John McCrae wrote his famous poem ‘In Flanders Fields’. At the time he was caring for the wounded near ‘Essex Farm’ in a small dressing post dug out of the canal bank. A small grave nearby inspired him to write ‘In Flanders fields the poppies blow / Between the crosses, row on row …’. On 27 April there was as yet no trace of an organised cemetery at Essex Farm. Five hundred metres to the north three rows of graves can already be seen at the Marengo Farm Cemetery.

» **SEE ALSO** 64 ESSEX FARM

↓ **VON KANNE**

Portrait of the German aerial photographer Freiherr Dietrich von Kanne, in the back of an observation plane.

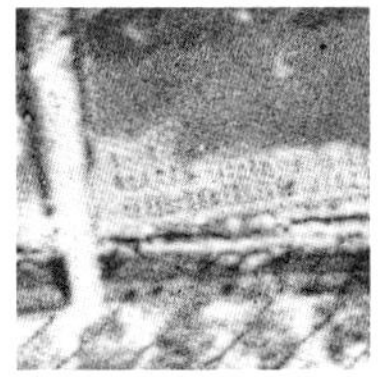

B3-C3
MARENGO FARM CEMETERY

Small cemetery with about forty graves near bridge 5. Graves are already visible in this aerial photograph.

H2
CANAL BANK

The elevated bank of the Ypres–Yser Canal – part of a seventeenth-century retrenchment designed by Vauban – was chosen as the location for a line of defence.

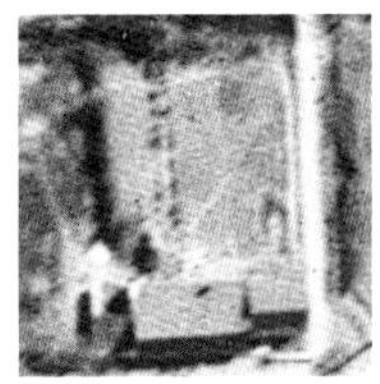

H2-H3
ESSEX FARM

Farm buildings named ‘Essex Farm’ by the Allies. To the right on the other side of the road is the future site of the Essex Farm Cemetery.

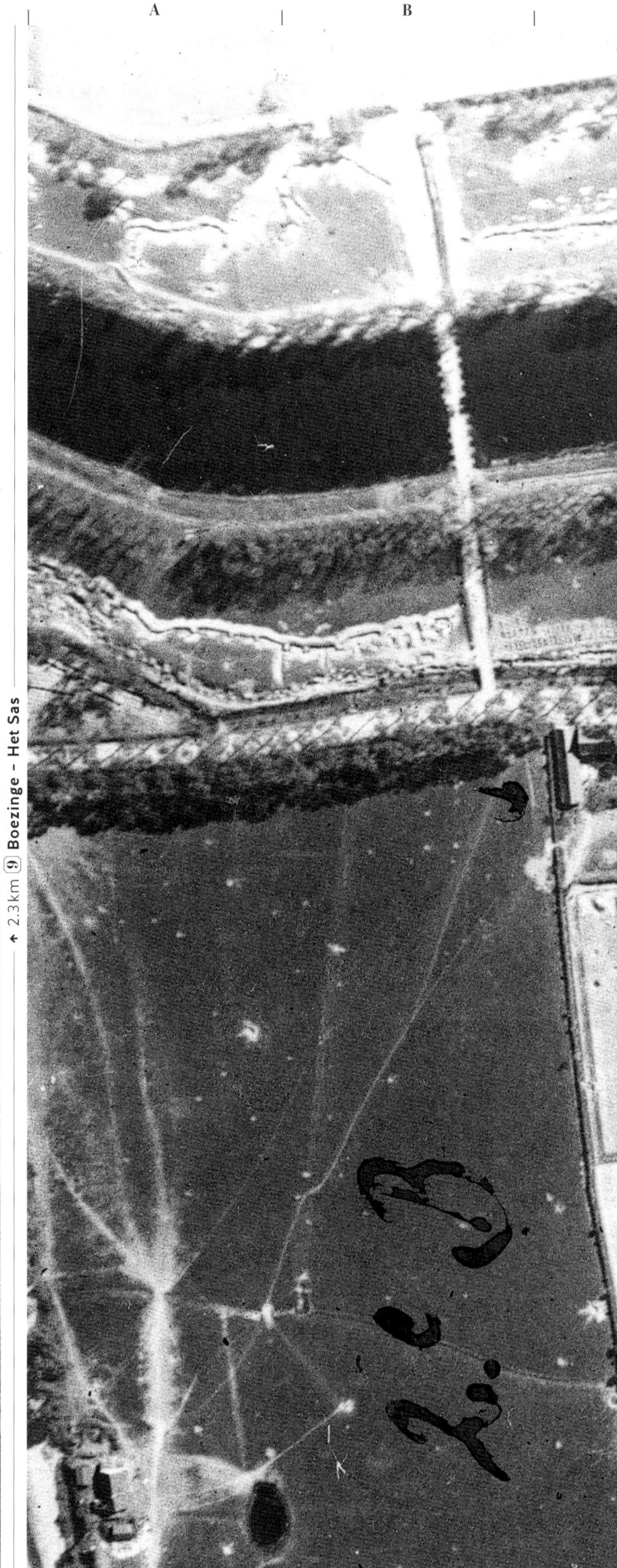

↑ 2.3km 9 Boezinge – Het Sas

GPS 50°52'15.22"N 2°52'24.19"E

D
↑ 1.2 km 10 Fusilier Farm
E
F
G
↓ wooden footbridge
I
J
Ieperlee
1
2
Diksmuideweg ↓
3
↑ 2.3 km 46 96 125 Ypres
5
6
100m
↓ 1.3 km Brielen
↑ Noordhofweg

12
BELLEWAARDE 29 MAY 1915

Bellewaarde Ridge, a strategic hill to the east of Ypres between the Menin Road and the Ypres–Roeselare railway, was taken by the Germans following a gas attack on 24 May 1915. This British photograph of 29 May 1915 shows the layout of the British and German trenches some days later. The British front line was set up west of Cambridge Road (Begijnenbosstraat, A2-E1), and the German troops dug themselves in between Railway Wood (F1-G1) and Y Wood (C4). The captured British trenches were reused but are recognisable by the angle of the traverses. The dark stripe (B6-E4) on the photograph is part of the aircraft's undercarriage.

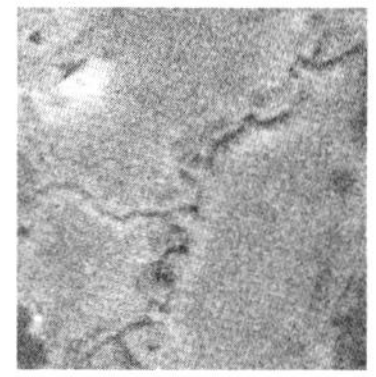

H5
BRITISH FRONT LINE BEFORE 24 MAY

The angle of the traverses in the trenches shows that this was the British front line before 24 May 1915.

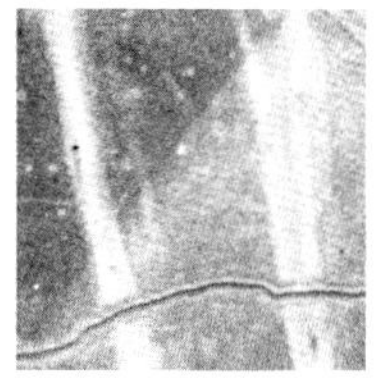

E5-E6
TROOP MOVEMENTS

The lightly coloured lines on the photograph are the traces of intense troop movements.

↓ TRAVERSED TRENCH

Diagram from a British field manual. The front of a trench was usually straight. The traverses jut out at the back.

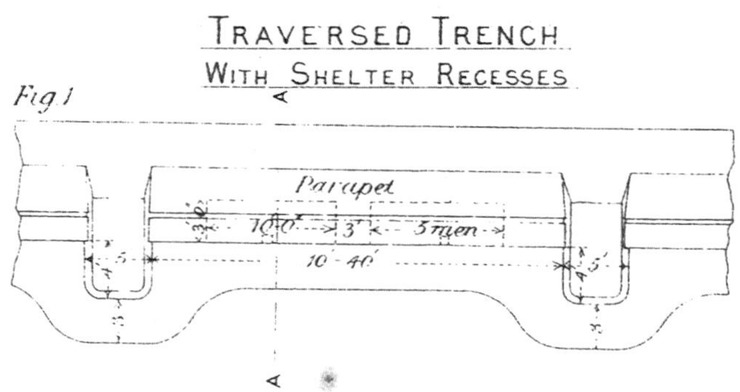

↓ BELLEWAARDE RIDGE

View of the Bellewaarde Ridge battlefield. The German front line is on top of the ridge (E3-G2). Railway Wood is to the left. Detail from a British photograph of 1 June 1915.

GPS 50°51'06.81"N 2°56'14.48"E

↑ 3km 46 96 125 Ypres

A

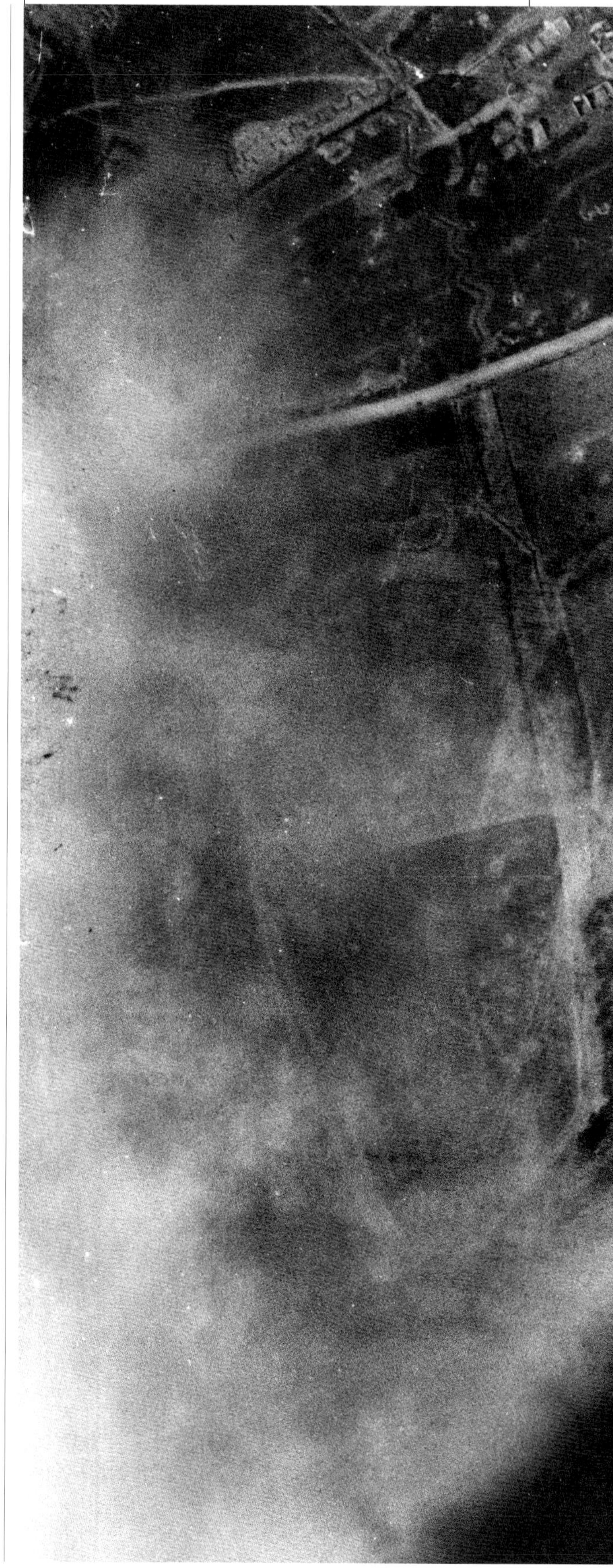

D
GB from 24 May 1915
E
F
Railway Wood
G
G from 24 May 1915
I
J
1
Ypres–Roeselare railway
3
GB before 24 May 1915
G before 24 May 1915
6
100m
300 m 14 22 43 129 Hooge
Bellewaerdestraat
GB before 24 May 1915
G before 24 May 1915

13

HOLLEBEKE 'DREIHÄUSER'

30 MAY 1915, 29 APRIL 1916 & 6 APRIL 1917

Many cemeteries were sited near hospitals or dressing posts in the front zone. Soldiers who succumbed to their wounds were often buried near by. In Hollebeke, in a little cluster of three houses behind the Ypres–Comines Canal, there was a German dressing post hardly a kilometre behind the front. It was called, appropriately, Dreihäuser ('Three Houses'). On 30 May 1915 a few rows of graves could already be seen in a field behind the buildings. Soon the cemetery next to the farm no longer sufficed. One year later (29 April 1916) another photograph shows burials in a second cemetery, also a simple one. This cemetery consists of three sections with what seems to be a memorial monument. The German cemetery at Dreihäuser grew month by month. The photograph on the extreme right dates from 6 April 1917. This series of photographs over a period of time bears tangible witness to the human suffering inflicted during the war.

GPS 50°48'34.43"N 2°56'39.49"E

↑ DREIHÄUSER

Photograph from 1915 of the farm buildings housing the dressing post of the 1st Sanitäts-Kompagnie (Medical Company) of the 105th Infanterie-Regiment. To the left of the farm can be seen the white crosses of the cemetery.

← BURIAL

German troops pose during the burial of a soldier in a cemetery near Dreihäuser.

→ THE DEVELOPMENT OF THE CEMETERY THROUGH THE WAR

From left to right: 20 May 1915, 29 April 1916 and 6 April 1917.

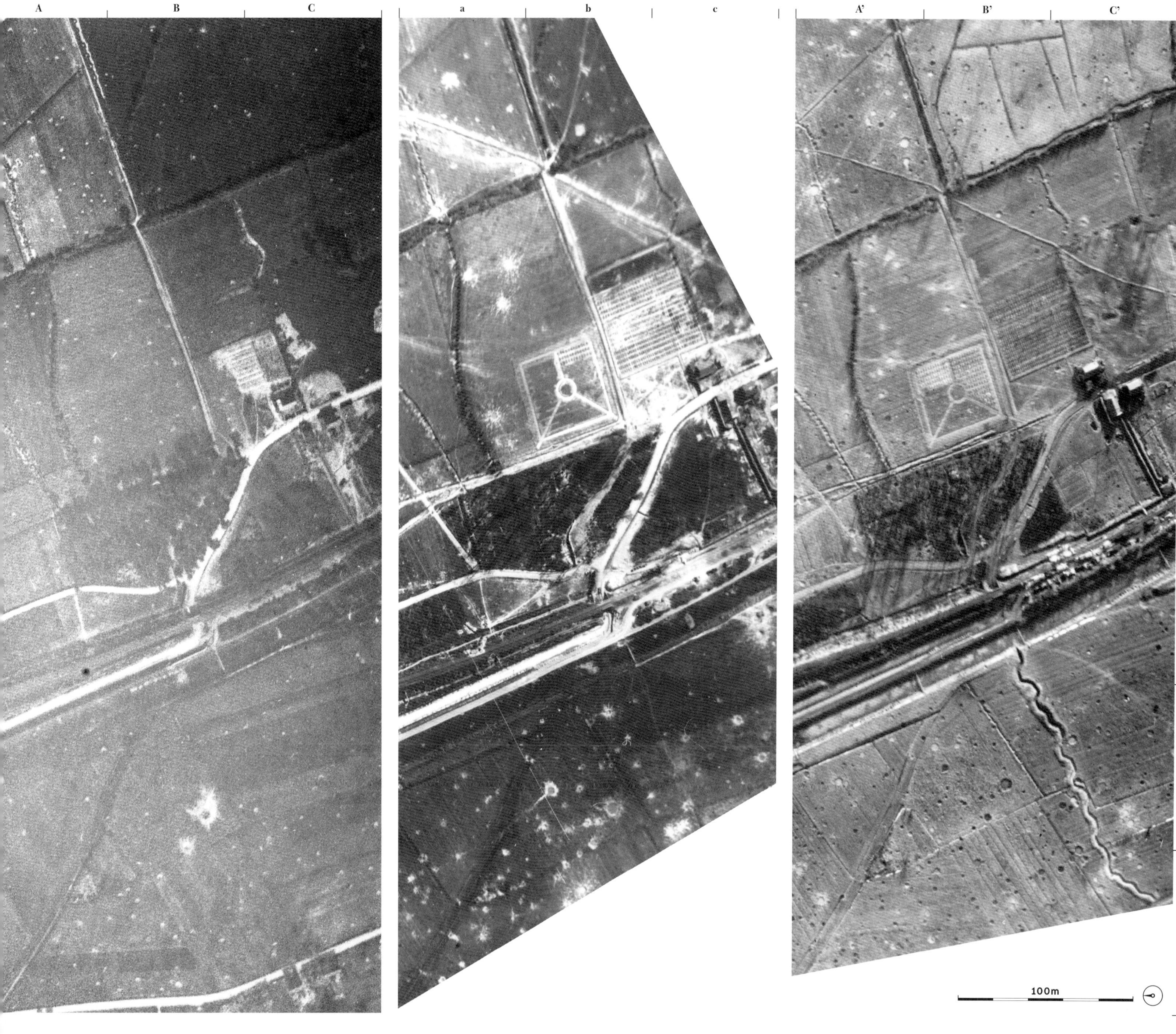

A
B
C
a
b
c
A'
B'
C'
1
2
3
4
5
6
Ypres-Comines Canal
2.7km Houthem
300m Kortewilde
100m

14

HOOGE 20 JULY 1915

In May and June 1915 there was heavy fighting for the high ground at Bellewaarde and Hooge. On 16 June 1915 the British 3rd division attacked, but failed to dislodge the German troops from their vantage points. From Hooge, the enemy still had a good view of the British lines. Under difficult circumstances a tunnel was dug to undermine the German positions. At about seven o'clock on 19 July an underground mine was exploded and the resulting crater was very quickly seized by the 4th Middlesex of the 3rd Division. Hooge, however, continued to change hands at various times in the following months, gaining notoriety as one of the most dangerous sectors on the Western Front.

→ MENIN ROAD

On 29–30 July 1915 the Germans took Château Hooge park and the Menin Road. After their recapture by the British 6th Division on 9 August 1915, the northern edge of the crater was equipped as a trench. The photograph dates from September 1915.

↑ HOOGE, JUNE 1915

Vertical view of Hooge just before the attack on Bellewaarde (16 June 1915). There were as yet no assembly trenches on the southern side of the Menin Road (cf. D1). The British occupy the area south of the road and the Château Hooge stables north of the road.

← HOOGE

View of the strategic high ground at the hamlet of Hooge, part of the panoramic picture taken on 6 June 1915.

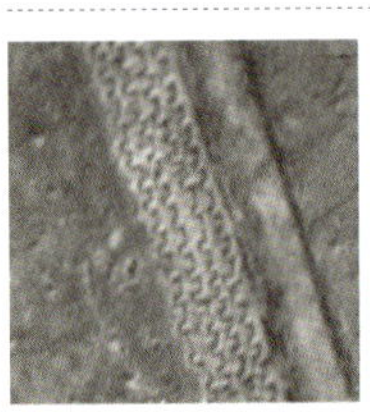

D1

ASSEMBLY TRENCHES

The purpose of the assembly trenches was to gather as many troops as possible at the front line – in this case to carry out an attack on the enemy lines on 16 June 1915 (first attack on Bellewaarde).

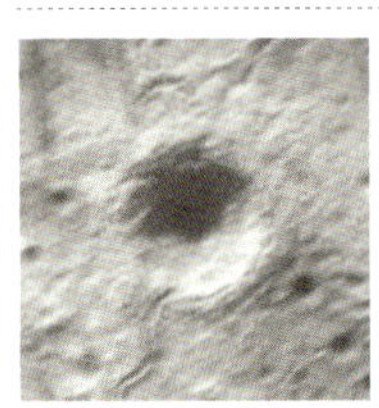

E3

CRATER, 19 JULY 1915

The 175th Tunnelling Company has just undermined the German lines. The photograph shows the crater, which is almost 40 metres wide.

SYMBOLS

- ALLIED TRENCHES
- GERMAN TRENCHES
- BELLEWAARDE LAKE
- WOOD
- CHÂTEAU HOOGE AND STABLES
- HOOGE CRATER

GPS 50°50'48.26"N 2°56'39.59"E

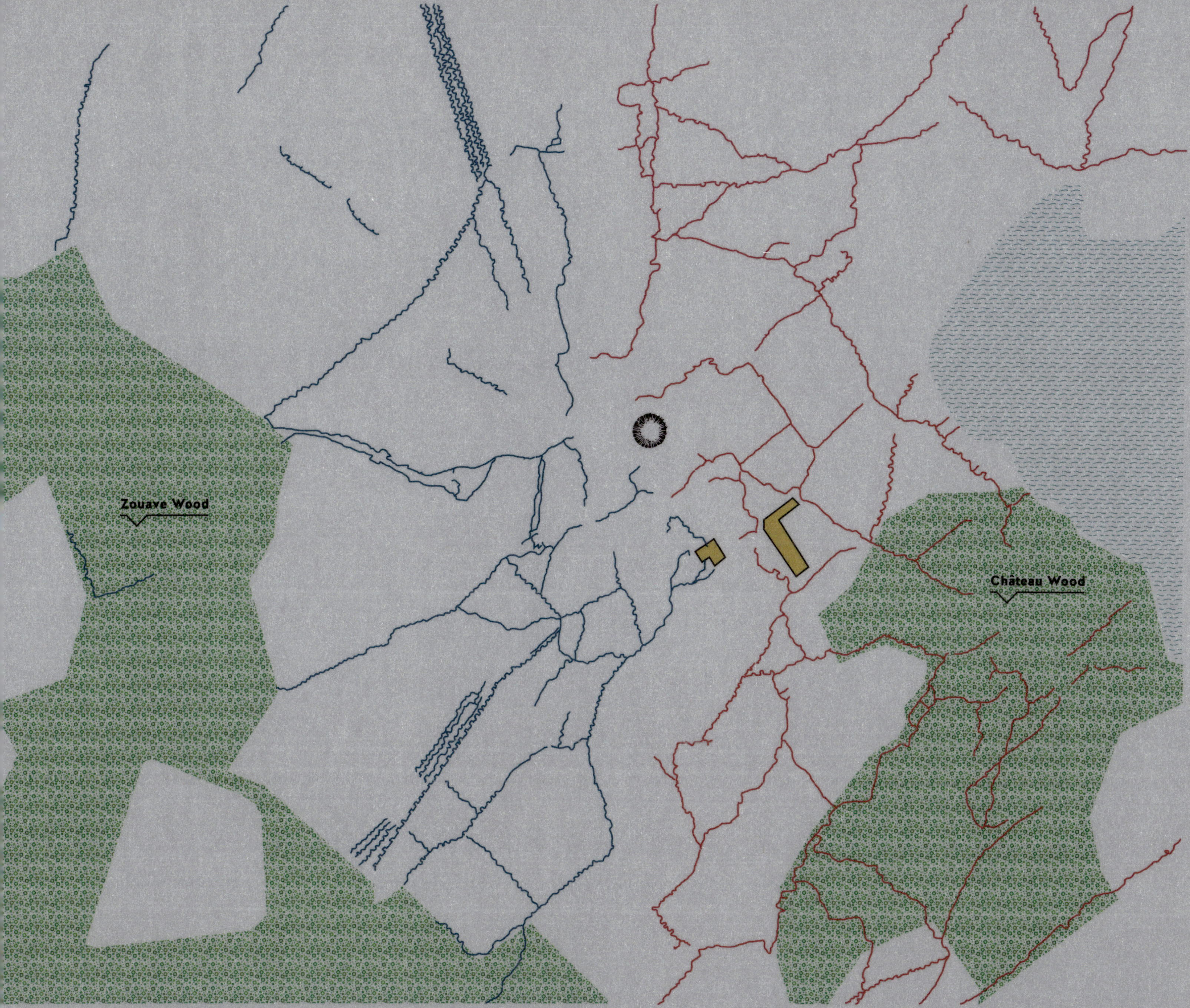
Zouave Wood
Château Wood

Château Wood
Zouave Wood

A
B
C
GB
↑ 3.5 km 46 96 125 Ypres
G
F
G
↑ 500 m 12 16 34 Bellewaarde
1
2
3
4
5
6
100m
GB
G
↑ Menin Road
Kasteeldreef ↖

15 WIJTSCHATE KRUISSTRAAT-HOEK 2 SEPTEMBER 1915

The front at Wijtschate and Mesen expanded at the start of the trench warfare into a genuine stronghold. In 1915 the military tacticians still attached great importance to the occupation of the foremost line, which was expanded, on the German side in particular. Dozens of shelters were dug and the first solid bunkers were built. Notable on the British side was the great concentration of communication trenches. The siting of the trenches was related to the contours in this sector: the difference between seeing and being seen was of vital importance. The communication trenches ran up to a plateau on the ridge of the hill (G4). At this point little account was taken of aerial reconnaissance.

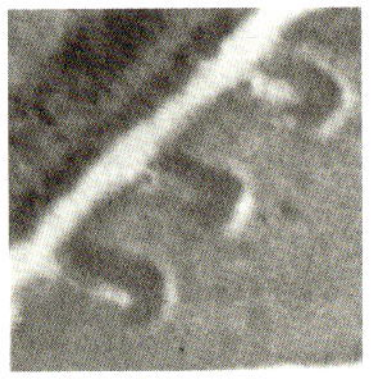

C5

ARTILLERY

Firing positions very near the front. Like the communication trenches, these were just out of sight of German observers.

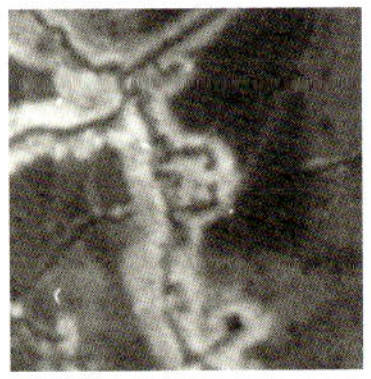

I4-I5

GERMAN BUNKER

Two small trench sections lead to the rear of an entrenched bunker.

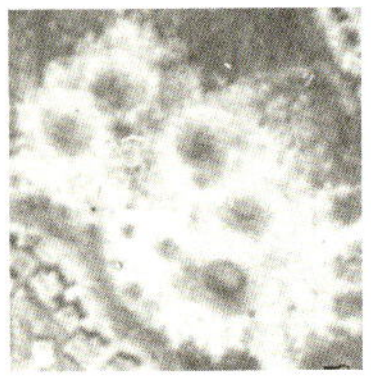

G4

MINE CRATERS

In the Wijtschate sector British tunnellers were pitched against German pioneers in an underground war. Evidence for this is provided by a dozen small mine craters in no-man's-land. These were the result of defensive mines exploded to make the enemy's tunnels collapse.

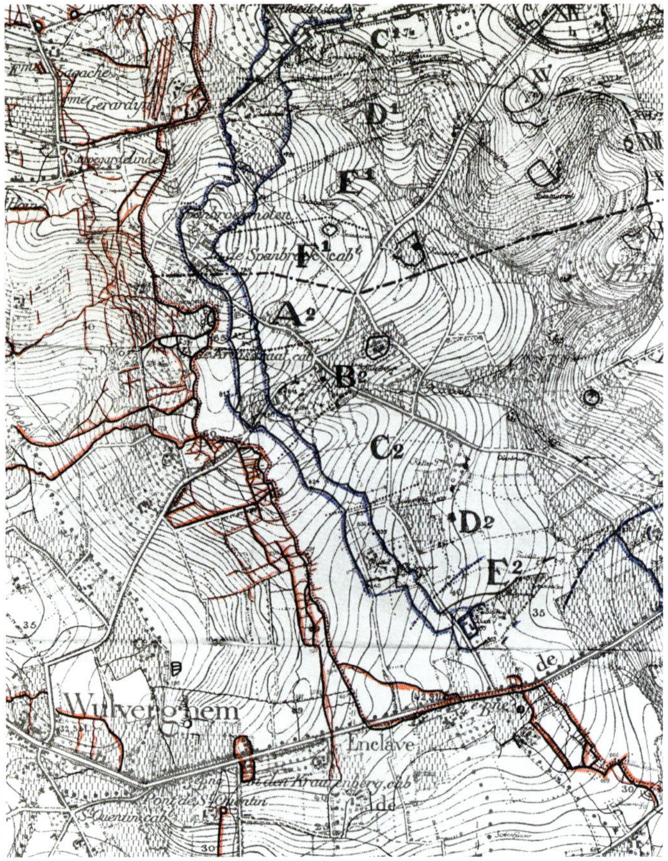

↑ **GERMAN TRENCH MAP**

Here we can see the ridge at Wijtschate, on a map from 1915. The Germans' own lines are marked in blue, the British positions in red.

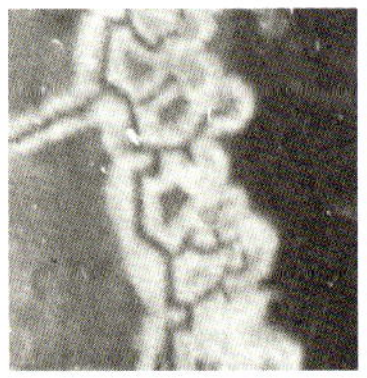

H1

SHELTERS

By 1915 the German second line had grown into a fort. On the rear side of the fighting trenches dozens of dugout shelters are visible.

B5-C5

R.E. FARM CEMETERY

British cemetery to the east of R.E. Farm, which was first used in December 1914. 179 British and Canadian soldiers still lie buried there today.

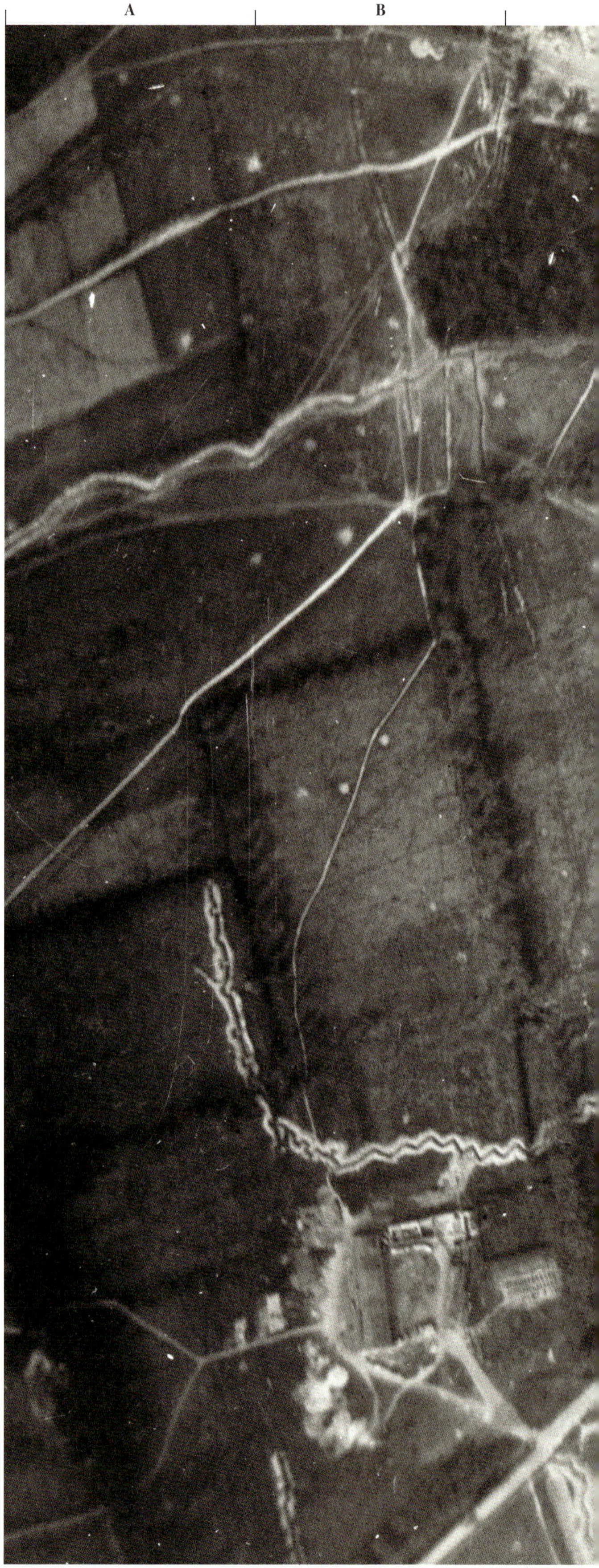

GPS 50°46'20.55"N 2°51'47.79"E

↙ 600 m **Wulvergem**

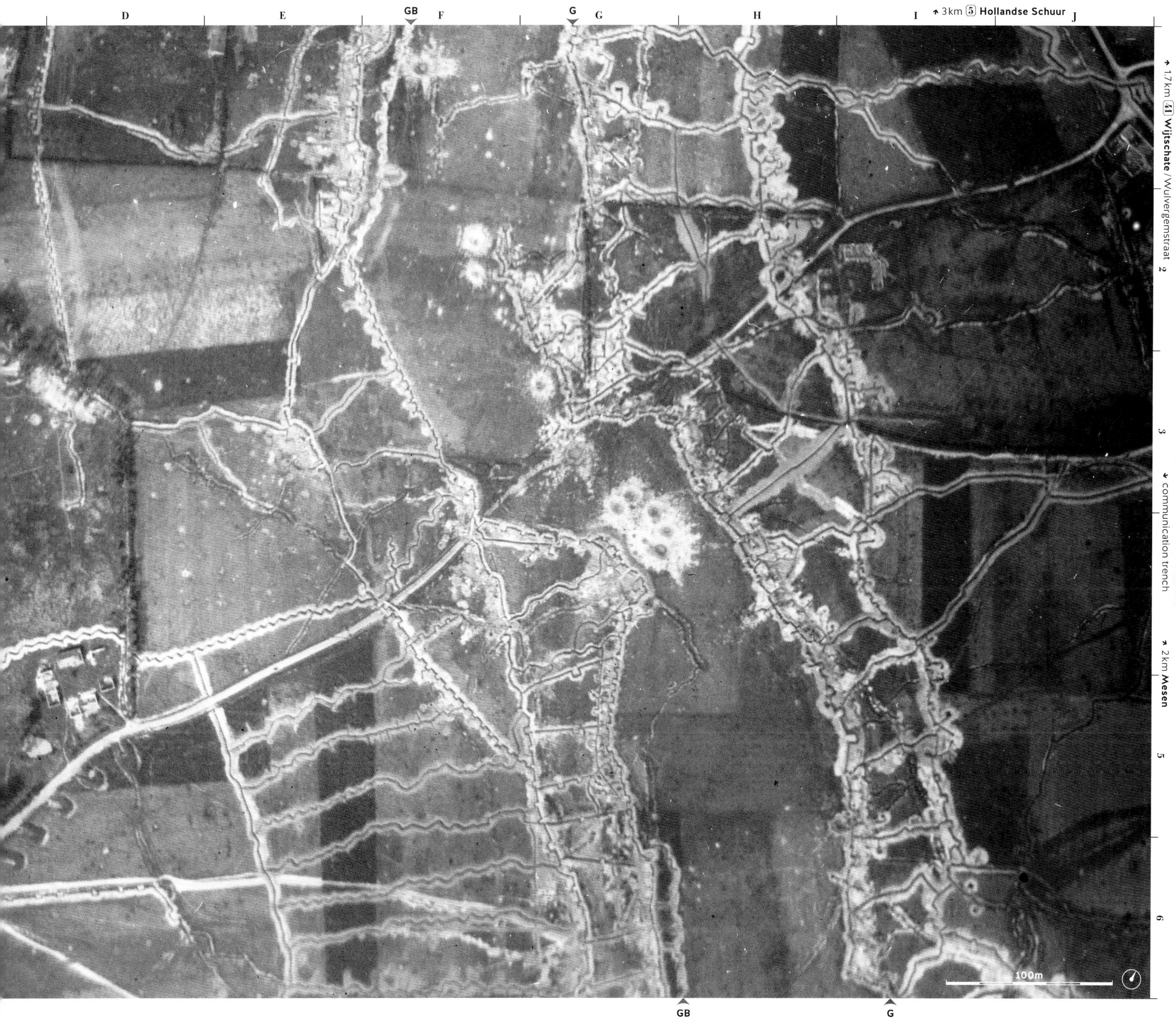

D
E
GB
F
G
G
H
I
↑ 3km 5 Hollandse Schuur
J
↗ 1.7km 41 Wijtschate / Wulvergemstraat
2
3
↙ communication trench
↗ 2km Mesen
5
6
100m
GB
G

16 BELLEWAARDE
2 AUGUST 1915

Following the German attack of 24 May (the Battle of Bellewaarde) both parties entrenched themselves on the ridge. Between 7 and 12 June eight parallel rows of assembly trenches were dug on both sides of the Cambridge Road. From here, British units mounted an attack on 16 June in an attempt to retake Bellewaarde Ridge. This was not an unqualified success: they chalked up only about 200 metres of territory. An aerial photograph of 2 August 1915 shows just for what more than a thousand soldiers died on that one day. It indicates three changing front lines during the tumultuous period between 24 May and 16 June. Up to 31 July 1917 the front hardly moved, though there was a remorseless underground war going on using deep mines.

» **SEE ALSO** 12 34 BELLEWAARDE

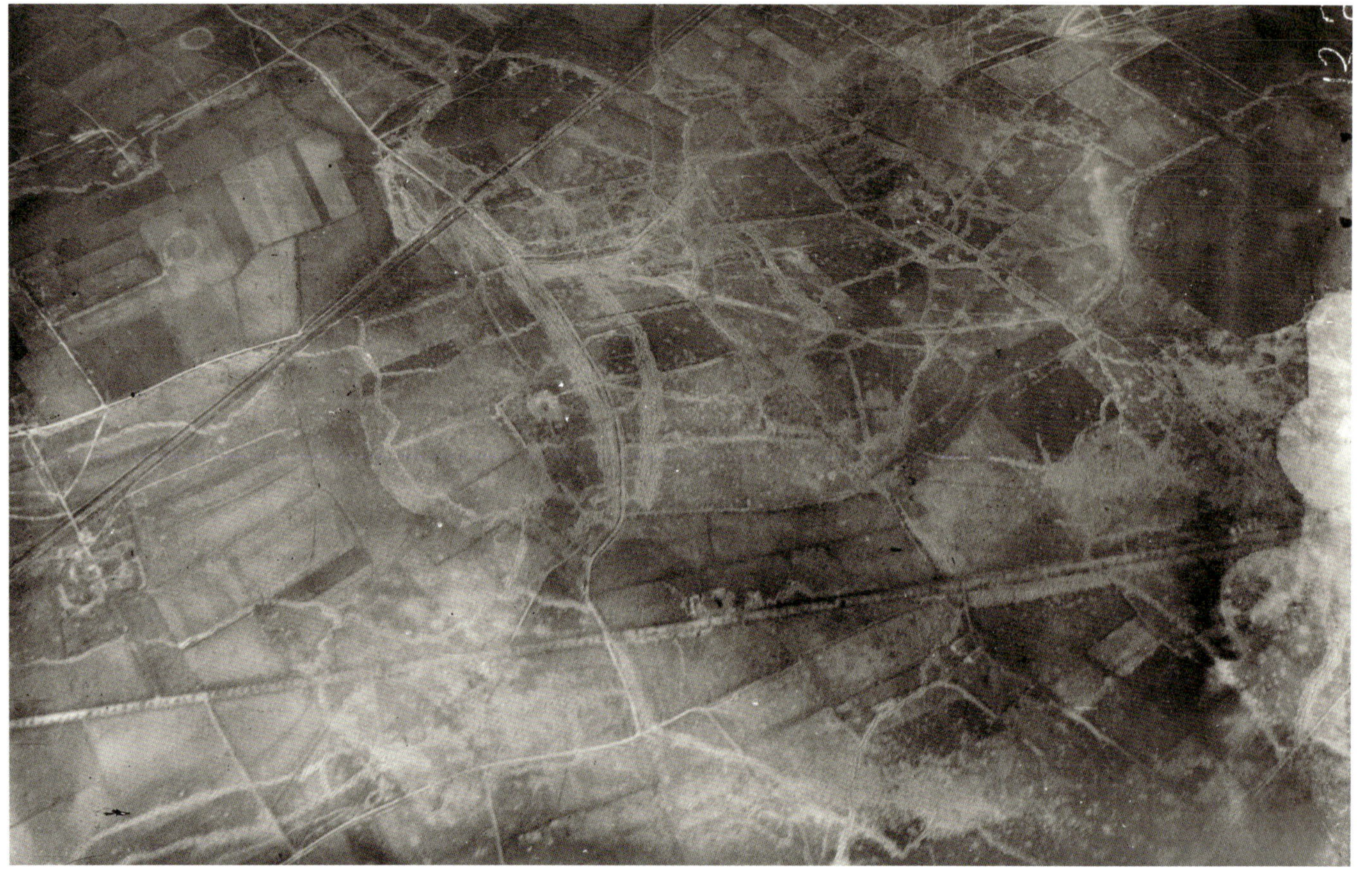

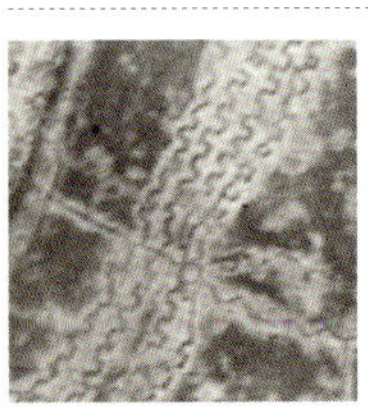

C5
ASSEMBLY TRENCHES

Assembly trenches were used to bring as many men as possible to the foremost line with the aim of mounting a massive attack. These examples were dug between 7 and 12 June 1915.

BELLEWAARDE, 16 JUNE 1915: PRIVATE FYFE

Photographs taken during the Liverpool Scottish attack on Bellewaarde Ridge on 16 June 1915. The photographer, Private Fyfe, lying wounded in no-man's-land, took a number of rare action photographs of the attack on the German positions. The attacking British troops are seeking shelter in front of a German front trench at Railway Wood.

SYMBOLS

- 1 BRITISH FRONT LINE BEFORE THE BATTLE OF BELLEWAARDE (24 MAY 1915)
- 1 GERMAN FRONT LINE BEFORE THE BATTLE OF BELLEWAARDE (24 MAY 1915)
- 2 BRITISH FRONT LINE AFTER THE BATTLE OF BELLEWAARDE (24 MAY 1915)
- 2 GERMAN FRONT LINE AFTER THE BATTLE OF BELLEWAARDE (24 MAY 1915)
- 3 BRITISH FRONT LINE AFTER AFTER THE FIRST ATTACK ON BELLEWAARDE (16 JUNE 1915)
- 3 GERMAN FRONT LINE AFTER THE FIRST ATTACK ON BELLEWAARDE (16 JUNE 1915)
- BRITISH FRONT LINE 1 AUGUST 1915
- GERMAN FRONT LINE 1 AUGUST 1915
- YPRES–ROESELARE RAILWAY
- MENIN ROAD
- CAMBRIDGE ROAD
- WATER
- WOOD

Railway Wood
Witte Poort Farm
Bellewaarde Farm
Y-wood
1
1
2
2
3
3

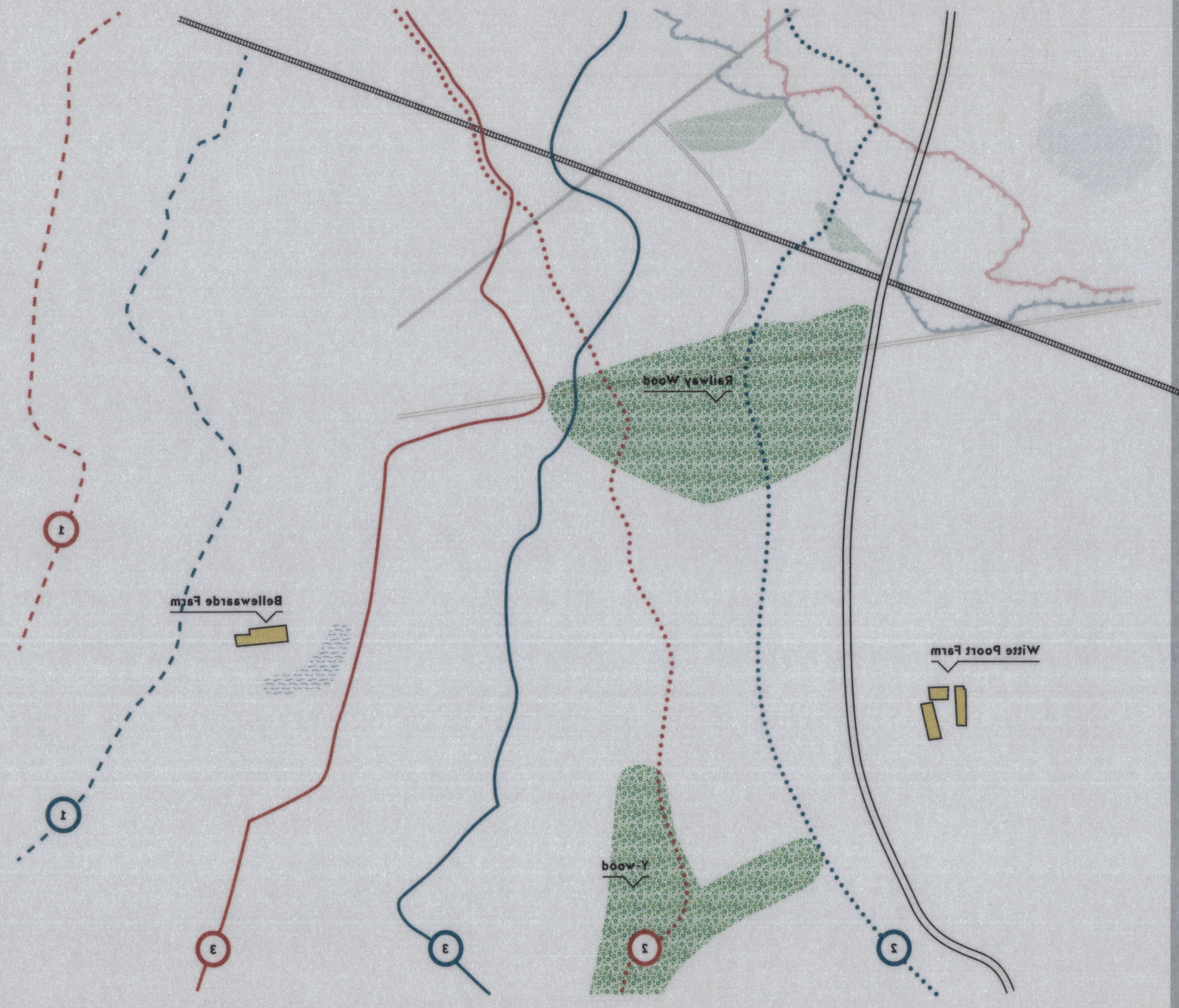
Railway Wood
Bellewarde Farm
Witte Poort Farm
Y-wood
1
1
3
3
2
2

Cambridge Road

14 22 43 129 **Hooge** 600 m

17

LE GHEER – THE BIRDCAGE

25 JANUARY 1916

Between the hamlets of Le Pelerin and Le Gheer (Ploegsteert, to the east of the wood), the Germans built a notorious position that the British called 'The Birdcage' on account of the large quantities of barbed wire in front of the trenches.[3] The small protruding salient was surrounded on three sides by British trenches, an unenviable and dangerous situation. Between June and September 1915 this sector was the theatre of an underground war in which the British and Germans sought to undermine each other's lines. A chronological series of aerial photographs illustrates the sequence of the mine explosions.

At the end of 1916 there were four more British mines under The Birdcage ready for the planned offensive on the Messines Ridge (7 June 1917). As they were ultimately outside the attack area, they were not exploded. One mine did eventually explode, during a storm on 17 July 1955, and left a 20-metre crater under the Chemin des Loups where it crossed Umbo Trench.

↓ THE BIRDCAGE

British trench map of 1 April 1917 with at the right bottom the German trenches known as 'The Birdcage' (between White Estaminet, Elger House and Le Pelerin), a salient in the Allied line.

→ SERIES OF AERIAL PHOTOGRAPHS

By analysing a series of aerial photographs taken over a period of time one can recapture the chronology of the mine explosions. These aerial photographs were taken on (from top to bottom) 24 May, 7 June, 12 July and 10 September.

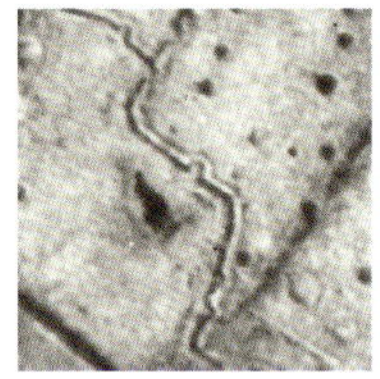

D4-D5

ABANDONED TRENCHES

Up to the middle of 1915 the German bulge protruded still further into the British lines. The trenches were abandoned in July 1915 in favour of a trench that was easier to defend, 120 metres eastwards.

F4

BRITISH CRATERS

Between 24 May and 7 June two mines were exploded under the German positions. After this the Germans strengthened the positions.

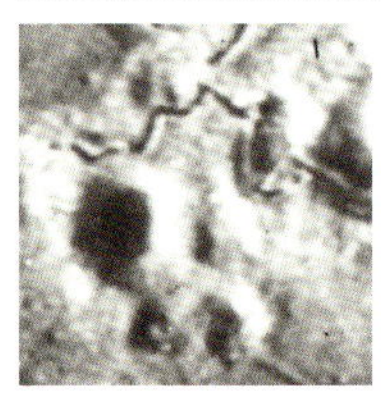

G3-G4

CRATERS

A large group of craters very near the British front line.

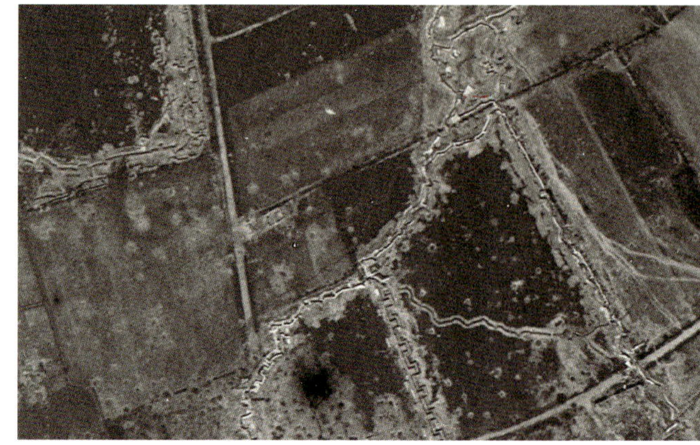

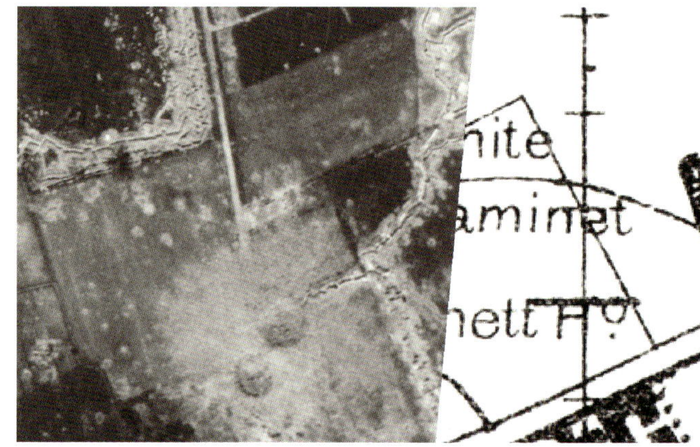

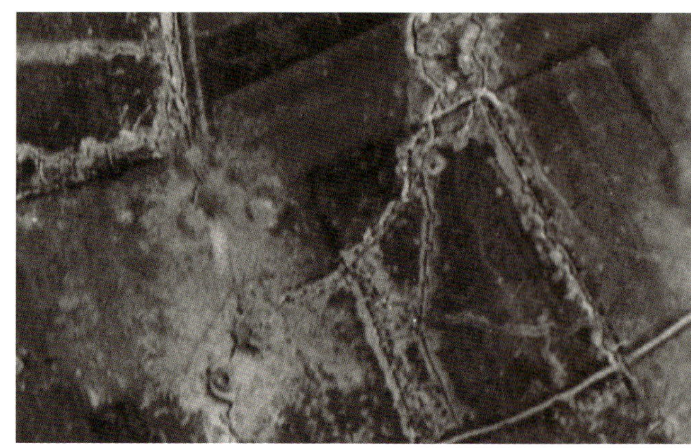

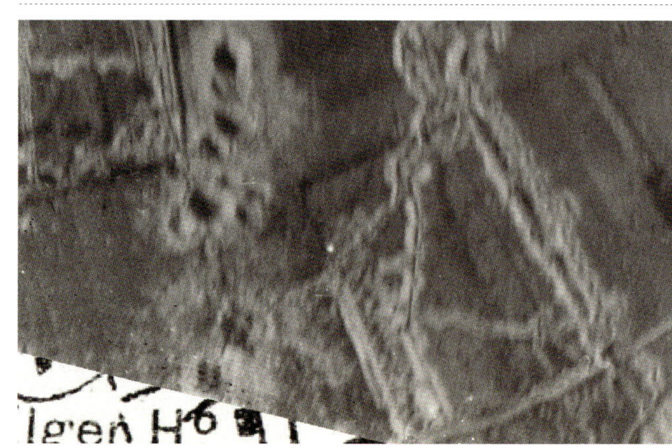

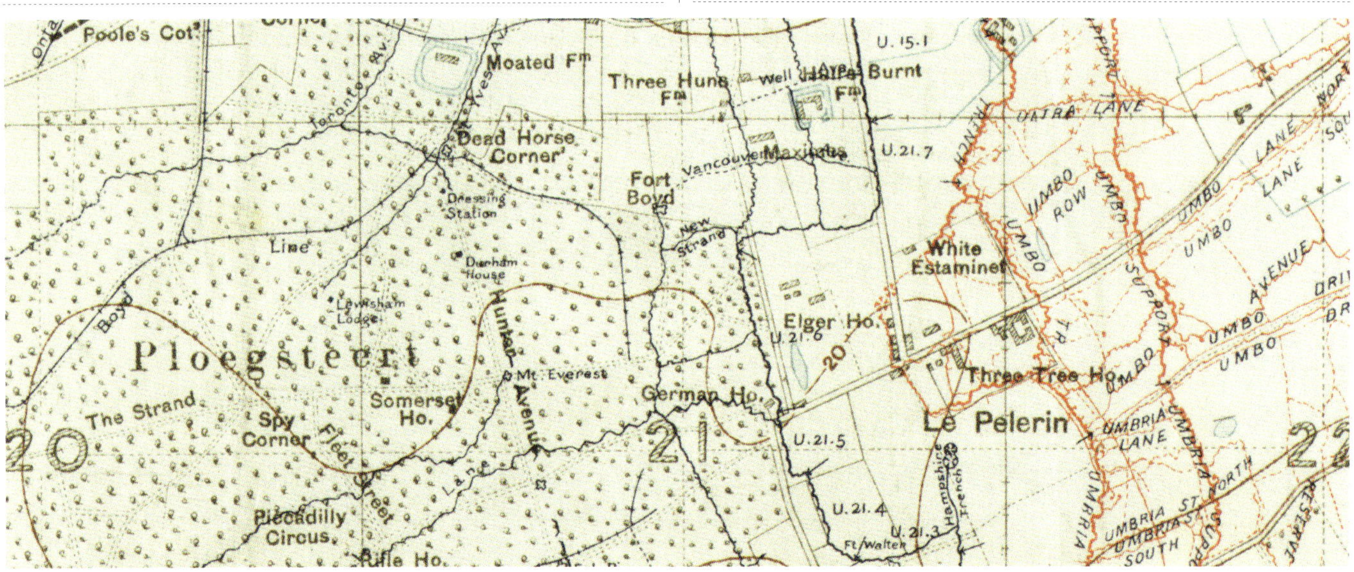

A
B
↓ Plugstreet Wood
C
D
↖ 2.2 km Ploegsteert
E
F
G
H
1
GB
2
3
G
4
5
Wolvenweg ↙
100m
GB
G

18
ZILLEBEKE - THE BLUFF
23 JANUARY 1916

South of Hill 60 the front crossed the Ypres–Comines Canal. Near to this point was a large, strategically situated heap of earth: 'The Bluff' – as the British called it – had been in Allied hands since 1914, much to the annoyance of the Germans. An aerial photograph of 23 January 1916 shows the British and German trenches to the north of the canal. The Bluff is recognisable from the dark shadow that it casts (B2-B3). On 21 January 1916 German mines blew a large crater in the side of the hill. On 14 February there followed a new mine attack, after which the German infantry succeeded in taking The Bluff together with the British front line to the north of it. This situation can be seen on an aerial photograph of 20 February 1916, which is reproduced as a tracing. There are two communication trenches (E1 and D4), running through no-man's-land, through which the Germans were able to safely access the captured position at The Bluff (B3-E1). On 3 March they were forced off the hill.

» **SEE ALSO** 39 THE BLUFF

↑ THE BLUFF, 1915
The Bluff from the German side, around May 1915. The artificial hill has not yet been blown up. In front of it next to the canal are the high piles of the parapet of the German front line.

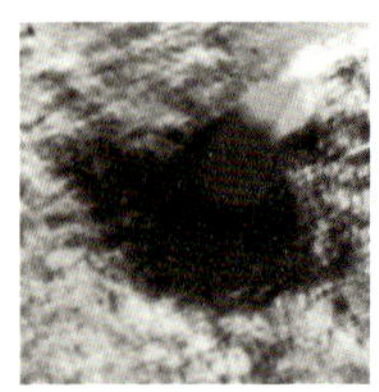

B4
GERMAN MINE CRATER
Elongated mine crater under The Bluff, dating from 21 January 1916 following the explosion of a group of German mines.

SYMBOLS
- 1 BRITISH FRONT ON 13 FEBRUARY 1916
- 1 GERMAN FRONT ON 13 FEBRUARY 1916
- 2 BRITISH FRONT ON 14 FEBRUARY 1916
- 2 GERMAN FRONT ON 14 FEBRUARY 1916
- GERMAN COMMUNICATION TRENCHES TO THE CAPTURED TRENCHES
- 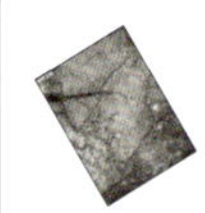 AERIAL PHOTOGRAPH OF 20 FEBRUARY 1916

↓ PANORAMA FROM THE BLUFF
British panoramic photograph taken from the top of The Bluff on 26 May 1915. The parapets of the German trenches on the other side of the no-man's-land contrast sharply with the high grass between the lines.

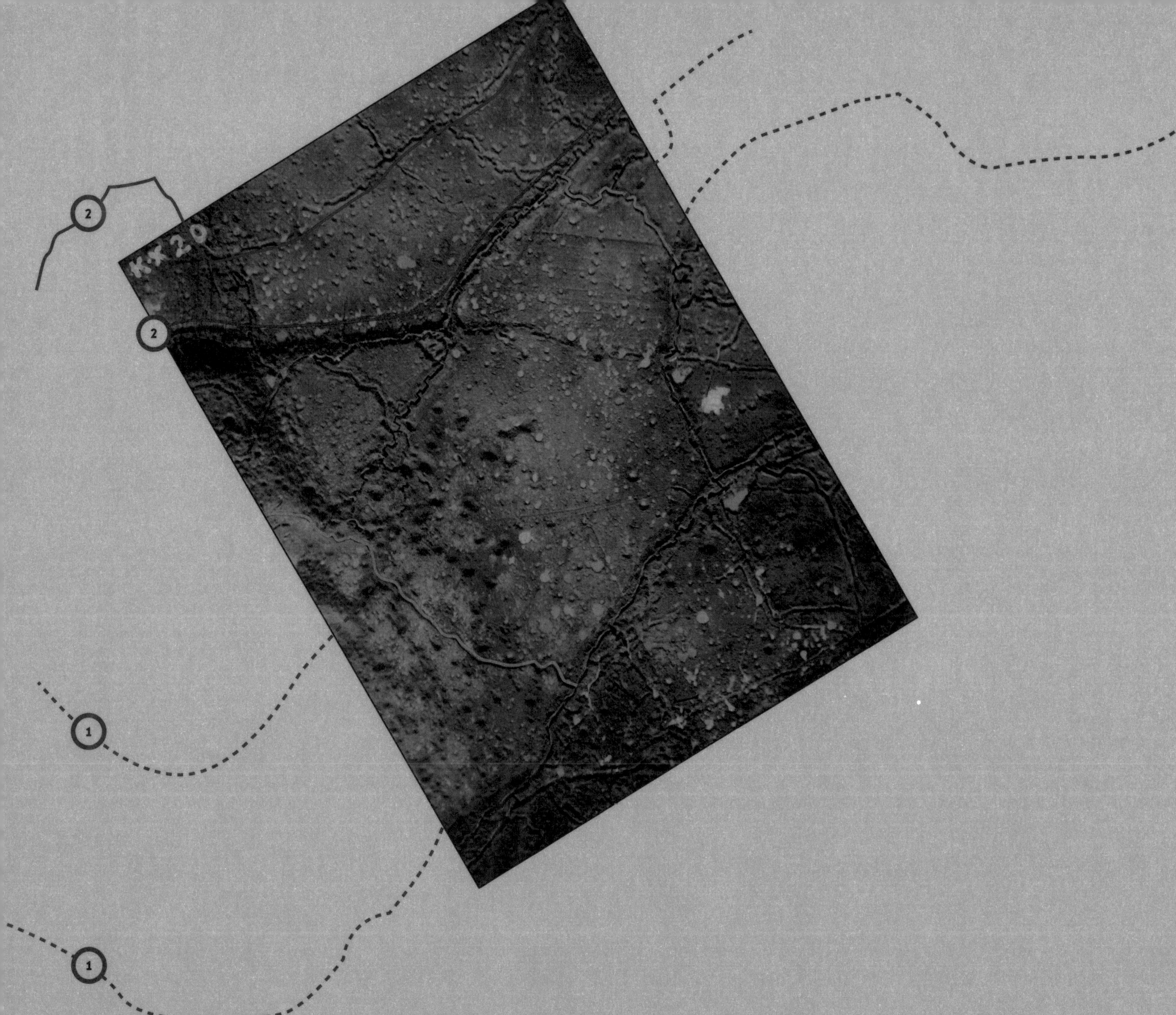
2
2
1
1

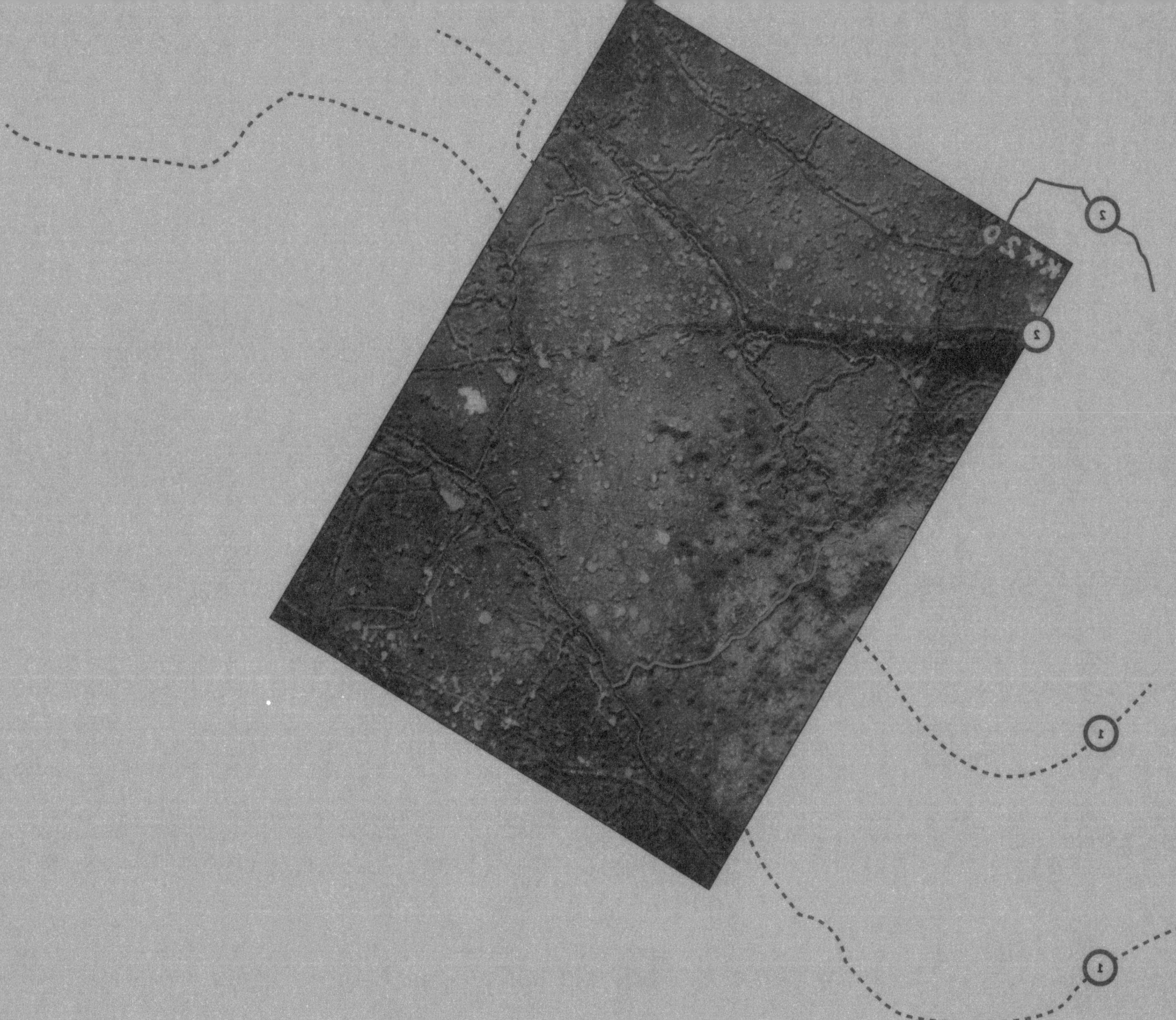

KX 20

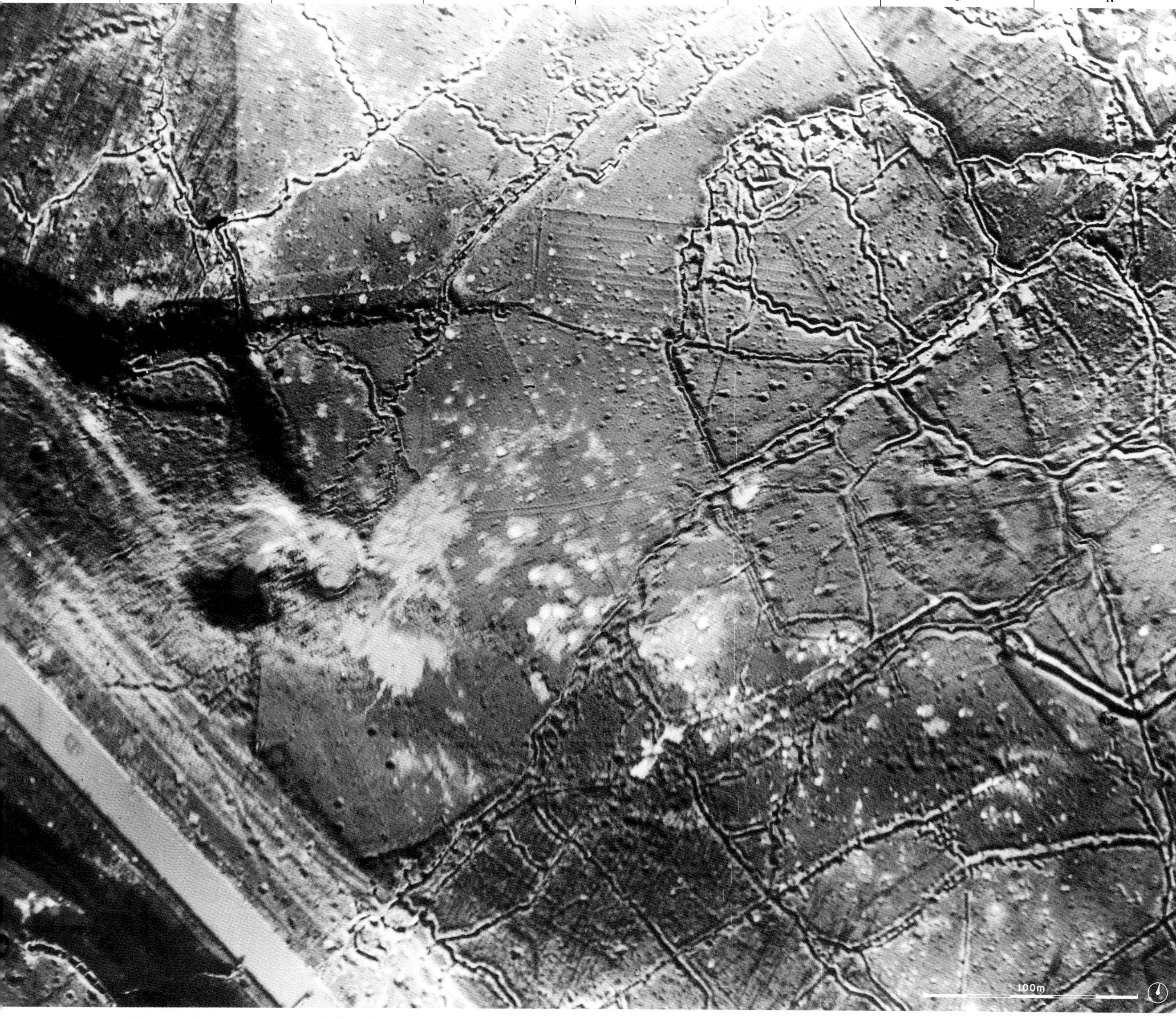

German trench

Ypres-Comines Canal

19

SINT-ELOOI 1 APRIL 1916

Sint-Elooi was, after 1915, the lethal theatre of an intensive underground war, mostly carried out in shallow dugouts. Between 1915 and March 1916, 33 mine explosions in four series transformed the village into a lunar landscape.[4] On 27 March 1916, at 6.15 a.m., British tunnellers detonated six deep mines simultaneously under the German trenches at Sint-Elooi. Once the debris from the explosions had finished falling, some one thousand soldiers of the British 3rd Division went on the attack in an attempt to adjust the Sint-Elooi Salient. A German soldier, W. Kindt, described the explosion thus: 'The air was totally obscured. Lumps of earth of all conceivable sizes rained down on us. At a complete loss, we were faced with a quite new phenomenon; it was a mine explosion of the largest dimensions …'[5] A German aerial photograph of 1 April 1916 shows the broader spatial context of the mine attack and includes annotations: the trenches that were in German hands at the time are shown in blue; the enemy position and the craters are in red.

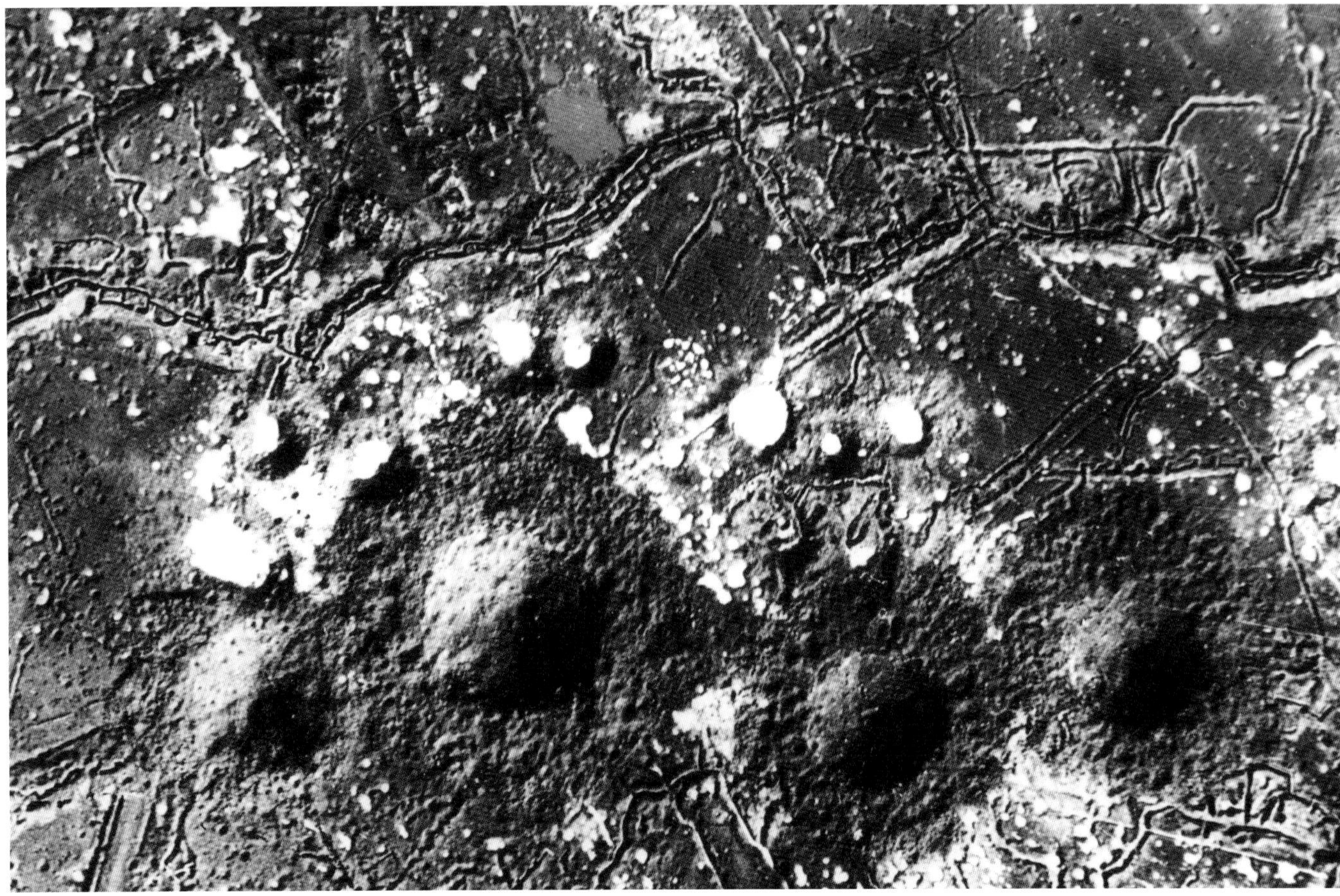

» **SEE ALSO** 6 32 SINT-ELOOI

↓ **GERMANS**

German soldiers in a trench at Sint-Elooi.

↑ **BRITISH CLOSE-UP OF MINE CRATERS**

A detailed British aerial photograph shows the situation after the mine attack. Craters 2, 3, 4 and 5 are clearly visible at the bottom of the photograph as wide open scars.
To the north of them are numerous craters from 1915 filled with water.

← **MINE EXPLOSION**

A British mine exploding at Sint-Elooi. Great clumps of earth are flung into the air.

→ **GERMAN AERIAL PHOTOGRAPH**

German aerial photograph taken by the Bavarian Artillery Flier Detachment 102 on 1 April 1916. This picture puts the close-up into context and has been annotated by a German observer. The blue lines mark the trenches and craters that were in German hands.

GPS 50°48'33.71"N 2°53'30.98"E

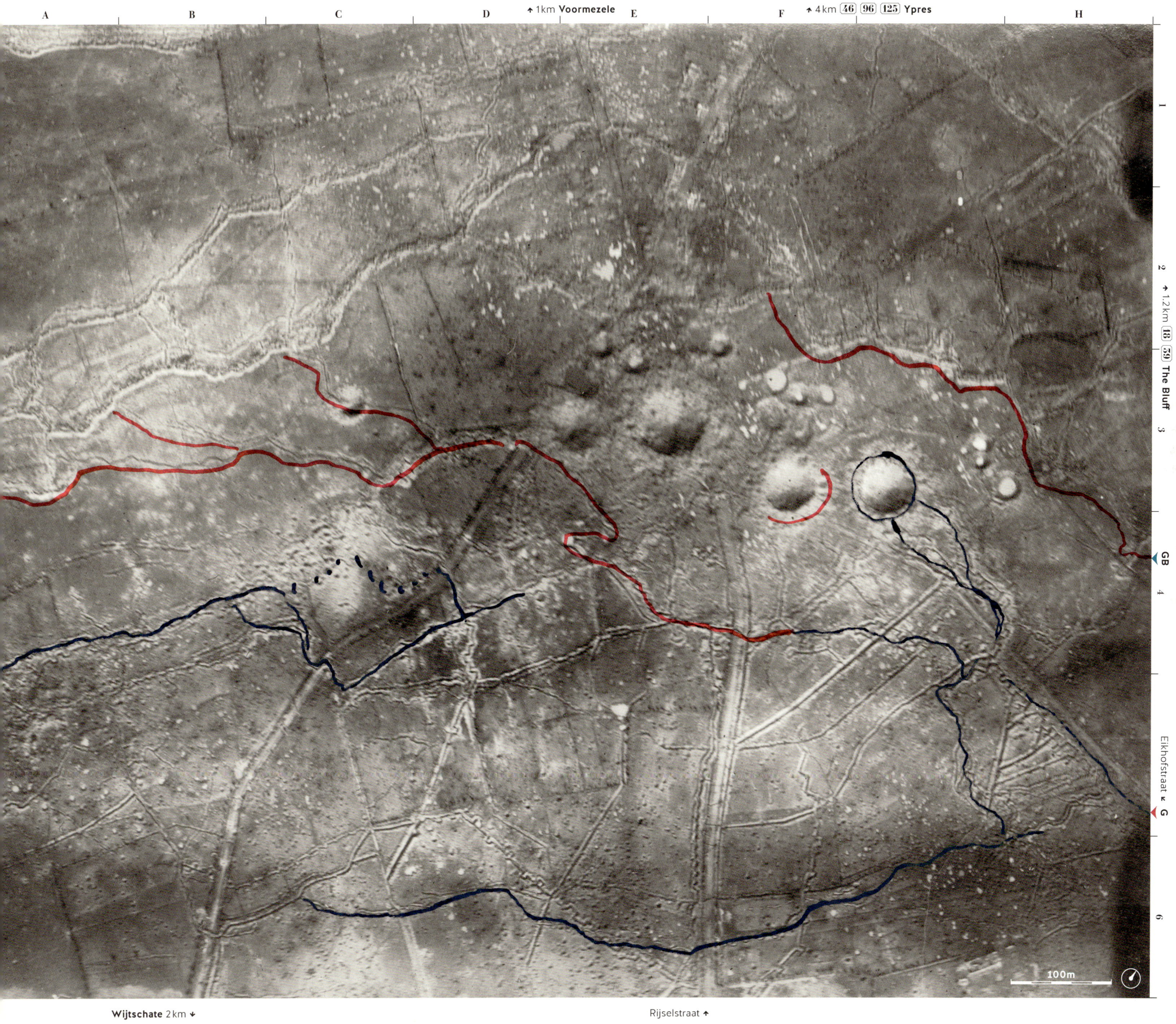
A
B
C
D
1km Voormezele
E
F
4km 46 96 125 Ypres
H
1
2
1.2km 18 59 The Bluff
3
GB
4
Eikhofstraat G
6
100m
Wijtschate 2km
Rijselstraat

20
SCHORE – GERMAN ARTILLERY
24 APRIL 1916

During the First World War artillery was deployed on an industrial scale for the first time. On both sides of the front there were thousands of gun emplacements with which the sides continuously bombarded each other. At Schore, a little village on the Yser plain, stood a conspicuously large number of German batteries. To disguise their positions from Belgian observers, the fronts of the batteries were camouflaged. In the flat polders of the Yser front it was totally impossible to prevent the enemy's aerial photographers from seeing the batteries. Sometimes 'inverted' camouflage was used: a very large number of positions were built in order to make it difficult for observers to make out whether a position was in use or not.

→ **GERMAN ARTILLERY**

German gun emplacement in the open air. The earthen embankment typical of such features can be seen at the front.

E4
HORSESHOE POSITIONS
Artillery positions were very often betrayed by the presence of a horseshoe-shaped front earthen embankment.

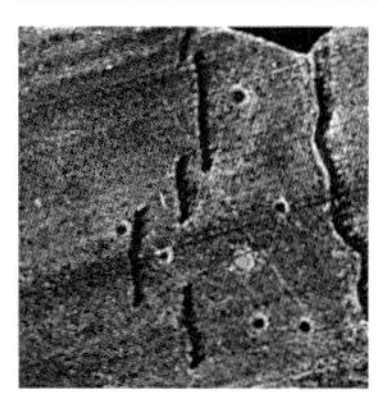

E5
BLINDS
Blinds could be made of wood, branches or canvas. Their purpose was to hide the flash of cannon being fired from observers on the ground.

F5-F6
GERMAN BATTERIES
A row of heavy artillery. The cannon are in the open air between two reinforced shelters, used for the storage of ammunition and protection of the gunners.

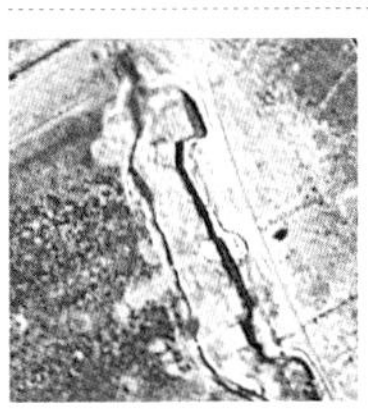

A5-A6
COVERED BATTERY
A large battery in which several cannon were stored under a roof. Ammunition was brought in by narrow-gauge railway.

F4
TRAFFIC
The heavy traffic of troops and ordnance left their traces on aerial photographs. The lighter lines on this photograph show which batteries were in use.

B5-B6
BATTERY
Battery with three pieces of artillery housed in an earthen shelter. The guns could be pushed into the shelter through the back.

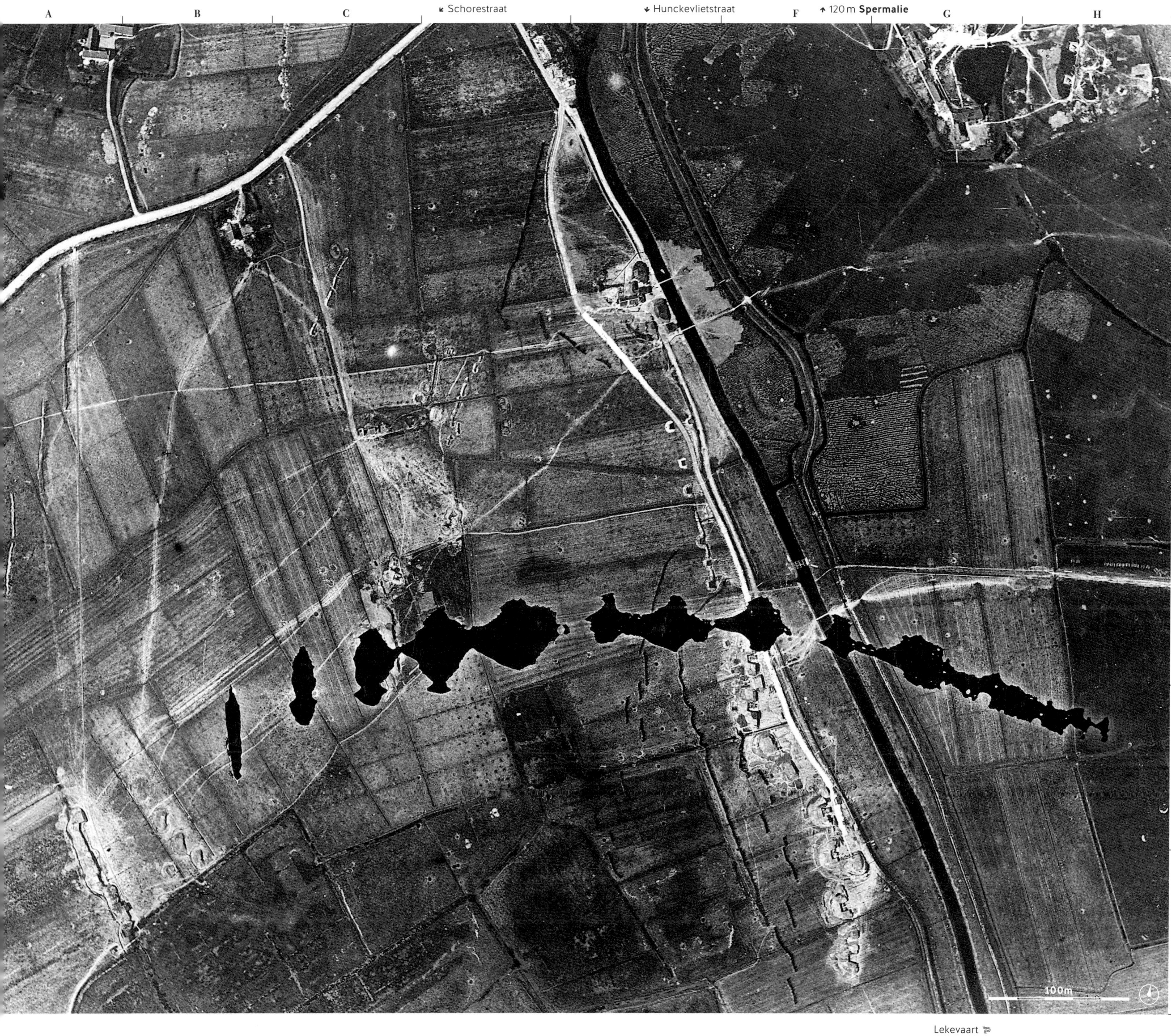

A
B
C
Schorestraat
Hunckevlietstraat
F
120 m Spermalie
G
H
1
2
3
4
6
stains on the photo negative
100m
Lekevaart

21

KOKSIJDE – 'MORT AUX BOCHES' 1916

As on the German side of the Belgian coastline, the Allied side of the coastal area behind the front was also a hive of industry. Trenches were dug in the dunes at Koksijde and various heavy artillery positions created. A railway branch line ran to two emplacements for long-distance cannon mounted on rail carriages. To create a diversion, the two cannon were fired at the precise moment that a heavy British battery at a secret site at Adinkerke opened fire on the German coastal battery known as 'Tirpitz'.[6] This German aerial photograph is significant evidence of the cat-and-mouse game played between the German aerial photographers and the Belgian or French soldiers who were constantly aware of being spied on from the air. The latter gave a clear message on the ground to the German reconnaissance planes: 'MORT AUX BOCHES' (Death to the Boches).

» **SEE ALSO** 25 TIRPITZ BATTERY

→ **RAILWAY CANNON**

Night-time firing of a heavy railway cannon.

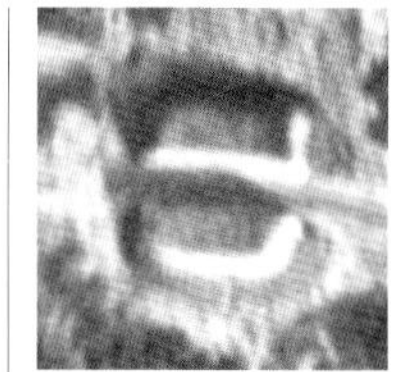

F4

RAILWAY CANNON

A railway branch line leads to a position for a French railway cannon capable of reaching targets far behind the front.

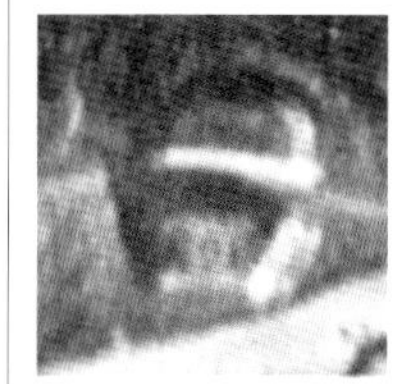

F5

RAILWAY CANNON

Identical railway cannon 150 metres south-west of the above.

G5

'MORT AUX BOCHES'

Next to a group of four barracks is the message, in letters 5 metres high, 'MORT AUX BOCHES'. There are several photographs of this area: on this one from 1916 the message is clearly visible but by May 1917 it had disappeared.

F1

TENNIS COURTS

Just to the north of the aerial photograph there was, before the war, a small seaside resort. Two tennis courts recall this pre-war period.

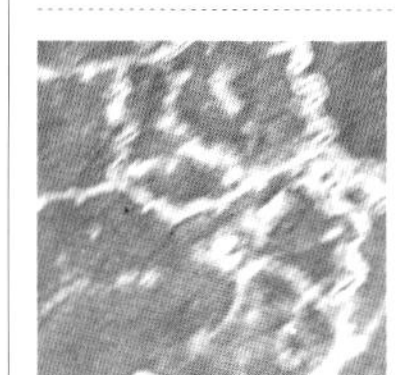

A3

TRAINING TRENCHES

The network of trenches shown on this part of the aerial photograph was presumably used for training. The position of the traverses indicates that this network was not a defensive construction.

GPS 51°06'51.05"N 2°38'37.36"E

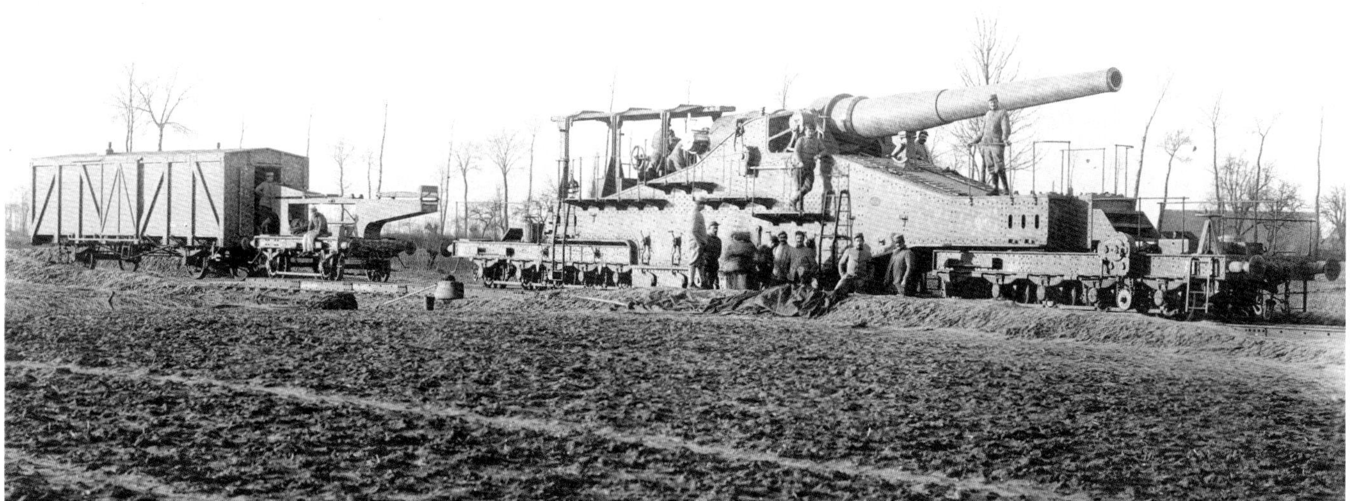

← **RAILWAY CANNON**

Carriages for a railway cannon. The projectiles were carried from the carriage on the left to the cannon.

A
B
Albert Bliecklaan
C
D
470 m North Sea
F
G
H
1
narrow-gauge railway
3
20 km 25 Tirpitz Battery
4
dunes
5
6.7 km 58 51 Nieuwpoort
AUX BOCHES
100m

22

HOOGE 7 JUNE 1916

Hooge was, from May 1915, a fiercely contended sector of the Ypres Salient. Following the first British mine explosion on 19 July 1915, the front changed frequently as a result of local actions. A further turbulent period commenced in June 1916. On 2 June the Germans launched an attack on the Canadians at Hill 62 and captured Mount Sorrel as well as Hill 62. For the anticipated counter-attack the Germans at Hooge held a trump card. Quite unexpectedly, four mines were exploded on 6 June. The next day Hooge was photographed through the clouds. The four mine craters are easy to see – the Canadian trenches have been pulverised. Despite heavy resistance, the Canadians retreated to their second position, 600 metres south-west of Hooge. Hill 62 would be recaptured, but Hooge remained in German hands until the Third Battle of Ypres (31 July 1917).

» **SEE ALSO** 14 45 129 HOOGE

→ **DUGOUTS AT HOOGE**

After the Third Battle of Ypres the craters at Hooge were used for underground dugouts. Here Australian tunnellers pump water out of the underground shelters (September 1917).

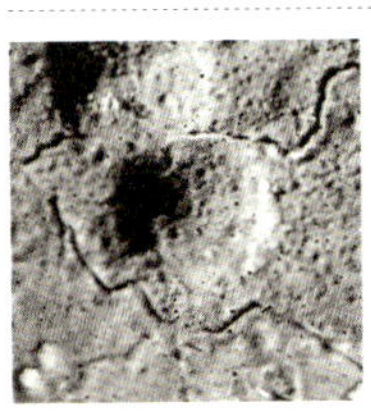

E5

COMMUNICATION TRENCH

Immediately after the mine explosions, communication trenches were dug to the craters so that they could be accessed safely.

D5-E5

MINE CRATER

The mine crater of 19 July 1915 is still clearly visible almost a year after the explosion. By the time the photograph was taken, it was full of water.

GPS 50°50'48.26"N 2°56'39.59"E

↑ **HOOGE, 18 MAY 1916**

Vertical aerial photograph of the Canadian–German front on 18 May 1916, just before the German mine attacks. At this time the old crater of 19 July 1915 (D5-E5, full of water) was in Allied hands.

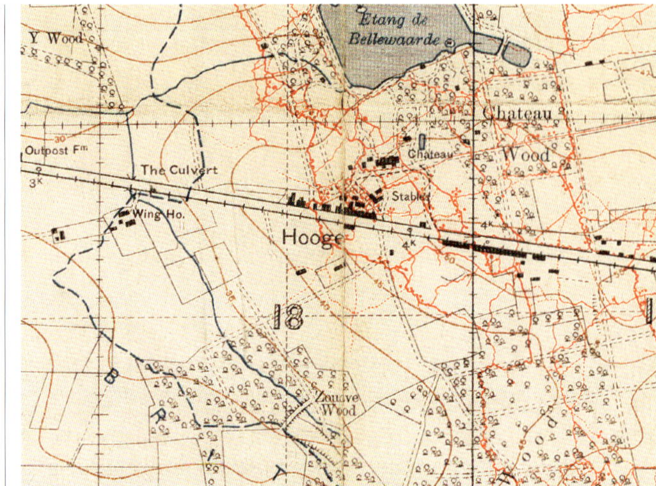

↑ **TRENCH MAP, 31 AUGUST 1916**

This British map shows the loss of terrain at Hooge in June 1916. Before the mine attack Hooge was partially in Canadian hands. After the strategic withdrawal the front line ran to the west of Zouave Wood (on this map dating from some months later indicated by a dotted blue line).

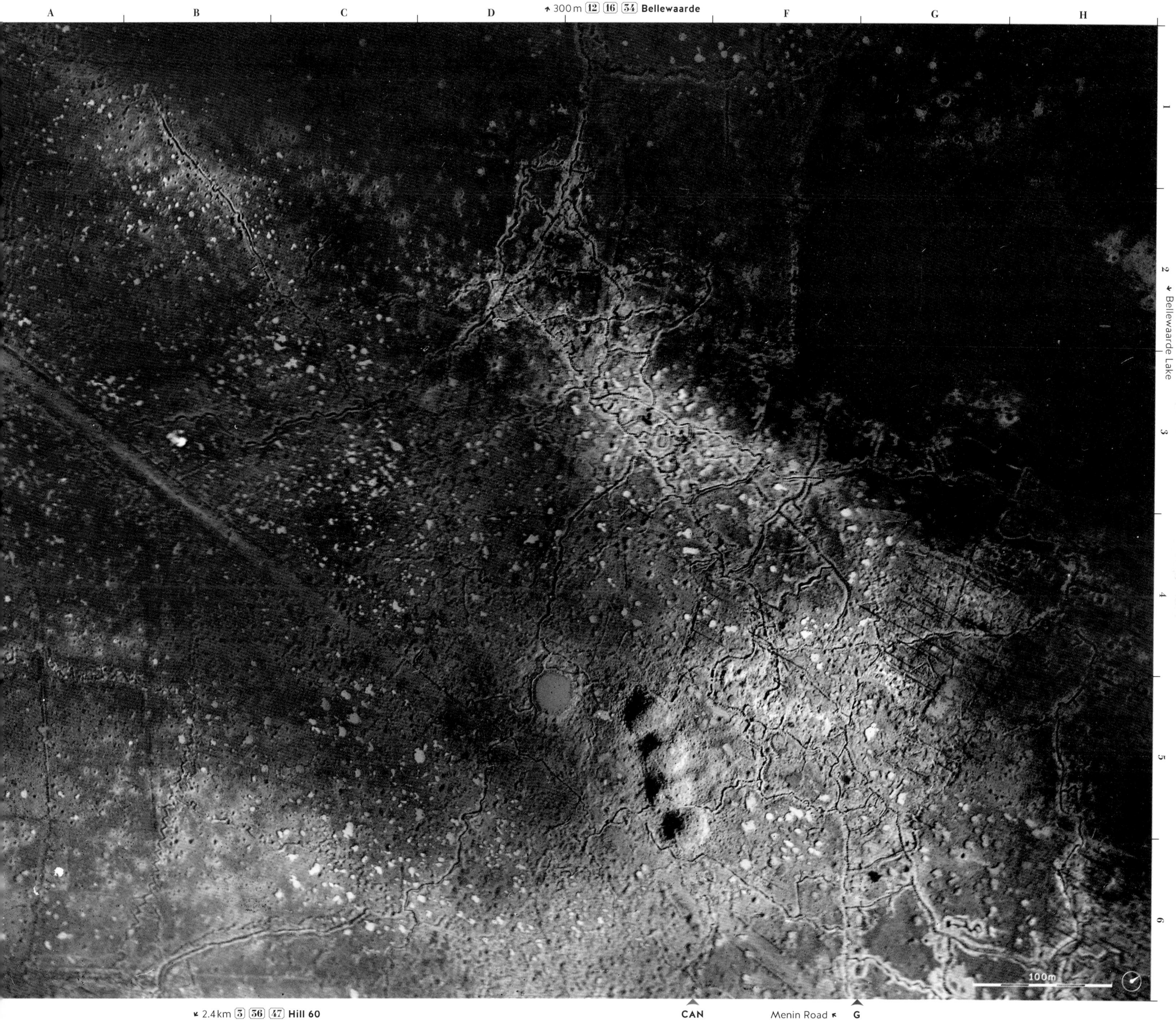

A
B
C
D
↑ 300 m 12 16 34 Bellewaarde
F
G
H
1
2
3
4
5
6
← Bellewaarde Lake
100m
↙ 2.4 km 3 36 47 Hill 60
CAN
Menin Road ↖ G

23 THE NORTHERN EDGE OF THE YPRES SALIENT 29 MAY 1916

After the gas attacks of the Second Battle of Ypres the front was 4 kilometres or so from the town and the Ypres Salient was formed. This marked the beginning of the so-called 'All Quiet on the Western Front' period. Apart from some local actions the front remained unchanged until the Third Battle of Ypres. The aerial photographs show that the Ypres Salient was anything but quiet, however. Artillery bombardment from the front line was a daily event.

» SEE ALSO 10 50 77

↓ RUDOLF LANGE SKETCH

The German officer Rudolf Lange was battalion commander in the 237th Reserve Infantry Regiment, which manned this sector for almost a year in 1915-16. He drew sketches of the German and British lines on Pilckem Ridge (J3).

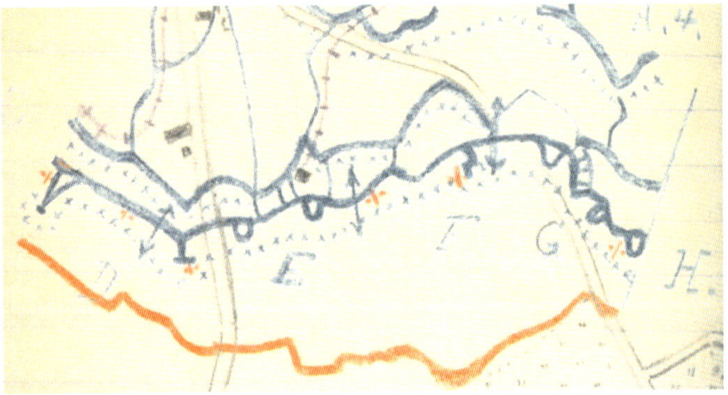

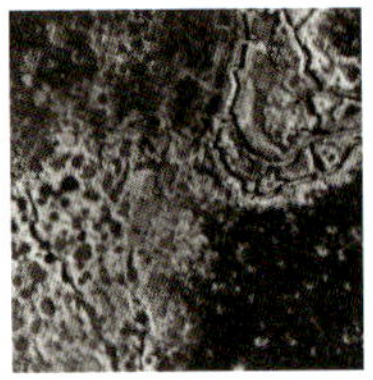

H3

CAESAR'S NOSE

At 'Caesar's Nose', a bulge in the German lines, the two lines were hardly 30 metres apart. The lower-lying Allied trenches bore the brunt of heavy fire in the spring of 1916.

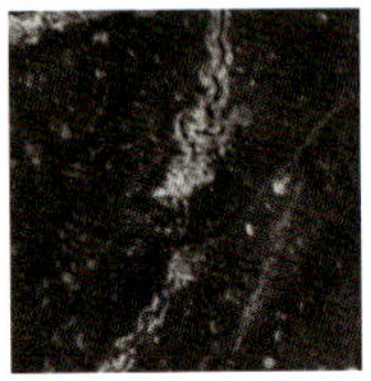

G3

SAPS IN NO-MAN'S-LAND

In both the Allied and the German front lines approach trenches and listening posts were set up.

GPS 50°53'22.68"N 2°52'36.90"E

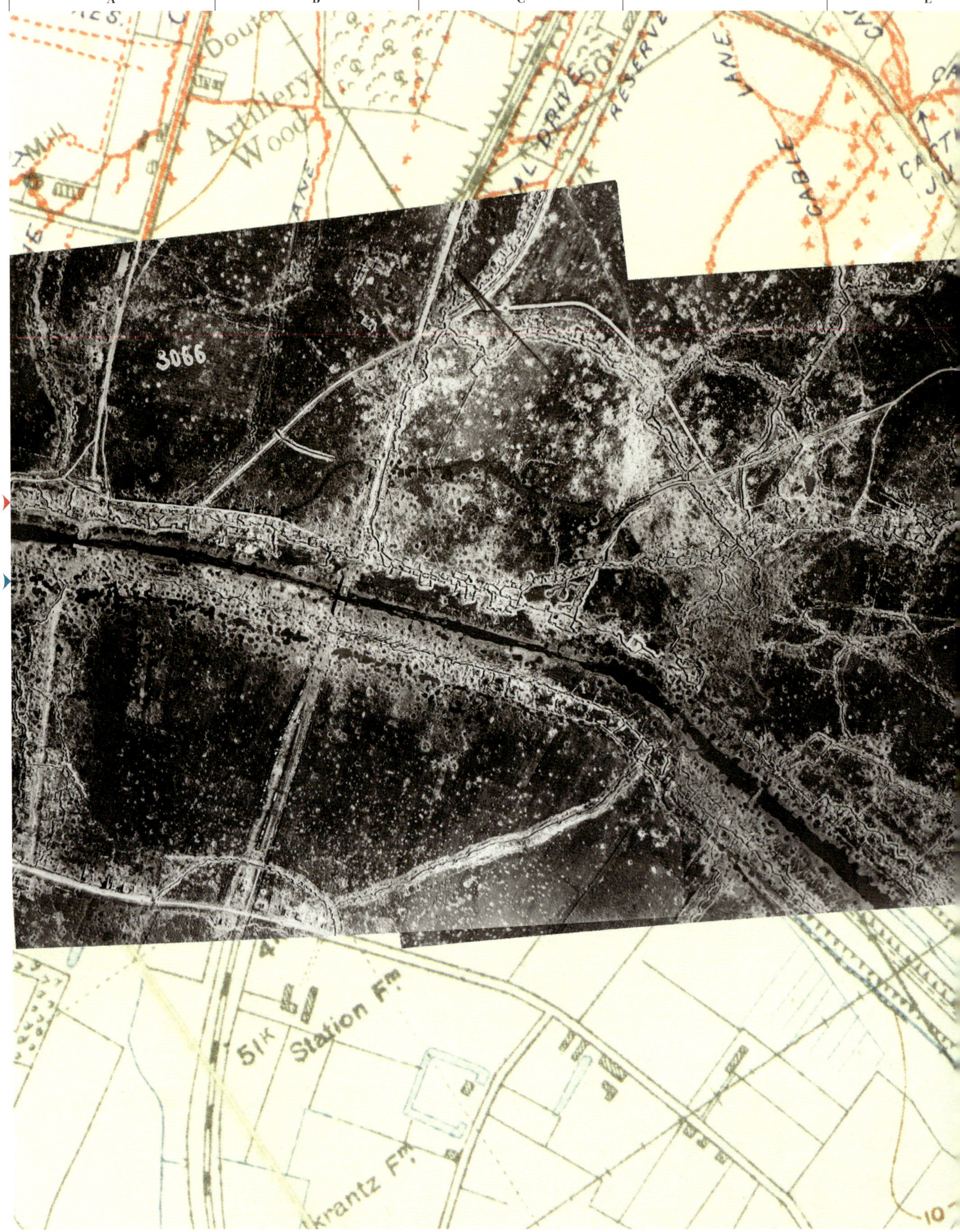

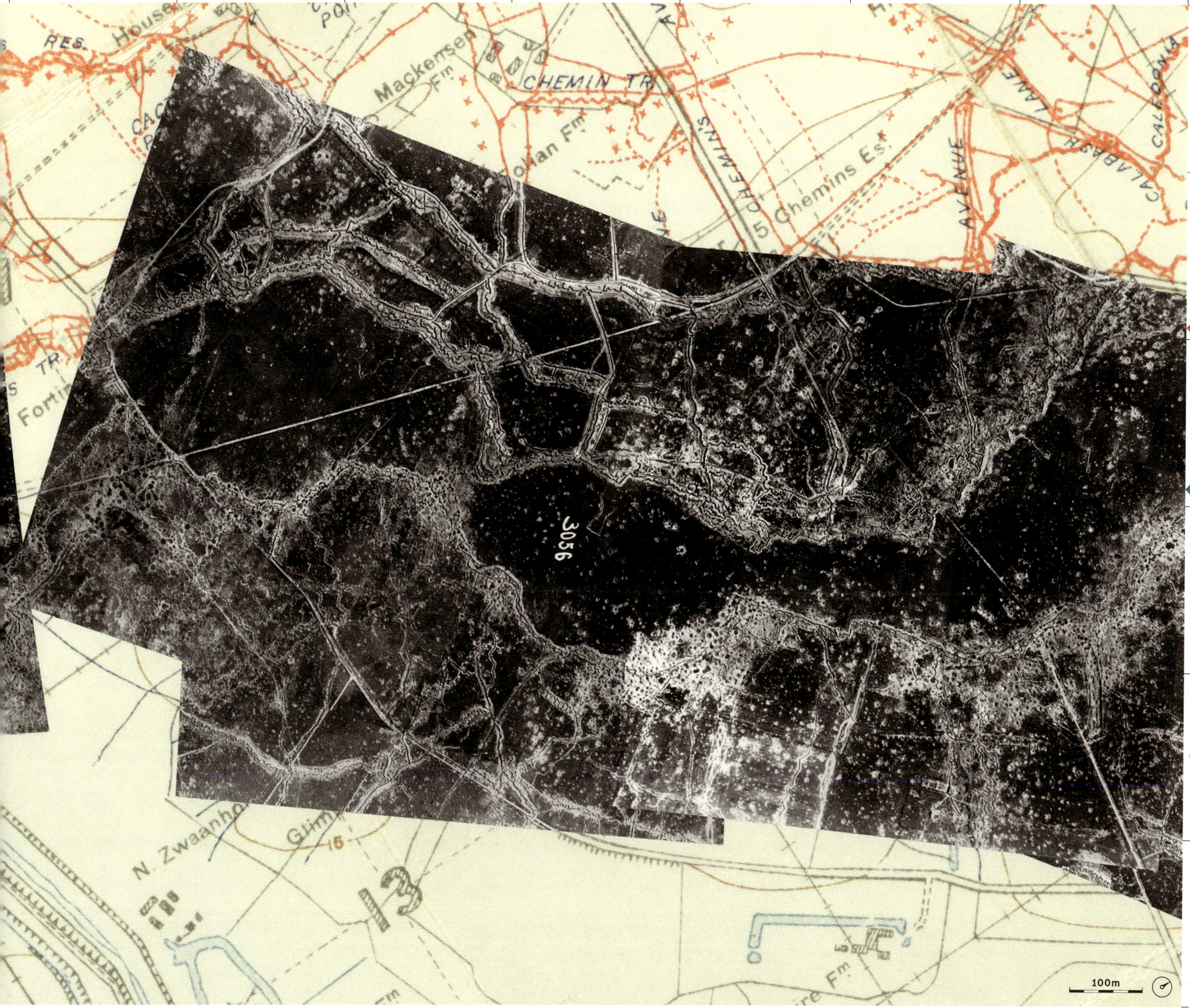

Moortelweg ↓
G
GB
Pilkemseweg ↓

24
STUIVEKENSKERKE 29 MAY 1916

The hamlet of Stuivekenskerke and the nearby Viconia Farm were situated on a small island in the flooded Yser plain. During the Battle of the Yser (18–31 October 1914) Stuivekenskerke fell into German hands and was made into a fortified outpost on the inundated plain. Long wooden footbridges connected it to the strengthened Yser dyke, which was set up as the leading German position in this area.

→ OBLIQUE AERIAL PHOTOGRAPH

This oblique aerial photograph with Viconia Farm in the centre shows the full extent of the inundation of the plain. In the foreground, the Belgian outpost known as the 'Ferme des Deux Pompiers' is visible.

↑ BELGIAN TRENCH MAP

Detail from a Belgian trench map indicating the Belgian (red) and German (blue) outposts on the Yser plain, 15 February 1917.

C2
LISTENING POST

To the west of the outposts, small listening posts were built in which soldiers kept guard. They are easy to detect on the photographs as they are linked to the outpost by wooden footbridges.

E2-F2
STUIVEKENSKERKE CHURCH

During the Battle of the Yser, Belgian soldiers set fire to the church in Stuivekenskerke, to prevent the tower being used as an observation post.

E2-E3
TRENCH PARAPETS

The defences on the Yser front consisted mainly of above-ground trenches built with sandbags. The high water level made it impossible to dig trenches in the ground.

H2
WOODEN FOOTBRIDGE

The outpost was reached via long wooden footbridges. Like important trenches, they were given a name on trench maps: Passerelle du Village, Passerelle du Château and Passerelle de la Statue.

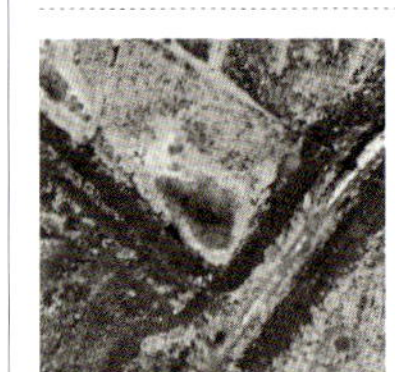

B3
INUNDATION

At the time this aerial photograph was taken, the level of the inundation was fairly low. Nonetheless, the ditches and property boundaries are clearly still full of water.

GPS 51°04'32.79"N 2°49'37.71"O

A
B
overflowing boundary ditch
D
E
G
F
G
inundation
H
778
1
2
Passerelle du Village
Tervate 1 700m
5
Passerelle du Château
150m Yser
100m
Belgian front line 400 m
G
Passerelle de la Statue

25
OSTEND – TIRPITZ BATTERY
JULY 1916

The Germans turned the occupied part of the coast into a fortified line, an Atlantic Wall *avant la lettre*. This had a dual aim: to ward off Allied landings and to protect the fleet and U-boat bases in Ostend and Zeebrugge. Behind the reinforcements on the beaches and in the dunes stood batteries of various calibres: the heaviest had a range of 47 kilometres.[7] The Tirpitz Battery to the west of Ostend, named after Admiral Alfred von Tirpitz, consisted of four 28-cm cannon and was capable of hitting targets both at sea and on land. Thanks to its long range (32 km), it could hit targets along large sections of the coastline.[8]

→ **TIRPITZ BATTERY, 1919**

One of the four cannon of the Tirpitz Battery in January 1919. The cannon are still protected by branches, a vestige of German attempts at camouflage.

D3-E3
FOUR 28-CM CANNON
At the beginning of July 1916 the battery consisted of four 28-cm cannon. Between and around the foundations five large bunkers are visible.

A4
AIRCRAFT HANGARS
To the west of the battery lay the airfield of Mariakerke. Two hangars are visible. The accuracy of the artillery fire could be aided from the sky.

E4
BUNKER
Here two narrow-gauge railways link a large ammunition storage bunker with the rest of the battery.

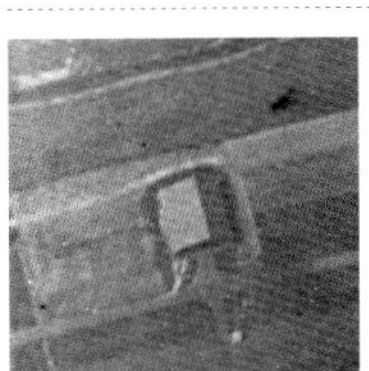

A1
AIRCRAFT
The planes taxied to a third hangar via a specially made carriageway.

D2
OLD FORT
The contours of a seventeenth-century fort can still be seen in the land divisions. Two small bunkers have been built on the south bastion, probably because the old fort stood on elevated terrain.

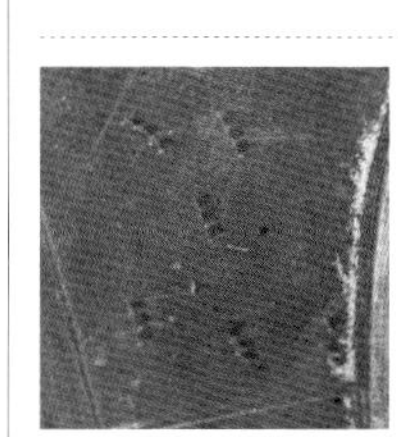

B4
SCREENS
Screens made of wood, canvas and sometimes even branches camouflaged the firing of the cannon, making it more difficult for Allied observers to pinpoint the position of the battery.

↑ 600 m North Sea
A
B
C
D
E
F
G
H
1
3
4
5
6
↖ H. Borgerstraat
↑ 8 km 57 Bredene
↖ Elisabethlaan
939
100m
Torhoutsesteenweg ↗

26

’S GRAVENTAFEL APRIL 1916

Aerial photographs from the first months of the trench warfare in the Westhoek are quite rare. Only from summer 1915 do more become available. To get an idea of the front lines and the kind of warfare conducted in the Westhoek during the earliest phases of the First World War, we have to turn to a mosaic of photographs taken in 1916 depicting the front in the period November 1914 – April 1915 and which show the front as a sort of petrified military landscape. Close study of these photographs (they date from April 1916) reveals an extensive network of trenches divided by a broad no-man’s-land. The now-unused trenches can hardly be made out, as they are no longer being maintained. Wild flowers and weeds grow in profusion over the parapets and almost blend into the surrounding greenery. Their last traces were eradicated during the Third Battle of Ypres.

→ **CASUALTIES DURING THE SECOND BATTLE OF YPRES**

An unsparing photograph of Allied corpses in a trench captured by the Germans during the Second Battle of Ypres.

↓ **PANORAMA**

British panorama taken on 17 April 1915 near ’s Graventafel. The German trenches are on the rolling hills and at the top of the ridge.

GPS 50°53'34.55"N 2°59'02.89"E

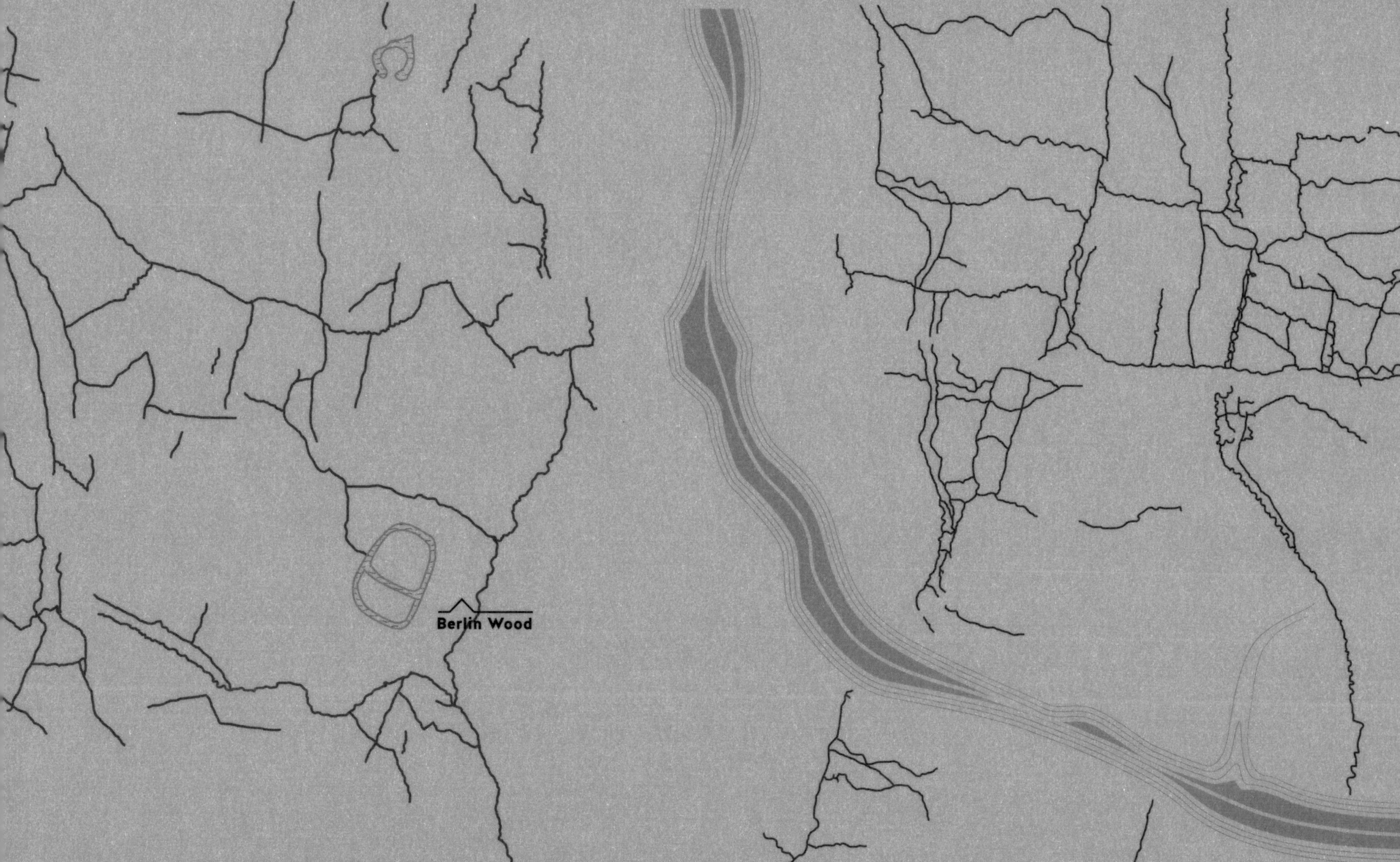
Berlin Wood

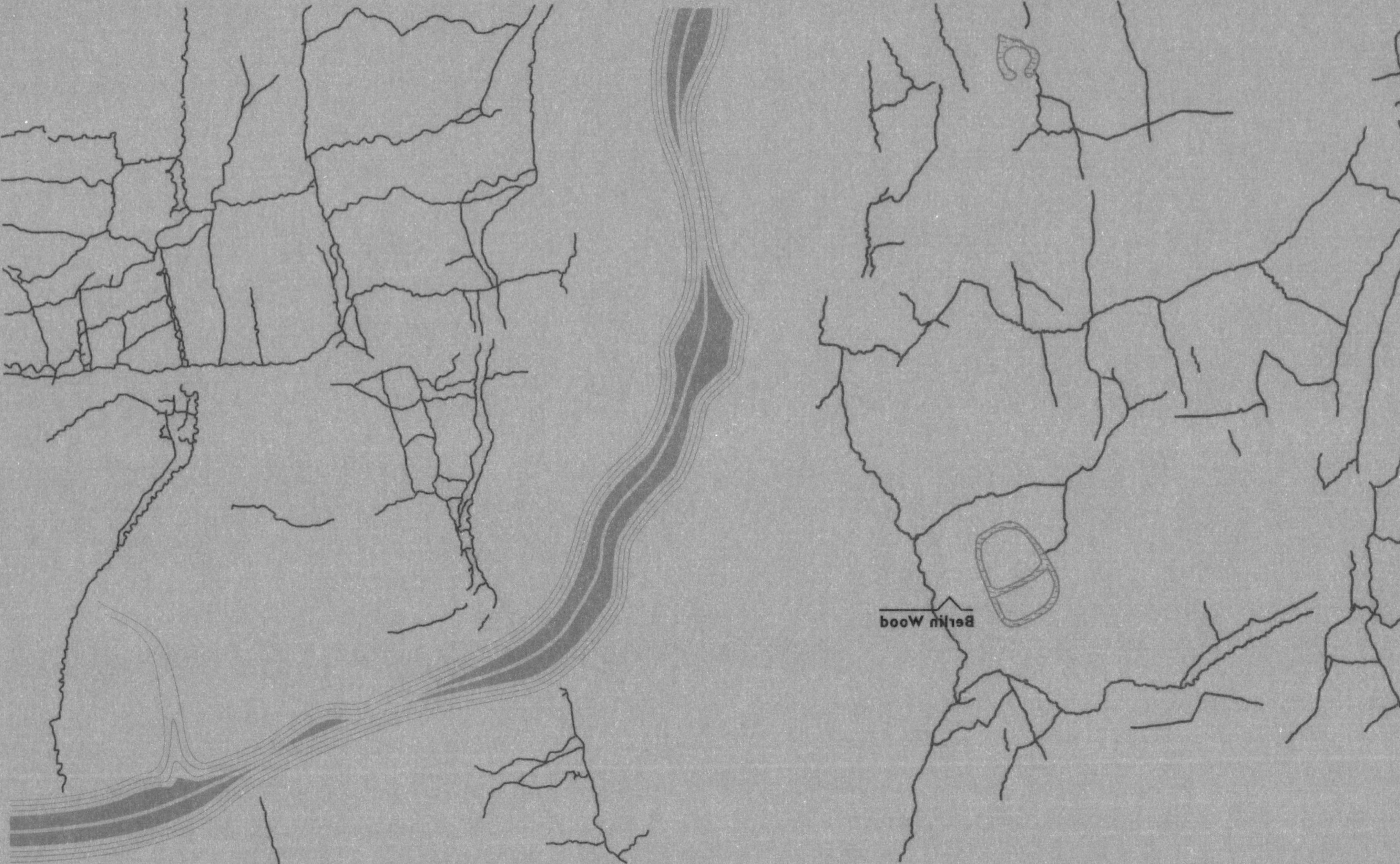
Berlin Wood

SYMBOLS

- ALLIED TRENCHES
- GERMAN TRENCHES
- MOATED SITE
- RAVEBEEK VALLEY

27

PREDIKBOOM 14 JULY 1916

Behind the lines, in the spring of 1915, the Germans built a special artillery emplacement less than 4 kilometres from the front, to the north-east of Klerken and near the hamlet of Predikboom. The emplacement was hidden from the direct view of Allied observers by its position to the east of the ridge between Klerken and Staden. It turned out to be an emplacement for a long-range cannon capable of shooting up to 38 kilometres. The cannon was fired for the first time on 26 April 1915, but was destroyed that same year by French artillery.[9]

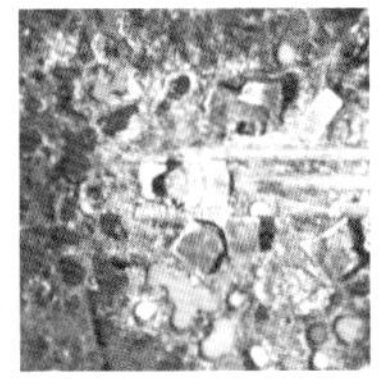

E4

CANNON AND BUNKERS

West of a triple narrow-gauge railway used for the assembly of the cannon are the cannon platform and a number of heavily reinforced bunkers.

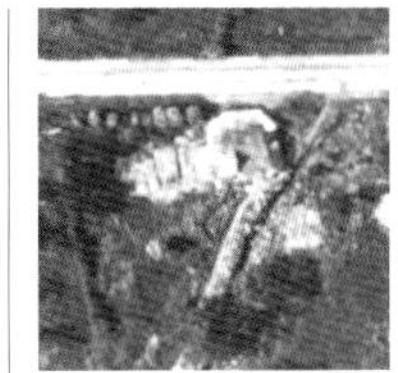

E3-F3

BUNKER

Large bunker next to the Steenstraat

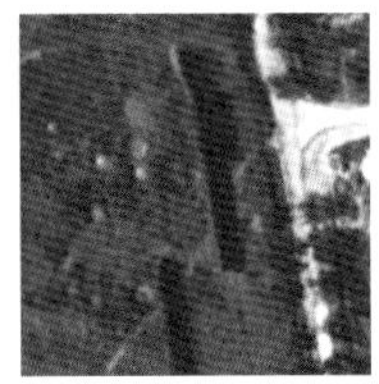

A3

CANVAS SCREENS

The canvas blinding visible here ensured that activities on the Steenstraat were not detectable from the Belgian lines.

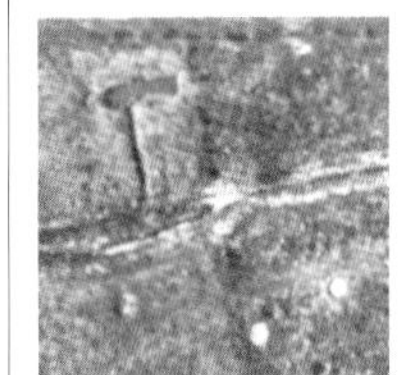

G3

BURIED CABLES

To reduce the risk of damage, communication cables were buried in thin channels.

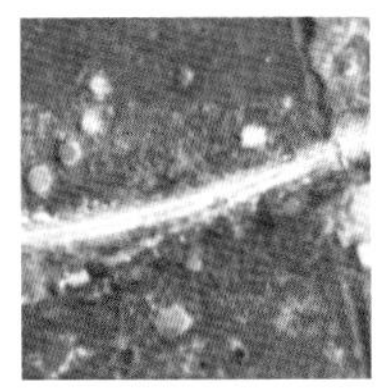

G4

NARROW-GAUGE RAILWAY

Supplies were transported to the Predikboom cannon site by narrow-gauge railway.

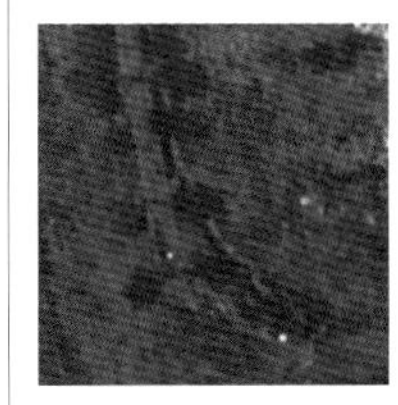

A4-A5

TRENCHES

The cannon is situated just behind the German third defence line running from Esen to Klerken and stands strategically on Klerken–Staden Ridge.

↓ **PREDIKBOOM, SPRING 1915**

Early Belgian aerial photograph taken in spring 1915. The emplacement is not yet ready, but the narrow-gauge railway line and a first large bunker have been built.

GPS 51°00'25.45"N 2°54'41.49"E

↓ Klerkenstraat | B | ↖ 36 km **Dunkirk** | C | D | ↑ 4 km (90) (126) **Diksmuide** | E | F | G | H

1

↗ 13km (58) **Koekelare Pommern Battery**

← Steenstraat

↓ narrow-gauge railway

5

6

↗ Esenstraat

↙ 16 km (46) (96) (125) **Ypres**

28

BOEZINGE – HET SAS

31 AUGUST 1916

After the French counter-attacks in May 1915, the Germans were pushed back to the eastern bank of the Ypres–Yser Canal. The water provided a natural line of defence. Hardly anywhere on the Western Front did the enemy trenches lie so near to each other as at Boezinge Sas. The western part was in Allied hands and on the other side, hardly 10 metres away, the Germans dug into the remains of the seventeenth-century St Nicholas Fort designed by Vauban. In this extremely detailed photograph of 31 August 1916, a Belgian aerial photographic interpreter has detected eight German bunkers. The ditches and walls of the fort are quite distinct. During the construction of bunkers 6, 7 and 8 the terrain conditions were fully exploited, with the bunkers concealed behind the old earthen walls.

» **SEE ALSO** 9 BOEZINGE – HET SAS

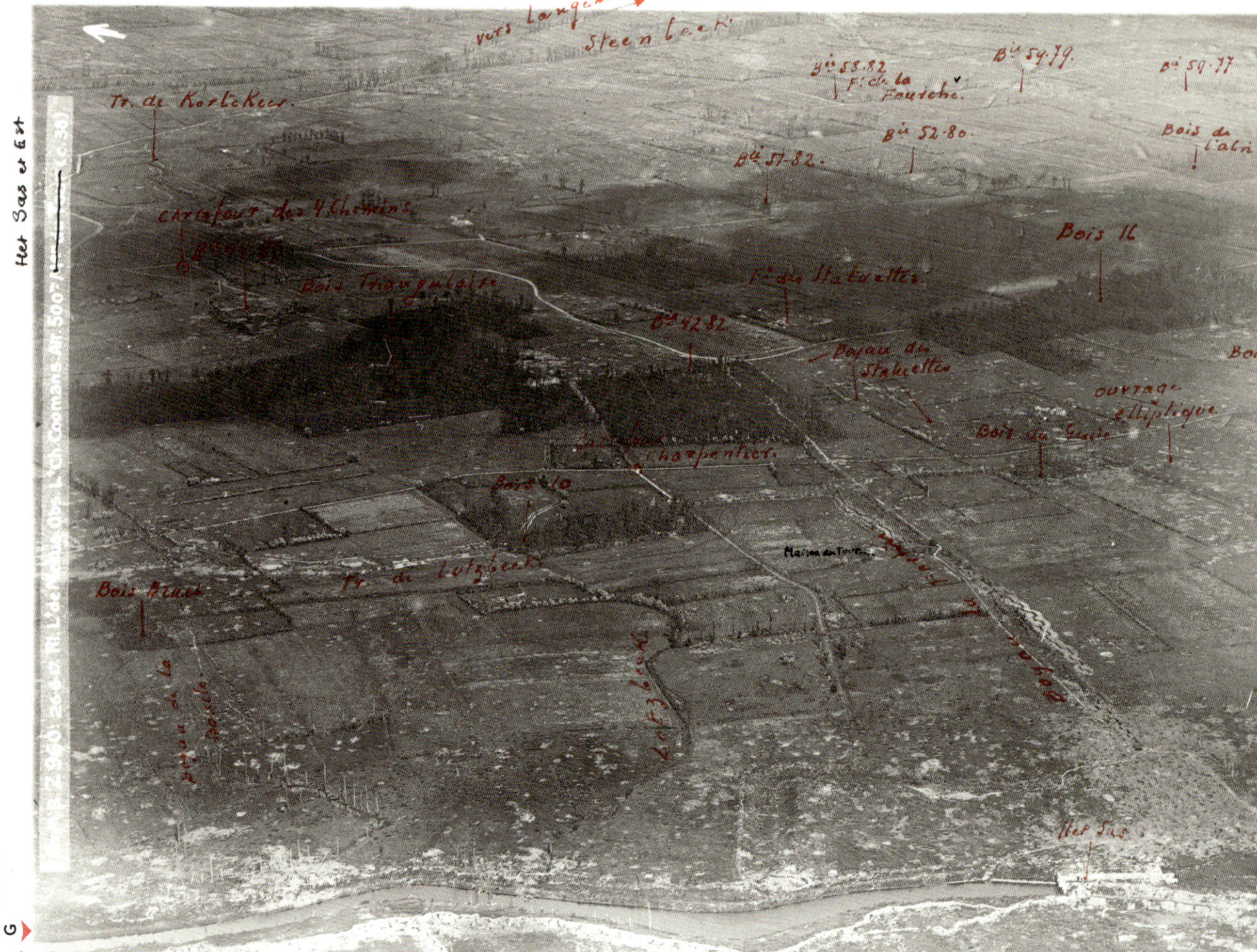

↑ **OBLIQUE VIEW OF BOEZINGE**

Oblique aerial photograph of Boezinge Sas taken on 26 June 1917. The lock and St Nicolas Fort are at the bottom right-hand corner. The Belgian front line lies on the west bank of the Ypres–Yser Canal, and the enemy front line is just on the other side of the lock and the canal. A Belgian photographic interpreter has marked the names of important trenches, woods, crossroads and a number of German artillery positions (e.g. see Bie 59–77).

← B5

BOEZINGE SAS

The lock seen from the Belgian front trench. Photograph taken north of the lock. The German first line is just a dozen metres further, on the other side of the Ieperlee.

GPS 50°54'38.16"N 2°51'02.67"E

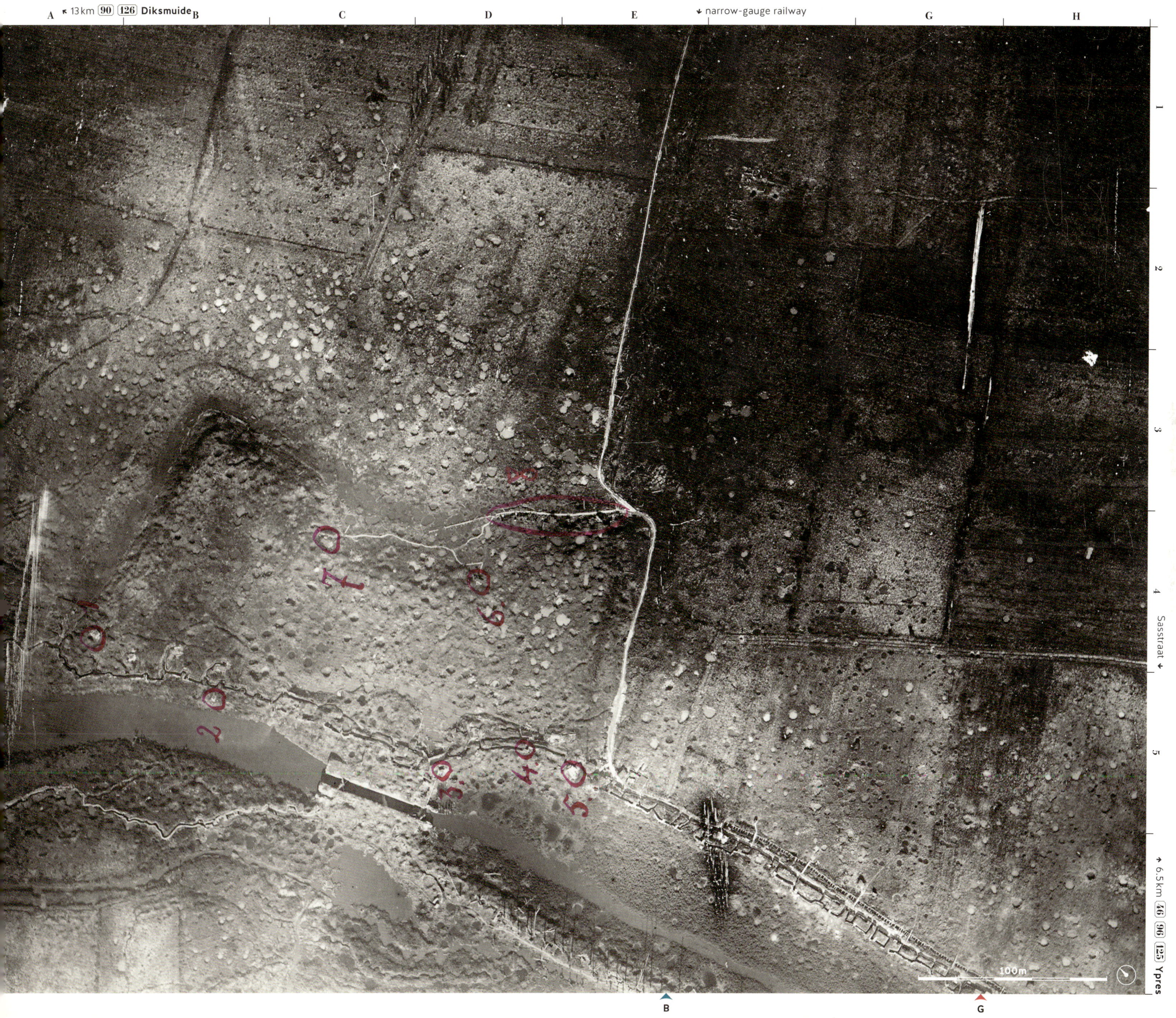
A
↖ 13 km 90 126 Diksmuide
B
C
D
E
↓ narrow-gauge railway
G
H
1
2
3
4
5
Sasstraat ↓
↑ 6.5 km 46 96 125 Ypres
100m
B
G

29

LANGEMARK-NORD

31 AUGUST 1916

In this *Soldatenfriedhof* (military cemetery) lie the mortal remains of more than 44,000 German soldiers. This is one of the four collective burial grounds where the German dead were reinterred after the war. The present cemetery has its origins in a smaller precursor, 'Langemark-Nord', of 1915, sited in approximately the same place.[10] A Belgian aerial photograph shows the cemetery as it was on 31 August 1916. Interments were still taking place in the southern part at that time. During the months before the Second Battle of Ypres, Langemark-Nord lay between the Allied and German front lines. Some remains of the shallow, weakly constructed French front line can still be seen on the left.

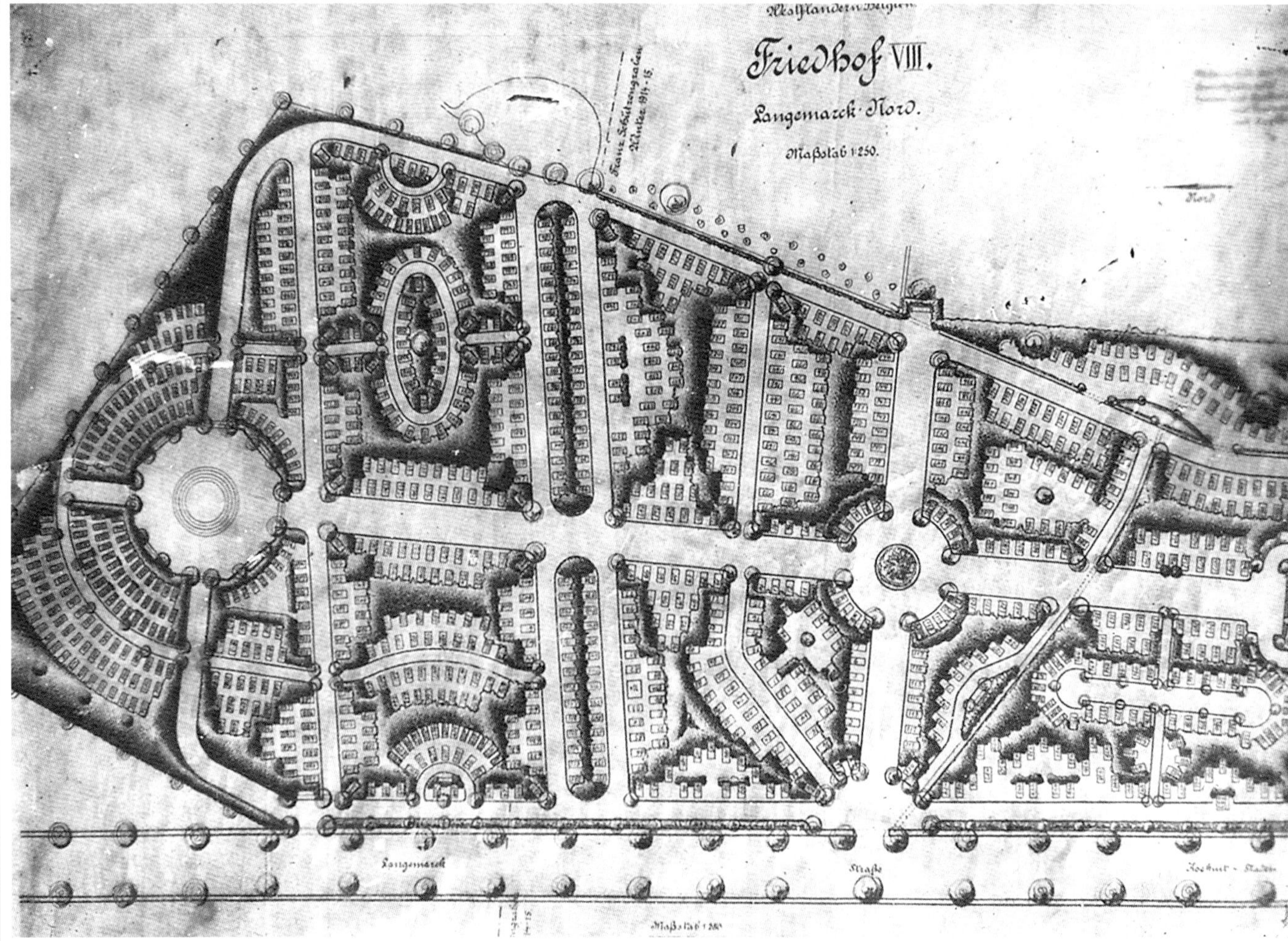

→ **GROUND PLAN OF LANGEMARK-NORD**

Original ground plan of the Langemark-Nord cemetery.

F6

LANGEMARK-NORD

Like so many other German cemeteries that have now vanished, the cemetery at Langemark-Nord has a complex design with a cross motif.

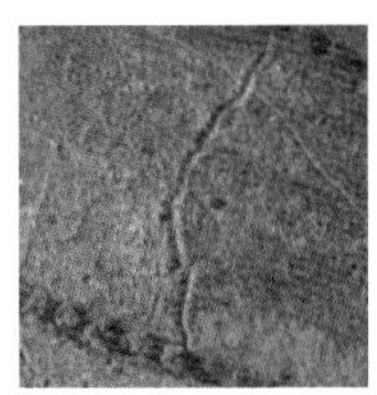

A4

FRENCH TRENCHES, 1914–15

Shallow French trenches. In contrast to the German lines, trenches on the French side were not always connected, consisting rather of unconnected short lengths.

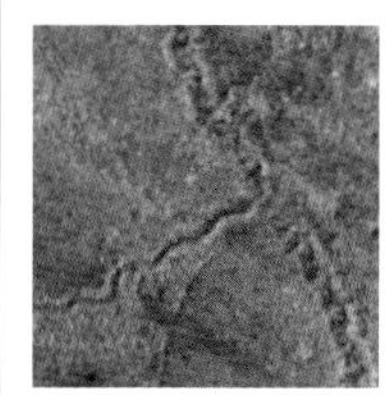

A3

FRENCH FRONT LINE, 1914 – APRIL 1915

Here, too, the French trenches are quite shallow and not accessible via communication trenches.

G6

CAMOUFLAGED BUNKERS

In the present-day cemetery are the remains of three large concrete shelters. They were built into the wide breastwork of a German trench. This trench dates from the beginning of 1915, but, presumably, the bunkers were added later. Thanks to expert camouflage, they were almost impossible to detect without prior knowledge. Nowadays, subtle differences in shades of colour betray their presence.

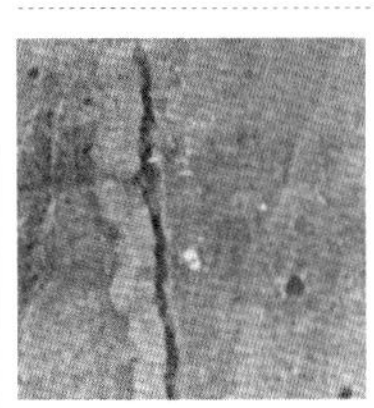

H2

CAMOUFLAGED ORDNANCE

After 22 April 1915 this area was 4 kilometres behind the front. The zone was dotted with positions for German cannon. Their camouflage was clearly quite successful in front: there are no sharp edges that could give the position away. However, the shadow at the back does reveal where they are.

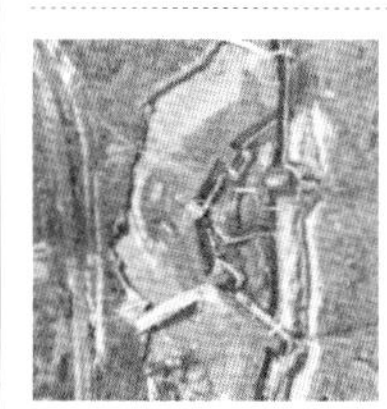

G1-G2

PARAPET

Trenches were not always dug in. In many places, and on both sides of the front, large above-ground earthen walls were used to house a trench. Here the necessary earth for the 13-metre-thick wall has been excavated from in front of the trench.

GPS 50°55'13.67"N 2°55'00.46"E

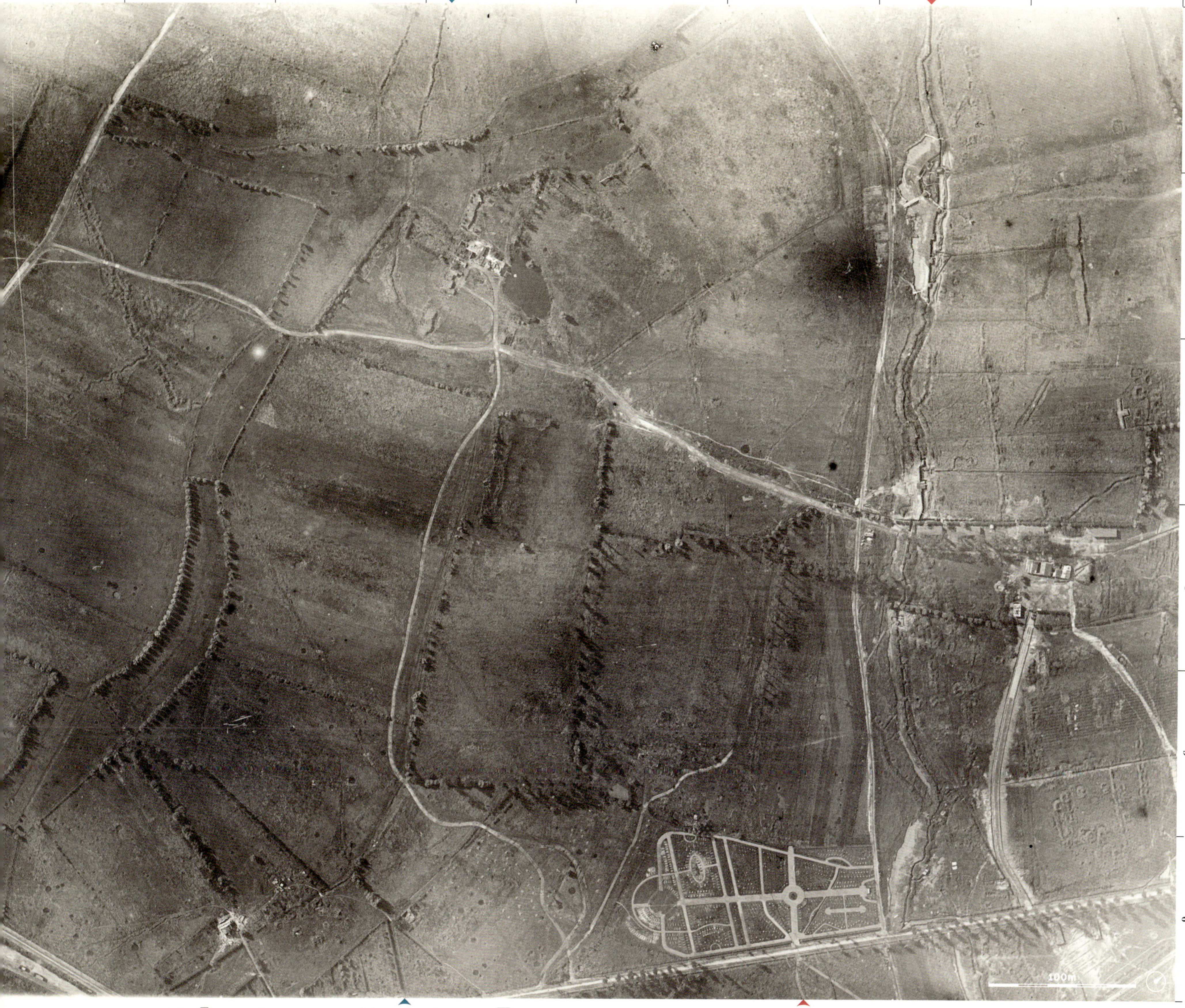
A
Bikschotestraat
C
F former front line
E
800 m 53 Broenbeek
F
G former front line
Broenbeek
1
2
3
4
5
Klerkenstraat
6
100m
350 m 8 Langemark
F former front line
500 m 70 Langemark
G former front line

30

WESTHOEK – GERMAN ARTILLERY 19 MAY 1916

The First World War was a pivotal moment in the history of warfare, not least because of the massive surreptitious deployment of artillery. At the hamlet of Westhoek, 1,500 metres east of Bellewaarde and Hooge, the Germans expanded their heavily fortified third line on the top of the ridge and just behind it. To the east of the hill, away from the direct view of the Allies, they constructed a large number of artillery positions. Hundreds of metres of buried cables provided a dense communications network for the relaying of orders.

» **SEE ALSO** 85 WESTHOEK 1918

↑ **21-CM MORTAR**

German gunners pose next to a heavy mortar. The cannon is housed in a bunker with an opening in the front through which it is fired.

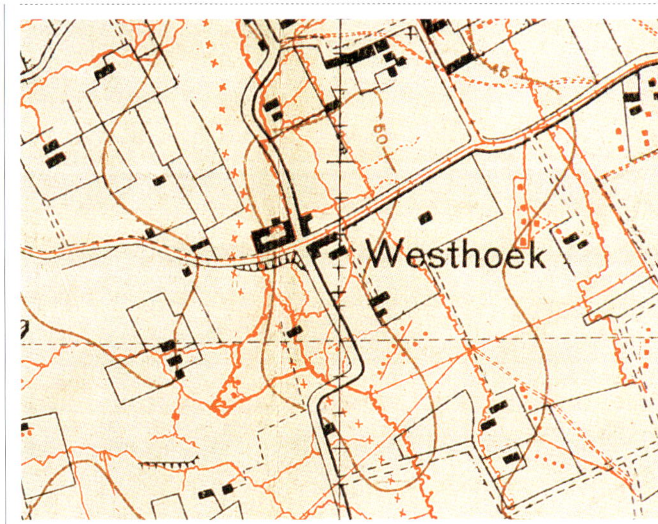

→ **BRITISH TRENCH MAP**

This British trench map of 31 August 1916 shows the German military structures at Westhoek. The artillery known of at that time is indicated by a line of red dots.

← **FIELD CANNON**

Concealed German field gun.

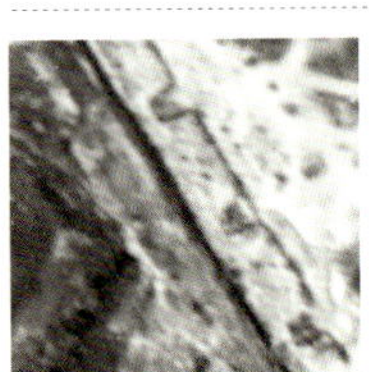

C1-D1

FIELD GUN

Elongated German artillery position. The guns stand in the open air in U-shaped earthen-walled bays with shelters between them for the ammunition and the gunners.

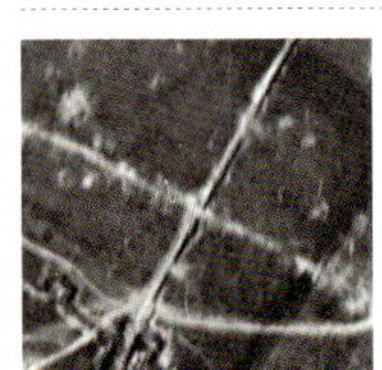

D2

CABLES

Telephone wires were laid in channels to protect them against artillery fire. Here cables in a filled-in channel and cables in an open channel cross each other.

SYMBOLS

- GERMAN TRENCHES
- BARBED WIRE
- BURIED CABLES
- FIELD GUN

GPS 50°51'06.19"N 2°57'43.96"E

A B ↙ Grote Molenstraat D E F G H

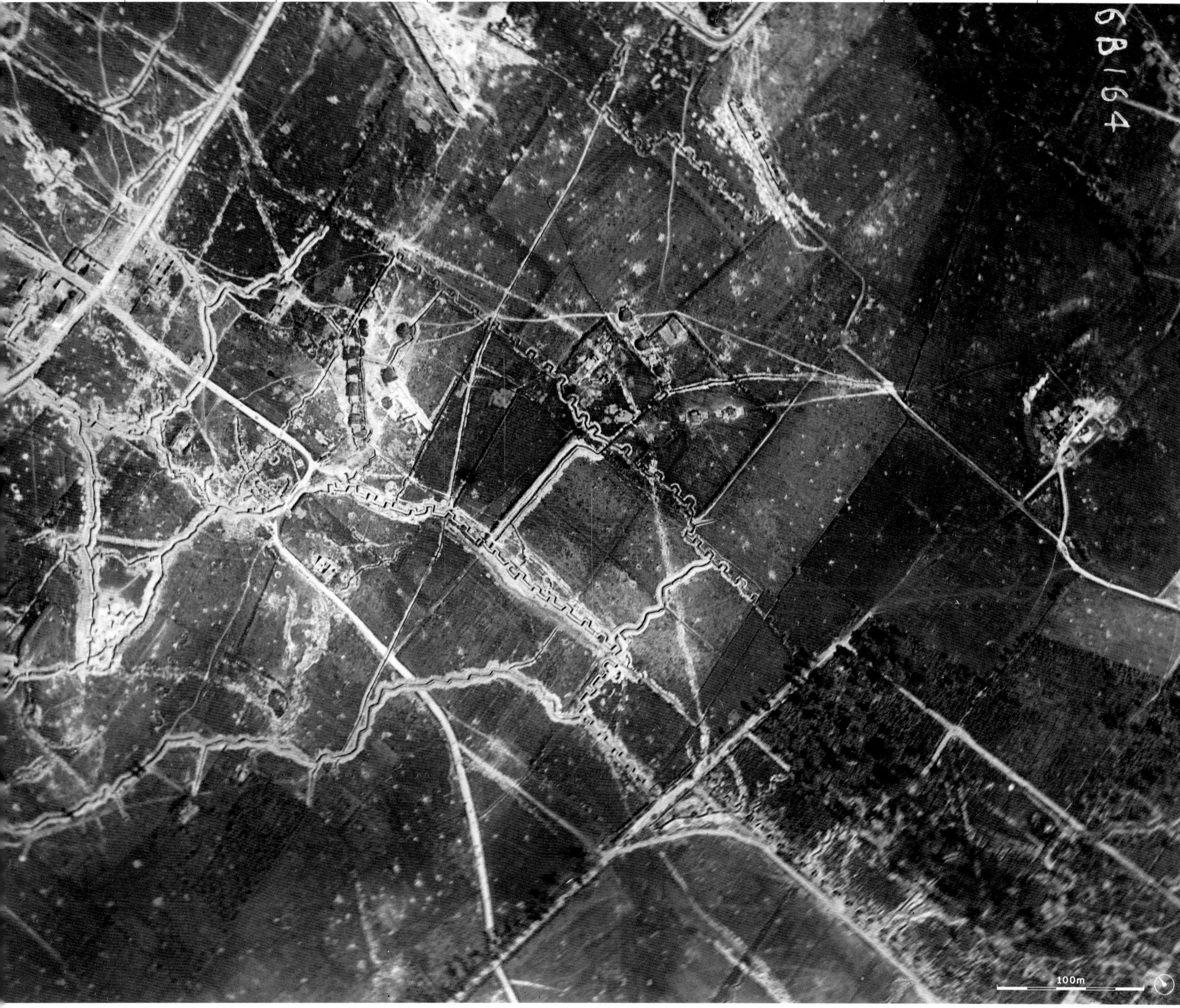

1
2
3
4
5
Nonnebossen-Zuid ↗6

↙ 1km 14 22 43 129 Hooge

31

MIDDELKERKE – ALBATROS C III

30 SEPTEMBER 1916

On 30 September 1916 the Belgian observer Captain Jaumotte took an astonishing picture of a German Albatros C.III reconnaissance aircraft to the south of Middelkerke above German-occupied territory. Aerial photographs of planes in full flight were not rare, but they were almost always of planes flown by colleagues. Taking a photograph of an enemy plane was dangerous and a technical tour de force: at a height of several kilometres one had to focus manually on the object and then, using a small lens aperture, to capture it in very clear detail on the sensitive plate. The observer in the back of the German plane was scanning the surroundings with the barrel of his machine gun pointing to the rear. He was probably not aware of the presence of the Belgians high above him.

Many copies were printed of this aerial photograph and it can be found in various archives and museums. This print is unique in that the names of the pilot and observer are written by hand on the photograph. It was possibly a war trophy.

↓ **CAPTAIN JAUMOTTE**

Both the airfield in Houtem and the one at De Moeren ran a photographic service. The director at De Moeren was Captain Jaumotte. In this picture he is working on a 52-cm camera.

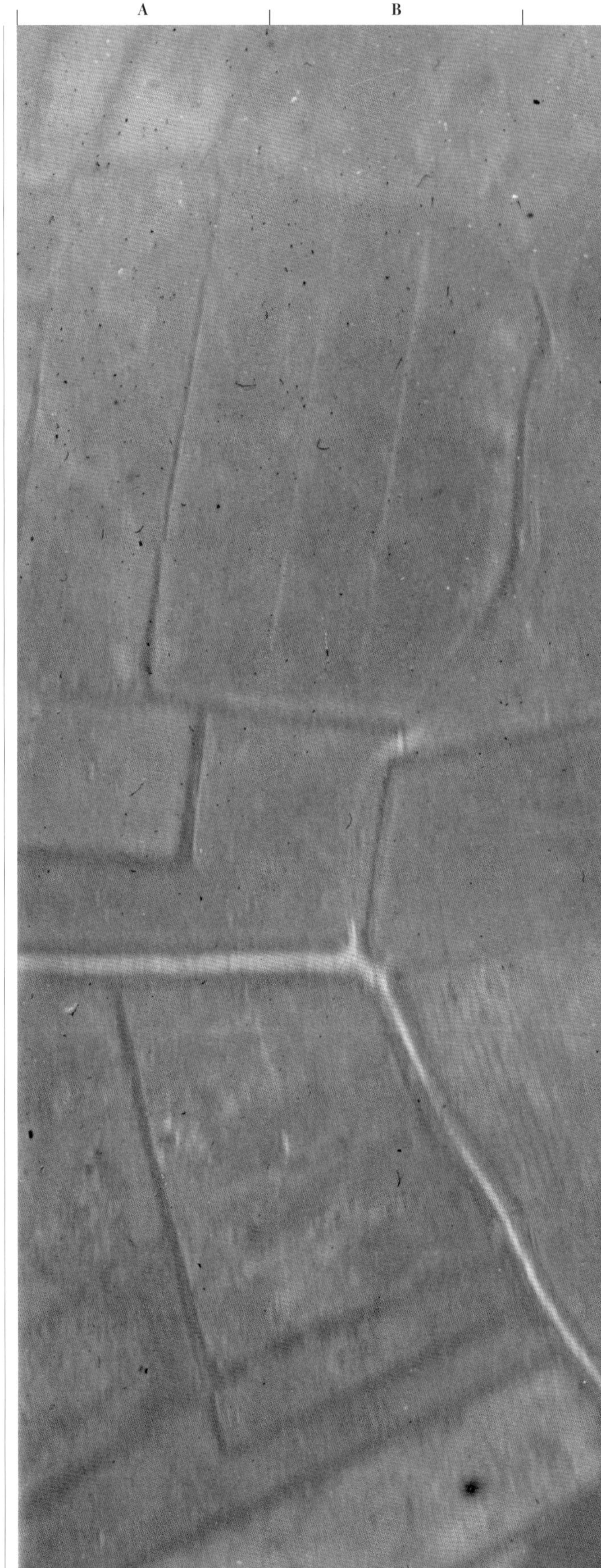

GPS 51°09'45.43"N 2°49'28.54"E

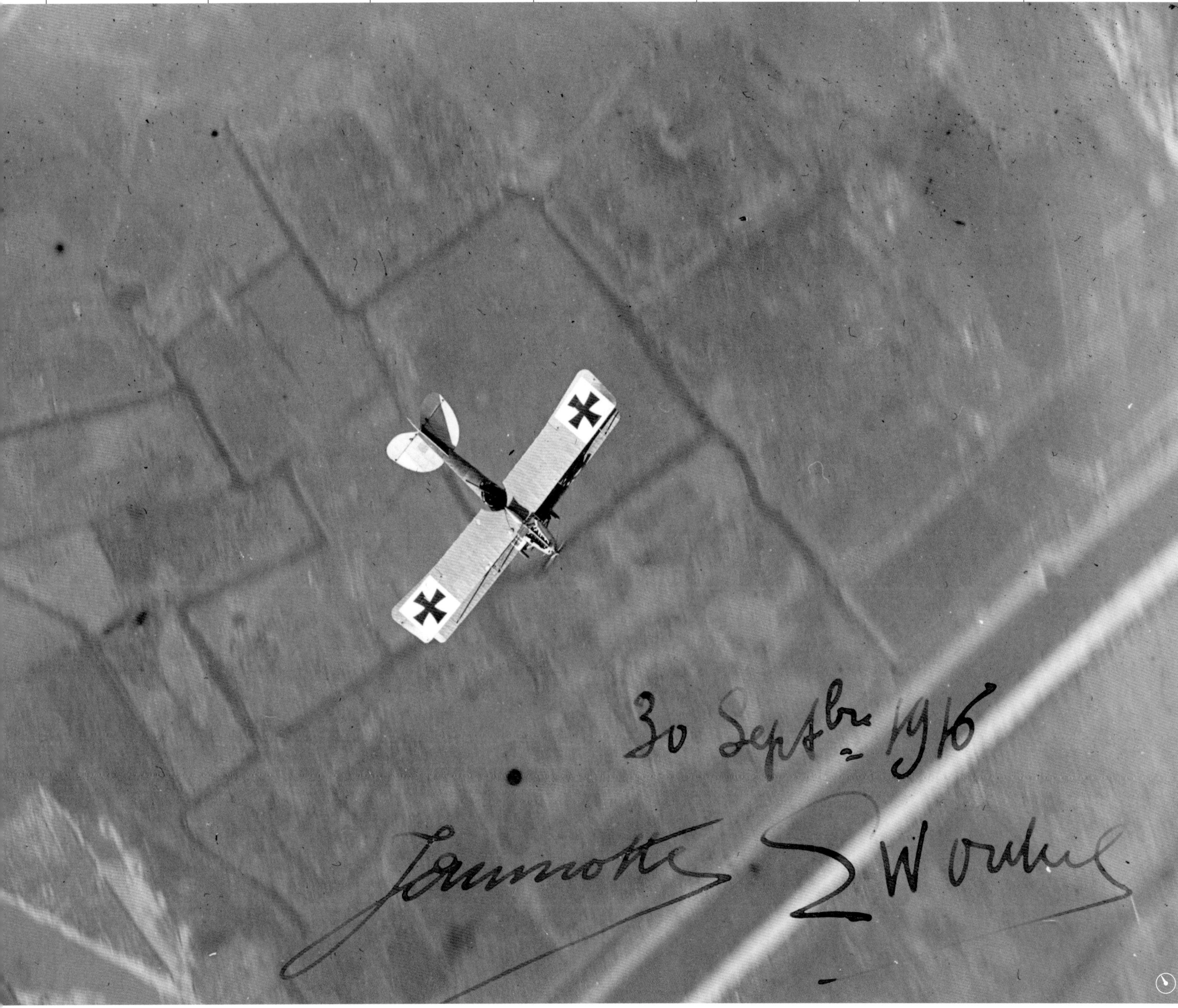

↗ Plassendale–Nieuwpoort Canal

↖ Kousestraat

Nieuwpoort 5.5 km ↙

32

SINT-ELOOI 15 SEPTEMBER 1916

Despite the initial success of the British attack at Sint-Elooi, the Germans recaptured their positions on 6 April 1916. They retook mine craters 2, 3, 4 and 5 and established the northern crater rims as solid fighting positions that once again came to dominate the Canadian and British lines. Numerous shelters were built into the wall as cover from artillery fire. Things would remain quiet in the Sint-Elooi sector until the Battle of Messines (7 June 1917).

» **SEE ALSO** 6 19 SINT-ELOOI

↓ **CANADIAN MAP OF NO-MAN'S-LAND**

Detailed sketch of the no-man's-land between the Canadian and German front lines. The map was used to prepare raids and shows where cover could be found. Craters 1 to 6 were the result of the action of 27 March 1916 when the British exploded six mines.

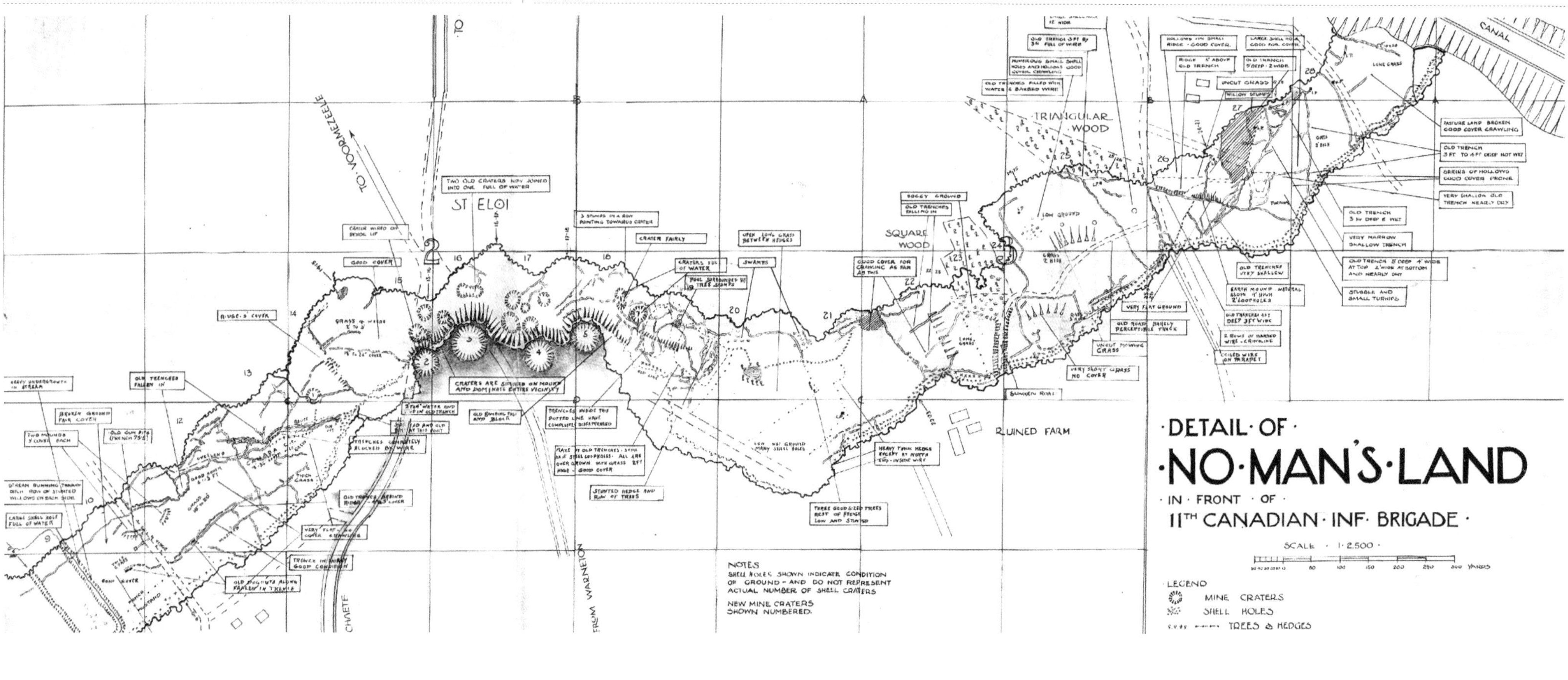

GPS 50°48'33.71"N 2°53'30.98"E

← C3
SHELTERS

Aerial photographs sometimes disguise the full horror of events on the ground. The immense dimensions of mine craters, for example, become clear only in photographs taken at ground level. In this German photograph one can see soldiers and shelters in the sides of the great crater at Sint-Elooi. Steps lead to a trench in the northern crater rim.

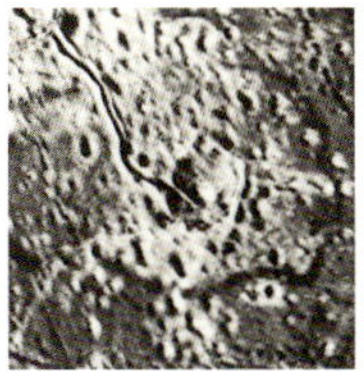

A3
CRATER 1

Part of the gallery of mine 1 caved in but, in order to create a position in British-held territory that would provide cover, the charge was exploded in no-man's-land.

C3
SINT-ELOOI MOUND

After the British mine attack little remained of The Mound, but the rim of the crater nonetheless remained the highest position in the whole surrounding area.

D3
CRATER 5

Craters 2 to 5 are here not only defended by a trench but are also equipped with numerous deep shelters in the walls.

↓ **SINT-ELOOI CRATERS**

Oblique view of the mine craters at Sint-Elooi, 20 October 1916. The terrain has clearly been totally devastated. The British front line was just 70 metres north of the large craters, which were held by the Germans. The crater rims have been converted into a trench.

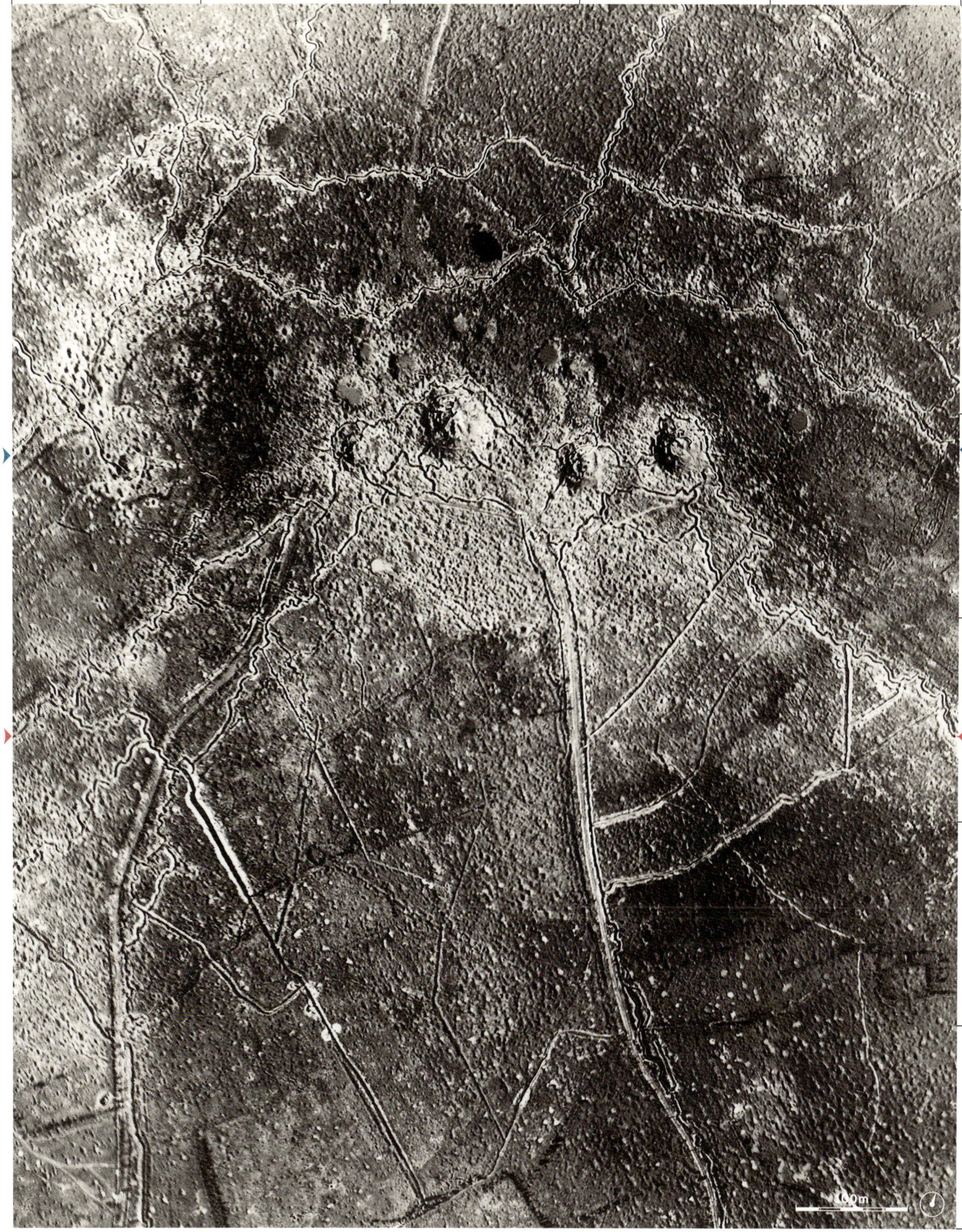

33
BROENBEEK - CEMETERY
31 JANUARY 1917

During the war, dead soldiers on both sides were buried in numerous military cemeteries near the front. In contrast to those of the Commonwealth, most of the German cemeteries have disappeared and the remains of German soldiers have been transferred to one of the four large collective cemeteries in Flanders: Langemark, Vladslo, Menen (Menin) and Hooglede. Some of the cemeteries disappeared in the years after the war, most of them (120 or more) in the 1950s. Thanks to aerial photographs, we still know where they were and what their often extensive geometric designs looked like. One of these 'lost' cemeteries – with one of the most beautiful designs – is Friedhof XII Weidendrift, designed in 1915 by Lieutenant Kemmer. This was a cemetery containing soldiers killed in October 1914. Their remains were transferred before 1932 to the existing military cemetery in Langemark.[11]

» **SEE ALSO** (29) LANGEMARK-NORD

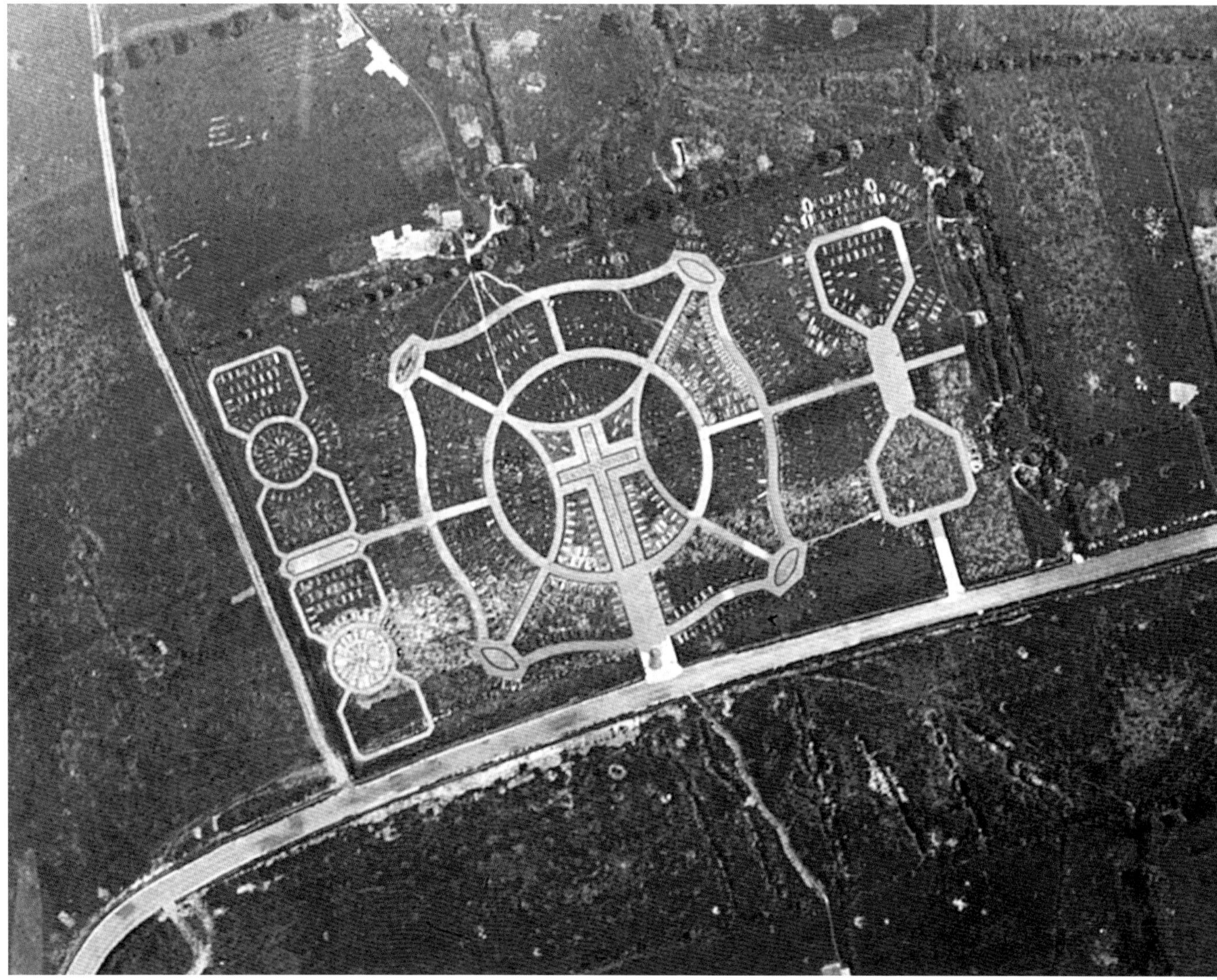

→ **CEMETERY**

Detail from a photograph of the cemetery taken on 20 July 1916. The individual graves are easy to make out.

F1-F2
WEIDENDRIFT CEMETERY

German cemetery with a large-scale design. Typical of German cemeteries is their frequent use of the cross design. Sites have been reserved in various places for memorial gardens and monuments.

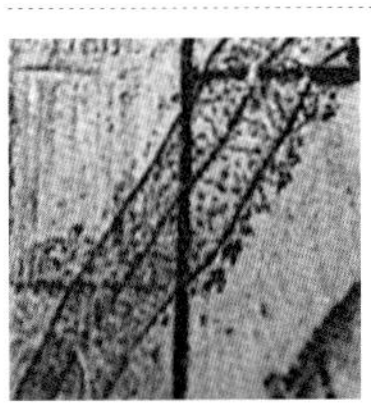

C1-C2
BARBED-WIRE BARRIER IN THE SNOW

Aerial photographs of snowy landscapes often reveal exceptional details. This barrier consists of three fences with barbed wire between them. Each black dot represents a post to which the barbed wire has been fastened.

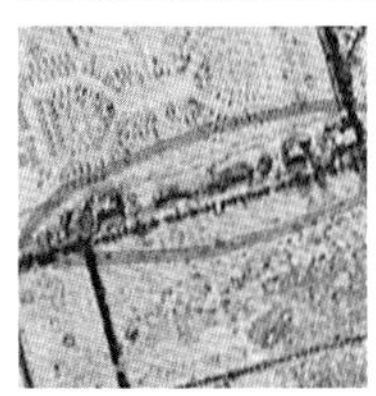

F2-F3
GERMAN ARTILLERY

Despite the proximity of the cemetery, a German firing position has been constructed just over a hedge. A Belgian photographic interpreter has spotted it and drawn a circle on the print with a pencil.

F3
REINFORCED POSITION

Reinforced position between lines of trenches surrounded by a barbed-wire fence that extends to the north-west and south-east.

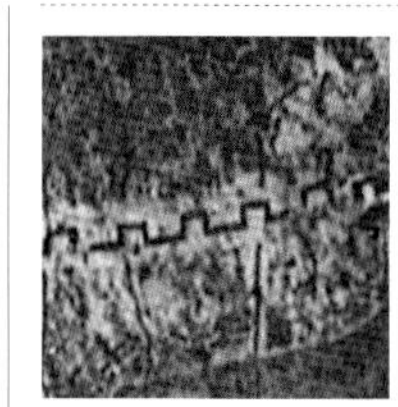

A2
TRENCH IN GOURBI WOOD

A German trench position was constructed behind Broenbeek stream in 1916. The course of the trench is clearly visible from the air, even through the wood. After the Battle of Langemark in 1917 this became the German front line.

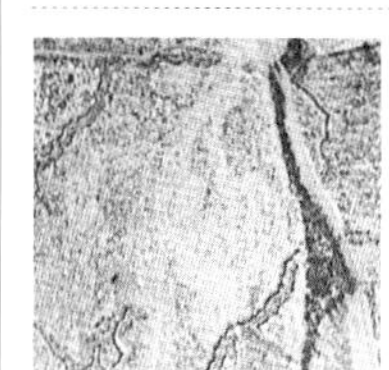

H6
GERMAN TRENCHES, NOVEMBER 1914 - APRIL 1915

Network of German front trenches from the period before the Second Battle of Ypres. The lack of shadow (in contrast to the trenches behind the Broenbeek) reveals that they were no longer maintained and were therefore no longer in use.

A
B
C
D
Broenbeek
E
F
G
H
800 m 29 Langemark
2
1.2 km Langemark
3
4
Mangelaarstraat
5
6
100 m
600 m Kortekeer

34 BELLEWAARDE 13 MAY 1917

After the attacks of 16 June 1915 an underground war raged beneath Bellewaarde Ridge. The German Pioneers and British tunnellers undermined each other's positions and exploded dozens of mines, sometimes, but not always, followed by infantry attacks. This British aerial photograph of 13 May 1917 shows the intensity of the mine war that lasted from September 1915 to July 1917.

↓ PLAN OF TUNNELLING ACTIVITIES

A British plan showing the progress of tunnelling activities beneath Bellewaarde Ridge: the trenches are in black and the British tunnels in red.

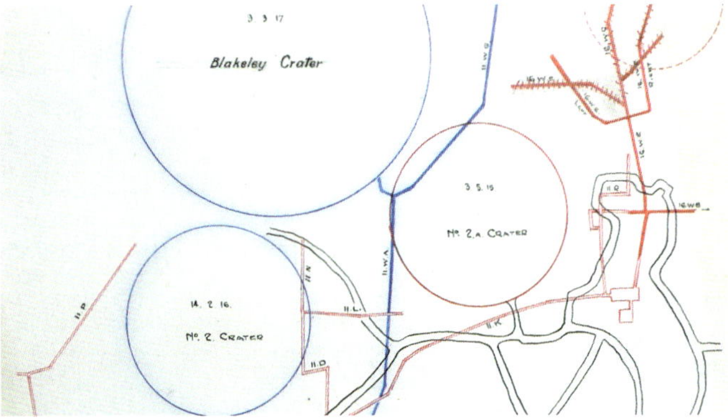

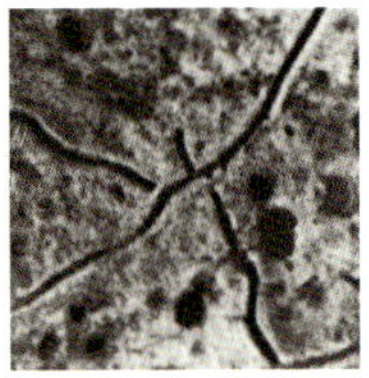

D5

ACCESS TO SHAFTS

British maps of the 177th Tunnelling Company show access points to the underground shafts and passages at this spot.

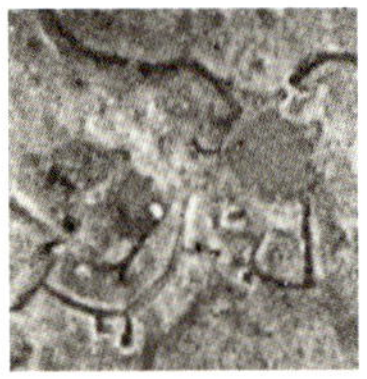

I5

REINFORCED CRATER

As soon as the mines blew craters in the landscape, they were stormed and strengthened as quickly as possible. The western crater rim shows several German fighting positions.

SYMBOLS

GERMAN TRENCHES, BUNKERS, NARROW-GAUGE RAILWAY
BRITISH TRENCHES
CRATER
BELLEWAARDE FARM MOAT
YPRES–ROESELARE RAILWAY

GPS 50°51'06.81"N 2°56'14.48"E

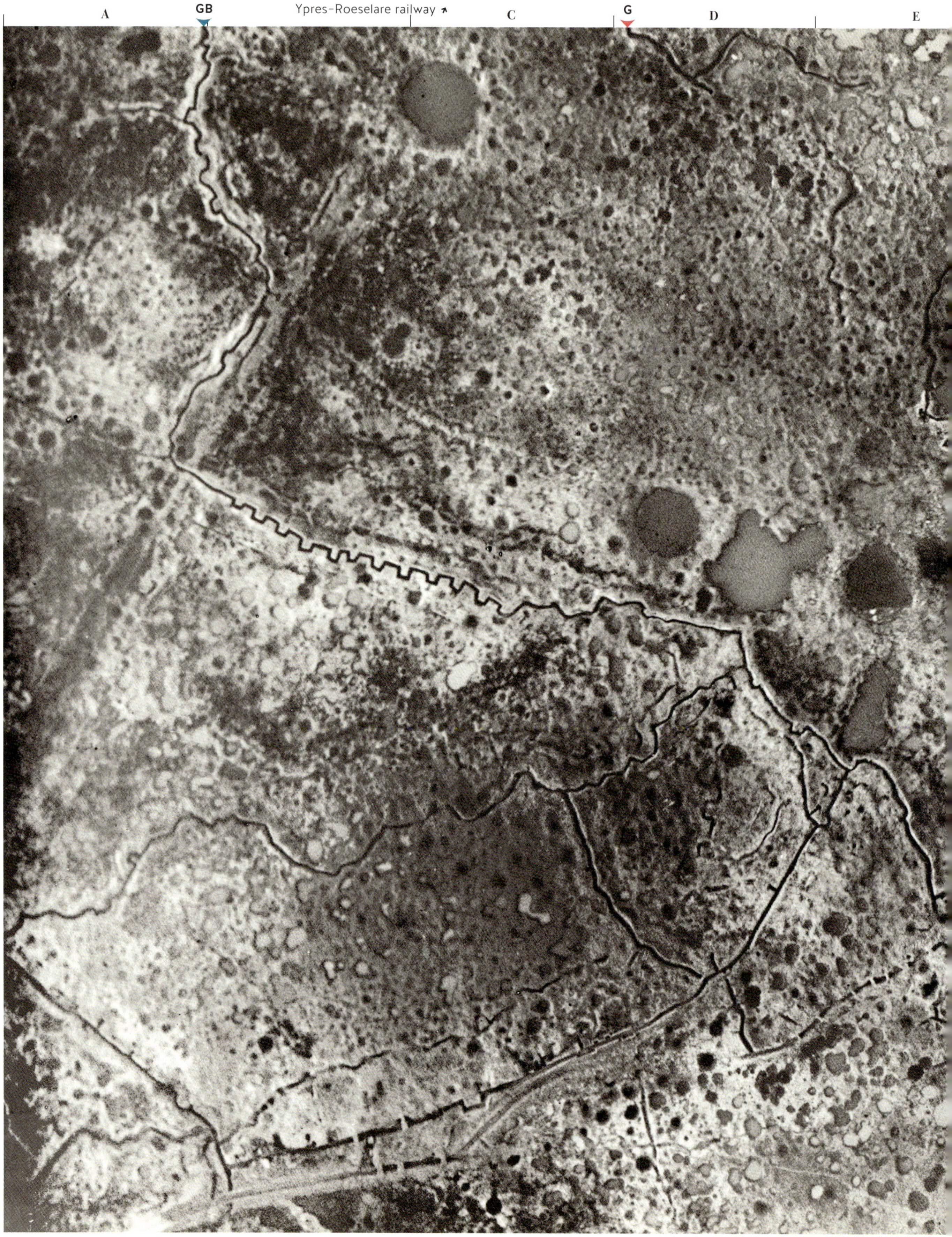

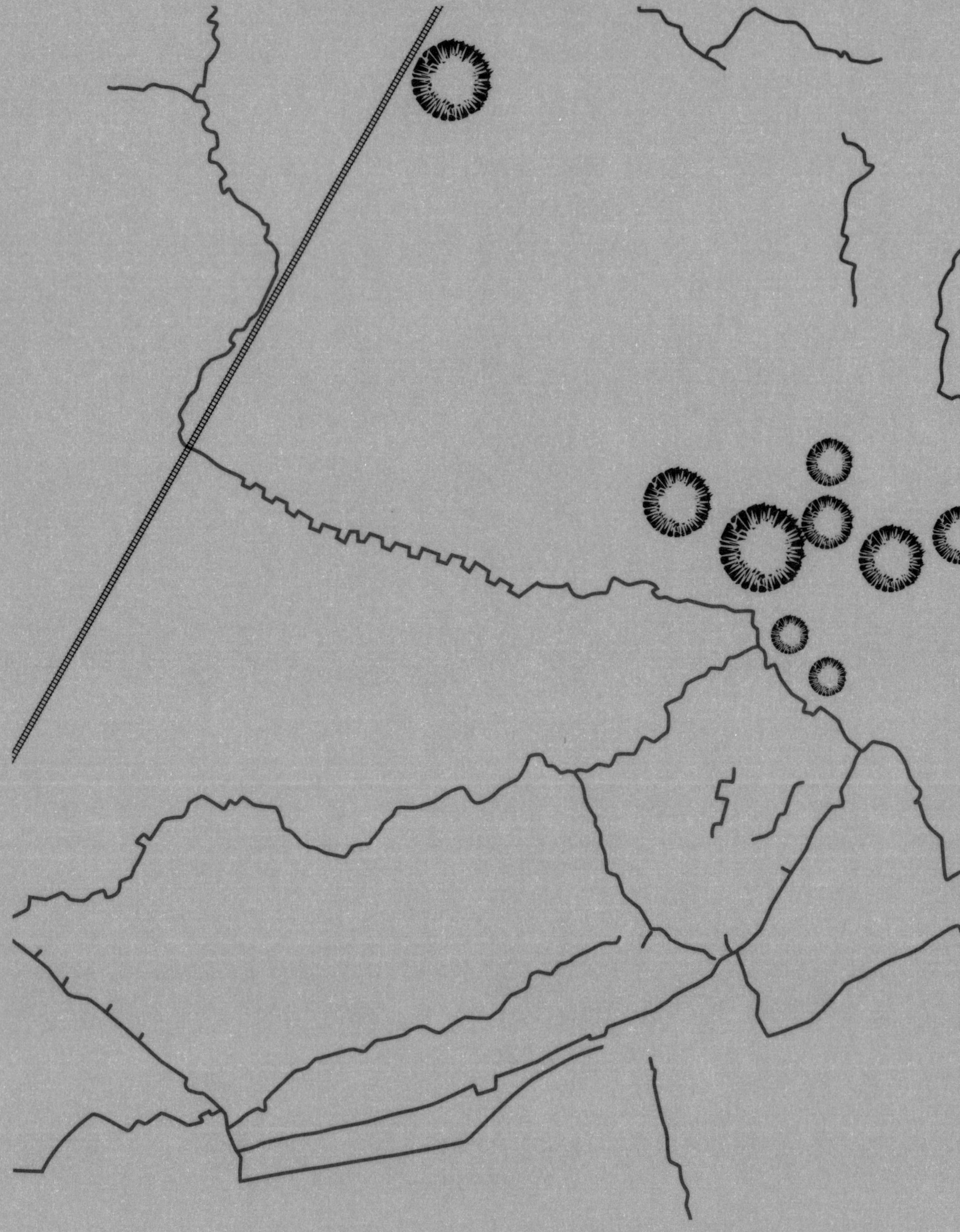

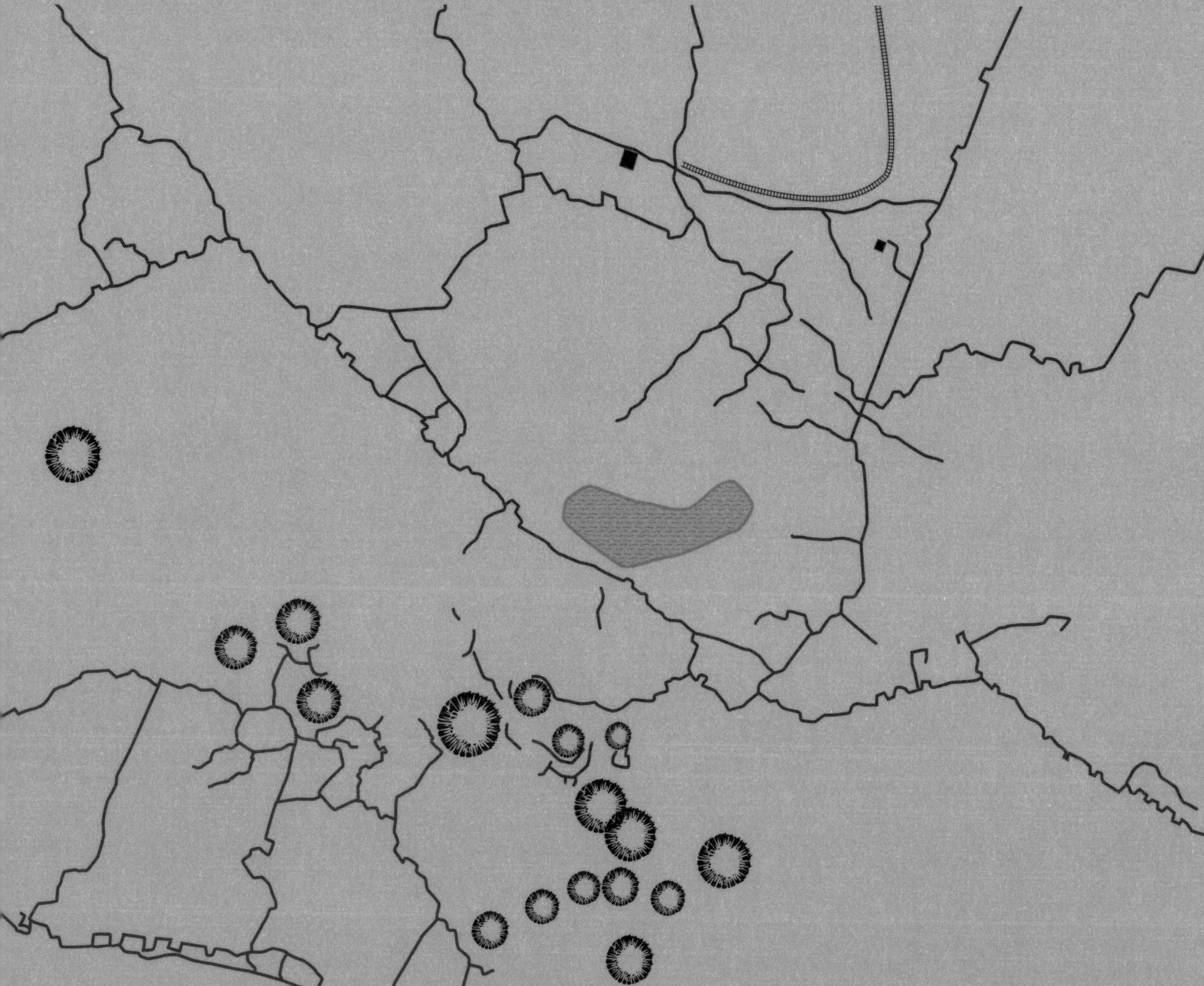

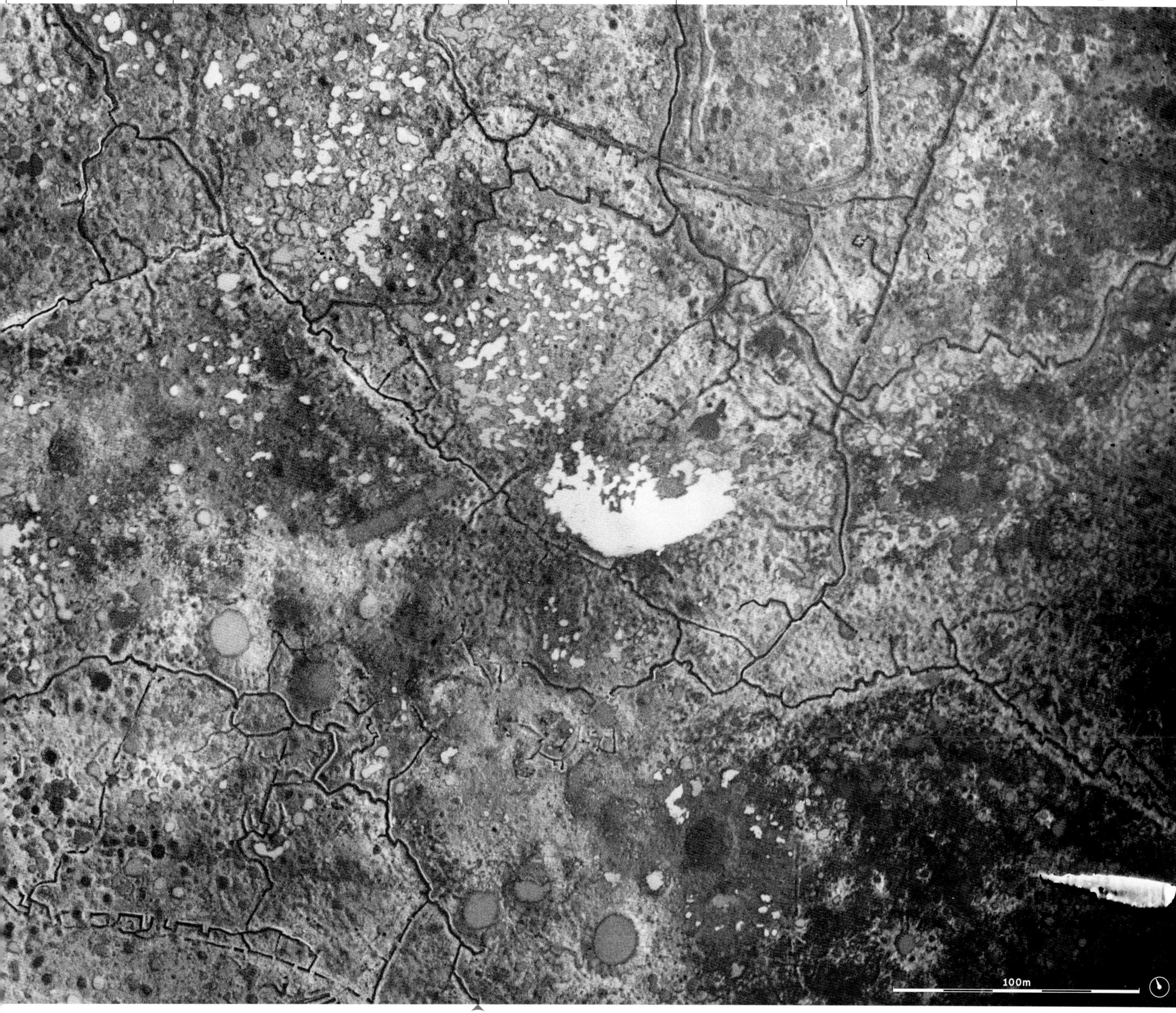
F
G
H
I
narrow-gauge railway
narrow-gauge railway
L
1
2
3
4
5
G 14 22 45 129 Hooge 450 m
100m
GB

35

DIKKEBUS – ARMY CAMP

24 APRIL 1917

A British aerial photograph of 24 April 1917 shows a typical Allied army camp at Dikkebus, less than 5 kilometres from the front. The soldiers were housed in small barracks, and on the west side of the camp there was an exercise field with a training trench and obstacle course. The camp was relatively undisturbed by the German artillery whose attention was focused on the British artillery a few hundred metres east of the farm.

↗ **CAMOUFLAGED POSITION**

Position for two anti-aircraft guns.

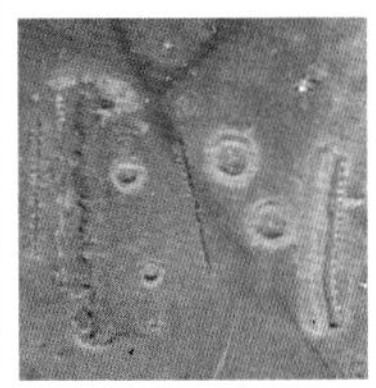

B4

ANTI-AIRCRAFT GUNS

West of the farm were four anti-aircraft guns. The guns could be turned quickly on their circular platforms.

↓ **DRAINAGE CHANNELS**

Musical entertainment in a British camp. Note the drainage channels in the foreground.

A6

SHALLOW TRENCHES

In contrast to the other trenches in this photograph, there is no shadow on the inner wall of this trench. It was possibly a shallow training trench.

D5

DRAINAGE CHANNELS

In these barracks preparations have clearly been made in case of excessive rainfall. To keep their feet dry, the men have dug drainage channels to direct the water to the farm dyke.

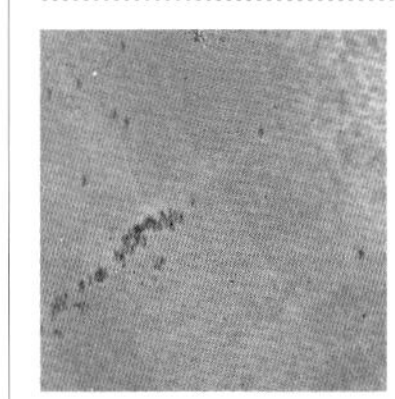

A5

SOLDIERS TRAINING

When this photograph was taken the silhouettes of dozens of soldiers were visible in the immediate vicinity. To the east of the training trench are more soldiers training.

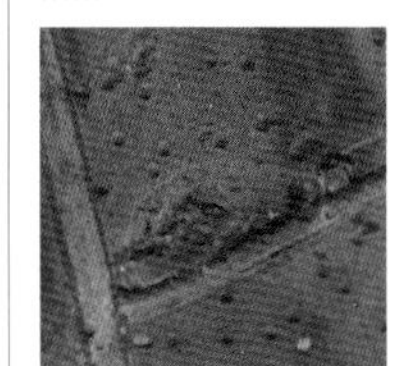

H4

ARTILLERY

Artillery set up under cover of a hedge, the simplest form of natural camouflage.

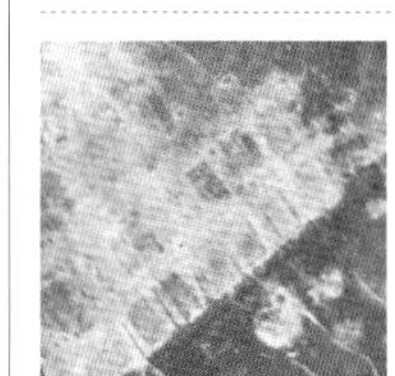

C2-C3

DESERTED BARRACKS

In November 1916 the fighting had intensified and there were some twenty barracks next to the farm. The contours of the barracks (which had meanwhile been removed) were still visible months later.

GPS 50°49'41.46"N 2°49'46.45"E

A B C D ↖ 2.4 km **Vlamertinge** E F G ↖ Groenejagerstraat

1 ↖ 4 km 46 96 125 **Ypres** 2 3 4 5 6

Steenakkerstraat ↗ ↓ 650 m 35 **Dikkebus** Zorgvlietstraat ↗

36

HILL 60 1 MAY 1917

After the fighting for Hill 60 in April and May 1915, the hill was still in German hands, and the front line would remain virtually unchanged until June 1917. The sector was one of the most heavily bombarded spots in the Ypres Salient. On the British side and on the German side, too, the earth was totally churned up. The degree to which German artillery fire was focused on the British positions on the hill is striking. A few hundred metres to the east of Hill 60, shooting at the British lines was much less fierce.

» **SEE ALSO** 5 7 47 HILL 60

→ **GERMAN TROOPS**

German troops in a well-maintained and robust trench on Hill 60. Sandbags and a wooden plank have been used to make a small shelter, offering some protection against rain, shrapnel and small shell fragments.

↓ **GERMAN PANORAMA OF HILL 60**

German photograph of the battlefield on Hill 60 at the end of April 1915. Sandbags, rolls of barbed wire and other refuse are scattered over the crater.

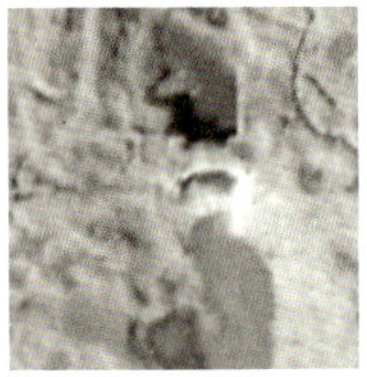

B1

RAILWAY BRIDGE

The bridge over the railway had formed part of the Allied front line since the beginning of 1915.

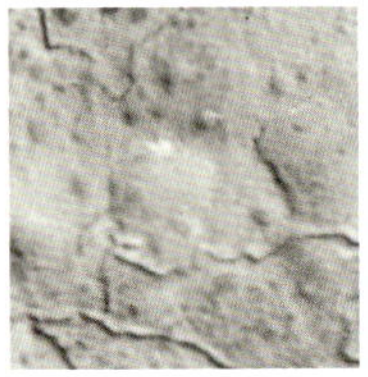

B2-C2

CHURNED-UP NO-MAN'S-LAND

The area just in front of the German lines was churned up by the old 1915 craters. Because of the persistent shooting they can only vaguely be seen on the photograph.

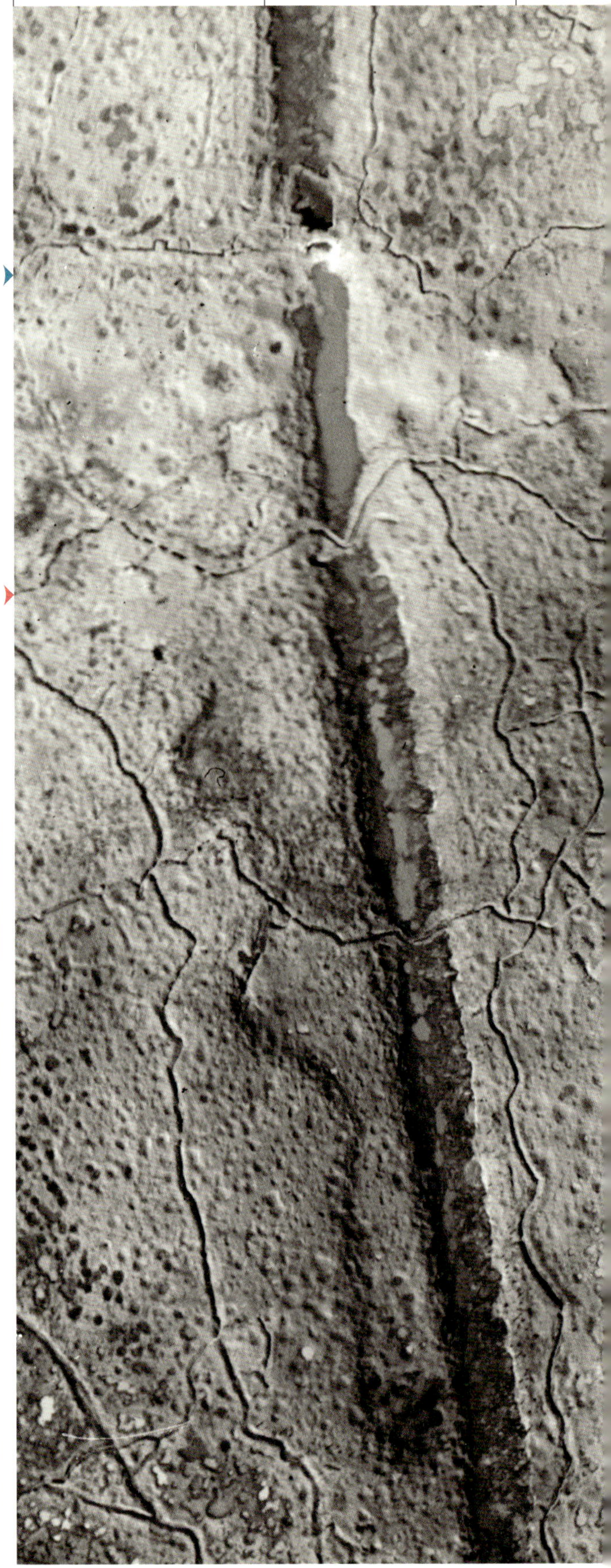

GPS 50°49'26.03"N 2°55'45.20"E

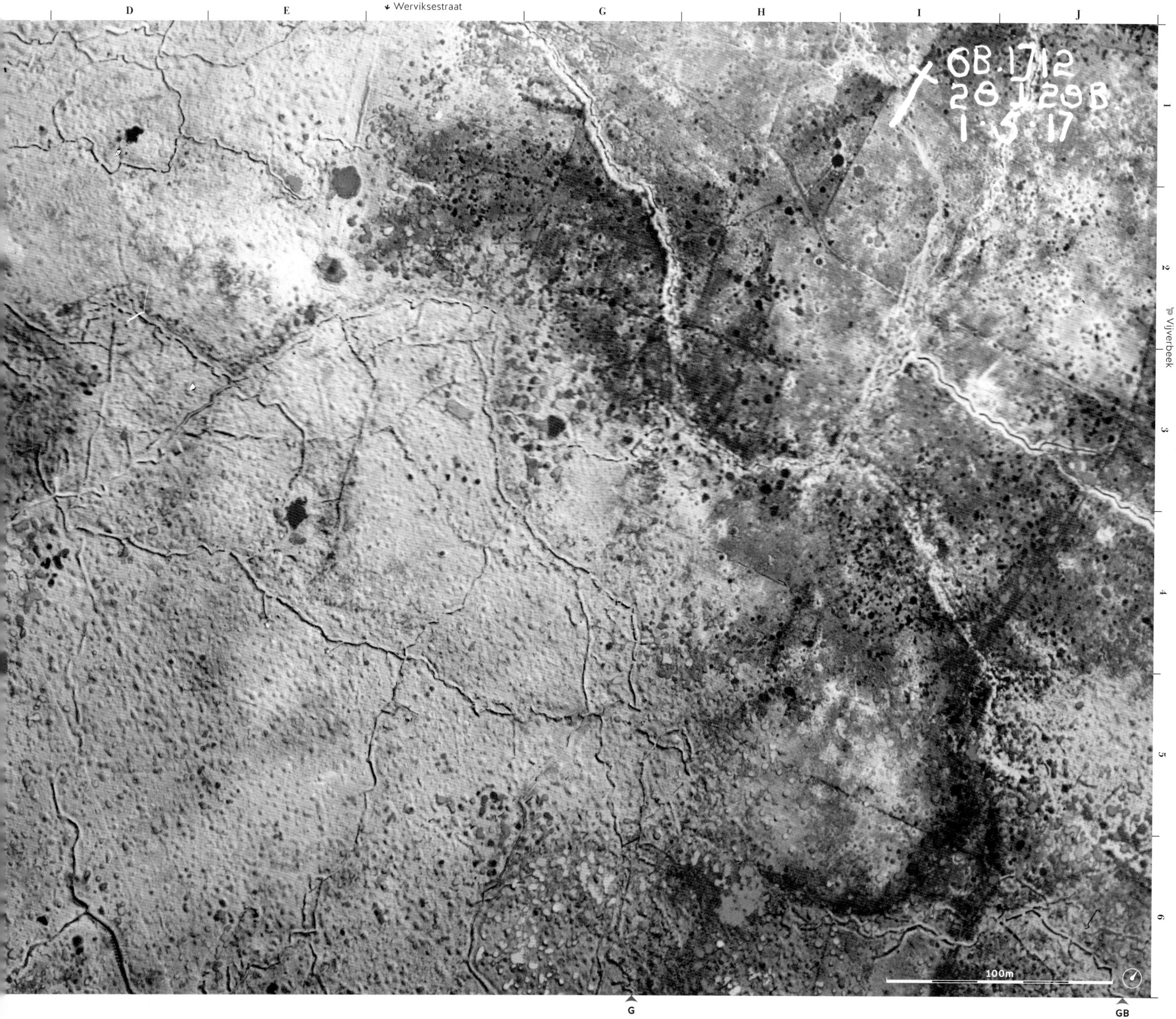

D
E
Werviksestraat
G
H
I
J
1
2
3
4
5
6
Vijverbeek
6B.1712
28.I.29B
1.5.17
100m
G
GB

37
LOMBARDSIJDE – START OF THE FRONT 28 MAY 1917

The Western Front stretched for more than 700 kilometres across Belgium and the north of France. It ran from the North Sea at Nieuwpoort to the village of Pfetterhouse on the Franco–Swiss border. On both sides of the no-man's-land were extensive defensive networks. After the Battle of the Yser the Allies established a bridgehead on the right bank of the Yser. An aerial photograph taken by the French 226th Squadron shows the clear-cut lines of the trenches in the sand dunes. On both sides shelters were dug into the high dunes. The Germans feared an Allied offensive towards the U-boat harbours in Ostend and Zeebrugge. This led to this sector becoming a theatre of war on 10 July 1917.

» **SEE ALSO** 81 NIEUWPOORT – OPERATION STRANDFEST

↑ **POSITIONS IN THE DUNES**

German sailors pose by their shelters in the dunes.

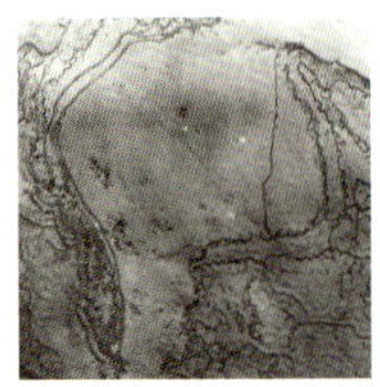

D1-F2

START OF THE WESTERN FRONT

The Western Front started at a dip in the dunes on a North Sea beach. The British called it 'The Pimple' while the Germans knew it as the Seekessel.

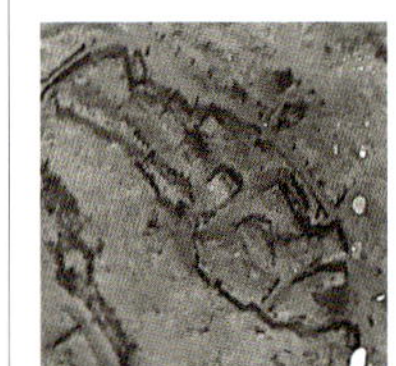

F4

GERMAN SHELTERS

At the back of the high dunes shelters were dug out of sight of the Allies.

↓ **POSITIONS IN THE DUNES**

Der Seekessel, watercolour sketch by Rudolf Lange, 17 July 1917. Lange painted this work a week after Operation Strandfest on 10 July 1917. By that point he was able to take his time observing the former no-man's-land without any danger to his life.

GPS 51°09'18.28"N 2°44'07.15"E

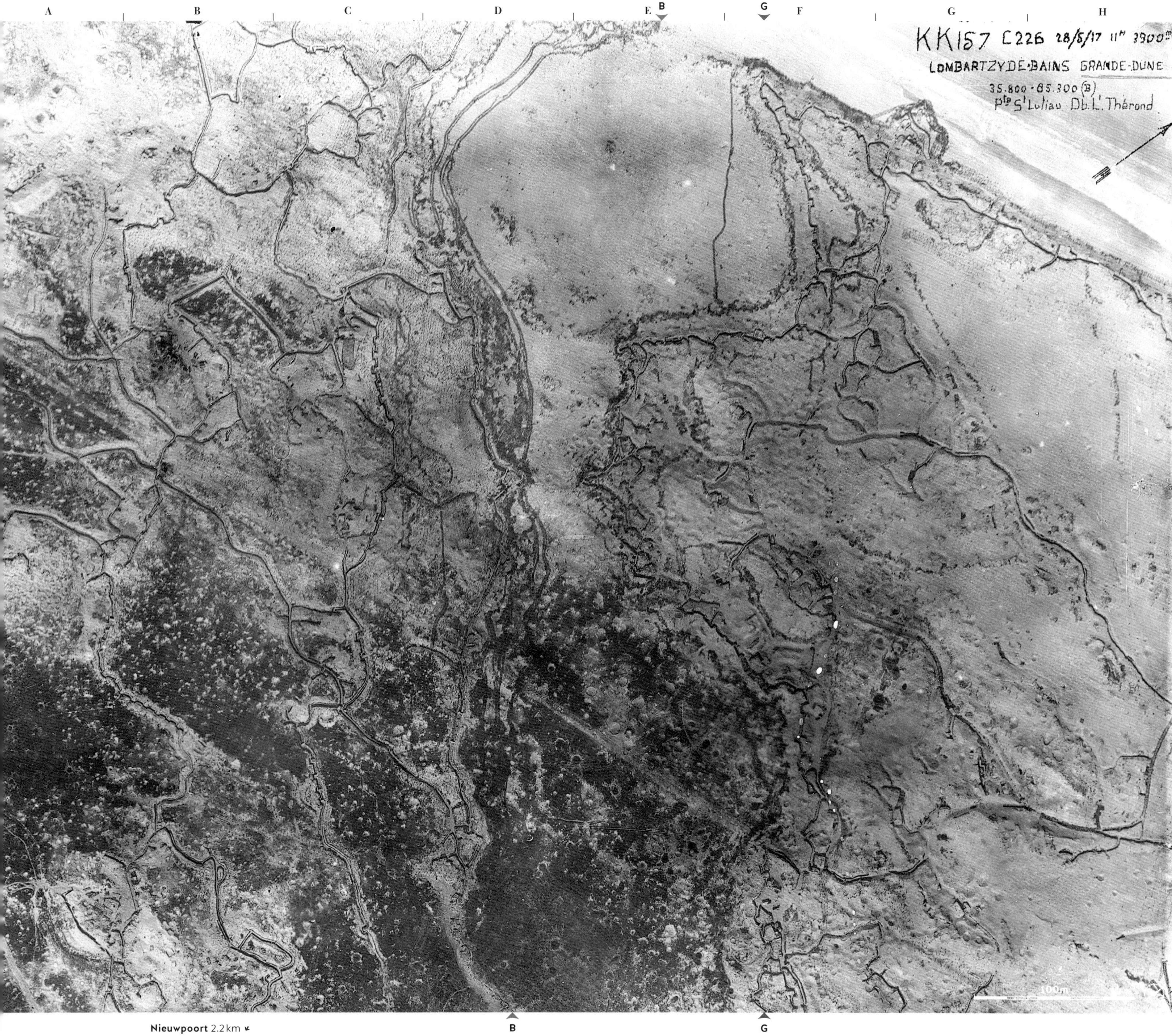
A
B
C
D
E
F
G
H
KK157 C226 28/5/17 11h 3900m
LOMBARTZYDE-BAINS GRANDE-DUNE
35.800 - 65.300 (B)
Pte S'Luliau Db. L'. Thérond
1
beach
2
3
4
5
6
100m
B
G
B
G
Nieuwpoort 2.2km

38
NIEUWPOORT – GANZENPOOT
5 MAY 1917

The sluice complex known as 'De Ganzenpoot' in Nieuwpoort has, since the second half of the nineteenth century, regulated the water level in the Yser basin. A system of sluices and waste weirs channels the excess water from watercourses and polders. At the climax of the Battle of the Yser, during the night of 29 / 30 October 1914, the overflow from the drainage sluice from the Noordvaart was opened. The rising water put an end to the German advance. The sluice complex remained in Allied hands for the rest of the war; from here water was drained or released to keep the inundation at the desired level. The Nieuwpoort sector was an international sector defended by the Belgian and French armies and, between June and November 1917, by the British army as well.

SYMBOLS

- ALLIED TRENCHES
- GERMAN TRENCHES
- INUNDATED AREA
- ARTILLERY
- BARBED WIRE

↑ OBLIQUE VIEW OF 'DE GANZENPOOT'

French oblique aerial photograph of 14 January 1916 showing, in the foreground, the northern edge of the town and the sluice system. The reflection of the midday light on the inundated area illustrates the marshy nature of the battlefields around Nieuwpoort. The front trenches were built on both sides of the narrow no-man's-land and consisted of above-ground trenches and shelters. The high water level in these low-lying polders made it impossible to dig into the soil.

C3-D3

FORT PALINGBRUG

Fort Palingbrug, a vestige from Nieuwpoort's past as a fortified town, was used as a bridgehead on the right bank of the Yser.

A5

BRITISH ARTILLERY

Heavily shelled British artillery position. Other firing positions were situated between Nieuwpoort and Oud-kanaal van Veurne.

↓ PANORAMA OF 'DE GANZENPOOT', NIEUWPOORT

Panoramic photograph of 'De Ganzenpoot' at Nieuwpoort. The sluices are on the extreme left while the ruins of Nieuwpoort can be seen on the horizon.

GPS 51°08'04.33"N 2°45'22.39"E

Canadalaan
B
C
D
E
F
Yser
G
H
B 1
800m
Lombardsijde 2
3
inundation
G
4
Lombarcsijde 2C0m
6
200m
Yser Canal
old Yser
Plassendale Canal
B
G

39

ZILLEBEKE – THE BLUFF

20 MAY 1917

'The Bluff' – the Germans called it simply 'die grosse Bastion' ('the big bastion') – was still, in 1916, a sector of very intensive underground warfare. A large part of its eastern flank was torn to shreds. Between the British and German front lines, at least ten mines had exploded, ploughing up the earth. By mid-1917 the battlefield had become a muddy lunar landscape, pockmarked with craters.

» **SEE ALSO** 18 ZILLEBEKE – THE BLUFF

↓ PANORAMA FROM THE BLUFF

View to the east from the top of The Bluff towards German lines. In the foreground lies one of the deep craters left by a mine exploded under the hill by the Germans in 1915.

C3-D3

'A-CRATER'

On 25 July 1916 the Germans simultaneously exploded four mines resulting in a large crater.[12]

C4

BRITISH FIGHTING POSITION

British fighting position on the rim of a crater.

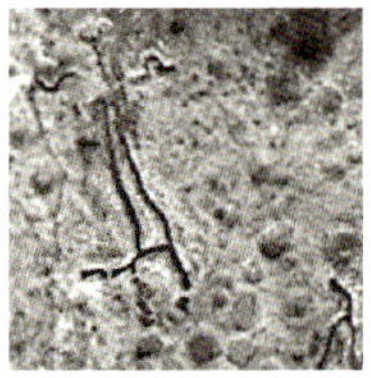

C5

GERMAN CRATER

Crater created by a German mine exploded to make the British underground shelters collapse.[13] The Germans have reinforced the crater and provided it with fighting positions.

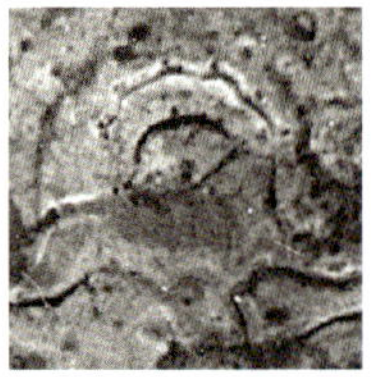

Ypres-Comines Canal

GPS 50°48'53.12"N 2°54'56.15"E

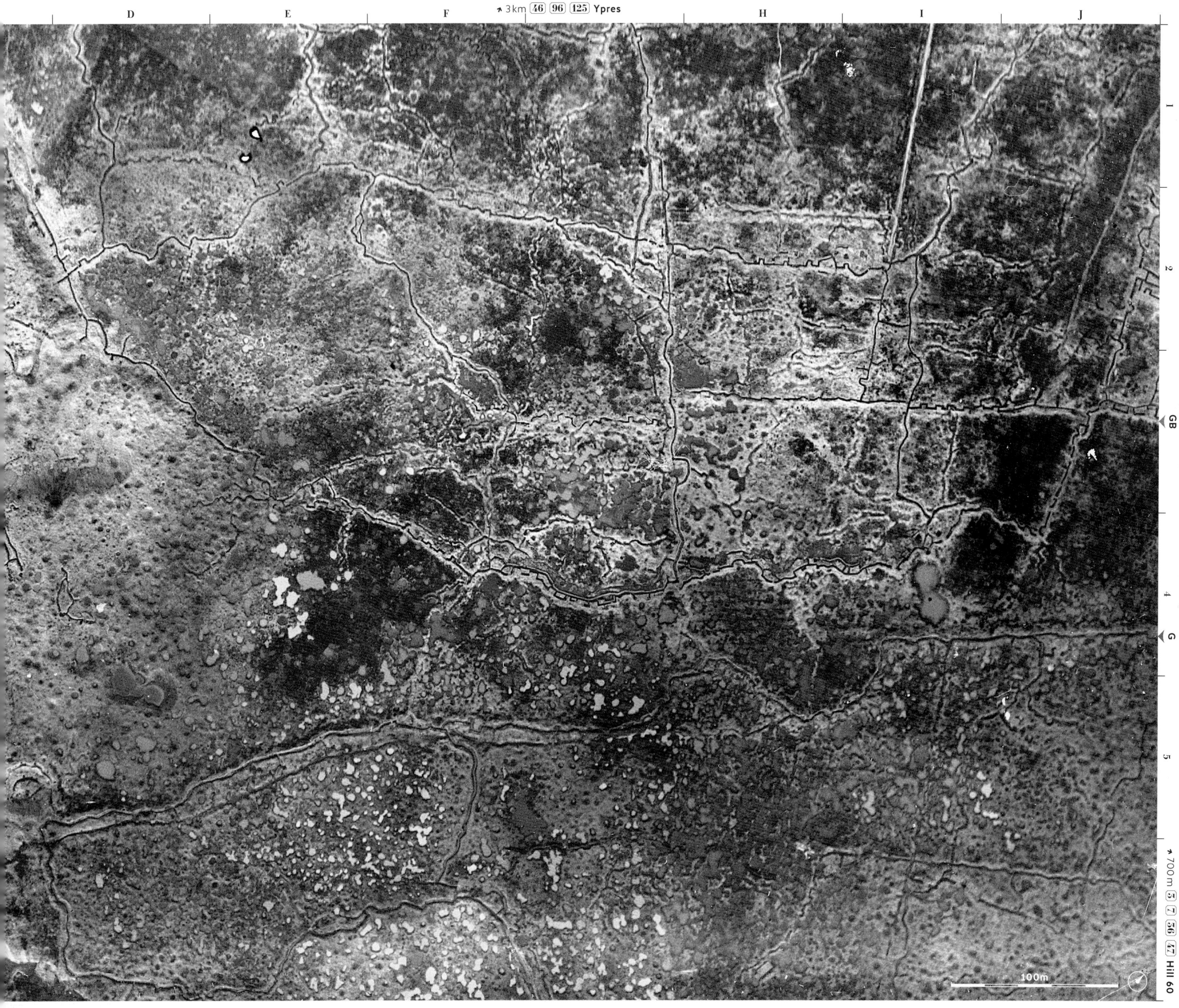
D
E
F
3km 46 96 125 Ypres
H
I
J
1
2
GB
4
G
5
700m 5 7 56 47 Hill 60
100m

40
OUDERDOM – TANK PARK
24 MAY 1917

At the beginning of May 1917 the first preparations were made for a special camp near the hamlet of Ouderdom to the north-east of Reningelst, 6 kilometres behind the British lines. Forty-five sheds stood in a conspicuous L-shape. Around the camp, carefully hung screens ensured that whatever happened inside them was concealed from the outside world. Vehicle tracks too wide for lorries or carts give the game away, however: this was a tank park. The British Captain William Watson described the 'tankodrome' at Ouderdom as follows: 'We drove first to Ouderdom, a vast and enticing railhead, which the enemy shelled methodically each night, much to the annoyance of "b" tank battalion, who lived, for reasons of state, at the edge of the railhead. Their tanks were housed with disarming naivety in a series of canvas stalls surrounded by a high canvas screen. The whole erection was perhaps three-quarters of a mile in circumference. The tanks were so obviously concealed that the enemy never suspected their existence.'[14]

» Continued on p. 134

→ CHRONOLOGICAL SERIES OF AERIAL PHOTOGRAPHS

The top photograph dates from 1 May 1917: the construction of the sheds has begun – the contours are visible but there are no roofs. The bottom photograph, taken a week later, shows the progress made on the project.

GPS 50°49'34.05"N 2°47'10.13"E

F2-F3
VEHICLE IN SHED

The tracks of incoming vehicles run towards the shed. One of the tanks seems not to have driven far enough inside. The tracks are more than 2 metres wide.

E4-E5
SHADOW OF CANVAS SCREEN

Screens were hung around the camp to deter prying eyes. However, they would have immediately caught the eye of anyone studying the photograph. The Germans seem to have had no idea of the purpose of the sheds, since they were not shelled.

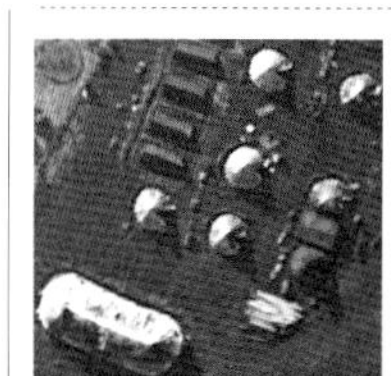

G5-H5
TENT ENCAMPMENT

To the south of the sheds, a tent encampment grew up. This was possibly the home of 'b' tank battalion, as described by Captain Watson.

1.2 km Reningelst
B
C
D
E
F
G
H
3.8 km Vlamertinge
tank sheds
tent encampment
2
3
4
5
6
6B1893
28 G30B
24·5·17
100m
Dikkebusweg
narrow-gauge railway

›› Continued from p. 132

The tanks arrived in Ouderdom by railway. From the railway there were caterpillar tracks leading to the sheds. Despite the secrecy, the arrival of the tanks did not escape the attention of the local population. Achiel van Walleghem, the assistant pastor of Dikkebus, whose diary provides an invaluable source of details about life in the front area at Ypres, notes on 24 May 1917: '[…] people say that tanks have already arrived and are standing in special storage facilities (packed in covering tents) in fields belonging to Cyriel Jacob at Ouderdom. […] 5 June 1917, Tuesday. I hear that in the night various tanks left Ouderdom over the fields and streams in front of and behind the farm of Cyriel Lamerant towards the front, and where the monsters pass all is pressed into the ground as if it were butter. Every day we await the attack.'[15] At ten past three on the morning of 7 June the mines exploded under the German lines – the attack had begun.

↑ **CHINESE LABOURERS AT ROLL-CALL**

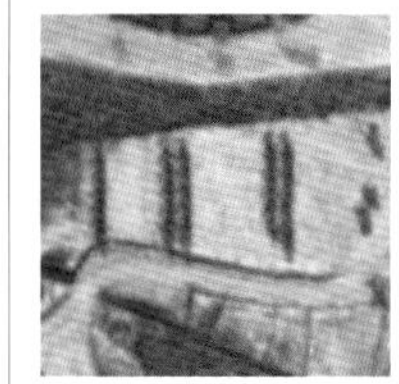

C4

ROLL-CALL FOR THE TROOPS

Just past the Goetmoet Mill (B4) the roll is called for a company of British soldiers. The various teams are lined up in rows.

↗ **OOSTHOEK WOOD**

A British soldier guides a Mark IV tank over the parapet of a trench. Photograph taken near Oosthoek Wood, 11 September 1917.

→ **TANKS ON A LOADING PLATFORM**

British tanks stand on a loading platform ready for transport through the Ypres region.

D1

SLOPING SURFACE

The tanks rolled down a ramp from their unloading platform to the British railway in Ouderdom.

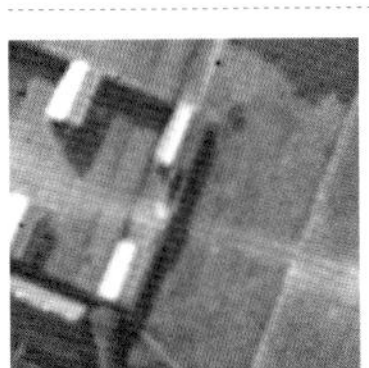

C1-C2

CATERPILLAR TRACKS

Tank tracks lead from the fenced-off sheds to the station.

GPS 50°49'34.05"N 2°47'10.13"E

A
B
C
D
E
F
G
disused trench
1
2
narrow-gauge railway
3
storage area
4
Bellestraat
5
6
100m
military road
narrow-gauge railway

41

WIJTSCHATE RIDGE

1 MAY 1917 & 3 JUNE 1917

The strategically important ridge at Mesen and Wijtschate, to the south of Ypres, had been in German hands since the end of 1914. To recapture the ground, a British mine offensive had been on the drawing-board since 1916. The Battle of Messines was preceded by a particularly heavy artillery bombardment of the German front line (more than 3,500,000 projectiles were fired).[16] An aerial photograph of 1 May 1917 shows a typical picture of the trench warfare on the Western Front in what was then a stable sector. On 3 June 1917 (see pp. 138-139) there was a lot of preparatory shooting. The myriad of smoke plumes show its intensity. There is a clear dividing line between the churned-up German line and the virtually untouched no-man's-land.

G

GB

→ **OBLIQUE VIEW OF WIJTSCHATE RIDGE**

British aerial photograph taken to the west of Wijtschate on 24 March 1917. In the foreground the British lines can be seen, together with the almost untouched no-man's-land. On the other side lies the German front line between Petit Bois and the Kemmel–Wijtschate road. Broad communication trenches run along and into Wijtschate Wood, towards Wijtschate (top left).

← **BOMBARDMENT OF MESEN**

View of Mesen from over the Douve Valley on 8 June 1917. Several grenades exploded in the village.

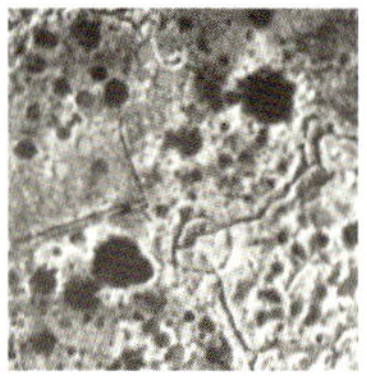

G1-F2

MINE CRATERS ON VANDAMME HILL

Before the Battle of Messines an underground mine war was already being waged in the sector, as witnessed here by several 10- to 15-metre-wide mine craters.

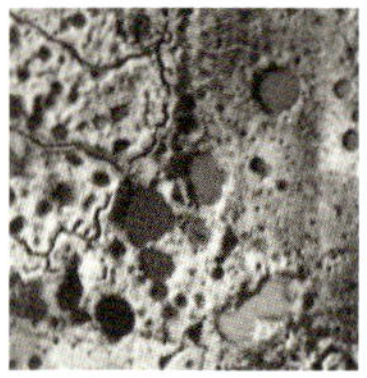

D6

MINE CRATERS AT PECKHAM FARM

At Peckham Farm a series of German mines were exploded under the British lines.

SYMBOLS

GERMAN TRENCHES

BRITISH TRENCHES

BURIED CABLES

CRATER

GPS 50°47'05.85"N 2°51'47.49"E

↓ Savaardlindestraat
B
C
D
E
F
GB
G
H
53 B 362.
28.N.23bd
24ac
1-5-17.
G
2
3
4
5
Wijtschate 675m ↗
100m
↗ Kruisstraat
GB
G

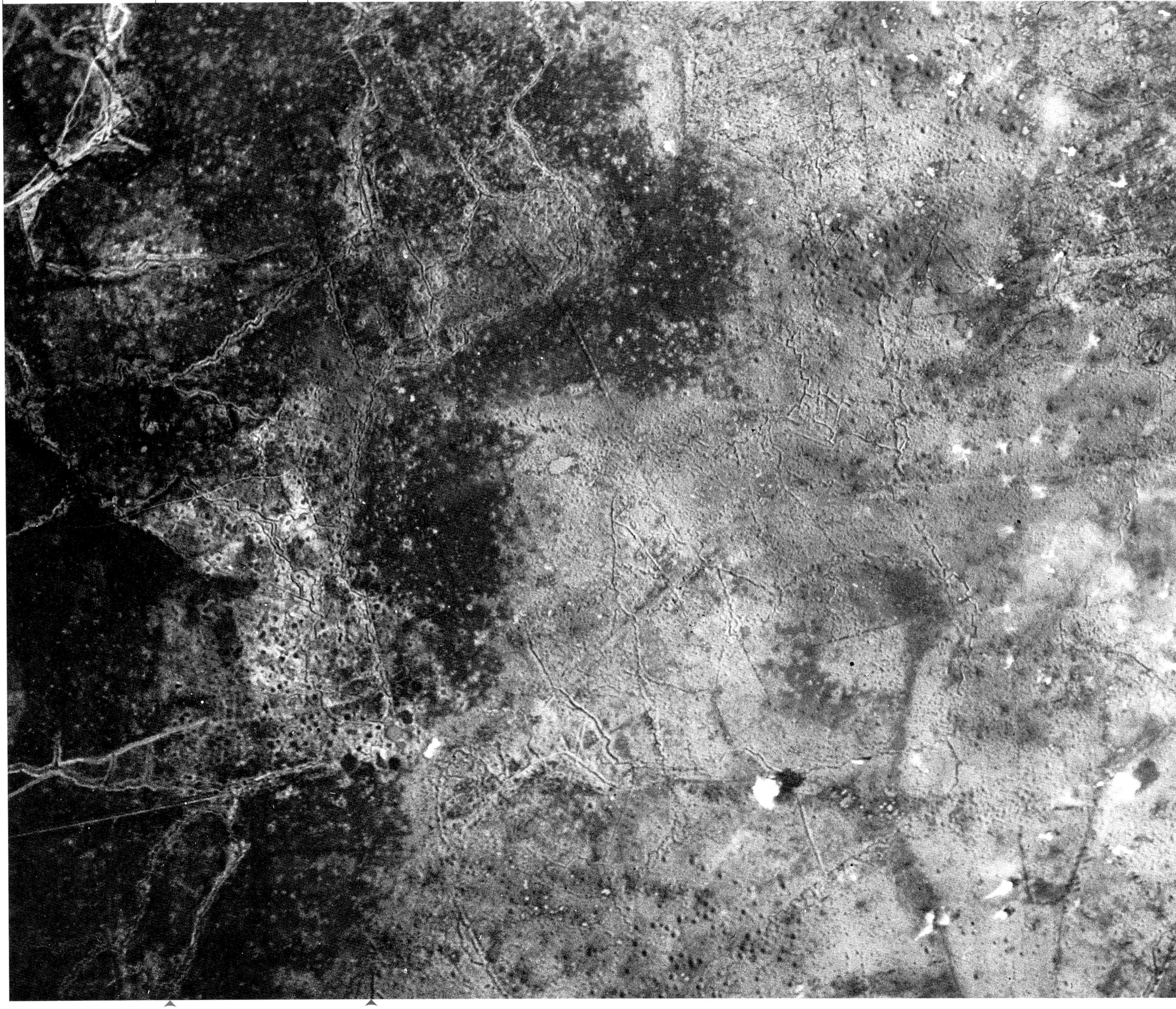
A
B
C
GB
G
E
F
G
H
GB
G
Kemmel 1.5 km
GPS 50°49'34.05"N 2°47'10.13"E
Wulvergemstraat

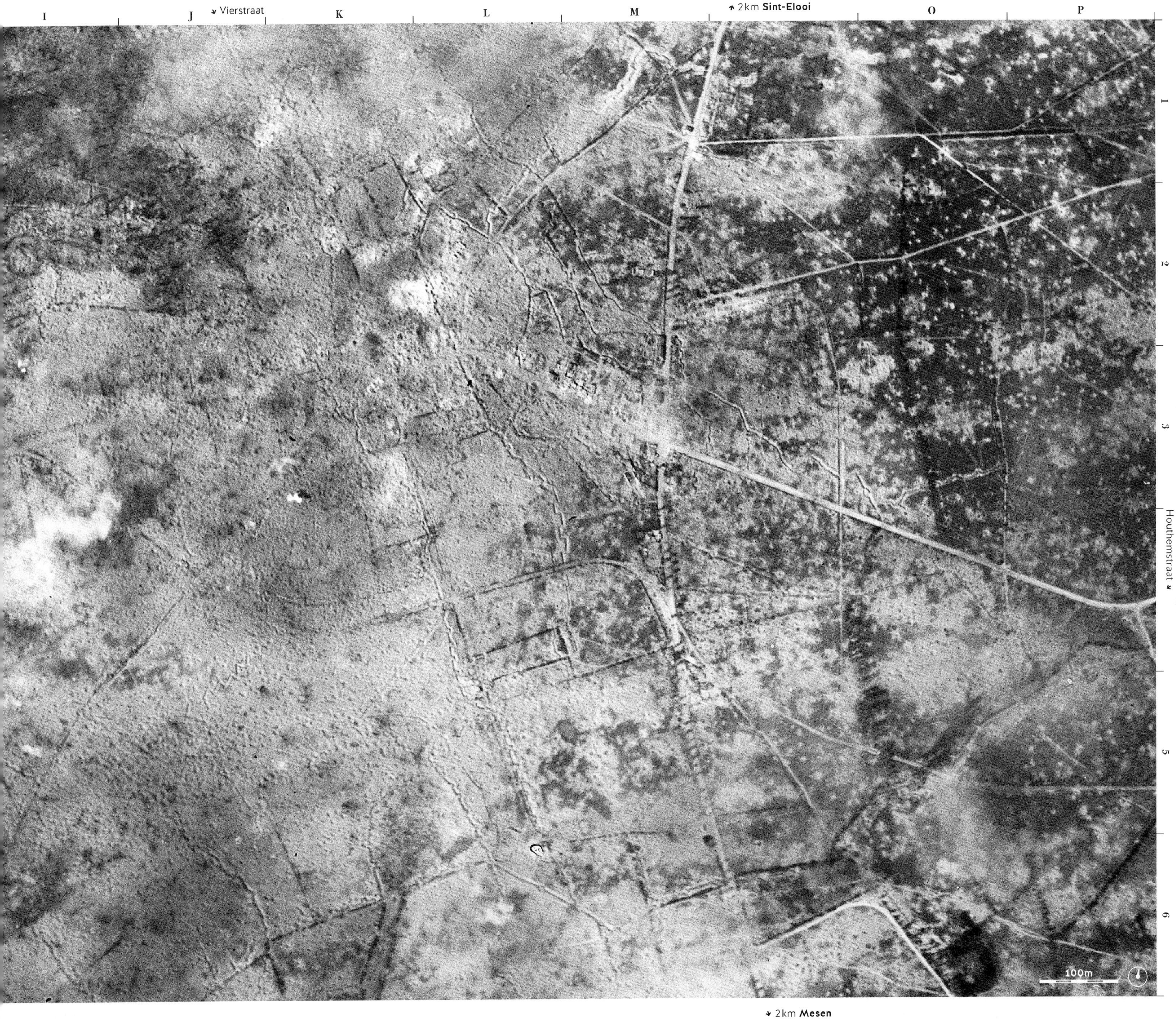

I
J
Vierstraat
K
L
M
2km Sint-Elooi
O
P
1
2
3
Houthemstraat
5
6
100m
2km Mesen

The British breakthrough attempts of 1917:

Messines, Passchendaele, Hush and Strandfest…

BRITISH PLANS WERE BEING DRAWN up from the end of 1915 for a major attack on Messines Ridge and Wijtschate. A series of heavy mine detonations was to open the attack over a distance of 15 kilometres. On 7 June 1917 the plan was successfully implemented and the mine war reached a climax. Nineteen mine explosions and artillery fire from more than 2,000 guns ensured the straightening of the front around Wijtschate and Mesen (Messines). It was to be the first step towards a breakthrough from the Ypres Salient to the coast.

During the Third Battle of Ypres, the British commander, Sir Douglas Haig, deployed an unprecedented arsenal of artillery and 750,000 troops from the whole of the British Empire. But failure soon threatened. After a hundred days of fighting the hardy attackers had made just one gain and an indefensible one at that – the village of Passchendaele – which, according to the plans, should have fallen after 72 hours, and which would be evacuated again after five months. The bloody offensive went on endlessly, and the terrain, churned up by the bombardments and the rain, made it impossible for the new Allied weapon, the tank, to move. There were more than 100,000 dead and many more wounded on the Allied side alone, sparking off a barrage of criticism in the Allied ranks. Passchendaele, or 'Passiondale', where the offensive ended on 10 November, became one of the major symbols for the waste of human lives in the First World War.

The attack should have been supported by a combined action from the sea and along the coast. Operation Hush, however, was a failure. Even before the British Fourth Army could go on to the attack, a German offensive in the dunes at Lombardsijde on 10 July 1917 pushed it back to the left bank of the Yser. Operation Strandfest silenced Operation Hush. The French 1ère Armée also took part in the offensive: to the north of the British, the army crossed the canal and moved in the direction of Houthulst Forest. Even further to the north, the Belgian army pushed on to Merkem. The battles of summer 1917 were the biggest ever to take place on Belgian soil. The scale of preparations in the hinterland of the front was gigantic.

The aerial observers recorded every element of this titanic clash. In the hinterland, the aerial photographs show the infrastructure: the roads, railways, camps, medical installations, artillery, airfields, training grounds, and the storage facilities for ammunition as well as the less explosive material. At the front, they recorded the destruction of towns, villages and the countryside.

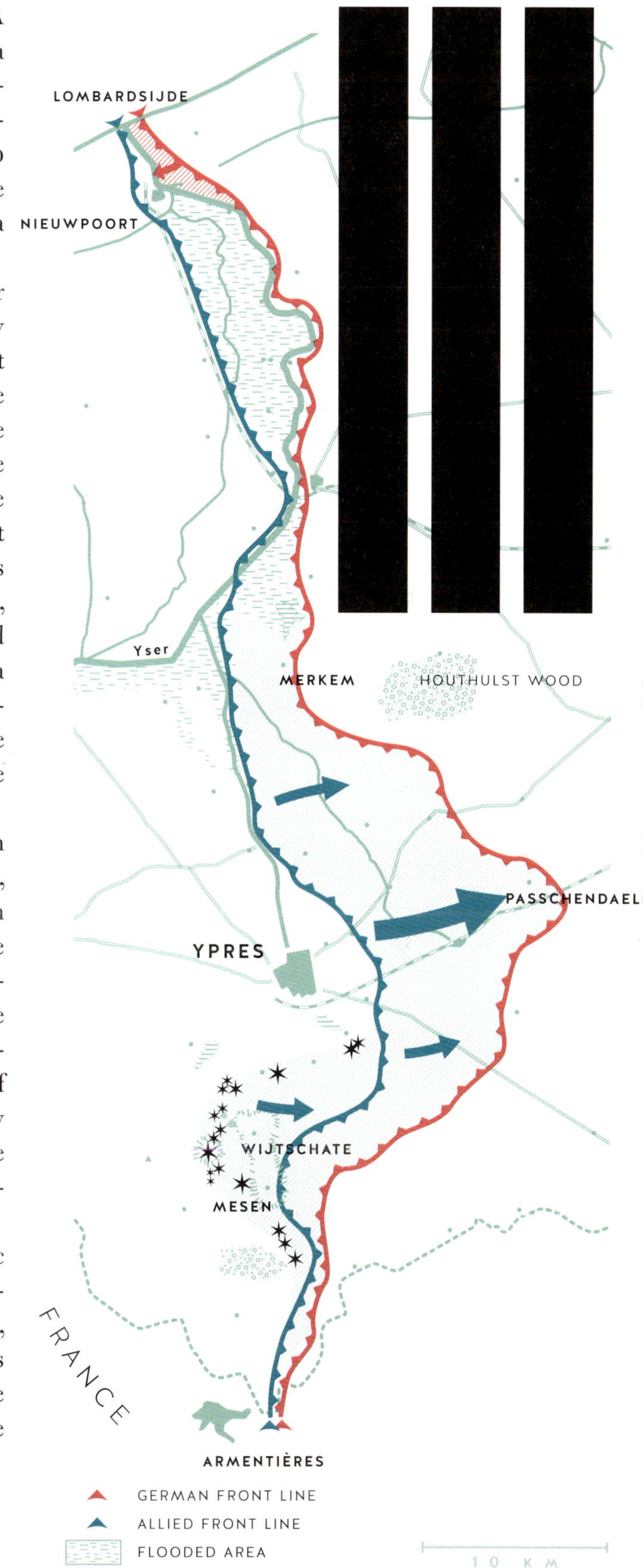

←

The Menin Road at Hooge.

42
MESEN – PREPARATION FOR THE OFFENSIVE 4 JUNE 1917

In the weeks preceding the Battle of Messines preparations were made at every level. The enemy lines were fired on, German batteries taken out and all kinds of provisions brought into the hinterland. The front hummed with activity. The German lines were situated on Messines Ridge and looked down on the Allied positions in the valley. The line occupied by the New Zealand division, facing the German fortifications at Mesen, was pushed forwards 150 metres. The aim was to make the intervening distance to be bridged in no-man's-land during the forthcoming attack as short as possible. The existing trenches were made larger, and between them new assembly trenches were constructed to accommodate the large number of attacking troops.

↑ MESSINES RIDGE

This aerial photograph has been laid over a relief model. The strategic ridge at Wijtschate and Mesen was over 80 metres high, and in some places the difference in height between the Allies and the German front line was more than 20 metres.

C2
DEVASTATION OF GERMAN LINES

Some days before the attack the German front was heavily bombarded with great accuracy. As the photograph reveals, the no-man's-land was not much damaged.

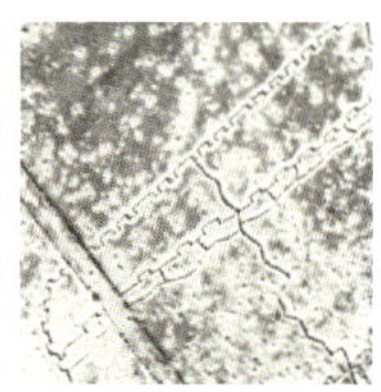

E5
THE ALLIED LINE

Just before the planned attack the Allied line was pushed forwards 150 metres.

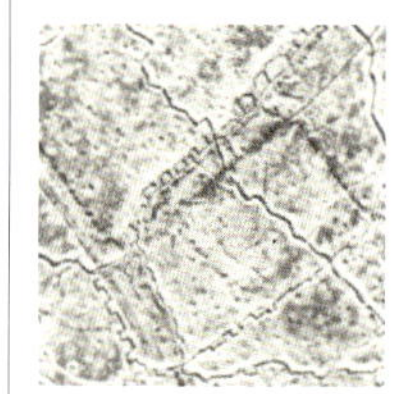

E6
ORIGINAL LINE

The original line lay further away from the German front.

↓ MESSINES RIDGE

Panoramic view of Messines Ridge from Le Rossignol. During the mine attack the Allies had to storm uphill from their trenches down in the valley.

GPS 50°45'39.03"N 2°53'09.26"E

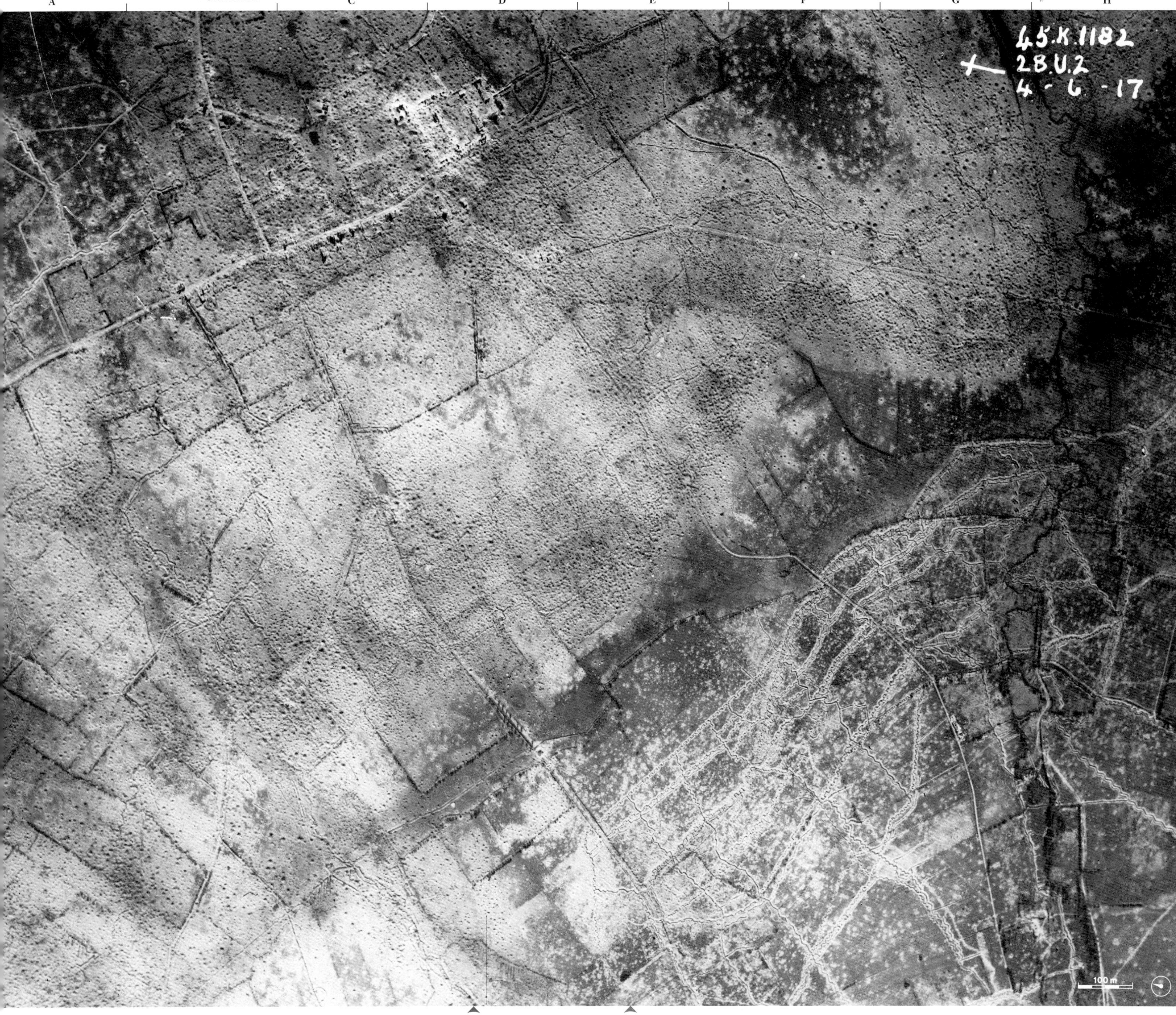

↓ 1.2 km 15 45 **Wijtschate** Steenbeek

Douvebeek

43

HOOGE 9 JUNE 1917

Because Hooge was already in German hands at the beginning of June 1916, it was possible to undertake the long-term consolidation of craters. The British crater of 19 July 1915 (J3-K3) was pumped dry, and on this aerial photograph from 9 June 1917 the entrances to underground shafts can be seen. A great deal of activity is also visible in the four German mine craters of 6 June 1916 (K4, K5). The aerial photograph also shows two mine craters that exploded in front of the German line in February or March 1917 (J2). The crater rim, from which there must have been an excellent view of the surrounding landscape, is equipped with four small fighting positions. On the British side we can see a newly dug trench to the north of Zouave Wood. The wood has been laid waste and the tree trunks are scattered around on the ground. The lighter shade of the parapet shows it is has only recently been dug, as there are no weeds on it. In anticipation of the imminent Third Battle of Ypres, the line was pushed forwards some 250 metres.

» **SEE ALSO** 14 22 HOOGE

SYMBOLS

- BRITISH TRENCH
- ABANDONED CANADIAN TRENCH
- GERMAN TRENCH, BUNKER, NARROW-GAUGE RAILWAY
- BARBED WIRE
- MENIN ROAD
- CRATER

BRITISH TROOPS

The Menin Road at Hooge on 1 October 1918. British troops of the 29th Division advance during the final offensive along this road, twisting and turning round the water-filled craters (see also p. 140).

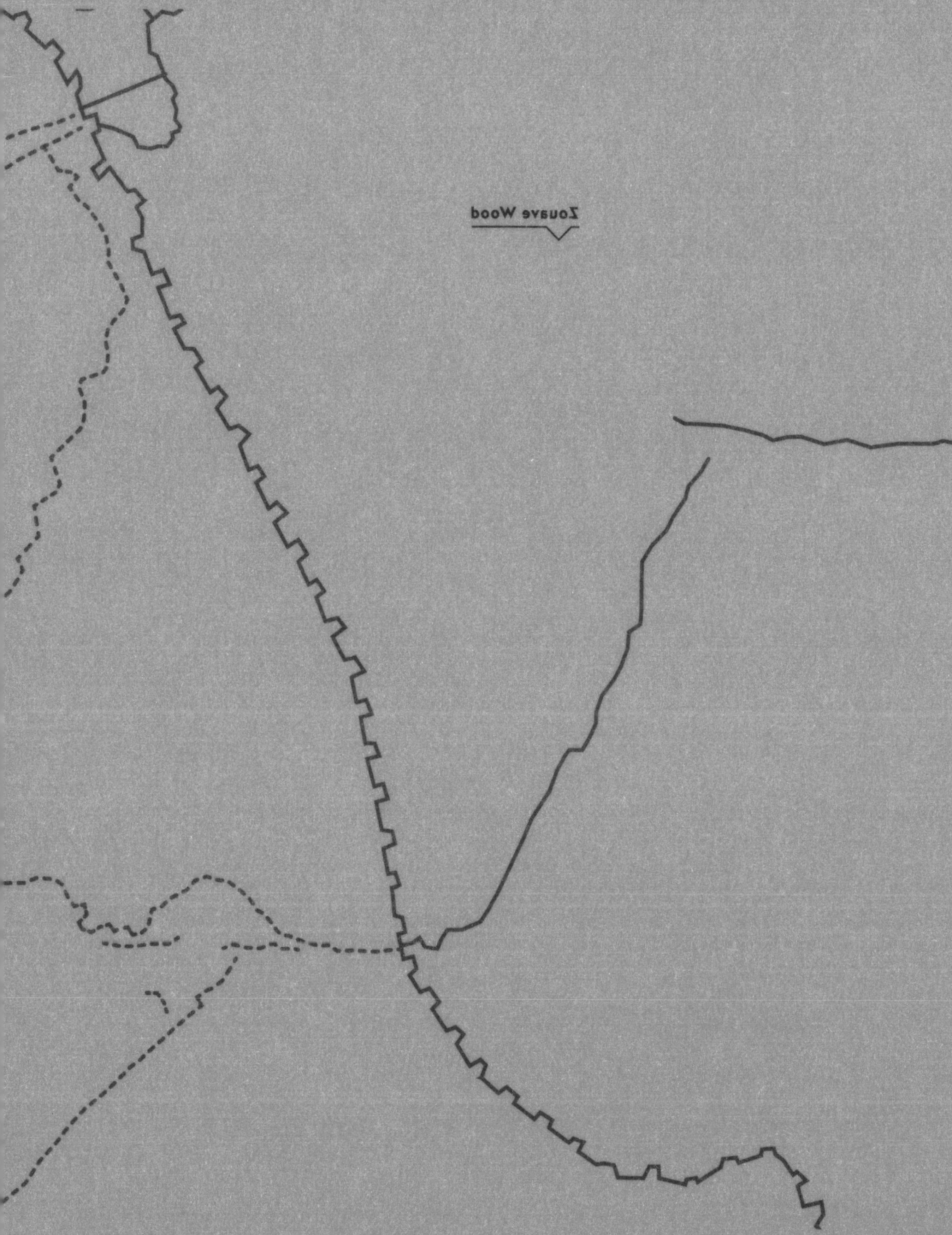
Zouave Wood

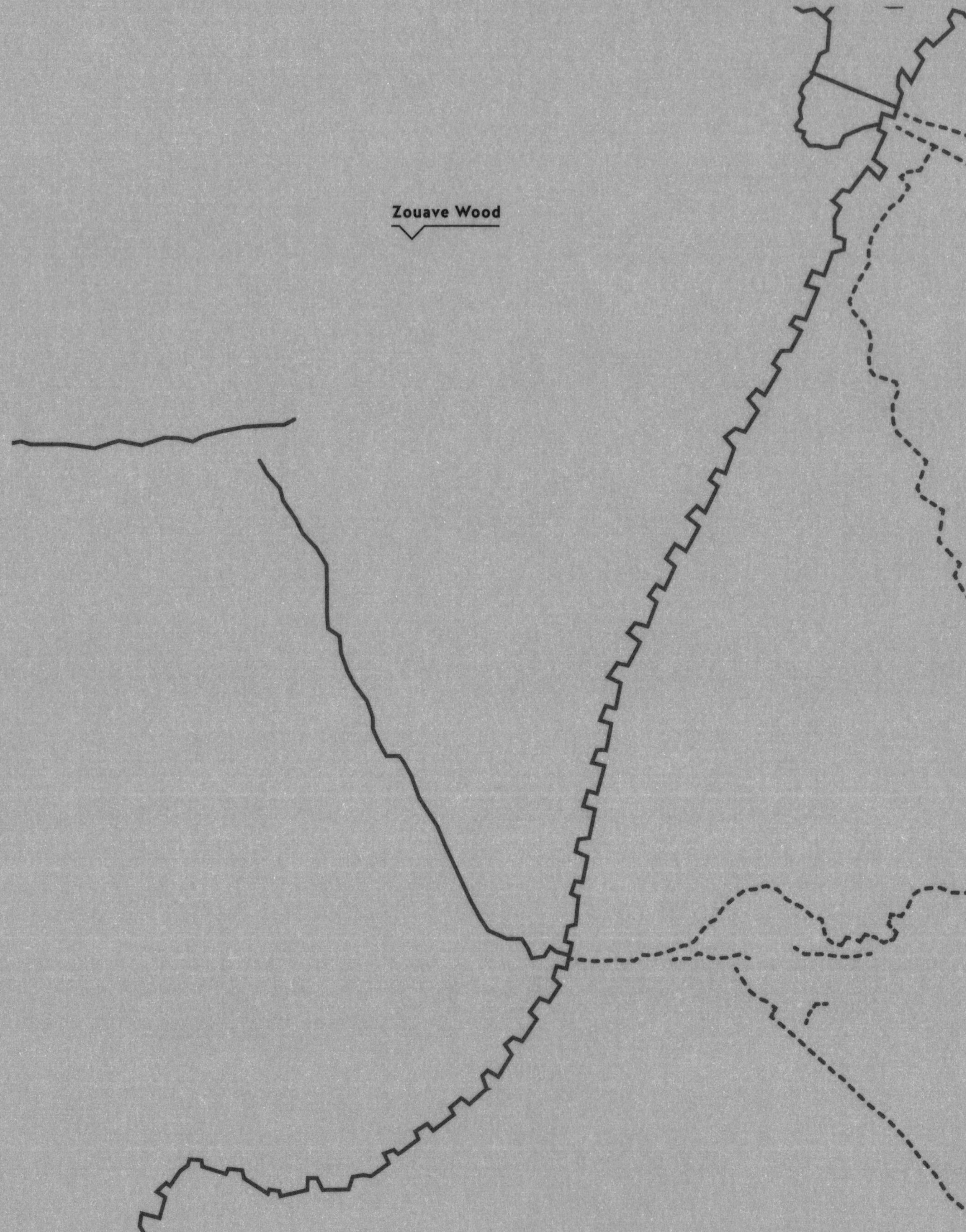
Zouave Wood

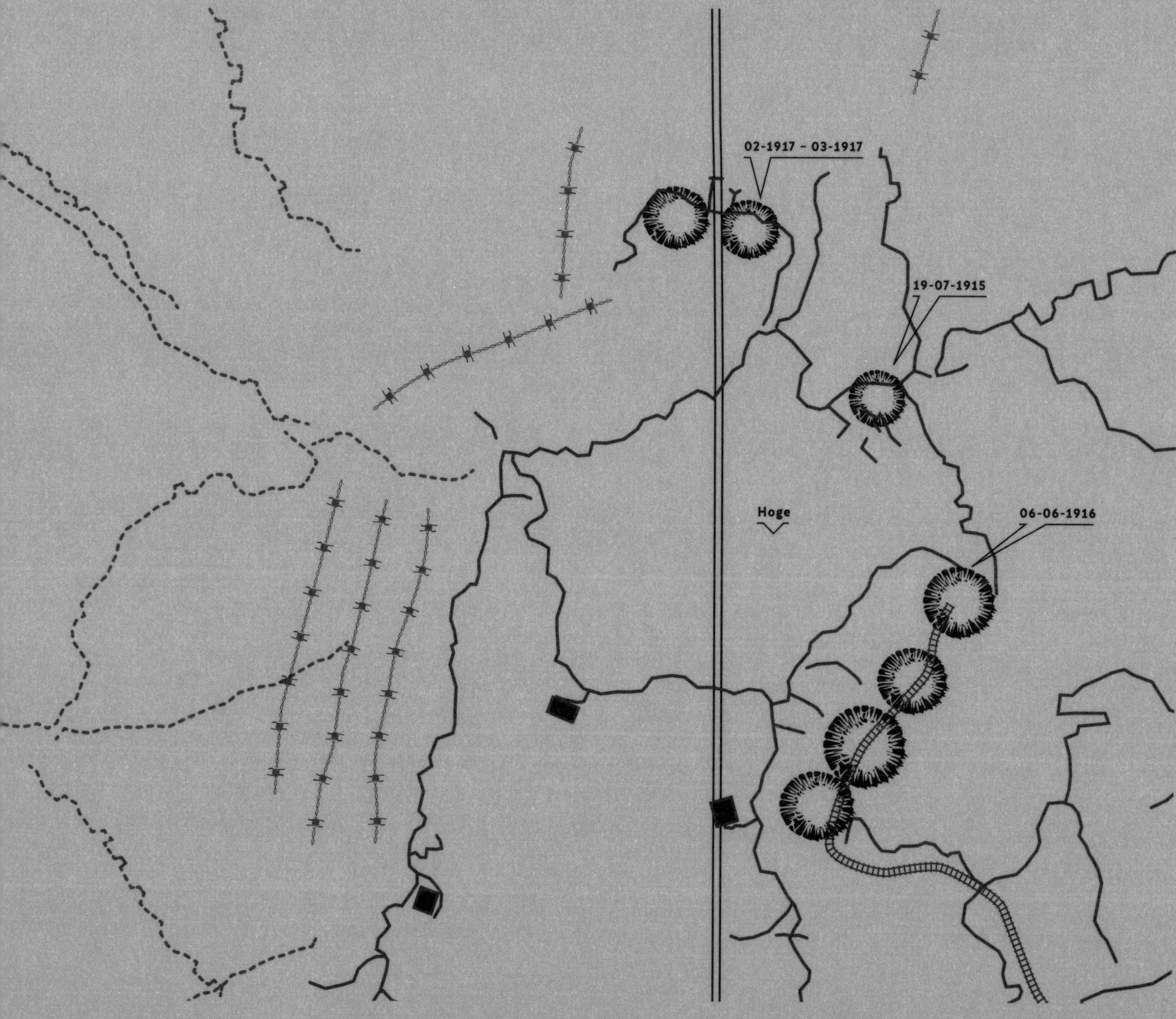
02-1917 – 03-1917
19-07-1915
Hoge
06-06-1916

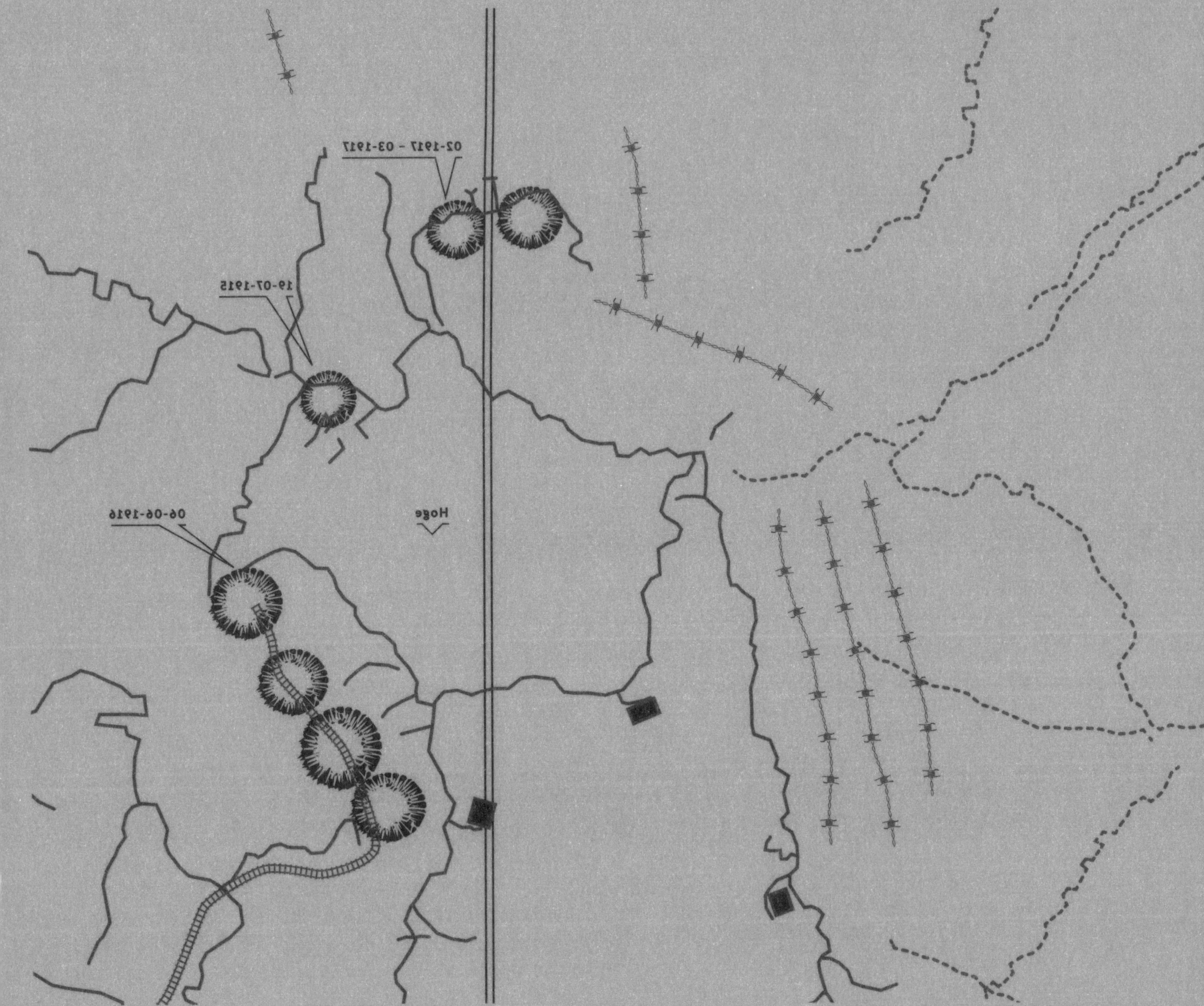
02-1917 - 03-1917
19-07-1915
Hoge
06-06-1916

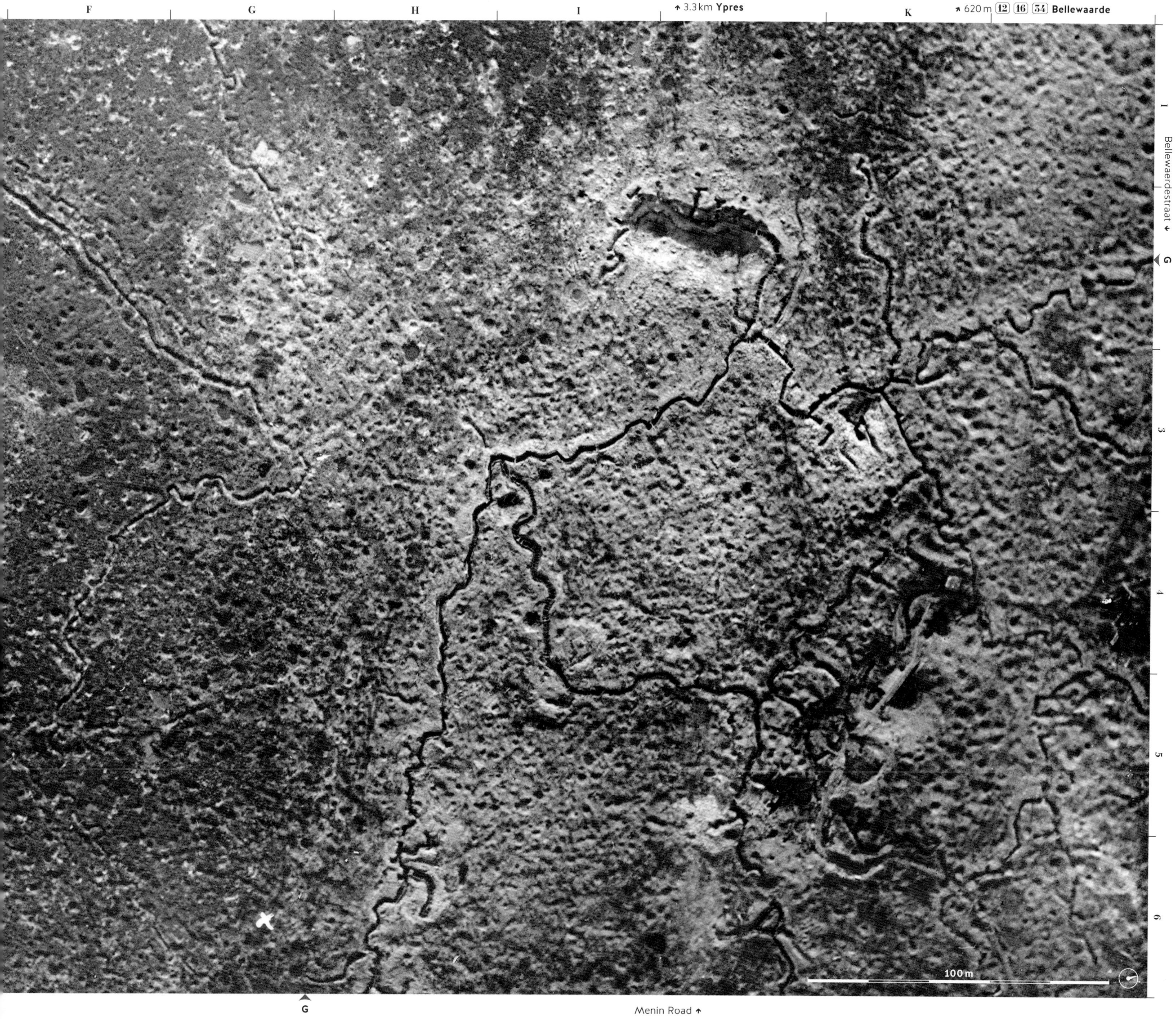
F
G
H
I
↑ 3.3 km Ypres
K
↗ 620 m 12 16 34 Bellewaarde
1
Bellewaardestraat ↓
G
3
4
5
6
100 m
G
Menin Road ↑

44 WIJTSCHATE - MINE CRATERS
2 JULY 1917

Zero hour for the Battle of Messines was ten past three in the morning of 7 June 1917. After a year and a half of underground digging, nineteen gigantic mines were exploded under the German lines between Hill 60 at Zillebeke and Trench 122 to the south of Mesen. It is said that the explosions were heard in London. The British, Australian and New Zealand attack was successful and its aims were soon achieved. Consolidation of the captured territory began immediately. A German aerial photograph of 2 July 1917 shows, as well as four of the nineteen enormous craters, new roads and railways laid straight through the abandoned battlefields to carry supplies to the new advanced front.

» **SEE ALSO** 45 128 WIJTSCHATE

→ **OBLIQUE AERIAL PHOTOGRAPH OF PETIT BOIS**

German oblique aerial photograph, summer 1918, taken over Wijtschate and with the two mine craters at Petit Bois. In the foreground are the splintered remains of Wijtschate Wood.

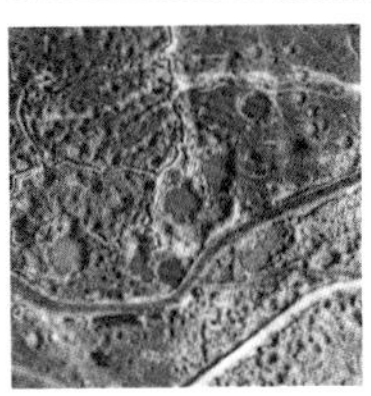

E5-F5
EARLY MINE CRATERS

A heavy underground war had been raging in the Ypres Salient as long ago as 1915. British and German mines regularly exploded. The small craters could still be seen in 1917. Their dimensions are nothing seen alongside the craters of 7 June 1917.

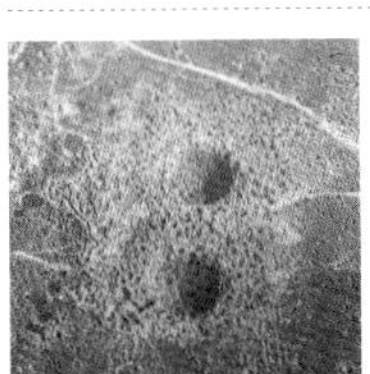

G1-G2
PETIT BOIS MINE CRATERS

Two large mines exploded at the end of a 30-metre-deep and more than 600-metres-long tunnel at Petit Bois. The craters have a diameter of 66 and 53 metres, respectively.[18]

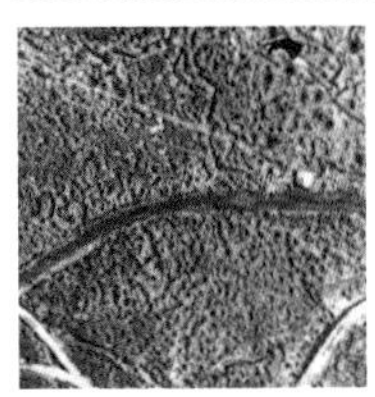

H4
NEW RAILWAY LINES

Railway lines were immediately laid straight through the captured territory to bring in materials, supplies and troops.

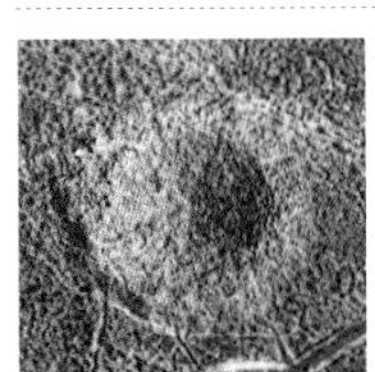

G4
MAEDELSTEDE FARM

The explosion of the underground charge at Maedelstede (Oosthoeve), 30 metres under the ground, left a crater 62 metres wide and 7 metres deep.[19]

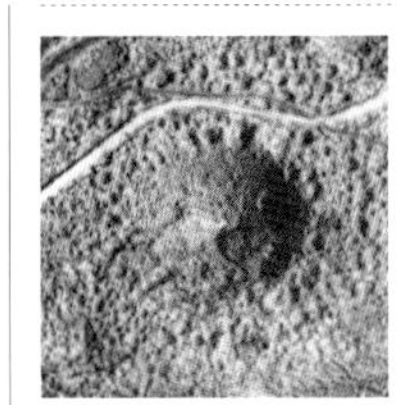

F5
PECKHAM CRATER

Nearly 40,000 kilograms of explosives were set off at a depth of 21 metres underneath the German line.[17] The result was an immense crater almost 80 metres wide.

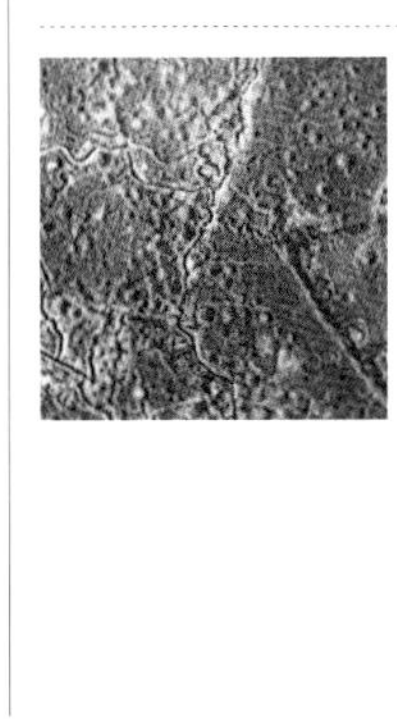

E4-F4
BRITISH FRONT LINE

Position of the British front line between December 1914 and 7 June 1917.

GPS 50°47'06.93"N 2°51'53.59"E

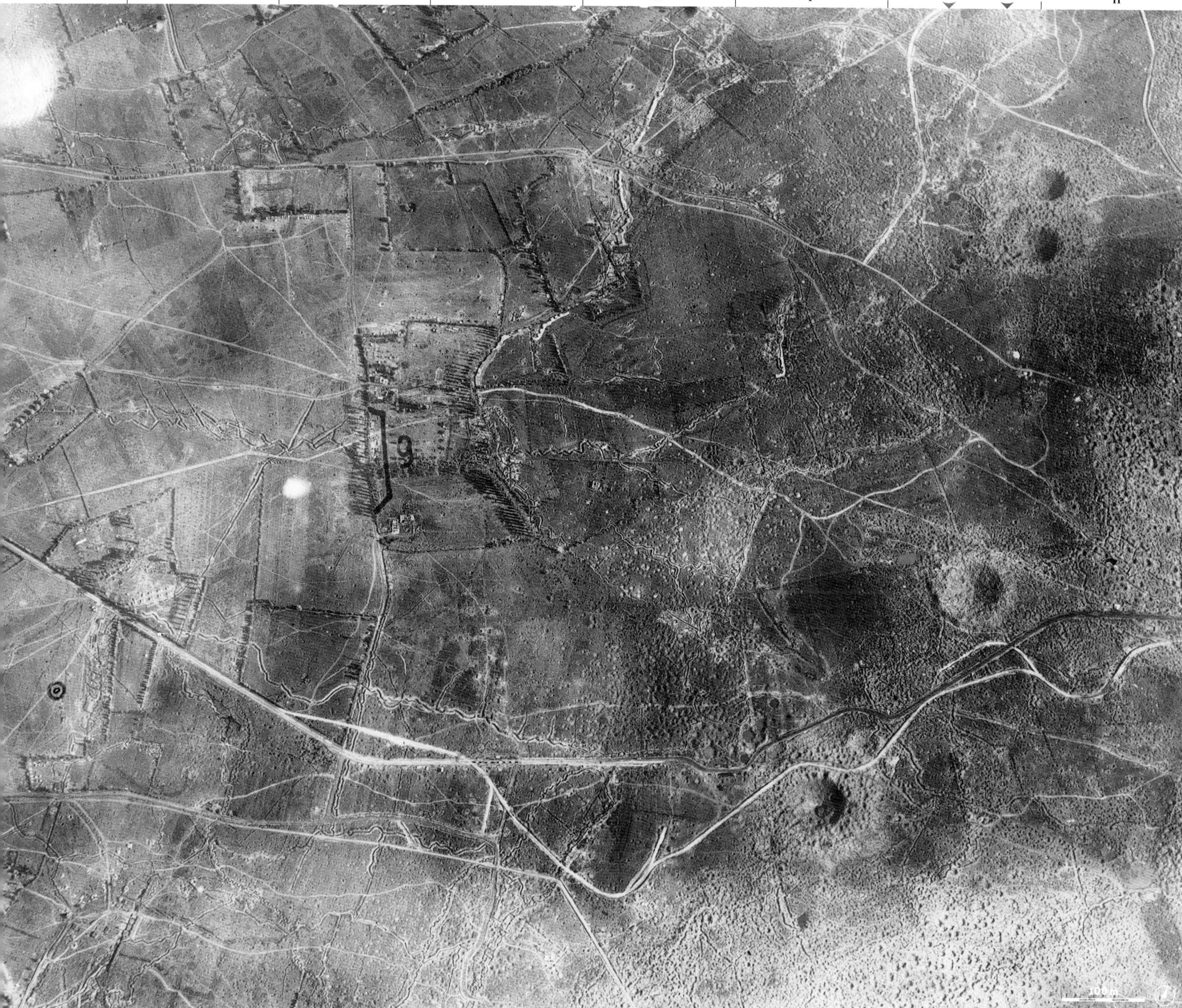
A
B
C
D
E
F
GB former front line
G former front line
H
1
← narrow-gauge railway
3
→ 2.6km front 2 July 1917
→ 800m Wijtschate
5
6
100 m
GB former front line
G former front line

45 WIJTSCHATE – SPANBROEKMOLEN 1 MAY 1917 & 16 SEPTEMBER 1918

The German lines were also undermined to the south-west of Wijtschate, at the former Spanbroekmolen and Kruisstraat. The front line at the mill was in a strategic position around a small hilltop, and the shape of the German line was determined by the local topography. The three mines at Kruisstraat targeted not only the German front line but also the trenches behind it. Comparison of the two aerial photographs shows the target and the craters caused by the underground mine explosions.

↓ OBLIQUE VIEW OF KRUISSTRAAT

Oblique view of the three Kruisstraat craters with, in the background, the Spanbroekmolen crater, today known as the 'Pool of Peace'. This aerial photograph dates from September 1918. Shelters have been dug into the crater walls.

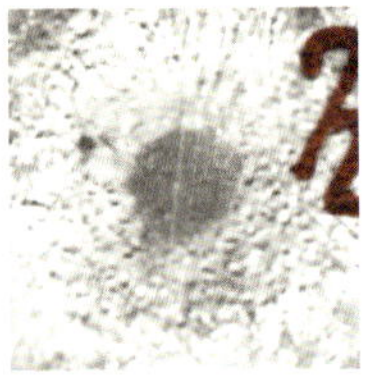

B2-C2

SPANBROEKMOLEN CRATER

Some 91,000 pounds of ammonal were detonated at a depth of nearly 27 metres under the German line. The result was a crater 76 metres wide and 12 metres deep.[20]

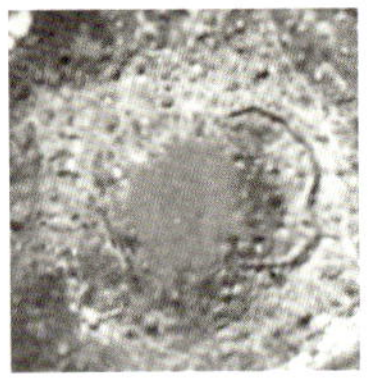

E5

KRUISSTRAAT MINE 3

The third Kruisstraat mine targeted the second line about 250 metres behind the German front.

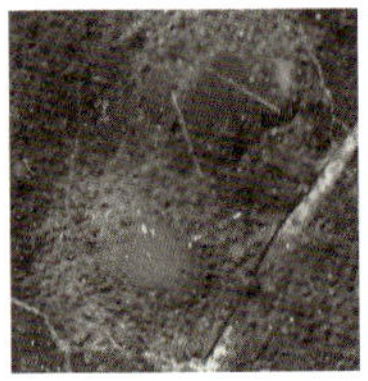

D6

KRUISSTRAAT CRATERS

Mines under the German positions at Kruisstraat.

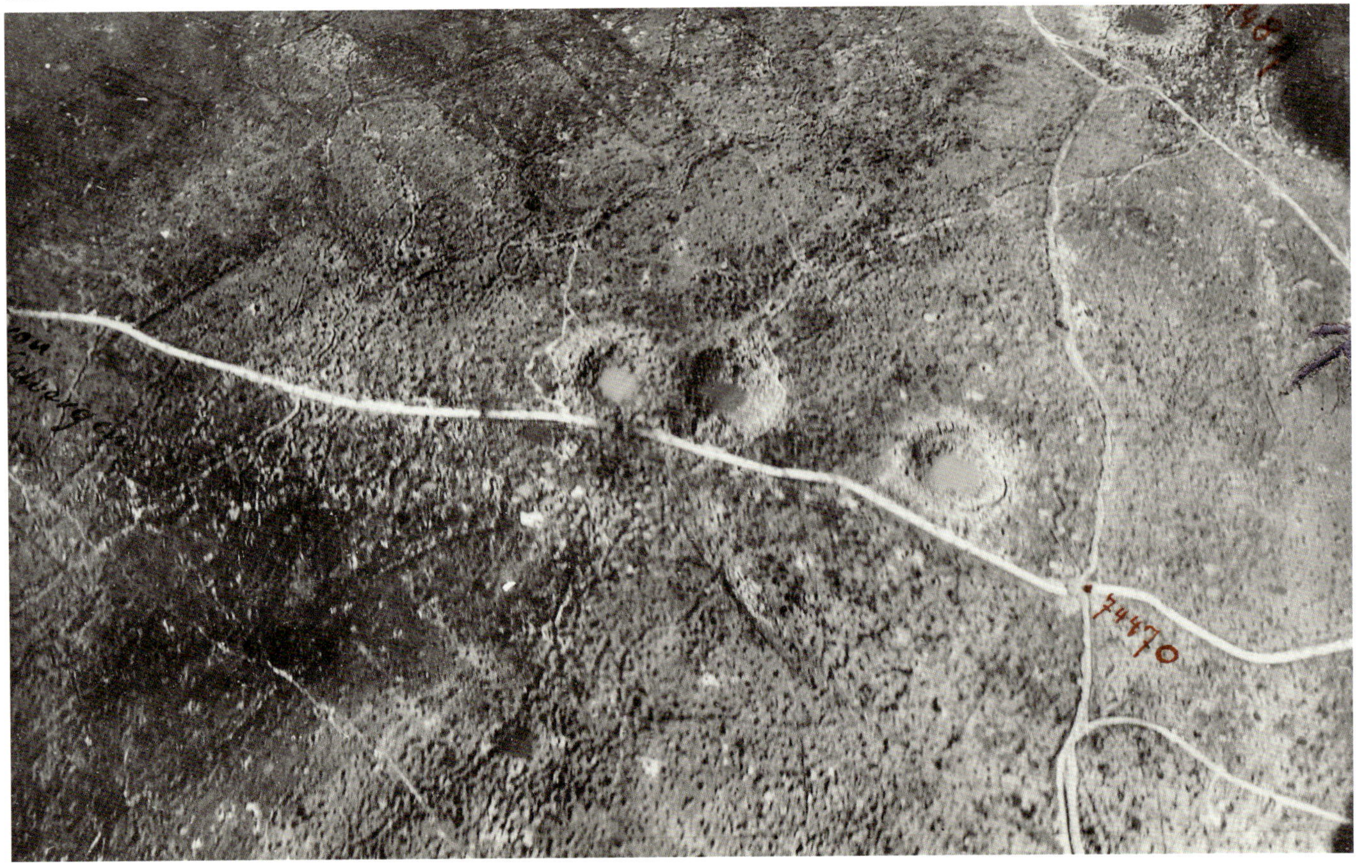

GPS 50°46'20.55"N 2°51'47.79"E

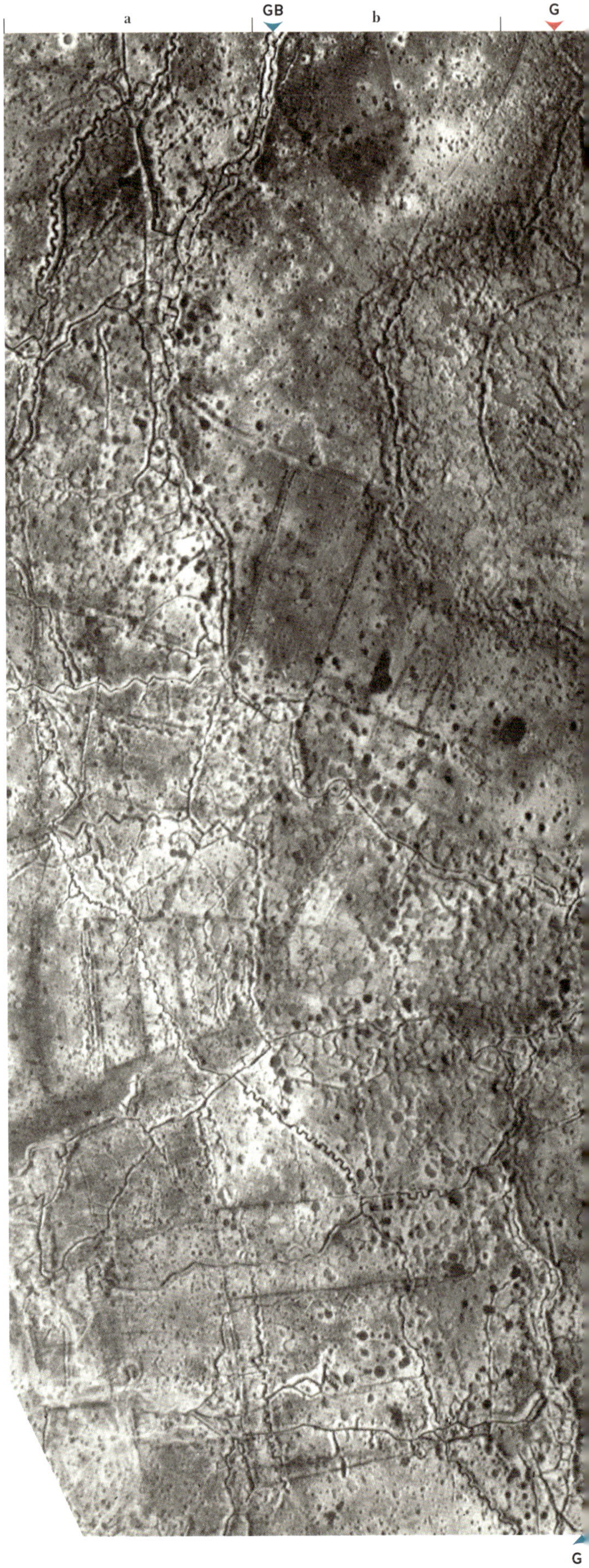

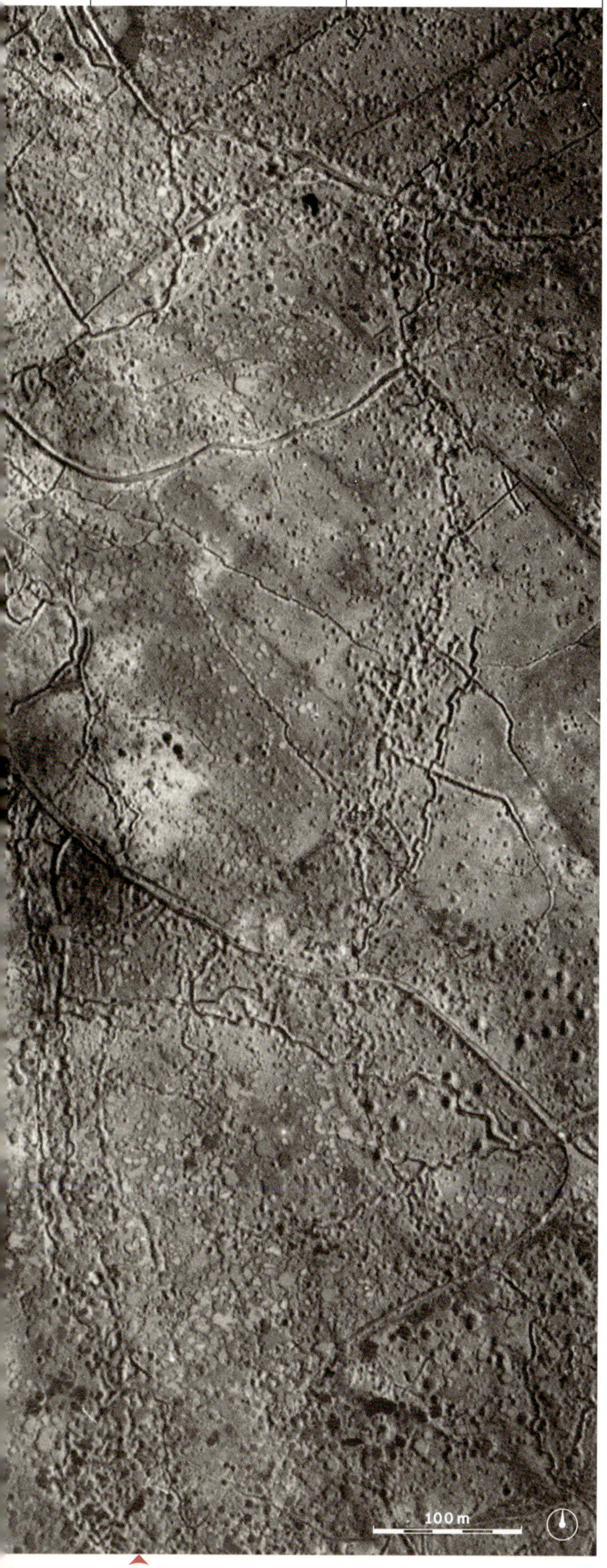
d
e
100 m
G

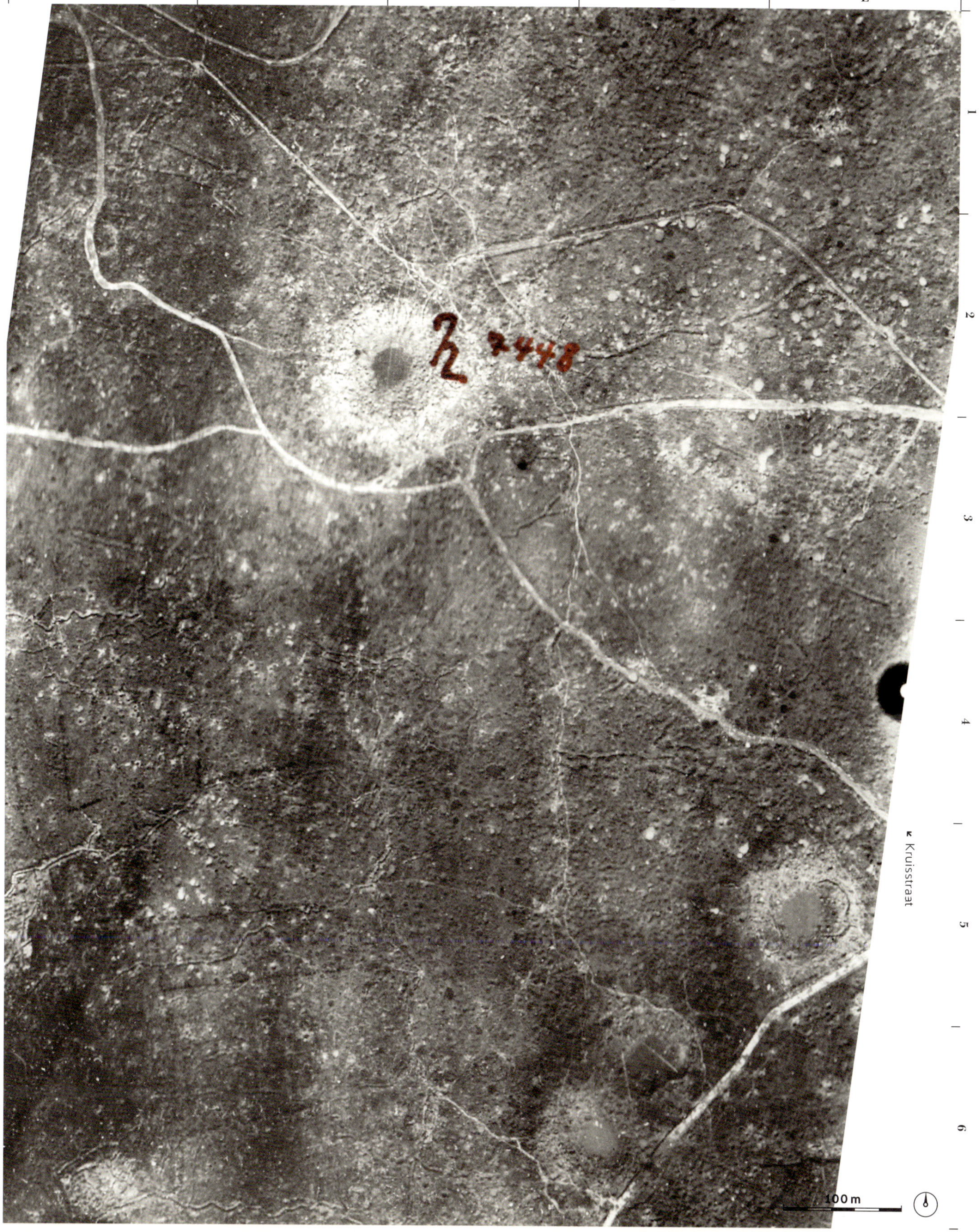
A
B
C
D
E
1
2
3
4
5
6
7448
100 m
Kruisstraat
Wulvergemstraat

46
YPRES 26 JUNE 1917

The Australian war photographer Frank Hurley described the view over the battlefields from an observation balloon near Ypres thus: 'The aerial view over the battlefield was inexpressibly wondrous and grand. It is just as one's imagination would photograph it. Although the visibility was bad, the misty atmosphere enhanced the terrible desolation and reality of this artificial hell, whereon thousands of lives are being expended and the resources of the world thrown.'[21] A Belgian crew took aerial photographs from the north.

» **SEE ALSO** 96 125 YPRES

→ **OBSERVATION BALLOON OVER YPRES**

Australian troops watching an observation balloon being released over the ruins of Ypres.

D5
YPRES RESERVOIR CEMETERY

British cemetery to the north of the prison and the reservoir – hence the name 'Ypres Reservoir Cemetery'.

G3-H3
INFANTRY BARRACKS

Infantry barracks built under Dutch rule (1820–22). During the war, men sheltered under the bomb-proof vaults.

A2-B2
THE ANTWERP HORNWORK

The outline of the Antwerp Hornwork, part of the Vauban fortifications around the town, is still visible in the property boundaries.

→ **OBLIQUE VIEW OF THE TOWN CENTRE**

Oblique view of the ruins of Ypres town centre, probably taken by the Australian photographer Frank Hurley or his assistant, Hubert Wilkins, in September 1917. In the foreground is the Dutch Infantry Barracks, which housed 2,000 soldiers in time of war.

50°51'03.94"N 2°53'07.46"E

↙ Menin Road
B
C
D
E
F
G
H
1
↙ Vauban fortifications around the town
3
4
5 Capronstraat ↙
Ypres–Comines Canal
Haiglaan ↗

47
MINE CRATER, HILL 60
12 JULY 1917

The two northernmost mines of the Battle of Messines exploded at Hill 60 (F2-F3) and the Caterpillar (C3-D3). These left terrible scars on the landscape that can still be seen today. Immediately after the explosion, the craters were stormed and trenches dug on the eastern crater rims so as to provide resistance to German counter-attacks. The enormous piles of earth thrown up by the explosion created an embankment several metres high, which was of considerable strategic importance.

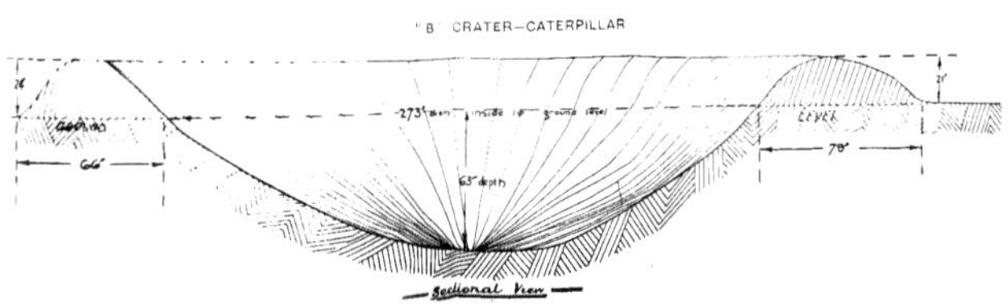

↓ **CATERPILLAR CRATER 1920**

The water-filled 'Caterpillar' crater to the south of the railway, with a battlefield tourist. On the horizon are the squatters' houses built by the first returning civilians.

↑ **MINE CRATER, HILL 60**

The devastated area at Hill 60 on 17 August 1917. An Australian soldier poses by the enormous, exceptionally deep mine crater at Hill 60. On the horizon is Zillebeke Lake.

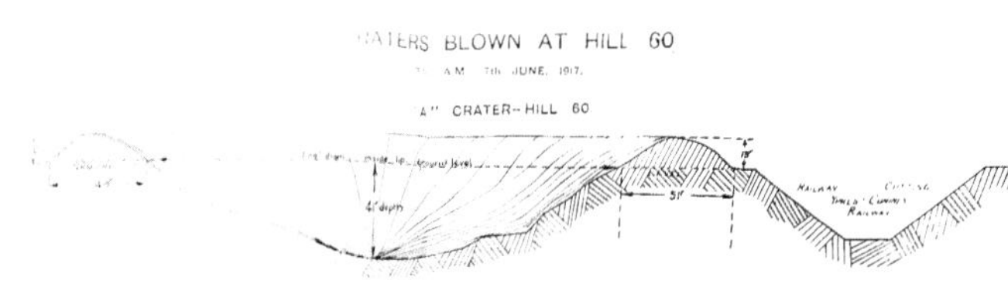

F2-F3
MINE CRATER, HILL 60

The mine explosion (for which more than 20,000 kilograms of ammonal and 3,175 kilograms of gun cotton were used) on 7 June 1917 blew a crater 18 metres deep and 60 metres wide.[22]

GPS 50°49'26.03"N 2°55'45.20"E

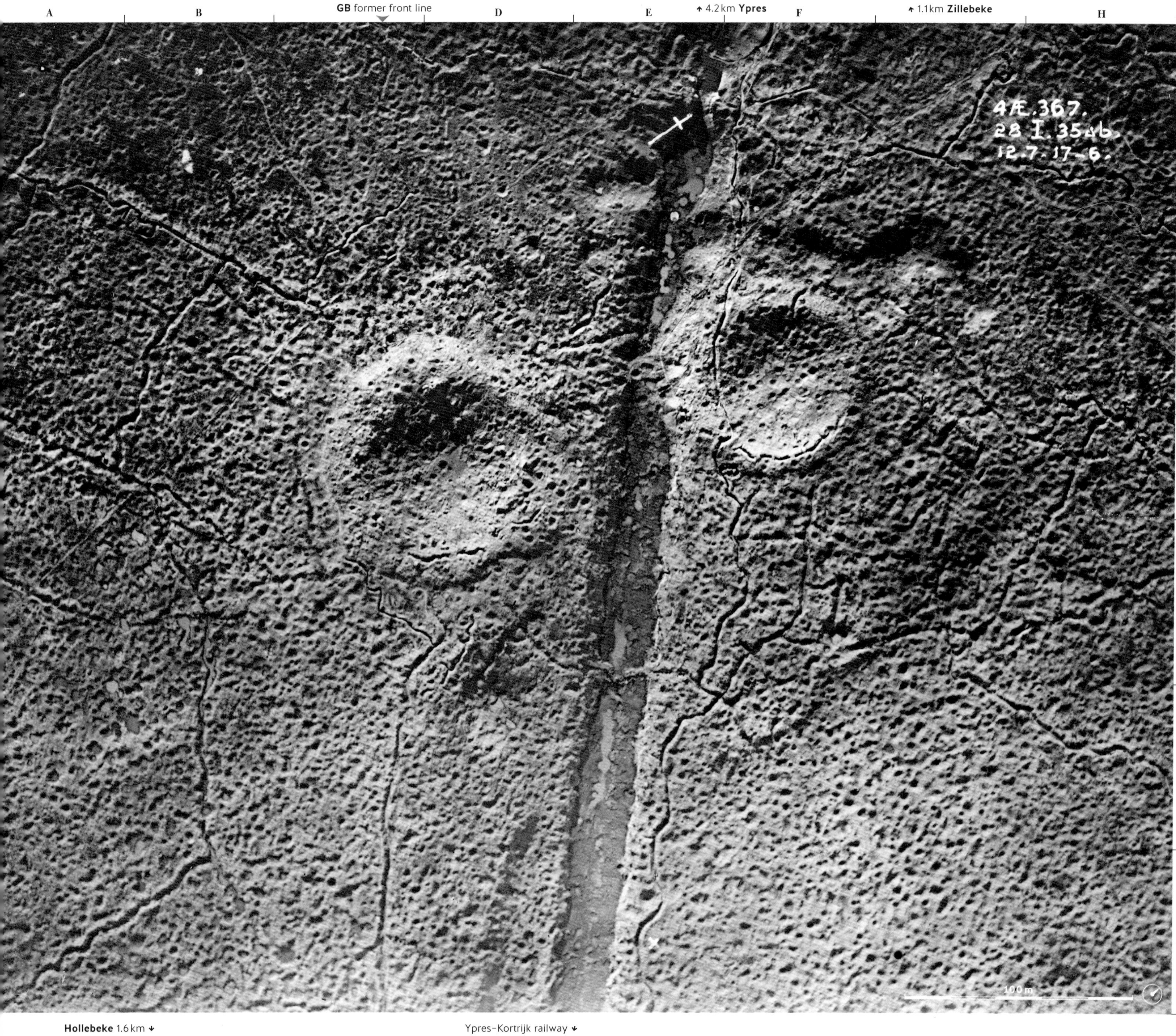

A
B
GB former front line
D
E
↑ 4.2 km Ypres
F
↑ 1.1 km Zillebeke
H
4Æ.367.
28 I.35ab.
12.7.17-6.
1
GB former front line
D former front line
4
5
6
100 m
Hollebeke 1.6 km ↓
Ypres–Kortrijk railway ↓

48
ESEN - HOOGLANDEKEN
22 JULY 1917

In the summer of 1917 hundreds of thousands of front-line troops and support units were stationed in billets just behind the front. On the Yser front alone, thousands of barracks were built. Most of these camps were situated between 4 and 8 kilometres behind the line,[23] far enough from the front to be out of range of artillery fire, but also near enough to ensure that transfers to the front were not unnecessarily long. To the south-east of Esen there was a concentration of German camps for units from the Diksmuide sector. These were made as comfortable as possible, and space was even reserved for little gardens and flower beds.

→ **GERMAN BARRACKS**
German troops resting in front of the Genter Barracks.

A3-B3
U-SHAPED CAMP
Nine barracks under cover of a broad row of trees. The idea of camouflaging barracks by setting them in the shade of the trees was undermined by the planting of flower beds in front of the barracks.

E5
CONCEALMENT
A German battery is hidden behind a hedgerow.

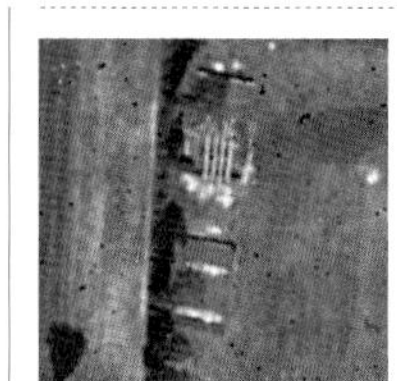

G2
OBSTACLE COURSE
Training camp for soldiers, with an obstacle course. Four balancing beams lie across a wide excavated ditch.

D1
FLOWER BEDS
This German camp is brightened up with three flower beds. In one of these is a heart motif.

B2
GERMAN CROSS
This barrack with its large front garden served as a headquarters or officers' quarters. On the ground is a typically German cross formed of large wooden beams.

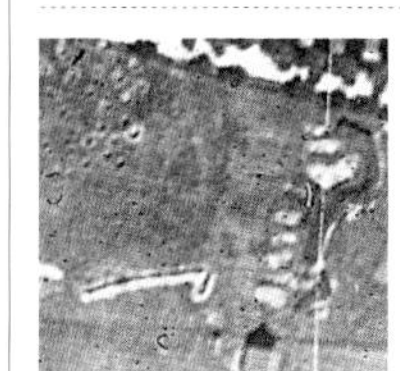

G6
TRAINING TRENCHES
Training trenches with specially dug bomb craters to simulate no-man's-land at the front.

GPS 51°01'24.71"N 2°55'17.49"E

A
B
Hooiweg
C
D
barracks
E
F
Roeselarestraat
G
H
1
2
Schoorlingstraat
4
5
Veldstraat
AMB1988.22
HOOGLAND
P: sLt Sauveu
100 m
27 Predikboom 1.2 km

49 BOEZINGE – PREPARATIONS FOR THE THIRD BATTLE OF YPRES 3 JULY 1917

In May and June 1917 it was uncommonly busy in the Ypres Salient owing to the intensive preparations for the imminent offensives. It was impossible, of course, to conceal this from the other side. One British soldier recorded: 'Apparently, we did not mind in the very least whether or not the enemy knew all about it. The countryside was stiff with light railways, enormous dumps, fresh sidings, innumerable gun-pits, new roads, enlarged camps. No advertisement of the impending attack was neglected.'[24] In the hinterland between Elverdinge and Boezinge the situation was the same. Railways were extended, cables buried to withstand bombardment and kilometres of road constructed to bring troops to the front line quickly.

↓ RAILWAY CONSTRUCTION

Just a few days before the start of the offensive, railways were still being built. Here British troops remove an obstructing tree near Boezinge.

SYMBOLS

- BRITISH TRENCH, NARROW-GAUGE RAILWAY
- GERMAN TRENCH
- BURIED CABLE
- NEW MILITARY ROAD
- HEAVILY BOMBARDED AREA

GPS 50°53'29.56"N 2°51'09.47"E

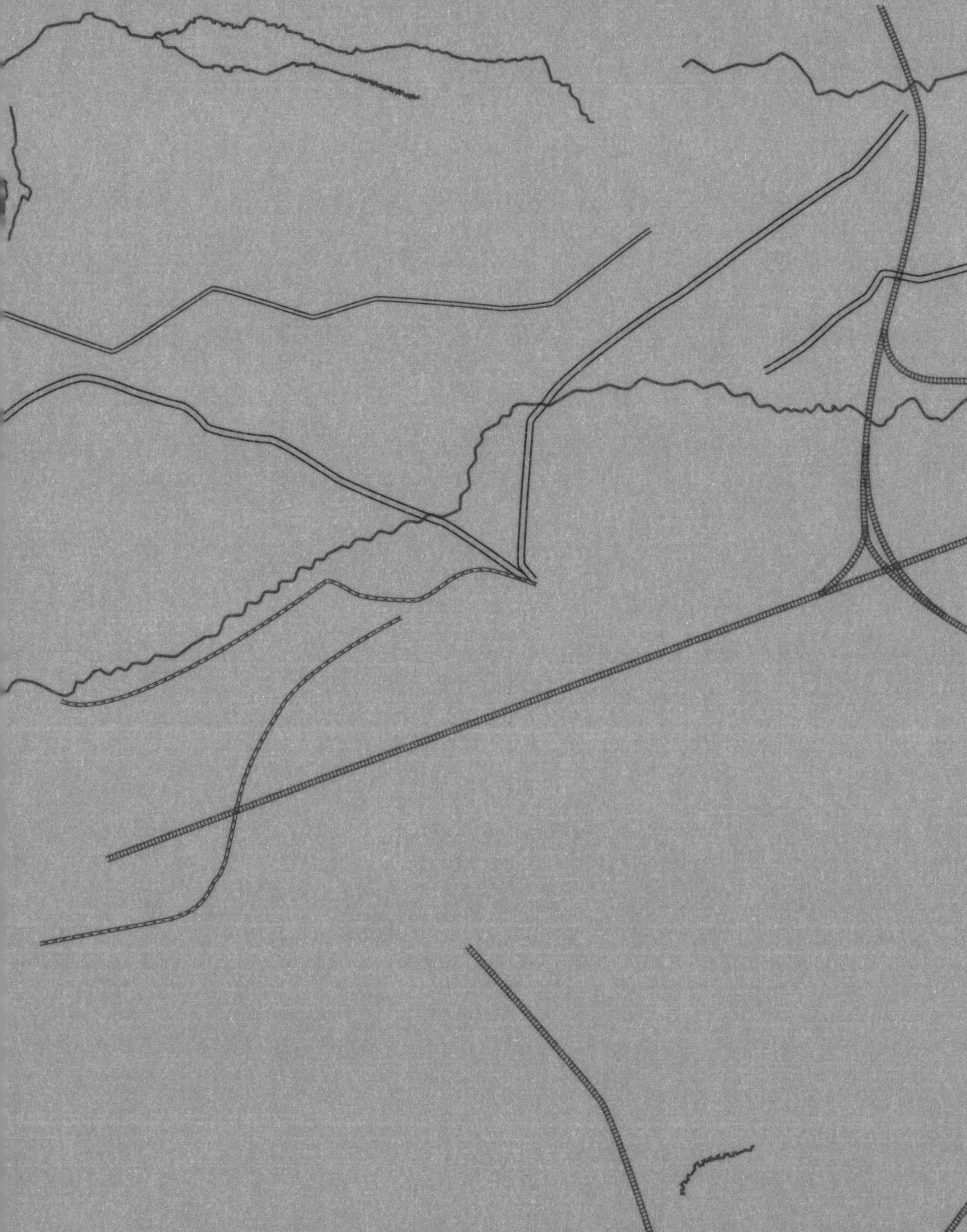

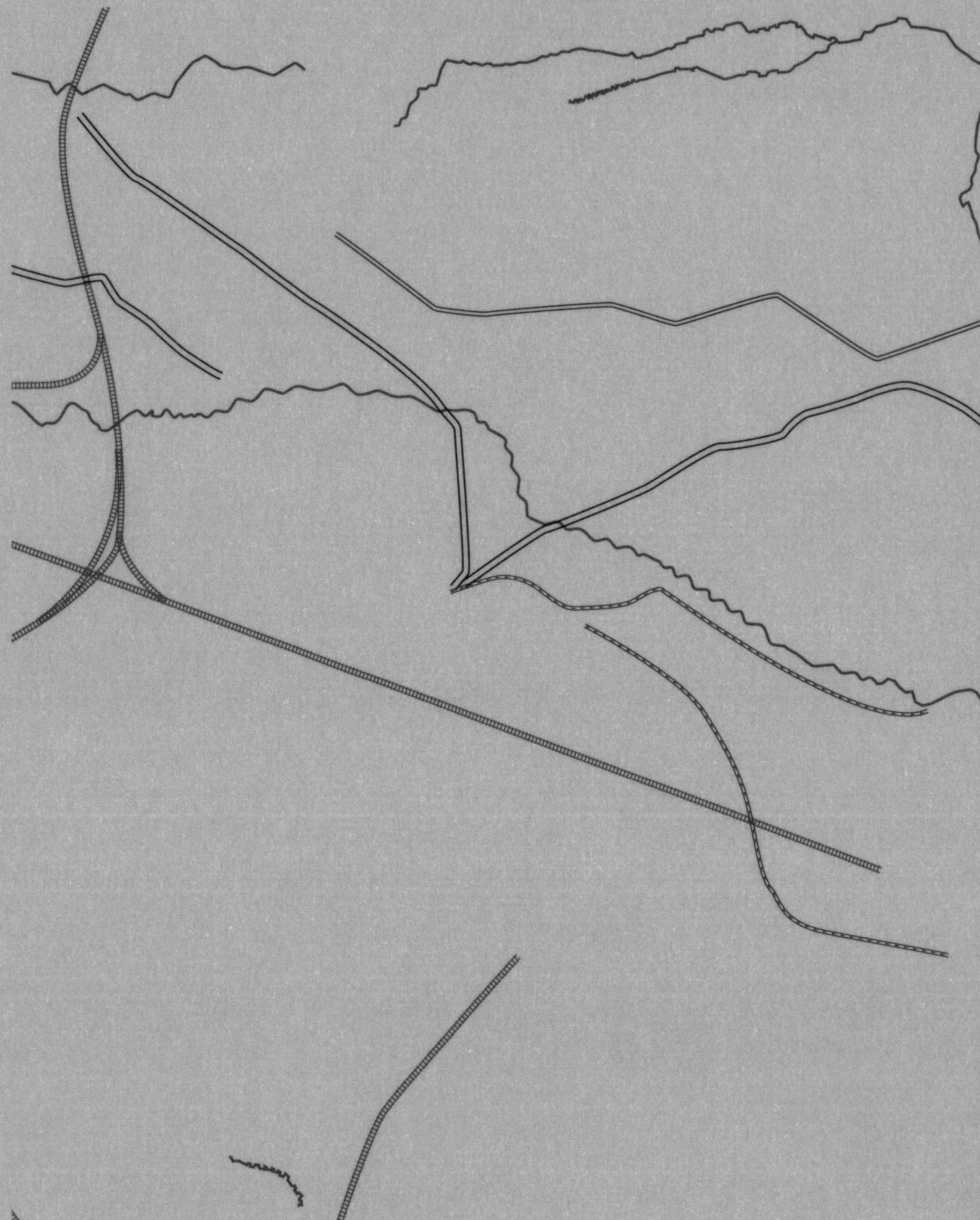

F
G
H
GB
G
I
J
K
L
1
2
3
4
5
6
Ypres–Torhout railway
9AE254.
28B.12.C.7.
3.7.17-2
9AE251.
28B.10D.11C.D.16.17.
3.7.17-2.
100 m
G
GB
Ypres 4 km
Ieperlee

50 THE NORTHERN EDGE OF THE YPRES SALIENT 22 JULY 1917

The British offensive, now known as the Third Battle of Ypres, started on 12 July 1917 with an intensive bombardment of the German front. The area shown in the aerial photograph partly overlaps that on the previous page (as well as with the area shown in [25]). While a few heavily bombarded patches are visible in the 3 July photograph, in the 22 July photograph the German front is churned up by thousands of bomb craters. Trench parapets have been shot to rags, barbed-wire fencing destroyed and many batteries knocked out.

» **SEE ALSO** [25] [77] YPRES SALIENT

→ **THREE DEAD GERMAN SOLDIERS**

German soldiers lie in their trench at Pilkem, 31 July 1917.

↓ **DESTRUCTION OF THE CANAL**

Ground photograph of the ruined German trenches behind the Ypres–Yser Canal, 5 August 1917.

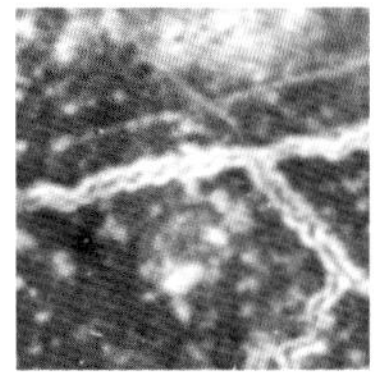

E3-E4

ADVANCED LINE

In June 1917 the British dug new trenches 150 metres from the German line. From here the troops of the 38th Welsh Division would attack on 31 July 1917, the opening day of the Third Battle of Ypres.

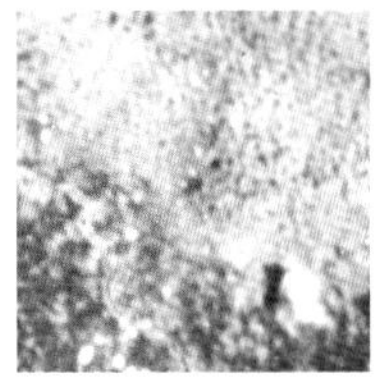

G3

CAESAR'S NOSE

The artillery fire was devastatingly accurate: the aerial photographs show a sharp contrast between the German lines and no-man's-land.

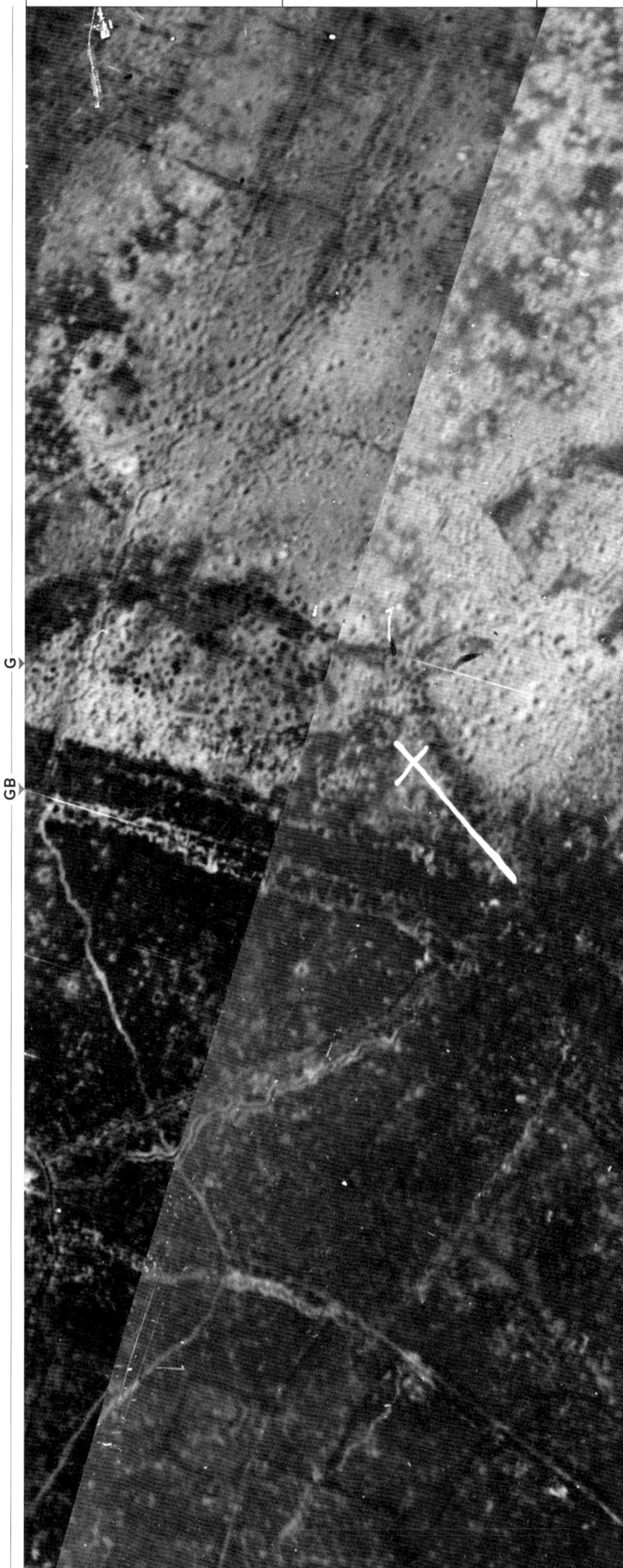

GPS 50°53'22.68"N 2°52'36.90"E

D
E
F
G
Pilkemseweg
H
I
J
Moortelweg
Von Kluck Cots
AVENUE
G
GB
100 m
Ieperlee

51

NIEUWPOORT 13 JULY 1917

During the whole war Nieuwpoort was less than 2 kilometres from the front lines and, like Diksmuide and Ypres, was heavily bombarded. The destruction wreaked upon the town was a disaster for the civilian population, who fled, but created favourable conditions for the Allies, for whom the ruins provided camouflage for bunkers and firing positions. By covering them with earth, bricks and other war detritus they merged into their surroundings. To the north of the Langestraat were six dug-in positions for shooting. In this image only the embrasure at the front is visible.

↓ COVERED TRENCH

An Australian tunneller in a cut-and-cover trench on Nieuwpoort beach.

E3-E4

UNDERGROUND FIRING POSITIONS

Two well-camouflaged firing positions. Their location is given away by the lighter shade of the concrete used. On photographs taken on other days the openings were camouflaged and were as good as invisible.

F6-G6

DUVETORRE

The Duvetorre was a vestige of medieval Nieuwpoort. The former church and fortification tower were used during the war as observation posts and thus suffered greatly from German bombardments.

E4

CUT-AND-COVER TRENCH

Covered zigzag communication trench. This has been dug out and then covered and was thus thought to be concealed from aerial photographs.

SYMBOLS

- TRENCH
- BUNKER
- BARBED WIRE
- COVERED TRENCH
- ARTILLERY POSITION
- SCREENS

↑ NIEUWPOORT 1916

Oblique aerial photograph of Nieuwpoort in 1916. The tallest buildings, such as the church and the Duvetorre, were the first to be fired on as they were used as observation posts.

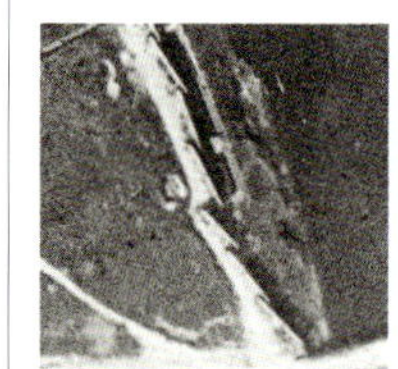

H6

SCREENS

Wooden screens on the Nieuwpoort–Dunkirk Canal conceal troop movements at this crossing point from the German observation points.

C4

COVERED TRENCH

Various covered trenches ran straight through the middle of the town. Despite the camouflage, this trench is recognisable by the darker shade of its roof, contrasting with the lighter colour of the street.

A2

SHADOWS

The opening of these two shooting positions was accentuated by the distinct shadow of the roof on the embrasure.

BIRGER STICHELBAUT
PIET CHIELENS

THE GREAT WAR *SEEN FROM THE* AIR

IN FLANDERS FIELDS, 1914–1918

MERCATORFONDS

IN COOPERATION WITH
IN FLANDERS FIELDS MUSEUM, YPRES
IMPERIAL WAR MUSEUMS, UNITED KINGDOM
THE ROYAL MUSEUM OF THE ARMED FORCES AND OF MILITARY HISTORY, BRUSSELS

DISTRIBUTED BY YALE UNIVERSITY PRESS, NEW HAVEN AND LONDON

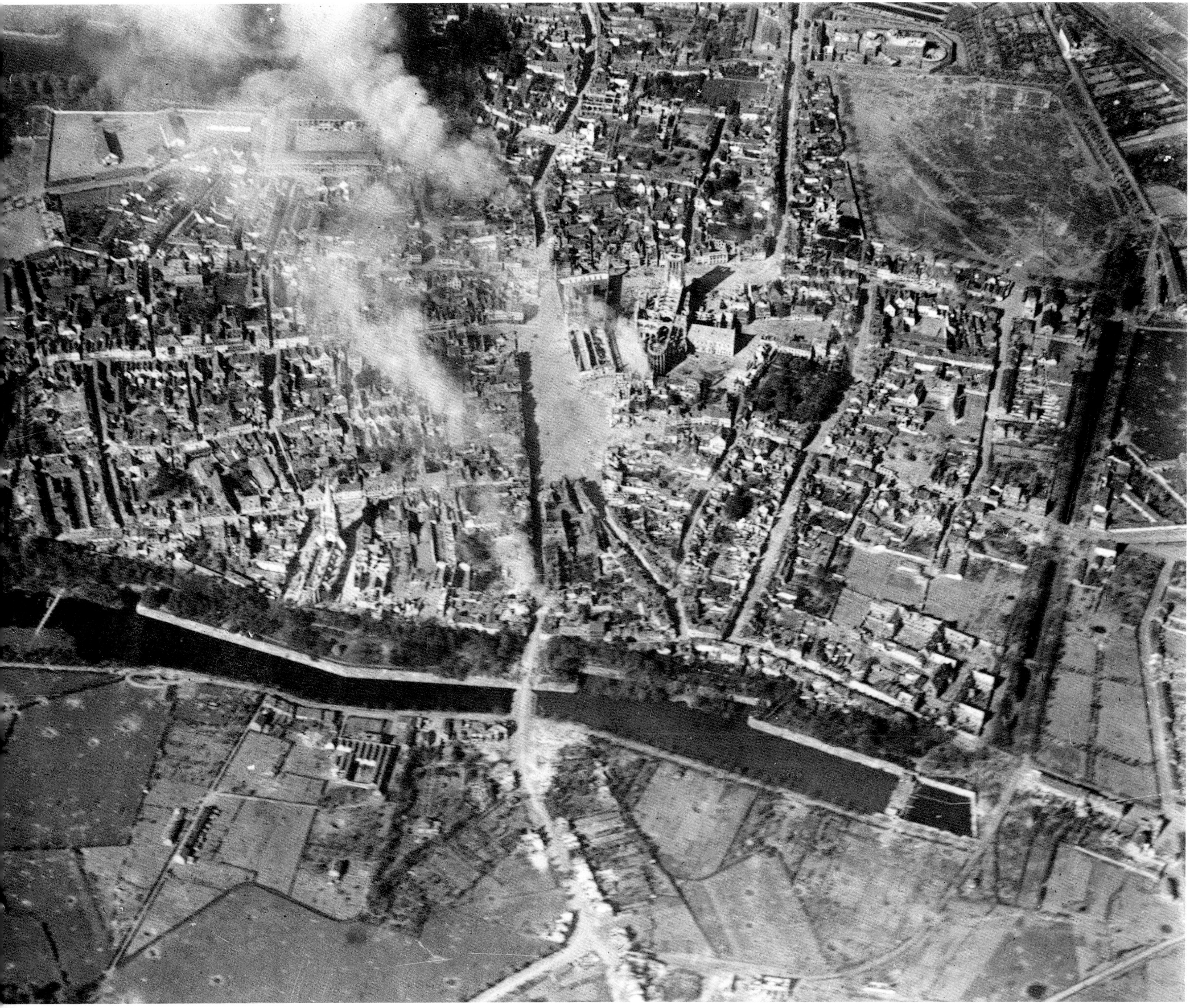

PUBLISHER
Mercatorfonds, Brussels
under the direction of Bernard Steyaert

IN COOPERATION WITH
In Flanders Fields Museum, Ypres
Imperial War Museums, UK
The Royal Museum of the Armed Forces
and of Military History, Brussels

AUTHORS
Birger Stichelbaut
Piet Chielens

TEXT EDITING AND TRANSLATION
First Edition, London

PROOFREADING
Kate Bell

DESIGN
Janpieter Chielens, Tijdgeest, Ghent

PRODUCTION
Tijdsbeeld & Pièce Montée, Ghent
under the direction of Ronny Gobyn and Rik Jacques

COORDINATION
Barbara Costermans, Tijdgeest, Ghent
Bregje Provo, Tijdsbeeld & Pièce Montée, Ghent
Ann Mestdag, Mercatorfonds, Brussels

PRE-PRESS, PRINT AND BINDING
New Goff, Ghent
Printed on LuxoArt Samt 150 g

TYPEFACES
Bulmer by William Martin
Halis by Ahmet Altun

www.mercatorfonds.be
www.inflandersfields.be
www.iwm.org.uk
www.klm-mra.be

ACKNOWLEDGMENTS

This book is based on research carried out since 2004 at Ghent University (Department of Archaeology), in close coordination, from 2009, with the In Flanders Fields Museum and the Province of West Flanders. The project was developed by Tijdsbeeld & Pièce Montée: thanks to Ronny Gobyn and Janpieter Chielens we are able to present the aerial photographs in this fine and beautifully designed book. We are also particularly grateful to Bregje Provo and Barbara Costermans for all their work, suggestions, and, above all, patience in the realisation of this complicated project.
Nor would this book have been possible without the support of the archive institutions and museums in which the aerial photos are kept. With their kind cooperation we have had full access to their rich collections. Our thanks also go to the following (in alphabetical order): Dominiek Dendooven, Anne Godfroid, Dominique Hanson, Sandrine Smets, Barry Smith, Lieven Stubbe, Annick Vandenbilcke, Alan Wakefield and Mark Whitmore.

BIRGER STICHELBAUT AND PIET CHIELENS

Distributed in Belgium, the Netherlands, and Luxembourg
by Mercatorfonds, Brussels
ISBN 978-94-6230-026-2
D/2013/703/35

Distributed outside Belgium, the Netherlands, and Luxembourg
by Yale University Press, New Haven and London
yalebooks.com/art
yalebooks.co.uk
ISBN 978-0-300-19658-0
Library of Congress Control Number: 2013955407

PHOTOGRAPHS COVER
FRONT: 'Trench of Death', Diksmuide, 4 November 1917 (see p. 187)
BACK: Captured German trenches, Boezinge,
5 August 1917 (see p. 158)

PHOTOGRAPH PAGE 3
Flight above Ypres, May 1915 (see p. 16)

PHOTOGRAPH PAGE 9
Gotha bomber over Flanders (see p. 302)

IN ASSOCIATION WITH
UNIVERSITEIT GENT
ArcLand
HERITAGE · DATA · KNOWLEDGE

CONTENTS

Preface

JEAN BOURGEOIS
Department of Archaeology, Ghent University

2014 will without a doubt be the year of remembrance. A century ago, after decades of mounting nationalism, a cataclysm was unleashed and for four long years, from Nieuwpoort to the Swiss border, and in numerous other parts of the world, the so-called civilised nations found the resources and energy for a display of incredible human stupidity which was to cost the lives of millions of men and women, civilians and military. This war, which some called the 'war to end all wars', made its mark on our memories as much as on our landscape.
The forms of commemoration will be legion, in our country and elsewhere, and it is to be hoped that they will stress the immense impact this war had on our world. Why then another project presenting the war – in a sense – from the air, at times even an almost sanitised version, since it overlooks the many dead or wounded soldiers, the animal carcases, the human and animal suffering? The aerial photographs this work takes as its starting point show the suffering of the countryside, the way in which it was affected by the war. It is another way of looking at the conflict, certainly no less dramatic than a collection of photographs taken on the ground.
From the North Sea to Comines-Warneton, Belgium saw the front line of the war take root in its countryside. Without wishing to minimise the importance of the human losses and suffering, which were the most tragic consequences of war, the four years of conflict also left a profound mark on the land, not only in the form of the linear traces of the trenches of the warring parties, but also in the depths of the country, dozens of kilometres behind the front. The troops in the trenches had to have places for supplies of arms and men; the wounded soldiers had to be moved out to be cared for in dressing stations and then hospitals or, too often, to be buried; as for the civilians, they had often already abandoned their farms and villages and even their towns that in certain cases – and here Ypres is their iconic symbol – had, so to speak, been razed to the ground; at the front trenches and dugouts were excavated, concrete shelters constructed and mines detonated in order to breach the enemy lines. These actions left deep scars on the landscape, many traces of which can be seen today. These vestiges of war are, to use the expression coined by a fine exhibition organised in 2006 – the 'last witnesses of the war'.
One of the effects of the first world conflict in our regions was the capture of the landscape on tens, or hundreds, of thousands, if not more, of photographic negatives or plates. Barely a decade after the first piloted and motorised flight by the Wright brothers in 1903, these photographs were taken from primitive aeroplanes with photographic apparatus that was continually improved throughout the war, ceaselessly creating 'superb' pictures of these war-torn landscapes, these landscapes of hell. It is hard to believe, but every inch of the front area and its hinterland was photographed at least once. It may seem heartless, but, thanks to the war, we now have an impressive documentation of the landscape of our regions as it was a century ago and of the development endured by this area during the conflict, which ultimately left parts resembling the Moon's surface rather than that of our Earth.
The photographs presented in this book are limited to 129 episodes. The aerial photographs have been deconstructed, analysed and, in a sense, brought alive again. The episodes chosen demonstrate the considerable documentary quality of aerial photography for those wishing to understand the landscapes of yesterday and today.
Whereas aerial photographs traditionally served above all as illustrations – numerous books on the First World War contain one or two aerial photographs but no more – thanks to digital imaging techniques and geographical information systems they have now come into their own as a documentary source of the first order. I would even say that they are a more objective source than the many photographs taken on the ground, since they were, for example, not of Allied bodies but only those of the enemy: more objective than the best novels or war diaries, refined by the filter of literary creation; more objective than trench maps, always of course drawn up without the

↑
Oblique aerial photograph of Polygon Wood, early 1915.

knowledge of the enemy. This book represents an important step in the appreciation of the value of these aerial photographs. Anyone who wishes to find out more should visit the In Flanders Fields Museum in Ypres, or consult the aerial photograph archives of the The Royal Museum of the Armed Forces and of Military History in Brussels or the Imperial War Museum in London.

This book gives us an impressive but tragic picture of the life on the war front in our regions, while showing us at the same time the extent to which the land can be altered by man, at a speed and on a scale unknown in its 'normal' evolution. Everywhere in the world landscapes tend to develop and change to the rhythm of the decades, centuries, even millennia. Here four years sufficed. Unimaginable. And if our minds can also visualise in this landscape living beings, allies or enemies, civilians or military, the idea of war becomes even more of a nightmare.

1

INTRODUCTION

'Aerial photographs were the eyes of our armies, as the cavalry had been in the past, but now how much more penetrating and precise!'[1]

GENERAL DUVAL, 1921

'The surface scars of the Great War are a secret language requiring knowledgeable translation.'[2]

D. WINTER, 1978

An untold wealth of wartime data

The First World War broke out in Europe in August 1914. What was expected to be a short, sharp series of military manoeuvres turned into a stalemate lasting years, not only in the trenches of the Western Front but, soon after, on many other fronts besides. Over time, war-torn terrain stretched from the North Sea in Belgium to the Franco-Swiss border and from the Black Sea in the south to the Baltic in the north. It encompassed parts of Italy and Slovenia, as well as more distant theatres of war, such as Gallipoli in Turkey and even Palestine.

An untapped resource

It was during the First World War that aerial photographs were first taken on a large scale. This was done on all fronts with the photographs serving as a source of military information – they were taken in order to obtain additional information concerning the enemy's position and intentions. Nowadays, these exceptional eyewitness records document territory under conflict during the First World War from a unique perspective. They depict a cultural landscape, remnants of which sometimes still remain as scars on the terrain, though often discernible only to eagle-eyed experts. These aerial photographs are now being revealed for the first time as a primary source of information for archaeologists, historians and landscape researchers.

In any story about the history and evolution of aerial photography, some reference is always made to the First World War. It is a story that has its beginnings in the nineteenth century – when the hot-air balloon was still the means of elevation – and which ends for now in the present day with high-resolution satellite photography. Many authors have already pointed to the importance of the First World War regarding the rapid, wholesale development of aviation, cameras and technology in general, but the subject is seldom studied in detail. In the eyes of the general public, the history of aviation in the First World War is dominated by heroic aerial battles performed by the famous 'flying aces', successful fighter pilots such as Albert Ball, Georges Guynemer and Manfred von Richthofen.[1] By comparison, aerial photography has all too often been treated as a somewhat lacklustre activity, quite literally lacking in colour.

When we look at the vast quantity of aerial photographs taken during the brief period between 1914 and 1918 – little more than a decade following the very first flight of an aeroplane on 17 December 1903 – the enormous significance of aerial photography soon becomes clear. There were quite literally millions of aerial photographs and to this day hundreds of thousands of these are still preserved in archives and museums throughout the world. These photographic archives hold an extraordinary and as yet unknown potential in terms of the information they contain.

About this book

The intention of this book is to awaken interest in these images and to reveal the wealth of information that they contain. As expressed by the scholars Bewley and Raczkowski: 'Unlocking these (historical) archives is perhaps the single most important development which would dramatically improve our understanding and knowledge of Europe's historical environment'.[2] At the end of the book (from p. 340 on), readers are provided with an appendix containing descriptions of the world's largest collections of First World War aerial photographs. By drawing attention to the museums and archives where these images can be viewed and studied, we aim to increase public awareness and access to these unique collections. Using this information, anyone with an interest will be able to consult aerial photographs of the Western Front for themselves in the original preserved archives. They are well worth being put at the disposal of the general public.

This book is divided into two parts. First, there is a general introduction concerning aerial photography during the First World War. We outline a succinct frame of reference and explain the context within which aerial photography appeared and developed during the war. This is not intended to be a complete history of aerial photography over the course of those four years. For such a study, we would encourage readers to consult Terrence J. Finnegan's *Shooting the Front*, the first and – at present – the only comprehensive review of the subject. Our own, more concise account of the birth of aerial photography begins with the first airborne photographic

↑
A crossroads in the vicinity of Kortrijk (Courtrai) in the German hinterland. This is a rare aerial photograph where the eye is drawn immediately to the presence of people on the ground.

experiments of the nineteenth century. This is followed by a deeper analysis of the use of aerial photographs for military intelligence and an outline of the most important ways in which the images have been used, both in the past and today. We will give brief explanations of what can be seen in the photographs, not only from an archaeological and topographical point of view, but also from a human perspective. Although aerial photographs may appear at first glance to be 'devoid of detail', stripped of any human presence, on closer inspection they reveal a complete overview of human activity in a war; what we see is invariably the record of humanity at work. When combined with other historical records, these images supply us with a unique insight into the fate of the people who lived, fought and died on and around the front.

All of this is substantiated in the second section of the book, which contains 129 case studies of the First World War in Belgium. For the first time, this historical subject will be approached from a bird's-eye view. Our intention is neither to rewrite the story of the First World War nor to provide a complete illustration of it. Far too many historical publications have employed aerial photographs simply for the sake of having some 'diverting pictures'. Very often these will include stereotypical images, such as overhead aerial views of the village of Passchendaele before and after heavy bombardment. This book adopts a reverse approach. The aerial photographs are the starting point. They supply information about a particular location or event. (That said, some images are so expressive or singular that they have been included purely for their visual impact.)

Wherever possible, we have placed the case studies in chronological order; they show the course and evolution of the First World War up to its conclusion. A conscious decision was made to adopt a geographically wide-ranging approach to the material. Not only do we highlight the trenches on the front lines and the no-man's-land lying in between, but we also focus attention on areas in the hinterland. The zones at the front are typified by the extraordinary density of trenches, bunkers and other military reinforcements. However, when we cast our gaze wider to take in areas extending well beyond the fields of combat, we are presented with a vast range of differing sites; a picture begins to emerge that includes airfields, storage depots, hospitals, port facilities and even a base for Zeppelins and bombers.

Furthermore, the armistice of 11 November 1918 did not signal the end of the story of the First World War from the air, even if the military dimension ceased from that moment. Some rare aerial photographs allow us to see reconstruction of the 'devastated region'. Even now, one hundred years later, the effects of the war remain tangibly present in the Westhoek region of western Belgium and northern France. Now that there are no longer any witnesses of the war still living, only the landscape is left to present its enduring, silent testament to the conflict.

The selection of the photographs

The aerial photographs selected for this book derive from a data set of more than 20,500 images that over the past few years has undergone academic research and study. We have the archives to thank for enabling us to bring these images together for this visual analysis. The wealth of material made it possible for us to select from among the most striking, fascinating and original photographs.

Interpreting an aerial photograph requires expertise and specialist knowledge. Consequently, to make them accessible to the layperson, we have annotated a large number of the photographs using transparent overlays that help to 'translate' our visual analysis. Often, it is the position of a piece of terrain in a photograph that is important; reference is made to the GPS coordinates[3] of the sites under discussion, thus making it possible to visit the location. Moreover, notes are provided in the margin to indicate distances from relevant population centres. We have also displayed several sites photographed at different times in order to show the development of the war and its impact on the landscape. Where it has seemed useful, aerial photographs have been included alongside photographs taken at ground level, historical maps and personal testimonies.

A town in its death throes

YPRES IN THE FIRST YEAR OF THE WAR

An intense feeling of presence

Somewhere within the pages of many of the personal photograph albums kept by German officers would be found an aerial photograph of Ypres. Very often, the town could be seen in the distance with the battle lines in the foreground. These photographs give us a sense of the feeling that must have weighed on any German commander who had been posted to that front for any length of time: so tantalisingly near and yet so frustratingly far.

Occasionally, there is a second photograph: a low pass over the town, never a vertical shot but, instead, oblique and quickly taken – a stolen glance at the devastation and suffering below. These are the most poignant of images, because aerial photographs give the impression of providing a view of reality caught in the here and now. It is the only medium to succeed in doing this. Time solidifies in photographs taken from the ground and thus they are always rooted in the past. Panoramas freeze the wind blowing across the landscape and turn the world into an icy stasis. However, aerial photographs are at once both far removed from what is happening and yet able to provide a bird's-eye view of it. And it is that bird's-eye view that is responsible for an intense feeling of presence in relation to the events that took place there. The distance means that, although you cannot, of course, see any motion, you still sense it as if it were there.

Visitors to the research centre at the In Flanders Fields Museum are sometimes in search of the place where an ancestor went missing in action or was given temporary burial. If an aerial photograph of that place happens to exist, taken perhaps only a few days or weeks after the date in question, such visitors will often remark that 'he's in the picture', even if a grave can hardly ever be discerned, let alone identified. This is not unusual for photographs taken at such a height. Nevertheless, they are right – 'he' *is* still *in* the picture.

Ypres: From bustling centre to ghost town

Aerial photographs of Ypres taken in the first year of war reveal the gradual death of the town as a result of the conflict. The oldest images date from after the burning of the medieval Cloth Hall and St Martin's Cathedral on 22 November 1914. The fire-ravaged buildings were left as skeletal shells among other structures that were still standing, where people had either taken shelter or continued to live.

→ **The centre of Ypres after the fire of 22 November 1914.**

→ **Oblique aerial photograph of a fragment of the Ypres Salient, autumn 1915. In the foreground is the front line at Bellewaarde and Hooge and in the distance the ruins of Ypres.**

Three photographs of Ypres from the south-west, spring 1915

The photographs of the south-western part of the town were taken between the First (19 October – 22 November 1914) and Second Battle of Ypres (22 April – 25 May 1915). As yet, the neighbourhood around the station square and the esplanade has hardly been damaged, apart from the unfortunate café Het Torretje (A2-B2) on the corner of the imposing neo-Gothic terrace along the north side of the park (B2). Fresh bursts of shelling evident in the photograph on p. 14 have already been extinguished in the one on p. 15, apart from in the public gardens. The popinjay mast (p.14, B4-C4) belonging to the venerable archers' guild, next to the gunpowder magazine (p.14, B4), is still standing bolt upright and ready for use.

←
Oblique general view from the south-west. The moat of the Vauban fortifications is quite easily visible. At the top is the market with the Cloth Hall.

↑

**Shell holes in C3 and C4 on the photograph above have been filled in on the photograph to the right (p. 15, B1 and p. 15, E1 respectively).
A smaller station building (B3) is shown intact on the photograph above and has bomb damage on the photograph to the right (p. 15, B1). In both cases the popinjay mast is untouched.**

The popinjay mast of the archery club
in the middle of the gunpowder magazine site.

Flight above Ypres by aerial observer Freiherr Dietrich von Kanne, 11(?) May 1915

The last of the town's inhabitants were evacuated a few days before this reconnaissance flight. A great many of the public buildings have already been gutted by fire, although most of the walls are still standing; St Martin's Cathedral and the Cloth Hall had already gone up in flames on 22 November 1914; St James's Church burned from 23 to 25 April 1915, St Nicholas's Church and the school behind it on 6 and 7 May. Moreover, in the weeks between 22 April and 8 May hundreds of soldiers and civilians in the town were killed by the bombardments. The last remaining citizens were evacuated by military order on 9 May 1915.

When Camiel Delaere, the pastor of St Peter's Church, and Gustave Delahaye, warden of the Sacred Heart Institute, returned to Ypres on 11 May with a few lorries from the Friends Ambulance Unit, to salvage any valuables still remaining, they observed that there were fires burning in five or six places and that – in contrast to the activity undertaken in previous weeks – nobody was taking the trouble to put them out any longer. The plumes of smoke in this series of photographs confirm this. In the days to follow a large part of the historic town centre would burn to the ground, street by street.

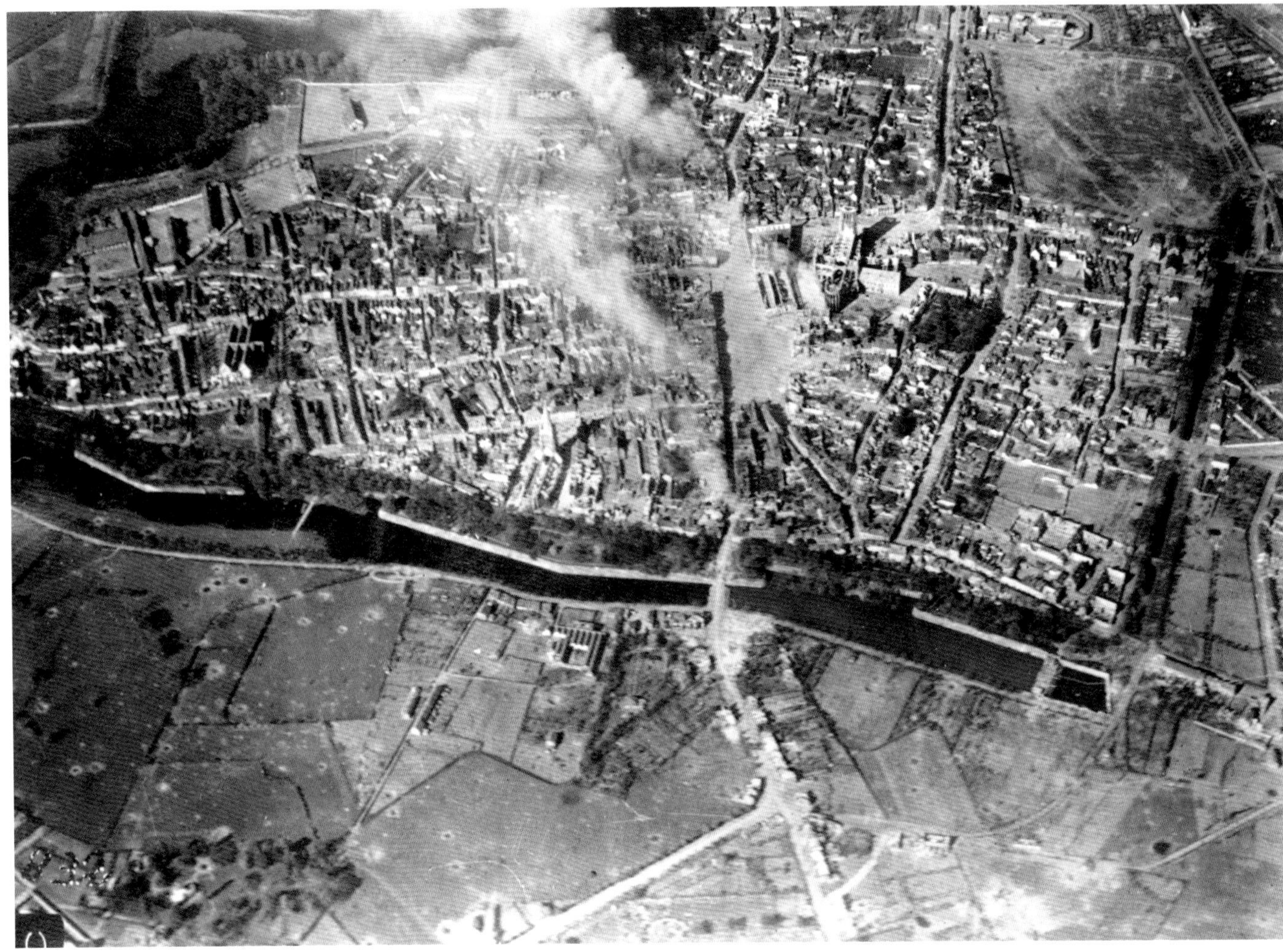

↖ **Bredene** 1.2 km B ↓ Zuid-Oostwijk C D ↑ 8 km (25) **Tirpitz** F G H

↖ coastline 850 m

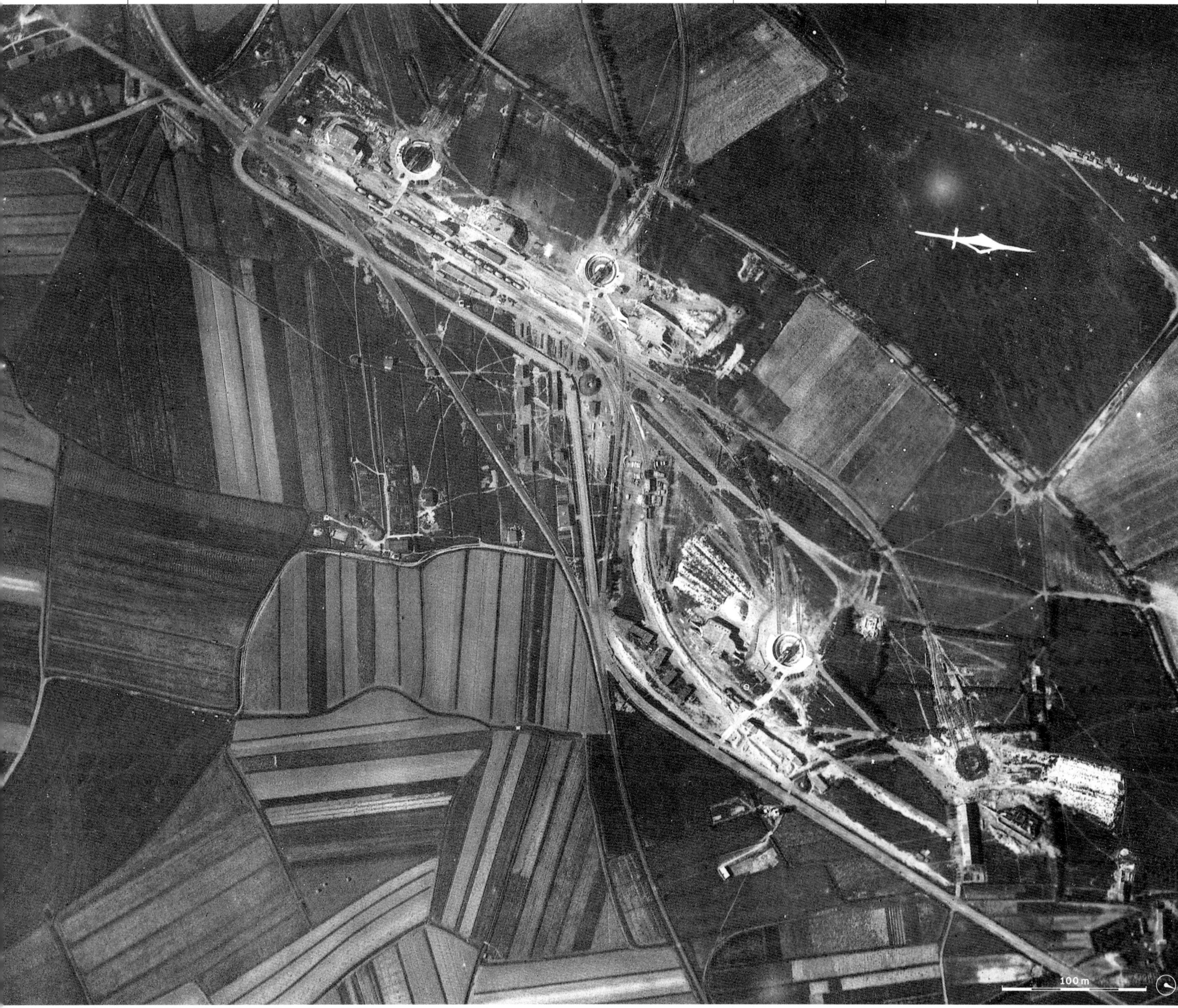

2 3 4 5 6

Klemskerke 1.4 km ↓

Wilhelm II Battery Knokke (86) 22 km ↓

Batterijstraat ↖

58

KOEKELARE - POMMERN BATTERY 28 SEPTEMBER 1917

On 7 May 1917 the Belgian Captain Jaumotte, on a reconnaissance flight over Koekelare, spotted the first signs of the construction of a new heavy German battery and photographed the site.[26] The cannon, known later as 'Lange Max', was in action for the first time on 27 June 1917 and was capable of firing 38-cm projectiles as far as Dunkirk. On 7 May 1917 (see photograph below) work was already in full swing – the sight must have caught the captain's eye because of the big railway line leading up to it. On 28 September the railway line was broken up in order to conceal the position. All in vain: the cannon had already been sighted and immediately afterwards it was bombarded by heavy artillery. But it was not possible to silence the cannon, which went on to sow death and destruction until 16 October 1918.[27]

» SEE ALSO 27 PREDIKBOOM

↑ **SIDE VIEW OF LANGE MAX**

View of the circular gun emplacement and the armour of the cannon. On both sides it is flanked by ammunition storage bunkers.

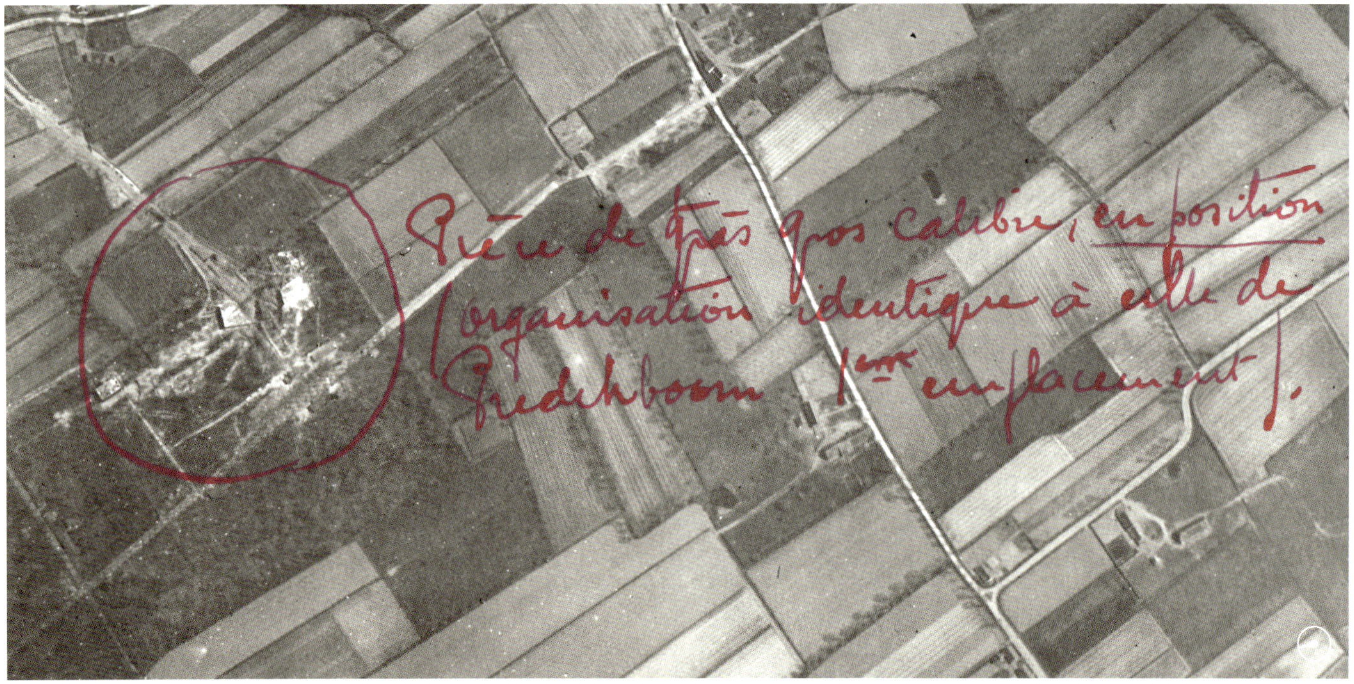

← **AERIAL PHOTOGRAPH OF 7 MAY 1917**

This photograph shows the cannon for the first time. There is a great deal of activity. Two large bunkers are clearly visible on both sides of the gun emplacement. Captain Jaumotte, the director of the Belgian military air force's aerial photography services, has annotated the photograph, remarking that the set-up is similar to the cannon at Predikboom.

GPS 51°07'11.39"N 2°58'52.11"E

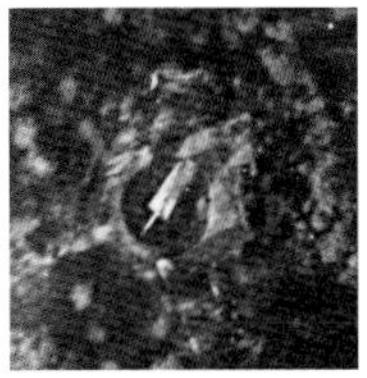

A4

LANGE MAX

The armoured 38-cm cannon 'Lange Max' is visible despite attempts to hide it beneath bundles of wood.

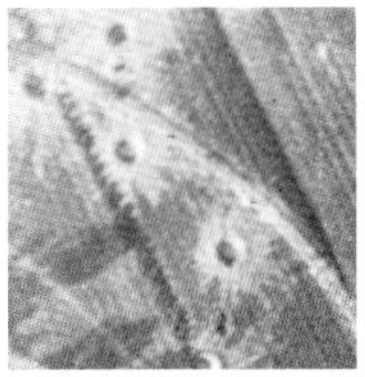

A1

RAILWAYS

The railway on the aerial photograph leads to a fake set-up in the north of the wood, intended to divert attention from the real position of the cannon.

B3/C3

BOMB CRATERS

Immediately after the discovery of the cannon, the battery was bombarded by projectiles fired by the French railway gun near Eggewaartskapelle.

↓ 'LANGE MAX' SEEN FROM THE FRONT

Frontal view of the enormous 38-cm cannon at Leugenboom. This 17.5-metre-long cannon stood on a large concrete emplacement. The damage to it was caused by an attempt to destroy it during the German withdrawal.

59

HOUTEM – BELGIAN AIRFIELD

21 OCTOBER 1917

From January 1915 the Belgian general headquarters were at the rectory at Houtem. In the autumn of 1917 the Belgian air force created an airfield near by, to the south of the village centre. Around it were six portable Bessonneau hangars and, at the southern end, a larger, more permanent shed. The aircraft used the central levelled area between the hangars as an unpaved runway for taking off and landing. Houtem was the home base of one of the aerial photographic services of the Belgian air force, which, from 1918, was under the directorship of Commander Jaumotte.

F3-F4

AERIAL PHOTOGRAPHIC SERVICE

The aerial photographic service at Houtem airfield was housed in this barracks.

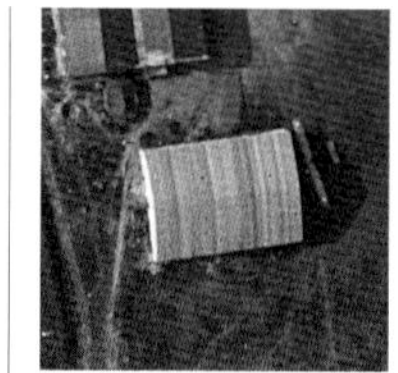

A4-B4

BESSONNEAU HANGAR

Belgian B.E.2c reconnaissance aircraft in front of a Bessonneau hangar. Just to the west of it, another plane of the same type is standing in front of the large shed.

← **AERIAL PHOTOGRAPHIC SERVICE, 1916**

Much of the history of aerial photography in the Belgian army was played out in this barracks in Houtem.

↓ **HANGARS AT HOUTEM**

Ground photograph of the Bessonneau hangars on the north side of the airfield.

↑ **DETAIL OF HOUTEM AIRFIELD**

Oblique view of the Belgian airfield at Houtem. The pale-coloured Bessonneau hangars were light constructions of wood and canvas. The many tracks on the ground are evidence of the great activity and traffic between the hangars and the aerial photography service. Immediately after a reconnaissance flight the glass negatives were unloaded and processed.

A
B
C
D
E
F
G
H
Heidenstraat
1
2
3
4
5
6
Dorpstraat
100 m
front line near Diksmuide 18 km
Houtemstraat

60
PASSCHENDAELE
31 OCTOBER 1917

After almost three years of relative peace in the German hinterland, very fierce fighting broke out in autumn 1917 in the Battle of Passchendaele, as the Allies fought for the ridge on which the village stands. The unprecedented intensity of the artillery bombardments, together with the persistent rain, turned the battlefield into a muddy swamp. 'Passiondale' became synonymous with the infernal war conditions, the bloody fighting in the mud and the hundreds of thousands of soldiers who left their lives in the fields of Flanders. A German oblique photograph taken only 500 metres above the scene shows the village centre of Passchendaele in the final stage of the battle. At this point it was still being defended by the Germans against constant Canadian attacks. A week later Passchendaele was taken and the first Allied trenches appeared.

›› Continued on p. 184

→ BEFORE

German aerial photograph of Passchendaele before the destruction. Comparison of the two oblique photographs is revealing.

G4-H4

CHURCH RUINS

Apart from some upright walls of the church, there is hardly anything left of Passchendaele.

↓ BATTLEFIELD

View of the battlefield at Passchendaele. The ruins of the church are prominent on the horizon.

↓ TRENCH MAP OF PASSCHENDAELE

This British trench map shows the progress of the battle on 1 November 1917. The front is shown as a blue line.

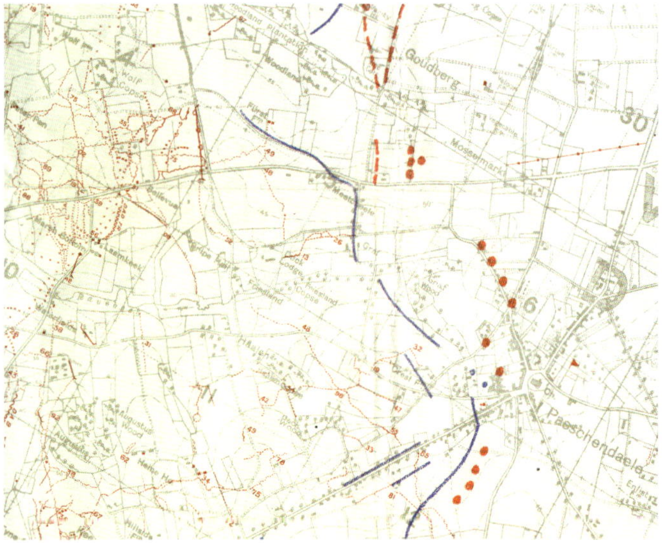

GPS 50°54'00.65"N 3°01'16.91"E

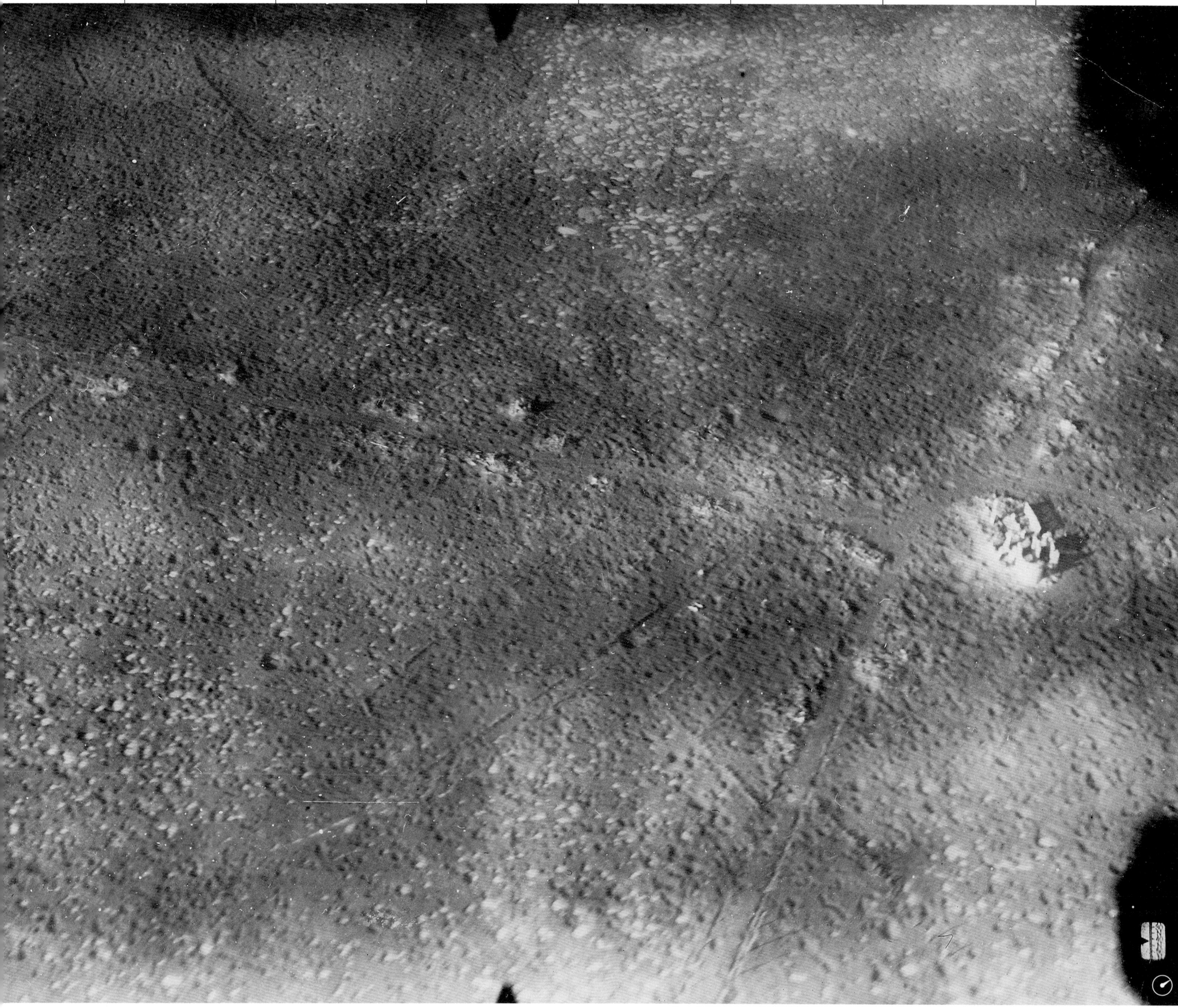
A
B
C
D
E
F
G
H
1
Vierde Regiment Karabiniersstraat
3
Molenstraat
4
5
6
Moorslede 79 2.6 km
Statiestraat

›› Continued from p. 182

A glance at this British aerial photograph of 12 November 1917, two days after the end of the battle, suffices to gain an impression of the ferocity of the bombardment and the difficult conditions in which the fighting took place. With the exception of the church, no more than a heap of stones remains – the village has been wiped off the face of the earth. The Allies have dug in in a circle round the village, using bomb craters and the fragmentary remains of trenches (E5, D5, B5). After only a few days some of trenches are already full of water (E3, E4).

PASSCHENDAELE BATTLEFIELD

Above: A desolate vista of the battlefield near Passchendaele, November 1917. Below: Wounded Canadian soldiers and German prisoners of war return from the battlefield through the mud, October/November 1917.

SYMBOLS

- BRITISH TRENCH, BUNKER
- GERMAN TRENCH, BUNKER
- BRITISH FRONT LINE (APPROXIMATE)
- GERMAN FRONT LINE (APPROXIMATE)
- CHURCH RUINS

PASSCHENDAELE, 1915

Vertical British aerial photograph of Passchendaele, taken on 19 November 1915. Comparison with the lunar landscape at the end of 1917 illustrates the intensity of the bombardment during the battle on the ridge.

GPS 50°54'00.65"N 3°01'16.91"E

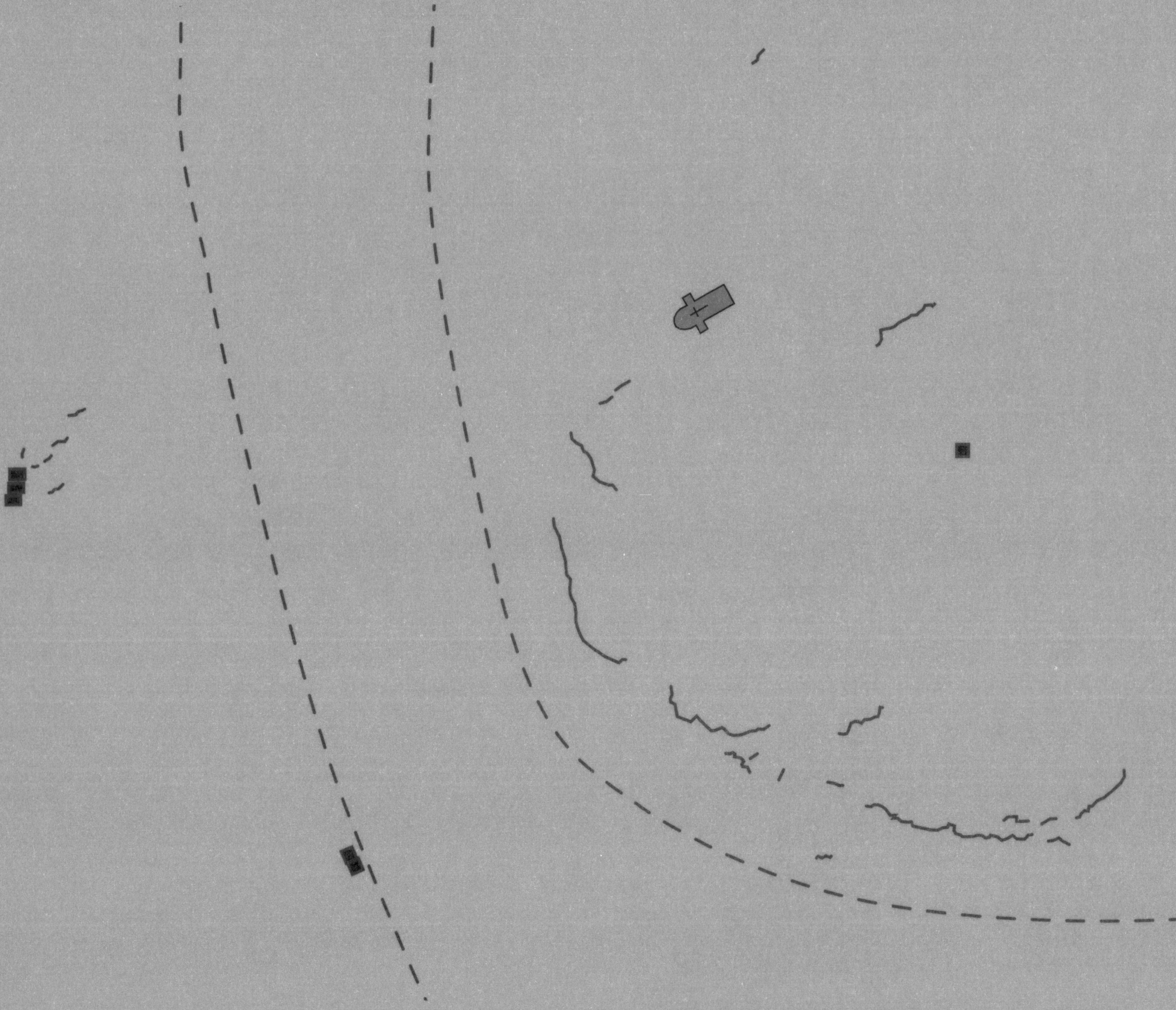

A
B
C
D
Molenstraat
GB/CAN
F
Doornkouterstraat
G
H
21.B.425.
28.D.62
12.11.17-11.
1
2
3
4
5
Oude Moorsledestraat
100 m
G
Statiestraat

61

DIKSMUIDE – 'TRENCH OF DEATH' 4 NOVEMBER 1917

The Dodengang ('Trench of Death') was a notorious trench to the north of Diksmuide, at the heart of the Yser front and in the dangerous, non-inundated part of the plain. The trench was dug in May 1915 as a Belgian approach trench in the Yser dyke, from which they intended to attack a German outpost on the same left bank (the 'petroleum tanks').[28] Gradually, it was established as a fire trench and made more robust. The two parallel trenches were dug out on the bank of the Yser. The eastern trench on the right was the fighting position; the western one on the left (set up in July 1915) served as a return trench with a light railway for the transport of materials. At one end stood the Ruiterschans ('Horseman's Redoubt'), a unique two-level fortification from which there was a good view of both banks and which would have improved the capacity for intercepting an enemy attack.

→ **RUITERSCHANS**

The back of the Ruiterschans with two narrow-gauge railway lines. From here the railway turns off and runs into the 'Trench of Death'.

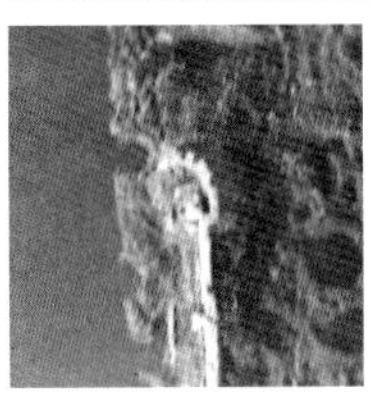

C5

BELGIAN OUTPOST

Outpost on the right bank of the Yser with only a parapet. There is no protective wall on the back (parados).

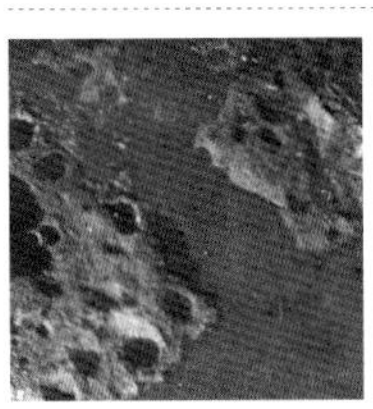

G1

DYKE BREACH

In October 1915 the 'Trench of Death' was shortened as some of the position was no longer tenable. To achieve this, engineers breached the dyke, causing a flood.

→ **'TRENCH OF DEATH', 1915**

Belgian aerial photograph, spring 1915. In the bend in the Yser the Belgian front line sheers off to join up with the Diksmuide–Nieuwpoort railway. The first excavation work for the 'Trench of Death' is visible along the Yser bank.

↑ F1

THE MOUSETRAP

At the extreme point of the 'Trench of Death' was a genuine booby-trap. In the open space between the bunkers, attackers could be harassed with grenades thrown through special openings and would have had no ghost of a chance.

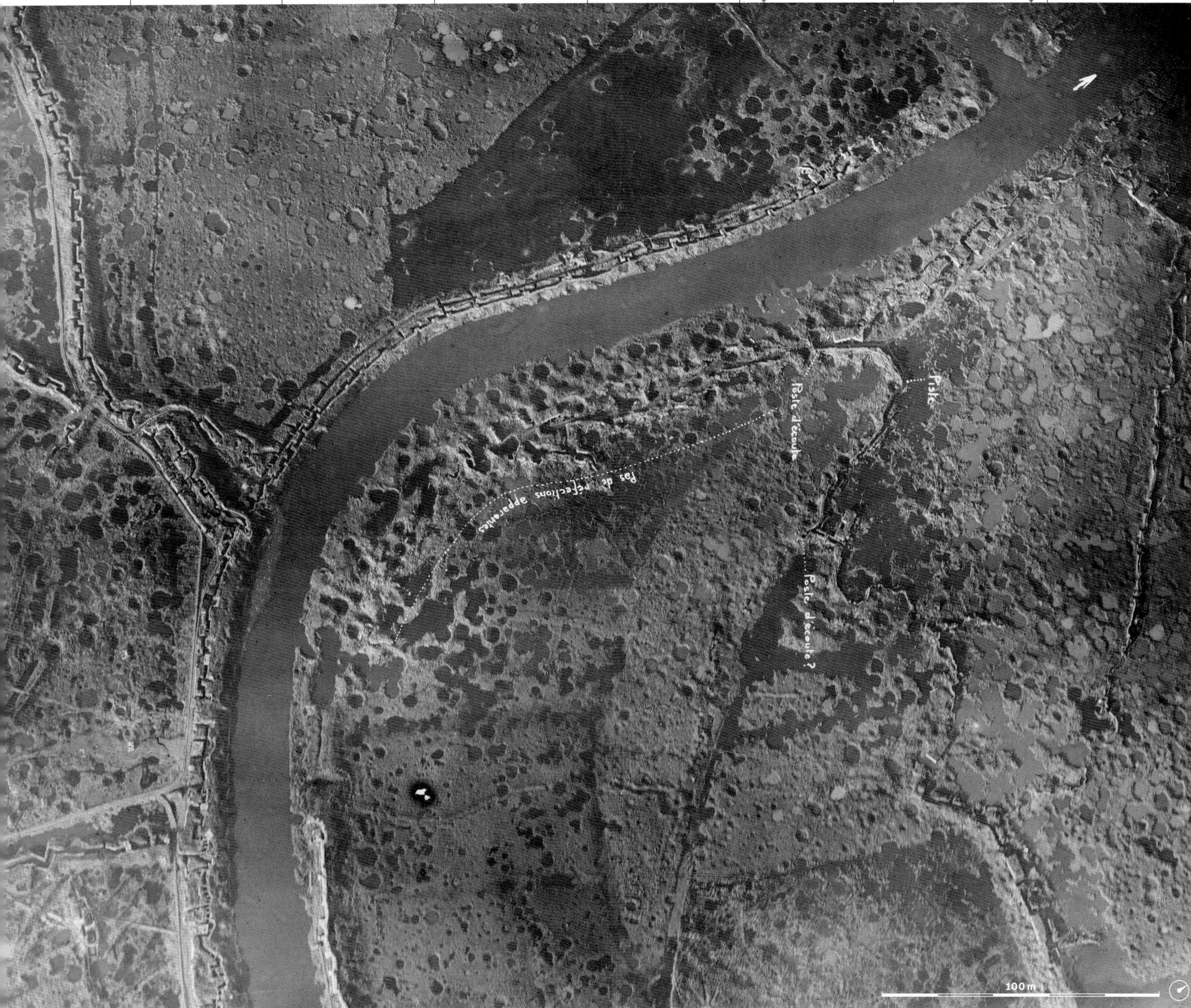

A
B
C
D
E
B
F
G
G
H
1
2
3
4
5
6
Pas de réfections apparentes
Poste d'écoute
Piste
Poste d'écoute ?
100 m
Yser
B
Diksmuide 1.7 km
G

62

DIKSMUIDE – 'TRENCH OF DEATH' 14 OCTOBER 1917

A Belgian aerial photograph of 14 October 1917 shows the Dodengang ('Trench of Death') in the foreground and, at right angles to it, the Ruiterschans with its two levels. The high groundwater level made it impossible to dig into the soil. Where there were no higher spots in the surrounding area, such as the Yser dyke or the embankment of the Nieuwpoort–Diksmuide railway, above-ground positions were made with sandbags and broad earthen walls. The land is marshy on both sides of the Yser. The intentional breach of the dyke (E4) led to part of the left bank being flooded.

↓ **'TRENCH OF DEATH'**

View from the 'Trench of Death' towards the enemy trenches on the left bank of the Yser. In the far distance, on the horizon, are the petroleum tanks.

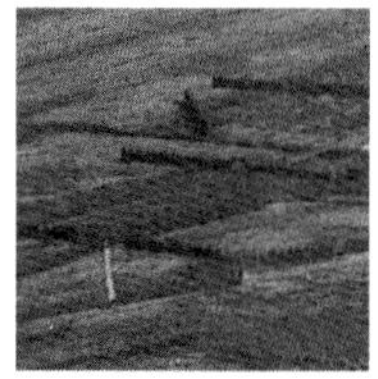

D2-E2

SCREENS

From Beerst a narrow-gauge railway ran for several kilometres to the German positions on the Yser. Wooden screens several metres high were needed to hide the transport from Belgian observers.

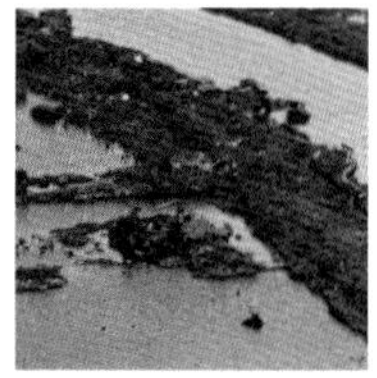

C3

PETROLEUM TANKS

German outpost by the petroleum tanks. From the ruins of the buildings and the storage tanks, the Germans had a good view of the Belgian trenches.

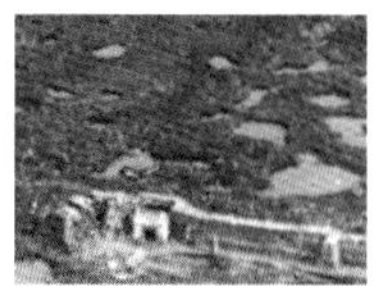

H6

BELGIAN OUTPOST

Between the Yser's *borne* (kilometre poles) 16 and 17 were some Belgian outposts on the right bank of the river. They could be reached only by using rafts.

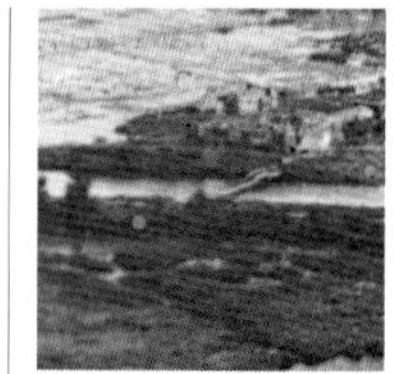

B2

FERME DE BORNE 15

Footbridges over the Yser near the ruins of a farm at the river's Ferme de Borne (kilometre pole) 15.

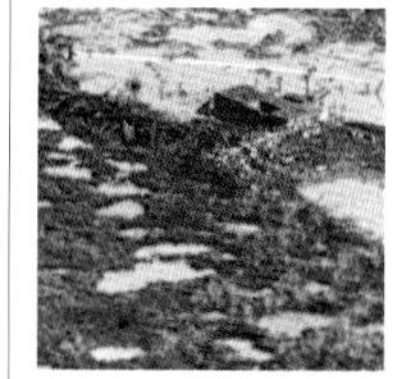

G5

TRENCH MORTAR

German bunker in Trench 111 with an opening in its roof for firing a trench mortar or a mortar.

E3

TRANCHÉE DU FOOTBALL ('FOOTBALL TRENCH')

In the German communication trench there is a narrow-gauge railway that runs via Ferme de Borne 15 into Beerst.

D4

GERMAN BUNKER

On the west bank of the Yser the Germans also have an approach trench, running from their outpost at the petroleum tanks towards the 'Trench of Death'. At the end of the Tranchée des Tanks stands a German bunker.

E6

RUITERSCHANS

The Ruiterschans is a unique two-level trench, featuring a covered way to the 'Trench of Death'. At the front a narrow-gauge railway line curves round into the 'Trench of Death'.

Yser

1.7 km **Diksmuide**

63

WOESTEN 28 DECEMBER 1917

Aerial photographs of snowy landscapes often reveal details that would otherwise be invisible. Manuals for photo-interpretation point out that, during wartime, enemy lines should, if possible, be photographed in snow in order to detect barbed-wire obstacles and artillery positions. This British aerial photograph of 28 December 1917 shows in particularly clear detail the positions around Woesten. From October 1914 to the end of July 1917 the village, some 4 kilometres behind the front, was set up as a fortified position. French, then British, and finally Belgian soldiers lived in the camps. The combination of snow and the shadows cast by the late-winter sun make it possible to see the posts to which the barbed wire is attached. Even more than other photographs, this example illustrates the quality of the work carried out by the aerial photographers.

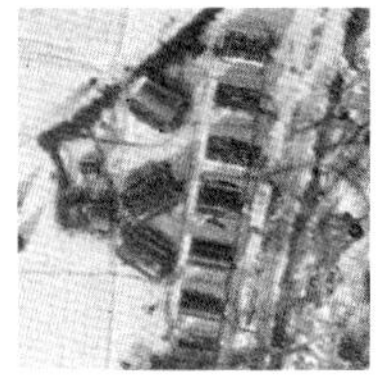

B3-B4

MELTING SNOW

Here the snow has melted as a result of intensive activity on the ground. It can thus be deduced which enemy bunkers and trenches are being used.

F2

FIRING POSITION

This U-shaped wall could be used as a gun emplacement.

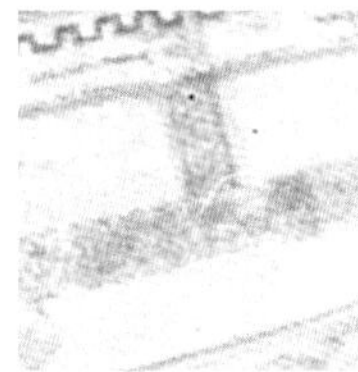

J4

BARBED-WIRE ENTANGLEMENT

The barbed-wire entanglement, several metres thick, consists of six rows of posts joined together, making them impenetrable.

↓ **BARBED WIRE**

A British soldier puts up barbed wire in the Ypres Salient, 8 January 1918.

GPS 50°54'01.98"N 2°47'23.71"E

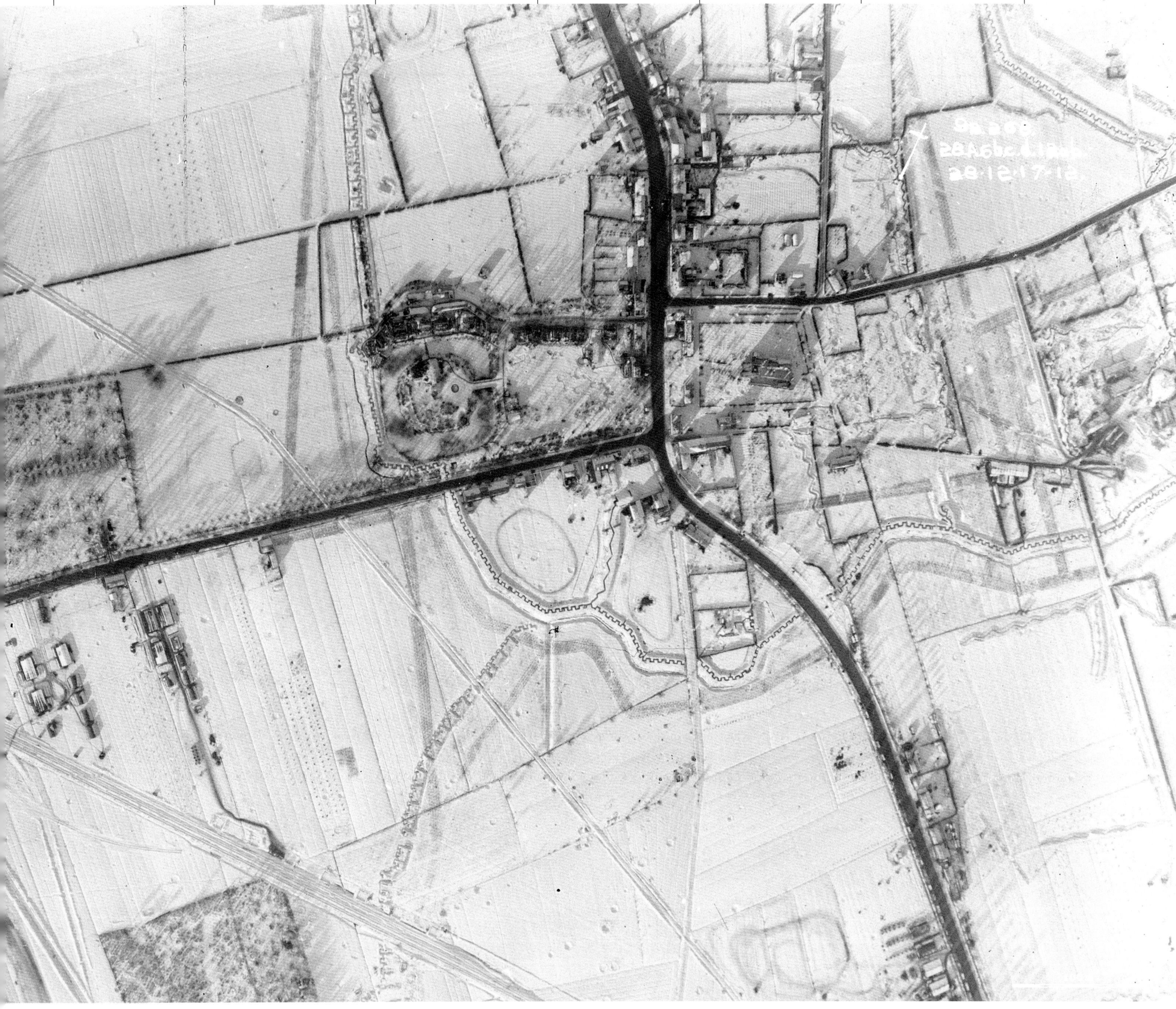

D
E
barbed wire
F
village of Woesten
G
H
I
barbed wire
J
1
2
trench
3
4
5
Boezinge 3.8km
6
railway
1.7km Elverdinge

64 ESSEX FARM AUTUMN 1917

After the Third Battle of Ypres the canal zone lay far inside the British hinterland. An oblique photograph (autumn 1917) shows the great activity behind the front. The burial grounds – Bard Cottage (D4-E4) and Essex Farm (H2) cemeteries – had grown exponentially to accommodate the many dead from the nearby medical stations during the British offensive. Dozens of underground shelters and bunkers had been dug into the high banks on both sides of the canal. To the east of the canal military camps had shot up like mushrooms from August 1917. A British photograph taken on 13 January 1918 (see right) shows the same area from a vertical viewpoint.

» SEE ALSO 11 ESSEX FARM

SYMBOLS

- TRENCH
- SHELTER, DUGOUT
- CANAL BRIDGE
- CEMETERY
- ARTILLERY POSITION
- BARRACKS, BARRACKS AREA
- TROOP MOVEMENTS
- RAILWAY

PANORAMA NEAR ESSEX FARM

A panoramic photograph of British shelters on the eastern side of the Ypres–Yser Canal. Bridge 4 (extreme right) was one of the solidly built canal crossing points.

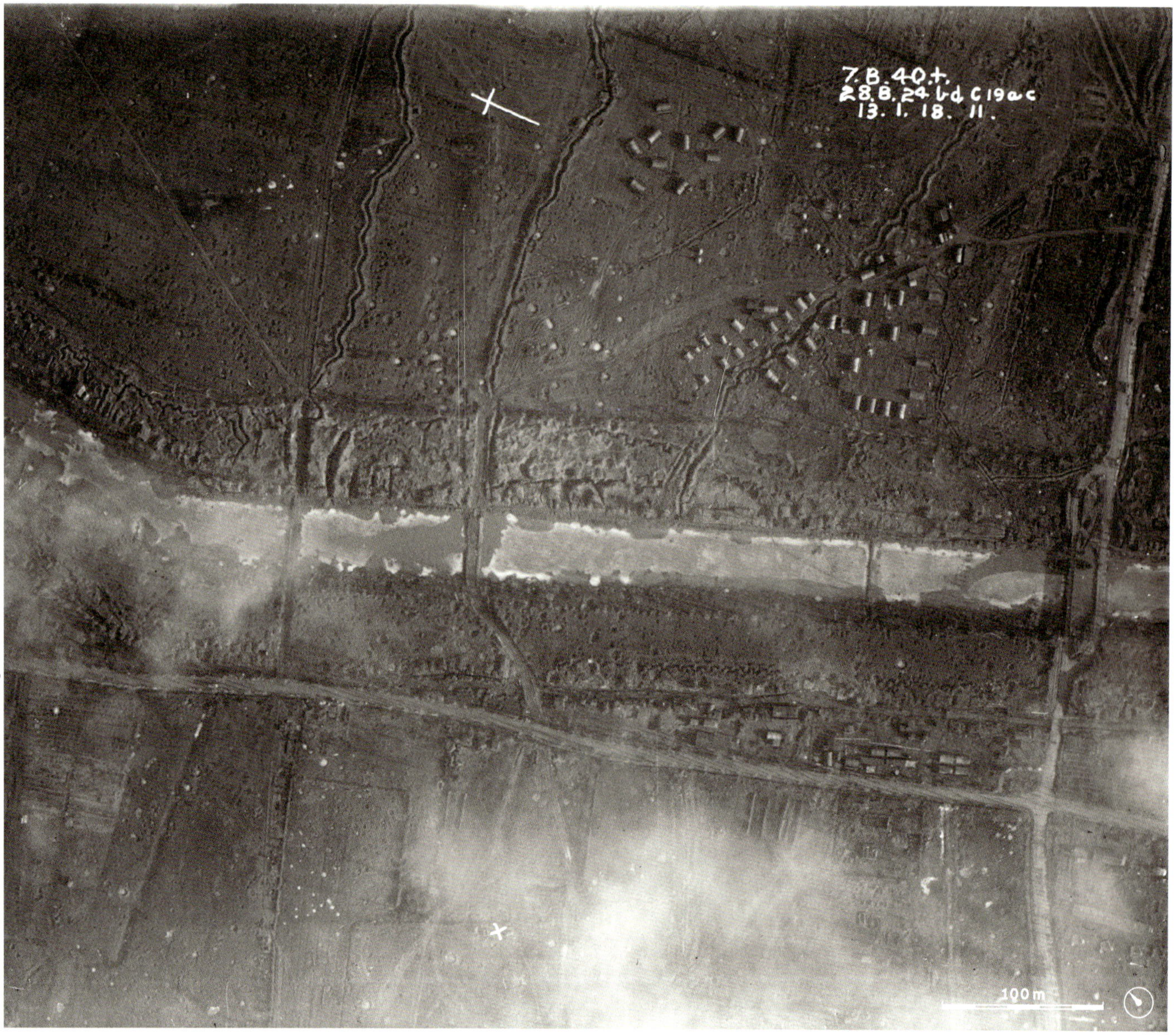

GPS 50°52'15.22"N 2°52'24.19"E

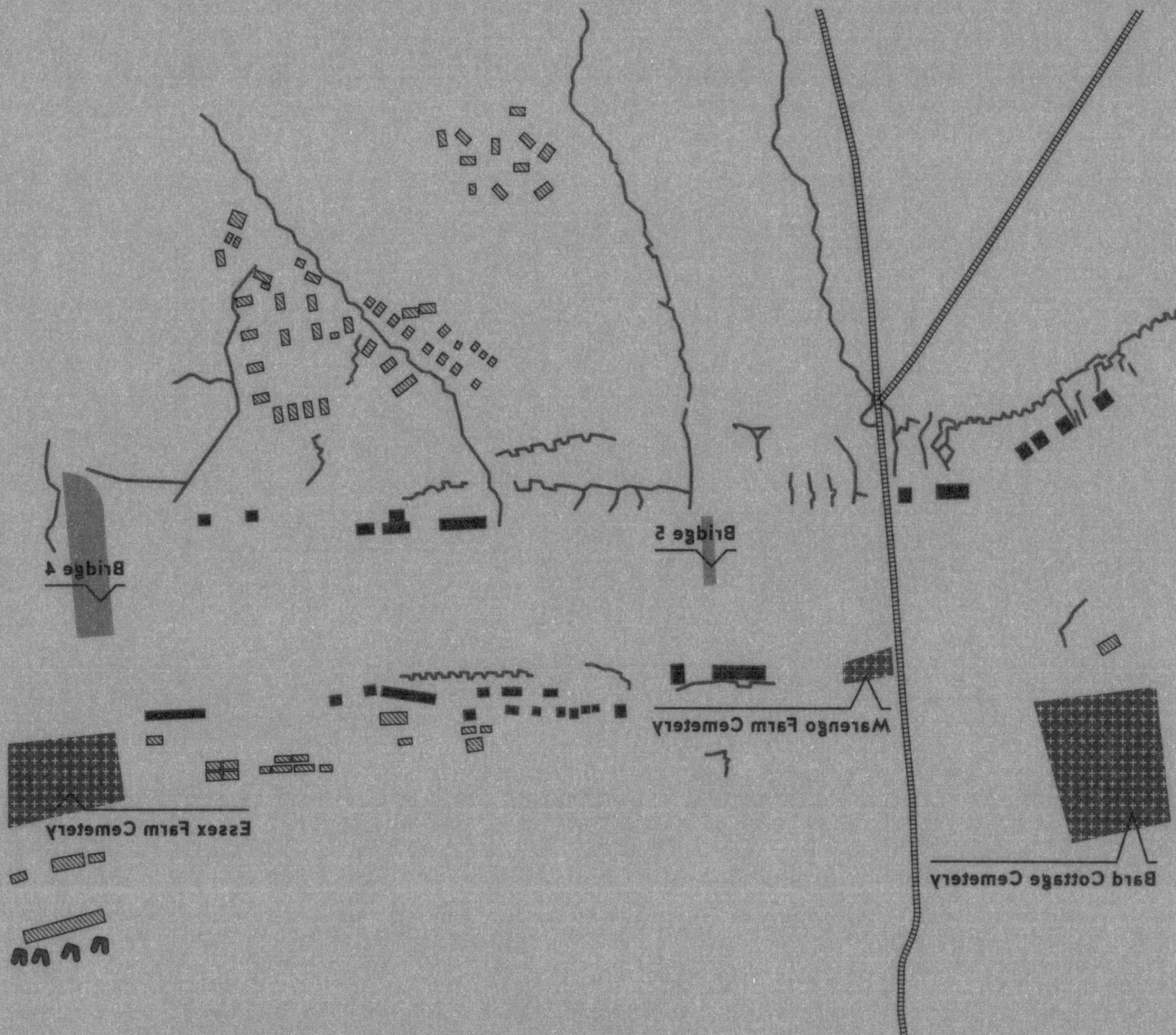
Bridge 4
Bridge 5
Marengo Farm Cemetery
Essex Farm Cemetery
Bard Cottage Cemetery

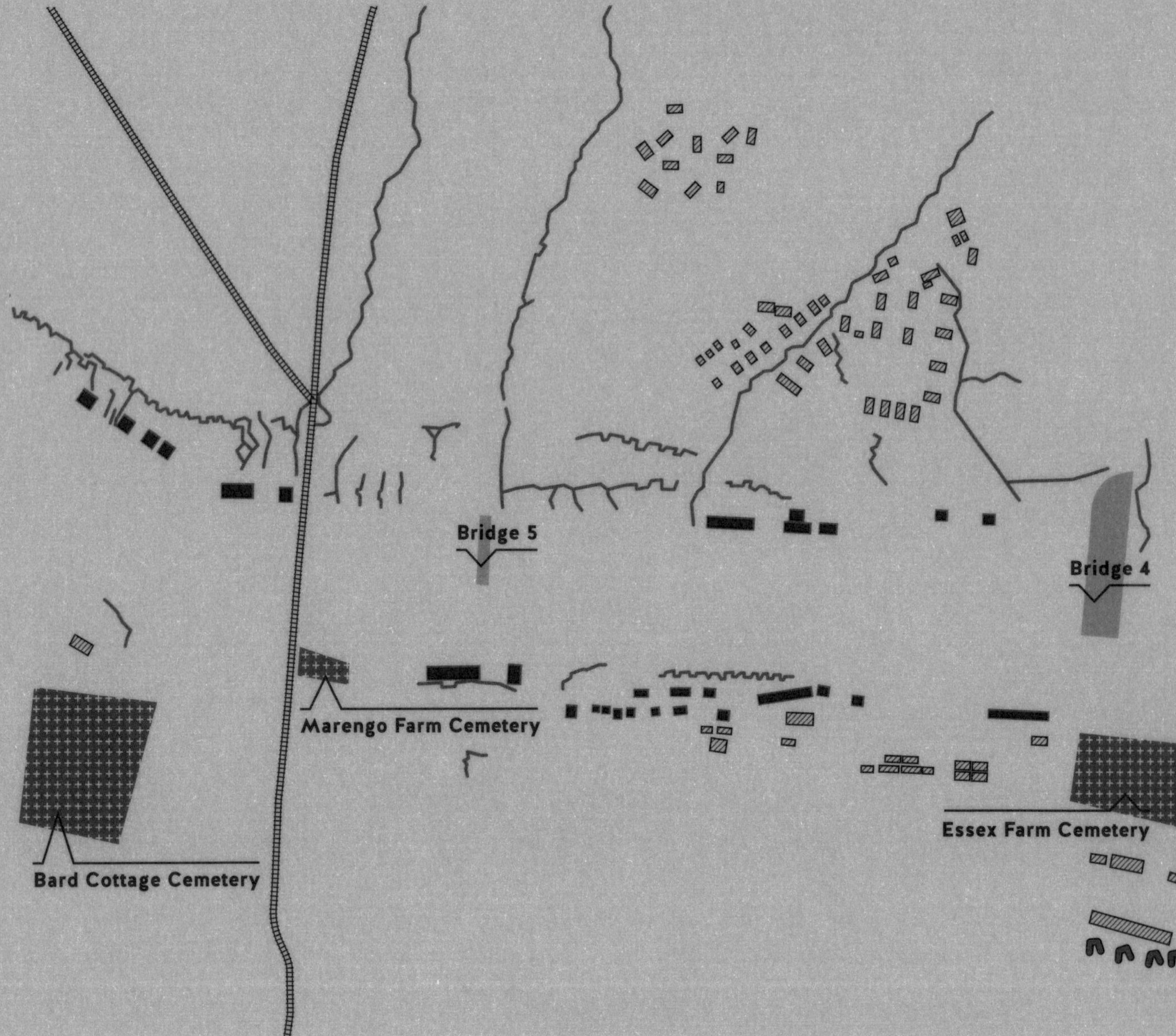

Bridge 5
Bridge 4
Marengo Farm Cemetery
Essex Farm Cemetery
Bard Cottage Cemetery

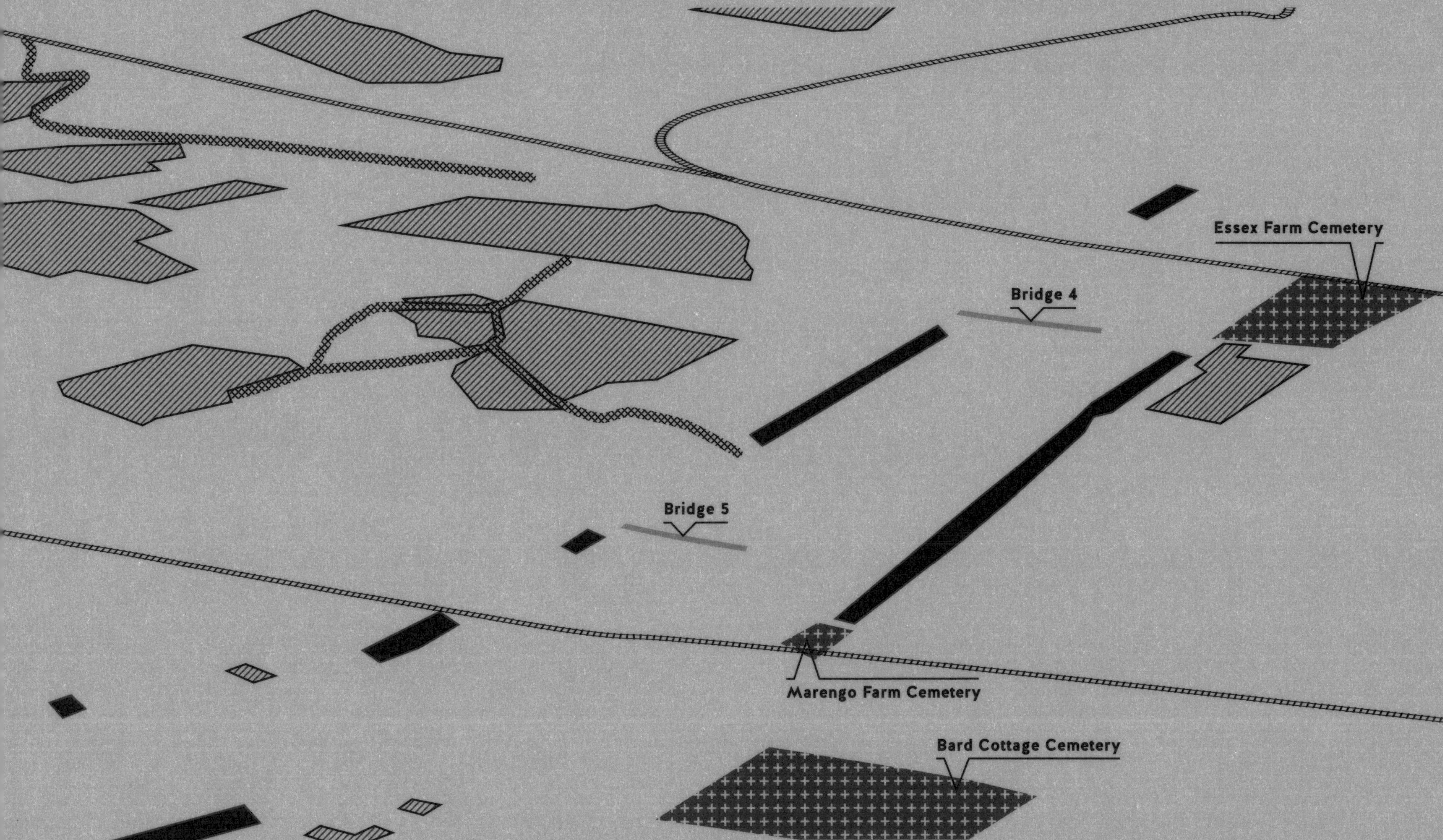
Essex Farm Cemetery
Bridge 4
Bridge 5
Marengo Farm Cemetery
Bard Cottage Cemetery

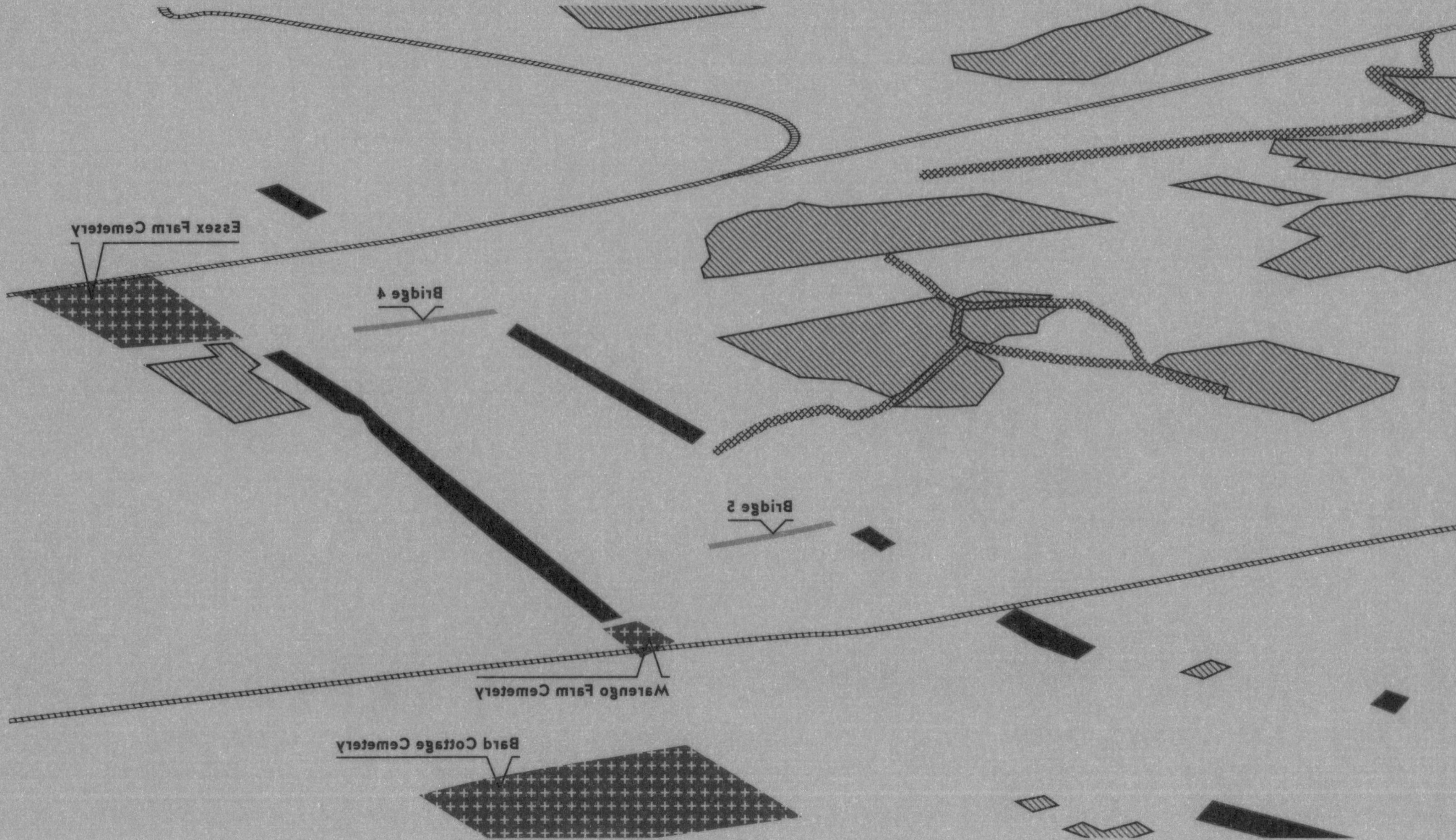
Essex Farm Cemetery
Bridge 4
Bridge 5
Marengo Farm Cemetery
Bard Cottage Cemetery

A
B
C
D
E
F
G
H
1
Ypres 2.2km
Noordhofweg
3
4
Diksmuidseweg

65

VINKEM – L'OCÉAN 2

SUMMER 1917

In De Panne, the Red Cross hospital L'Océan played a key role in the Belgian sector of the front. In spring 1917 it was decided to move it to another location since De Panne was now in the British sector. In Vinkem, a hospital was built around Torreelen Farm (E4-E5) under the direction of the surgeon Antoine Depage: this was L'Océan 2.[29] The hospital came into use from September 1917 and had a maximum capacity of 3,000 beds. When the photograph was taken, the central pavilion and the south wing had been completed. Work was still in progress on the northern wing.

→ **TENTED HOSPITAL**

The temporary tented hospital in Vinkem, erected pending the opening of L'Océan 2 in September 1917.

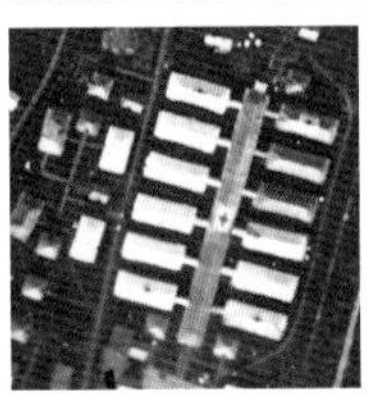

F3-F4

TENTS

During the first phase of construction (between May and September 1917) the temporary hospital consisted merely of a number of tents around the farm. Later they were replaced by more substantial barracks.

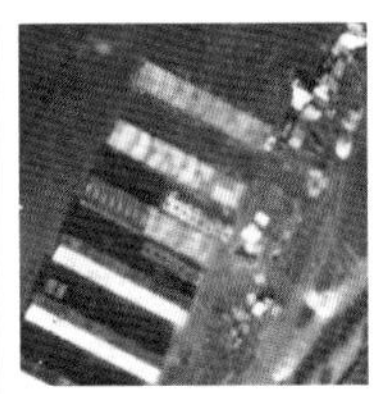

E2-F2

BARRACKS UNDER CONSTRUCTION

Barracks at various stages of construction.

C3

SUPPLY LINE

A double railway line brought supplies and patients to the hospital. Here final work on a terminus station is in full flow.

D1

THE NORTH WING

Work is still underway on the construction of the north wing of L'Océan 2. The wooden frame for the barracks is ready.

← **HOSPITAL**

The central pavilion of the hospital in Vinkem. This was where the casualties were brought and admitted to the hospital.

GPS 51°00'44.34"N 2°38'39.65"E

↗ **De Panne** 9 km | B | C | D | E | F | **Wulveringen** 250 m ↗ | **Vinkem** 700 m ↗

1 2 3 4 5 6

↗ Joe Englishstraat | Houtemstraat ↗

66
DRIE GRACHTEN
10 DECEMBER 1917

At the Third Battle of Ypres French troops captured the German outpost at Drie Grachten on 16 August 1917. Adjustments were made to make the post defendable and a double bridge was built to facilitate the supply of provisions for the front.

» **SEE ALSO** 54 DRIE GRACHTEN

B4-C4
CONVERSION OF BUNKERS
In the bunkers, which were originally constructed by the Germans, access was now on the side the enemy fired from. Conversion was necessary to make them safe to enter. The parapet was moved to the other side.

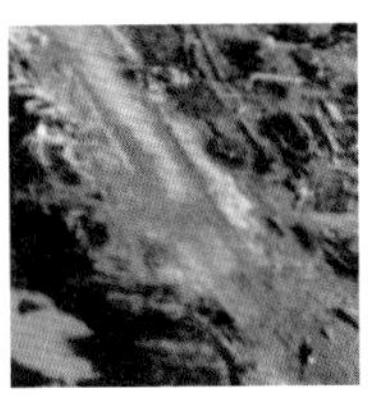

F2
ROAD INFRASTRUCTURE
The German communication trench was levelled off to make the Noordschote–Luigem road passable again.

↓ **BELGIAN SOLDIERS**

Belgian soldiers pose next to captured bunkers in Drie Grachten.

GPS 50°57'33.27"N 2°49'21.22"E

F
G
H
I
J
K
L
1
2
3
4
5
6
Ypres 12km
Ieperlee
Noordschote 800 m

67
GROTE HEMME
28 DECEMBER 1917

Although the Belgian army inundated the Yser plain in October 1914, it could not be called a large expanse of water. The depth of the flooding was variable, and in some places dry islands emerged in the inundated area. The warring sides made good use of these to install small advanced posts. In the centre of the oblique aerial photograph the course of the Yser can be seen. To the west of the river the areas totally under water are recognisable by their darker hue (H3, D4), which contrasts starkly with the surrounding snow-covered fields and meadows. Visible in the foreground are Belgian (B5-D6) and German positions (B4-F5) near the Grote Hemme Farm (G5).

Violettestraat ↓ G

B

B G

GPS 51°06'41.56"N 2°47'55.49"E

↑ AERIAL PHOTOGRAPH OF GROTE HEMME FARM

Vertical aerial photograph taken to the north of Grote Hemme Farm (G5) on 5 August 1916. The Belgian and German outposts are 300 metres apart. The lines consist of nothing more than small reinforced positions with room for one or two soldiers, built entirely above ground using sandbags. The density of defensive structures in this sector was very low as neither party could undertake offensive action on the marshy ground.

← FOOTBRIDGE IN THE YSER PLAIN

A barricaded footbridge in the middle of the inundation on the Yser front line.

A B C D E F G H
1 2 3 5 6
AvMB_2684_28-12-17_1500m_14h
YSER. B. 4.500 - P: Adj. Ledure. O: Lt Verelst.
nouv. piste
nouv. passerelle
nouveaux reseaux
Brugsesteenweg
Yser
Schoorbakke 1.3km
G
Grote Beverdijk
Hemmestraat
B

68

TYNE COT 3 JANUARY 1918

On 3 January 1918 a British reconnaissance aircraft climbing away from La Lovie Airfield at Poperinge photographed a snowy landscape in the Ypres Salient, a good kilometre behind the front line at Passchendaele. The area had just come under fire from German artillery and fifty or so hits were still smouldering; in this image taken during the flight dark clouds of smoke stand out against the crater-riddled fields. The target of the bombardment was a communication trench that the 3rd Australian Division had captured from the Germans on 4 October 1917. In one bunker an advanced dressing station was being set up, along with a small but growing cemetery at Tyne Cot. The small scale of the photograph means that the graves are not visible. After the war Tyne Cot Cemetery became the largest cemetery in the British Commonwealth, the last resting-place of almost 12,000 soldiers.

» **SEE ALSO** 4 TYNE COT 1915

↓ **MAP – 1 MARCH 1918**

This British trench map shows the situation at the front in this sector. The two westernmost bunkers were called 'Irksome' and 'The Barnacle' and can still be seen at Tyne Cot Cemetery.

↑ **TYNE COT CEMETERY**

Post-war photograph of Tyne Cot Cemetery, with the large bunker in the background.

C5

TYNE COT BUNKER

The bunkers at Tyne Cot were part of the German Flanders II position. After the war, when the cemetery was landscaped, the cross of sacrifice of Tyne Cot Cemetery was built on top of the central bunker.

SYMBOLS

TRENCH

DUCKBOARD TRACK

BUNKER

TYNE COT IN 2013 WITH TWO PRESERVED BUNKERS AND THE CROSS OF SACRIFICE

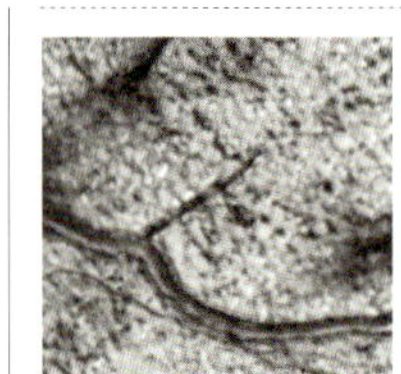

E6-F6

INVERARY AVENUE

From Tyne Cot a long communication trench ran eastwards to the front at Passchendaele.

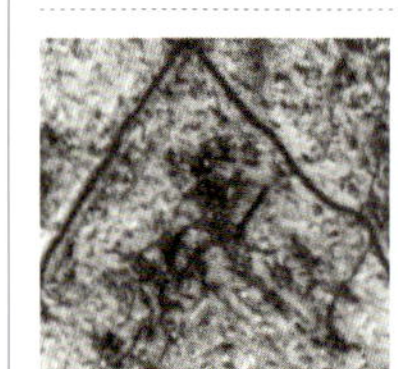

C4

WOODEN PLANKS

The battlefield had become scarcely accessible after the bombardment of the Third Battle of Ypres. In order to make troop movements possible, a network of duckboard tracks (wooden planks) was laid down.

GPS 50°53'13.83"N 2°59'57.17"E

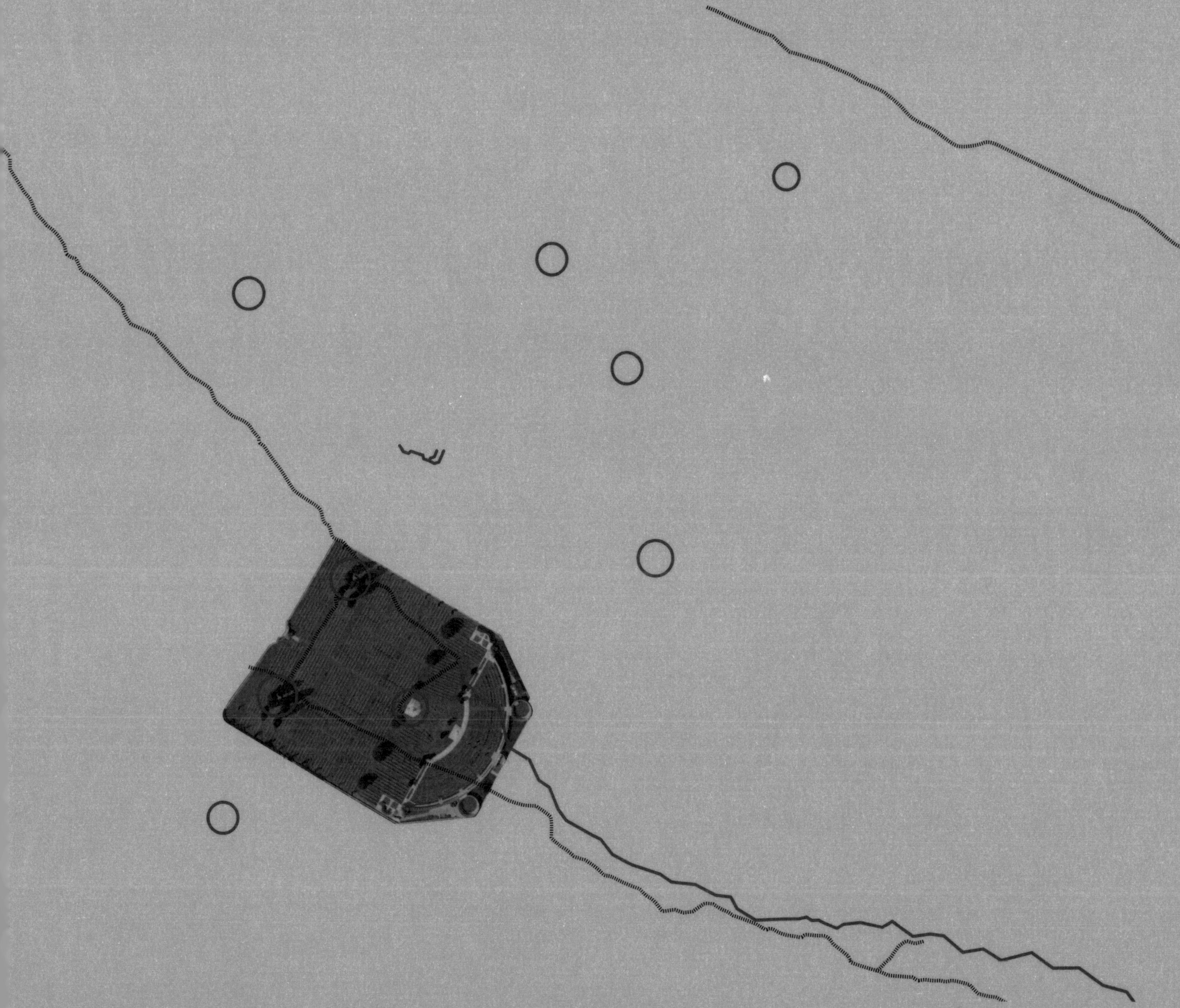

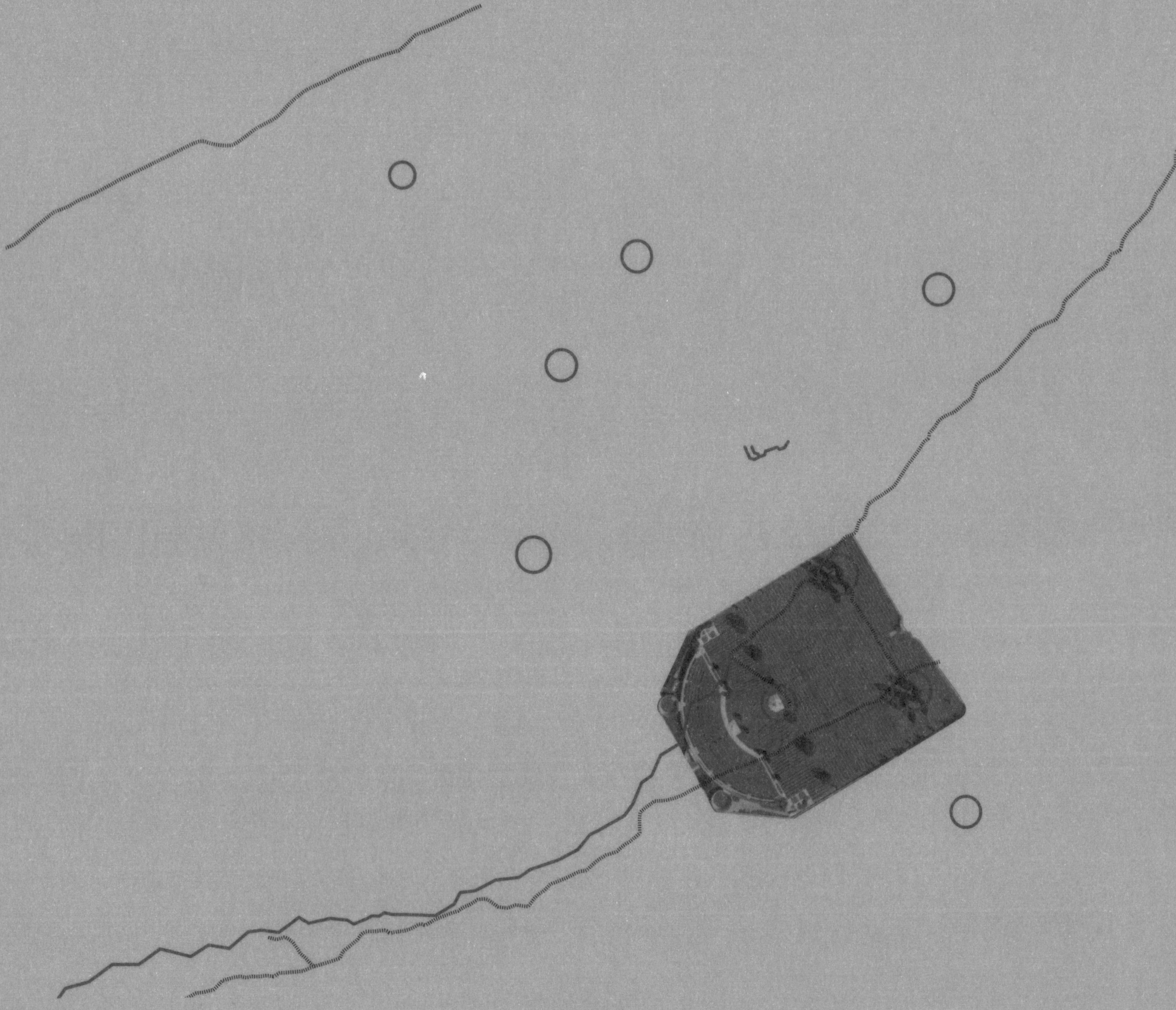

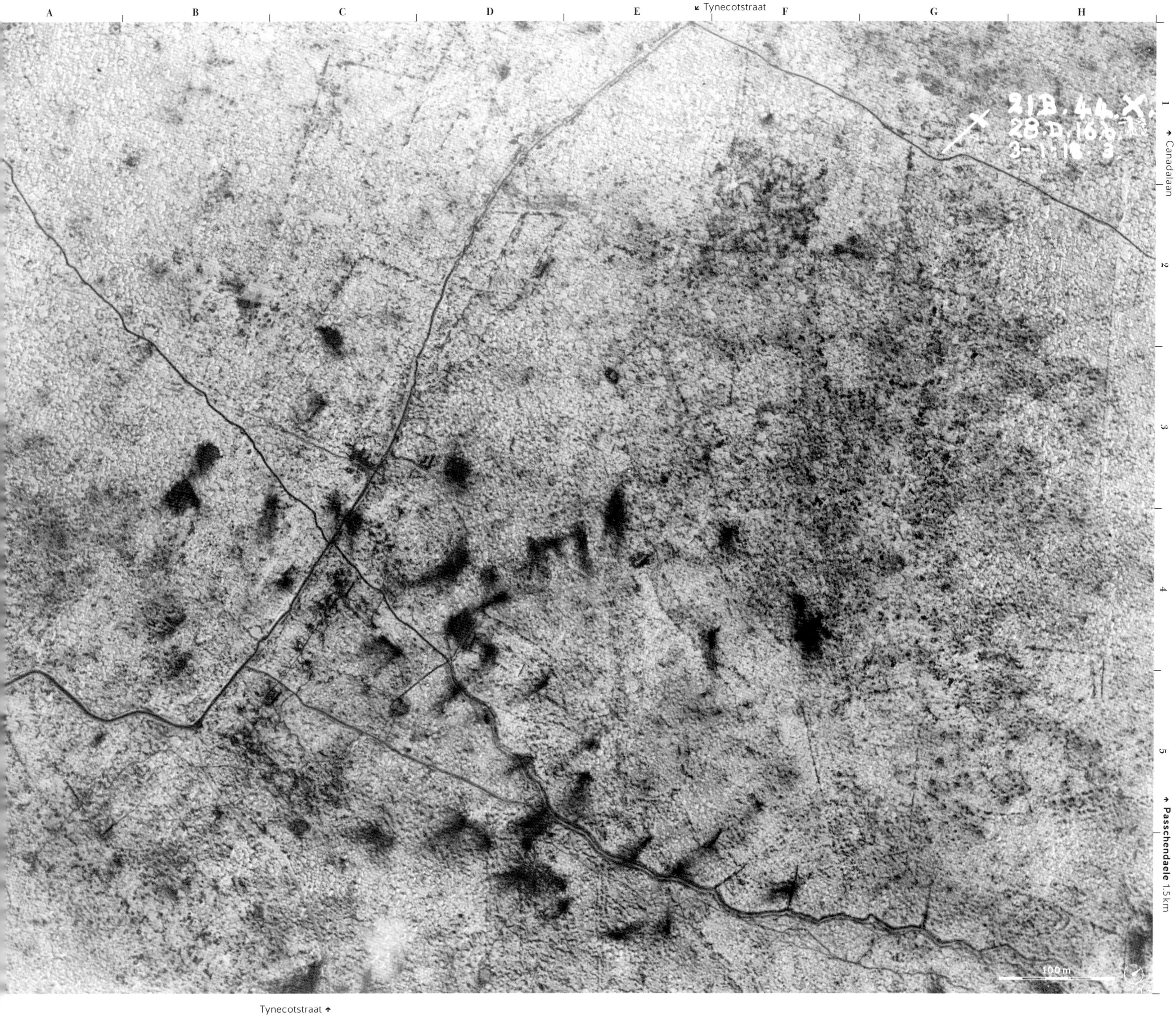

A
B
C
D
E
F
G
H
Tynecotstraat
1
2
3
4
5
Canadalaan
Passchendaele 1.5 km
100 m
Tynecotstraat

69

MERKEM – GRANDFATHER FARM 26 DECEMBER 1917

After the Battle of Merkem the Allied offensive came to a halt on 27 October 1917, on a line between De Blankaart and Kippe-Aschhoop. Winter was coming and the Allies gratefully made use of the captured German bunkers to build up their positions. On both sides, the foremost line consisted of nothing more than the few bunkers that had been able to withstand the bombardments, together with an unbroken line of bomb craters guarded by sentries. On the aerial photograph of 26 December 1917 the Belgian–German front line can be seen to the north of the Kippe crossroads. The fine, irregularly placed barbed-wire barriers can be seen only because of the strong contrast provided by the snow. Soldiers on sentry duty in bomb craters unwittingly made the snow melt and thus betrayed their position on aerial photographs.

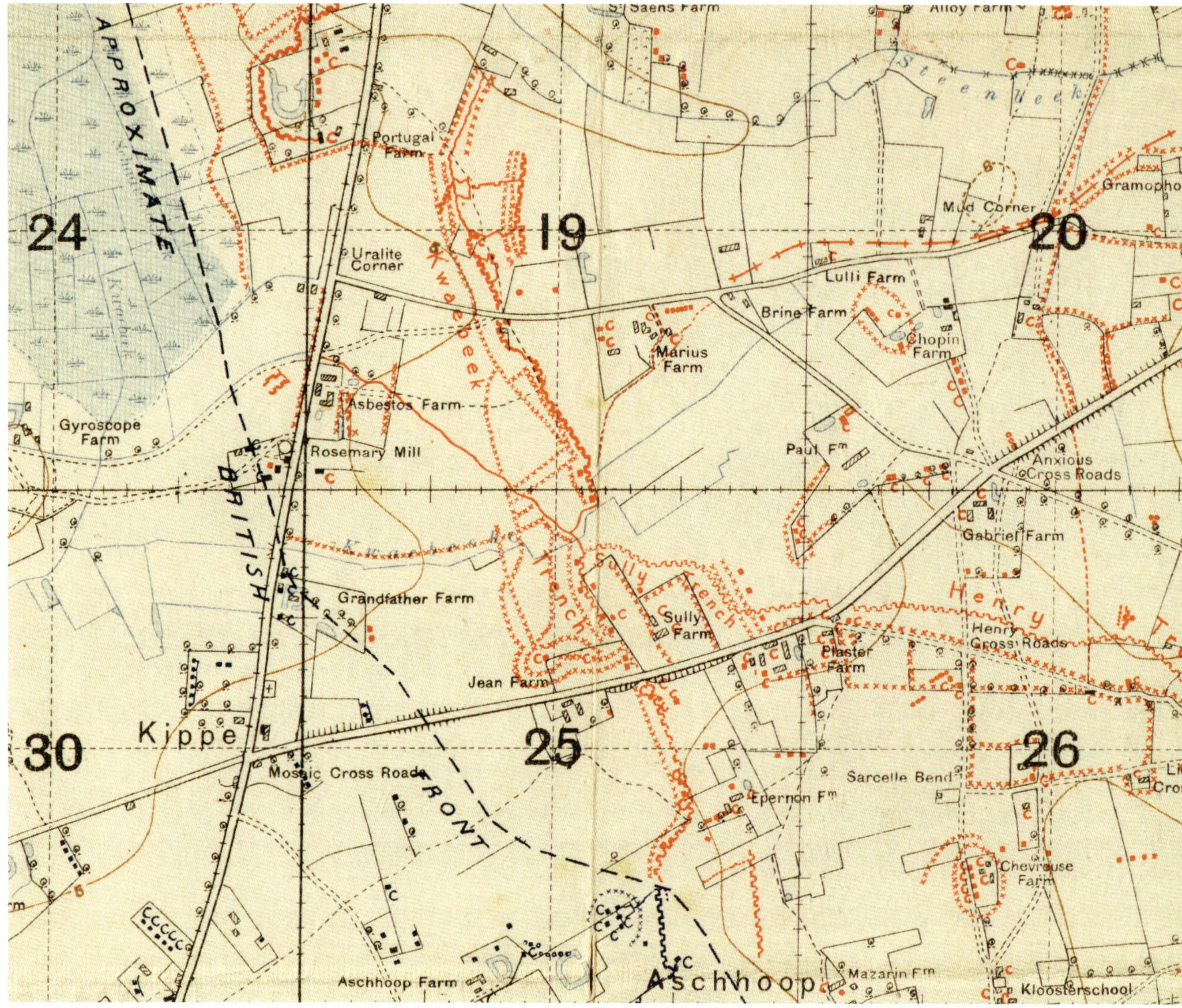

→ **BRITISH TRENCH MAP**

This trench map shows the front line near Kippe. The British front line is marked with a dotted blue line, German structures are in red.

G5

BUNKER

Large bunker just west of Grandfather Farm. The snow on the roof has melted, making it easy to see.

G5-H5

GRANDFATHER FARM

The moat round the farm has thick ice on it, which in turn has been covered by snow.

E5

TRENCH

As a result of a change in military tactics, the front line did not need to be strengthened at all times in 1917: defence in depth and the hinterland were prioritised.

D3

BARBED WIRE

On the other side of no-man's-land are German barbed-wire fences.

F4

OCCUPIED OUTPOST

Outpost in a bomb crater just behind a barbed-wire fence.

B1

GERMAN TRENCH

German trench between Sully Farm and Asbestos Farm (see trench map above).

GPS 50°57'30.23"N 2°52'00.71"E

A
B
C
D
E
F
G
H
G
2
B
3
4
5
Iepersteenweg
6
Kwadebeek
B

70
LANGEMARK – ELDORADO
3 JANUARY 1918

During the Third Battle of Ypres many village centres in the Ypres Salient were reduced to ruins. The centre of Langemark became little more than an ill-defined spot in a desolate landscape of craters. Most of the hundreds of bomb craters in the photograph were full of water and what remains of Langemark church was hardly more than a heap of rubble. There are no military structures to be seen in the ruins of the village centre – with the exception of a British tank: the *Eldorado* became stranded on 23 September 1917 in the vicinity of Langemark church on the way to its intended starting point.[30]

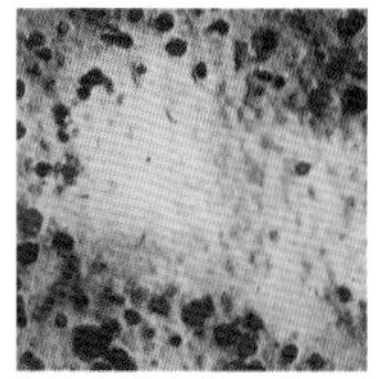

D2
LANGEMARK CHURCH

From the air, the ruins of the church are only recognisable as a light-coloured blur of stone fragments.

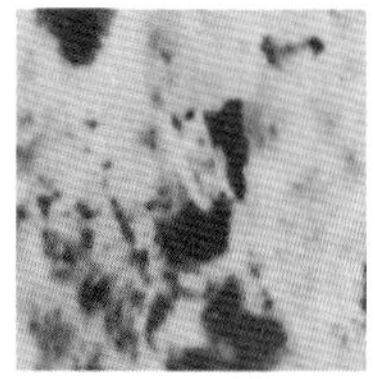

E5
ELDORADO

The outline of the British Mark IV tank *Eldorado* and the shadow cast by its carcase. The tank is some 8 metres long, giving an idea of the size of the hundreds of craters in the vicinity.

↓ **ELDORADO**

Three soldiers pose next to the shell of *Eldorado*, a Mark IV tank, originally equipped with five machine guns.

↑ **LANGEMARK CHURCH, 1919**

GPS 50°54'48.61"N 2°55'09.30"E

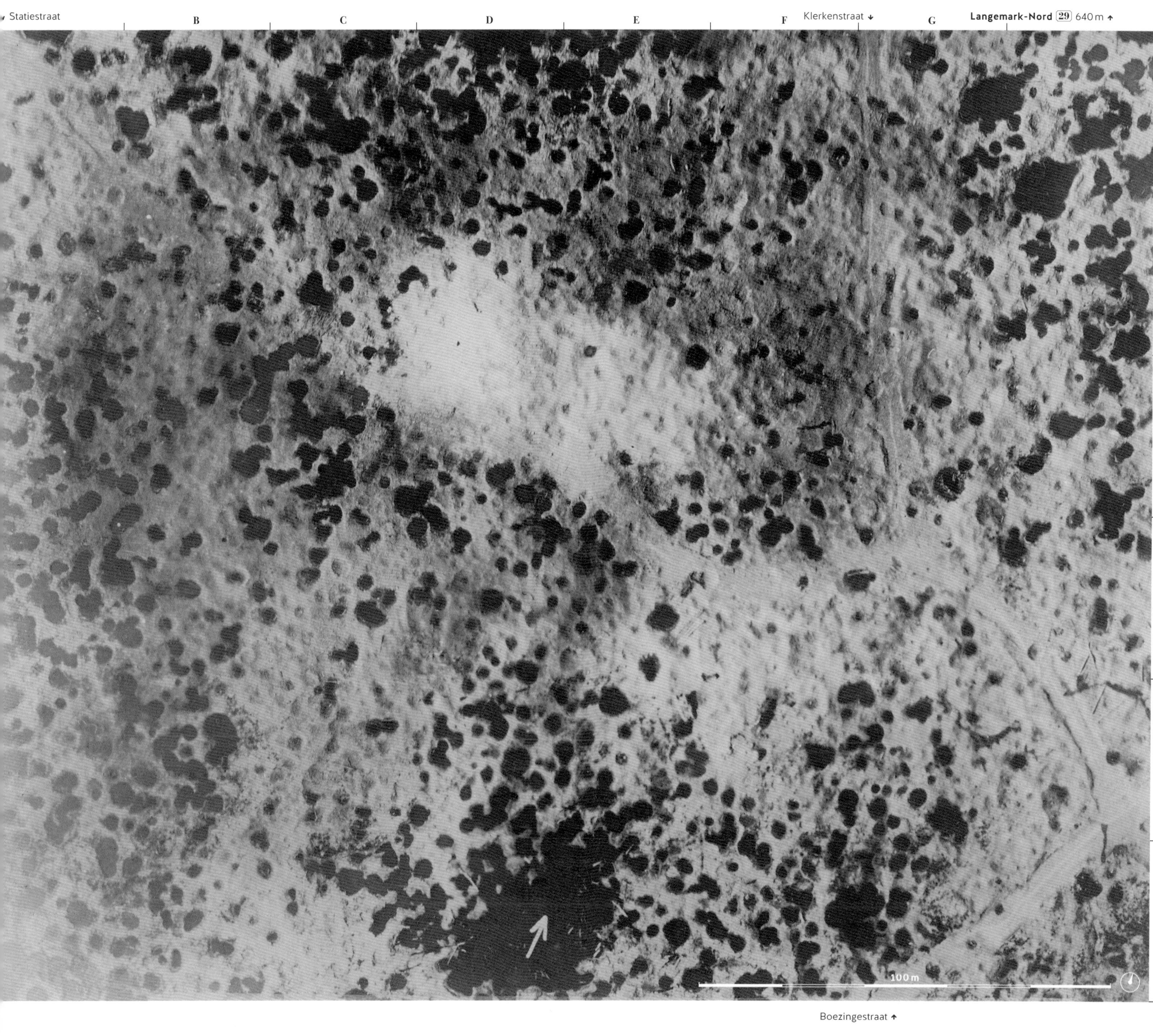

Statiestraat
B
C
D
E
F
Klerkenstraat
G
Langemark-Nord 29 640 m
1
2
3
4
5
6
100 m
Boezingestraat

71
ONDANK – STORAGE DEPOT
4 JANUARY 1918

The war machinery at the front required enormous logistical support. At Wippe, to the west of Woesten, there was a storage area containing large amounts of wood, supplies and construction components for trenches. It was criss-crossed by a network of narrow-gauge railway tracks. The materials were then sent via the main railway connection to Elverdinge and Boezinge and towards the front.

GPS 50°53'44.13"N 2°46'37.96"E

D3
WOOD AND PLANKS
Immense piles of wood and planks were stored.

E6
A-FRAMES
A-frames were prefabricated trench components that facilitated drainage. Duckboards were laid in the A-frames and the water ran off underneath.

← A-FRAMES IN YORKSHIRE TRENCH
A-frames found during excavations in the industrial zone at Boezinge.

↑ STORE
British troops stacking ammunition in a storage area. In the background there are large piles of wood.

E1 F1
WAGONS
A group of eight small wagons standing on a branch of a narrow-gauge railway.

E1/F1
CIRCULAR HORSE TRACKS
These large round tracks were made by horses going round in a circle.

A
Groenestraat ↘
C
D
E
F
Woesten 65 800 m ↗
G
H
1
↑ Elverdinge 3 km
2
3
4
5
6
100 m
cart tracks ↑
Canada Farm 87 870 m ↘

72 SCHOUTHOEK – AMMUNITION DUMP 4 JANUARY 1918

A British aerial photograph of 4 January 1918 shows the area behind the second German line at Moorslede. Just beyond range of the artillery was an ammunition dump. Stacks of projectiles lay spread out on both sides of the road to Moorslede. From the large depots in the hinterland, the munitions were distributed along a distribution chain to the lower echelons, until the projectiles ended up at the artillery batteries on the front. With some effort the Flandern III Stellung (Flanders III position) of the Germans can be made out. This German defence system was developed in depth; various positions followed one after the other, deep into the hinterland. This position consisted mainly of wide barbed-wire barriers with bunkers strategically placed behind.

GPS 50°52'40.22"N 3°06'17.48"E

→ **SCHOUTHOEK**

Belgian aerial photograph of the munitions store at Schouthoek during the final offensive. The photograph has been taken sideways from the cockpit and the photographer has caught part of the wing in the picture.

Papelandbeek

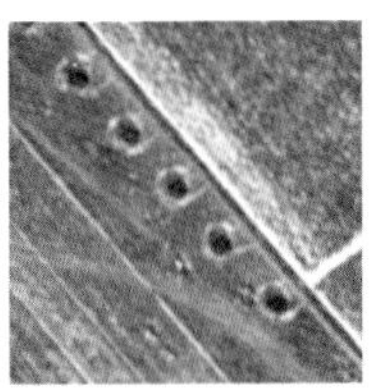

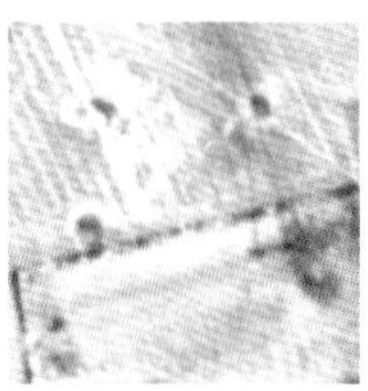
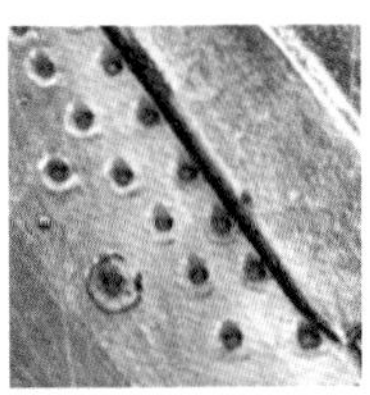
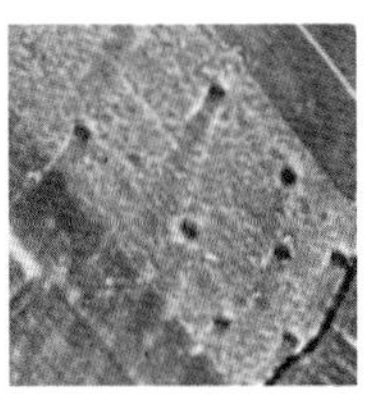

A3-G2-I2
B4-A6-H5
MUNITIONS

Between the farm in the foreground of the oblique aerial photograph and the main road between Roeselare and Menen (Menin) lay dozens of piles of munitions, often surrounded or covered by an earthen wall.

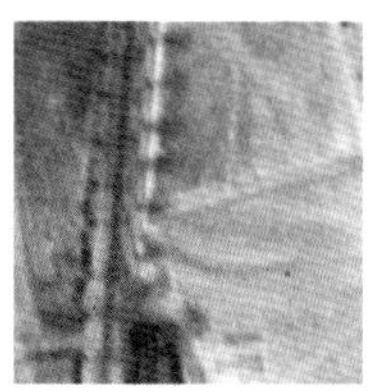

I2, I4, H1
BARBED WIRE

Here and there on the photograph can be seen indistinct barbed-wire fences of the Flandern III Stellung.

E6-F6
TRENCH

Shallow, zigzag communication trench.

Schouthoek
Beitem 1km
D
E
F
G
H
I
J
1
2
3
4
5
6
Groene Jagerstraat
100 m
Oude Heirweg
Provinciebaan

73

PROVEN – CCS 'MENDINGHEM'

29 JANUARY 1918

Casualties were taken via an evacuation route to field hospitals far behind the lines. One of the last links in the chain was the casualty clearing station (CCS), where the soldiers received more extensive care than they did at the medical aid posts at the front. From mid-1916 the 46th CCS was in action at Proven, nicknamed 'Mendinghem'. Later it was joined by the 64th and the 12th CCS in the run-up to the Third Battle of Ypres. The field hospital stood next to a large railway link built by German prisoners of war. The line carried the wounded to the CCS in ambulance trains. The American neurosurgeon Harvey Cushing carried out operations in Mendinghem and described the hospital in his diary: 'The place, as I have said somewhere before, is called "Mend-inghem". This was originally a joke and was to have been "End-inghem"; but this on second thought was changed as being too much even for the Tommy. The army has a professional name maker, I may add. Mendinghem is already on the printed maps, and there is in this district a "Bandagehem" and "Dosinghem" which I have not located as yet.'[31]

↑ **MENDINGHEM MILITARY CEMETERY, 1919**

Post-war photograph of the cemetery to the west of the field hospital.

↑ **DR CUSHING'S STAFF**

Staff of the American neurosurgeon Harvey Cushing in CCS Mendinghem No.46.

↓ **SKETCH OF CCS MENDINGHEM**

This sketch of the interior of Casualty Clearing Station No.64 Mendinghem was drawn by the British artist C.W. Allen (alias 'Ubique') on 17 May 1917.

D3

MENDINGHEM MILITARY CEMETERY

The many soldiers who died as a result of their wounds were buried in Mendinghem Military Cemetery, where 2,442 soldiers still lie.

E3

HOSPITAL TENTS

The Red Cross emblem on a central barracks showed that this was a hospital. CCS Mendinghem had standard accommodation for 200 beds, but the capacity could easily be increased to 1,200 or 1,300.

E2-E3

VEHICLE PARK

The wounded were brought in by ambulances, which parked in the hospital vehicle park. The hospital was also linked to the front by a railway.

British railway to Bergues (FR)
Bandagehem 1.4 km
Roesbrugge-Haringe 2.2 km
British railway
La Lovie 76 3.8 km
Proven 700 m
Dosinghem 3.5 km
100 m

74

ANTWERP - STABROEK FORT

31 JANUARY 1918

In 1914 the string of forts round Antwerp could not halt the German advance, and on 7 October the Réduit National (National Redoubt) at Antwerp was evacuated. In 1916 the German army decided to incorporate the old fortifications into a ring of positions around Antwerp, extending along the Dutch border to Turnhout (the so-called Antwerp–Turnhout position). The line continues the Holland position between the Zwin estuary and the River Scheldt. In the northern part of the Antwerp–Turnhout position the Brialmont forts were connected by a network of barbed-wire fences, trenches and some 500 bunkers.[32] The trenches have now disappeared, but remains of the impressive rows of bunkers still survive.

» SEE ALSO 105 HOLLANDSTELLUNG

↓ **STABROEK FORT**

German photograph of the fort at Stabroek near Antwerp, taken shortly after the fall of Antwerp in October 1914.

GPS 51°20'31.54"N 4°21'09.04"E

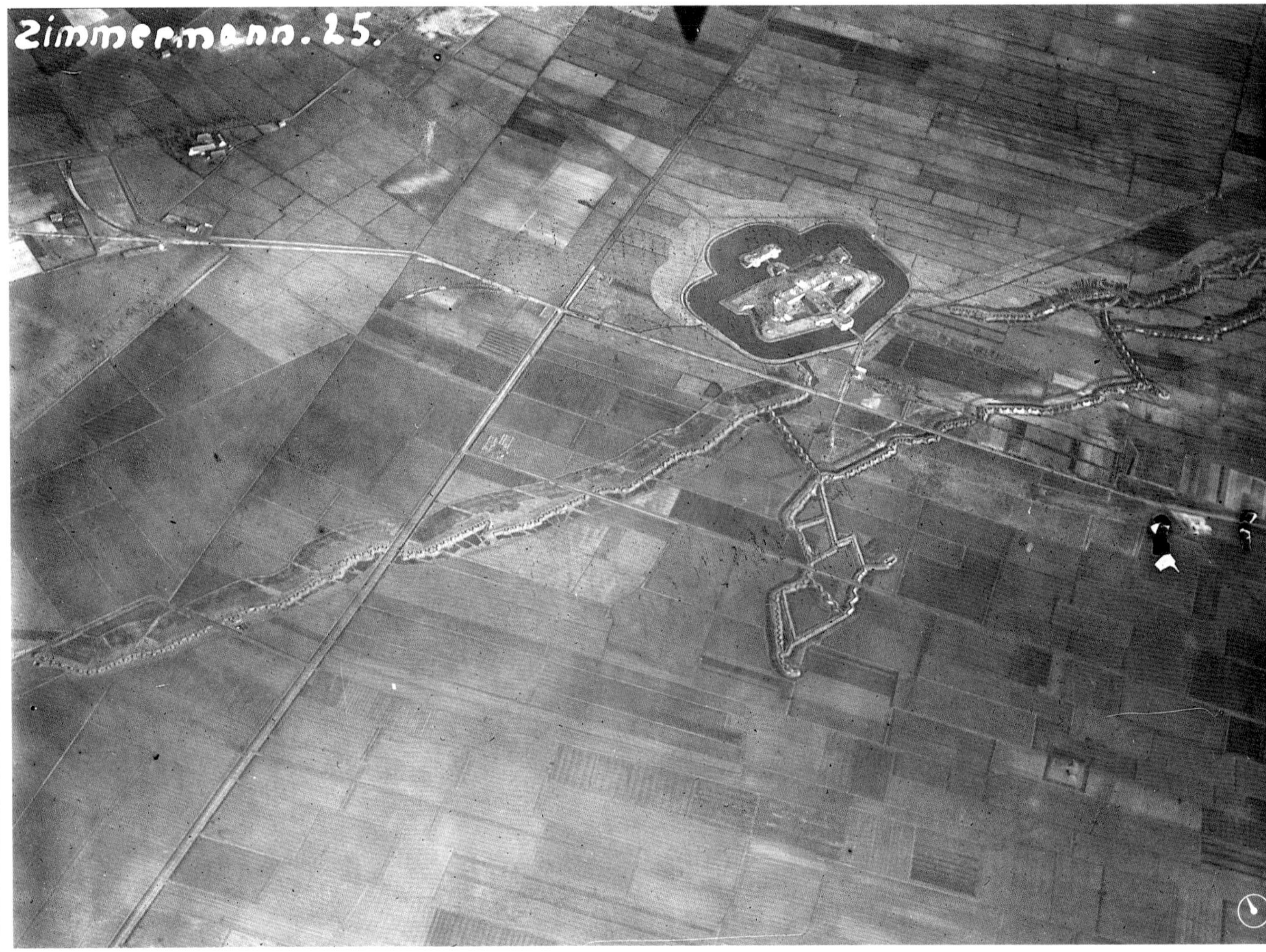

↑ **OBLIQUE VIEW OF STABROEK FORT**

General view of the German position between the Brialmont forts, north of Antwerp. In the centre is Stabroek Fort (built 1902), with extensive trenches on both sides and above-ground parapets.

H4

ELECTRIC FENCE

An electric fence ran along the whole length of the Belgian–Dutch border, to prevent citizens of the occupied area fleeing into the neutral Netherlands.

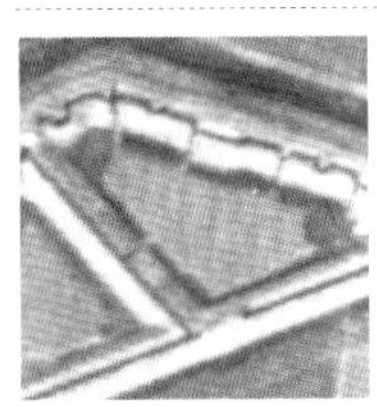

B2

BUNKER

A large number of bunkers were built into the massive parapets. They are as good as invisible from the air and only recognisable where there are breaks in the regular pattern of trenches.

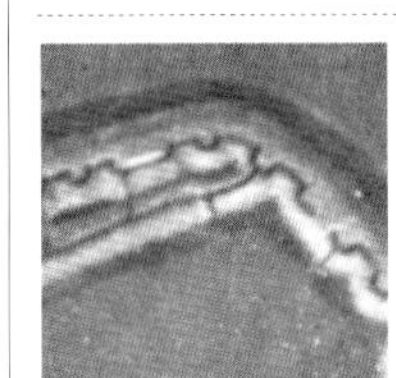

A2

BUNKER

Some bunkers are visible due to the light colour of the concrete. These have been built into the parapets, with only the back part, in the trench, exposed.

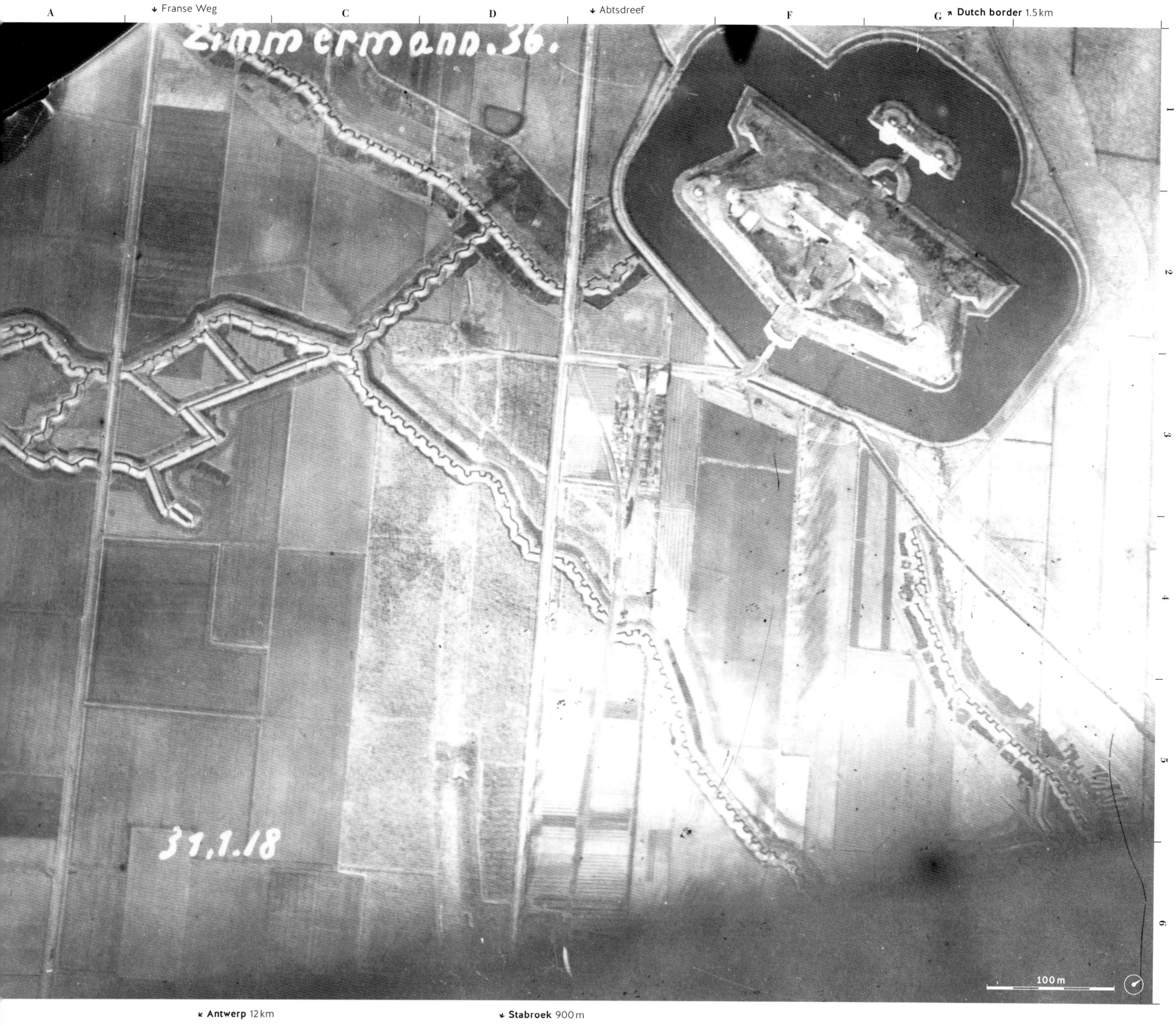
A
↓ Franse Weg
C
D
↓ Abtsdreef
F
G ↗ Dutch border 1.5 km
1
2
3
4
5
6
Zimmermann.36.
31.1.18
100 m
↙ Antwerp 12 km
↓ Stabroek 900 m

75
YPRES - VERLORENHOEK
17 FEBRUARY 1918

During the Third Battle of Ypres the Allies achieved some hard-won territorial gains and the ravages of war slowly encroached on Zonnebeke and Passchendaele. A British photograph taken on 17 February 1918 of Verlorenhoek, a hamlet east of Potijze, shows very clearly how very little remained of the earlier battlefield. What was the no-man's-land between the British and German fronts is still sharply defined. After the offensive, dozens of shelters were put up for soldiers to take cover in. Many aerial photographs were taken at a great altitude, so people are rarely visible, giving the misleading impression of 'empty' landscapes. This photograph is a rare exception. A column of troops moving to the front throws a distinct shadow in the bright winter sunlight. The troops are circumnavigating a large crater, created by an explosion in spring 1917.

↑ **VERLORENHOEK, 1915**

The front at Verlorenhoek on 21 September 1915. From the British line, approach trenches run to a ruin in no-man's-land named the 'Oder House'.

D1-D2-E2
ARTILLERY

Six pieces of artillery lined up on the former no-man's-land.

↓ **CONVOY IN WIELTJE**

A full cartload of troops passing through the ruins of Wieltje, just north of Verlorenhoek.

GPS 50°51'50.66"N 2°55'50.53"E

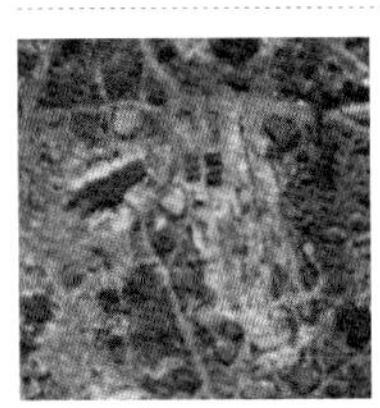

E5
AEROPLANE CEMETERY

A small cemetery in the middle of what was no-man's-land between the British and German lines. After the war it was greatly extended, and today 1,105 dead lie buried there.

F5-G5
CAMEROUN TRENCH

German front line until 31 July 1917. A bunker dug into the parapet of Cameroon Trench.

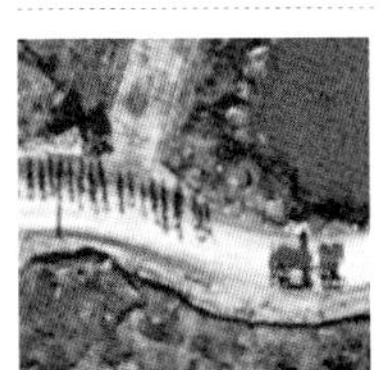

F4
CONVOY

Thirty or so soldiers moving along a road. Next to them is a horse and fully laden cart with driver atop. The road winds round a 20-metre-wide mine crater.

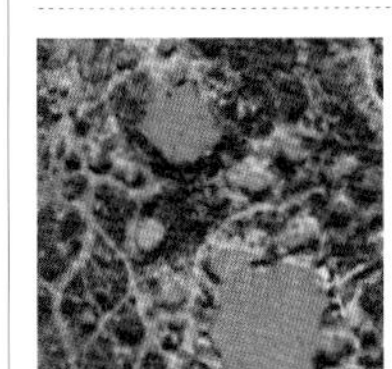

F5
MINE CRATERS

Five small mine craters (only four are visible here) in front of the German trenches. They are presumably the result of defensive mines detonated by the Germans to destroy putative British tunnels.

A
Wieltje 700 m
B
C
D
E
F
G
narrow-gauge railway
H
1
2
front 5 km
3
Zonnebeekseweg
5
6
100 m
Ypres 3 km
GB former front line
traces of troop movements
G former front line

76

POPERINGE – LA LOVIE AIRFIELD 18 FEBRUARY 1918

The area round Poperinge was dotted with Allied airfields. One of them was set up next to Château De Lovie, which for a long time served as British headquarters. It lies 3 kilometres north-west of 'Pops', as Poperinge was called by the Allies. A British reconnaissance plane of the 21st Squadron of the Royal Flying Corps photographed its own base station on 18 February 1918. The airfield had eight large hangars (each 25 x 20 m). Aircraft took off from an unpaved but well-drained runway, here recognisable by its fishbone pattern.

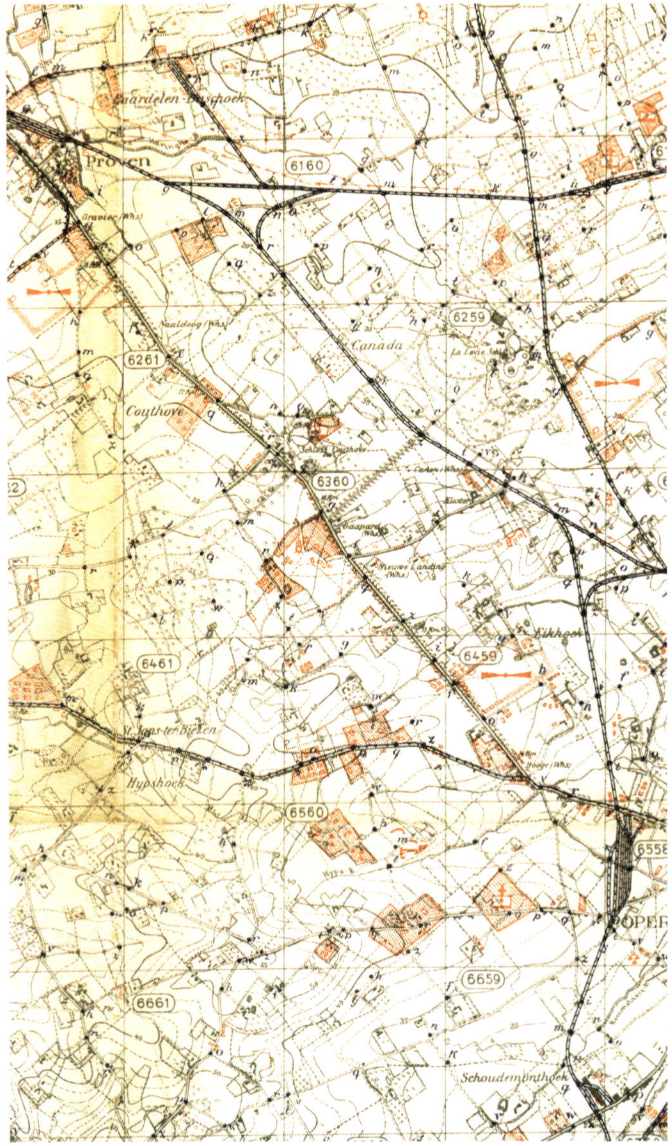

→ **GERMAN TRENCH MAP**

German trench map of the area between Proven and Poperinge, 15 April 1918. The airfields are indicated by a pictogram: a two-bladed propeller.

↓ **PANORAMA FROM CHÂTEAU DE LOVIE**

This photograph was taken on the roof of the château in 1917.

GPS 50°52'54.57"N 2°42'12.11"E

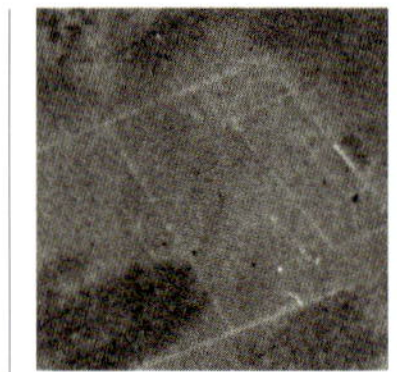

B3
FOOTBALL FIELD

Football field in the grounds of Château De Lovie. The château is at the top of the picture.

D6
AIRCRAFT

These are probably reconnaissance planes with which the 21st Squadron was equipped for photo-reconnaissance duties.

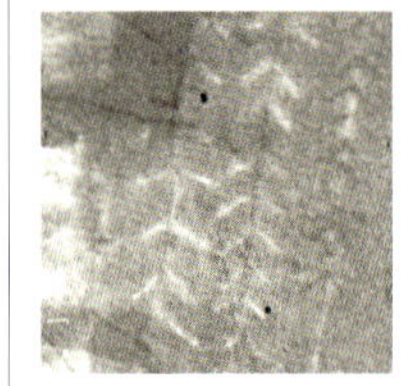

D4
FISHBONE PATTERN

The fishbone patterns on the airfield runway were part of the drainage system. The runway had to be as dry as possible to ensure that the aircraft did not get stuck in the soggy subsoil.

C4
AIRCRAFT HANGARS

On the west side of the airfield were eight large aircraft hangars and to the west of these a vehicle park.

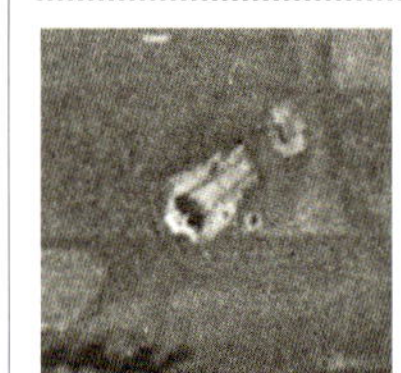

H5
SHOOTING STAND

Shooting stand with a stop butt at the far end, used for the adjustment of aircraft machine guns.

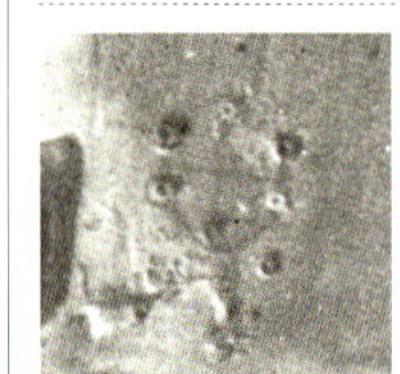

E6
AIR DEFENCE

Anti-aircraft batteries protected the airfield against air attacks. This battery next to the hangars had four guns.

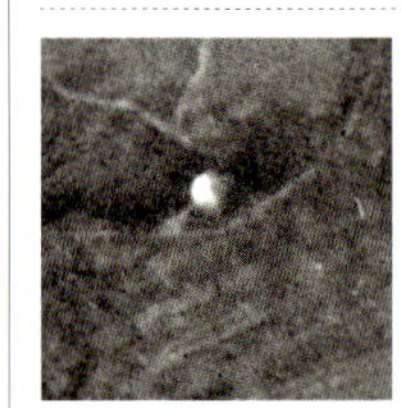

C3
DROGENBROODBERG

To the south of the football field is Drogenbrood Hill, on top of which, on an ornamental mound, stands the easily visible dome of a parkland folly.

Krombeekseweg
A
B
C
D
F
G
H
1
2
3
4
5
6
100 m
Poperinge 2.6 km

77 THE NORTHERN EDGE OF THE YPRES SALIENT 21 FEBRUARY 1918

Following the Battle of Pilkem (31 July – 2 August 1917) the northern edge of the Ypres Salient was no longer part of the theatre of war, but this did not mean there was any let-up in activity. On the contrary, immediately following the advance, the Royal Engineers and working parties from the infantry started constructing bridges over the canal. Ruined roads were made accessible again and railways were built to bring artillery, troops and supplies to the front. In the midst of this pockmarked landscape there arose military camps with small barracks and tents.

» **SEE ALSO** 25 50 NORTHERN EDGE YPRES SALIENT

B5
BOEZINGE RAILWAY STATION
Boezinge railway station reassumed its logistical function. Here large stocks of materials for transport are visible.

G3
HUDDLESTON CAMP
British barracks (in the form of Nissen huts) on both sides of a narrow-gauge railway. Huddleston Camp was situated between the former British and German lines.

↓ CANAL BRIDGE
British infantrymen erect a bridge over the canal at Boezinge, 5 August 1917.

GPS 50°53'22.68"N 2°52'36.90"E

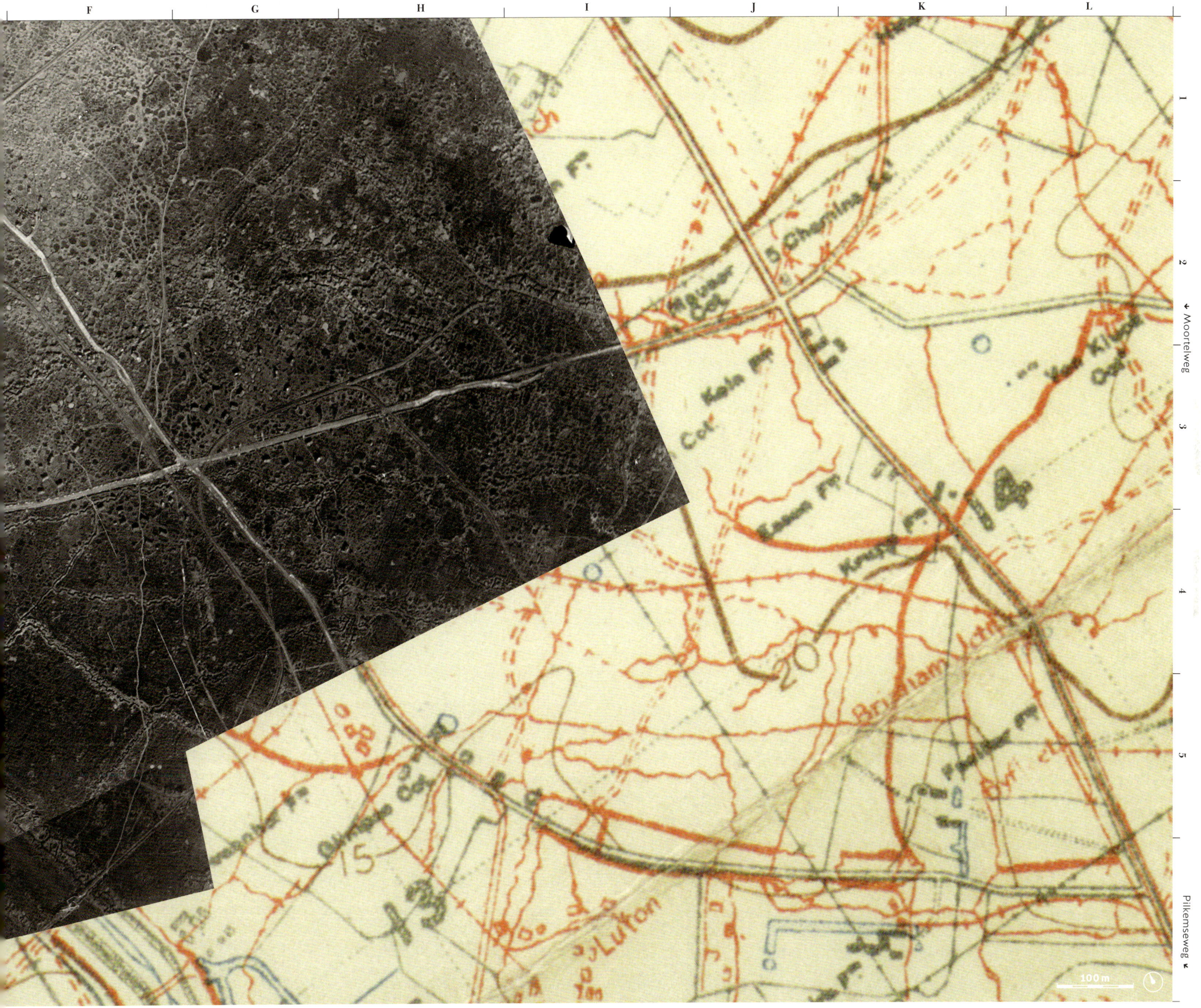

Ieperlee

Ypres 3.8 km

Lancashire Farm

78
ELVERDINGE – RAILWAY GUNS
21 FEBRUARY 1918

Heavy-calibre guns were often mounted on train wagons. Railway guns were easily transported and were consequently more difficult for enemy observers to spot. Once this kind of gun had discharged its deadly load, it could be moved to a safer location behind the front. Railway guns were often fired from the sidings of railway lines. Typically, the sidings were curved, so that by driving forwards or backwards the direction of fire could be changed.

» **SEE ALSO** 27 PREDIKBOOM

↓ **305-MM CANNON**

A French 305-mm cannon on a railway undercarriage, used on the Belgian front at Isenberge. This photograph was taken during shelling of the German long-range cannon at Predikboom.

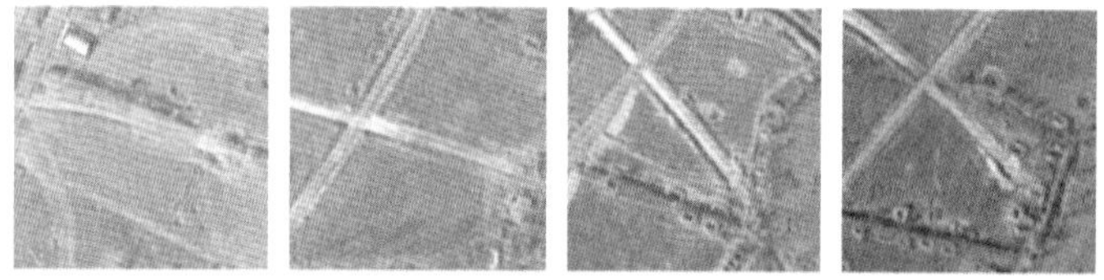

E1 / F3 / E3 / D4
RAILWAY GUNS
Deployment of a battery of four sets of railway guns

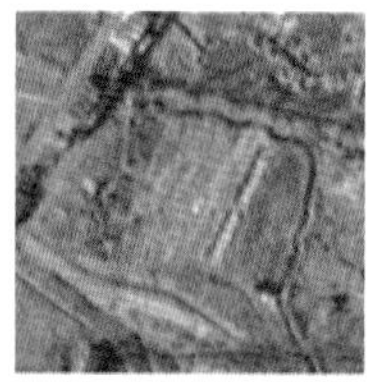

B4-B5
BLEUET FARM CEMETERY
This small British cemetery was originally a dressing station in the nearby farm.

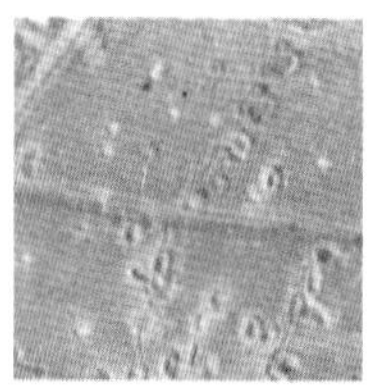

H2
FIELD GUNS
A row of positions for light field guns. In this photograph they are not in use.

↑ British railway

British railway ↑

GPS 50°53'26.21"N 2°49'48.30"E

Oude Boezingestraat
D
E
F
G
H
I
J
1
2
3
4
5
6
communication trench
100 m
Reningestraat
Boezinge 850 m

79 MOORSLEDE 8 MARCH 1918 & 28 SEPTEMBER 1918

Until the start of the Third Battle of Ypres, Moorslede was a dozen kilometres from the front. In May 1916 (photograph top right) the village had still hardly been touched by the war. During the battle, however, the front moved 2 kilometres away. Moorslede lies just to the east of Passchendaele and suffered heavy bombardments in autumn 1917 and spring 1918. Towards the end of the war, in September 1918, only a few walls remained standing in the village.

F1 and Fi

CONVENT AND MILITARY HOSPITAL

The only two buildings that are still standing in this oblique photograph are parts of the convent of Our Lady of Bunderen. A German military hospital was housed here until September 1917.

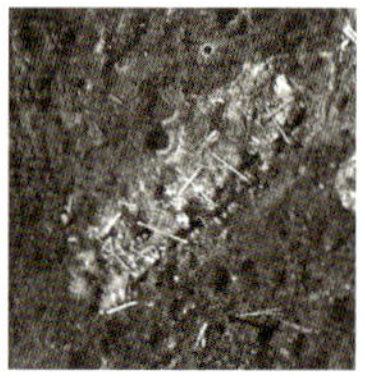

E1-F1 and Ei-Fi

UNFINISHED SCHOOL WING

The only sign of destruction visible in this photograph of May 1916 seems to be the long roofless building (E1-F1). In fact, this was the new wing of the convent school, which could not be finished because of the arrival of the war in 1914. By March 1918 there was nothing left of it (Ei-Fi).

GPS 50°53'27.58"N 3°03'47.28"E

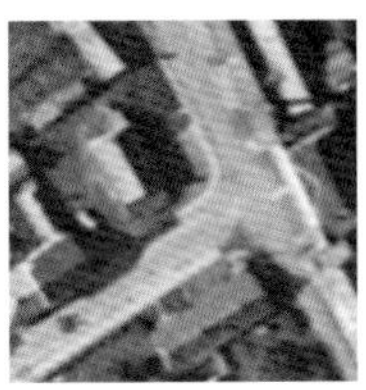

H1 and Hi
BARRACKS

September 1918: ruined houses have made way for a row of German barracks.

← OBLIQUE PHOTOGRAPHS OF MOORSLEDE

These photographs were taken with a 25-cm wide-angle lens at an altitude of barely 150 metres on 8 March 1918. At the time the German second line lay just east of the village. The German aerial photographic interpreters marked a number of surveyed points on the ground in red ink.

80

VLAMERTINGE – ABANDONED TENT CAMP 6 MARCH 1918

Soldiers sleeping in tents in military camps were vulnerable to artillery fire. One way of protecting themselves was to stack sandbags round the tents to form a barrier against shrapnel. When a camp was abandoned the sandbag walls remained. Months later they still marked the camp position. The impact of military structures on the landscape of the hinterland was considerable. In the winter of 1917–18 the landscape behind the Allied lines was still dotted with hundreds of abandoned camps.

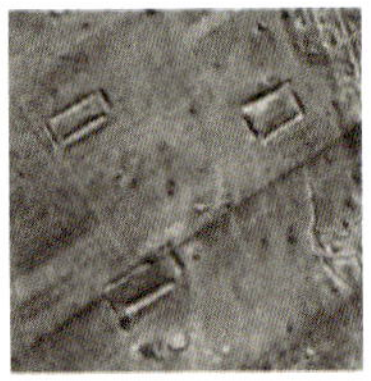

G3-H3

ABANDONED TENT CAMP

When the tents that had sandbags round them were taken away, the sandbags remained and thus marked where the abandoned, and often very temporary, camps had stood. To the west in this photograph is a camp that was still in use.

↑ CAMOUFLAGE

Camouflaged tent with sandbag protection.

SYMBOLS

- BARRACK, TENT
- TRENCH
- ABANDONED BARRACK AND TENT CAMP
- MOATED FARM
- RAILWAY
- VLAMERTINGHE MILITARY CEMETERY

GPS 50°51'35.24"N 2°49'06.52"E

Elverdinge 1.6 km ↗ Vlamertingsestraat ↓

↗ Kasteelweg ↑ Vlamertinge church

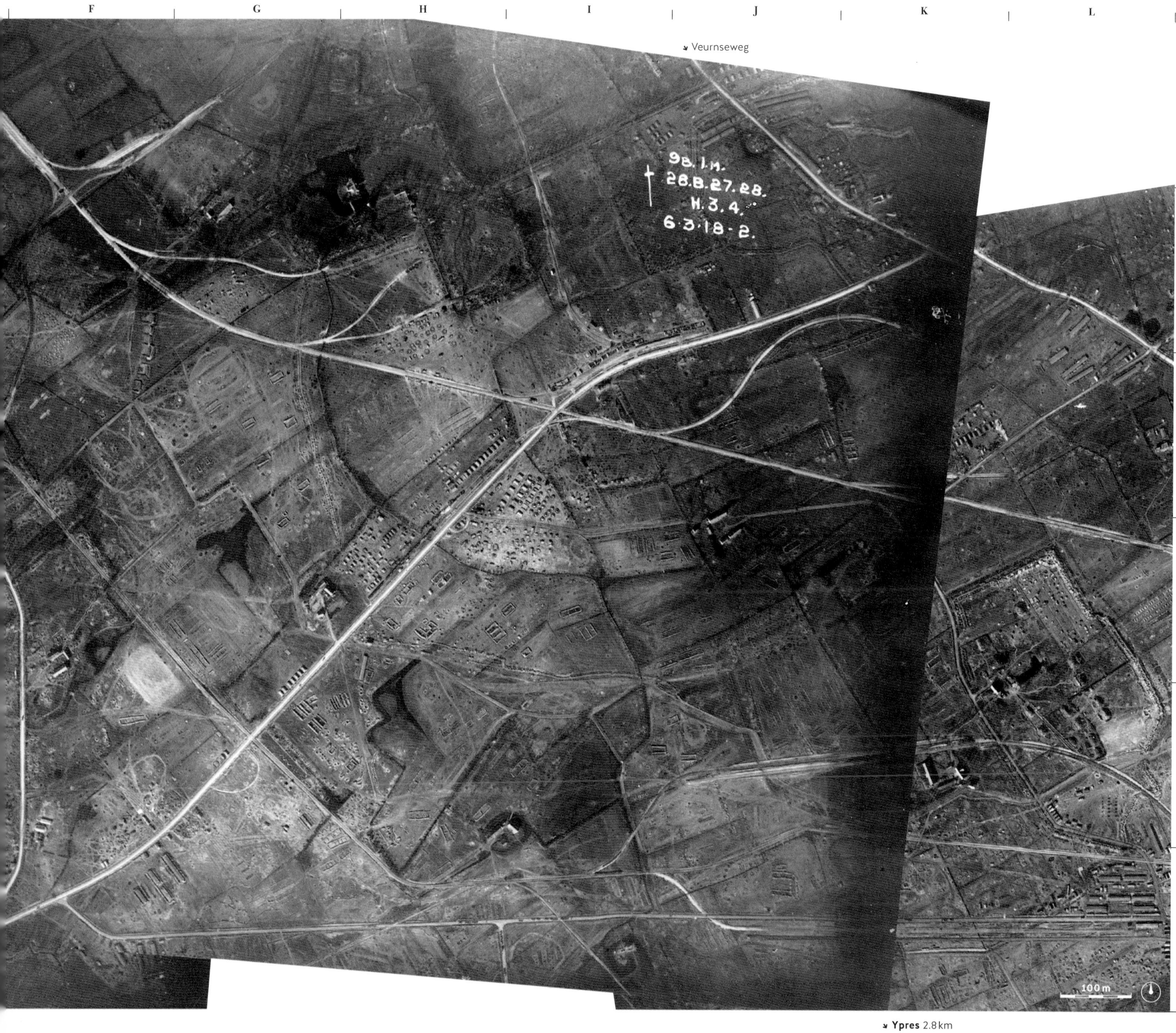

F
G
H
I
J
K
L
1
2
3
4
5
6
Veurnseweg
9B.1.M.
28.B.27.28.
H.3.4.
6.3.18-2.
100 m
Ypres 2.8 km

81
NIEUWPOORT – OPERATION STRANDFEST 9 MARCH 1918

The Yser front was a quiet sector, because the inundation left, quite literally, little room for any offensive action. One exception was Operation Strandfest in the summer of 1917. On 10 July units of the German Marine Corps attacked the Allied bridgehead on the east bank of the Yser at Nieuwpoort. This was a pre-emptive strike, as the Germans were expecting a British offensive from Nieuwpoort, and there were indeed plans for an Allied amphibian attack on the coastline targeting the U-boat bases in Zeebrugge and Ostend (Operation Hush).[33] To prevent this, and to exploit to the full the Yser estuary as a natural line of defence, the Germans decided to take the bridgehead. The attack was a great success. After this, both warring parties dug in, one on each side of the Yser estuary.

» SEE ALSO 57 LOMBARDSIJDE

↑ BARREL POST

The last man on the Western Front, a soldier of the 4th East Lancashire Regiment, watches the German front through his periscope over the parapet. In the background is the jetty.

↓ BRITISH MAP, 25 JULY 1917

The British trench map shows the situation following the successful German Strandfest offensive (German trenches are shown in red). After the offensive the Allied positions were reset and a new front line dug on the west bank of the Yser estuary at Nieuwpoort. The attack won the Germans an advance of 800 metres and deprived the British of a strategic bridgehead.

GPS 51°09'18.06"N 2°44'00.33"E

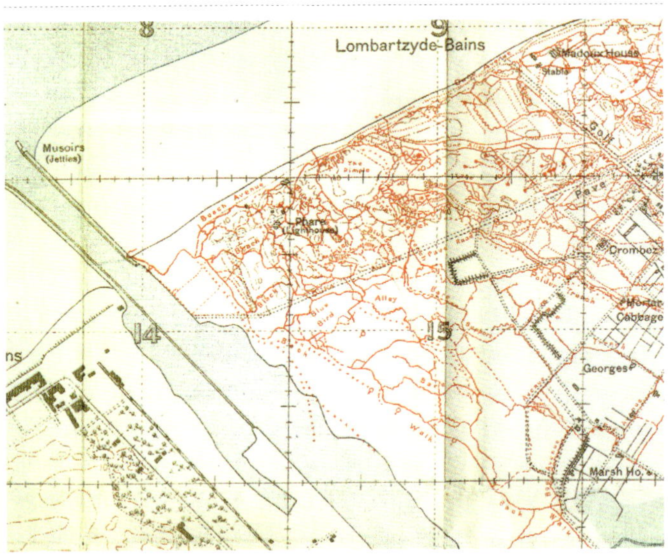

← JETTY

Oblique aerial photograph of the jetty at Nieuwpoort.

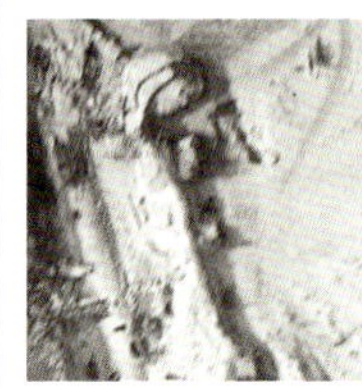

F3
THE BLACK WALK TRENCH

Between 10 July 1917 and the start of the liberation offensive in 1918 the front was situated on the Yser estuary to the north of Nieuwpoort. This was the most northerly post on the Western Front.

B1
FOOTPRINTS

Footprints of the Allied patrols run towards the jetty in the North Sea.

C2
THE BARREL POST

The very furthest post of the Western Front lies behind a wall of piled-up sandbags.

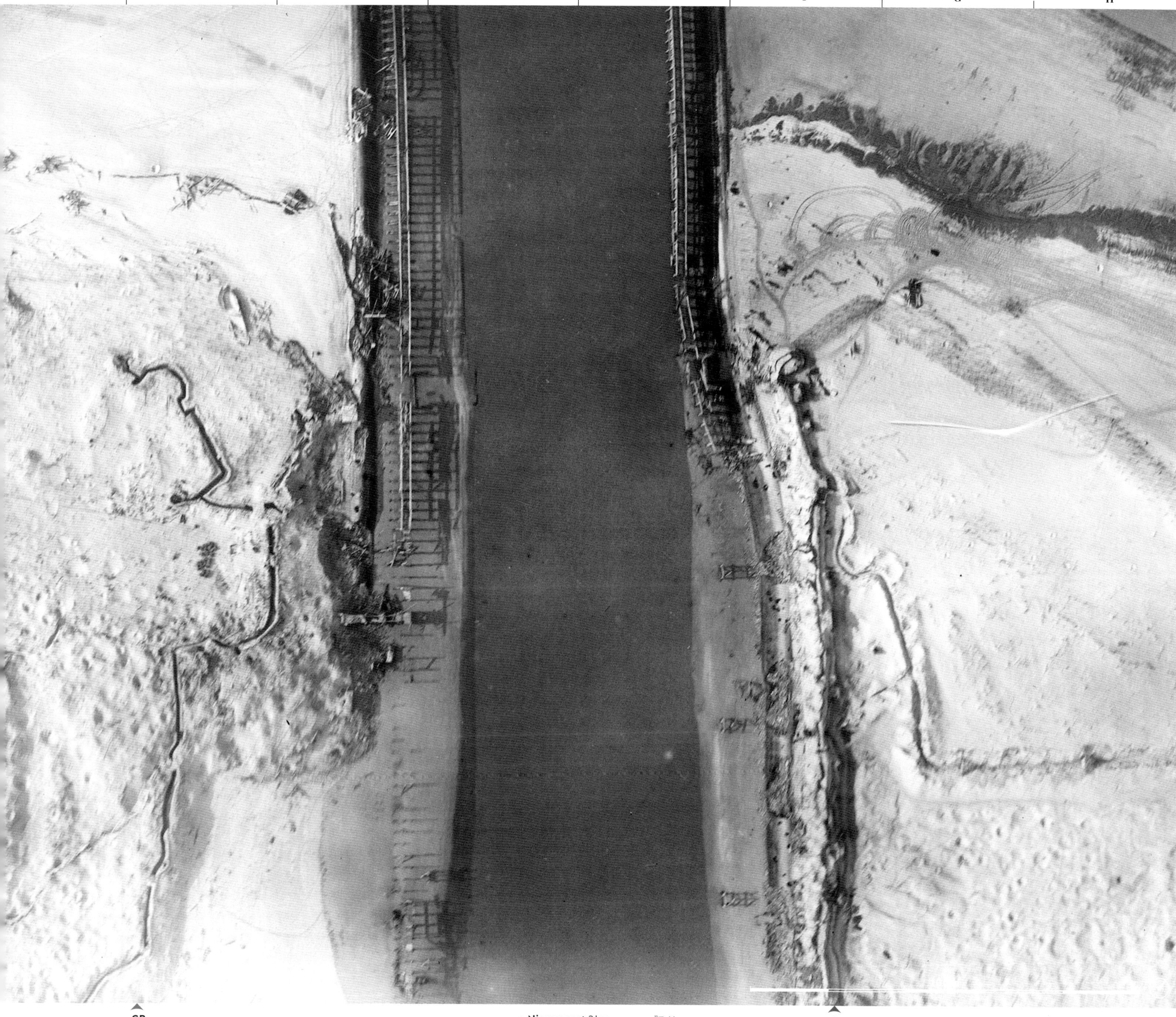

A
B
C
↓ shadows of the jetty
E
↓ jetty
F
G
H
1
coastline ↓ 2
start of the front 57 800 m ↗
4
5
6
GB
↓ Nieuwpoort 3km
Yser
G

82

ZONNEBEKE – POLYGON WOOD

12 MARCH 1918

During the Battle of Polygon Wood (26 September – 3 October 1917) the wood was recaptured from the Germans and both parties dug themselves in again. The nature of trench warfare did, however, change for good as a consequence of new tactics and the condition and lie of the battlefield. Instead of closely connected lines of trenches, the lines were now made up of reinforced posts with short sections of trench and, mainly, bunkers. Hardly anything recognisable remained of the once-extensive wood.

↓ **'BUTTE'**

A photograph of the notorious 'butte' (artificial mound) of Polygon Wood in 1921. By this time the memorial obelisk of the 5th Australian Division had already been erected on top of the mound.

↑ D3

POLYGON WOOD

The spiky stubs of the Polygon Wood with, at the back, the big 'bullet-stopper', or butte.

→ E2

TROOPS

Soldiers move up to the front along the 'Oversea Avenue', a communication trench just to the north of Polygon Wood.

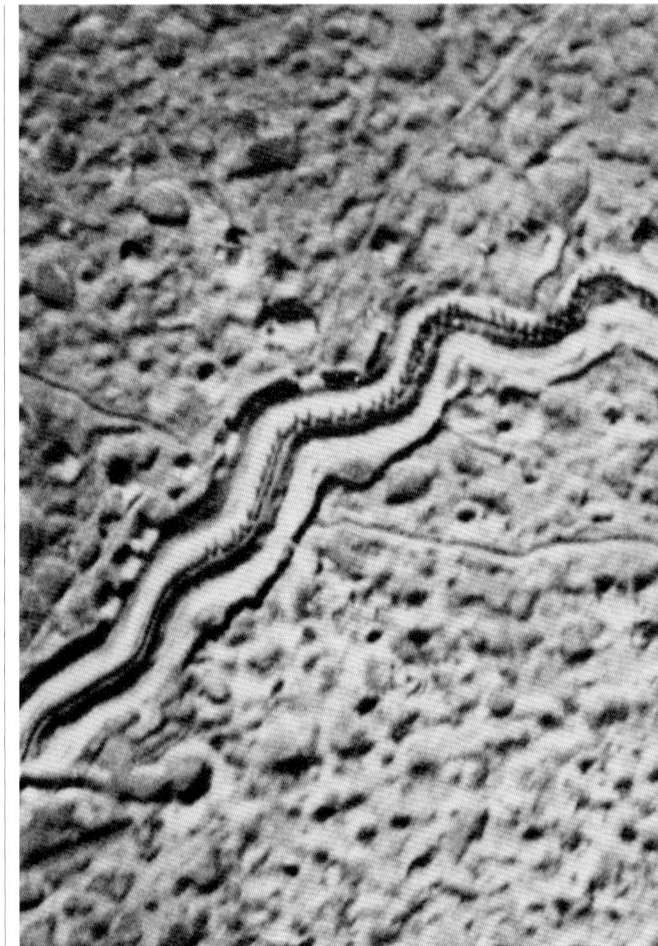

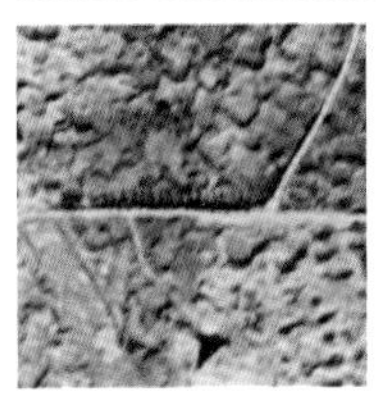

D3

TROOPS

Shadows of soldiers moving through the war landscape over a duckboard track.

B2

REDOUBT

A small pentagonal redoubt made it possible to offer resistance against attack from any direction.

B3

NARROW-GAUGE RAILWAY

A narrow-gauge railway partially buried in the ground. In the junction, which was also the end of the line, materials have been stored.

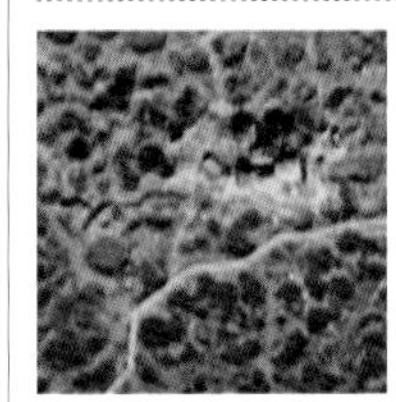

B5

BUNKERS

This small group of bunkers is accessed via wooden duckboards in the devastated war-torn landscape.

H4-H5

POLYGON 'BUTTE'

Before the war Polygon Wood had been used for military exercises and was equipped with an artificial mound, or 'butte', to stop the bullets from a firing range. During the war, shelters were dug into its sides.

D4

BUNKER

The distinct shadow of a 5-metre-wide bunker.

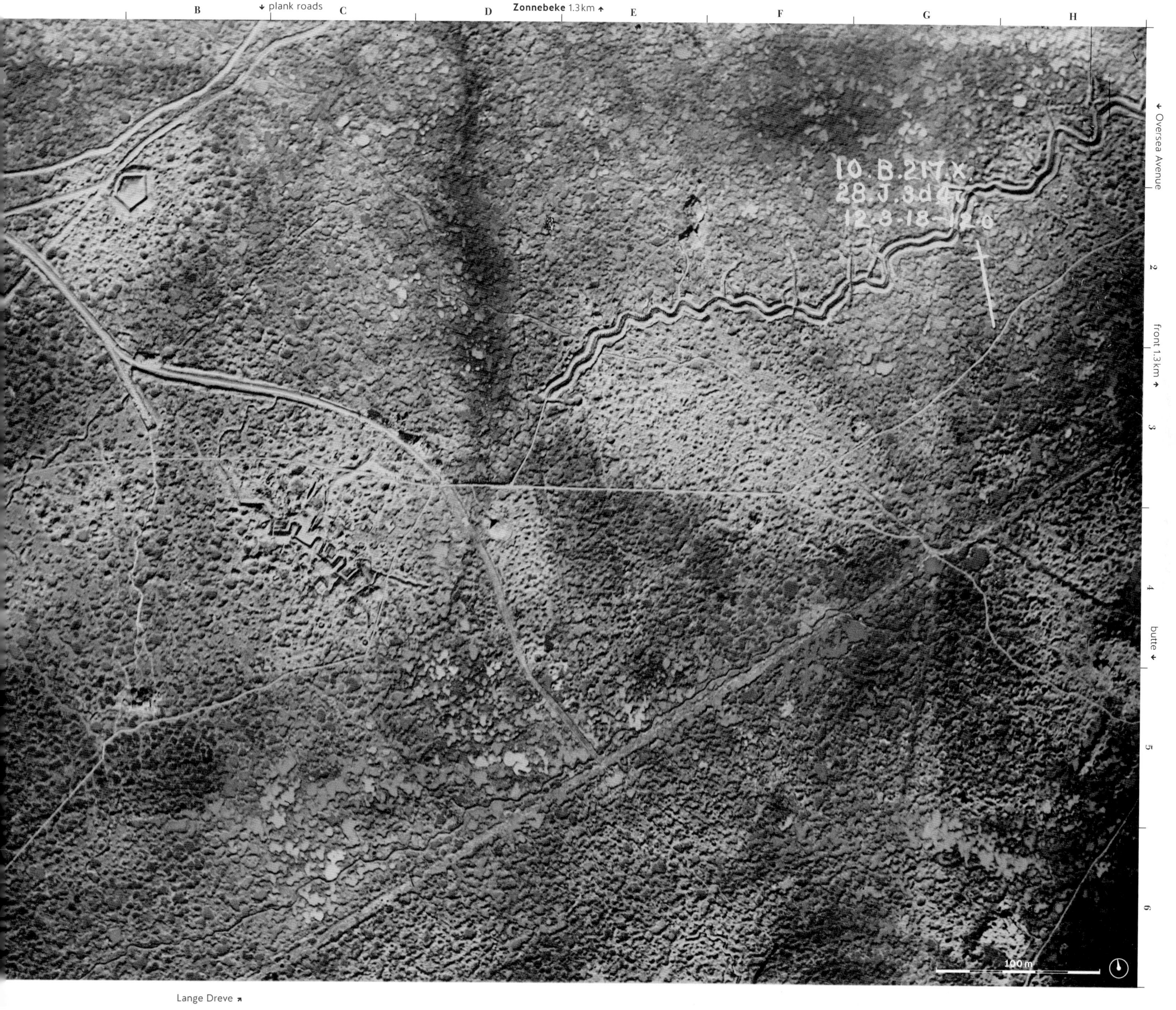

↓ plank roads
Zonnebeke 1.3km ↑
B
C
D
E
F
G
H
← Oversea Avenue
front 1.3km →
butte ←
2
3
4
5
6
10. B. 217. X
28. J. 3d 4c
12-8-18-12.0
100 m
Lange Dreve ↗

83
WARNETON - QUATRE-ROIS
12 MARCH 1918

During the Battle of Messines, which began on 7 June 1917, units of the II Anzac Corps reached their final destination on 14 June – the German Oosttaverne Line – and set up the first outposts on the ridge at Quatre-Rois, opposite the former German third line, the Warneton Line; there they dug in again.[34] Originally, the Warneton Line had been a rather weakly built trench behind a double barbed-wire fence. It was gradually strengthened and by September 1917 the line had already been joined by second trench, built parallel to it. Some months later it was further strengthened with an extra barbed-wire fence and a third trench 100 metres further forward. This region remained the front line until it was recaptured during the German Spring Offensive in 1918.

» **SEE ALSO** 52 WARNETON

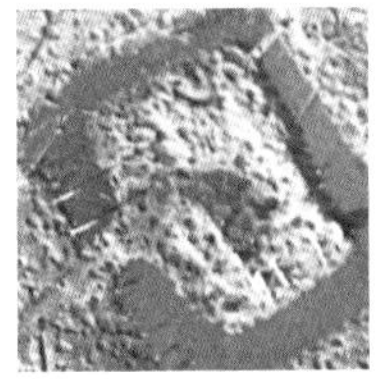

I1-I2
BURG HOF - KIWI FARM
The Germans called the farm 'Burg Hof' while Allied trench maps give it the name 'Kiwi Farm'.

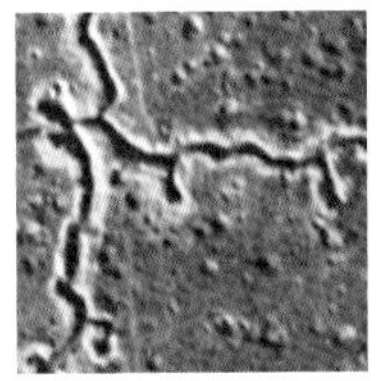

H5
SHELTERS
Visible here are the shelters and niches in the side of trenches in which mortars and machine guns could be set up.

↓ **WARNETON LINE**

German aerial photograph taken by Fliegerabteilung 6 on 3 September 1917. The line, which had originally consisted of only the front trench, had now been expanded into a double line.

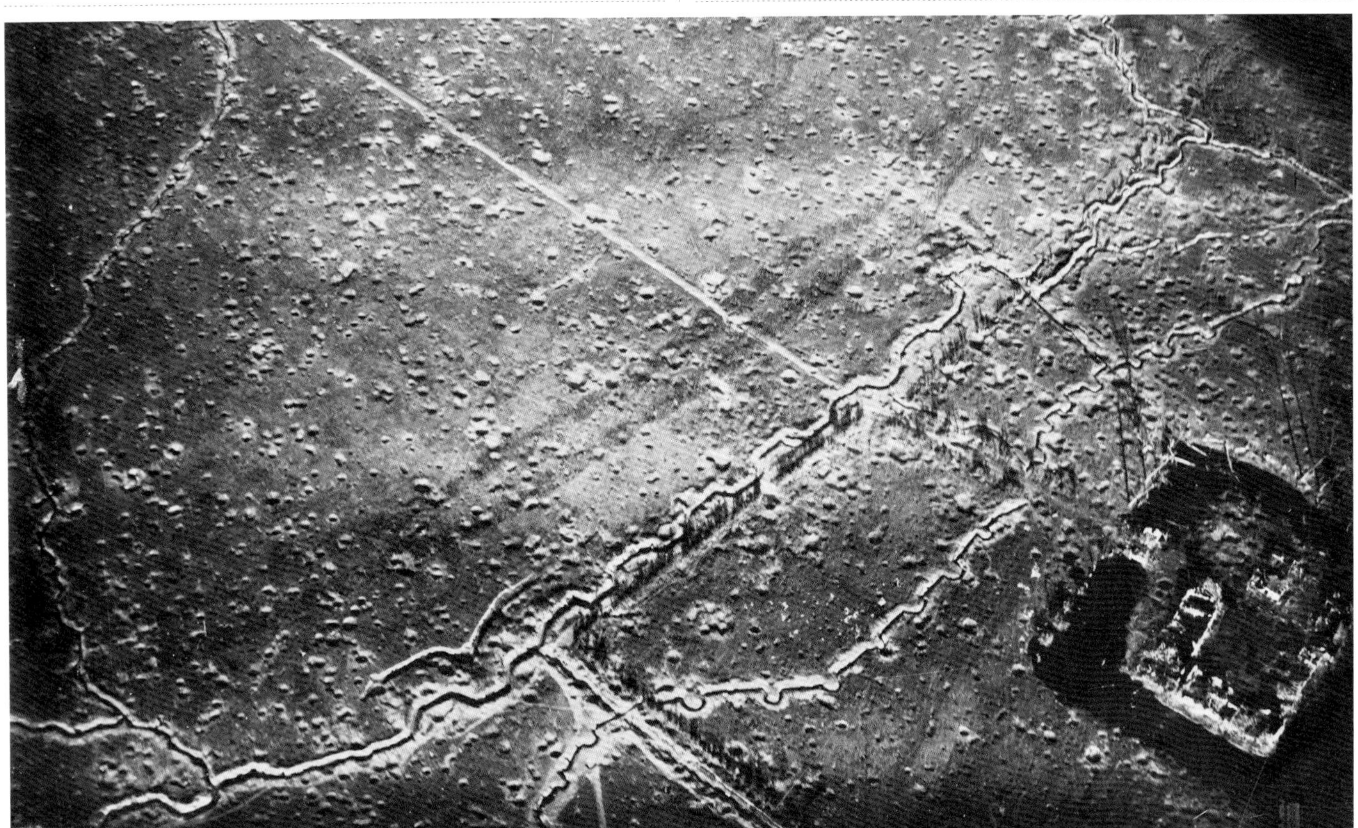

GPS 50°45'54.19"N 2°56'17.76"E

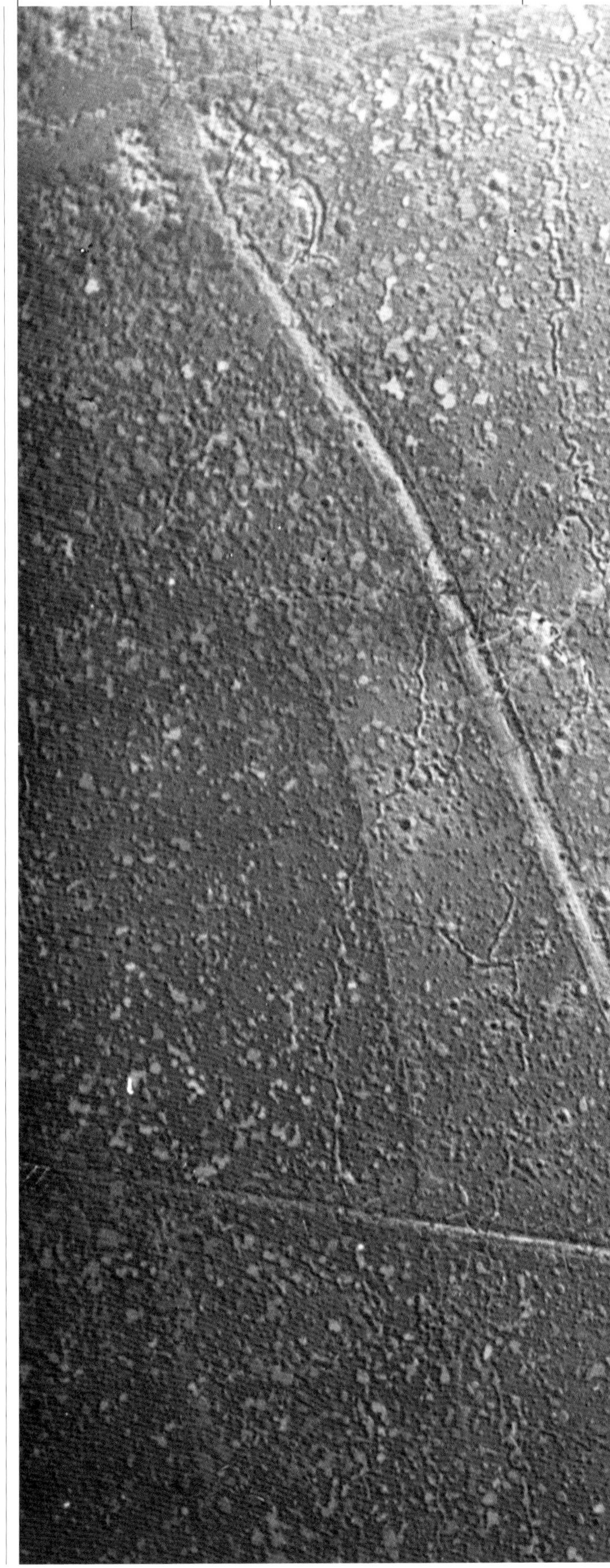

Warneton 52 900 m ↘

D
GB
E
F
G
G
H
I
J
1
2
3
4
5
6
100 m
Warneton 1.35 km
GB
G

84

ZILLEBEKE – CLAPHAM JUNCTION 12 MARCH 1918

A new weapon was deployed from 1916 to break the deadlock created by trench warfare: the tank. The shape and size of tanks meant they could be driven over trenches and big craters and right through barbed-wire fences. However, the bombardments and the persistent rain had turned the battlefields into mudbaths and tanks proved much too heavy for the terrain. In various places they got bogged down and this produced so-called 'tank cemeteries'. One of these was to the east of Hooge at Clapham Junction and Stirling Castle. Numerous tanks were stranded at the Battle of Menin Road. This aerial photograph of 12 March 1918 shows at least 11 tank 'carcases'. At the time the front lay several kilometres to the east.

→ DESOLATE LANDSCAPE

Crater landscape with two wrecked tanks at Clapham Junction (Zillebeke). This photograph was taken from the Menin Road looking towards Sanctuary Wood in September 1917.

GPS 50°50'37.44"N 2°57'40.36"E

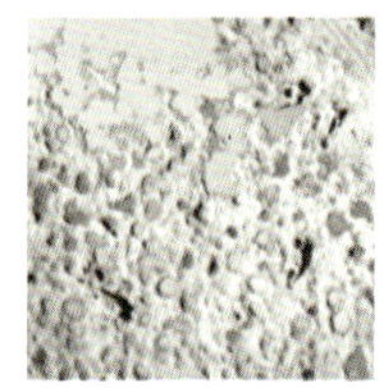

E5

GROUP OF TANKS

During the Battle of Menin Road in September 1917 a group of tanks was stranded just south of the Menin Road.

B2

BRITISH ARTILLERY POSITION

In March 1918 the Menin Road area lay a couple of kilometres behind the front and artillery support was offered from firing positions.

SYMBOLS

TRENCH, BUNKER, ARTILLERY

STUCK TANK

ROAD

← TANK

Australian troops in the shade of a tank stuck on a tree-stump, Clapham Junction, 27 September 1917.

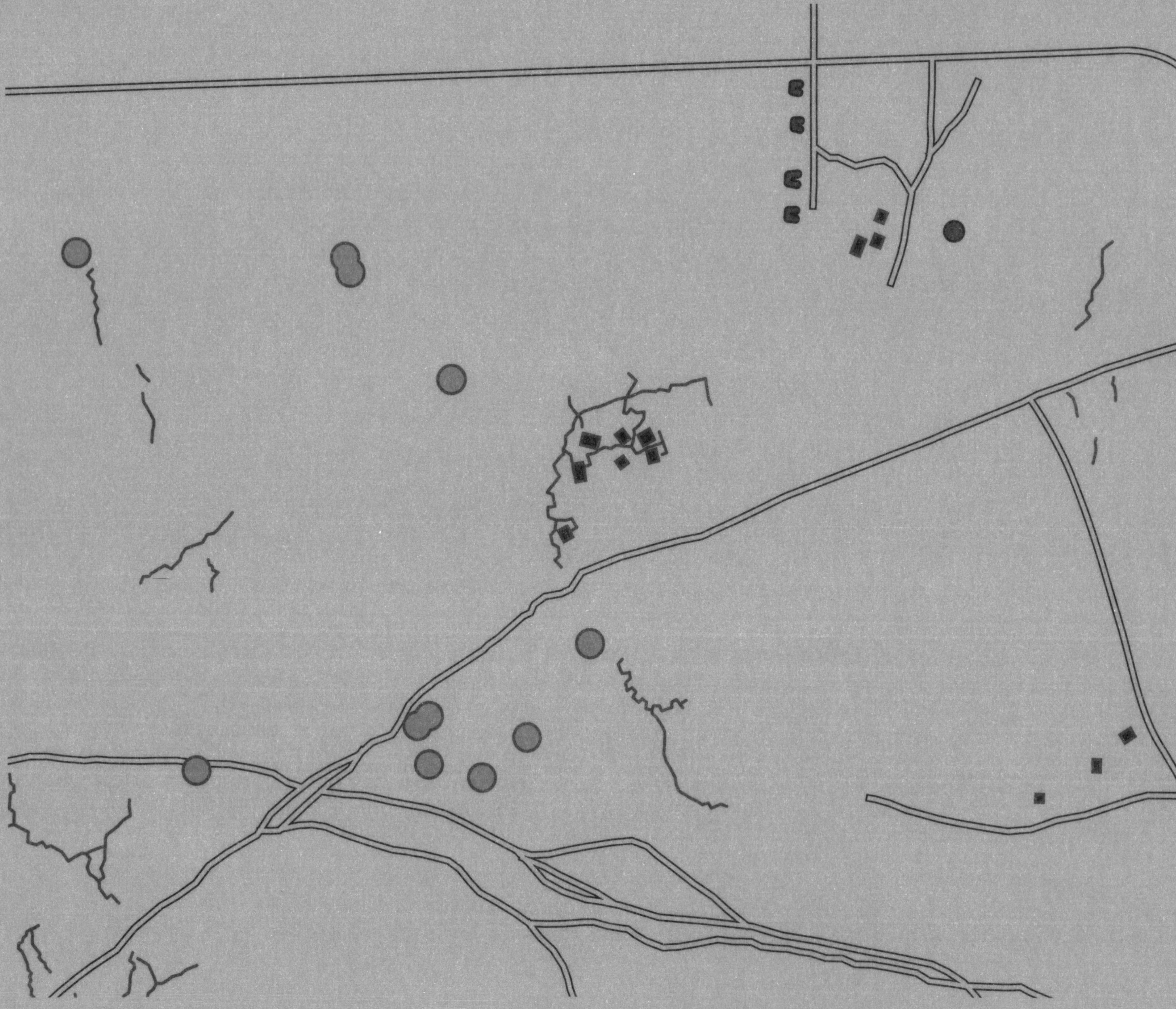

A
↖ Bellewaarde lake 250 m
B
C
D
E
F
↑ 600 m 30 85 Westhoek
G
H
10.B.968
28.J.13 a.b
27.5.18-4.45
F-8½"
← Kasteeldreef
2
3
4
5
→ front 2.3 km
6
Menin Road ↖

85 WESTHOEK 12 MARCH 1918

A British aerial photograph of 12 March 1918 shows how gunners were again making intensive use of the ridge at Westhoek. The light area in the centre shows the top of the ridge. The lower areas are much wetter and therefore much darker. At Westhoek, dozens of Allied artillery positions were constructed, this time on the western side of the hilltop so as not to be visible to German observers further up on the front. In this bleak landscape, guns were very difficult to camouflage and hide from aerial observation. To make the movements of artillery and troops over the muddy terrain possible, new roads were laid down with planks on the top.

» SEE ALSO (30) WESTHOEK 1916

D3
ARTILLERY
Two firing positions under an earthen embankment.

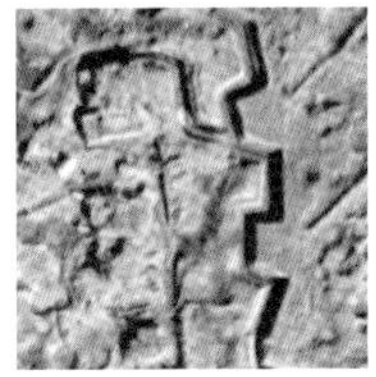

H2
FIGHTING POSITION
A fighting position extended over a group of captured German shelters, the remains of a German firing position of 1916.

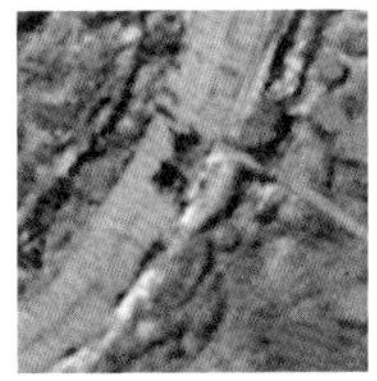

C3
HORSE AND CART
A horse pulls a cart along a wooden plank road towards Ypres.

↓ **WESTHOEK RIDGE, 1917**
Troops on their way to the front along a plank road, Westhoek Ridge, 1917.

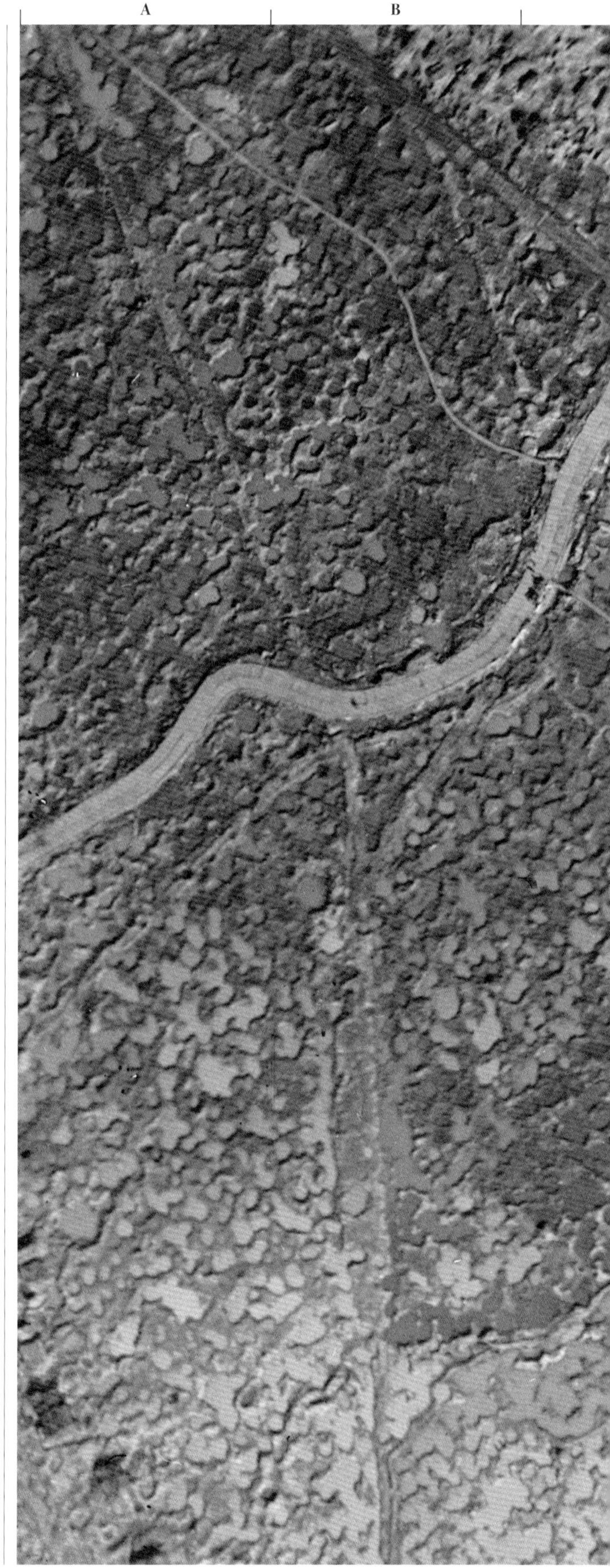

plank road ↑

GPS 50°51'06.19"N 2°57'43.96"E

Clapham Junction 84 500 m ↓

86

KNOKKE - WILHELM II BATTERY

13 MARCH 1918

Between Knokke-Heist and Duinbergen was the Wilhelm II Battery, named after the German Kaiser. It formed part of the German coastal defences and consisted of four 30.5-cm guns on open concrete circular emplacements (Kesselbettungen).[35] Next to each gun stood ammunition bunkers. The complex was dotted with narrow-gauge railway tracks for the transport of ammunition. The belt of dunes around the battery was protected by extensive barbed-wire fences (B6-C6), and contained bunkers, trenches and an exercise course with artificial bomb craters (E4-E5) and even a 200-metre-long shooting-range (D6), very near to the still-standing watertower (F6).

→ **WILHELM II BATTERY CANNON**

One of the four cannon of the Wilhelm II Battery. It had armour plating and could be turned on a circular platform. To the left of the cannon is a front view of one of the ammunition storage bunkers covered with earth.

F1

30.5-CM GUN

One of the four cannon of the Wilhelm II Battery in its open emplacement.

F1

AMMUNITION BUNKERS

Ammunition bunkers between the guns.

D6

FIRING RANGE

A 200-metre-long firing-range with, at the back, a mound to catch the bullets.

GPS 51°20'38.19"N 3°16'48.36"E

↑ **AMMUNITION BUNKERS**

Each gun had its own storage bunker with a narrow-gauge railway running to it. Another narrow-gauge railway connected the bunkers and ran straight through the concrete structures.

↑ **TROOP BUNKER**

The back of one of the troop bunkers of the Wilhelm II Battery in Knokke.

↓ North Sea
B
↓ dunes
C
D
↑ Knokke 400 m
E
F
G
Knokkestraat ↓
H
1
2
3
4
5
6
100 m
barbed wire ↑
'The Mole' Zeebrugge 107 108 5 km ↓
Heist 2 km ↓

87

ELVERDINGE – CANADA FARM

16 MARCH 1918

The war machine at the front required an enormous support infrastructure. In the areas behind the front line the soldiers could rest and relax. Dressing stations were also set up just behind the front for the reception and treatment of wounded soldiers. One of these was housed in Canada Farm and was in use during the Third Battle of Ypres. Soldiers who did not pull through were buried in the nearby Canada Farm British Cemetery.

→ **CANADA FARM**

Sketch of Canada Farm, the temporary 'home' of the British artist C.W. Allen (alias 'Ubique'), 5 July 1917.

↓ D3

DESERTED FARM

Sketch of the Deserted Farm, to the south-east of Canada Farm, 24 June 1917.

F3

VEHICLE PARK

Here some 15 parked vehicles are visible.

B2

CANADA FARM BRITISH CEMETERY

In this cemetery lay 907 soldiers for whom medical treatment in Canada Farm had come too late. Most of them were victims of the Third Battle of Ypres.

C3

CANADA FARM HOSPITAL

A dressing station in the buildings of Canada Farm and the surrounding barracks. The Red Cross emblem has been painted on the roof to ensure that the site is not bombarded.

E1-D2-E2

CARDOEN CAMP

Some of the smaller barracks (9 x 5 m) at Cardoen Camp were used as accommodation for the troops. The larger sheds to the east of Elzendammestraat were presumably used for some other purpose (perhaps as workshops).

E5

SIRIUS HOUSE CAMP

Sometimes military camps were abandoned. Remains of embankments around barracks and tents endured and could sometimes still be seen months later on aerial photographs.

B1-B2

FOOTBALL PITCH

Space was made for relaxation. In between the battles a football pitch has been marked out; this stayed in use for months.

← **RELAXATION**

Soldiers playing football behind the front.

A
650 m 63 Woesten
B
C
D
Elverdinge 1.6 km
F
G
H
98.295 X.
28.A.17.18.23.24.
16.3.18.2.
1
2
4
5
6
Gasthuisstraat
military railway
100 m
military railway
Steentjesmolenstraat

88
CHÂTEAU COUTHOF
12 MARCH 1918

A British aerial photograph shows an example of activities behind the front, with military camps and hospitals stretching far into the hinterland. Near Zoom Farm (F5) and to the south of Château Couthof was a military camp with extensive training facilities. In March 1916 sappers of the 177th Tunnelling Company began digging an experimental mine near their quarters for training purposes. On 20 June 1916 this was detonated and a training area was subsequently built around the crater to prepare soldiers for the mine war in the Ypres Salient. Behind this, in the château gardens, stood the wooden barracks of the Elisabeth Hospital for Belgian citizens and soldiers. This mixed hospital had been evacuated from Poperinge in August 1915 and was established in the gardens in June 1916.

F6
EXPERIMENTAL MINE PROFILE

The 177th Tunnelling Company dug out a gallery in the clay soil and filled it with 700 kilograms of ammonal. The explosion of the experimental mine on 20 June 1916 created a 25-metre-wide crater.

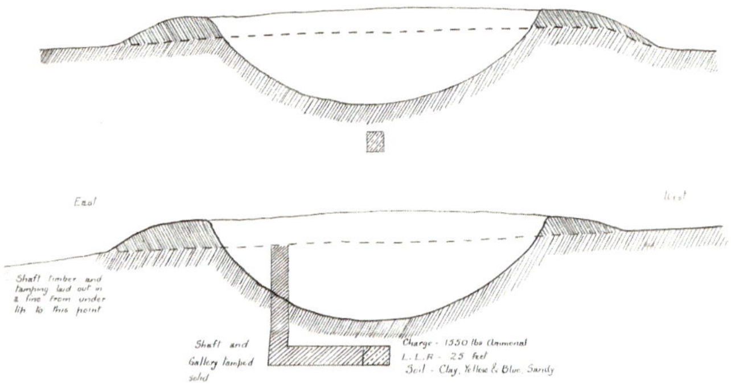

GPS 50°52'09.09"N 2°40'24.88"E

SYMBOLS

- TRENCH, BARRACK, TENT
- ABANDONED TENT CAMP
- OBSTACLE COURSE
- ELISABETH HOSPITAL
- VEHICLE PARK
- EXERCISE CRATER

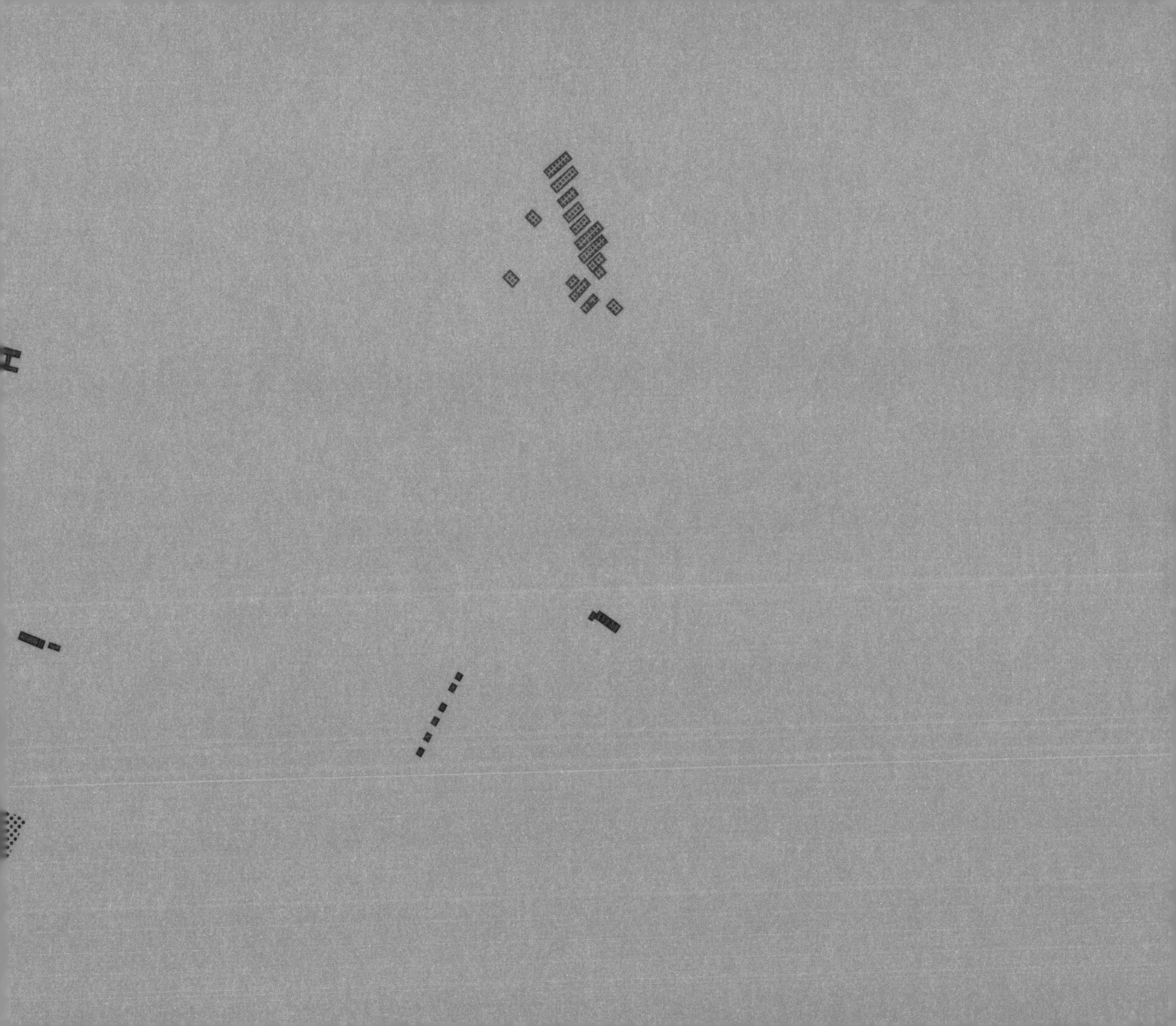

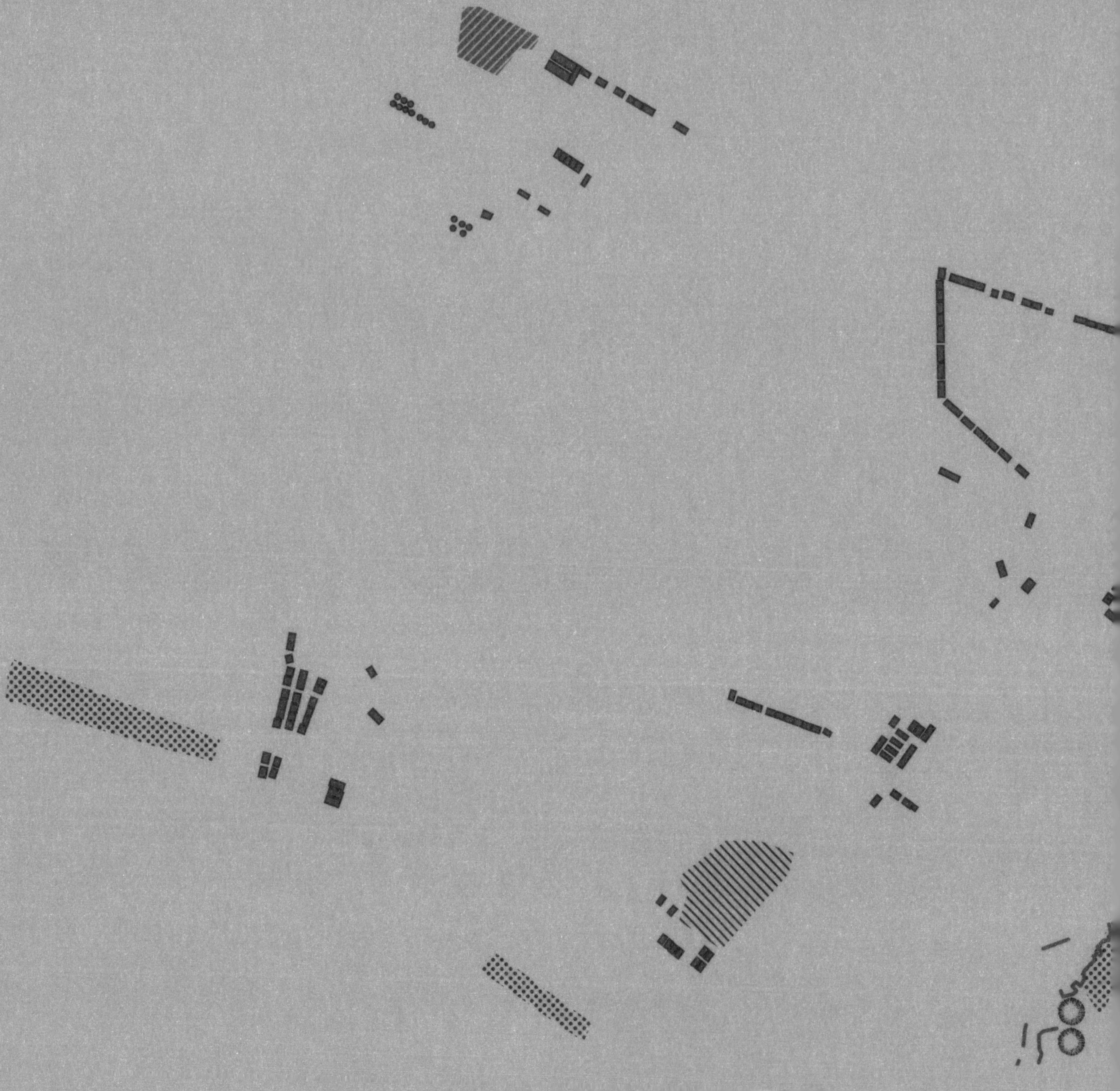

F
Loviestraat
G
H
I
Provenseweg
J
K
L
1
2
3
4
5
6
100 m

89 DIKSMUIDE – RAID
18 MARCH 1918

A Belgian aerial photograph of 18 March 1918 captured a moment in time after the German raid at Diksmuide by the 2nd Bavarian Reserve Infantry Regiment. The Belgian army had occupied the western bank of the Yser while the German positions were sited on the opposite bank. Since it was impossible to wade through the 25-metre-wide river, the Germans stormed the Belgians using flat-bottomed boats, rafts and gangplanks on wooden floats. The attackers destroyed a number of positions in the Casbah Trench (D1-D6) and took prisoners of war.[36] This aerial photograph was taken at 10 a.m. by which time the attack had been wrapped up and the Germans had returned in their sloops to the eastern bank near the Schünemann Stellung (G3). In the photograph their helmets glisten in the sun.

H6
GERMAN BUNKER

Reinforced German bunker on the peninsula between the Yser and the Handzamevaart. The footbridge appears to be full of German troops.

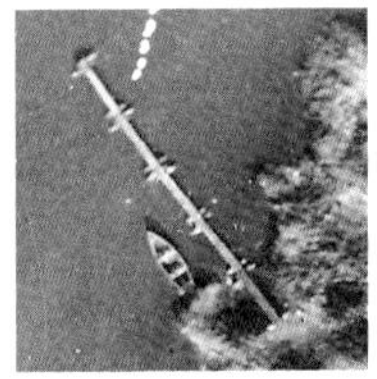

E6
FOOTBRIDGE

The attackers crossed the Yser with the help of a floating footbridge. They managed the last few metres by wading through the water.

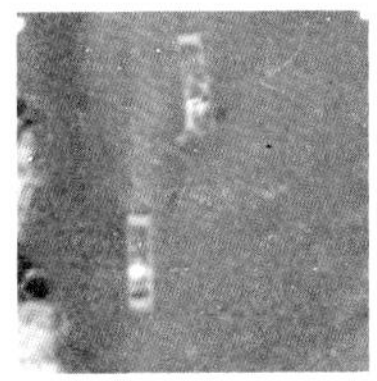

E3
SUNKEN CRAFT

During the attack some craft were sunk by mortar grenades. Their shapes are visible in the shallow waters of the Yser.

→ **CASBAH TRENCH**

Belgian soldiers at a first-aid station in the Casbah Trench.

↓ **CONFLUENCE**

The confluence of the Yser and the Handzamevaart seen from the Casbah Trench. This was where the German makeshift 'fleet' advanced on the Belgian positions.

GPS 51°02'08.86"N 2°51'19.87"E

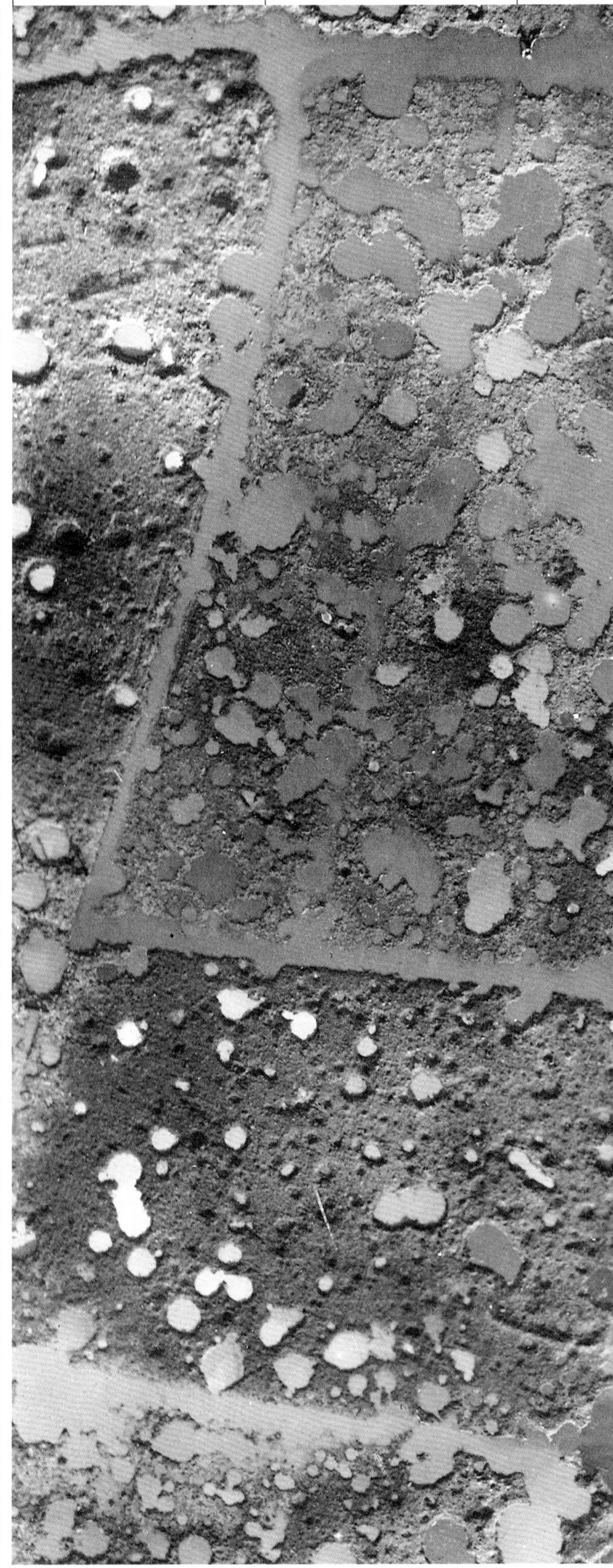

D B E Yser G F G H I J

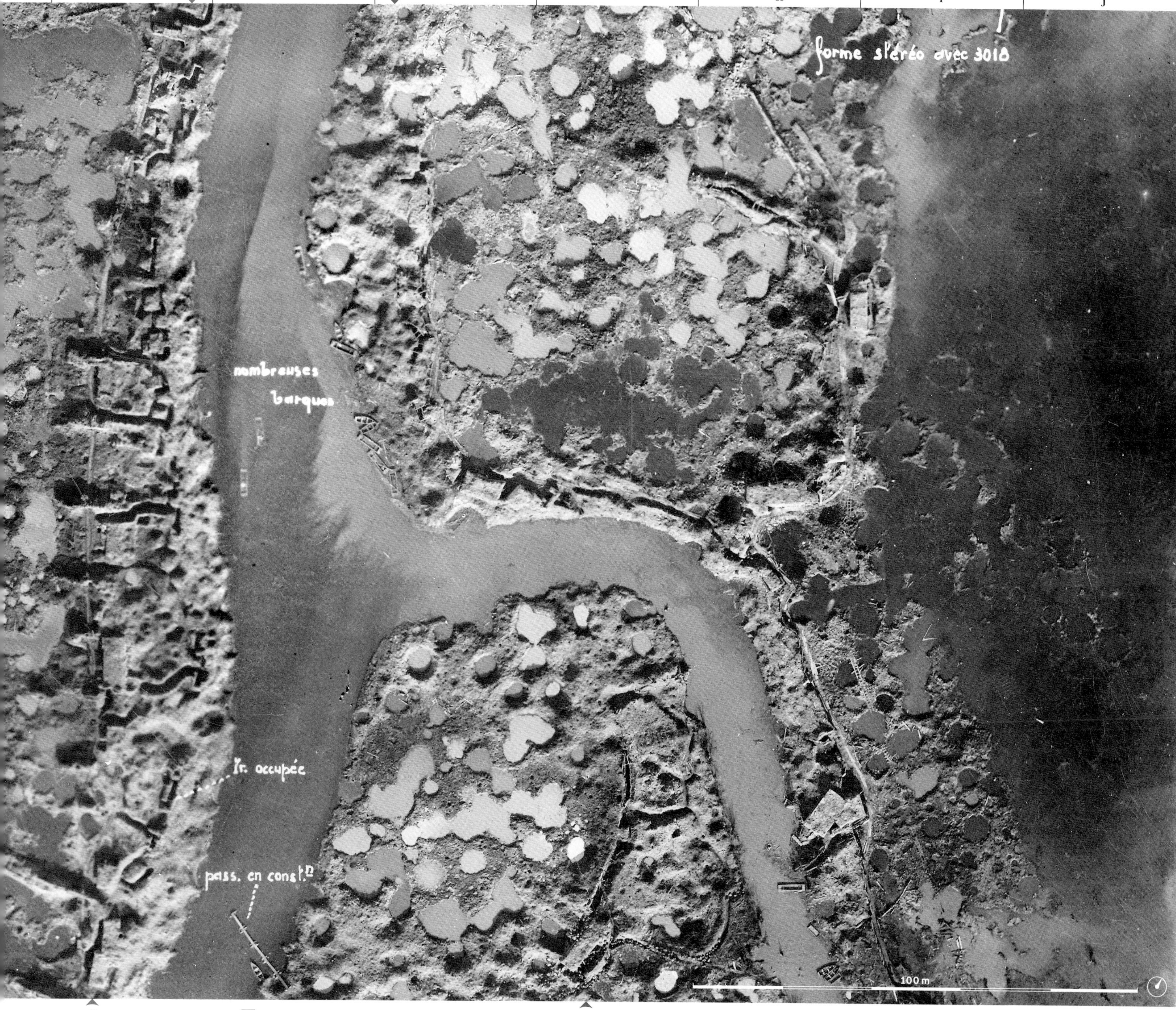

B ↓ 450 m 90 Diksmuide – railway bridge G Handzamevaart ↓ 91 centre of Diksmuide 580 m

90

DIKSMUIDE – RAILWAY BRIDGE

18 MARCH 1918

The area between the railway bridge over the Yser and the confluence of the Yser and the Handzamevaart, 600 metres further north, was one of the most dangerous and heavily bombarded places on the Belgian front. Belgians and Germans dug themselves in solidly, each on their respective bank of the Yser. On 18 March 1918 a Belgian reconnaissance aircraft photographed the area in detail. The German Kück position, called 'Trench 16' by the Belgians, was in a very poor state and virtually nothing was left of the railway bridge over the Yser (E2).

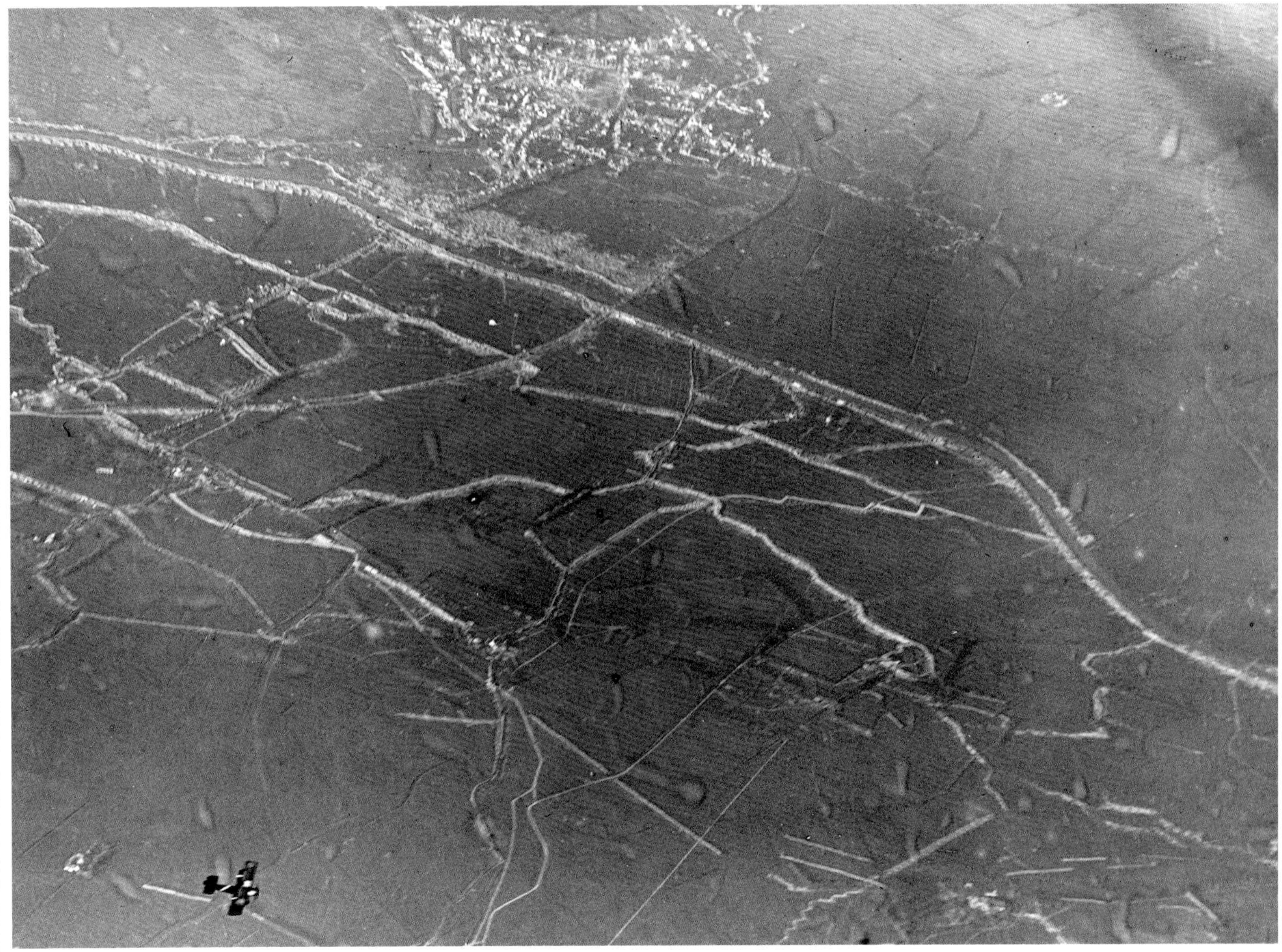

→ **OBLIQUE VIEW OF DIKSMUIDE**

Oblique view of Diksmuide from above Oudekapelle. The intensity of the Belgian bombardments of the German Yser front can be deduced from the lighter shade of the recently churned-up earth.

G1-G2

TRENCH 16

The earthern parapet of German Trench 16 has been shot to pieces. Only the concrete bunkers that were originally embedded in the parapet have survived the heavy Belgian bombardments.

B2

BUNKER IN THE 'BOYAU DU RAIL'

The 'Boyau du Rail' (Railway Trench) running westwards away from the Belgian front. Use was made of a former railway embankment so that there was no need to build a trench above ground in the muddy crater landscape.

↑ E2-E3

BELGIAN BUNKER

A massive Belgian bunker built of large concrete blocks. In the foreground, dug into the bank of the Yser, a narrow-gauge railway runs parallel to the Belgian front line. The bank keeps it hidden from German observation.

↑ **THE YSER**

Belgian trench on the Yser at Diksmuide.

GPS 51°01'47.65"N 2°51'14.24"E

A
B
C
D
B
E
↑ 450 m 89 Diksmuide - Raid
G
91 centre of Diksmuide 600 m ↑ H
remains of Nieuwpoort-Diksmuide rai way
1
3
4
5
6
Av.M.B. 3021. 18.3.18. 1000m. 10h30.
PONT. RAIL. C.31.
P. Adjt. Ledure. O. Lt Colin.
forme stéréo avec 3022
100 m
B
Yser

91
DIKSMUIDE 22 MARCH 1918

Once the French marine fusiliers, the Belgian line soldiers and the Senegalese Tirailleurs had tried in vain to defend Diksmuide during the Battle of the Yser, withdrawing to the west bank of the Yser on 10 November 1914, the front remained unchanged for four years. Then, in the spring of 1918, the medieval town was almost completely destroyed. Virtually the only structures left standing were a large number of bunkers, which the Germans had camouflaged within ruined houses. The severity of the bombardments made them visible again.

F2-G2
BUNKER

An enormous German shelter more than 55 metres long.

G5
MORTARS

Small German bunker with two openings in its roof, perhaps for the firing of trench mortars.

↓ **DESTRUCTION**

Belgian soldiers in the ruins of Diksmuide after the recapture of the town at the end of September 1918.

GPS 51°01'58.82"N 2°51'34.82"E

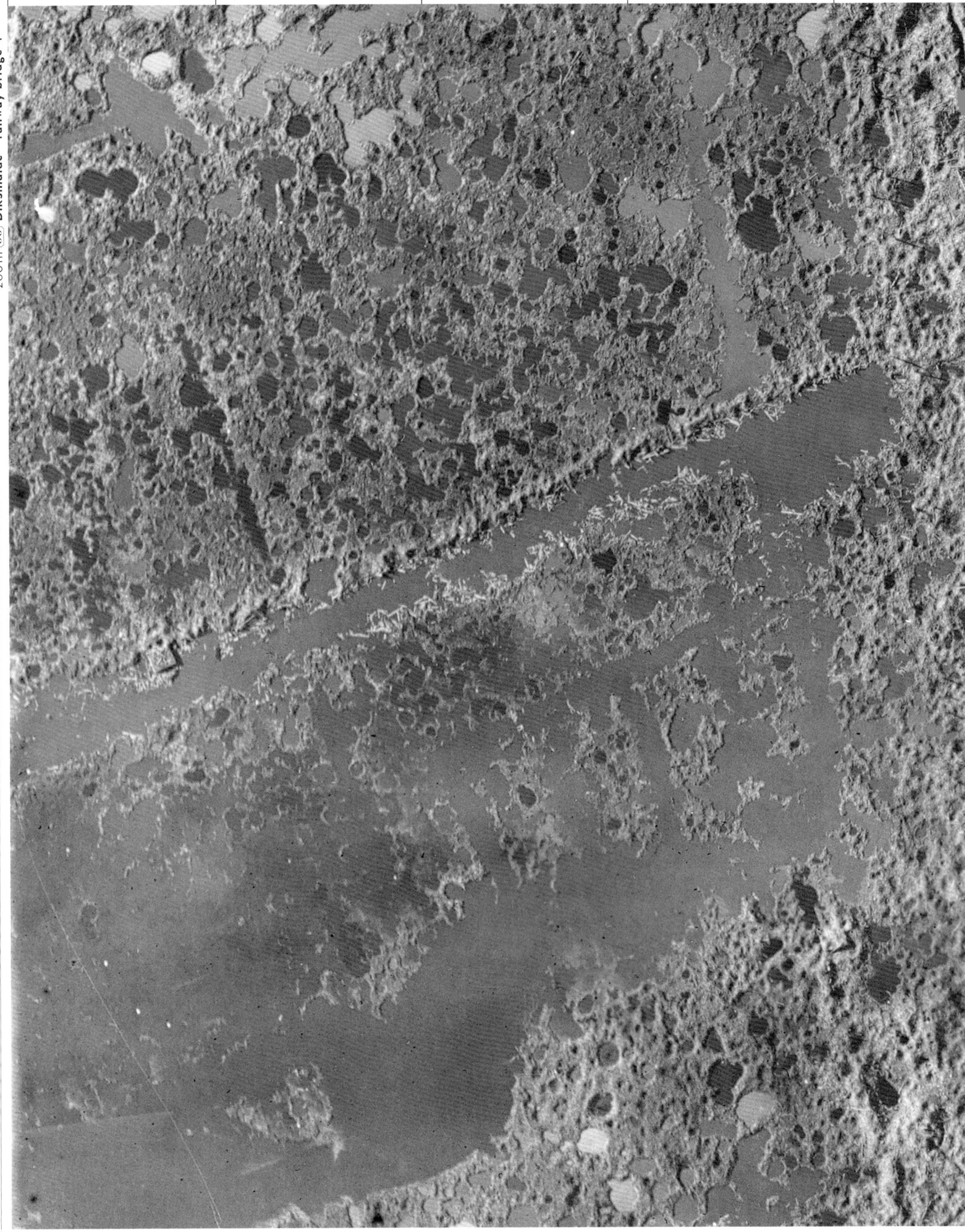

F
G
H
Handzamevaart
I
J
inundated area
L
traces of the medieval moat around Diksmuide
Kleine Dijk
4
5
6
100 m
Generaal Baron Jacquesstraat
Wilgendijk

92
INUNDATION OF THE YSER PLAIN 18 MARCH 1918

At the end of October 1914 the Yser plain to the north of Diksmuide was flooded, a centuries-old tried-and-trusted method of halting an enemy advance. The zone between the left bank of the Yser and the Diksmuide–Nieuwpoort railway embankment was inundated. Here and there islands of dry land remained above water and the marshy plain. Belgians and Germans used these as outposts. The so-called 'railway inundation' was followed on 10 November 1914 by the 'Blankaart inundation' to the south of Diksmuide. During the whole of the war both inundations were maintained by Belgian engineers and the daily briefing to the units at the front included a report on the water level in the flooded areas. Where necessary, measures were taken to correct it.

SYMBOLS

- TRENCH, BUNKER (OR SHELTER)
- INUNDATED AREA
- FOOTBRIDGE
- BARBED WIRE

GPS 51°06'18.82"N 2°46'21.34"E

↑ BELGIAN TROOPS AT AN OUTPOST

A small group of Belgian soldiers pose at an outpost in the inundation. Many of the small islands in the flooded Yser plain were farms built on higher ground in the polder.

C3
BUNKERS

Two bunkers project from the railway embankment. In the event of an attack they could form the base for harassing the enemy with enfilade fire.

D5
SHELTERS

The railway embankment was built up to become the main Belgian line on the Yser front. The embankment contained hundreds of brick or concrete shelters.

← OBLIQUE VIEW OF THE INUNDATION

A Belgian oblique aerial photograph taken at the start of 1915 shows the inundation to the east of the railway embankment at Ramskapelle.

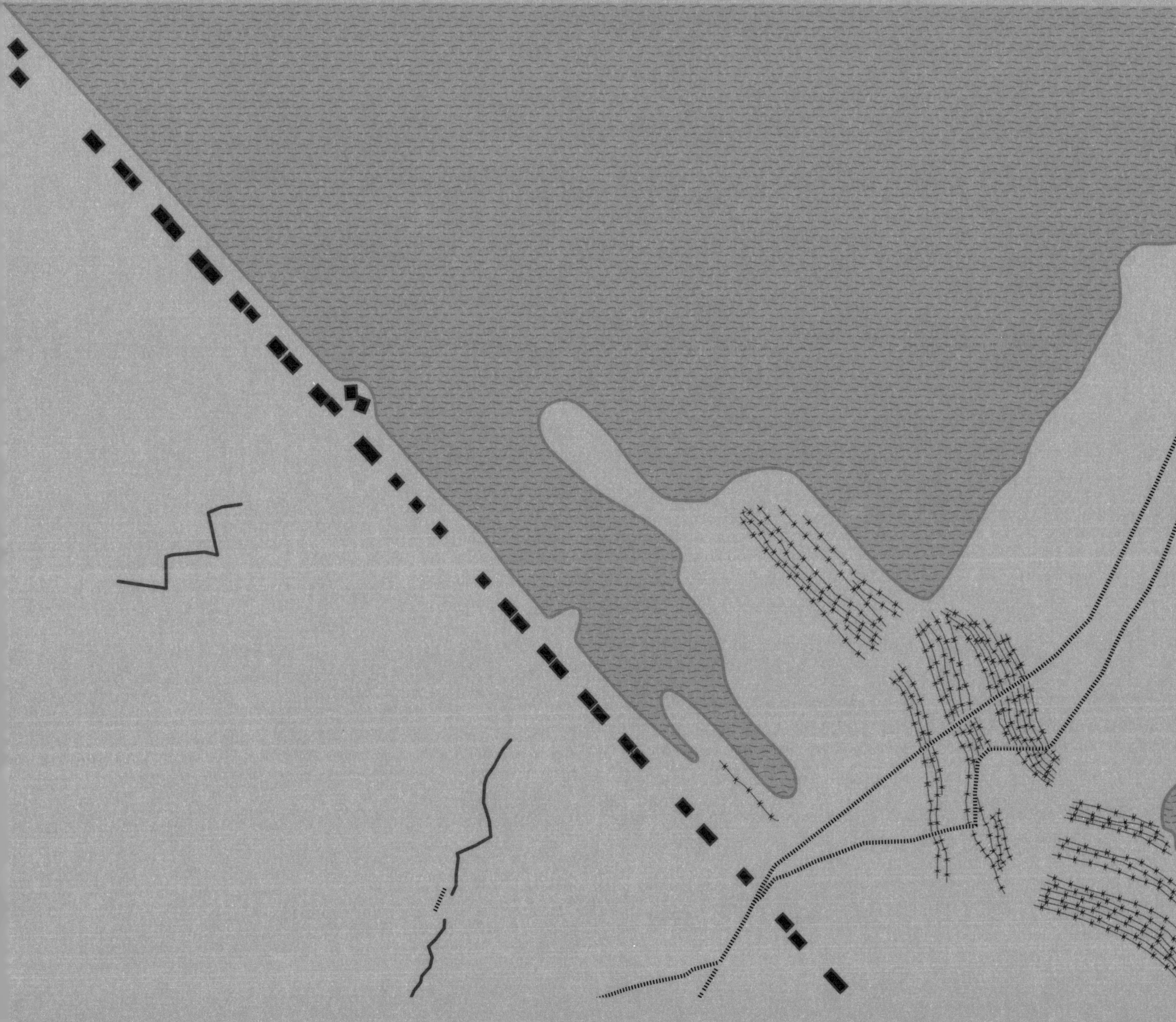

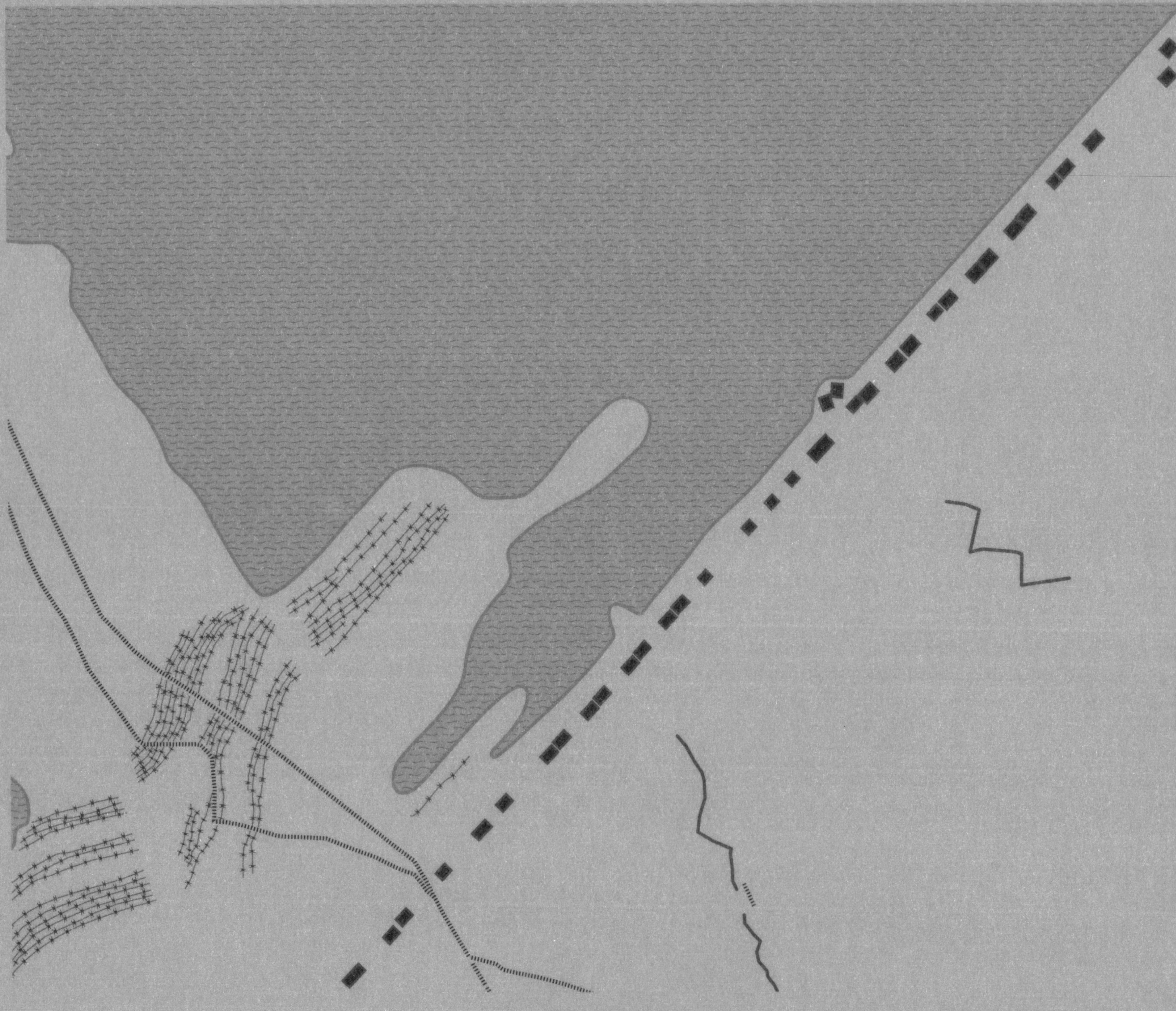

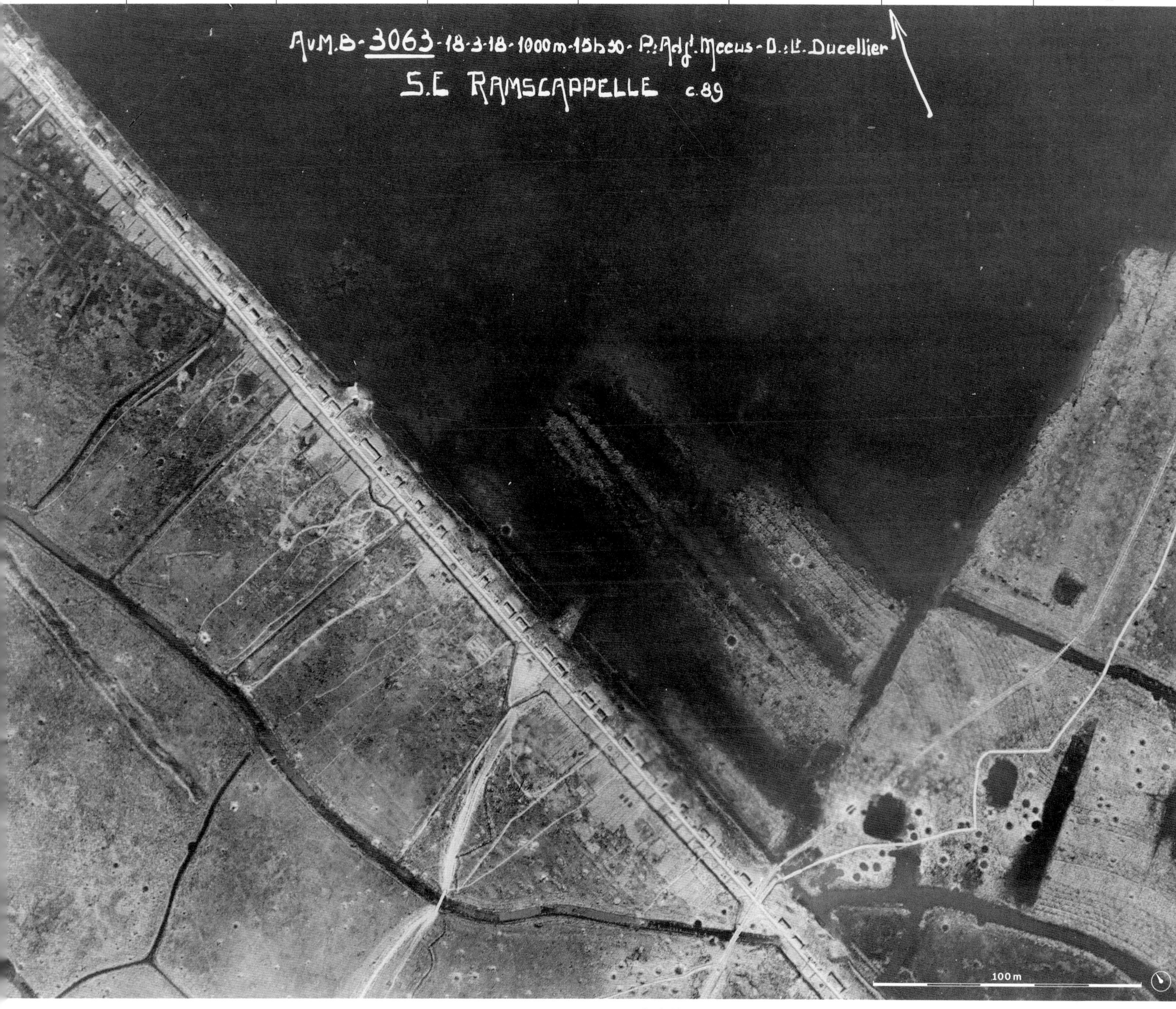

Nieuwpoort 3 km
Ramskapelle 640 m
inundated area
AvM.B-3063-18-3-18-1000m-15h30-P: Adj^t Mecus-O: Lt. Ducellier
S.E RAMSCAPPELLE c.89
1.8 km 67 Grote Hemme
footbridge
barbed wire
100 m
footbridge
Frontzate / Diksmuide-Nieuwpoort railway embankment

93

KORTEKEER – BREGUET 14

1 APRIL 1918

A Belgian Breguet 14 photographed at a height of 4 kilometres above Kortekeer, between Bikschote and Langemark, by the Belgian aerial photographer Lieutenant Gilles. The conditions in which aerial photographs were taken were very challenging. Aerial scouts were dispatched to photograph objects over enemy territory. At altitudes of several kilometres, they took photographs from an open cockpit. The exposure had to be set manually and after every shot the glass negative had to be replaced and stored away. Meanwhile, the observer photographer combed the skies for enemy fighter planes looking for observation planes to shoot down. In brief, good aerial photographs were almost always the result of dangerous feats and highly professional expertise.

» **SEE ALSO** [31] MIDDELKERKE

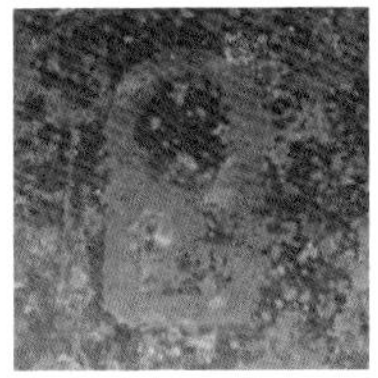

E6

MEDIEVAL MOATED SITE

Aerial photographs from the First World War are a dream come true for archaeologists searching for clues to archaeological sites. Artillery bombardments destroyed drainage systems and, as a result, depressions in the landscape, such as the long-hidden moats of medieval farms or castle mottes, were often revealed.

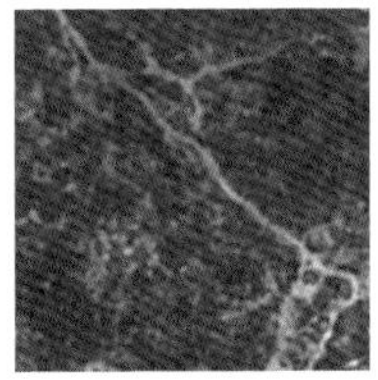

F3

POSITIONS

At an altitude of 4 kilometres, the positions can be identified only by the lighter shade of the built-up parapets and the dozens of paths and footbridges running towards them.

↓ BREGUET RECONNAISSANCE AIRCRAFT

French Breguet type 14 A.2, a common two-seater reconnaissance aircraft.

GPS 50°55'28.35"N 2°53'17.28"E

Bikschote 900 m
D
E
F
G
H
Broenbeek
I
GB
J
1
2
G
3
4
Broenbeek
5
400 m
Broenbeek
6
M.B. Z 2827. 1.6.18. Pil. Adj. Stampe. Obs. Lt Gilles. Alt. 4000 m E. Fme Mondovi (c. 69) Ech. 1/8000
100 m
Langemark 2.25 km
GB
G

94

PLOEGSTEERT – HILL 63

1 APRIL 1918 & 7 SEPTEMBER 1918

Between Ploegsteert, 'Plugstreet' to the British, and Mesen lies the Mont de la Hutte, or, in terms of military contours, Hill 63. The topography of this hill was ideally suited to the digging of underground shelters. Since 1 August 1916 the 1st Australian Tunnelling Company had been digging a deep, extensive system of galleries in which two full battalions (up to 2,000 soldiers) could be safely accommodated. The official name of the system was the 'Hill 63 dugouts', but the soldiers called the complex 'The Catacombs'. A German aerial photograph of 1 April 1918, taken at an altitude of more than 5 kilometres, shows the entrances to the catacombs to the north-west of Ploegsteert Wood.

» Continued on p. 254

↑ **PLOEGSTEERT WOOD**

A German oblique aerial photograph taken above the wood at Ploegsteert on 5 September 1918 shows why an underground network of tunnels was dug under Hill 63 (in the centre, with woods on its southern flank). The excavation work took place out of view of the enemy, and from the foot of the hill it was possible to dig deep galleries underneath.

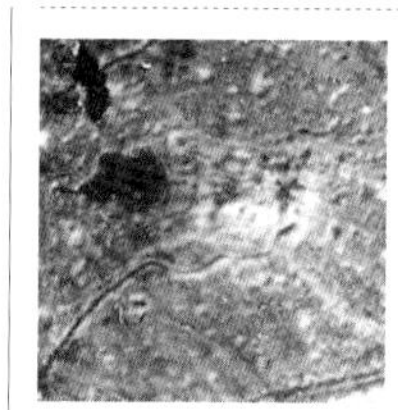

D2

CHÂTEAU DE LA HUTTE

On top of the hill, on its northern side, stand the ruins of the Château de la Hutte, with the outlines of the paths and ornamental pond of the château gardens still visible even after three and a half years of war.

↓ **HYDE PARK CORNER**

Troops of the Australian 2nd Division pass 'Hyde Park Corner'. The entrances to The Catacombs are just over the road.

GPS 50°44'22.52"N 2°52'59.16"E

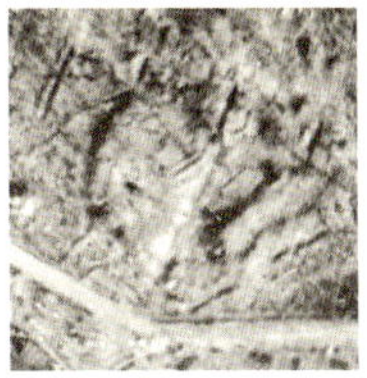

B3
ENTRANCE TO 'THE CATACOMBS'

Just north of Hyde Park Corner there is much activity, and most of the trees in the wood have disappeared. This reveals a large entrance area. The dark stripes are the shadows cast in the entrances to the dugouts.

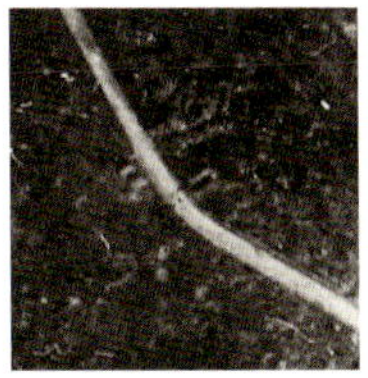

A2
ENTRANCES

Two smaller entrances to The Catacombs under Hill 63.

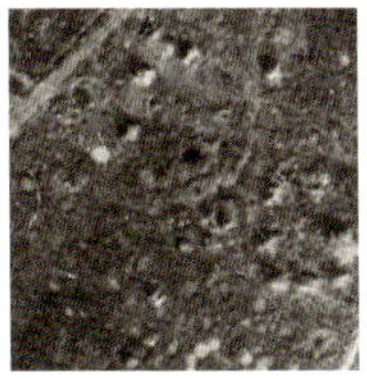

A4
SHELTERS

In and around Ploegsteert Wood were dozens of shelters. In many cases they were made of semicircular sheets of corrugated iron covered with earth or concrete.

↓ TRENCH MAP, HILL 63, 22 MARCH 1918

German trench map of the area north of Ploegsteert Wood. British trenches are marked in red, shelters and bunkers with square dots, and Allied batteries with a blue symbol and code letter.

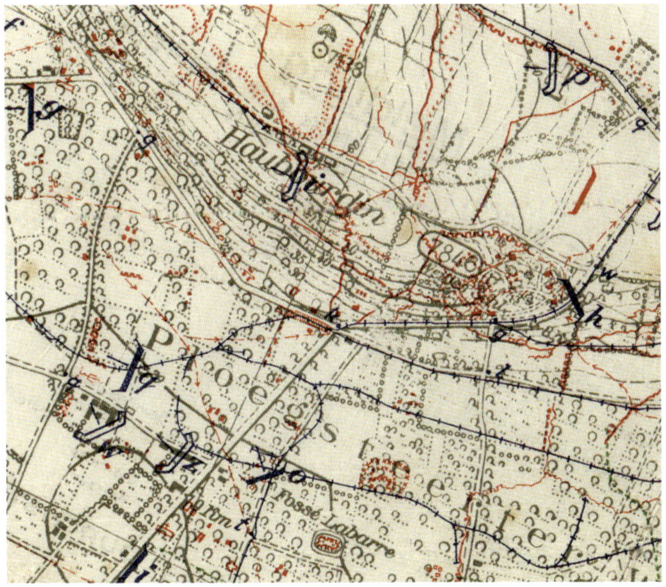

›› Continued from p. 252

This oblique German aerial photograph was taken at barely 500 metres. At the time it was taken, Hill 63, with The Catacombs beneath, was in the German hinterland. The entire area from Warneton to Loker had been captured during the German Spring Offensive. In the foreground, at least two entrances to the underground tunnels can be seen. Four years of war have battered the wood beyond recognition. It is summer, but the trees are bare.

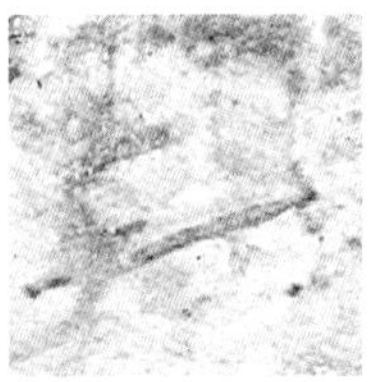

D6
ENTRANCES

Two horizontal corridors lead to the dugouts under Hill 63. The Australian troops called it 'Wallangarra'.[37]

C5
TUNNEL

A third entrance to the Hill 63 dugouts.

B3
SHELTERS

Spread throughout the Bois de la Hutte were reinforced shelters.

→ **DUGOUT ENTRANCES**

Soldiers of the 7th Field Company of the Australian Engineers pose in front of one of the entrances to the dugouts under Hill 63. The entrance is decorated with a kangaroo.

Bois de la Hutte
A
B
C
D
E
F
G
H
1
2
3
4
5
6
Rue du Petit Pont

95

HOUTHULST – TRAINING COMPLEX BECOMES THE FRONT 2 APRIL 1918

Just a few kilometres behind the front, to the south of Houthulst Forest, a large German training complex, including trenches, was built in the summer of 1916. In some instances, such training facilities were replicas of front trenches, so that soldiers could practise specific trench-related exercises. In the second half of October 1917 the post marking the front was moved to the former training trenches. Remains of the German exercise trenches were used as outposts. A chronological sequence of photographs shows one such site during the war. This series shows that an interpretation does not only give a picture of the evolution; it also reveals important functional modifications.

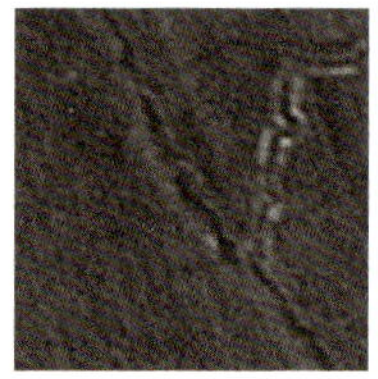

B5
TRENCHES 1915

The training ground was laid out next to former German front trenches dating from before the Second Battle of Ypres. The evolution in the way trenches were built over barely eighteen months is enormous.

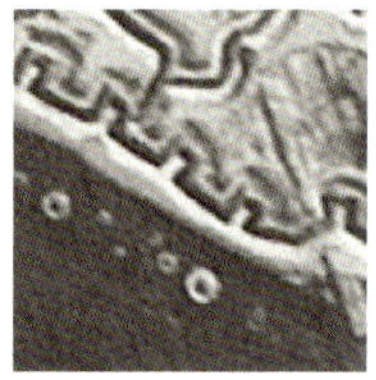

D3
'CRATERS' AND BARBED WIRE

To make the training more true to life barbed-wire fences were laid in front of the trenches and an imitation no-man's-land was created with 'bomb craters'.

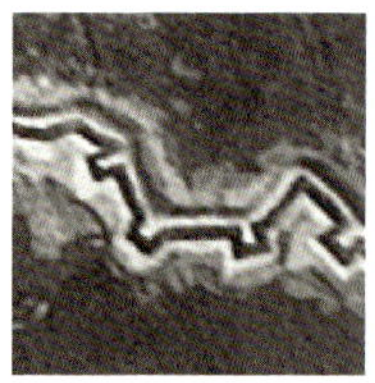

D5 and C4
WIDE PARAPET

The practice trenches were built with an above-ground parapet. Despite heavy bombardments, some were still recognisable two years later.

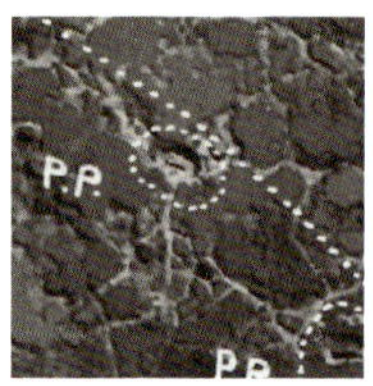

d3
'HOUTHULST SUPPORT'

The Allied front line in the spring of 1918 consisted of linked, small, reinforced posts only a few metres wide. The erratic light-coloured lines indicate intense troop traffic.

↓ BRITISH TRENCH MAP

British trench map showing the front on 17 December 1917.

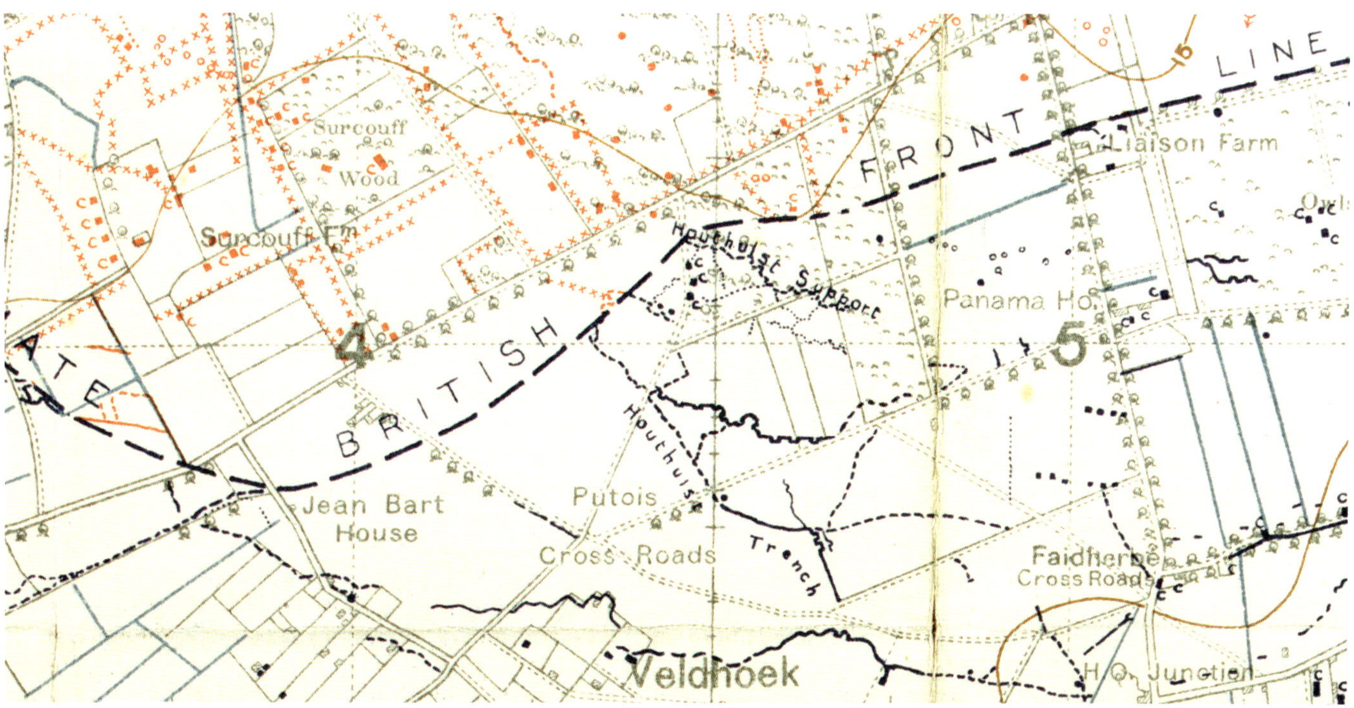

GPS 50°56'30.95"N 2°55'20.06"E

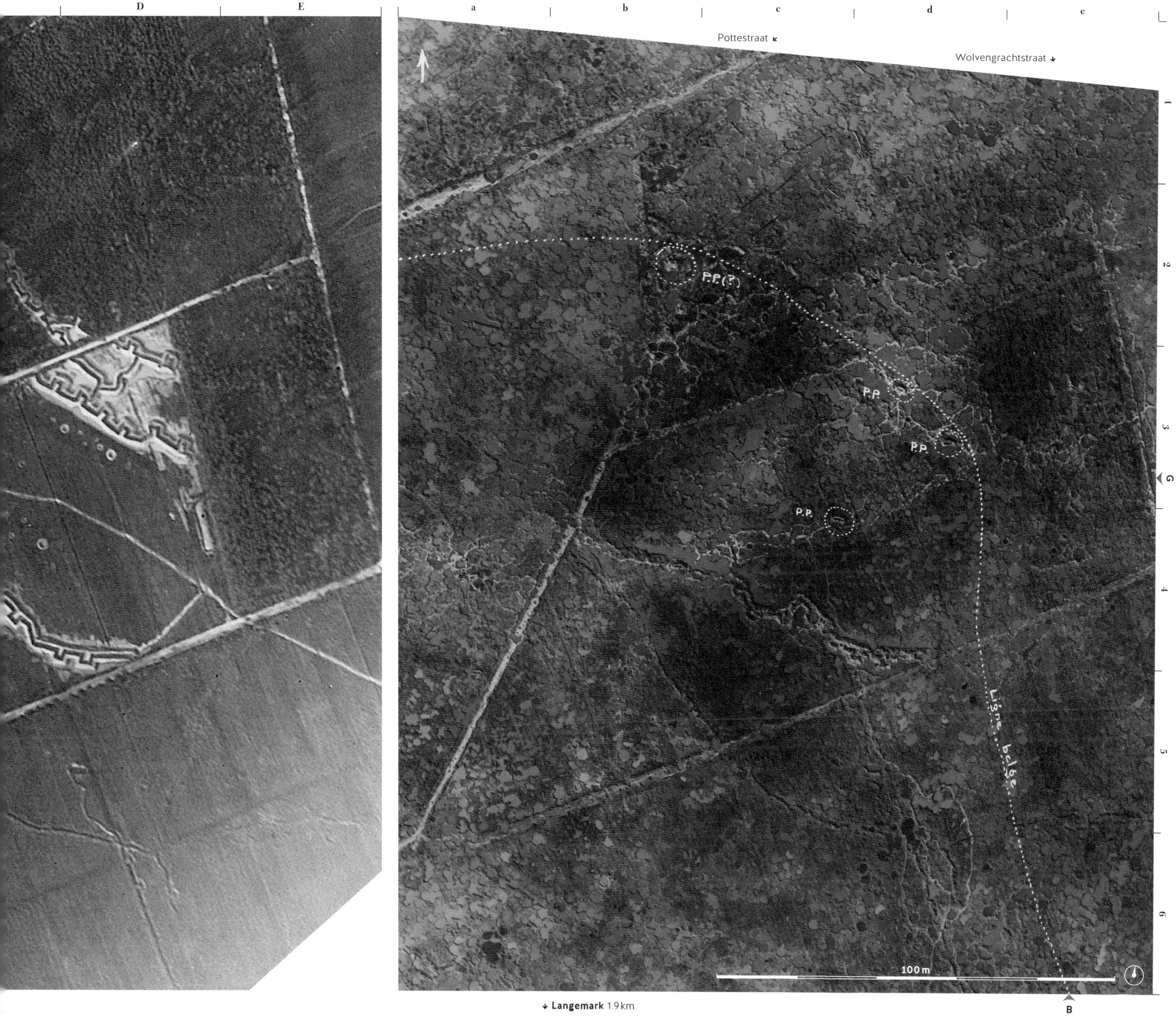

D
E
a
b
c
d
e
Pottestraat
Wolvengrachtstraat
1
2
3
4
5
6
G
P.P.(?)
P.P.
P.P.
P.P.
Ligne belge
100 m
Langemark 1.9 km
B

1918: Spring Offensive and Liberation Offensive

BY THE END OF 1917 all parties were exhausted. On 6 April 1917 the United States finally declared war on the German Reich and its allies but the American troops had not yet reached the Western Front. The first troops arrived in France in December 1917 and in Belgium only in May 1918. Before they could be deployed in any numbers, Germany exploited the coming to power of the Bolsheviks in Russia in November 1917. On 3 March 1918 a peace treaty was signed in Brest-Litovsk, and the Eastern Front was shut down. The German Reich could now concentrate all its forces on the West.

This was the last opportunity for the German commanders Hindenburg and Ludendorff to force a break-through. Their Spring Offensive, first on the Somme and then in Flanders, followed by three attempts on the Marne, were all failures, but demanded particularly heavy sacrifices from the Allied troops. The offensive ground to a halt in West Flanders at the end of April and beginning of May, in what was left from the previous year of the military infrastructure in the Allied hinterland. New lines were drawn between railway tracks, camps and cemeteries. By this time the war had virtually annihilated everything in the area of the front. The German hinterland was still relatively intact. British raids on the harbours of Zeebrugge (22 April) and Ostend (10 May) attempted in vain to cripple the German U-boat bases.

On 18 July 1918 a new counter-offensive started up in France and on 28 September 1918 the Liberation Offensive also started in Flanders. The last six weeks were among the bloodiest of the war. The combined offensive by the Belgians and British, together, at a second stage, with the French and Americans, forced the German troops to retreat, but at great cost. The last phase of the war took place in hitherto undamaged country where civilians still lived and were often surprised and killed by the cruel storm of the approaching force of war. The fighting continued unabated until 11 November 1918 when the Armistice was at last signed.

The aerial photographs taken during the last year of the war show us how observation from the air was being increasingly taken into account. From now on the camouflaging of positions on the ground and the creation of smoke screens to hide certain sectors and activities soon became a permanent feature of day-to-day warfare.

IV

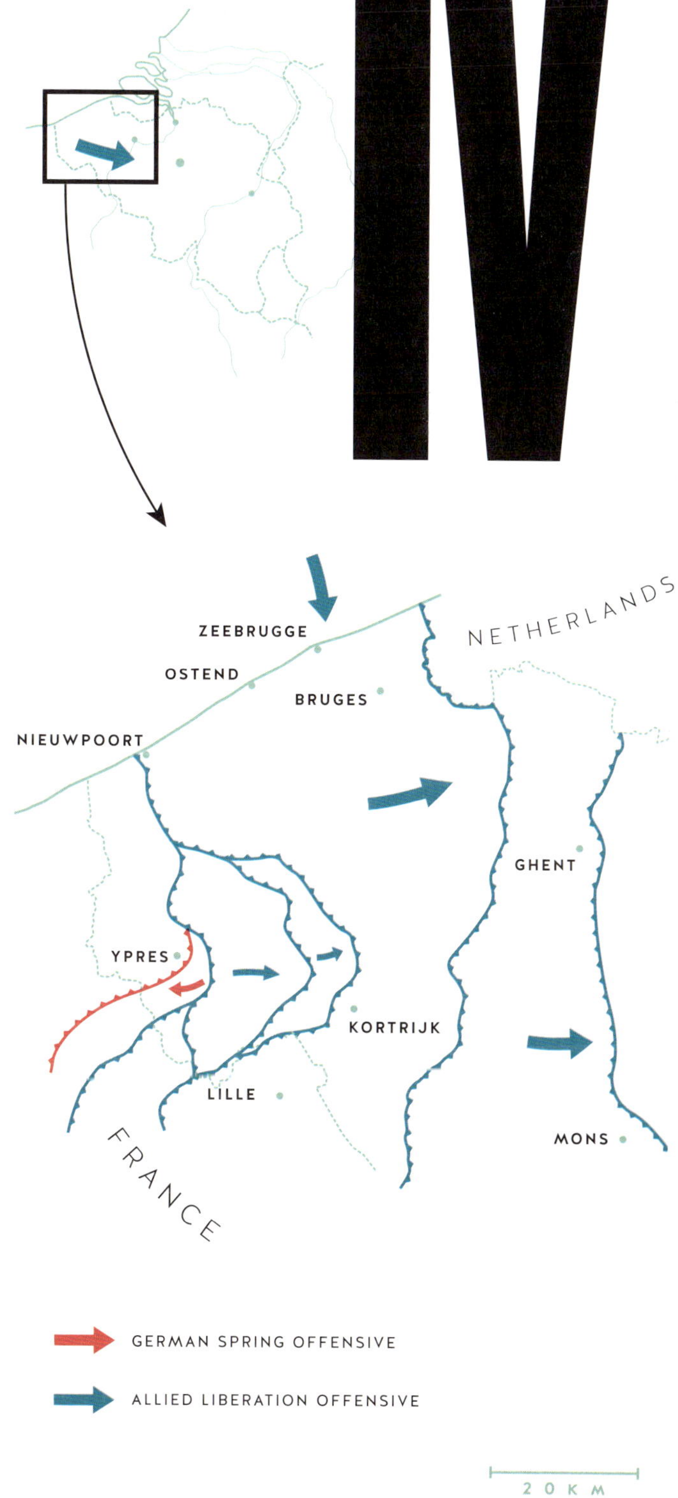

←

Smokescreens near the hamlet of Le Bizet, south of Ploegsteert (7 September 1918). This German oblique aerial photograph was taken from an altitude of just under 500 metres.

96
YPRES 8 MAY 1918

It was on 28 October 1914 that the first German shells fell on Ypres, thenceforth to be in the firing line of the German troops entrenched in a semicircle around the town. For four years Ypres suffered intense bombardment and its historic buildings were steadily annihilated. In 1915, soon after the town had first been devastated, plans were already being made for its reconstruction. At the time no one knew what the final extent of the damage would be. The shadows on this aerial photograph of 8 May 1918 indicate that, apart from a few groups of buildings, hardly any walls were left standing. Eveything else had literally been swept off the map, first by the constant bombardment, then by the British army's clearance services. The picture on the following page shows the whole town (31 July 1918). At no time during the war did the front come so near to the town as after the German Spring Offensive of 1918 (p. 145, P1-P6), when German soldiers advanced to within one and a half kilometres of the town wall.

D5-E4
THE CLOTH HALL
The Cloth Hall was all but destroyed, with the exception of parts of the south façade and the belfry tower.

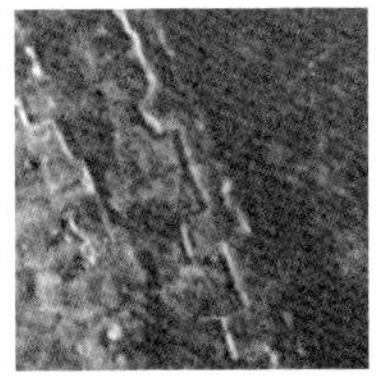

H1
TRENCHES IN THE FORTIFICATIONS
British trenches were dug into the Vauban fortifications. From here there was an excellent view of the lower-lying surroundings.

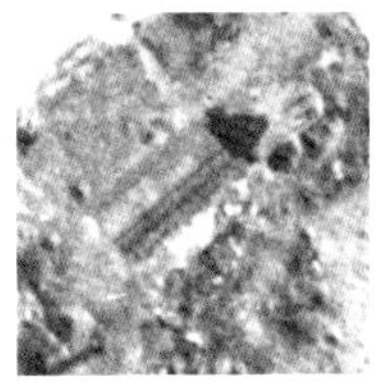

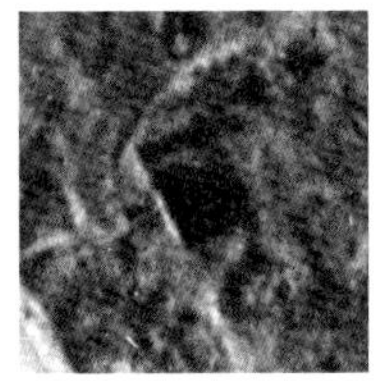

D6 and E2
SHELTERS
Barracks and shelters were built in various places in the town.

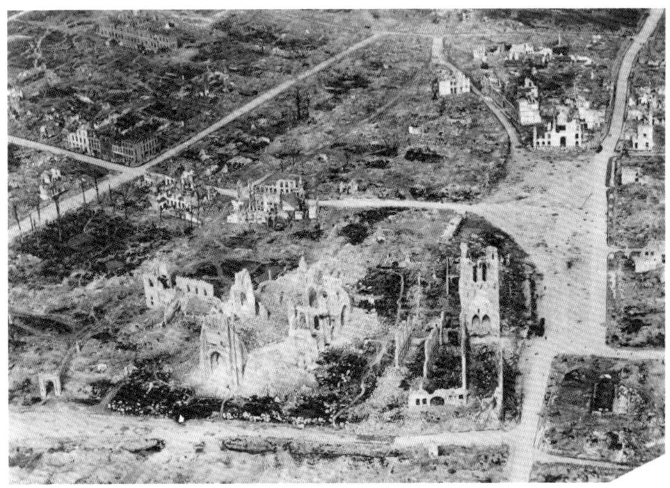

→ **YPRES 1918**

Oblique view of Ypres. From left to right: St Martin's Cathedral, the Cloth Hall and the market square.

↓ **VIEW OF THE CLOTH HALL**

Panoramic photograph with a view of the belfry tower.

GPS 50°51'03.94"N 2°53'07.46"E

D
↓ Diksmuidestraat
E
F
G
Vauban fortifications
I
J
↙ Frenchlaan
1
2
3
→ front 1.5 km
4
5
6
100 m
Rijselstraat ↖

A
B
C
D
↑ Elverdinge 5 km
F
G
Boezinge 5 km ↑
↑ Vlamertinge 2.8 km
GPS 50°51'03.94"N 2°53'07.46"E
↓ Dikkebus 3.8 km

I
J
K
L
M
Zonnebeekseweg
O
P
GB
1
12 16 54 Bellewaarde 1.5 km
3
4 Menin Road
5
2.6 km 5 56 47 Hill 60
6
E88
100 m
Sint-Elooi 3.6 km
GB no-man's-land

97 LOKER

3 MAY 1918 & 31 JULY 1918

For most of the war Loker (Locre) lay at a safe distance from the front and numerous military rest camps were set up in its vicinity. In April 1918 things changed when the Germans advanced during their Spring Offensive far beyond their old lines at Mesen and Wijtschate. On 25 April the Kemmelberg (Mount Kemmel) was captured and German storm troops entered Loker. The next fortnight saw heavy fighting for the village and parts of Loker changed hands several times. A British aerial photograph shows the situation shortly after the final recapture of the heavily battered village by French troops. In the rolling landscape there are few traces to be seen of the battle. Dozens of foxholes reveal where some lines have been hastily dug to halt the German attack. A single French trench forms the front line, and there is as yet no trace of German field reinforcements. The photograph was taken at midday and the ruined church is bathed in sunshine.

›› Continued on p. 266

→ **TRENCH MAP, 21 AUGUST 1918**

This German trench map shows the changes on the front after the German Spring Offensive. At this time the French defenders had once again been replaced by their British allies.

GPS 50°46'48.61"N 2°46'22.73"E

← **LOKER**

The centre of Loker at the end of the war (2 September 1918). In the space of a few months this village had been reduced to a heap of ruins.

C5-D5

GALOOIE-MOTTE

The motte is all that remains of a medieval motte-and-bailey castle (a mound of earth with a tower on top of it).

SYMBOLS

FRENCH TRENCH, BARRACK

GERMAN FRONT LINE

GALOOIE-MOTTE

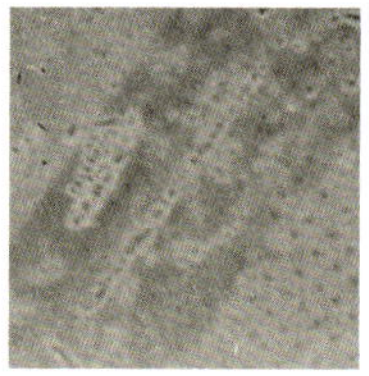

C6

FOXHOLES

French foxholes: the earth from these shelter holes was piled up on the south side, facing the German attacks.

D1-E1

LOKER

The shadow cast by the tower of St Peter's Church shows the indignities heaped upon the building by artillery fire.

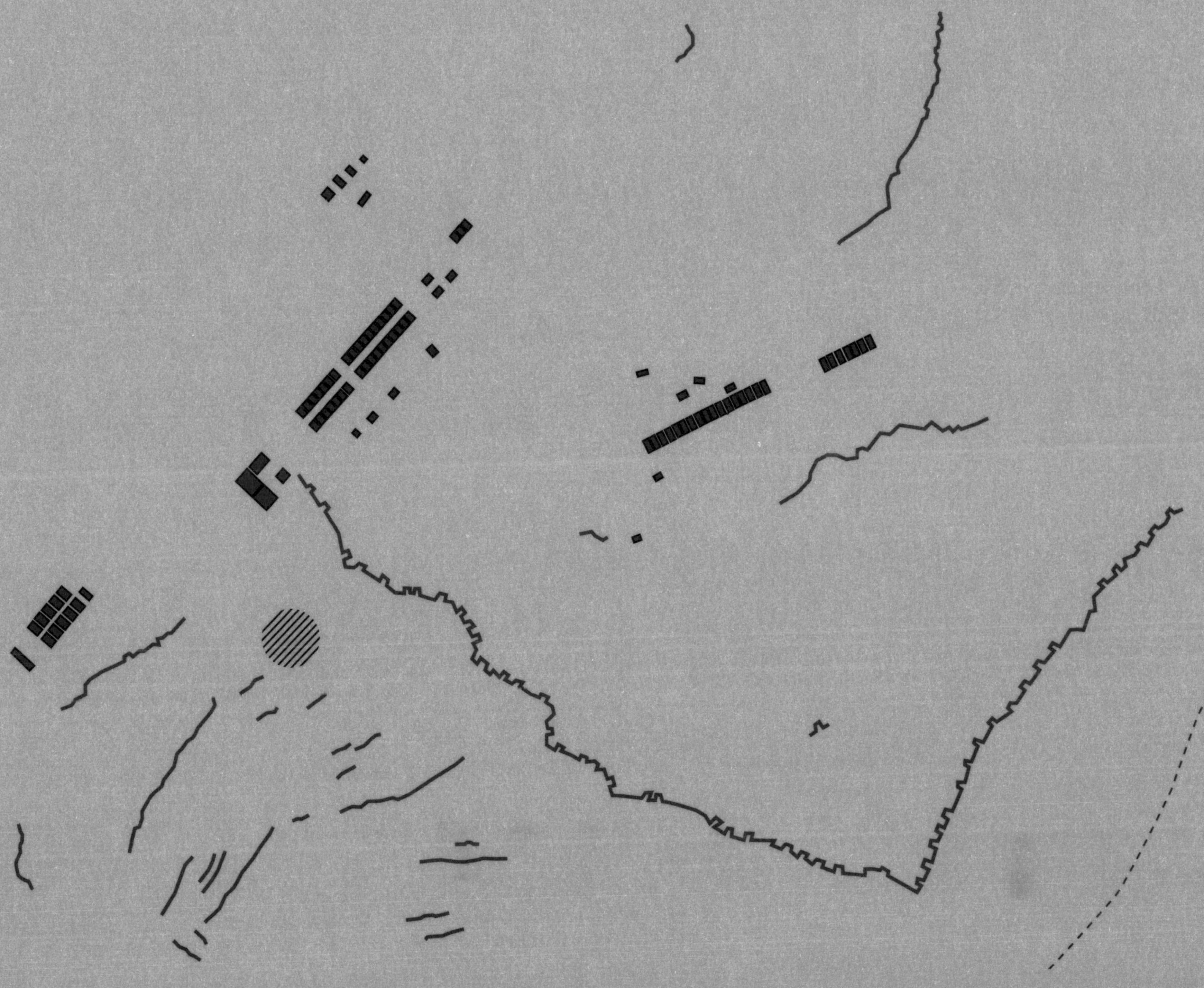

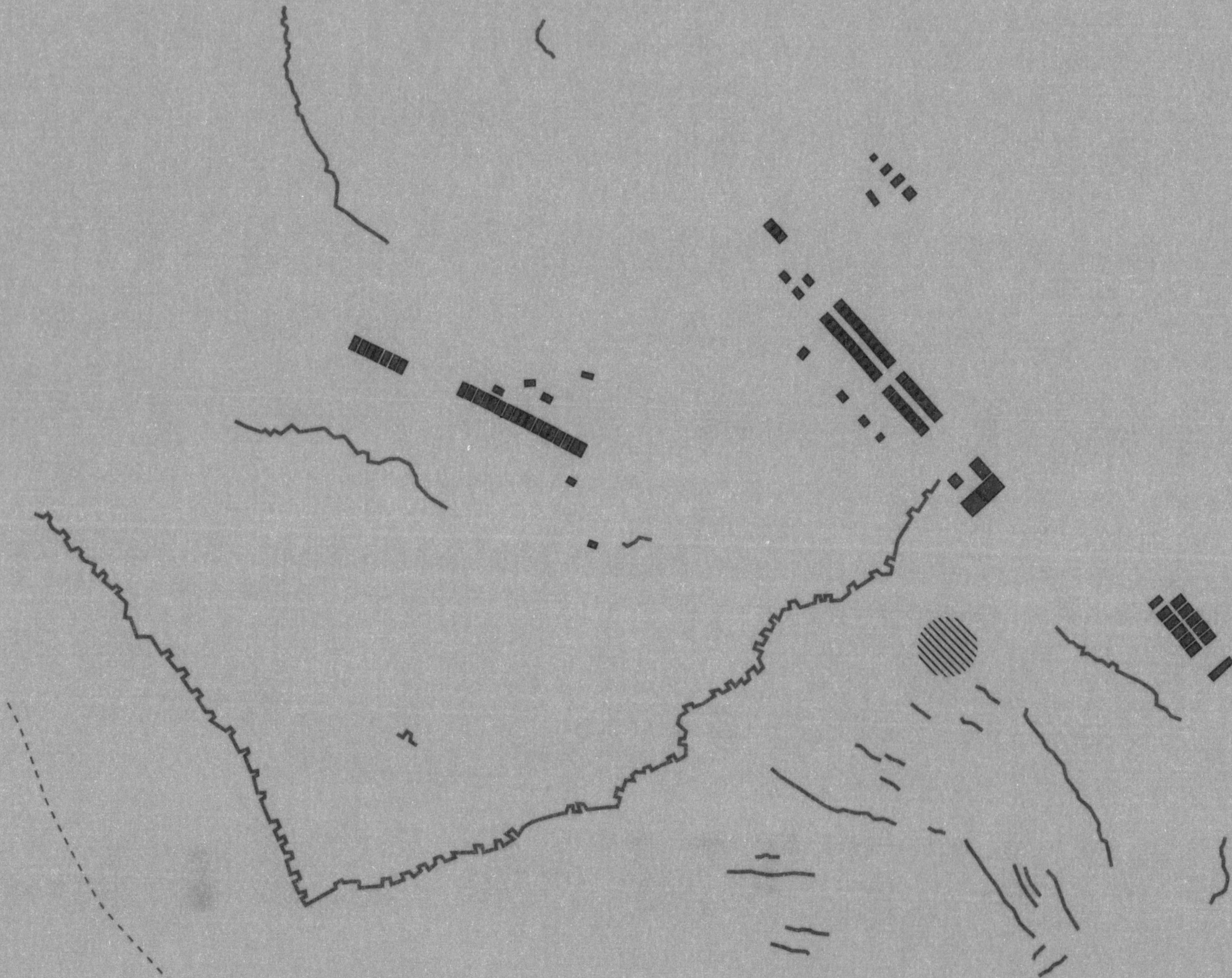

A
B
C
D
E
F
G
H
1
2
3
5
6
Ypres 10km
Kemmelberg 2.3km
Bailleul 4.8km
Dranouter 1.1km
F
G
53B 2017
28 M 22·23·28·29
3·5·18: 12 PM
100 m

›› Continued from p. 264

A British aerial photograph of 31 July 1918 shows how the front settled down after the Loker attacks. The French trench to the east of Loker is still in use and some work has been done on the development of the positions. The German front line is more lightly fortified, with their defences more developed to the rear. On both sides, outposts are situated in no-man's-land, their location revealed by the numerous fine lines leading towards them, indicating paths.

→ **SIGNALLING STATION**

German troops at a captured signalling station on the Mont de l'Hospice between Loker and Kemmelberg.

↓ **AERIAL PHOTOGRAPH OF LOKER HOSPICE 7 MAY 1918**

The front line runs right up to the hospice's garden wall (ciii-diii), behind which William ['Willie'] Redmond lay buried (ciii), veers to the right and hugs the wall until just before Loker Hospice Cemetery (diii). Respect for the dead came first, even in wartime.

GPS 50°46'48.61"N 2°46'22.73"E

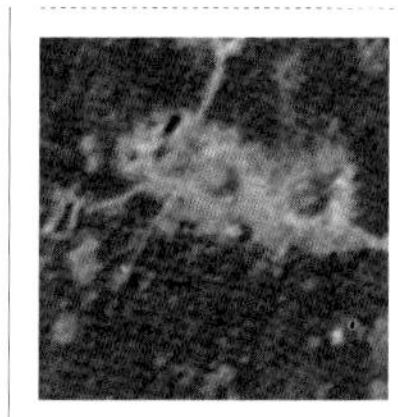

H3

GERMAN OUTPOSTS

Paths reveal the location of a line of outposts in no-man's-land.

D6-E6

BARRACKS IN RUINS

As Loker lay far behind the front line for most of the war, it was home to a number of military rest camps. Most of them were reduced to ruins in the spring of 1918.

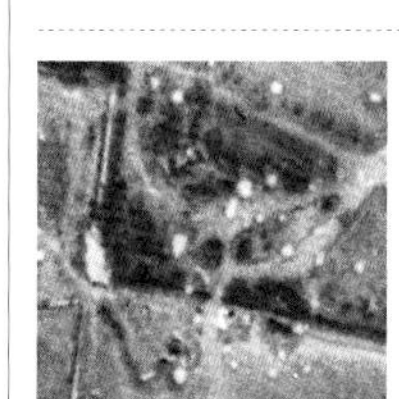

ciii / F1

GRAVE OF WILLIAM REDMOND

The Irish politician William Redmond (1861–1917) was a protagonist in the struggle for Irish independence. He died during the Battle of Messines, 7 June 1917.

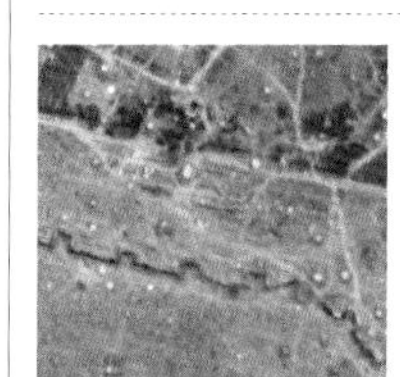

diii

LOKER HOSPICE CEMETERY

Between June 1917 and April 1918, 246 soldiers were buried behind the garden of the convent of St-Antoine.

A
B
C
↙ Dondeyneweg
E
↓ the hospice's garden wall
G
GB
H
1
G
2
3
↘ Hofstraat
4
5
6
100 m
↘ 1km Dranouter

98

SINT-JAN – SUPPLY HUB

7 MAY 1918

To keep the wheels of the war machine turning, an enormous logistical apparatus ensured that the stream of supplies reached its proper destination. As the Allied Summer Offensive of 1917 shifted eastwards, this apparatus moved with it. One of the challenges faced by the Allies was the rapid conversion of old battlefields into supply hubs. Trenches and bomb craters were filled in with earth, and miles of roads and railway lines were built. During the 1918 Spring Offensive the Germans recaptured much of the area lost in 1917, and the war was subsequently fought in this 'reconverted' military hinterland.

→ E2
SINT-JAN 1918

Activity in the railway complex at Sint-Jan, photographed from the east on 22 February 1918.

C1
NEW IRISH FARM CEMETERY

A British cemetery with some 70 graves. After the war it was extended to become a collective cemetery in which 4,715 Commonwealth soldiers were laid to rest.

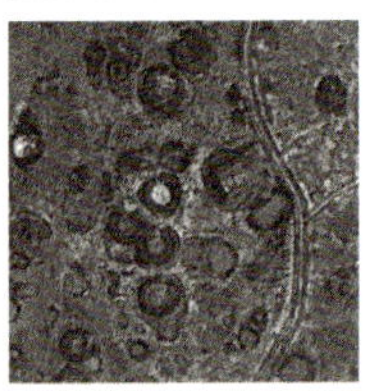

G3
ROUND MARKS

Owing to the proximity of the front, the tented camps in Sint-Jan disappeared in May 1918. The round marks, where they are not bomb craters, are the remains of sandbags heaped around tents as protection against stray shrapnel.

A4
GRAVES

Just past the bend in 'Buffs Road' (Hogeziekenweg) are the 86 graves of the Divisional Collecting Post, set up between August 1917 and January 1918.

↓ E6
SINT-JAN 1918

The western part of the distribution hub at Sint-Jan, 22 February 1918.

↓
THE FRONT, SPRING 1918

At the time this photograph was taken, the front was less than 2 kilometres away and many barracks and shelters were within firing range.

A
Hogeziekenweg
B
C
D
front 1.7 km
E
F
G
H
1
Briekestraat
2
3
4
5
6
Ypres 1.7 km
100 m
railway lines

99

MONT NOIR – SAND QUARRY

8 MAY 1918

An aerial photograph reduces the landscape to two dimensions. In reality, the seemingly 'flat' landscape shown in this photograph was in fact a hill ridge more than 150 metres high. Raw materials were needed to support the building work at the front and in the hinterland. The sand strata on the flanks of the south-western Flemish hills offer rich resources for this. The American Harvey William Cushing, who worked as a surgeon in CCS Mendinghem, describes the imposing excavations as follows: 'Between this landmark and Kemmel lies Mont Noir – almost levelled for its product of sand to fill bags, to make road beds and concrete.'[38] In the bottom left-hand corner of the photo (A5) can be seen the country house of Michel Cleenewerck de Crayencour who lived there from 1903 to September 1914 with his daughter, the (future) French author Marguerite Yourcenar.

» **SEE ALSO** 73 CCS MENDINGHEM

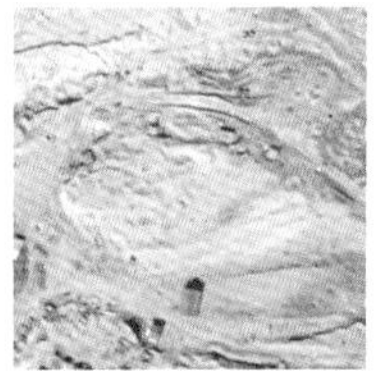

E3

SANDSTONE QUARRY

The flanks of the top of Mont Noir were exploited as a sand quarry by the Allies.

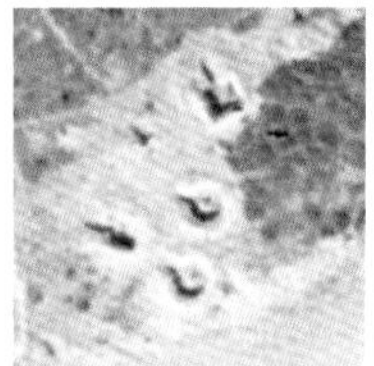

E2

'ARCHIE'

Set-up for an Allied anti-aircraft gun, also known in military jargon as an 'archie'.

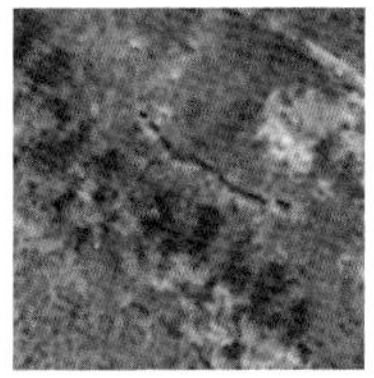

F4-G4

TRENCH AT TOP OF MONT NOIR

Following the German Spring Offensive the front was situated just one and a half kilometres away from the hill. On the top of it, a small trench offered a commanding view in the direction of the front.

↓ TRANSPORT OF SAND AND CEMENT

Raw materials and building supplies were transported to the front by trains. Here a train full of sand and cement is being unloaded at Ypres, 7 January 1918.

GPS 50°46'49.06"N 2°44'07.84"E

D
E
F
G
H
I
J
1
2
3
4
5
6
97 Loker 2.5km
Route du Parc
100 m

100

BISSEGEM & MARKE – AERIAL BOMBARDMENT 17 MAY 1918

As the war moved on, the role of military aviation changed. Initially, the aircraft were the 'new eyes' of the war leaders and were principally used for reconnaissance flights. As the war progressed, the air force was also used for aerial bombardment. Aircraft could bomb strategic points far behind enemy lines. During such missions aerial photographs were taken to give a picture of the 'hits'. On 17 May 1918 Bissegem airfield (A1-B1) and Marckebeke airfield (F3-F6) came under fire, but a large proportion of the bombs missed their targets. It was from Marckebeke airfield that the famous German ace Manfred von Richthofen, better known as the 'Red Baron', and his fighter squadron ruled the air over the Ypres Salient in 1917.

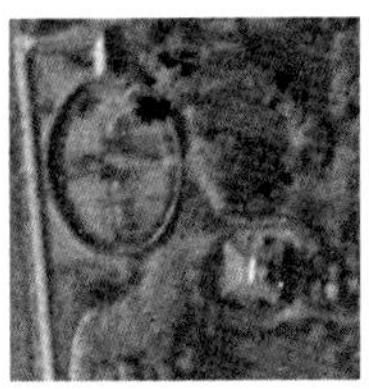

H4

CHÂTEAU MARKEBEEK

This house was the headquarters of Manfred von Richthofen. His 'Flying Circus', as the Allies called his fighter unit, Jagdgeschwader 1, was housed here.

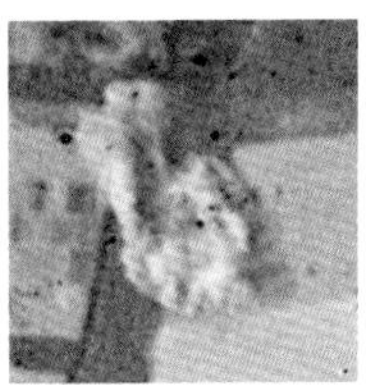

H5

EXPLOSIONS

Aeroplane bombs exploding to the east of the airfield.

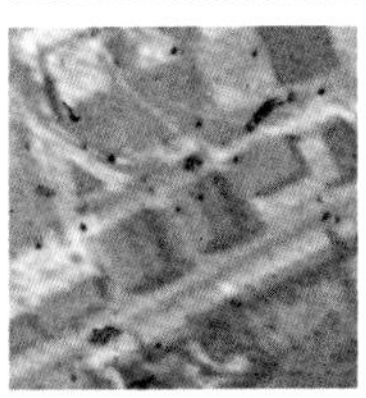

G6

MARCKEBEKE AIRFIELD

The hangars at Marckebeke airfield.

↑ **AIRCRAFT**

A row of German aircraft at an airfield on the Western Front. In the background are a number of hangars.

A1-B1

HANGARS

Large aircraft hangars at the German airfield at Bissegem.

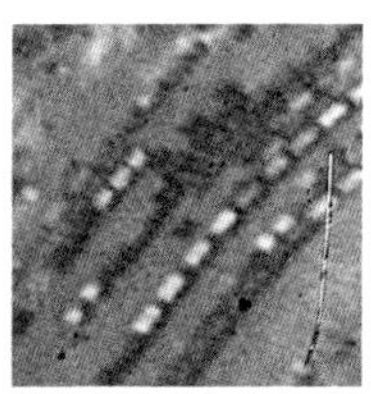

J6

STATION

Wagons at Kortrijk station.

GPS 50°49'02.72"N 3°14'19.61"E

↑ Bissegem 100 m
E
F
G
H
I
J
29. M. 6. MARCKE.
17. 5. 18
Lys 1
2
Kortrijk 1,5 km ↑
3
4
5 ↓ Marksesteenweg
6
100 m

101
PERVIJZE – RAILWAY EMBANKMENT
18 MAY 1918

A British aerial photograph of 1918 shows the Diksmuide–Nieuwpoort railway embankment, used by the Belgian army as its first line. To the east are outposts in the inundation that could only be reached along wooden walkways. The darker-coloured areas are submerged fields and meadows.

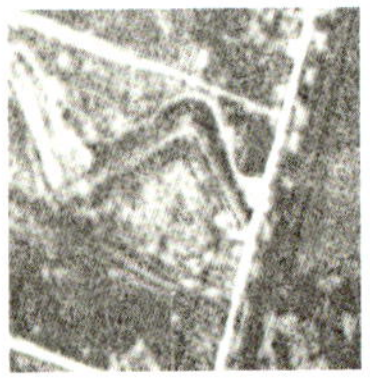

B1
RAILWAY EMBANKMENT
The embankment above the Yser plain was equipped with trenches and concrete shelters. A zigzag trench led from there to the line at the rear.

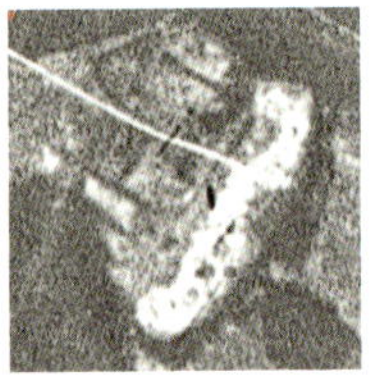

E4
BERKELHOF
Major watch-post (Grand Garde 4) in the inundation. It consisted of a few trenches built around the ruins of Berkelhof Farm.

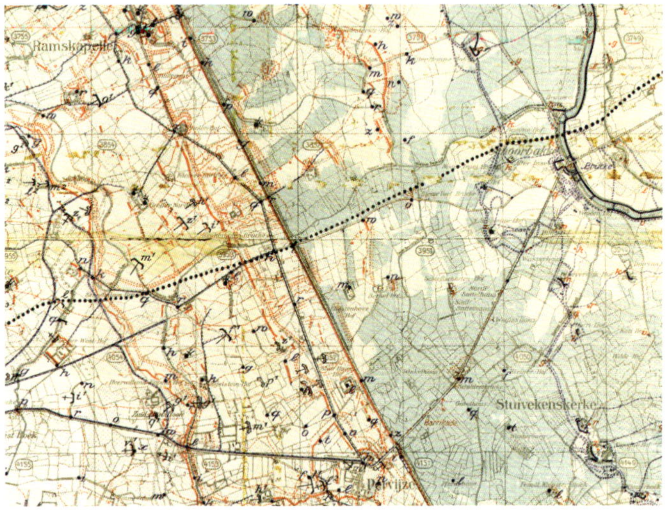

↑ GERMAN TRENCH MAP
A German trench map of 10 October 1918 shows the flooded area between the Yser and the railway.

↓ PANORAMA
Panorama of the flooded Yser plain taken from coordinate B2 on the aerial photograph. From the railway embankment wooden walkways or footbridges ran to the farm buildings on the horizon, which served as Belgian outposts.

GPS 51°05'16.60"N 2°47'22.13"E

D
E
F
B
G
H
I
G
J
1
Schoorbakke 1.2 km ↗
2
3
inundation ↓
4
100 m
B

102
PANORAMA POTIJZE-YPRES-DE KLIJTE 21 MAY 1918

During the First World War it was mainly planes that were used to carry the cameras that took oblique and vertical aerial photographs. Throughout the war, however, captive balloons were also used for observation purposes. These high observation posts were also used for aerial photographs taken, not above enemy lines, but from a distance using lenses with a long focal length. This German panoramic photograph was taken on 21 May 1918 by a photographer of the Feld-Luftschiffer-Abteilung (Balloon Detachment 36) and records the area between De Klijte and Potijze. An aerial photographic interpreter has marked the position of the front following the German Spring Offensive of 1918 with a white dotted line.

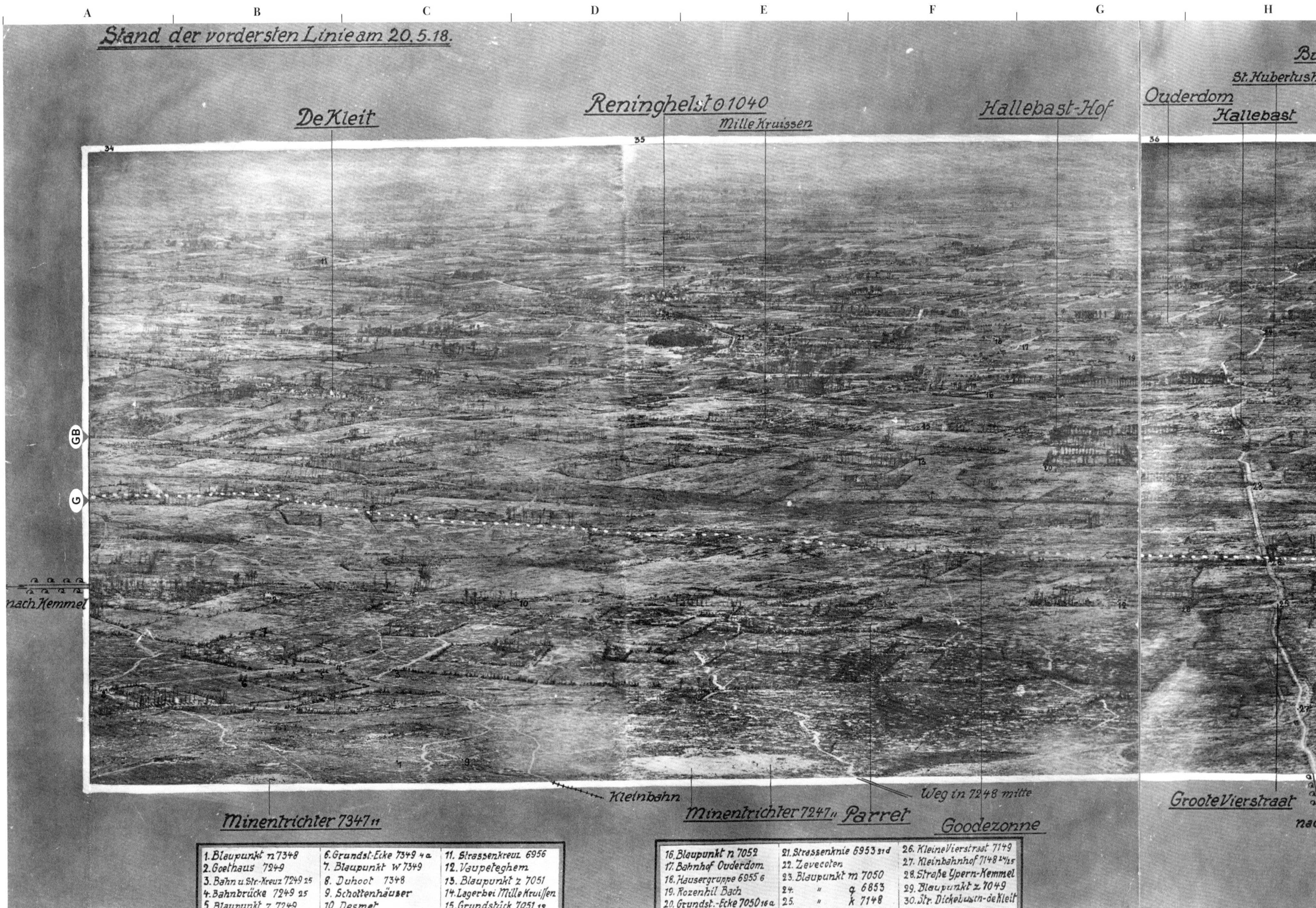

→ BRITISH TRENCH MAP

Fragments of a British trench map of 19 May 1918. These correspond to the places that are visible on the oblique aerial photograph below.

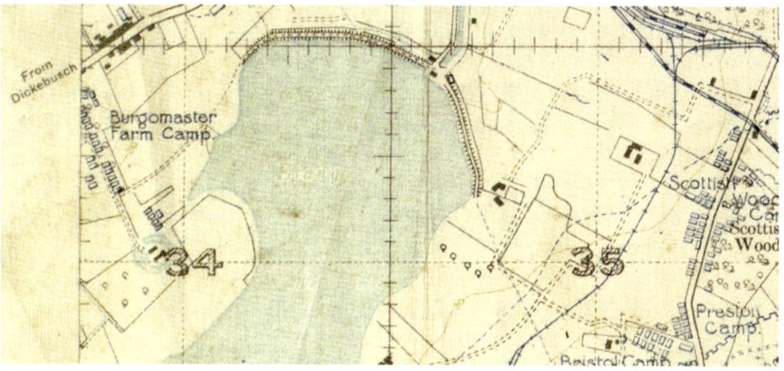

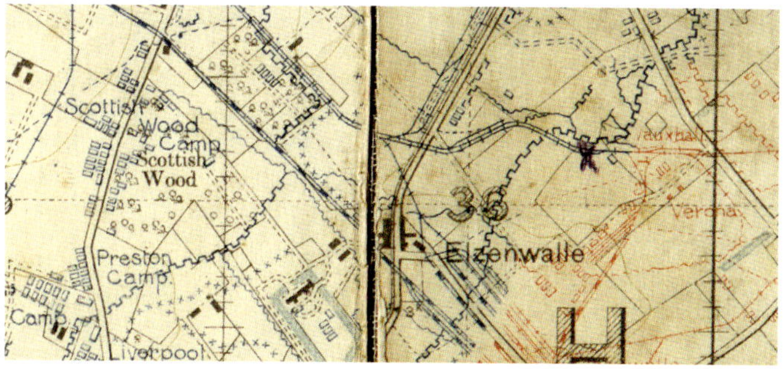

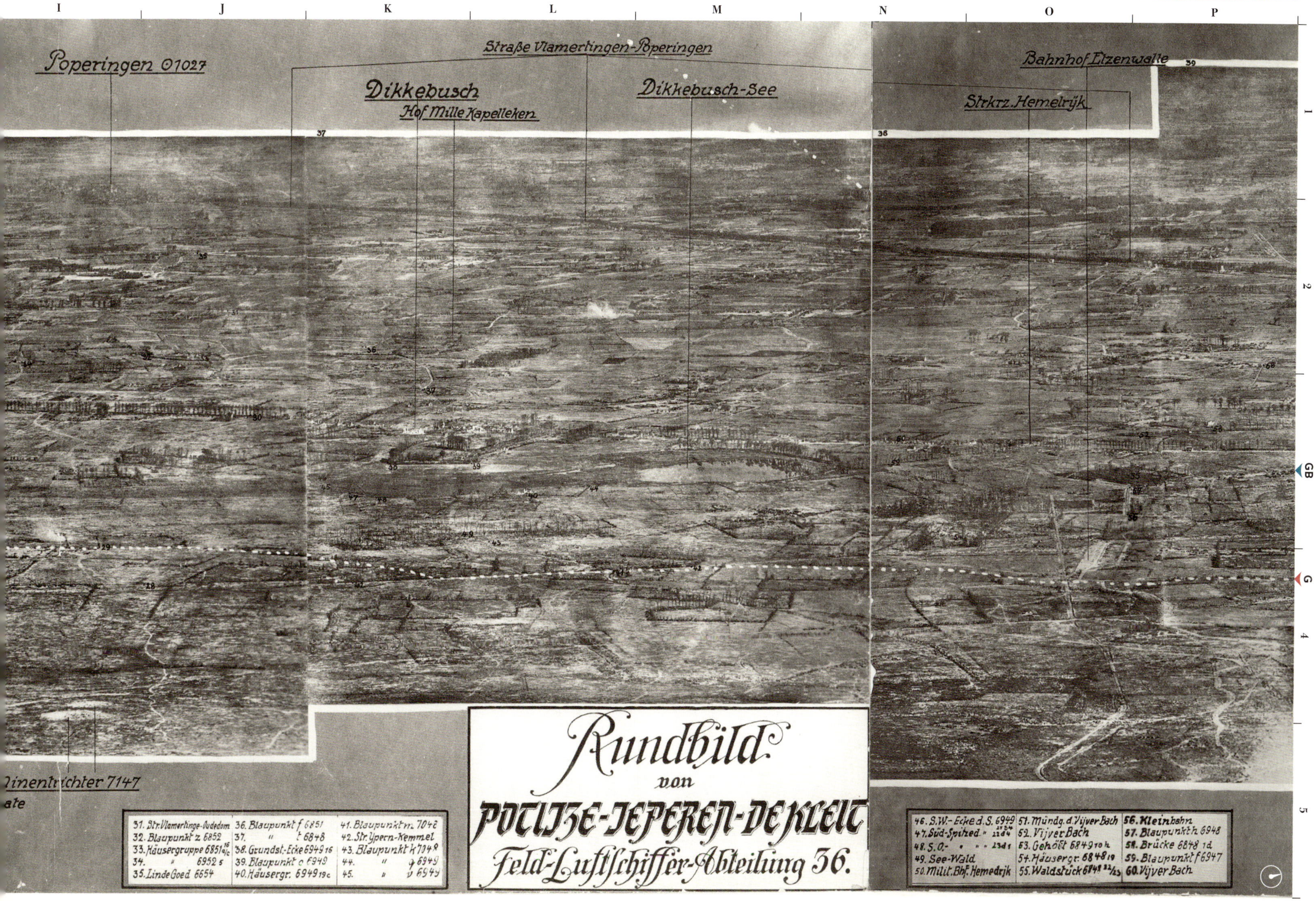

← **OBSERVATION BALLOON**

A German observation balloon released over Flanders. The observer sat in a basket hanging under the balloon.

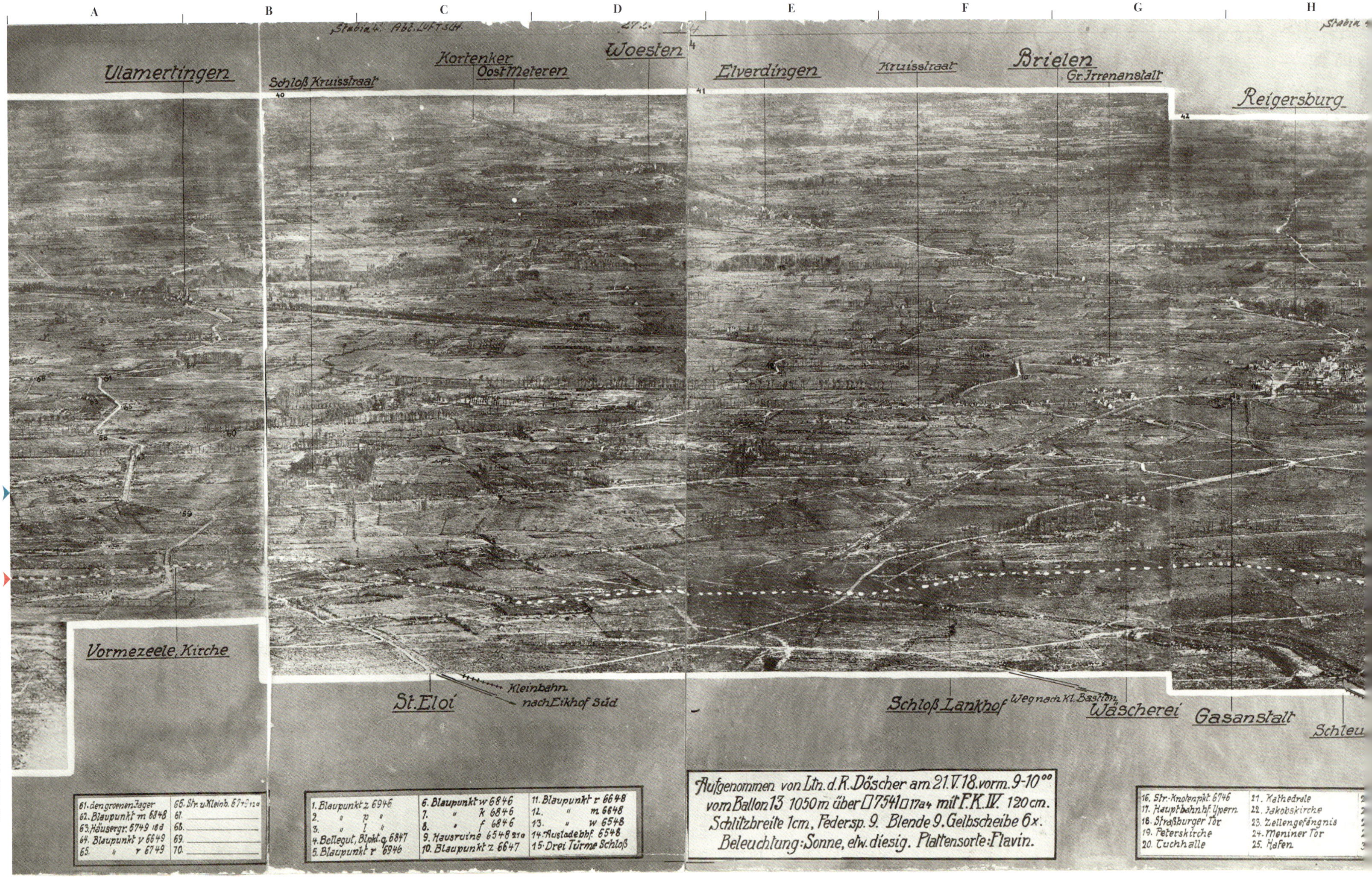

YPRES
Zillebeke Jctn.
C3 Line
Zillebeke Tunnel
Zillebeke

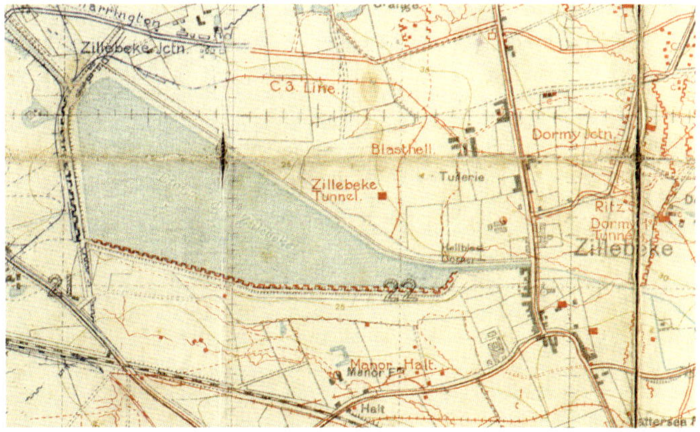

Potijze
Gibraltar Fm
Dragoon Farm Camp.
Dragoon Fm
James Fm
Cavalry Road
(Duckboard)

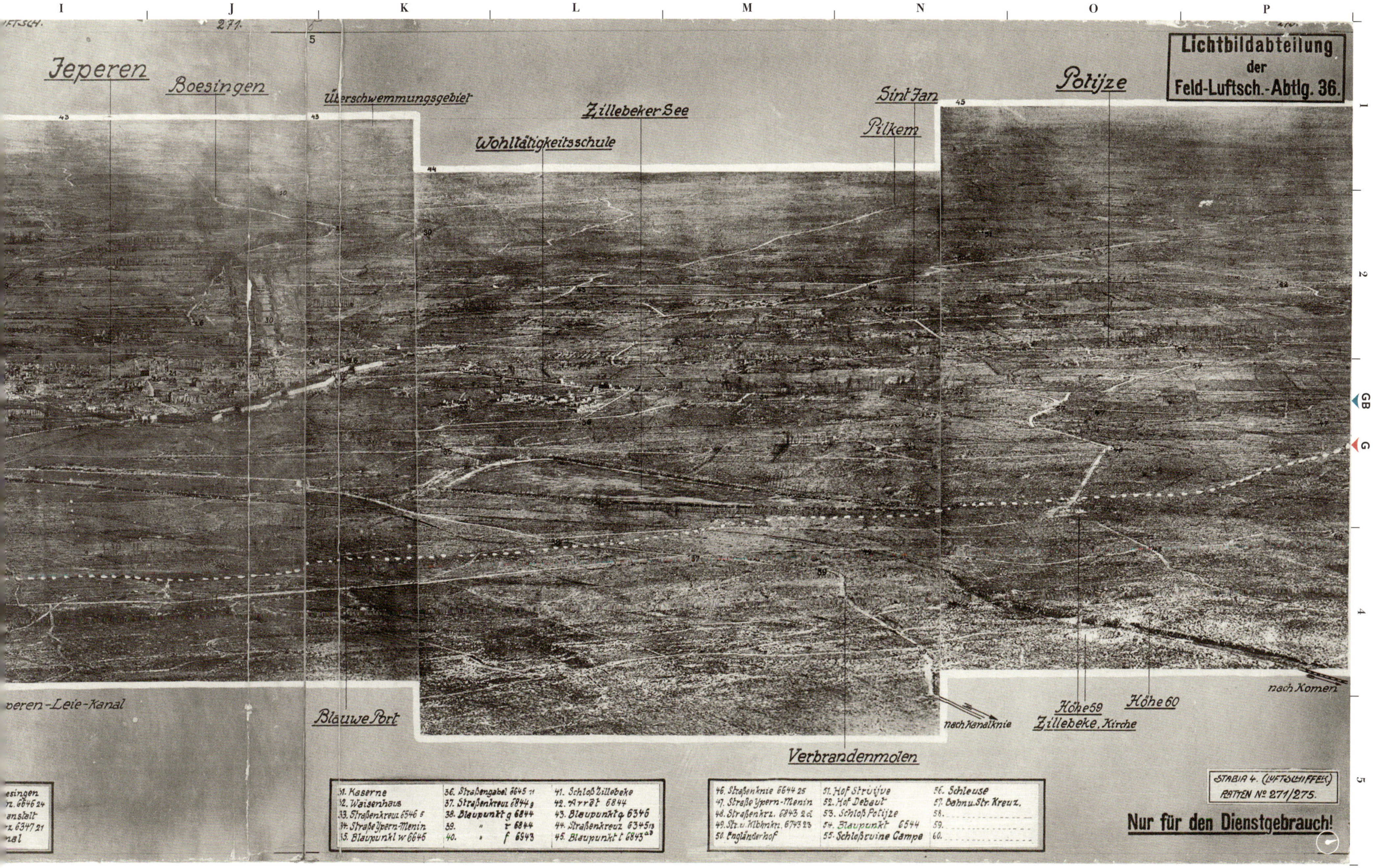
Lichtbildabteilung der Feld-Luftsch.-Abtlg. 36.
Ieperen
Boesingen
Überschwemmungsgebiet
Zillebeker See
Wohltätigkeitsschule
Sint Jan
Pilkem
Potijze
eperen-Leie-Kanal
Blauwe Port
Verbrandenmolen
nach Kanalknie
Höhe 59
Zillebeke, Kirche
Höhe 60
nach Komen
31. Kaserne
32. Waisenhaus
33. Straßenkreuz 6546 5
34. Straße Ypern-Menin
35. Blaupunkt w 6645
36. Straßengabel 6645 11
37. Straßenkreuz 6844 g
38. Blaupunkt g 6844
39. " r 6844
40. " f 6943
41. Schloß Zillebeke
42. Arrêt 6844
43. Blaupunkt q 6346
44. Straßenkreuz 6345 13
45. Blaupunkt t 6843 ab
46. Straßenknie 6644 25
47. Straße Ypern-Menin
48. Straßenkrz. 6843 2d
49. Str. u. Klbhnkr. 6743 23
50. Engländerhof
51. Hof Strüijve
52. Hof Debaut
53. Schloß Potijze
54. Blaupunkt 6544
55. Schloßruine Campe
56. Schleuse
57. Bahn u. Str. Kreuz.
58.
59.
60.
STABIA 4. (LUFTSCHIFFER) RATTEN No 271/275.
Nur für den Dienstgebrauch!

103

BRUGES – IMPERIAL SHIPYARD

30 MAY 1918

The port of Bruges (Kaiserliche Werft Brügge / Bruges Imperial Shipyard) was connected by canal to the North Sea. Bruges was an important centre for the German navy because, unlike ports in northern Germany, it had easy access to the North Sea. Its geographical situation inland and regional network of deep canals made Bruges a relatively safe haven for submarines. The port had workshops, floating dry docks, barracks and concrete U-boat bunkers to protect them against air attacks. In the vicinity of the port infrastructure, in this image, are dozens of craters, the result of Allied aerial bombardment.

→ **U-BOAT BUNKER**

German U-boat bunker (F2) at the entrance to the first dock in the port of Bruges. A little further away is a second, similar construction (F2-F3).

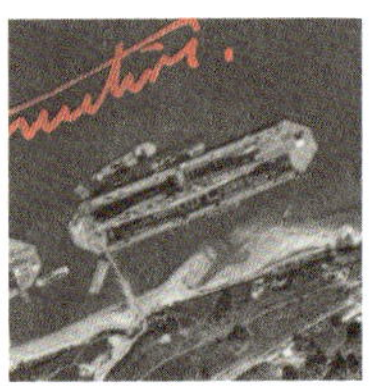

E4

U-BOAT IN DRY DOCK

In one of the dry docks a U-boat is awaiting repairs.

D2-D3

U-BOAT BUNKERS

At the time the picture was taken six of the eight U-boat bunkers (the so-called 'Eight Beatitudes') had been completed.

C4-C5

CONSTRUCTION YARD

Construction is underway for a new U-boat bunker.

SYMBOLS

- GERMAN SHED, BUNKER
- U-BOAT BUNKER
- BOMB CRATER
- AMMUNITION STORE
- FLOATING DRY DOCKS
- RAILWAY

GPS 51°13'59.98"N 3°13'14.51"E

↓ **THE 'EIGHT BEATITUDES'**

The eight concrete U-boat bunkers in the first dock of the port of Bruges – known familiarly as the 'Eight Beatitudes' – at the end of the war.[39]

↓ **OBLIQUE VIEW**

The port infrastructure in Bruges with the northern outskirts of the city in the background.

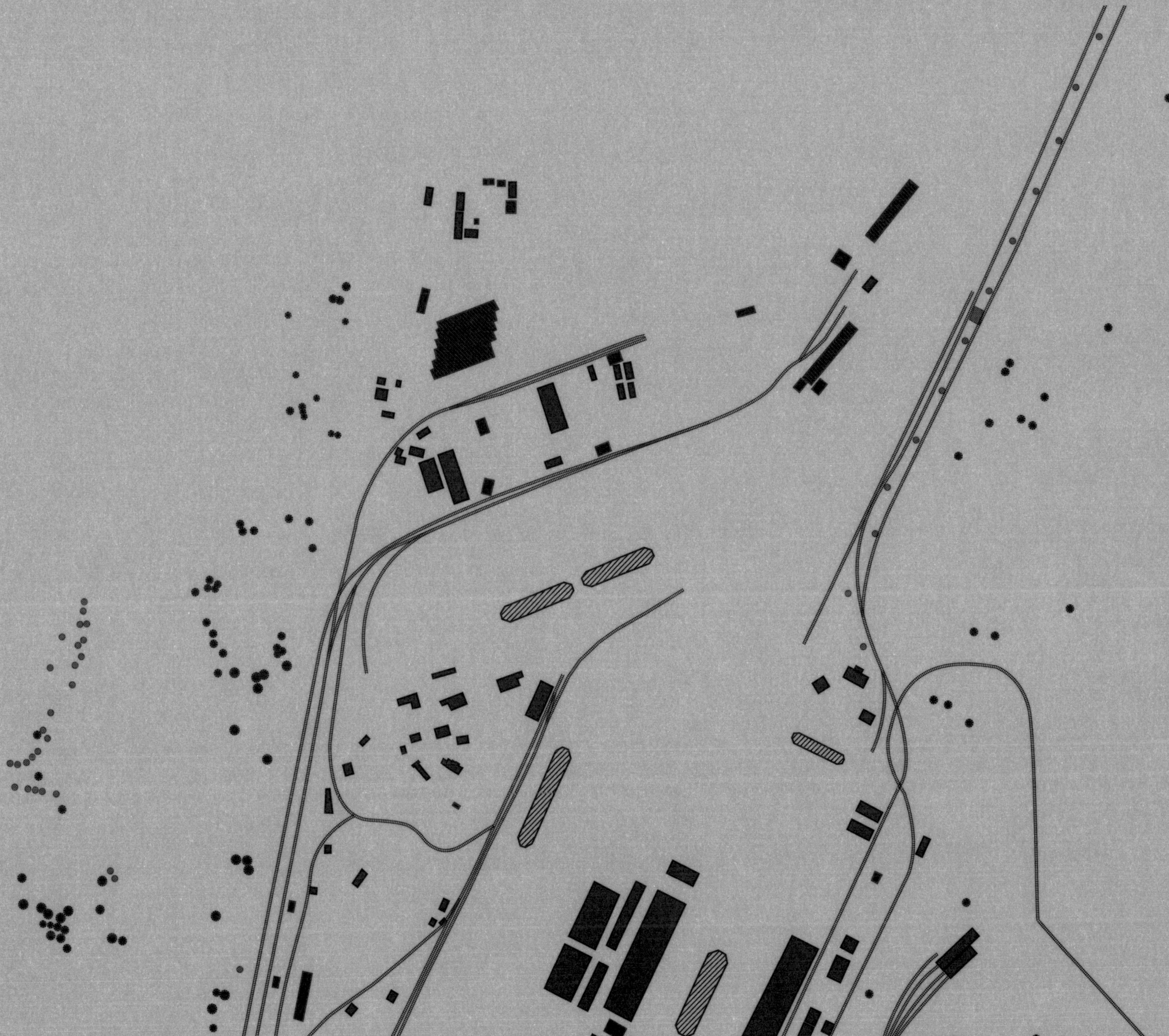

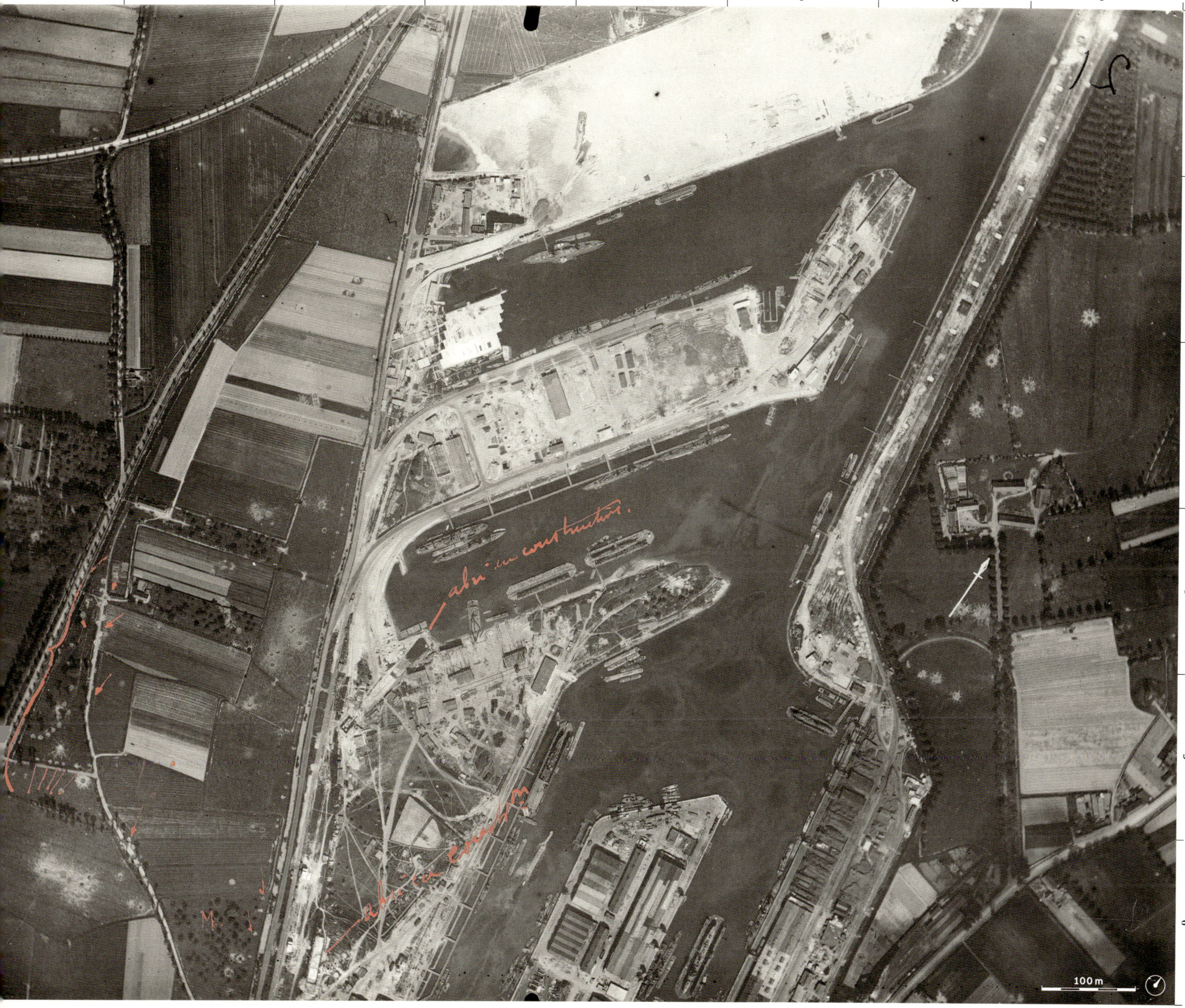
A
B
C
D
E
F
G
North Sea-Bruges Canal
1
2
3
4
5
6
100 m
centre of Bruges 1.6 km
Groot Handelsdok
Klein Handelsdok

104
SINT-JANSMOLEN – CAMOUFLAGE 20 MAY 1918

The difference between seeing and being seen could make the difference between life and death. One of the earliest and simplest ways of not being seen was to set up guns under stands of trees. The foliage and the shadows cast by the trees often made the guns invisible. Attempts were made to cover artillery with branches and leaves, painted covers and camouflage nets. But it was extremely difficult to ensure that nothing betrayed the position of an artillery gun. The cat-and-mouse game between ground camouflage and aerial photography was often settled in favour of the latter. An effective new technique made this possible: stereoscopy. This enabled the aerial photographic interpreter to detect what might at first seem to be perfectly camouflaged positions. This Belgian aerial photograph of Belgian gun positions near Sint-Jansmolen was possibly taken to investigate the effectiveness of camouflage. There are six firing positions to be seen, two of which have been the subject of serious attempts at camouflage.

GPS 51°02'29.83"N 2°46'09.50"E

↓ **BELGIAN ARTILLERY**

Belgian artillery troops pose by their camouflaged gun emplacement.

G3

ARTILLERY BATTERY

There seems to have been little attempt to camouflage these four gun emplacements bounded by a horseshoe-shaped wall.

B5

BARBED WIRE

Barbed-wire entanglement round Sint-Jansmolen, which had been set up as a reinforced position and surgery station.

E2

CAMOUFLAGED POSITIONS

To the west of the Oude Zeedijkstraat are two camouflaged but still visible heavy gun emplacements. Despite every effort to cover them with coloured screens, the emplacement catches the eye because of the difference in shade between the screens and the surrounding grass and because of the footpath around it. The emplacement was marked on German artillery maps, so the enemy, too, was clearly not taken in by the camouflage.

↓ **GERMAN ARTILLERY MAP, 10 OCTOBER 1918**

Despite the camouflage, the emplacement has nevertheless been recognised by German aerial photographers. They have marked the spot with an 'r'.

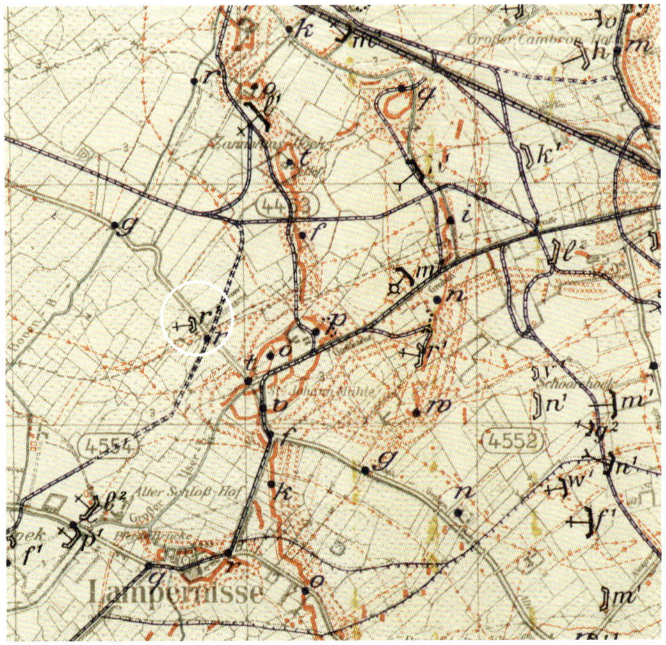

↑ barbed wire

Diksmuide 6.3 km   front 5 km   Oostkerke 1.8 km

105
HOLLANDSTELLUNG
30 MAY 1918

Between Knokke and Turnhout the German 4th Army and the Marine Corps Flanders built an extensive defensive line along the Belgian–Dutch border.[40] The fear was that the Netherlands would abandon its neutrality and allow the Allies passage through its territory, thus enabling them to circle round to attack the German army from behind. The Germans' counter-plan was a network of defences that comprised the Hollandstellung (stretching 80 kilometres from the North Sea to the River Scheldt), the Antwerp Stellung (round Antwerp, 48 km) and the Turnhout-Kanalstellung (from Antwerp to Turnhout, 34 km).[41] Construction of the Hollandstellung was begun in 1916 and was completed in the summer of 1917. The line consisted mainly of enormous barbed-wire barriers behind which were hundreds of concealed bunkers. Between the old St Isabella and St Donaas Forts the Hollandstellung followed the path of the Cantelmo Line of 1632, a Spanish line built during the Eighty Years' War. The Germans incorporated the 300-year-old redans and redoubts, perhaps in order to profit from the slight elevations they provided in the flat polder landscape.

GPS 51°19'01.15"N 3°21'04.59"E

» **SEE ALSO** 74 ANTWERP - STABROEK FORT

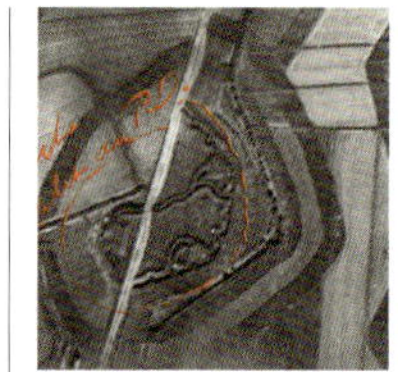

C4
CANTELMO LINE REDANS

The Cantelmo Line formed an elevation in the landscape. When they constructed the Hollandstellung the Germans made use of the redans as part of their trenches.

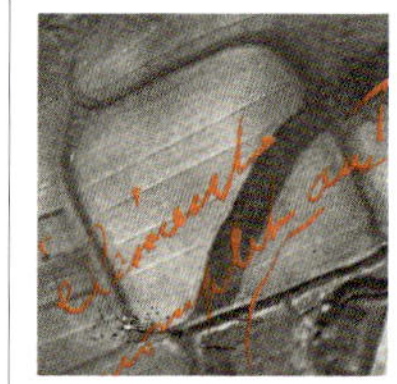

B3/C3
SEVENTEENTH-CENTURY REDOUBT

Behind the redan there are recognisable traces in the property boundaries of a seventeenth-century redoubt, a kind of field earthwork.

← **GREVENINGE POLDER (30 MAY 1918)**

General view of the German Hollandstellung, virtually running along the seventeenth-century Cantelmo Line.

→ **ELECTRIC WIRE FENCE**

In 1915 the Germans had already built an electric wire fence along the Belgian–Dutch border in an effort to stop spies, civilians and war volunteers from fleeing occupied Belgium.[42]

A
B
C
↑ North Sea 4.8 km
D
↑ St Isabella Fort
E
↓ barbed wire
F
↓ barbed wire
G
H
1
2
3
4
5
6
211.F.E.1401
5.0.27.33.
26.9.18–11.30
F–20
100 m
↓ Sluis (NL) 2 km

106

ZEEBRUGGE – U-BOATS

19 MAY 1918

The harbour infrastructure of Zeebrugge, Bruges and Ostend was an important asset for the German navy. From spring 1915 the U-Bootflotille Flandern (Flanders U-boat flotilla) operated out of Zeebrugge and Ostend, patrolling the waters of the North Sea,[43] and sinking a wartime total of more than 2,500 ships.[44] The Zeebrugge inner harbour offered a safe haven for U-boats, thanks to two large submarine bunkers on the eastern side of the Old Ferry Dock. They offered protection in the event of aerial bombardment.

» **SEE ALSO** 115 OSTEND

→ **OBLIQUE AERIAL PHOTOGRAPH OF U-BOAT BUNKERS**

A post-war aerial photograph from the early 1920s shows the two 70-metre-long concrete U-boat bunkers and a wooden landing-stage for boats.

F5

U-BOAT BUNKERS

Berth and two concrete U-boat shelters at the side of the Old Ferry Dock in Zeebrugge inner harbour.

A5

MOORED SHIPS

German naval ships in the dock.

G4

FORTIFICATION

To the east of the concrete U-boat shelters is a bunker with a small trench next to it. The dark line at top left is a 10-metre-wide barbed-wire barrier.

GPS 51°02'46,08"N 2°50'34,57"E

→ **SUBMARINE**

German submarine of the U-Bootflotille Flandern in one of the West Flemish canals.

↑ 1.9 km 107 108 Zeebrugge

Bruges 103 9.5 km ↙

107
ZEEBRUGGE – RAID 23 APRIL 1918

In 1918 the British came up with a plan to block submarine access to the North Sea by sinking old ships in the harbour entrances. On the night of 22 to 23 April they carried out a raid on the harbours of Ostend and Zeebrugge. The HMS *Vindictive*, *Daffodil* and *Iris* brought British landing troops to the Zeebrugge harbour breakwater where they took out the German battery on the end of it (I1). Meanwhile, three old cruisers (the *Intrepid*, the *Iphigenia* and the *Thetis*), fully loaded with concrete, were sunk in the entrance to the canal that led into Bruges. The raid on Ostend, by contrast, was a failure and a further attempt had to be made on 9 May.

SYMBOLS

- GERMAN TRENCH, SHED
- GERMAN BUNKER, U-BOAT BUNKER
- FLYING-BOAT HANGAR
- OBSTACLE IN THE HARBOUR CHANNEL
- BRITISH BLOCKSHIP
- BREACH CAUSED BY EXPLODING BRITISH SUBMARINE
- BARBED WIRE
- CANNON

GERMAN AERIAL PHOTOGRAPH OF THE CANAL ENTRANCE

Oblique view of the three British blockships, with the harbour breakwater in the background. In the foreground are the *Intrepid* and the *Iphigenia* and, further out, the *Thetis*.

GPS 51°20'46.21"N 3°10'15.39"E

↑ harbour breakwater

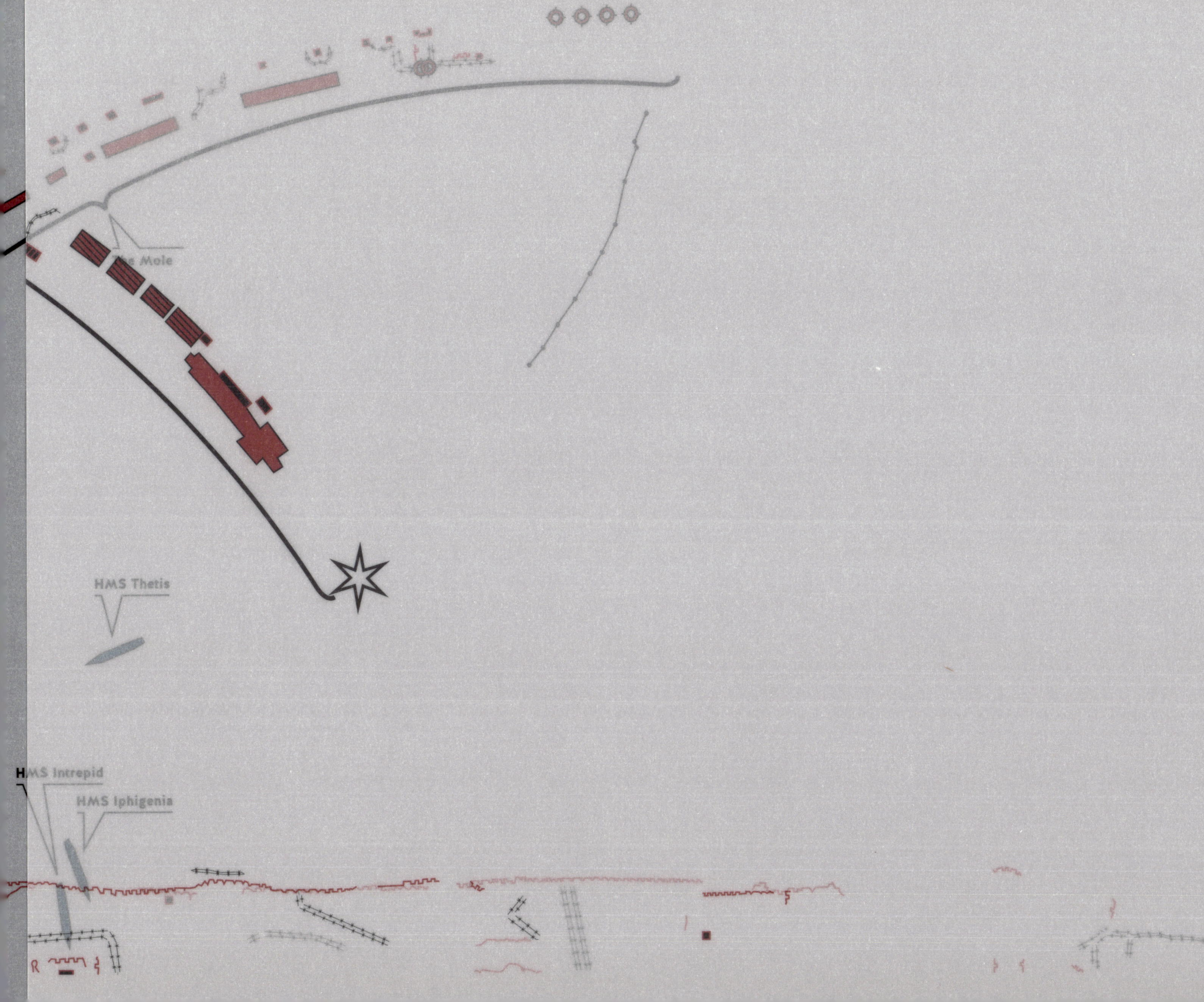

The Mole
HMS Thetis
HMS Intrepid
HMS Iphigenia

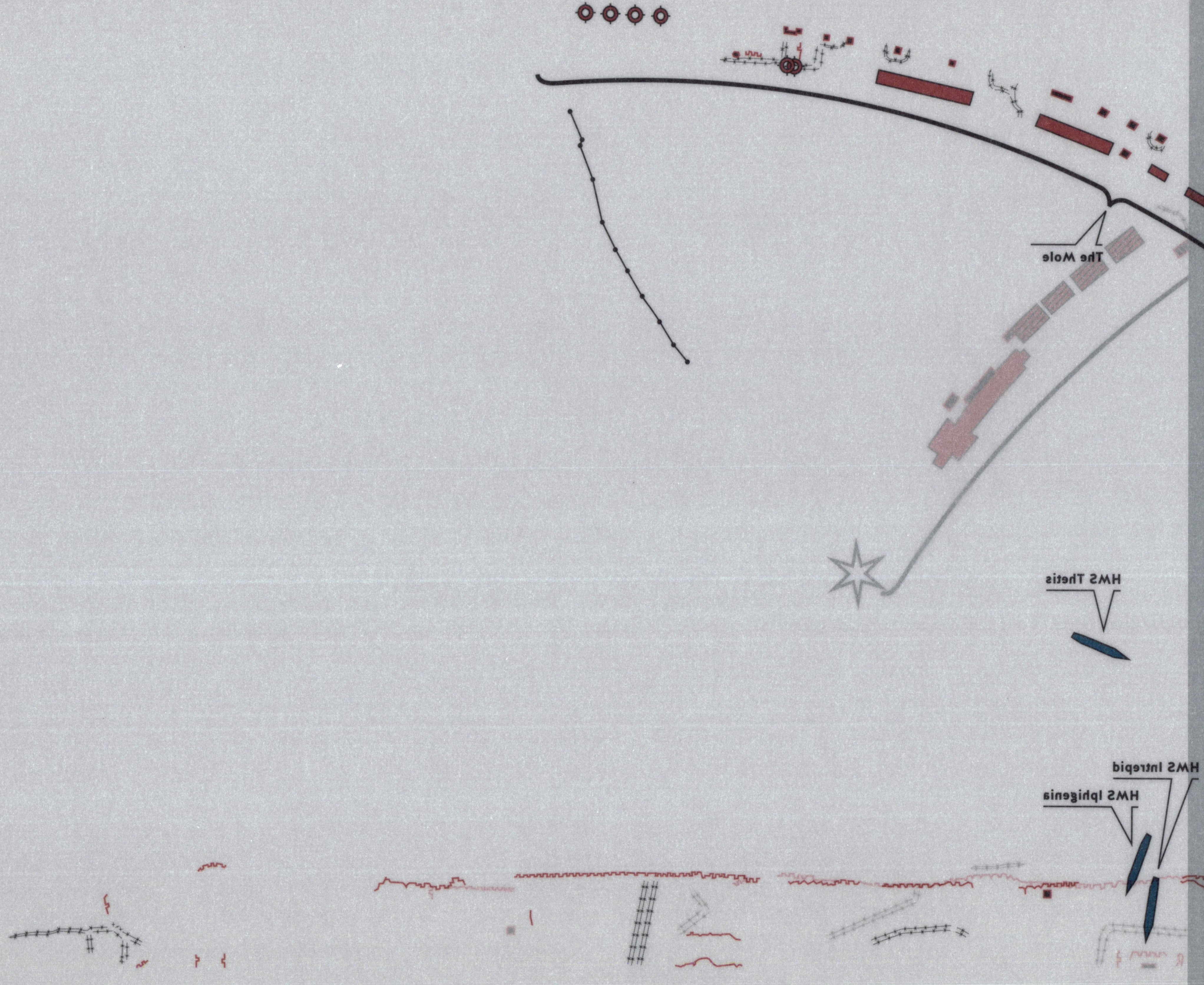
The Mole
HMS Thetis
HMS Intrepid
HMS Iphigenia

North Sea–Bruges Canal

Lys Drainage Canal

108
ZEEBRUGGE - SEEFLUGSTATION FLANDERN I 27 MAY 1918

From the end of 1914 the Zeebrugge breakwater was used as the base for the Seeflugstation Flandern I of the German navy. From here the Germans bombed Great Britain. On 6 December the first flying boats arrived.[45] A special base was constructed on the breakwater: harbour cranes hoisted the craft out of their sheds and into the water. On the inner side of the high breakwater the Imperial Navy's ships were protected. From here torpedo boats and torpedo-boat destroyers operated in the Channel and the North Sea. The breakwater was like a fort, with bunkers and barbed-wire fences.

» **SEE ALSO** (113) SEEFLUGSTATION FLANDERN II

↗ C3 and D3
FLYING-BOAT CRANE

German flying boats were lowered into the water using giant cranes.

→ **DIRECT HIT**

Direct hit on one of the German submarine shelters on 'The Mole'. These shelters were built on a metal frame with an armour-plated roof. As the photograph shows, they were not completely proof against attack.

→ **FLYING-BOAT HANGARS**

Ground photograph of the flying-boat base on the Zeebrugge Mole.

C3-D3
FLYING BOATS

Various types of flying boat standing on the harbour wall in front of their sheds.

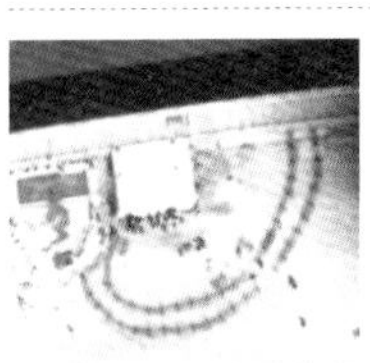

I1
HARBOUR DAM FORTIFICATION

Bunker on the outer side of the harbour dam surrounded by a double barbed-wire fence.

GPS 51°20'53.89"N 3°10'14.69"E

D
E
F
G
H
I
J
1
2
3
4
5
6
harbour breakwater
100 m

109
MIDDELKERKE 5 JUNE 1918

The German Marinekorps Flandern converted the coastline between Lombardsijde and the Dutch border at Knokke into a position for repelling Allied landings and protecting the harbour infrastructure. Numerous defensive structures were built in the dunes and in the town centres.

» **SEE ALSO** 37 START OF THE FRONT

→ D5
CASINO

The ruins of the casino hid a German observation bunker. The trenches in the dyke are visible at bottom left.

↓ **OBLIQUE VIEW**

On 27 October 1917 a British air scout ventured close to the coastline to take a panoramic picture of Middelkerke.

D5
TRENCHES

Trenches were built on the sea wall, from which the beach could be raked with enfilade fire.

G3
DRESSING STATION

Set among the buildings still standing in the Kerkstraat, the Red Cross symbol indicates the location of a German dressing station or hospital.

G6
ANTI-AIRCRAFT POST

The round emplacement of an anti-aircraft gun just behind the coastline.

GPS 51°11'16.24"N 2°48'47.45"E

A B C D E **Ostend** 8 km ↑ F G H

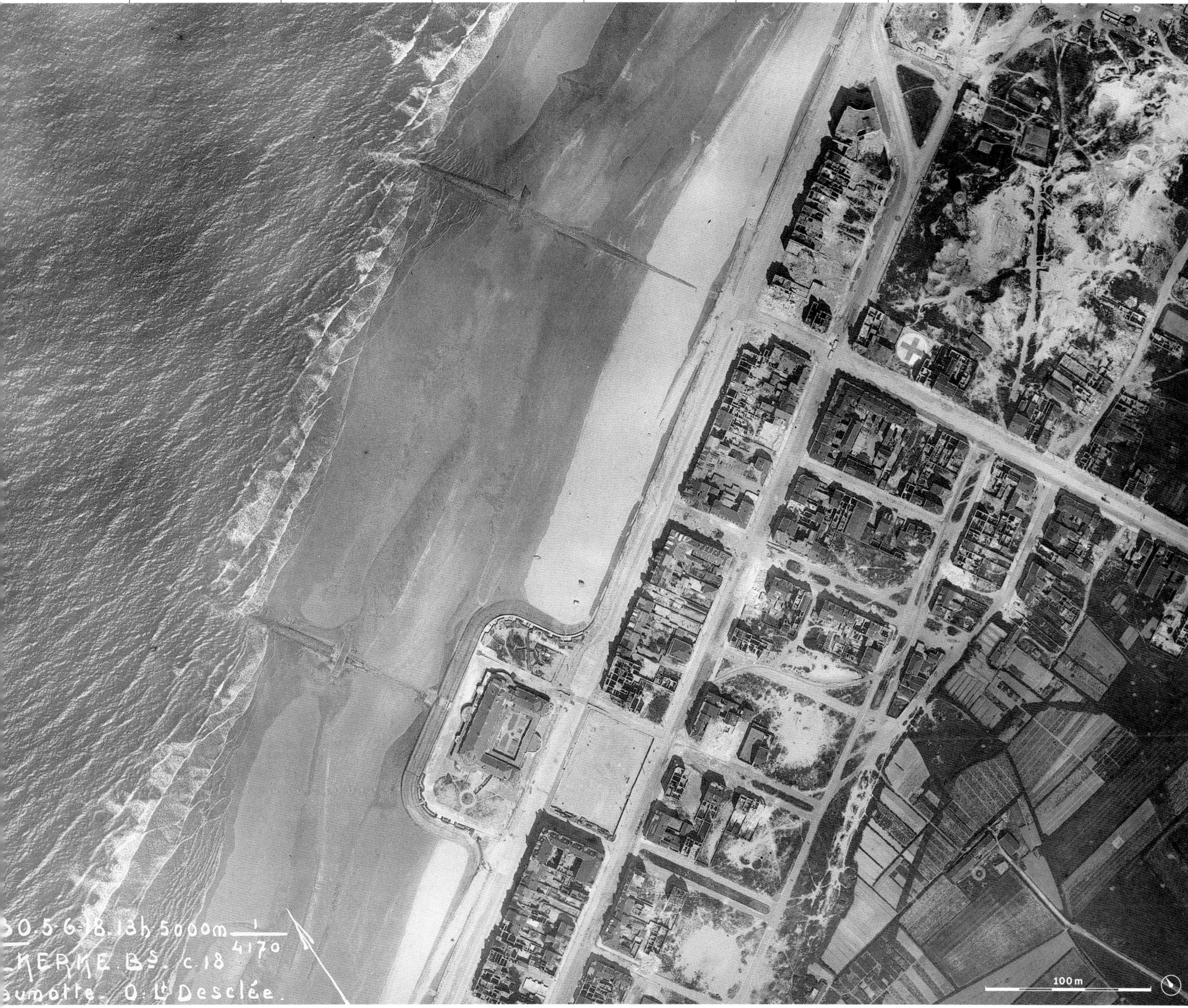

1 2 3 Kerkstraat ↙ 4 5 barbed wire ↓ 6

start of the front 37 7.2 km ↙ Koninginnelaan ↗ ↑ barbed wire

110
MALDEGEM 17 JUNE 1918

The accelerated development of both aeronautical and photographic technologies led to a remarkable increase in reconnaissance flights during the war. In the period 1914–16 it was the front that was the main subject of photography. Gradually, the range and altitude of flights increased and tactical reconnaissance flights were undertaken far beyond the front. One example resulted in the aerial photographs of the German installations at Maldegem, 50 kilometres behind the front. The curious forward-pointing arrow can be seen only from the air – this was doubtless intentional. Perhaps the purpose of this construction was to give pilots signals from the ground.

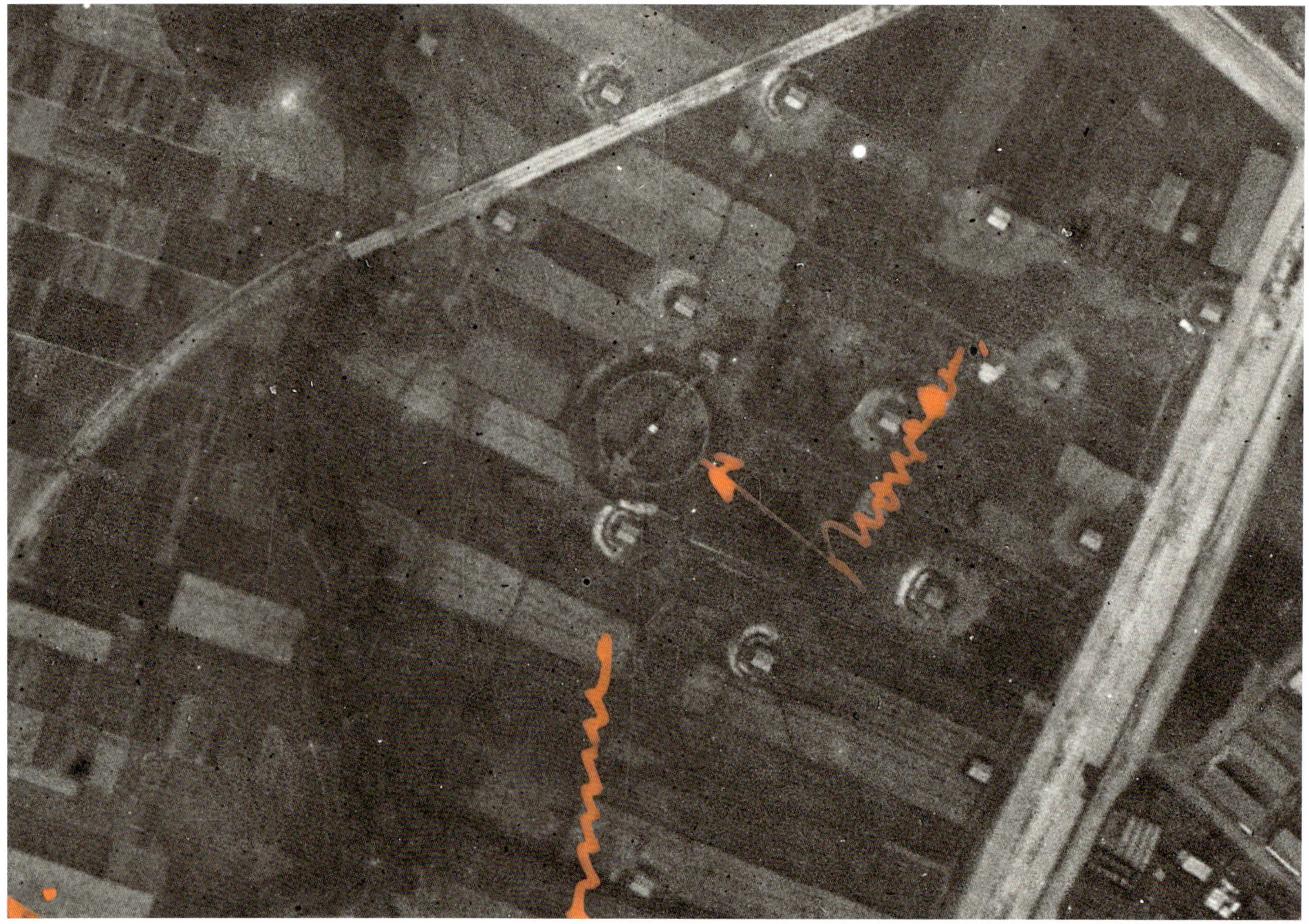

→ **ARROW**

On 16 July 1918 the arrow pointed in a different direction from that of a month earlier.

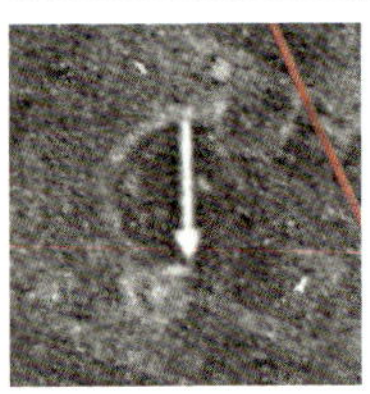

G2
ARROW
In the centre is a 30-metre-long arrow that could be rotated on a circular platform.

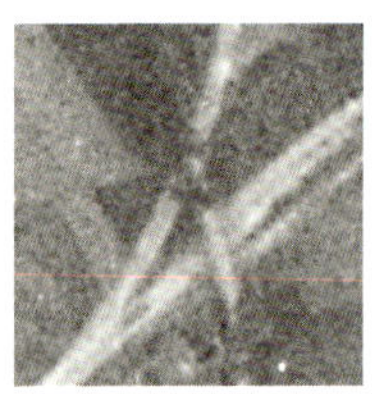

F5
NARROW-GAUGE BRANCH LINE
A branch of the Bruges-Eeklo railway line leads to the ammunition store in Maldegem.

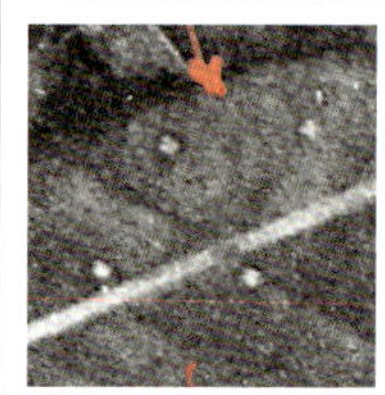

G1/H1
AMMUNITION STORE
The area between the railway and the centre of the village serves as an ammunition store. A score of ammunition piles lie scattered here and there.

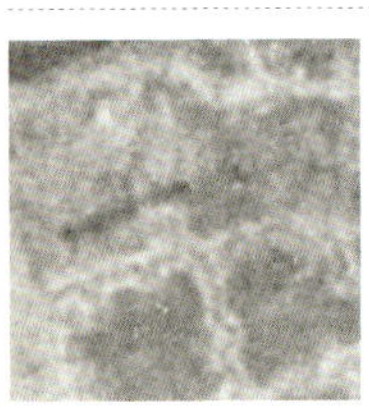

G6
EXERCISE TRENCHES
Dozens of trench systems were laid down far beyond the front, well into the countryside, for tactical practice and drill training.

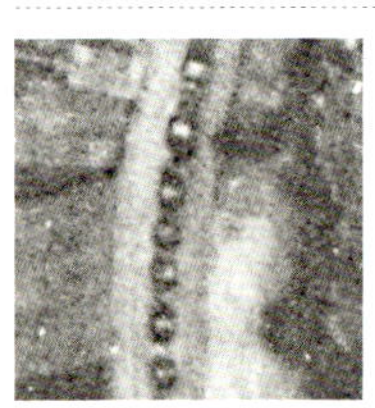

F3
AMMUNITION STORE
Next to a narrow-gauge railway track lie large piles of ammunition.

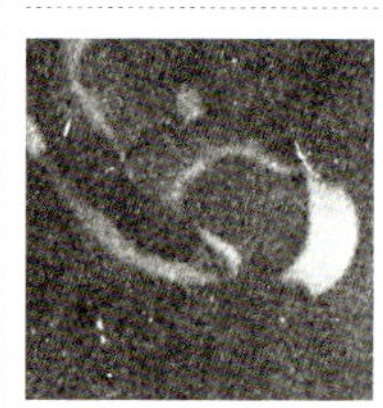

B5
REESINGHE MANOR
A nineteenth-century neo-Gothic country house and estate.

A
B
C
D
E
Westeindestraat ↓
F
G
H
1
2
↖ railway to Eeklo
3
4
5
6
100 m
↓ Ypres 55 km

111

JABBEKE 1 JULY 1918

In January 1917 a Pioneer Park was opened for the Gruppe Nord of the German 4th Army.[46] Such parks were an important link in the logistical supply chain. From here, building materials, provisions and ammunition were distributed to smaller supply points nearer the front. Railway lines connected the Pioneer Park to the front and to the hinterland. It also had a loading quay for materials to be sent via the Bruges–Ostend Canal. The western section was used mainly for the storage of ammunition in small wooden barracks (E3-F4), set at some distance from each other for safety reasons. To the north of the canal, ammunition was stored in piles in the open air (B4).

G1

NAVAL SHIP

A German destroyer or torpedo boat skulking in one of the canals in the country behind the coastal area.

F2

STORAGE OF MATERIAL

Large piles of supplies lying in the open air.

E4

AMMUNITION

Ammunition stored in wooden barracks. Narrow-gauge railways run through the Pioneer Park.

↓ **SHELLS**

German troops unloading shells from a goods train.

A B

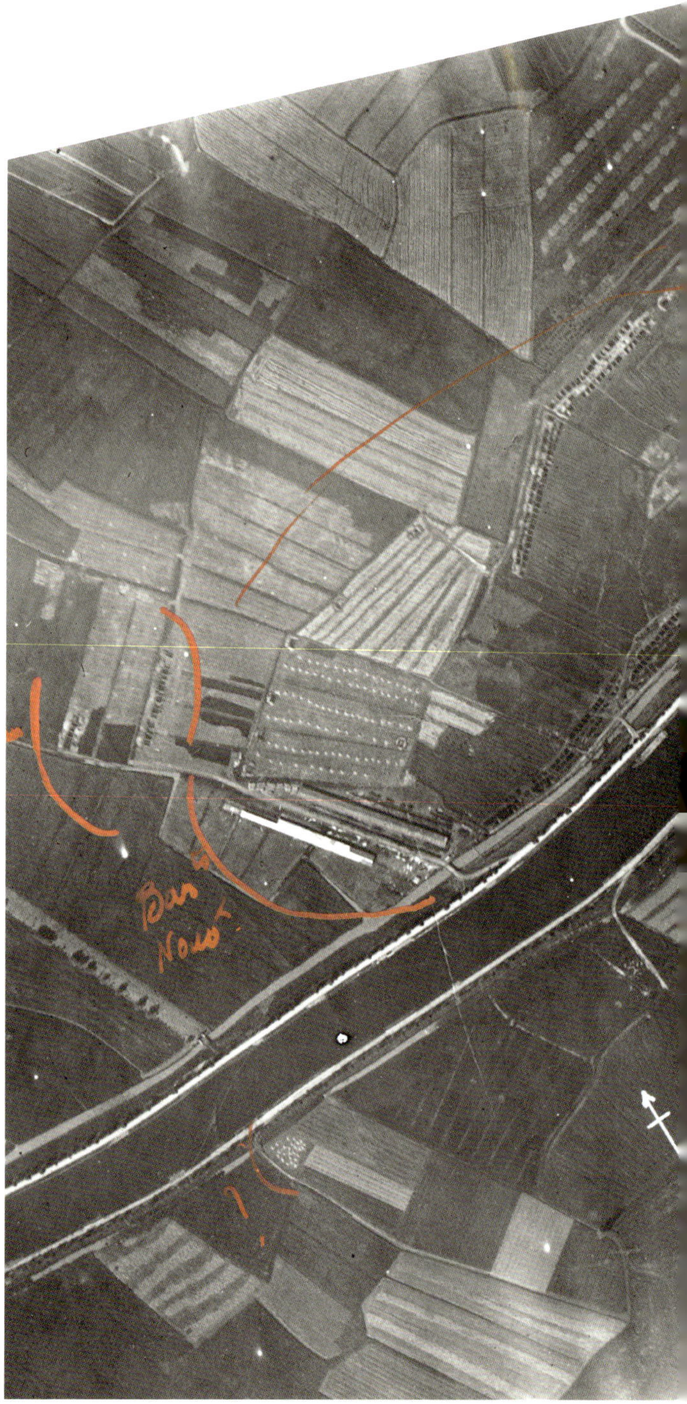

D
E
F
G
H
Bruges-Ostend Canal
J
railway to Bruges (9km)
Stationstraat
railway to Ostend (11km)

112

HANDZAME 4 JULY 1918

Near the front were training compounds where infantry techniques were practised and soldiers drilled. The siting of training areas, often within range of enemy artillery, made the training true to life, with cannon roaring in the background. This photograph of a typical German training area of this kind was taken at an altitude of almost 5 kilometres with a 120-cm lens. The training trenches catch the eye, as do the ditches, holes and low walls spread over the area forming an assault course. A conspicuous feature is the presence of round bomb craters in front of the training trench. To make the training as realistic as possible craters have been dug out by hand to make an artificial 'no-man's-land', providing a realistic imitation of conditions at the front.

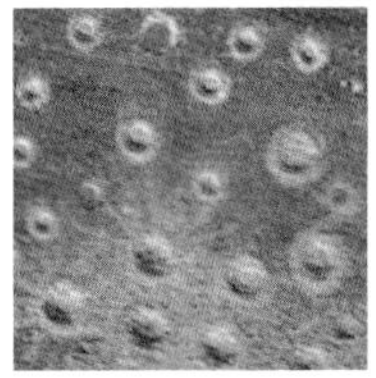

E3

ARTIFICIAL BOMB CRATERS

Unlike genuine craters, those dug by hand were perfectly round and showed no trace of an explosion. Scattered throughout this aerial photograph are dozens of genuine bomb craters.

E3/E4

TRAINING TRENCHES

These trenches are easily recognisable as training trenches because of their isolated location and the angle of the traverses.

F3

ASSAULT COURSE

The fine light lines show how and in what sequence the various obstacles of the assault course were tackled. Soldiers had to climb over walls, manoeuvre round bomb craters, and run through pools filled with water and across ground pitted with shell holes.

↓ **ASSAULT COURSE**

British troops take part in an obstacle race.

GPS 51°01'17.06"N 2°59'54.70"E

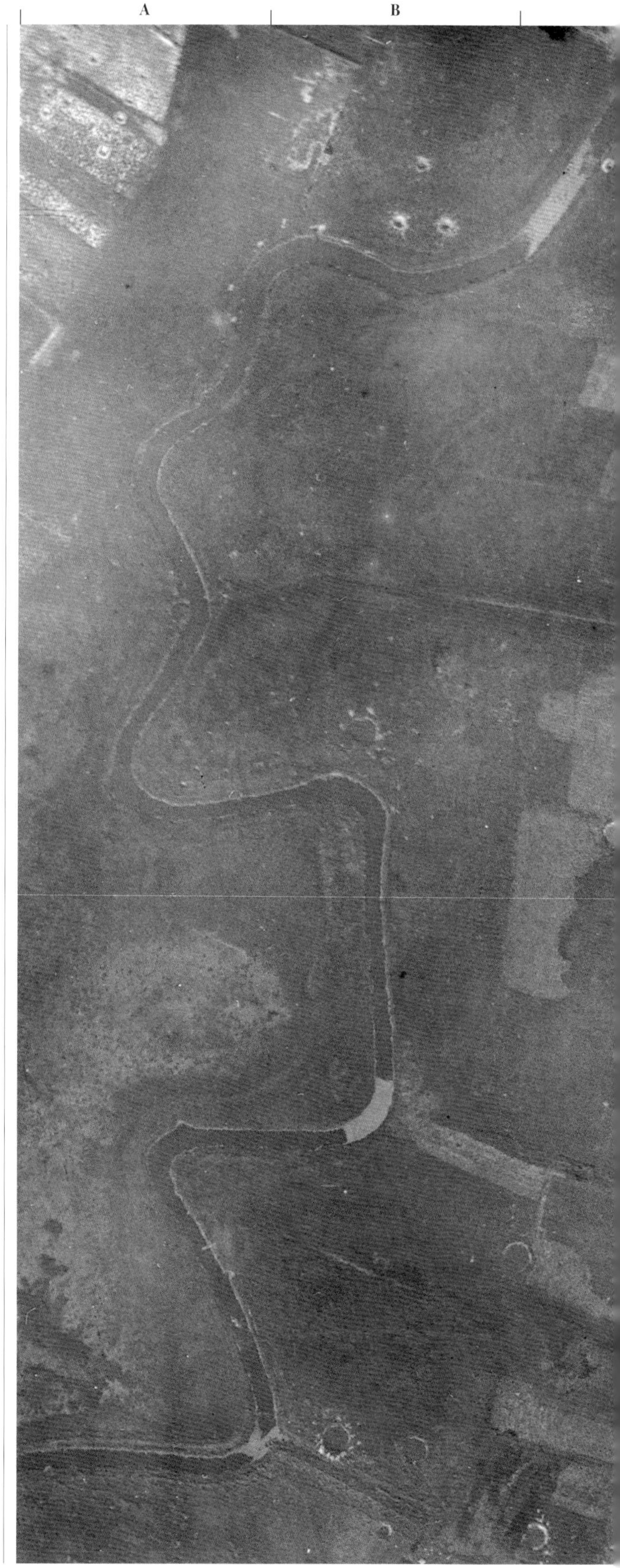

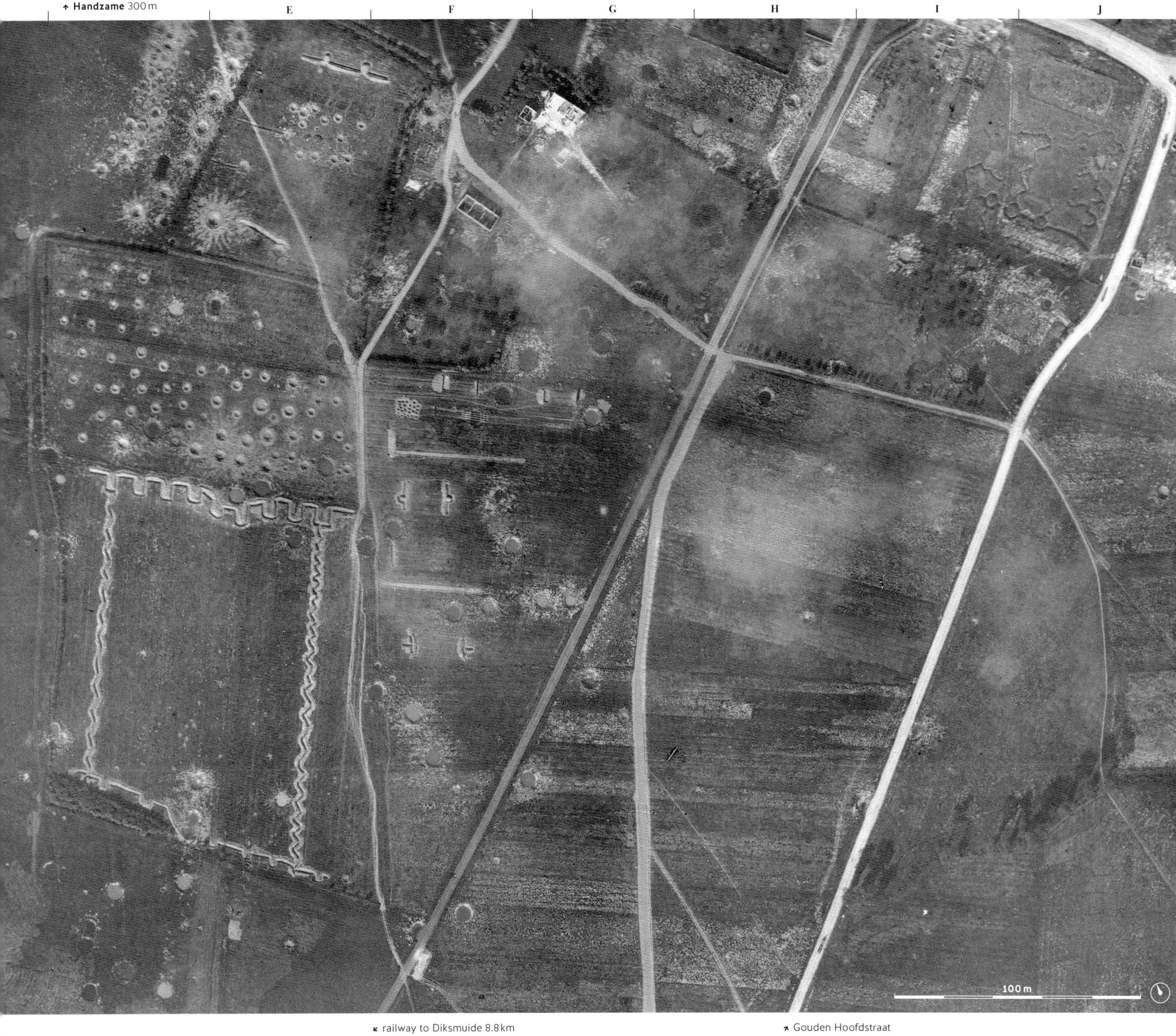

↑ Handzame 300 m
E
F
G
H
I
J
1
2
3
4
5
6
100 m
↙ railway to Diksmuide 8.8 km
↗ Gouden Hoofdstraat

113
OSTEND – SEEFLUGSTATION FLANDERN II 7 JULY 1918

A second German base for flying boats was created in the Spuikom at Ostend in 1916.[47] From here, flying boats of the Seeflugstation Flandern II operated in the North Sea. They were used to bomb targets in Great Britain and France, but their main job was to be the eyes of the coastal defence and to help provide bearings for the coastal artillery.[48] The Spuikom base had six hangars for flying boats. They were lowered into the water with the aid of a crane and a slipway. The base was connected with Bredene and Ostend by a narrow-gauge railway network.

» **SEE ALSO** 108 SEEFLUGSTATION FLANDERN I

↓ **BASE FOR FLYING BOATS**

Three hangars can be seen in the foreground, with a slipway on the left to help the planes into the water; in the background is a hoisting crane.

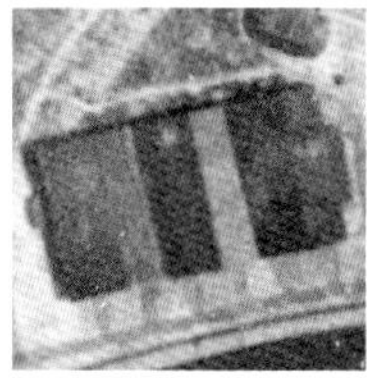

C5-D5

AIRCRAFT HANGARS

On the banks of the Spuikom stand six hangars providing accommodatation for the flying boats.

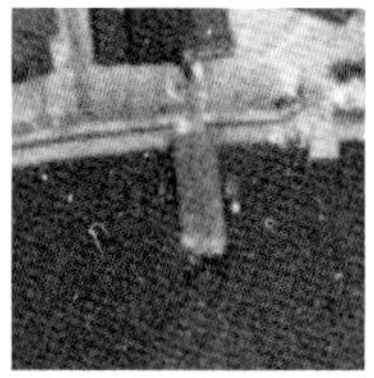

D5

SLOPING SURFACE

The aircraft were guided into the water down a slipway.

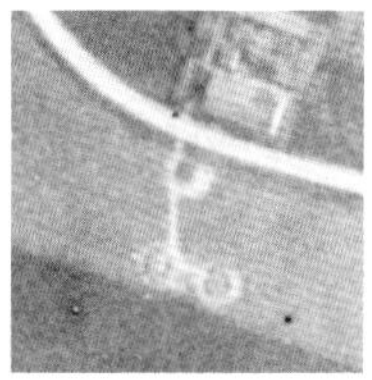

B4

AIR DEFENCE

An air defence battery with two guns mounted on a round platform helped to make the air space round the base safe.

GPS 51°14'19.78"N 2°55'16.12"E

↑ Bredene 400 m
D
E
F
G
H
I
J
1
2
3
4
5
6
100 m
↑ Spuikom
↖ Fritz Vinckelaan

114

GONTRODE - AIR BASE

22 AUGUST 1918

The Germans were already using airships for reconnaissance and bombing when they invaded Belgium. In Belgium, they immediately built five bases for Zeppelins from which they could carry out bombing raids on French and British towns. One of these bases was set up at Gontrode in November 1914 and included a 180-metre-long shed to provide shelter for Zeppelins.[49] The raids were intended mainly as a deterrent and were ultimately stopped. From May 1917 Britain faced a new threat: aircrew from the 'England Geschwader' carried out missions from the Gontrode and Sint-Denijs-Westrem airfields using Gotha bombers, later backed up by R-planes (*Riesenflugzeuge* – 'giant aeroplanes' manufactured by Zeppelin-Staaken).[50] On 25 May, 22 bombers flew across the Channel and dropped bombs on Folkestone.[51] The airfield at Gontrode had now become much larger than just one airship hangar. There were aircraft hangars, barracks, air defence guns, ammunition bunkers and hard-surfaced runways for the bombers.

↑ **NIGHT PHOTOGRAPH OF THE ZEPPELIN SHED**

German photograph of the large hangar on the Gontrode airfield. The hangar seems to be lit inside while on the right are the traces of nocturnal artillery fire.

↓ **INSPECTION**

Autumn 1917. The Commanding General of the German air force, Lieutenant-General Ernst von Hoeppner, inspects the 'England Geschwader' in Gontrode. The Gotha bombers are lined up in front of the large airship hangar.

→ **GOTHA BOMBER**

Gotha bomber over Flanders.

GPS 50°58'55.94"N 3°47'13.71"E

F2
BOMBER

A German bomber parked in the vicinity of the runway.

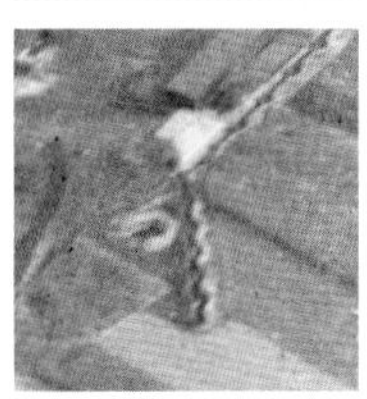

E3
SHELTER TRENCH

Short zigzag shelter trench offering refuge during bombing raids.

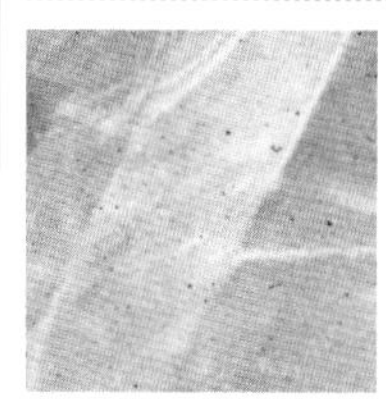

G2
RUNWAY

Large sections of the runway in Gontrode had hard surfaces, which made it easier for the heavy bombers to take off and land.

GPS 50°58'55.94"N 3°47'13.71"E

I J K L M N O P

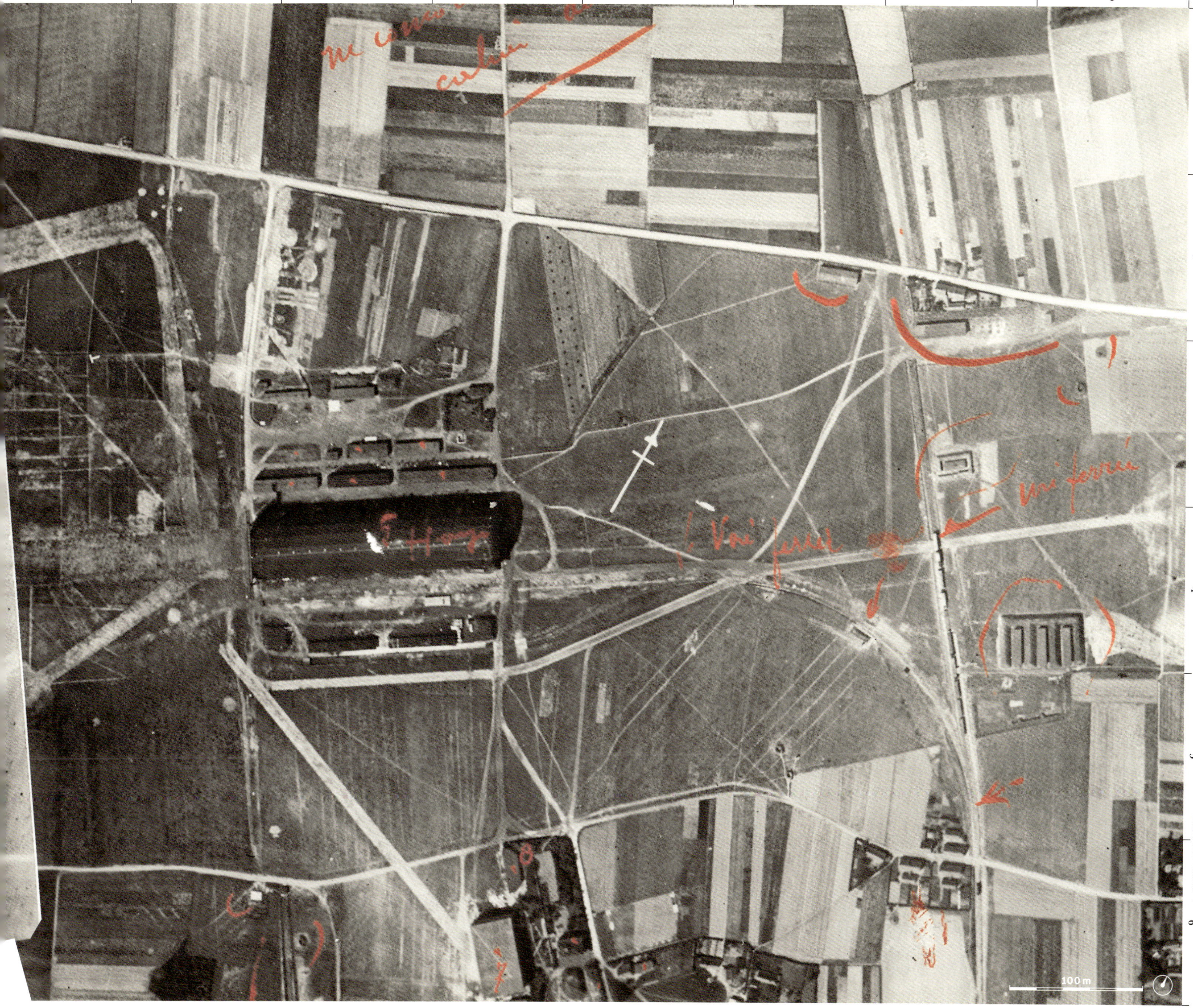

1 2 3 4 5 6

← Scheldeweg ↑ 2.2 km (119) Kwatrecht

Gontrode 100 m →

115
OSTEND 11 AUGUST 1918

After the first failed attempt on 23 April 1918, the British cruiser HMS *Vindictive*, filled with concrete, was sunk in the harbour mouth during a raid on Ostend harbour on 10 May. It was not an unalloyed success. Although the cruiser sank, it blocked the harbour mouth only partially. Just like Zeebrugge harbour, Ostend was of strategic importance for the German navy owing to its position on the North Sea.

›› Continued on p. 308

» **SEE ALSO** 107 ZEEBRUGGE RAID

→ **HMS VINDICTIVE**

HMS *Vindictive* in Ostend, October 1918.

↓ C3

CASEMATES

Rear view of the Halve Maan casemates.

GPS 51°14'19.78"N 2°55'16.12"E

A3-B3

HMS VINDICTIVE

HMS *Vindictive* by the jetty in Ostend.

F6

ANTI-AIRCRAFT BATTERY

The German Grossherzog anti-aircraft battery protected the harbour infrastructure and coastal positions against low-flying Allied aircraft.

E2

FORT NAPOLEON

This Napoleonic fort (1810–14) was adapted in the First World War as a military headquarters and as accommodation for German officers. To the east is a small garden with paths.

E5

U-BOAT BUNKERS

Just as at the Bruges inner harbour, in Ostend shelters and bunkers afforded protection to the U-boats of the Flanders fleet. The roof visible here consists of a three-part stepped structure.

E2-F2

HINDENBURG BATTERY

The German coastal Hindenburg battery. The guns of this 28-cm battery were armour-plated. From the easternmost part a communication trench runs to Fort Napoleon.

A5

BATTERY GNEISENAU

This German coastal battery consisted of four guns on the Ostend sea dyke.

A-4567. 11-8-18-16h 3600m. E 1/11200
OSTENDE.
A
B
C
D
E
F
H
1
2
4
5
6
coastline
↑ Bredene-aan-Zee 1km
Seeflugstation Flandern II (II) 1km
100 m
↑ centre of Ostend
Bruges–Ostend Canal

116
LANGEMARK – AU BON GÎTE
4 SEPTEMBER 1918

In autumn 1918 the landscape at the front could hardly be compared to the situation the year before. Between 1915 and 1917 two major offensives had devastated the region near Langemark. In spring 1918 the German Spring Offensive came to a halt on a level with the Au Bon Gîte Farm on the Steenbeek. To frustrate any attempt at an enemy breakthrough along the more or less intact roads, some strategic access roads were blown up – such as these two crossroads just south of Langemark – leaving deep craters.

GPS 50°54'39.66"N 2°55'11.84"E

» **SEE ALSO** 8 LANGEMARK

→ OBLIQUE VIEW OF LANGEMARK

Here we can see the area around Langemark as it was on 20 September 1918, with one large crater on the crossroads to the left and, in the background, another crossroads destroyed in the same way. At the front is the German foremost line, featuring bunkers and occupied bomb craters.

F1
CRATER

An explosive charge was detonated at the junction of Boezingestraat and the Korte Ieperstraat, producing an 18-metre-wide crater that quickly filled with water.

H1
BUNKER

This large concrete bunker measuring about 4 by 12 metres was originally built by the Allies after the Third Battle of Ypres. When this photograph was taken it was in German hands.

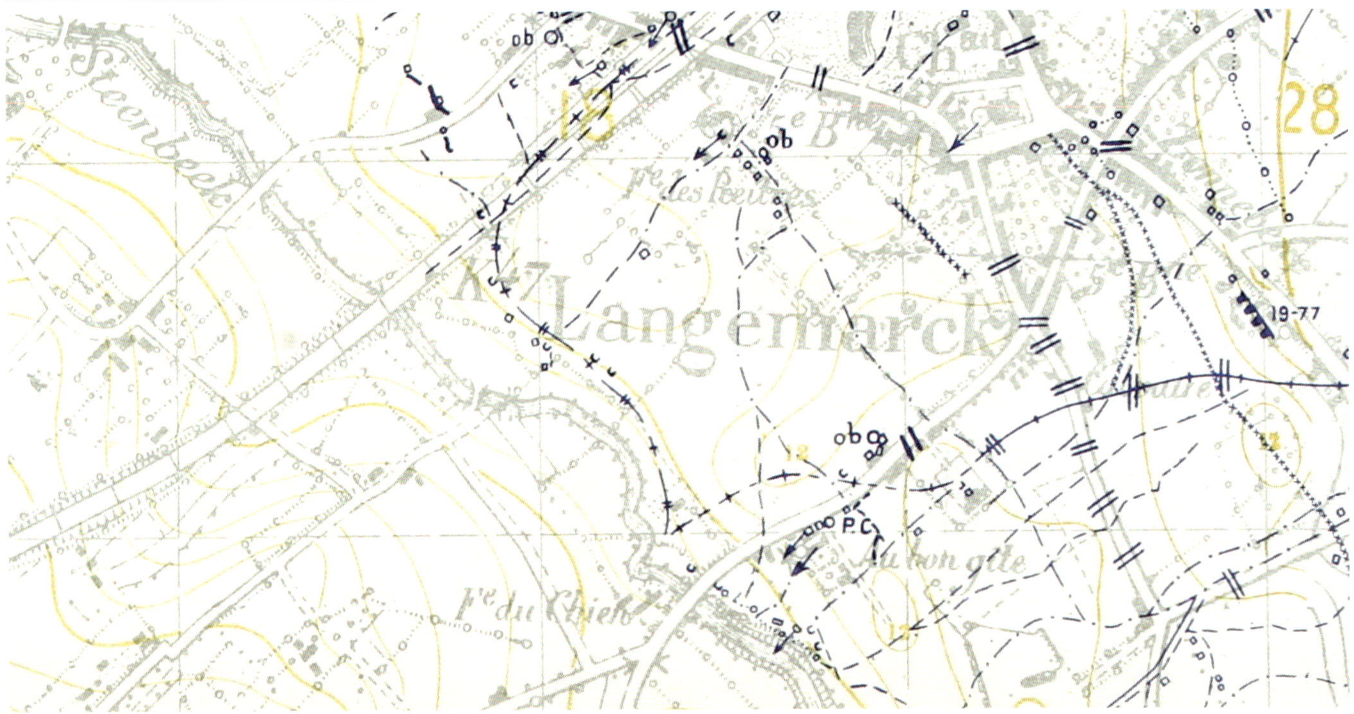

→ LANGEMARK TRENCH MAP

Fragment of a Belgian trench map of the Langemark region, dated 20 September 1918, with the foremost German line just to the east of the Steenbeek.

A
B
C
D
E
F
G
8 Langemark 130 m
Boezingestraat
1
2
3
4
5
6
B.535 - 24-9-18 P.Adj. Wittevrongel. O.Lt. Van Thorenburg Alt. 1800. 1/3600 Au bon Gite (R17)
100 m
Sint-Juliaan 2 km
Cayennestraat

117

SINT-JULIAAN – CANOPUS TRENCH 31 AUGUST 1918

Between 1915 and July 1917 the German Canopus Trench formed part of the German second line between Pilkem and Fortuin, to the south of Sint-Juliaan. It had well-camouflaged bunkers integrated into the parapet. On 31 July 1917 the British 39th Division captured Canopus Trench and the position remained in British hands until the German Spring Offensive. Between the end of April and the end of September 1918 the front was crossing this trench. Belgian soldiers restored the trench's western end. On the other side of the no-man's-land the Germans reoccupied their old trench and bunkers.

→ **BUNKERS AT SINT-JULIAAN**

The remains of a German line of bunkers at Sint-Juliaan – British photograph of 12 October 1917, after the bunkers had been captured during the Third Battle of Ypres.

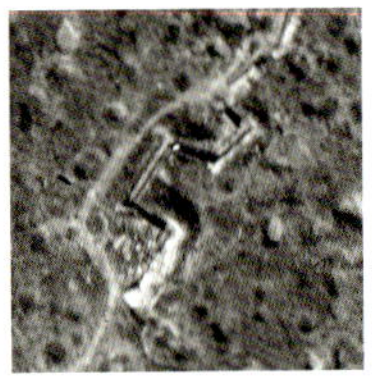

D5

CONNECTING PATH

A path from the Canopus Trench provided a connection with other outposts along the front line.

F4

NO-MAN'S-LAND

The central part of the trench has been shot to smithereens and has become part of no-man's-land.

SYMBOLS

- GERMAN TRENCH, BUNKER
- BRITISH TRENCH, BUNKER
- GERMAN FRONT LINE
- BRITISH FRONT LINE
- MOAT OF OBLONG FARM
- BARBED WIRE

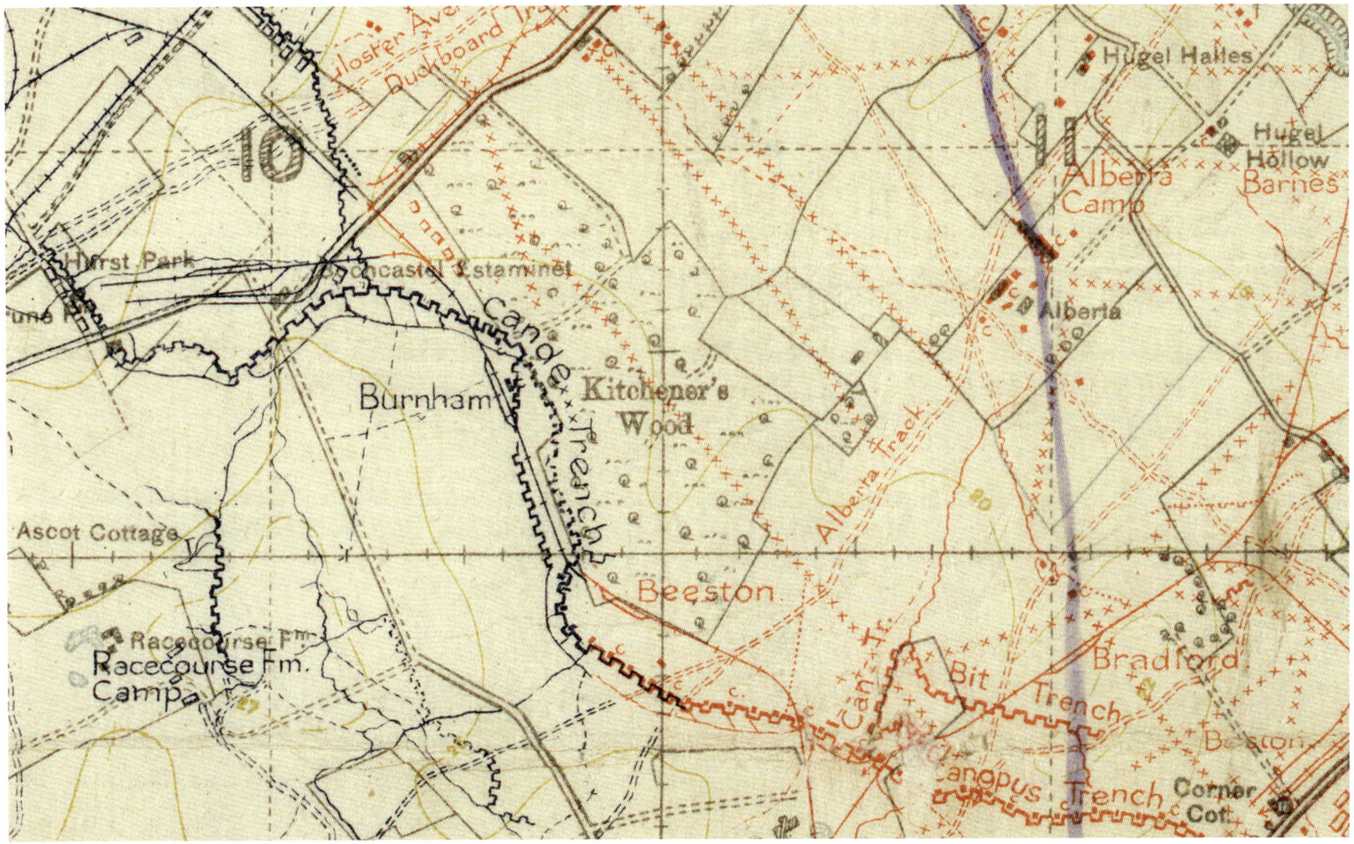

→ **TRENCH MAP**

This British trench map shows the front line on 13 May 1918. On the aerial photograph nothing remains to be seen of Kitchener's Wood.

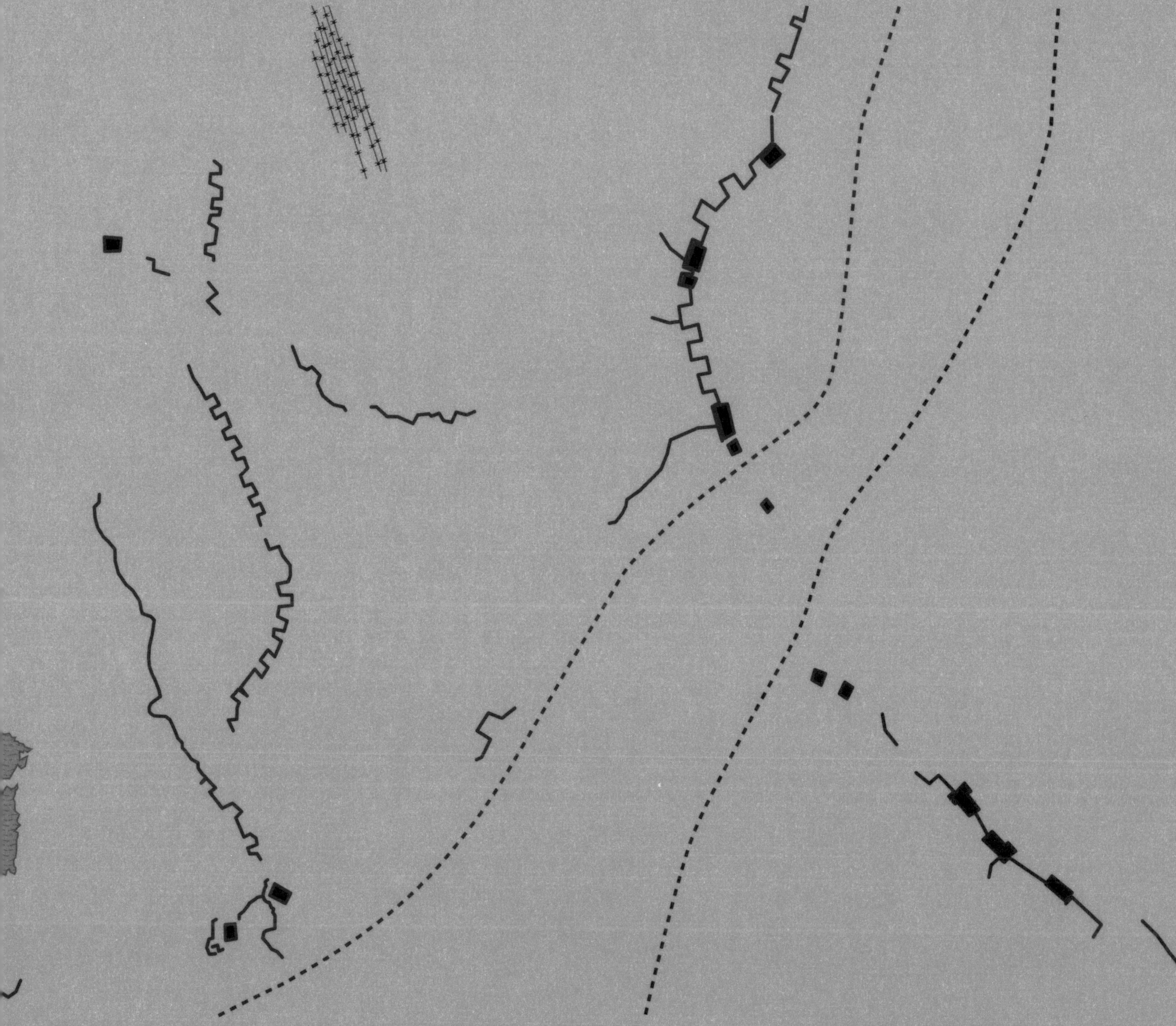

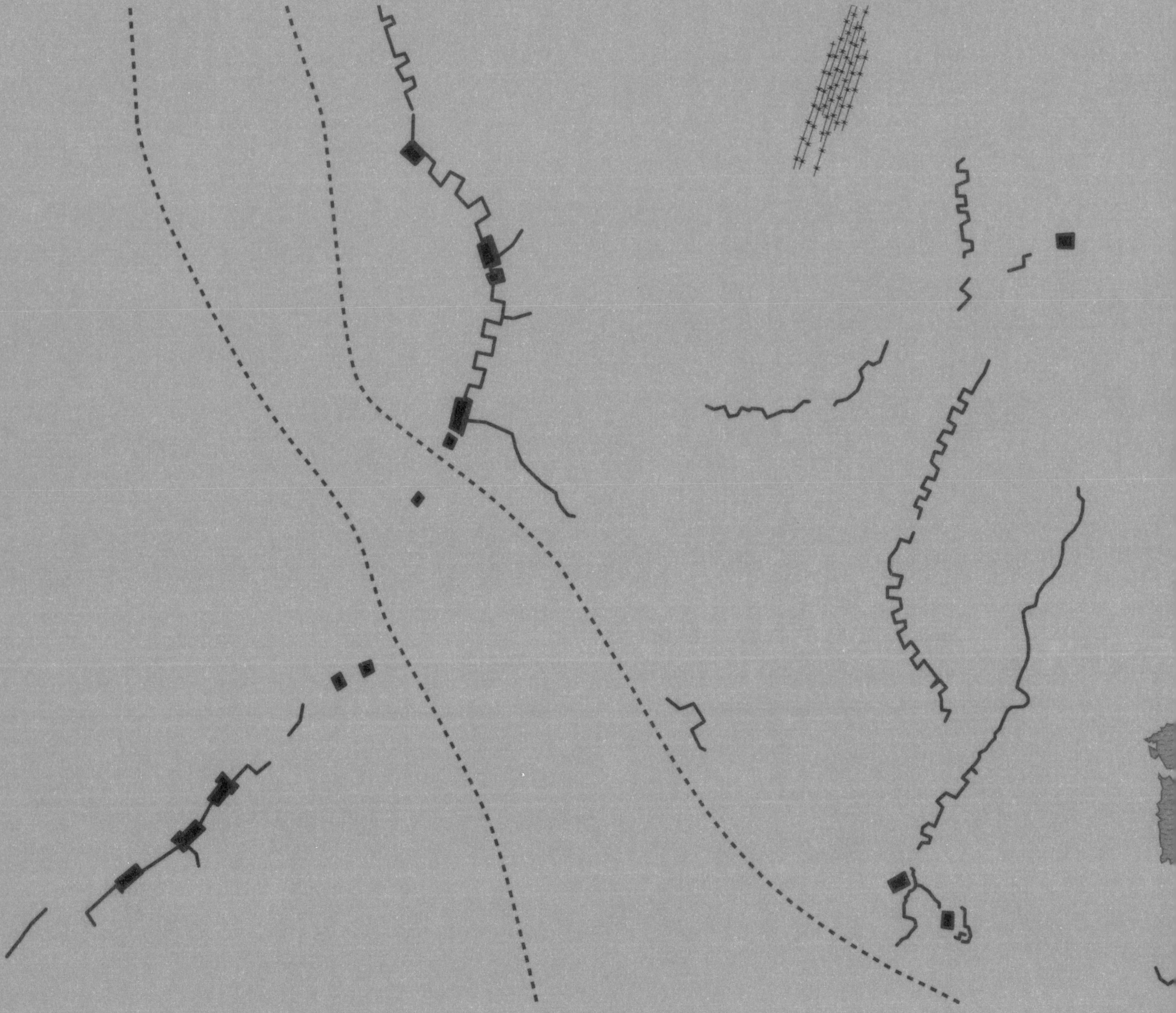

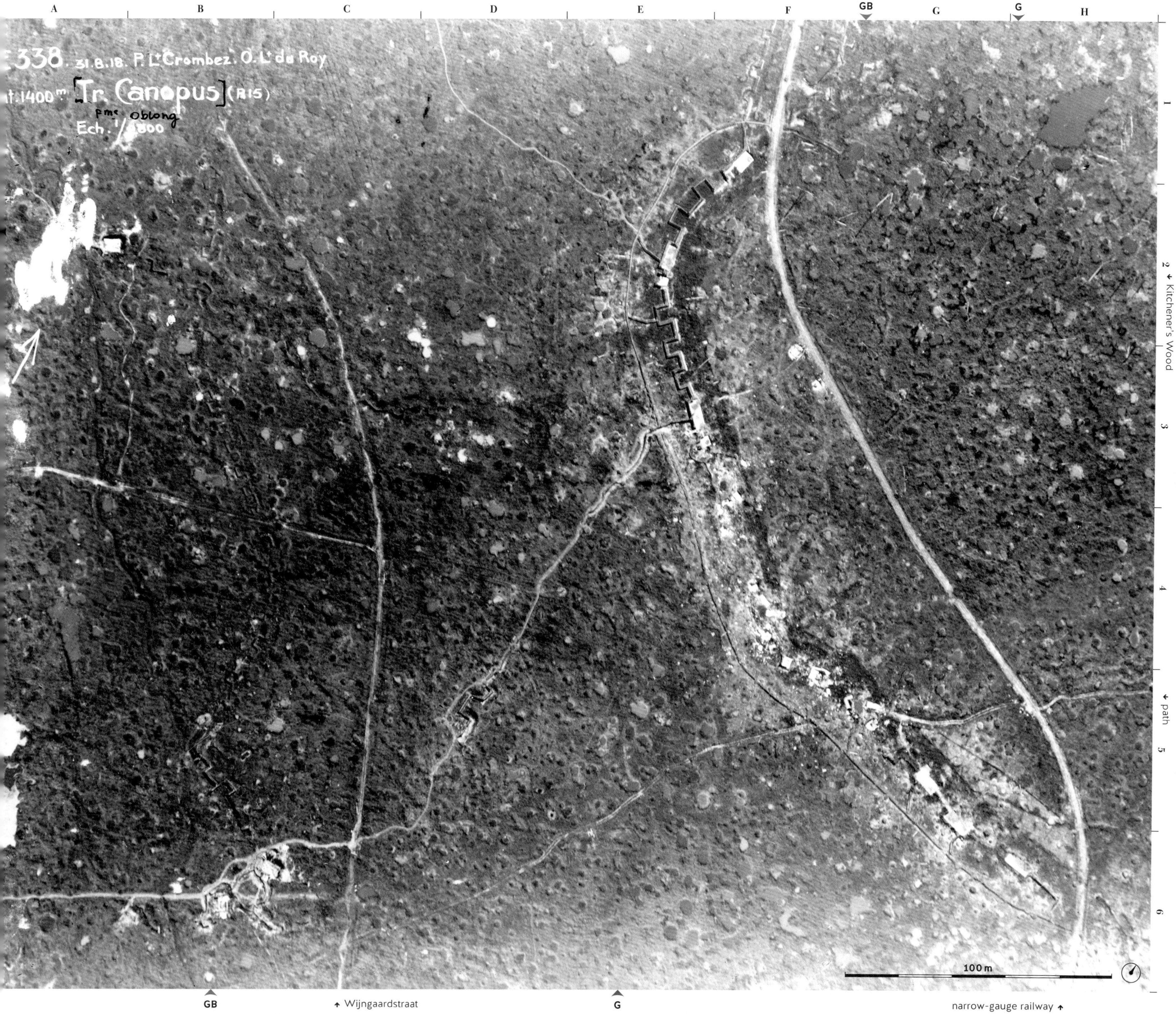

A
B
C
D
E
F
GB
G
G
H
338. 31.8.18. P. Lt Crombez. O. Lt de Roy
t.1400m [Tr. Canopus] (R15)
Fme oblong
Ech. 1/
1
2 ← Kitchener's Wood
3
4
← path
5
6
100 m
GB
↑ Wijngaardstraat
G
narrow-gauge railway ↑

118

ZILLEBEKE – RAILWAY DUGOUTS CEMETERY 13 SEPTEMBER 1918

In the embankment of the Ypres–Comines railway dugout shelters were used as an advanced medical station. The Railway Dugouts burial ground is situated alongside. Interments took place here from April 1915 until the end of the war. A German aerial photograph of 13 September 1918, taken at an altitude of hardly 100 metres, shows the cemetery in detail (F2). Hundreds of soldiers lay buried there under characteristic white crosses. After the German Spring Offensive of 1918 the foremost British line was now only a few hundred metres to the east. In some places graves had been destroyed by grenade attacks.

↑ **6 MAY 1917**

Aerial photographs of the same place. On this photograph of 6 May 1917 the burial ground can be seen in the centre.

↑ **2 FEBRUARY 1918**

This aerial photograph shows what the cemetery was like on 2 February 1918. The layout of the burial ground is no longer recognisable and the surroundings are dotted with dozens of bomb craters.

B2-C2

SHELTERS

The entrances to the concrete shelters can be seen in the railway embankment.

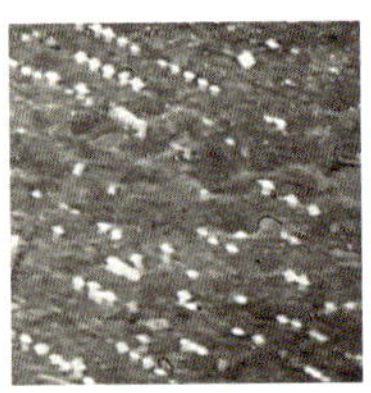

F3-G3

BURIAL GROUND

Much of the burial ground has been destroyed by artillery fire.

G5

BUNKER

This concrete shelter in the railway embankment lay barely 200 metres from the front in the second half of 1918.

→ **RAILWAY DUGOUTS CEMETERY**

Close-up of the British cemetery.

GPS 50°50'05.78"N 2°54'07.48"E

A
B
C
D
Ypres 1.5 km
E
F
G
H
1
Komenseweg
2
3
4
Hill 60 5 56 47 1.8 km
Ypres–Comines railway

119

KWATRECHT – MUNITIONS PARK 29 SEPTEMBER 1918

Starting in 1915, a huge munitions park was built on two sites in Kwatrecht, more than 65 kilometres behind German lines.[53] Branch lines were built from the Ghent–Aalst railway to transport the munitions to small storage areas, situated at some distance from each other in wooden barracks. The complex was vulnerable to aerial bombardment, hence the anti-aircraft batteries around it. Unexploded ammunition is still unearthed there today during excavation and building work.

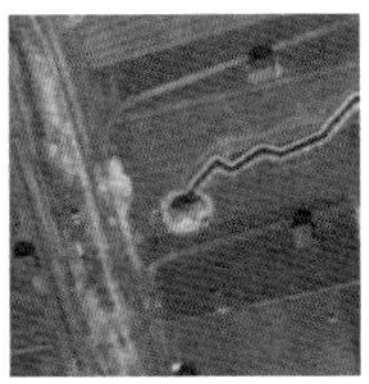

K4

BUNKER

In the middle of the munitions park is a concrete bunker linked to zigzag trenches, providing shelter during air attacks.

↓ D5

GERMAN ANTI-AIRCRAFT GUN

German gunners wearing gas masks while operating the anti-aircraft gun.

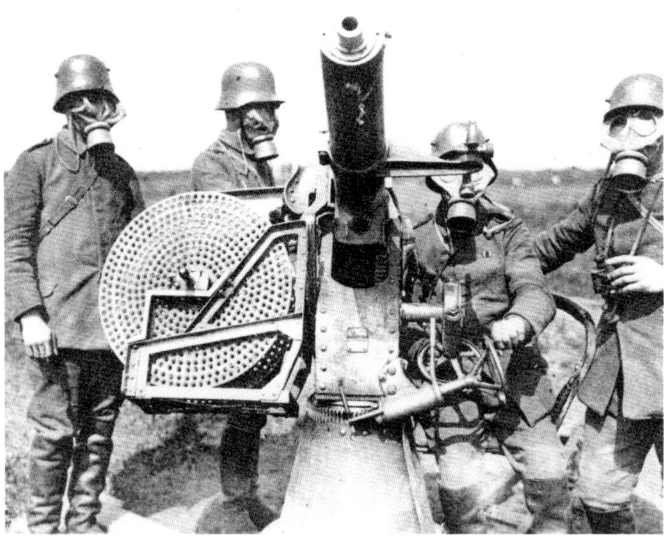

GPS 50°59'23.95"N 3°50'37.00"E

A B C D E

Brusselsesteenweg ↖

Scheldt
F
G
H
I
J
K
L
1
2
3
4
5
6
Ghent–Aalst railway
100 m
Zuidlaan

120

VELDHOEK 2 OCTOBER 1918

The final offensive at the end of 1918 broke the years of stalemate and changed the conflict back into a mobile war. The supply of materials and provisions through a severely damaged landscape was sometimes difficult. At the beginning of October 1918 the roads in the region of Veldhoek were choked with lorries and carts. The fields were full of bomb craters and criss-crossed by little paths that indicated intensive troop movements.

→ **CONVOY**

An aeroplane flies over a French transport convoy in the region of Kortrijk, 18 October 1918.

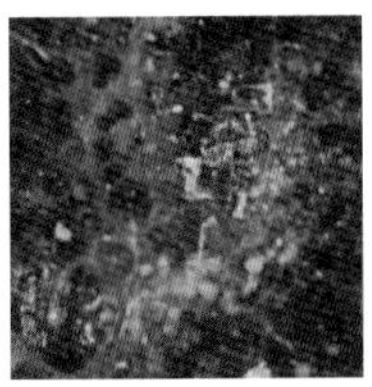

A3

RUINS OF A BUNKER

Traces of a devastated German bunker. The concrete debris is scattered far and wide and can be recognised by its lighter shade.

D3

LORRIES AND CARTS

The roads are chock-full: some seventy carts and lorries advance eastwards.

D4

BROKEN RAILS

Along the road lie the remains of a German narrow-gauge railway.

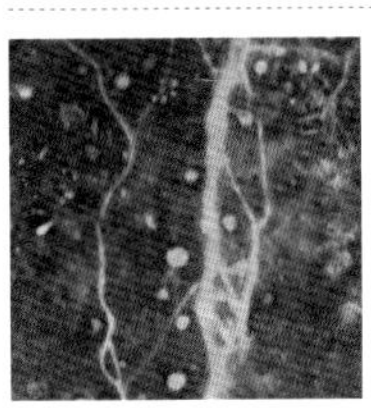

B5

GROUP OF SOLDIERS

The hundreds of faint lines are little tracks made by intensive troop movements. On this broad path we can see a group of soldiers.

→ **A QUEUE**

Belgian soldiers taking part in the final advance in Flanders.

PRECISE LOCATION UNKNOWN

A
B
C
D
E
F
G
H
1
2
3
4
5
6

121
WAREGEM – FINAL OFFENSIVE
14 OCTOBER 1918

In October 1918, during the final advance in Flanders, the fighting reached Waregem. Trenches were no longer being dug in this phase. In various places the Germans had defensive lines that consisted simply of foxholes providing cover for one or two soldiers. In 1914 such foxholes had been extended into much larger trench systems. In contrast to the Westhoek, the warfare left few traces on the landscape here. In many places, houses, fields and roads were left intact.

» **SEE ALSO** 1 TERVATE

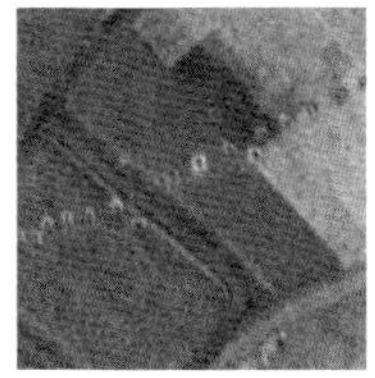

H3
FOXHOLES

Here some thirty foxholes have been dug to offer resistance to an Allied attack from the west.

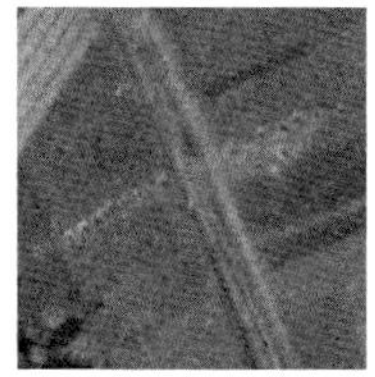

F2
FOXHOLES

A second line of foxholes extends away from the road on both sides.

D3
FOXHOLES

Here the foxholes are scarcely visible.

↓ **BOMBARDMENT OF RAILWAY AT WAREGEM**

On 14 October 1918 the Kortrijk–Ghent railway came under Allied artillery fire at Waregem. Plumes of smoke rise up from the targets.

GPS 50°53'18.32"N 3°27'39.72"E

D
E
F
G
H
I
J
2
3
4
5
6
82. B. 218.
29. D. 17. 23.
28. 10. 18. (11.
F = 8 1/4"
100 m
Driekavenstraat
Nokerseweg

122

ANZEGEM – GERMAN RETREAT

26 OCTOBER 1918

During the liberation offensive the retreating Germans systematically destroyed railway lines so that the Allies could not use them. Among the railways damaged were the lines from Waregem to Oudenaarde, Kortrijk to Oudenaarde and Oudenaarde to Ronse. This aerial photograph of 26 October 1918 shows how explosives detonated under the track at regular intervals left deep craters (A3-F1).

→ **RAILWAY AT LEUPEGEM**

At Leupegem, a small village south of Oudenaarde, the railway was also systematically disabled.

↓ **KORTRIJK-OUDENAARDE RAILWAY**

The nearby Kortrijk–Oudenaarde railway to the south of Anzegem has similar craters.

GPS 50°50'03.15"N 3°27'13.37"E

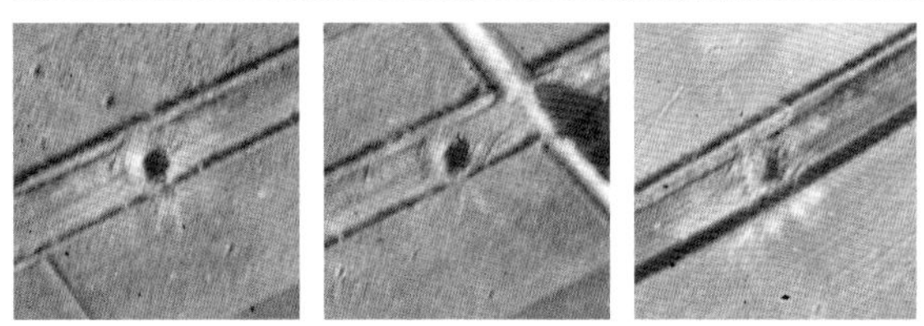

A3, C3, D2

RAILWAY DESTRUCTION

The explosions leave deep craters, making the railway unusable.

G4

ZWIJNSTEERT MILL

The Zwijnsteert Mill was destroyed in the bombardment in October 1918. Bomb craters can be seen to the west of the mill.

Waregem–Oudenaarde railway
A
B
C
D
E
G
H
1
2
3
4
5
82.B.169.
29.J.22.28.
26.10.18. (13.00)
F = 8 1/4"
Stientjesstraat
100 m

123
NIEUWPOORT 9 OCTOBER 1918

Detailed photograph of the sluices at Nieuwpoort at the end of the war. In order to prevent the Allies from assembling large forces to the north of Nieuwpoort, the Germans also decided to utilise the hydrological complex connected to the Ganzepoot, which itself was in Allied hands.[54] Intensive bombardment had inflicted heavy damage on the northernmost lock in autumn 1917. At high tide this allowed sea water to flow unhindered into the area between Nieuwpoort and Lombardsijde, inundating a large part of the remaining area, which had fallen into British hands after Operation Strandfest (10 July 1917). The water flowed back when the tide went out, leaving a marshy area where large-scale troop movement was impossible. After the Germans had been pushed back, there was no longer any danger for air reconnaissance units: this photograph was taken at a low altitude (1,500 metres), presumably to measure the damage to the hydrological complex.

GPS 51°07'45.56"N 2°45'01.89"E

↑ **OBLIQUE AERIAL PHOTOGRAPH OF NIEUWPOORT**

German oblique photograph taken at a very low altitude on 16 January 1918. The consequences of the destruction of the first sluice are very clear. The parapets of the British trenches protrude from the inundated polder. The photograph was taken as the tide was going out.

→ **SLUICE COMPLEX 1916**

German aerial photo (23 April 1916) of the then still completely intact sluice complex at Nieuwpoort.

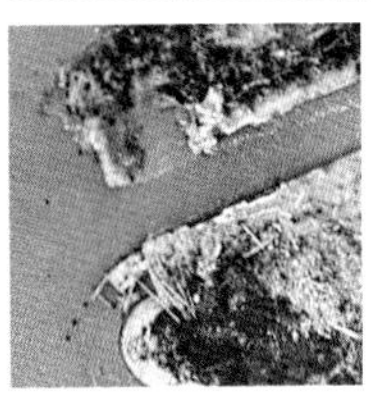

D4-D3

OVERFLOW AT THE NIEUWBEDELF AND GRAVENSAS

The destruction of the sluices of the overflow from the Nieuwbedelf and the Gravensas meant that part of the British front was covered with water every day.

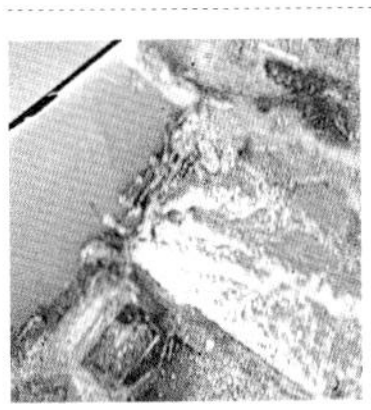

D5

YPRES LOCK

Aerial photograph taken at high tide. Water flowed into the Yser Canal from the Ypres sluice.

A4

BUNKER

Various trenches lead to a bunker that is easily recognisable by its light concrete.

A
B
C
D
E
F
Lombardsijde 1.6 km
G
inundation
H
A5320.-9.10.18.-15h30.-1500m. E 1/3000
ECLUSES NIEUPORT A23.
P.1r Sgt Bastin. O. Lt De Groeve.
front 1.3 km
Nieuwbedelf
2
Plassendale Canal
old Yser
5
6
100 m
Nieuwpoort 300 m
Noordvaart
Yser Canal

V

Reconstruction and the last witness

WHEN THE FIRST people returned home to the front area in 1919 they were faced with nothing but destruction. Where they had once lived had been declared a 'devastated region'. From Nieuwpoort to the French border at Armentières an area of almost one thousand square kilometres had been destroyed. There had been major destruction in other parts of the country, too. The Belgians rebuilt their country relatively quickly. Aerial photographs from the early 1920s show how rapidly the reconstruction proceeded. Towards the end of the decade most of the rural areas had also been restored. Buried beneath the surface were innumerable pieces of evidence that bore witness to the war, including human remains, structures and also dangerous ammunition. In the Westhoek, industrial development for a long time lagged behind that of the rest of the country.

Reconstruction eradicated many of the traces of the First World War. However, the landscape still bears marks of commemoration: the cemeteries and monuments; the pilgrims and visitors visiting the former battlefields; rituals such as the Last Post and the IJzerbedevaart (Pilgrimage of the Yser), and identity-forming symbols of remembrance such as the poppy and Anzac Day. The history of the war has become an essential part of the region. Of the more than 600,000 soldiers and civilians who lost their lives in Belgium as a result of the First World War, more than 550,000 fell in West Flanders.

The war's victims came from all over the world. In recent decades there has been a growing realisation that the region itself has to take on responsibility for its globally significant heritage. And, with the disappearance of the generation who lived through First World War, the heritage is increasingly vested in the places where the war once raged, rather than in its people. Modern visual analysis of the military aerial photography from the war is an essential instrument for bringing to light the 'DNA' of the former front region as a 'last witness'. There is perhaps no better or more exact medium for detecting the countless traces of the war. This amounts to a rehabilitation of the aerial observers, who always remained in the shadow of the so-called 'genuine' heroes during the pioneering age of flight. Having once been the eyes of the armies in the conflict, it would seem that the PBOs, the 'poor bloody observers' as they were called, are destined to become increasingly the eyes of remembrance.

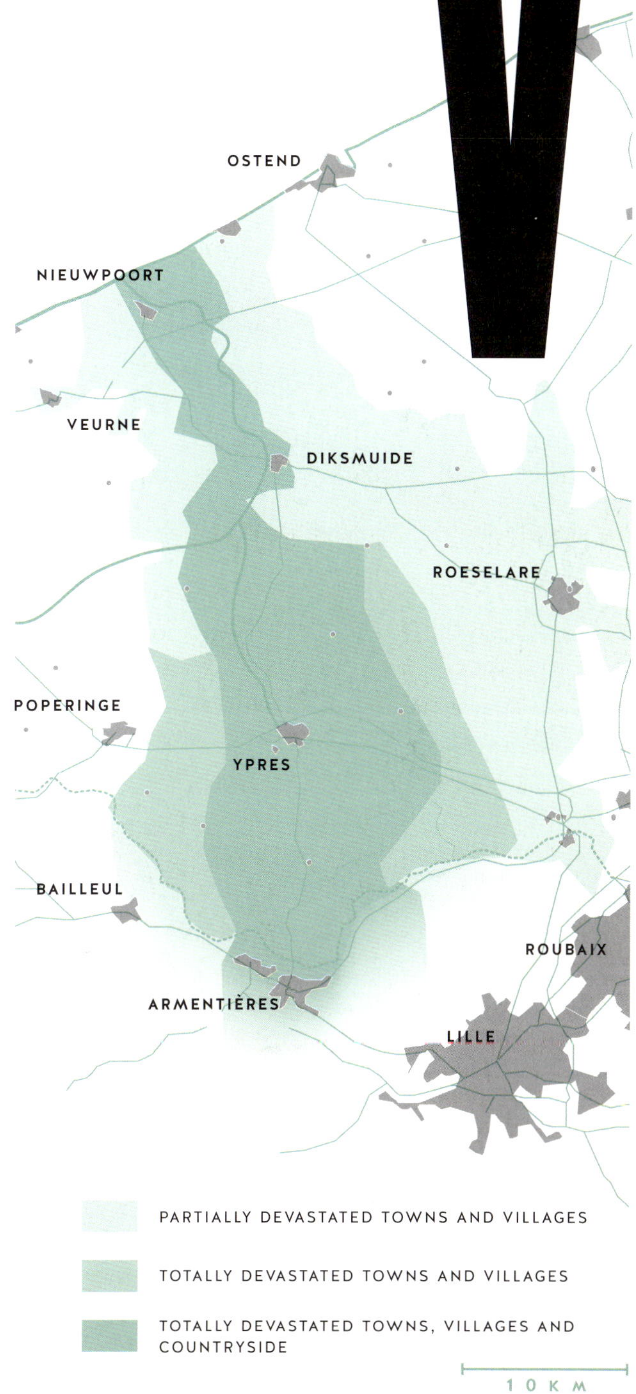

←

An Australian soldier looks out over the ruins of Ypres, autumn 1917.

124
LIÈGE – LONCIN FORT
20 JULY 1921

Loncin Fort was one of the twelve forts of the Liège Fortified Position, a ring of forts around Liège designed by General Brialmont in 1888. At the beginning of the First World War it was not adapted for recent artillery developments. The unreinforced concrete could only withstand shells of up to 210 millimetres. When the German army invaded Belgium on 4 August 1914 Liège was their first target. The city was captured on 7 August, but the forts remained in Belgian hands. The Germans called in a new weapon to break their resistance: the 'Big Bertha' cannon with shells of 420 millimetres. On 15 August 'Big Bertha' was turned on the Loncin Fort. Five shells weighing 810 kilograms were fired, the ammunition store exploded and part of the fort collapsed. Some 350 soldiers died. After the collapse it was decided not to rebuild the fort and to leave the site as a memorial and necropolis.

→ **CANNON TURRET**

Post-war photographs of a cannon turret and the destruction caused by the explosion of the ammunition store.

E6
CANNON
The fort had four gun turrets each housing a rapid-fire 5.7-cm cannon for close defence.

B4
COLLAPSE
The ammunition store explosion was so powerful that the centre of the fort collapsed.

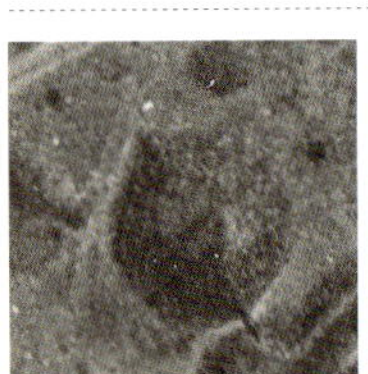

A2
SHELL HOLES
Giant shell holes show the impact that 420-mm shells could have.

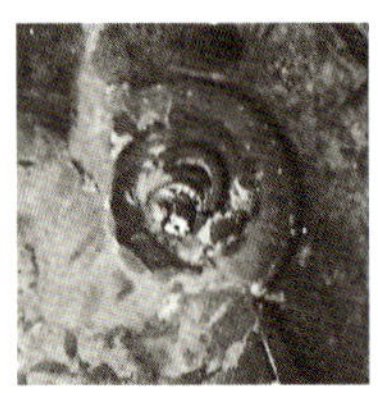

C4
CANNON DOME
The fort's heaviest firepower consisted of 210-mm howitzers under an armour-plated dome.

A4
TRENCHES
On the outside of the central body of the fort were trenches dug on two sides that could be manned in the event of an infantry attack.

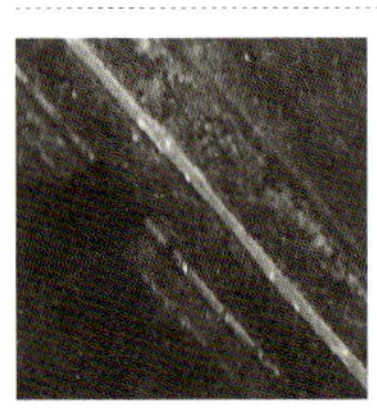

D3
DRY DITCH
Outside the fort there was a dry ditch that could be defended with 5.7-cm cannon kept ready in casemates in the corner of the fort.

SYMBOLS
- TRENCH
- CANNON TURRET
- ENTRANCE TO THE FORT
- CASEMATE WITH 5.7-CM CANNON
- DITCH
- GLACIS (EARTH BANK AROUND THE FORT)
- CRATER
- DESTROYED AREA

GPS 50°40'28.38"N 5°29'33.01"E

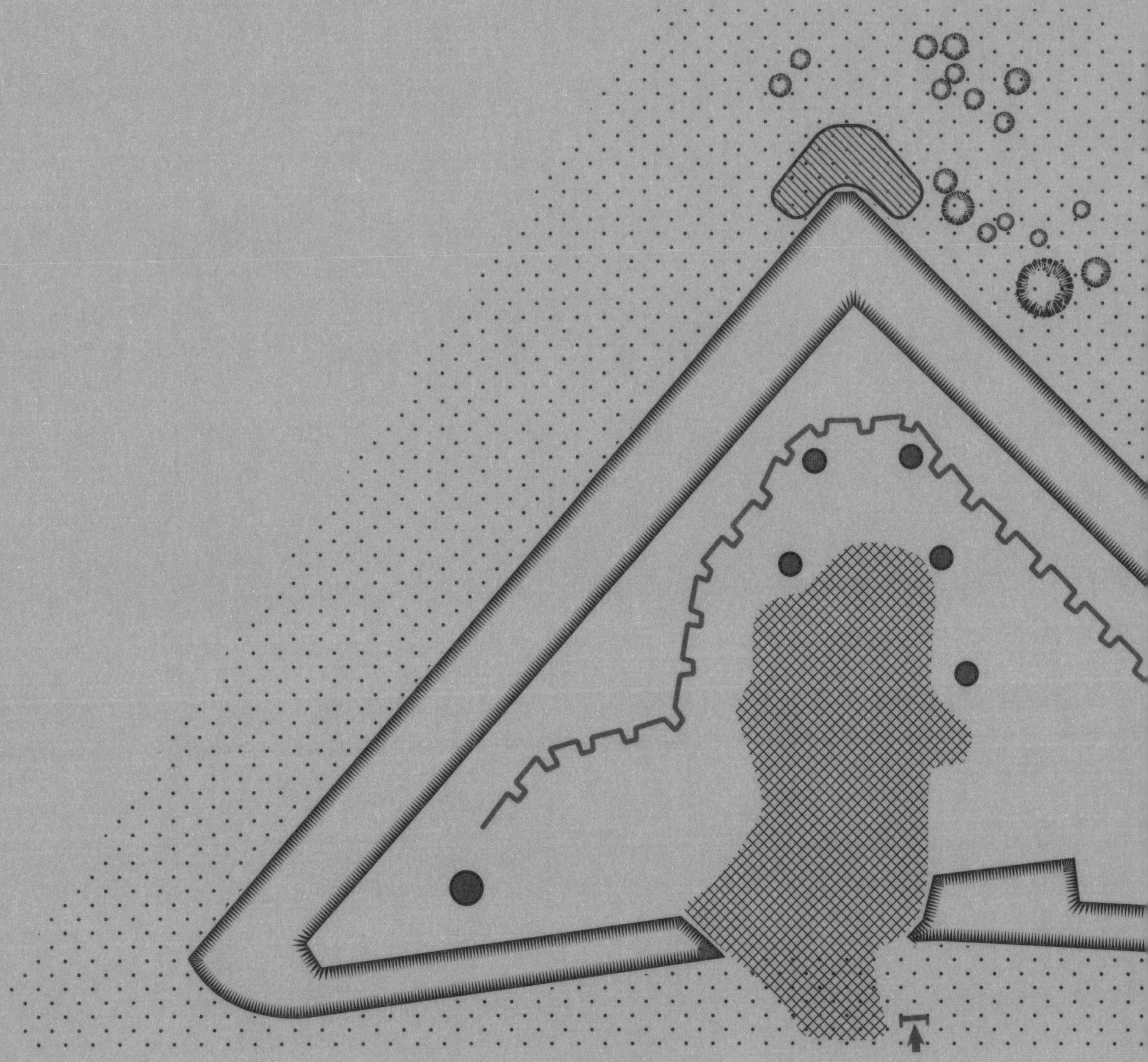

Av. M.B. G. 129. - 20-7-21. 12h30. 800m.
FORT. de LONCIN.
Pt sy. Lt Tollet. O Lt Martens.
A
B
C
D
E
F
G
H
1
2
3
4
5
6
100 m
Rue du Cheval d'Or
Liège 7km
Loncin 1.1km

125

YPRES – RECONSTRUCTION 1923

During the four war years the front towns of Nieuwpoort, Diksmuide and Ypres had been virtually wiped off the map. After the war there were various visions of how the 'devastated regions', as the front area was called, should be rebuilt. Even during the war voices were heard urging that the towns be rebuilt on an entirely new basis, or that the ruins of Ypres be preserved as a memorial. In 1919 Winston Churchill proposed: 'I should like us to acquire the whole of the ruins of Ypres. A more sacred place for the British race does not exist in the world.'[55] Ultimately, the vision of a rebuilt Ypres based on its pre-war appearance won the day and Ypres was restored under the direction of the town architect Jules Coomans. This aerial photograph taken in 1923 shows a town with its major buildings under scaffolding (D3) and with much of its private housing already rebuilt. From 1919 temporary housing and barracks were erected on the town outskirts to provide accommodation for the returning population (A3). Many middle-class houses were built between 1922 and 1924. It was only in 1967 that the Cloth Hall, an important symbol of the suffering inflicted by the war and of the town's renaissance, was completed.

↑ **YPRES 1917**

Oblique view of the destruction in the centre of Ypres, 31 January 1917. Many houses have been reduced to ruins. Only parts of St Martin's Cathedral, the Cloth Hall and the belfry are still standing.

← **MENIN GATE**

The Menin Gate, the first Memorial to the Missing, under construction around 1926. The monument was inaugurated on 24 July 1927.

GPS 50°40'28.38"N 5°29'33.01"E

Zonnebeekseweg
Menin Road
A
B
C
D
E
F
G
1
2
3
4
5
6
Vauban fortifications
III Gr. 1011
Elverdingestraat
Boterstraat

126 DIKSMUIDE – RECONSTRUCTION 1923

In 1919 only a few of the streets in Diksmuide were passable and the centre was in ruins. The railway, having been rebuilt fairly rapidly, was very useful for bringing in building materials. The war had left its mark everywhere on the landscape. There was only sparse emergency accommodation for the first civilian returnees. In 1923 the agricultural areas around the town were a wasteland: in the foreground is an overgrown German trench (C6). Gradually, as the reconstruction effort got under way, the building of emergency barracks was superseded by the construction of long-term housing.

» **SEE ALSO** 91 DIKSMUIDE

→ **DIKSMUIDE 1919**

↓ **DIKSMUIDE 1917**

↘ **DIKSMUIDE 1918**

GPS 50°51'03.94"N 2°53'07.46"E

A
B
C
D
E
F
G
Esenweg
1
2
3
4
5
6
IJzerlaan
Yser

127
NIEUWPOORT – RECONSTRUCTION 1923

The return of local residents who had fled the region during the war created a crisis of homelessness. With help from the State, emergency accommodation was provided in the first instance by the Albert Fund and by using army barracks. Only later was the reconstruction started. Between 1920 and 1925 Nieuwpoort was rebuilt by Joseph Viérin. A historicising approach was chosen, based on the pre-war street layout and aspect of the town, and on the reconstruction of buildings for which there was sufficient documentation. Two oblique aerial photographs show the progress made between 1919 and 1923. Apart from the district with emergency accommodation in the foreground, the reconstruction is clearly well advanced. Here and there in the town a number of wooden barracks remain. The meadows and fields have been cleared and crops have been sown again.

» **SEE ALSO** 51 NIEUWPOORT

↑ **NIEUWPOORT 1919**

View of Nieuwpoort in 1919. Emergency accommodation and barracks were being built to the west of the town, between the devastated area and the Oude Veurnevaart, on sites where no reconstruction was needed.

↓ **NIEUWPOORT 1917**

Oblique view of the ruins of Nieuwpoort in 1917. This picture was taken from the south-west, in the direction of the sluice complex.

GPS 51°07'45.56"N 2°45'01.89"E

A
B
Plassendale Canal
D
E
F
G
Yser Canal
1
2
3
4
5
Oude Veurnevaart
III Gr. 1008
Canadalaan

128
WIJTSCHATE – THE LAST WITNESS 2012

Although the war ended almost one hundred years ago, not all traces of it have vanished from the Westhoek landscape. Numerous scars are still apparent to the attentive visitor. Now that the survivors have left us, the landscape remains as the last witness to this bloody episode. The 'evidence' is diverse: from subtle traces, such as overgrown shelters and buried archaeological heritage, to the enormous craters blown in the landscape by the underground war and the endless rows of white tombstones dominating the countryside as palpable reminders of the enormous loss of human life.

» **SEE ALSO** 44 45 WIJTSCHATE

↗ **CROP MARKS**

On modern-day aerial photographs, taken in the right conditions, archaeological traces from the war (and earlier periods) can be seen as differential growth in crops. On this aerial photograph, taken between Scherpenberg and Reningelst, we can see the trace of a British zigzag communication trench dug in May 1918.

↗ B6
CRATERS

In various places the water-filled mine craters remain as reminders of the underground war in the Ypres Salient. Two of the three craters at Kruisstraathoek created by explosions on 7 June 1917 can still be seen in the landscape.

→ D4
BUNKER ON THE MESSINES RIDGE

An Allied bunker on the Messines Ridge. Thousands of bunkers were built during the war, on both sides of the front. This kind of relic is a valuable physical reminder of what happened a century ago in the Westhoek. In recent decades dozens of bunkers have been destroyed. The anti-war mindset of the 'reconstruction' generation kept fighting against the war, as a result also destroyed much of the war heritage.

GPS 50°46'47.99"N 2°52'24.317"E

D2
WYTSCHAETE MILITARY CEMETERY
In this post-war cemetery lie the remains of 1,003 soldiers.

B1
PETIT BOIS MINE CRATERS
To the north of Petit Bois lie two large mine craters full of water. Following the German front line southwards, we can also see the craters of Maedelstede (East Farm), Peckham, Spanbroekmolen and the Kruisstraat.

B2
MAEDELSTEDE FARM
The crater at Maedelstede Farm was partially filled after the war.

B3-B4
PECKHAM CRATER
Crater created by one of the nineteen mines detonated beneath Messines Ridge.

A/B-4/5
SPANBROEKMOLEN CRATER
The Spanbroekmolen crater (also known as the 'Pool of Peace' or 'Lone Tree Crater') owes its existence to one of the nineteen mines detonated during the mine war.

B4
SPANBROEKMOLEN MILITARY CEMETERY
Small cemetery for soldiers killed at the Battle of Messines.

B6
KRUISSTRAAT
Two of the three craters at the Kruisstraat can still be made out in the landscape.

SYMBOLS
ALTITUDE 35 M — 85 M

129
HOOGE – THE LAST WITNESS
2012

The former Western Front is one of the world's largest archaeological sites. Buried beneath the surface are thousands of kilometres of trenches and many bunkers; the remains of tens of thousands of soldiers still lie buried in the Westhoek. This recent aerial photograph shows the location of all the traces of war, regardless of nationality or date, seen on 490 aerial photographs taken between May 1915 and September 1918. This mapping method provides a new insight into the density, diversity and geographical spread of the potential subterranean military heritage. It also shows that aerial photographs, besides being fascinating illustrations of a history of war, are also new historical sources that can play a part in the scientific investigation on which policy decisions may be based.

» SEE ALSO 14 43 HOOGE

↓ B2
ARCHAEOLOGICAL HERITAGE
Archaeological excavation of a German trench on the Bellewaarde Ridge carried out by the Agentschap voor Onroerend Erfgoed (Flanders Heritage Agency).

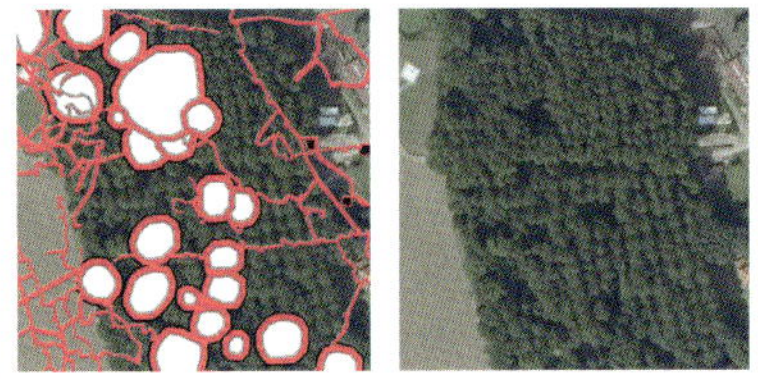

B2
MINE CRATERS
Some areas were never restored during the reconstruction period. On Bellewaarde Ridge a wood has been planted over the mine craters many metres beneath.

C4
HOOGE CRATER CEMETERY
After the war a small British cemetery at Hooge grew to become the Hooge Crater Cemetery, where almost 6,000 soldiers lie buried.

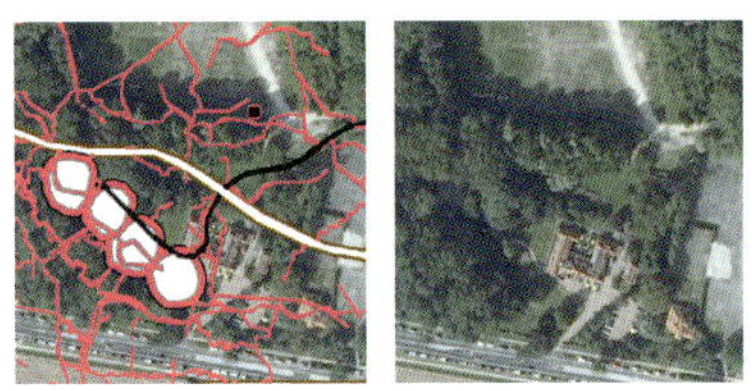

D4
CHÂTEAU HOOGE
In the gardens of the Château Hooge lie craters from mines that exploded on 6 June 1916.

SYMBOLS
- TRENCH
- ARTILLERY POSITION
- BUNKER OR SHELTER
- RAILWAY
- ROAD
- CRATER

A
↓ 250 m Bellewaarde 12 16 34

D
E
F
↓ 50 m Westhoek 50 85
H
I
J
1
A19 highway ↙
2
3
Clapham Junction 84 400 m ↙
5
Menin Road ↙
100 m
↑ Drieblotenbos

Lost and forgotten? Aerial photographic collections

From the end of 1915 photo-reconnaissance units were systematically sent out along the Western Front. They took photographs on an almost industrial scale and half a million of them have survived. A survey of accessible collections of aerial photographs dating from the First World War has revealed that many have been forgotten or hidden away in filing cabinets. Surprisingly, however, literally hundreds of thousands of pictures have survived. Largely unaffected by the ravages of time, they are currently kept in miscellaneous archives. The large numbers of extant pictures are astonishing and are an indication of the real importance of aerial photography during the First World War. The collections are spread out across Europe, the United States and Australia. In the study of First World War landscapes and battlefields, the importance of the archives should be emphasised because this forms the starting point for any further research. The aerial photographs can be found in a variety of different archives, private collections and museums. The number of photographs, their quality but most of all their accessibility varies enormously. In this part of the book we deal with some of the most important, accessible and interesting collections.

IMPERIAL WAR MUSEUM (IWM)

The collection of aerial photographs in the Imperial War Museum in London is probably the most famous in the world and is usually referred to as the 'Box Collection'.[1] Its origins lie in the reconnaissance work done by the British Royal Flying Corps (RFC, later Royal Air Force – RAF). The Box Collection consists, not of paper prints, but of original glass-plate negatives. The IWM is the only museum in the world where such a considerable number of valuable negatives of the Western Front have survived. All other major archives possess only paper prints. The collection is believed to have been transferred from the Royal Air Force (RAF) School of Photography at Farnborough to the IWM at some point between 1932 and 1935.[2]
The Box Collection is physically divided between two locations: departments of the Imperial War Museum at London and Duxford. The London branch of the museum keeps a card index of the negatives stored at the Duxford location. At the IWM in London, the collection is searchable via a map card index, keyed to the 1:40,000 GSGS (Geographical Section of the War Office General Staff) map sheets. Because of their tactical and strategic use, the maps were provided with a reference grid (24 squares, each 6,000 yards wide) allowing the accurate positioning of photographs. The entire collection has been quantified by counting the index cards, and this has resulted in an estimate of 133,288 unique glass-plate negatives of vertical aerial photos (*1915:* 2,472; *1916:* 14,001; *1917:* 52,737; *1918:* 64,078) covering France and Belgium.[3] Vertical photographic coverage from 1915 to 1918 is available for vast swathes of the British sectors of the Western Front in Belgium and northern France.

AUSTRALIAN WAR MEMORIAL (AWM)

The Australian War Memorial (AWM) comprises a memorial, a museum and the largest military archive in Australia. The Memorial was developed out of the Australian War Records Section –this latter organisation started collecting paper records, maps, photographs and war relics as early as 1917, thereby forming the basis of the AWM.[4] The archival department contains an important collection of aerial photographs covering the various theatres of war. The most extensive is the Western Front collection of aerial photographs. Other – more limited – coverage is related to Gallipoli and to the Palestine Front. The Western Front collection, which comprises 16,030 aerial photographs, is accessible in the same way as the Imperial War Museum's Box Collection, by means of the contemporary GSGS trench map sheet references. The principal part of this collection consists of aerial photographic prints, although there are some negatives as well. The collection was set up to document the Australian battlefields in Belgium and France. Consequently, they start only in 1916 when Australian troops were sent over from Gallipoli and Egypt. Although not comparable with the huge Box Collection of the IWM as regards quantity, it is nonetheless an important source for the engagements in which the Australian units fought. The collection consists mainly of British photographs taken by the RFC and RAF, together with Australian, French and even some captured German aerial photographs.

ROYAL ARMY MUSEUM BRUSSELS (KLM-MRA)

The collection of First World War aerial photographs, the Collection Photos Aériennes '14–'18, at the KLM-MRA is the largest in Belgium. Because the majority of the aerial photographs were taken by the Aviation Militaire Belge (AvMB) during the First World War, the geographic coverage of the photographs is broadly limited to the area between Nieuwpoort on the North Sea and the northern part of the Ypres Salient, the front held by the Belgian Army.

The KLM-MRA collection consists of 365 boxes of aerial photographs, containing 48,511 photographic prints. The aerial photographs can be consulted though a sizeable geographic card index with entries for 1,935 place names, the latter deriving from the captions of the aerial photographs (for example Diksmuide, Ferme de la Nouvelle Batterie, Carrefour Wagner, etc.). It is one of the three largest collections of aerial photographs taken during the First World War. The large quantity of photographs is made even more significant because they cover a relatively small sector of the Western Front.

In addition to the Collection Photos Aériennes '14–'18, aerial photographs can also be found in other departments of the KLM-MRA. The Collection '14–'18 Aviation-Aérostation also deserves some mention. The aerial photographs in the Collection '14–'18 Aviation-Aérostation in certain respects complete the Collection Photos Aériennes '14–'18. The collection relates mainly to the *ordres journaliers* (day orders), since numerous orders and reports of the day were accompanied by supporting aerial photographs, especially between 1915 and 1916. This is therefore an important source for the early stage of Belgian aerial photography.

IN FLANDERS FIELDS MUSEUM (IFFM)

The In Flanders Fields Museum holds a rich collection of more than 2,000 aerial photographs covering the Western Front in Belgium. The collection is very diverse and includes many unique images. Unlike those in the more conventional archives found in London and Brussels, for example, the aerial photographs are displayed in photo albums that were composed during or shortly after the war and are thus a reflection of the personal war experience of the maker. An example of this is the Collection of Freiherr Dietrich von Kanne, a German Oberleutnant (First Lieutenant) who served in Feldflieger Abteilung 41 (Field Flyer Detachment), based in Gits. The album contains many unique images taken in early 1915 just before and during the Second Battle of Ypres. Besides aerial photographs, von Kanne's albums contain photographs of the aerodromes and observation balloons, battlefield scenes, group portraits and also important observation maps. Other private albums are similarly illuminating. These often include unique aerial photographs that were collected in albums because they showed special scenes (e.g. the reconstruction of Ypres, Nieuwpoort and Diksmuide shortly after the war) or specific actions (e.g. German aerial photographs of British raids on Zeebrugge), or simply for their aesthetic value (e.g. reflections of clouds in flooded terrain) or illustrative value (e.g. many aerial photographs of flying aircrafts). The 2,100 images of the IFFM collection are generally of locations in the western part of Belgium. The origins of the photographs are diverse, and interestingly a third of the collection consists of German aerial photographs. Almost a quarter of the images are oblique; this is typical for compiled collections because oblique aerial photographs are much easier to read for a layperson.

Many museums, archives and libraries all over the world have similar collections. Because the photographs in them have sometimes been selected for a specific reason – as opposed to the bulkier, less discriminating holdings of the large and more official collections – they are often very interesting.

NATIONAL ARCHIVES AND RECORDS ADMINISTRATION (NARA)

Compared to the air services of its allies, the Aviation Section of the US Signal Corps (the US military aviation) was still in its infancy when the US joined the Allies in 1917. The Americans also used aerial photography on the Western Front, but only after a learning period based on British and French examples, simply because they had virtually no experience of aerial photography prior to the declaration of war.[5] The National Archives and Records Administration (NARA) in Washington DC has a substantial collection of aerial photographs. The guide to the archives refers to the records of the American Expeditionary Forces as Record Group 120.[6] Within the records of the 2nd Section of the General Staff (GHQ AEF), the Intelligence section, an aerial photographic collection is succinctly described as 'American, French, and some German aerial photographs and index maps relating to the Western Front, 1917–19 (16,291 items)'.[7] The aerial photos of the American Expeditionary Forces are divided into 124 box files. A concise index to these files is available as an addition to the preliminary inventory of the cartographic records of the AEF.[8] In January 2007 a one-page description of the aerial photographs became available, and this estimates the size of the collection at approximately 26,000 aerial photographs.[9] The collection contains printed aerial photographs taken by American Air Service and French reconnaissance units. Most of the coverage is restricted to France, and more specific areas involving American troops, such as the Second Battle of the Marne, the Battle of St-Mihiel and the Meuse–Argonne campaign.[10] There is also some post-war coverage available, mostly related to the Allied occupation of the German Rhineland, the principal points of interest being watercourses and connecting roads.

BAYERISCHES HAUPTSTAATSARCHIV – KRIEGSARCHIV

The Bavarian War Archive supposedly houses the largest collection of First World War aerial photographs in the world. However, surprisingly little appears to be known about its contents. Occasionally, the collection is briefly mentioned in publications, mostly in connection with its size.[11] Fuchs summarises the collection, for instance, as: '… aerial photographs taken during military missions … the number of photos is in the six figures, but many exist in duplicate and triplicate. They are mostly from the Western Front. Most are paper prints, but from the Bavarian units there are about 10,000 glass negatives.' This collection is known at the Bavarian War Archive as the Bildsammlung-Aufklärung, the pictorial collection of reconnaissance photos. The BS-Aufklärung is archived according to provenance. For the aerial photographs this means that the photographs are arranged according to the unit that took the photographs. The majority of the units are of Bavarian origin, although occasionally Prussian and occasionally even Württemberg units also show up. The collection is only sketchily described to a certain degree in the reference guide. In total, the BS-Aufklärung consists of 127 box files, each of which contains large numbers of aerial photographs. The search tool to the collection describes the contents per box file, including the unit responsible for taking the photographs, a general location of the aerial photographs based on several keywords, a selection of place names for which coverage is available and sometimes even a map reference to a 1:25,000 map. Sizeable series of photographs from the same photo-reconnaissance flight are kept together. Consequently, large areas are covered with photographs of the same date, allowing an overview of complete front sectors rather than individual sites. Additionally, this facilitates the selection of overlapping photographs that can be used for stereoscopic research. The geographic coverage of the BS-Aufklärung is divided over distinct theatres of war. The large majority are photographs of the Western Front, but some imagery of other theatres of war such as the Eastern Front, Transylvania, Macedonia and the Isonzo Front is also available.

COVERAGE OF THE WESTERN FRONT, 1914–18

From the above we can see that it would be possible to track several hundred thousand First World War aerial photographs through archival research. These collections form an archival patchwork of aerial coverage. Some archives have unique aerial photos for certain areas, while others overlap to a large extent. The map on page 343 is a basic map of Europe showing which areas were photographed from the air. This not only gives us an idea of how photographs were dispersed across Europe but also enables us to identify blind spots and hot spots, thereby providing us with a realistic assessment of future research possibilities.[12] To understand the distribution of the entirety of accessible Western Front aerial photo collections, it is important to find a suitable way of representing the data. Because the classification system used at the Australian War Memorial and Imperial War Museum is based upon the GSGS trench map referencing method and forms a regular grid, the distribution of the Belgian Army Museum and the US National Archives has also been converted to this system.

The map shows the location of approximately 500,000 historical aerial photographs. Almost 200,000 Allied photographs are represented within 6,000-yard squares. Some squares are covered only by one image while the most densely covered areas contain up to 5,651 First World War aerial photographs. The collection of the Bayerisches Hauptstaatsarchiv is, on the other hand, indicated by triangles representing place names mentioned in the search tool of the BS-Aufklärung. The size of the triangle depends on the number of entries.

→ **Overview of the coverage of the five largest collections of First World War aerial photographs along the Western Front.**
Source: Birger Stichelbaut

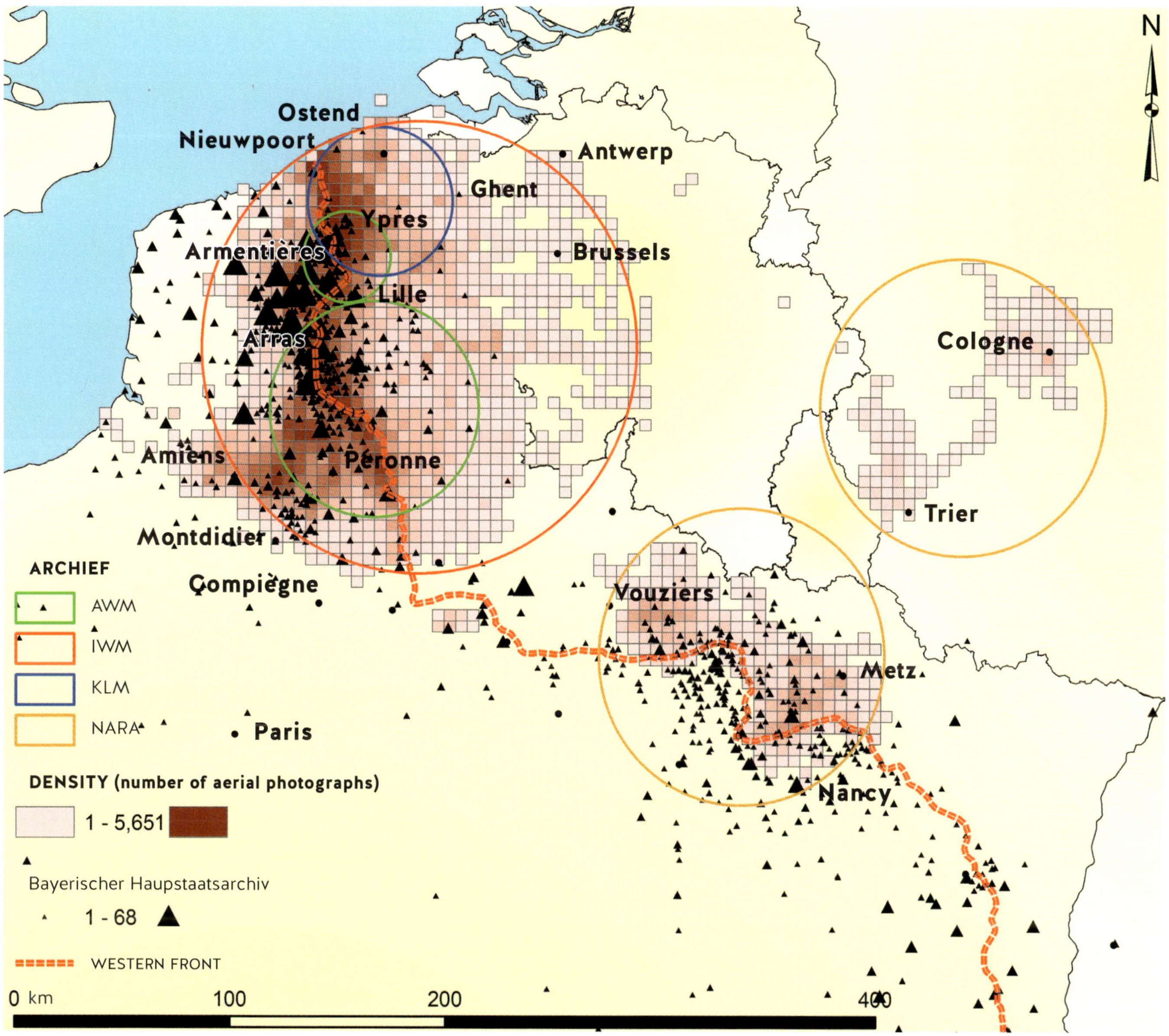

Three clusters are immediately apparent. The first, and largest, group extends from the North Sea in Belgium to Montdidier. This cluster consists of pictures taken by both warring parties and covers the Belgian provinces of West and (to a lesser degree) East Flanders and the French regions of Nord-Pas-de-Calais and Picardy. The centre of gravity of the Bavarian photographs lies at the midpoint between Armentières and Arras (France). The second cluster is located mainly in Lorraine with some very limited coverage in the neighbouring regions (Champagne-Ardenne, Franche-Comté and Alsace). These areas are covered only by German and American aerial photos. The eastern limit of the cluster is covered only in the German archival collections. The third group has its focus in the Rhineland. These pictures are of American origin and were taken in 1919 as part of the American occupation of this region.

Equally important are the areas where aerial coverage is lacking. It is noticeable that there is a gap between the largest clusters, between Compiègne and Vouziers. Both the Allied and German collections focus on other areas. This gap is linked to the absence of Bavarian army operations in the region.[13] From the Allied point of view, the French front line ran from the Somme to the east. Since the French aerial photographic collections are inaccessible and extremely dispersed, these areas can be considered as relatively empty zones.[14]

Notes

Introduction *(p. 8)*

1 General Duval, cited in Carlier 1921: preface.
2 Winter 1978: 264.

An untold wealth of wartime data *(pp. 10-11)*

1 Streckfuss 2009.
2 Bewley & Raczkowski 2002: 5.
3 Coordinates using the World Geodetic System of 1984 – the coordinate system for Google Earth.

Aerial photography and the war: a brief history *(pp. 20-31)*

1 Leggat 2000.
2 Musson et al. 2005: 18.
3 Deuel 1969: 30-31.
4 Carlier 1921: 7.
5 Porter 1921: 159.
6 Porter 1921: 165; Gojda 2007: 18; Deuel 1969.
7 Porter 1921: 165.
8 Finnegan 2006: 8.
9 Newhall 1982: 59-60.
10 Ibid. 123.
11 Dumarche 1988: 8.
12 Reeves 1927: 3.
13 Chasseaud 2009: 105.
14 Lampaert 1997: 35-36.
15 Carlier 1921: 4.
16 Wrigley 1932: 53.
17 Grand Quartier Général des Armées 1916.
18 Anon. 1916.
19 Finnegan 2009: 56.
20 Cooksley 2000: 142.
21 Hauser 2008: 34.
22 Pepin 1917; Goussot 1923.
23 Parry 2003: 3.
24 Cooksley 2000: 141.
25 Parry 2003: 7.
26 Finnegan 2006: 360.
27 Wash 1925: 3.
28 Finnegan 2006: 475.
29 Braun 1987: 80; Gorrell 1961; Carlier 1921.
30 Anon. 1918: 33.
31 Finnegan 2006: 353-354.
32 Porter 1921: 167.
33 d'Hendecourt 1935.
34 Chevallier 1971: 13; General Headquarters 1918.
35 Défense Nationale 1925: 12.
36 Dalman 1925: 116.
37 Défense Nationale 1925: 14.
38 Royal Air Force GHQ Mesopotamia 1918: 14.
39 Vrancken 1999: 163.
40 Carlier 1921: 190.
41 Grand Quartier Général des Armées 1916: 2.
42 Carlier 1921: 193.
43 General Headquarters 1918: 37.
44 Ibid. 47.
45 Collier 2002: 159.
46 Chasseaud 2009: 87.
47 Goussot 1923: 113; Labussière 1919: 172.
48 Chasseaud 2009: 100-101.
49 De Bissy s.d.: 1.
50 Ibid.
51 Desmet 1922: 41.
52 Grand Quartier Général des Armées 1916: 47.
53 General Headquarters 1918: 35.
54 Ibid.
55 Pieters 1998: 24.
56 Goussot 1923: 91.
57 Défense Nationale 1925: 6.
58 Ibid.
59 Carlier 1921: 126.
60 General Headquarters 1918: 12-13.
61 Défense Nationale 1925: 8.
62 Ibid. 16.
63 Ives 1919: 352-353.
64 Anon. 1918: 3-4; Great Britain Army General Staff 1918.
65 General Staff British Army 1918: 9.
66 Winchester et al. 1928: 149.
67 Deuel 1969: 30.
68 Royal Air Force GHQ Mesopotamia 1918: 15.
69 Carlier 1921: 112.
70 General Headquarters 1918: 20.
71 Jaumotte 1919; Anon. 1918; Défense Nationale 1925.
72 Duchatelet 1938: 5.
73 Finnegan 2006: 446.

Multi-layered landscapes *(pp. 32-45)*

1 Saunders 2009: 32.
2 See also Stichelbaut et al. 2013.
3 See also Gheyle et al. 2013.
4 Decoodt 2013.
5 Decuypere 1998.

The war seen from the air *(pp. 46-339)*

1 Lampaert 2000: 68.
2 Journal de Marche et des Opérations de la 42ème Division d'Infanterie, GR 26 N 342 - p 38, Service Historique de l'Armée de Terre.
3 Spagnoly 1997: 26.
4 Lampaert 2000: 70.
5 Bastanier, Von Jacobi and Mangel 1933: 179.
6 Deseyne 2007: 158.
7 Jäger 2001: 108.
8 Deseyne 2007: 161.
9 T'Sas 1973: 186-194.
10 Höwe, Missinne and Verbeke 2011: 3-5.
11 Höwe, Missinne and Verbeke 2011: 120.
12 Institution of Royal Engineers 1922: 24.
13 Lampaert 2000: 67.
14 Watson 1920: 104-105.
15 Van Walleghem 1965: 204.
16 Edmonds 1948: 49.
17 Institution of Royal Engineers 1922, plate XVIII.
18 Ibid.
19 Ibid.
20 Ibid.
21 Frank Hurley, cited in O'Keefe 1986: 64.
22 Institution of Royal Engineers 1922, plate XVIII.
23 Stichelbaut 2011: 65.
24 Watson 1920: 104-105.
25 Watson 1920: 141.
26 Armée belge 1922 : 66.
27 T'Sas 1973: 187.
28 Debaeke 2008: 69.
29 De Munck 2012: 100-102.
30 Baccarne 2007: 49.
31 Cushing 1936: 165.
32 Gheyle, Dossche, Bourgeois, Stichelbaut and Eetvelde 2013: 5.
33 Kommandeur der Flieger des Marinekorps Marine-Stabsbild-Abteilung 1918: 17.
34 Bean 1938: 677-678.
35 Ryheul 1996: 159.
36 Helbling, von Brunner and von Dittelberger 1926: 118-122.
37 Spagnoly 1997: 73.
38 Cushing 1936: 121.
39 Ryheul 1996: 32.
40 Sakkers, den Hollander and Murk 2011: 35.
41 Gheyle, Dossche, Bourgeois, Stichelbaut and Eetvelde 2013: 5.
42 Sakkers, den Hollander and Murk 2011: 20.
43 Deseyne 2007: 54.
44 Ryheul 2010: 29.
45 Neumann 1920: 63.
46 Verdonck et al. 2011: 379.
47 Deseyne 2007: 62.
48 Ryheul 1996: 110.
49 Dhanens 2008: 89.
50 Dhanens 2008: 118.
51 Kennett 1991: 60.
52 Kedar 1999: 14.
53 Van Heden and Trio 2011: 12.
54 Kommandeur der Flieger des Marinekorps Marine-Stabsbild-Abteilung 1918: 19.
55 Archives CWGC, Maidenhead. Minutes of meeting of the Imperial War Graves Commission, 21 January 1919.

Lost and forgotten? Aerial photographic collections *(pp. 340-343)*

1 Imperial War Museum 2007; Watkis 1999.
2 Watkis 2006; NAPLIB 1999: 49.
3 Stichelbaut et al. 2010.
4 Bean 1917.
5 Finnegan 2006: 221.
6 Matchette 1995.
7 NARA 2008.
8 Burch 1966.
9 NARA 2007.
10 Toulmin 1927: 337–388.
11 Fuchs 2000: 133.
12 Stichelbaut and Bourgeois 2009: 238.
13 See Haupt 2009 for an overview of other German collections.
14 Beylot 2009.

Bibliography

Anon. 1916. De l'étude des organisations allemandes par le moyen des photographies aériennes, *Bulletin du Service de la photographie aérienne aux armées*, 3: 3–39.

Anon. 1918. *Das Raumbild*, Berlin, n. publ.

Anon. n.d. Les photographies aériennes et leur étude au point de vue militaire, *Revue militaire française* XX: 1–22.

Armée belge 1922. *Notices sur les sites de guerre conservés: Brochure illustrée d'une carte au 100.000e, de quatre croquis et de treize gravures du Service photographique de l'Armée*, Brussels, Ministère de la Défense nationale.

Atkinson, C. 1927. *The Seventh Division, 1914–1918*, London, John Murray.

Baccarne, R. 2007. *Poelcapelle 1917: a trail of wrecked tanks*, Poelkapelle, n. publ.

Baccarne, R. & Steen, J. 1979. *Boezinge 1914–1918: gasaanval 2e slag om Ieper*, n.p., Bank van Roeselare en West-Vlaanderen.

Baker, C. 2011. *The Battle for Flanders: German defeat on the Lys, 1918*, Barnsley, Pen & Sword.

Barton, P. 2005. *The Battlefields of the First World War: the unseen panoramas of the Western Front*, London, Constable and Imperial War Museum.

Barton, P., Doyle, P. & Vandewalle, J. 2006. *Beneath Flanders Fields: the tunnellers' war, 1914–1918*, Brimscombe Port, The History Press.

Bastanier, H., Von Jacobi, E. & Mangel, H. 1933. *Geschichte des Großherzoglich-Mecklenburgischen Reserve-Infanterie-Regiments Nr. 214: unter Benutzung des amtlichen Materials des Reichsarchivs und von Tagebüchern und Aufzeichnungen vieler Kameraden*, Dessau, Selbstverlag des Offiziervereins R.I.R. 214.

Bean, C. 1917. Australia's records: preserved as sacred things – pictures, relics and writings, *The Anzac Bulletin* 40.

Bean, C. 1938. *Official History of Australia in the War of 1914–1918. Volume IV: The Australian Imperial Force in France 1917*, Sydney, Angus & Robertson.

Bewley, R. & Raczkowski, W. 2002. Future development of aerial archaeology. In: Bewley, R. & Raczkowski, W. (eds), *Aerial Archaeology: developing future practice*, NATO Science Series 337, Amsterdam, IOS Press, 1–8.

Beylot, A. 2009. Military Aerial Photographs, from 1914 to the Present: a survey of the French sources. In: Stichelbaut, B., Bourgeois, J., Saunders, N. & Chielens, P. (eds), *Images of Conflict: military aerial photography and archaeology*, Newcastle upon Tyne, Cambridge Scholars Publishing, 135–50.

Braun, R. 1987. *Bayern und seine Armee: eine Ausstellung des Bayerischen Hauptstaatsarchivs aus den Beständen des Kriegsarchivs*, Munich, Bayerisches Hauptstaatsarchiv.

Burch, F. 1966. *Preliminary Inventory of the Cartographic Records of the American Expeditionary Forces, 1917–21*, Washington DC, The National Archives.

Carlier, A. 1921. *La Photographie aerienne pendant la guerre*, Paris, Librairie Delagrave.

Cave, N. 1998. *Hill 60*, Yorkshire, Leo Cooper.

Chasseaud, P. 2009. Imaging Golgotha: photogrammetry on the Western Front, 1914–18. In: Stichelbaut, B., Bourgeois, J., Saunders, N. & Chielens, P. (eds), *Images of Conflict: military aerial photography and archaeology*, Newcastle upon Tyne, Cambridge Scholars Publishing, 87–120.

Chevallier, R. 1971. *La photographie aérienne*, Paris, Librairie Armand Colin.

Chielens, P., Deknudt, A. & Jahr, C. 2004. *Rudolf Lange 1874–1918: oorlogsgetuige*, Bruges, Van de Wiele.

Chielens, P., Dendooven, D. & Decoodt, H. (eds) 2006. *De Laatste Getuige. Het landschap van Wereldoorlog I in Vlaanderen*, Tielt, Lannoo.

Collier, P. 2002. The impact on topographic mapping of development in land and air survey, 1900–1939, *Cartography and Geographic Information Science* 29(3): 155–74.

Commonwealth War Graves Commission 2013. Commonwealth War Graves Commission website (http://www.cwgc.org).

Cooksley, P. 2000. *The RFC/RNAS Handbook, 1914–1918*, Midsomer Norton, Bookcraft.

Cushing, H. 1936. *From a surgeon's journal, 1915–1918*, London, Constable & Co.

Dalman, G. 1925. *Hundert Deutsche Fliegerbilder aus Palästina*, Gütersloh, Bertelsmann.

Debaeke, S. 2008. *Het drama van de Dodengang. De hel van het IJzerfront*, Koksijde, De Klaproos.

de Bissy, J. n.d. *Illustrations to Accompany Captain de Bissy's Notes regarding the Interpretation of Aeroplane Photographs*, n.p., n. publ.

Decoodt, H. 2013. Duits elektriciteitsgebouw uit de Eerste Wereldoorlog, Inventaris van het Bouwkundig Erfgoed, https://inventaris.onroerenderfgoed.be/dibe/relict/208944, 14 April 2013.

Défense nationale 1925. *Notice sur l'étude des photographies aeriennes*, Brussels, Défense nationale.

De Munck, L. 2012. *Het hospitaal van de Koningin. Rode Kruis, L'Océan en De Panne, 1914–1918*, De Panne, Gemeentebestuur De Panne.

Dendooven, D. 2006. De wederopbouw. In: Chielens, P., Dendooven, D. & Decoodt, H. (eds), *De Laatste Getuige: Het landschap van Wereldoorlog I in Vlaanderen*, Tielt, Lannoo, 97–102.

Deseyne, A. 2007. *De kust bezet: 1914–1918*, Bruges, Provincie West-Vlaanderen.

Desmet, J. 1922. Rôle des aviations belge et française sur le front occidental pendant la grande guerre (III), *Bulletin des sciences militaires* (1922): 343–52.

Deuel, L. 1969. *Flights into Yesterday: the story of aerial archaeology*, Harmondsworth, Penguin Books.

de Vos, L. 2003. *De Eerste Wereldoorlog*, Leuven, Davidsfonds.

Dhanens, P. 2008. *Een Eeuw Luchtvaart boven Gent. Deel I: 1785–1939*, Erembodegem, Flying Pencil.

d'Hendecourt, R. 1935. *Heures inoubliables*, Brussels, Wellens-Pay.

Edmonds, J. 1948. *History of the Great War based on Official Documents by Direction of the Historical Section of the*

Committee of Imperial Defence. Military Operations. France and Belgium, 1917: [vol. II] *Messines and Third Ypres (Passchendaele) 7 June – 10 November*, London, Macmillan.

Faulkner, N. & Duranni, N. 2008. *In Search of the Zeppelin War: the archaeology of the first blitz*, Stroud, Tempus Publishing.

Finnegan, T. 2009. Shaping 20th-century Military Intelligence through a Static Battlefield: aerial photography's impact. In: Stichelbaut, B., Bourgeois, J., Saunders, N. & Chielens, P. (eds), *Images of Conflict: military aerial photography and archaeology*, Newcastle upon Tyne, Cambridge Scholars Publishing, 55–68.

Finnegan, T.J. 2006. *Shooting the Front: Allied aerial reconnaissance and photographic interpretation on the Western Front – World War I,* Washington DC, National Defence Intelligence College Press.

Freytag, A. & Van Driessche, T. 2011. Die Deutschen Soldatenfriedhöfe des Ersten Weltkriegs in Flandern, *Relicta* 7: 163–238.

Fuchs, A. 2000. The Bavarian War Archive in Munich, *Over the Front* 15(2).

General Headquarters 1918. *Study and Exploitation of Aerial Photographs*, Washington DC, Government Printing Office.

General Staff British Army 1918. *Notes on Observation from Aeroplanes*, n.p., Army Printing and Stationery Services.

Gheyle, W., Dossche, R., Bourgeois, J., Stichelbaut, B. & Eetvelde, V.V. 2013. Integrating archaeology and landscape analysis for the cultural heritage management of a World War I militarised landscape: the German field defences in Antwerp, *Landscape Research* DOI (Digital Object Identifier): 10.1080/01426397.2012.754854 and being printed).

Gojda, M. 2007. *Flights into the Past*, Prague, Národní Muzeum.

Gorrell, E. 1961. *Col. Gorrell's History of the U.S. Army Air Service*, Washington DC, The National Archives.

Goussot, C.-M. 1923. *Précis de photographie aerienne*, Paris, Librairie Aéronautique.

Grand Quartier Général des Armées 1916. *Notes sur l'interprétation des photographies aeriennes*, n.p., n. publ.

Great Britain Army General Staff 1918. *Illustrations to Accompany Notes on the Interpretation of Aeroplane Photographs*, n.p.

Haupt, P. 2009. Great War Aerial Photographs in German Archives: a guide to the sources. In: Stichelbaut, B., Bourgeois, J., Saunders, N. & Chielens, P. (eds), *Images of Conflict: military aerial photography and archaeology*, Newcastle upon Tyne, Cambridge Scholars Publishing, 151–64.

Hauser, K. 2008. *Bloody Old Britain: O.G.S. Crawford and the archaeology of modern life*, London, Granta Books.

Helbling, L., von Brunner, E. & von Dittelberger, M. 1926. *Das K.B. Reserve-Infanterie-Regiment nr. 2: Unter Verwendung der amtlichen Kriegstagebücher für das Regiment bearbeitet*, Munich, Bayerisches Kriegsarchiv.

Heyvaert, B. 2006. The Last Witness: the war landscape of the Ypres Salient. *In Flanders Fields* 8: 8–9.

His Majesty's Stationery Office 1914. *Manual of Field Engineering 1911*, London, His Majesty's Stationery Office.

Höwe, H., Missinne, R. & Verbeke, R. 2011. *De Duitse begraafplaats in Langemark*, Bruges, De Klaproos.

Imperial War Museum 2007. Box Collection Vertical Photographic Coverage. London, Imperial War Museum. Unpublished document.

Institution of Royal Engineers 1922. *The Work of the Royal Engineers in the European War, 1914–19, Military Mining*, Chatham, Mackay & Co.

Ives, H. 1919. *Airplane Photography*, Philadelphia & London, Lippincott.

Jäger, H. 2001. *German Artillery of World War One*, Ramsbury, The Crowood Press.

Jaumotte, J. 1919. Conférence du Commandant J. Jaumotte du Génie. *La conquête de l'air – Bulletin officiel de l'Aéroclub de Belgique* 14 (1919): 163–6.

Kedar, B. 1999. *The Changing Land between the Jordan and the Sea: aerial photographs from 1917 to the present*, Jerusalem, Yab Ben-Zvi Press.

Kennett, L. 1991. *The First Air War, 1914–1918*, New York, The Free Press.

Kommandeur der Flieger des Marinekorps Marine-Stabsbild-Abteilung 1918. *Nieuwpoort. Beigabe zum 100. Blatt der Nachrichten-Sammlung der Gruppe Nord*, n.p., Marine-Stabsbild-Abteilung.

Labussière, M. 1919. La photographie aérienne. In: de Brunoff M. (ed.), *1914–1918 L'aéronautique pendant la Guerre mondiale*, Paris, M. de Brunoff, 186.

Lampaert, R. 1997. *België in Oorlog. Van Pionier tot Luchtridder*, Erpe-Mere, Uitgeverij De Krijger.

Lampaert, R. 2000. *De mijnenoorlog in Vlaanderen*, Erpe, Uitgeverij De Krijger.

Leggat, R. 1995–. *A Hypertext History of Photography, from Earliest Times to the the 1920s*. Available at http://www.rleggat.com/photohistory/ (14 August 2008).

Longworth, P. 1967. *The Unending Vigil: a history of the Commonwealth War Graves Commission, 1917–1967*, London, Constable.

Matchette, R. 1995. *Guide to Federal Records in the National Archives of the United States*, Washington DC, National Archives and Records Administration.

Maurer, M. 1978. *U.S. Air Service in World War I. Vol 1.*, Washington DC, Government Printing Office.

Musson, C., Palmer R. & Campana, S. (eds) 2005. *In volo nel passato: aerofotografia e cartografia archeologica*, Siena, All'Insegna del Giglio.

NAPLIB 1999. *Directory of Aerial Photographic Collections in the United Kingdom*, Toftwood, NAPLIB.

NARA 2007. *RG 120: Records of the American Expeditionary Force. Aerial Photographs*, Washington DC, NARA.

NARA 2008. Web Version Based on Guide to Federal Records in the National Archives of the United States. Compiled by Robert B. Matchette et al. Washington DC, National Archives and Records Administration. Available at: http://www.archives.gov/research/guide-fed-records/groups/120.html (6 February 2008).

Neumann, P. 1920. *The German Air Force in the Great War*, London, Hodder & Stoughton.

Newhall, B. 1982. *The History of Photography from 1839 to the Present*, New York, The Museum of Modern Art.

O'Keefe, D. 1986. *Hurley at War: the photography and diaries of Frank Hurley in two world wars*, Broadway, The Fairfax Library.

Parry, D. 2003. Descriptions of aerial reconnaissance cameras used, or evaluated for use by the Royal Flying Corps and Royal Air Force, *Aerial Archaeology E-mail newsletter.*

Pepin, E. 1917. 'A lecture on the study and interpretation of aerial photographs', n.p., n. publ.

Pieters, W. 1998. *Above Flanders' Fields*, London, Grub Street.

Porter, H.E. 1921. *Aerial Observation*, New York, Harper & Brothers Publishers.

Pyner, A. 1988. Air Cameras RAF and USAAF, 1915–1945. Unpublished document, Crouch.

Reeves D. 1927. *Aerial Photographs: characteristics and military applications,* New York, Ronald Press.

Royal Air Force GHQ Mesopotamia 1918. *Notes on Aerial photography Part II: the interpretation of aeroplane photographs in Mesopotamia*, Baghdad, Air Ministry.

Ryheul, J. 1996. *Marinekorps Flanders 1914–1918*, Aartrijke, Decock.

Ryheul, J. 2010. *Marinekorps Flandern: de Vlaamse kust en het hinterland tijdens de Eerste Wereldoorlog*, Erembodegem, Flying Pencil.

Sakkers, H., den Hollander J. & Murk, R. 2011. *De Hollandstellung van Knokke tot Antwerpe: Stille getuige van de Eerste Wereldoorlog*, Antwerp, Witsand.

Saunders, N. 2009. Ulysses' gaze: the panoptic premise in aerial photography and Great War archaeology. In: Stichelbaut, B., Bourgeois, J., Saunders, N. & Chielens, P. (eds), *Images of Conflict: military aerial photography and archaeology,* Newcastle upon Tyne, Cambridge Scholars Publishing, 27–40.

Smets, M. (ed.) 1985. *Resurgam: De Belgische wederopbouw na 1914*, Brussels, Gemeentekrediet.

Spagnoly, T. 1997. *A Walk round Plugstreet: South Ypres Sector, 1914–1918,* London, Cooper.

Stichelbaut, B. 2011. The first thirty kilometres of the Western Front, 1914–1918: an aerial archaeological approach with historical remote sensing data. *Journal of Archaeological Prospection* 18(1): 57–66.

Stichelbaut, B. & Bourgeois, J. 2009. The overlooked aerial imagery of World War One: a unique source for conflict and landscape archaeology. *Photogrammetrie – Fernerkundung – Geoinformation* 3: 231–40.

Stichelbaut, B., De Clercq, W., Herremans, D. & Bourgeois, J. 2013. First World War aerial photographs and medieval landscapes: moated sites in Flanders. In: Hanson, W. & Oltean, I. (eds), *Archaeology from Historical Aerial and Satellite Archives*, New York, Springer, 69–86.

Stichelbaut, B., Gheyle W. & Bourgeois, J. 2010. The Imperial War Museum's Box Collection. In: Standring, R.A., Cowley, D.C. & Abicht, M.J. (eds.), *Landscapes through the Lens: aerial photographs and the historic environment*, Oxford and Oakville, Oxbow Books, 225–36.

Streckfuss, J. 2009. Why the air war really mattered: a guide to understanding the significance of aviation in World War I. In: Stichelbaut, B., Bourgeois, J., Saunders, N. & Chielens, P. (eds), *Images of Conflict: military aerial photography and archaeology*, Newcastle upon Tyne, Cambridge Scholars Publishing, 41–54.

T'Sas, F. 1973. La pièce de 38,1cm SK. L/45 de l'artillerie allemande de marine, 1914–1944. À propos des canons de Leugenboom, Predikboom et de Paris, *Revue belge d'histoire militaire* 10(2): 179–95.

Toulmin, H. 1927. *Air Service, American Expeditionary Force 1918*, Nashville, The Battery Press.

Van Heden, R. & Trio, J. 2011. *Het munitiepark in Kwatrecht,* Wetteren, Gemeentebestuur Wetteren.

Van Walleghem, A. 1965. *De oorlog te Dickebusch en omstreken, deel 2*, Bruges, Geldhof.

Verdonck, A., Vermeiren, E. & Troubleyn, R. 2011. Zeldzame reminiscenties van de Grooten Oorlog: archivalisch en bouwtechnisch onderzoek van de legerbarakken in Jabbeke (prov. West-Vl.), *Relicta* 8: 377–418.

Wash, C. 1925. 'Lecture on aerial photography', n.p., n. publ.

Watkis, N. 1999. *The Western Front from the Air,* Wiltshire, Redwood Books.

Watkis, N. 2006. The Box Collection of the Imperial War Museum, London, *Conference on Military Aerial Photography and Archaeology, Ypres, 19 October 2006.*

Watson, A. 1920. *A Company of Tanks*, Edinburgh, William Blackwood.

Winchester, C., Cobham, A. & Clutterbuck, P. 1928. *Aerial Photography: a comprehensive survey of its practice and development*, Boston, MA, American Photographic Publishing.

Winter, D. 1978. *Death's Men: Soldiers of the Great War*, London, Allen Lane.

Wrigley, H. 1932. *The Battle Below: being the history of No. 3 Squadron A.F.C.*, Sydney, Errol Know.

Index

Names on maps and aerial photographs are not indexed.

Photographic credits

AGENTSCHAP ONROEREND ERFGOED, MARC DEWILDE
p. 338 bottom

BAYERISCHES HAUPTSTAATSARCHIV – KRIEGSARCHIV, MUNICH
p. 39, p. 60 bottom left, pp. 60-61, p. 62 top left, p. 62 top right, p. 63, p. 164 top, p. 164 bottom right, p. 230 left, p. 252 top, p. 253 right, p. 255, p. 258

CENTRUM VOOR HISTORISCHE DOCUMENTATIE VAN DE KRIJGSMACHT, EVERE
p. 103, p. 180 top left

IMPERIAL WAR MUSEUMS, UK
p. 9, p. 21, p. 30, p. 31 top left, p. 37, p. 38 bottom, p. 43, p. 52 top, p. 52 bottom, p. 54 top, p. 54 bottom left, p. 55, p. 59, p. 64 middle, p. 64 bottom, p. 66, p. 76 left, pp. 76-77, p. 79 left, p. 79 middle, p. 79 right, p. 80 top left, p. 80 top right, p. 81, pp. 82-83, p. 84 top, p. 84 top, p. 84 bottom left, p. 84 bottom right, p. 85, p. 86 top right to bottom right, p. 87, p. 89, p. 89 tracing, p. 90 top, p. 90 bottom left, p. 96 top left, p. 96 bottom, p. 97, p. 105 top, p. 113, p. 116 top, p. 117 right, pp. 120-121, p. 122 bottom, p. 123, pp. 124-125, p. 130 left, pp. 130-131, p. 132 top, p. 132 bottom, p. 133, p. 134 bottom, p. 134 top left, p. 134 top right, p. 135, p. 136 bottom, p. 137, pp. 138-139, p. 140, p. 141 top, p. 143, pp. 144-145, pp. 148-149, p. 150 top, p. 150 bottom, p. 152 top, p. 153, p. 156 left, pp. 156-157, p. 158 bottom left, p. 158 top left, pp. 158-159, p. 160 bottom left, p. 162 (aerial photo), p. 163 (aerial photo), p. 166 left, p. 174 top, p. 174 bottom, p. 182 bottom left, p. 184 top, p. 184 middle, p. 184 bottom, p. 185, p. 192 top, p. 207, pp. 208-209, p. 211, p. 214 bottom, p. 214 top, p. 215, p. 216 bottom, p. 216 top left, p. 217, p. 218 left, pp. 218-219 (aerial photos), pp. 220-221, p. 223 top, p. 224 left, pp. 224-225, p. 226 top, p. 228 top right, p. 229, pp. 230-231, p. 231 top, p. 232 bottom, p. 232 top, p. 234 left, pp. 234-235, p. 239, pp. 240-241, p. 250 left, p. 252 bottom, p. 254, p. 260 bottom, pp. 260-261, p. 264 left, p. 265, p. 266 bottom, p. 266 top , p. 267, p. 268 top, p. 268 bottom left, p. 270 left, pp. 270-271, pp. 272-273, p. 296 left, p. 298 left, p. 302 top, p. 302 bottom left, p. 302 bottom right, p. 303, p. 306 bottom left, p. 312 top, p. 314 top right, p. 318 top, p. 320 left, pp. 320-321, p. 322 left, p. 323, p. 326

GIS WEST-VLAANDEREN, BRUGES
p. 201 (tracing), p. 337, pp. 338-339 (aerial photo)

IN FLANDERS FIELDS MUSEUM, YPRES
pp. 2-3, pp. 6-7, pp. 10-11, p. 12 top, p. 12 bottom, p. 13, p. 14, p. 15, p. 16 top, p. 16 bottom left, p. 16 bottom middle, p. 16 bottom right, p. 17 top, p. 17 bottom, p. 18, p. 19, p. 24, p. 25 bottom, p. 26, p. 27 bottom, pp. 32-33, p. 34, p. 35, p. 36 top, p. 36 bottom, p. 38 top, p. 43 bottom left, p. 43 bottom right, p. 44, p. 50, p. 53, p. 54 bottom right, p. 56 top, p. 56 bottom, p. 57, p. 58, p. 62 bottom left, p. 64 top left, p. 64 top right, p. 65, p. 68 top, p. 68 bottom, p. 69, p. 70 top, p. 71, p. 72 top, p. 73, p. 74, pp. 74-75, p. 78 top, p. 80 bottom left, p. 82 top left, p. 86 bottom left, p. 88 top, p. 88 bottom, p. 90 bottom right, p. 91, p. 92, p. 95, p. 96 top right, p. 98 left, pp. 98-99, p. 100 left, p. 104 top, pp. 104-105 bottom, p. 109, p. 111, p. 112 top, p. 112 bottom left, p. 112 bottom right, p. 115, p. 116 bottom, p. 117 left, p. 121 top, p. 124 top left, p. 124 bottom left, p. 126 bottom, p. 128 bottom, p. 136 top, p. 142 bottom, p. 144 bottom left, p. 146 top, p. 148 left, p. 149 right, p. 152 bottom left, p. 154, pp. 162-163 (map), p. 164 left, p. 165, pp. 166-167, p. 168 left, p. 170 top left, p. 170 bottom left, p. 172 bottom left, p. 172 bottom right, p. 175, p. 176 top, p. 178 top, p. 180 top right, p. 181, p. 182 bottom right, p. 183, p. 186 top, p. 186 bottom right, p. 193 top, p. 194 top, p. 194 bottom, p. 195, p. 196 left, pp. 196-197, p. 198 bottom, p. 199, p. 200 bottom, p. 200 top, p. 202, p. 203, p. 204, p. 205, p. 206 left, p. 206 right, p. 210 bottom left, p. 210 top left, pp. 218-19 (map), p. 222, p. 226 bottom left, p. 226 bottom right, p. 227, p. 228 bottom left, p. 228 top left, p. 238 top, p. 238 bottom left, p. 238 bottom right, p. 242 top left, pp. 242-243, p. 244 top, p. 248 top, p. 253 bottom left, p. 256 left, p. 260 top, p. 264 top, p. 268 bottom right, p. 272 left, p. 274 top left, pp. 274-275 bottom, pp. 276-277, p. 277 top, p. 278 top left, p. 278 top right, pp. 278-279, p. 279 top left, p. 279 middle top, p. 279 top right, p. 280 bottom left, p. 280 bottom right, p. 282 left, p. 282 middle, p. 286 top, p. 288 left, pp. 288-289, p. 290 top left, p. 290 middle left, pp. 290-291, p. 306 top, p. 307 top, p. 309, p. 312 bottom, p. 314 top left, p. 314 bottom, p. 315, p. 316, p. 319, p. 322 right, p. 323 top, p. 323 bottom, p. 328 top, p. 328 bottom, p. 329, p. 330 bottom, p. 331, p. 332 top, p. 332 bottom left, p. 333, p. 334 top, p. 335 top, p. 335 right

KONINKLIJK MUSEUM VAN HET LEGER EN DE KRIJGSGESCHIEDENIS, BRUSSELS
p. 22, p. 25 top, p. 28, p. 29, p. 30 bottom right, p. 93, p. 94 top, p. 94 bottom, p. 100 right, p. 101, p. 102, p. 106, p. 107, p. 108 top, p. 108 bottom, pp. 114-115, p. 118, p. 119, p. 126 top, p. 127, p. 128 top, p. 129, p. 147, p. 151, p. 155, p. 160 top, p. 161, pp. 168-169, pp. 170-171, p. 172 top, p. 173, p. 176 bottom left, p. 176 bottom right, p. 177, p. 178 bottom, p. 179 left, p. 179 right, p. 180 bottom, p. 182 top, p. 186 bottom left, p. 187, p. 188, p. 189, p. 190, pp. 190-191, p. 198 top, p. 208 left, p. 212 left, p. 212 right, p. 213, p. 220 left, p. 223 bottom, p. 236 top, p. 236 bottom left, p. 236 bottom right, p. 237, p. 242 bottom left, p. 244 bottom left, p. 244 bottom right, p. 245, p. 246 left, pp. 246-247, p. 248 bottom, p. 249, pp. 250-251, pp. 256-257, p. 257 right, pp. 262-263, p. 269, pp. 274-275 top, p. 280 top, p. 281, pp. 282-283, p. 284 top, p. 284 bottom, p. 285, p. 286 bottom, p. 287, p. 290 bottom left, p. 292 top, p. 292 bottom, p. 293, p. 294, p. 295, pp. 296-297, pp. 298-299, p. 300 left, pp. 300-301, pp. 304-305, p. 307, p. 308 left, p. 308 bottom right, p. 310 top, p. 310 bottom, p. 311, p. 313, pp. 316-317, p. 318 bottom, p. 325, p. 330 top, p. 332 bottom right

NATIONAL ARCHIVES (UNITED KINGDOM), KEW
p. 120 left, p. 240 left

PRIVATE COLLECTION P. WOETS, HOLLEBEKE
p. 78 bottom

PRIVATE COLLECTION A. VERBRIGGHE, POPERINGE
p. 216 bottom right

PRIVATE COLLECTION P. OOSTERLINCK, MENEN
pp. 192-193 bottom

SERVICE HISTORIQUE DE LA DÉFENSE, VINCENNES
p. 72 bottom left

UGENT VAKGROEP ARCHEOLOGIE, B. STICHELBAUT
p. 336 top, p. 336 middle, p. 336 bottom, pp. 338-339 (mapping aerial photo), p. 343

US NATIONAL ARCHIVES AND RECORDS ADMINISTRATION, COLLEGE PARK
p. 23, p. 27 top, p. 30 bottom left

VOLKSBUND DEUTSCHE KRIEGSGRÄBERFÜRSORGE, KASSEL
p. 110

SOURCES OF ILLUSTRATIONS FROM PUBLISHED LITERATURE:

Cushing H. 1936. *From a surgeon's journal 1915-1918,* London, Constable & Co.
p. 210

His Majesty's Stationery Office 1914. *Manual of field engineering 1911,* London, His Majesty's Stationery Office
p. 76 middle

Institution of Royal Engineers 1922. *The work of the Royal Engineers in the European War, 1914-19, Military Mining,* Chatham, Mackay & Co.
p. 152 top left, p. 152 bottom right

Willers H. & Mangels M. 1926. *Königlich Preussisches Reserve-Infanterie-Regiment Nr. 215,* Berlin, G. Stalling
p. 70 bottom